6년간 아무도 깨지 못한 기록

합격자 수 1위
에듀윌

KRI 한국기록원 2016, 2017, 2019년 공인중개사 최다 합격자 배출 공식 인증 (2022년 현재까지 업계 최고 기록)

에듀윌을 선택한 이유는 분명합니다

편입 교육 브랜드만족도 **1**위	3년 연속 서성한반 서울소재 대학 합격 **100**%
합격 시 업계 최대 환급 **500**%	업계 최초 불합격 시 환급 **100**%

에듀윌 편입을 선택하면 합격은 현실이 됩니다.

3년 연속 서성한반 서울소재 대학 100% 합격자 배출[*] 교수진

합격까지 이끌어줄 최정예 합격군단
에듀윌 편입 명품 교수진을 소개합니다.

기본이론부터 문제풀이까지 6개월 핵심압축 커리큘럼

기본이론 완성	핵심유형 완성	기출심화 완성	적중실전 완성	파이널
기본이론 압축 정리	핵심포인트 집중 이해	기출문제 실전훈련	출제유력 예상문제 풀이	대학별 예상 모의고사

* 서성한반(P사) 교수진 전격입성 | 2019~2021년 서성한반(P사) 수강생 합격자 서울소재 20개 대학 기준 3년 연속 100% 합격자 배출
(서울소재 20개 대학: 연세, 고려, 서강, 성균관, 한양, 중앙, 이화, 한국외, 경희, 서울시립, 건국, 국민, 동국, 숭실, 홍익, 숙명, 세종, 명지, 광운, 서울여)

에듀윌 편입 시리즈
전격 출간

3년 연속 100% 합격자 배출* 교수진이 만든 교재로
합격의 차이를 직접 경험해 보세요.

* 본 교재 이미지는 변동될 수 있습니다.
* 여러분의 합격을 도와줄 편입 시리즈 정보는 에듀윌 홈페이지(www.eduwill.net)에서 확인하세요.

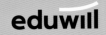

노베이스 수험생을 위한
편입 스타터팩 무료혜택

편입 영어 X 수학 입문강의
한 달이면 기초 탈출! 신규회원이면 누구나 신청 가능!

24만원 상당

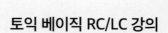

24만원 상당

노베이스
토익커도
RC 단기졸업
#이은희 #최영주

가장 쉬운
토익 LC
왕초보 탈출
#이은희 #셀다

편입 영어 X 수학 입문 강의

· 한 달이면 기초 탈출 입문 강의
· 짧지만, 이해하기 쉬운 기초 탄탄 강의
· 1타 교수진 노하우가 담긴 강의

토익 베이직 RC/LC 강의

· 첫 토익부터 700+ 한 달이면 끝
· 편입 공인영어성적 준비를 위한 토익 기초 지원

합격비법 가이드

· 대학별 최신 편입 전형 제공
· 최신 편입 관련 정보 모음
· 합격전략 및 합격자 수기 제공

기출어휘 체크북

· 편입생이 꼭 알아야 할 편입 어휘의 모든 것
· 최신 기출 어휘를 빈도순으로 구성

편입 합격!
에듀윌과 함께하면 현실이 됩니다.

스타터팩
무료 이벤트

* 본 혜택과 경로는 예고 없이 변경되거나 대체될 수 있습니다.

에듀윌 편입의
독한 관리 시스템

전문 학습매니저의 독한 관리로
빠르게 합격할 수 있도록 관리해 드립니다.

독한 담임관리

· 진단고사를 통한 수준별 학습설계
· 일일 진도율부터 성적, 멘탈까지 관리
· 밴드, SNS를 통한 1:1 맞춤 상담 진행
· 담임 학습매니저가 합격할 때까지
　독한 관리

독한 학습관리

· 학습진도 체크 & 학습자료 제공
· 데일리 어휘 테스트
· 모의고사 성적관리 & 약점 보완 제시
· 대학별 배치상담 진행

독한 생활관리

· 출석 관리
· 나의 학습량, 일일 진도율 관리
· 월별 총 학습시간 관리
· 슬럼프 물리치는 컨디션 관리
· 학원과 동일한 의무 자습 관리

eduwill

에듀윌
편입영어

핵심유형 완성

독해

머리말

PREFACE

독해를 잘하려면 어떻게 해야 하는가에 대한 질문은 수험생들이라면 누구라도 하는 질문이다. 편입에 처음 입문하는 학생들뿐 아니라 심지어는 외국에서 10년을 살다 온 학생들마저도 편입 시험에 출제되는 독해의 난도에 혀를 내두를 정도이다. 그렇다면 어떻게 해야 독해를 잘할 수 있을까?

제대로 영문을 이해하기 위해서는 영어의 이해, 사회와 문화의 이해, 그리고 진정한 글의 이해로 나눠서 생각해 볼 수 있다. 영어의 이해는 어휘와 문법과 구문 실력이 필요한 단계이며, 학습 초기에는 어휘와 문법만 알면 글을 이해할 수 있을 것 같지만, 어느 정도 난도가 높아지면 이 단계로는 해결이 안 된다. 그다음이 바로 사회적 · 문화적 이해인데, 여기에는 영미권의 사회와 문화를 이해해야만 알 수 있는 부분이 상당수 있으며, 많은 글을 읽으면서 어느 정도 해소되어 간다. 마지막으로 이 단계를 넘어서면 진정한 글의 이해로 개인 각자의 지적인 이해 능력이 필요한 단계이다. 읽어도 알 수 없고, 추상적인 글을 구체화하지 못했던 기억들이 있다면 바로 이 단계의 문제인 셈이다.

이렇게 상상 이상으로 어려운 독해 영역을 정복한다는 것은 어불성설이며, 원어민들조차도 모든 글을 이해할 수는 없다. 마치 우리가 한국어 원어민이지만, 자신의 전공과 무관한 어려운 논문을 이해할 수 없는 것과 마찬가지 이치이다. 그렇다면 시험에 나오는 정도의 글을 이해하고 해결해 나갈 수 있는 독해력을 갖춘다는 것은 가능한 일일까? 시험에 관한 한 가능하다는 게 저자의 생각이다. 물론 올바른 학습법을 통해 수많은 노력을 한다는 전제하에서 그러하다.

가장 올바른 학습법은 체계적으로 독해력을 향상시킬 수 있는 프로그램과 이에 적합한 교재들, 그리고 이러한 방법을 일관성 있고 논리적으로 전달할 수 있는 교수법이 동반되어야 한다. 이 책은 독해의 4단계(기본–유형–심화–실전)의 두 번째 단계에 해당한다. 구문 독해를 거쳐 체계적인 편입 독해에 들어서서 먼저 [기본 독해]에서 글의 구성과 전개 방식에 대한 이해를 바탕으로 가벼운 문제 유형을 정리하고, [유형 독해]에서 좀 더 체계적으로 편입시험의 독해 영역에 나오는 다양한 유형의 문제들을 분석하고 훈련하는 과정이다. [유형 독해]에서는 지난 15년간의 독해 지문과 문제들을 분석하여 가장 최적화된 유형 연습 문제들로 구성하였고, 향후 출제 가능한 모든 문제 유형을 망라하여 다루었다.

유형 편의 내용을 간략하게 살펴보면 기존의 책들과는 다르게 전체적인 이해를 요하는 문제, 세부적인 이해를 요하는 문제, 논리적인 이해를 요하는 문제 등 크게 세 부분으로 나눈 후에 각각의 핵심적인 유형을 파악하여 정리한 후 종합 문제까지 총 19개의 Chapter로 구성하였다. 물론 각각의 Chapter에 세부적인 유형까지 더하여 훨씬 더 정교하게 분석을 하였으며, 이를 통해 2019년 이후의 신경향을 파악할 수 있도록 구성하였다. 가령 시험에 출제되는 밑줄 문제만 하더라도 막연한 문제가 아니라 이를 철저히 분석하여, 밑줄을 의미 파악과 지시어구를 묻는 문제로 나누고, 의미 파악도 1차적인 의미를 묻는 경우, 본문과의 관련성을 바탕으로 2차적인 의미를 묻는 경우, 그리고 이렇게 밑줄을 이해했다면 다른 문장으로 paraphrase해도 이해할 수 있는지를 묻는 문제 등으로 세분화하여 설명해 두었다. 이 책을 완독하고 나면 편입시험의 독해 분야에 출제되는 어떠한 문제라도 풀 수 있는 올바른 문제 해결 능력을 충분히 배양할 수 있을 것이다. 이 과정이 끝나면 [심화 독해]에서는 인문학, 사회과학, 자연과학, 문화와 예술 등 주제별로 독해를 기출문제 중심으로 연습하게 된다. 이후 [실전 독해]에서 최근의 실제 경향을 반영한 장문을 포함하여 다양한 예상 문제들로 독해력을 향상시키는 프로그램으로 구성된다. 에듀윌 편입 독해 교재를 차근차근 따라가면 원하는 대학에 갈 만큼의 충분한 실력을 얻을 것이라 자신한다. 편입에서 독해가 가장 중요한 영역인 이유는 대학에서는 원서를 해독할 수 있는 능력을 갖춘 학생을 선발하고 싶어 하며, 경쟁률이 높기 때문에 독해 영역의 난도는 점점 높아져 간다. 이런 상황에서 가장 필요한 것은 글을 해독하고 이해하는 능력이다. 이러한 실력을 갖추는 길은 올바른 학습법으로 체계적인 학습으로 꾸준하게 나아가야 한다. 지금 당장 쉬운 길이 합격을 보장하는 것이 아니고 어렵지만 정도를 걷는 것만이 합격을 보장해 준다는 사실을 명심하고 한걸음씩 차근차근 글을 읽고 이해하는 독해 연습을 해 나가길 바란다. 그렇게 하다 보면 어느 순간 독해의 길이 열리고 읽는 재미를 느낄 수 있을 것이다. 수험생 여러분의 건투를 빈다.

독해력의 체계적인 향상을 기대하며

저자 홍준기

독해를 장악하는 4단계 핵심 학습법

GUIDE

01 기본이론 완성 독해

글의 구성과 전개 방식을 살펴보고, 문제 유형들을 간단하게 점검한다. 초·중급 난도의 독해 지문의 연습을 통해 문장을 이해하고, 단락을 이해하는 연습을 통해 독해의 확실한 기본을 정립할 수 있다. 독해에 대한 기본적인 훈련을 통하여 어려운 지문으로 나아갈 수 있는 발판을 만드는 과정이며, 이 과정에서 편입 독해에 대한 방향을 정립할 수 있도록 구성하였다.

02 핵심유형 완성 독해

지난 20년간의 학교별 편입 독해를 철저히 분석하여, 출제되는 문제 유형을 분석한 교재이다. 향후 편입 독해 교재의 표준이 되어 줄 이 책은 유형을 좀 더 세분화하고 새로운 유형을 추가하여 향후 편입 독해의 유형을 예측할 수 있다. 추론 등의 복잡한 문제를 해결하는 요령 등을 상세히 서술하였고, paraphrase 유형 해결 방안도 살펴본다. 최근의 새로운 문제 유형에 대해서도 소개하였다. 최신 경향을 반영하여 다양한 문제에 대한 접근법을 소개하였으므로, 추론과 같은 문제들뿐 아니라 순서 연결과 같은 논리적 전개 등 특정한 유형에 약한 수험생들에게 역시 도움이 될 것이다.

03 기출심화 완성 독해

2002년부터 2021년까지의 20년간의 기출문제를 철저히 분석하고, 분야별로 나눠 시험에 출제된 핵심적인 지문들을 수록하였다. 철저한 해설과 분석을 바탕으로 한 난도가 높은 지문들을 학습하고 나면 편입 기출문제에 대한 두려움은 사라질 것이다. 더불어 다양한 소재의 수많은 지문으로 구성되어 있으므로 배경지식에 대한 두려움도 어느 정도 극복될 것이다.

04 적중실전 완성 독해

총 20회로 구성되는 난도 높은 예상 문제집으로 회당 10개 지문에 20~30문제씩 구성되어 있다. 매년 마무리 특강으로 자료를 만들고 마무리 수험생들을 대상으로 그 결과를 비교 분석하여 실전에 가장 근접한 문제들로 구성하였다. 실제보다 다소 어려운 문제들도 있지만, 이렇게 훈련한 학생들이 시험에서 좋은 성과를 거두었고, 이제는 입소문으로 실전 독해를 찾는 독자들이 많아졌다. 단순한 문제와 해설뿐 아니라, 문제의 보기 하나하나까지 출제 원리에 근거해 가장 최적화된 예상 문제로 준비하였다.

구성과 특징
FOREWORD

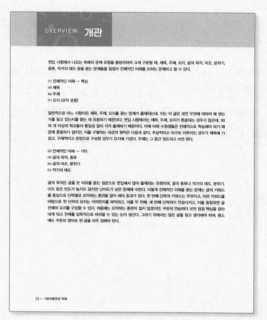

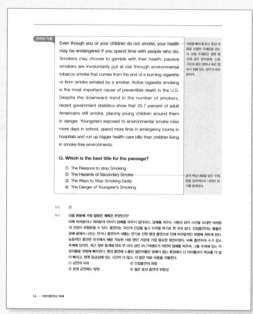

1 OVERVIEW

각 PART에서 학습할 유형의 정의, 출제 빈도 및 경향을 소개하여 수험의 강약을 조절할 수 있도록 하였다. 구체적인 유형에 접근하기에 앞서 학습의 방향성을 파악하고자 하였다.

2 유형 가이드와 전략의 적용

각 유형의 대표적인 질문 유형을 단원별로 4개 정도로 구성하여 살펴보도록 하였고, 문제에 대한 접근법과 풀이 전략을 제시하여 효과적으로 문제를 풀 수 있도록 하였다. 각 단원마다 대표 예제를 제시 · 분석하여 문제 풀이 전략을 어떻게 적용할 수 있는지 살펴볼 수 있도록 하였다.

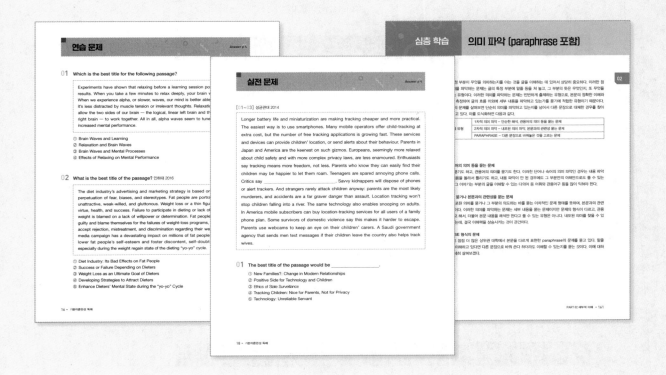

3 연습 문제와 실전 문제

단원별로 문제 유형을 익힐 수 있도록 연습 문제를 2~3개 정도씩 수록하였다. 그리고 실전 감각을 키울 수 있도록 지난 20년간 출제된 중요한 주제들을 중심으로 다양한 문제를 실전 문제에 수록하였다.

4 심층 학습

의미 파악, 추론, 문장 완성의 경우 더 깊이 있는 분석을 위하여 심층 학습으로 구성하여 관련 부분에 수록하였다.

차례

CONTENTS

PART 01 전체적 이해

OVERVIEW	개관	12
CHAPTER 01	제목	13
	연습 문제	16
	실전 문제	18
CHAPTER 02	주제	40
	연습 문제	43
	실전 문제	45
CHAPTER 03	요지	56
	연습 문제	59
	실전 문제	61
CHAPTER 04	글의 목적과 어조 등	76
	연습 문제	78
	실전 문제	80

PART 02 세부적 이해

OVERVIEW	개관	94
CHAPTER 01	내용 일치	95
	연습 문제	98
	실전 문제	100
CHAPTER 02	특정 정보	123
	연습 문제	125
	실전 문제	127
CHAPTER 03	문법성 판단	146
	연습 문제	148
	실전 문제	150
CHAPTER 04	의미 파악	158
	[심층 학습] 의미 파악의 이해(PARAPHRASE 포함)	161
	연습 문제	163
	실전 문제	165
CHAPTER 05	재진술(paraphrase)	176
	연습 문제	178
	실전 문제	180

CHAPTER 06	지시어구	194
	연습 문제	197
	실전 문제	199
CHAPTER 07	단어와 숙어	211
	연습 문제	215
	실전 문제	217

PART 03   논리적 이해

OVERVIEW	개관	230
CHAPTER 01	순서 연결	231
	연습 문제	234
	실전 문제	236
CHAPTER 02	연결 구조	255
	연습 문제	257
	실전 문제	259
CHAPTER 03	문맥과 흐름	268
	연습 문제	271
	실전 문제	272
CHAPTER 04	전후 관계	278
	연습 문제	281
	실전 문제	283
CHAPTER 05	추론	295
	[심층 학습] 추론의 이해	298
	연습 문제	300
	실전 문제	302
CHAPTER 06	유사 추론	326
	연습 문제	329
	실전 문제	331
CHAPTER 07	어휘형 논리	346
	[심층 학습] 문장 완성의 이해 – 문제 해결의 원리	349
	연습 문제	352
	실전 문제	354
CHAPTER 08	독해형 논리	368
	연습 문제	371
	실전 문제	373

• • •   정답과 해설

PART 01

전체적 이해

OVERVIEW   개관

CHAPTER 01   제목

CHAPTER 02   주제

CHAPTER 03   요지

CHAPTER 04   글의 목적과 어조 등

편입 시험에서 나오는 독해의 문제 유형을 총망라하여 크게 구분할 때, 제목, 주제, 요지, 글의 목적, 어조, 분위기, 종류, 작가의 태도 등을 묻는 문제들을 일컬어 전체적인 이해를 요하는 문제라고 할 수 있다.

(1) 전체적인 이해 — 핵심
(a) 제목
(b) 주제
(c) 요지 (요약 포함)

일반적으로 어느 시험이든 제목, 주제, 요지를 묻는 문제가 출제되는데, 이는 이 글은 과연 무엇에 대하여 왜 썼는가를 알고 있는지를 묻는 데 유용하기 때문이다. 편입 시험에서는 제목, 주제, 요지가 혼동되는 경우가 많은데, 30여 개 이상의 학교들이 통일성 없이 각자 출제하기 때문이다. 이에 비해 수험생들은 전체적으로 학습해야 하기 때문에 혼동하기 쉽지만, 이를 구별하는 대강의 원칙은 다음과 같다. 추상적이고 어구로 이루어진 경우가 제목에 가깝고, 구체적이고 문장으로 구성된 경우가 요지에 가깝다. 주제는 그 중간 정도라고 보면 된다.

(2) 전체적인 이해 — 기타
(a) 글의 목적, 종류
(b) 글의 어조, 분위기
(c) 작가의 태도

글의 목적은 글을 쓴 이유를 묻는 질문으로 편입에서 많이 출제되는 유형이며, 글의 종류나 작가의 태도, 분위기, 어조 등은 빈도가 높지도 않지만 난이도가 낮은 문제에 속한다. 이렇게 전체적인 이해를 묻는 문제는 글의 키워드를 중심으로 단락별로 요약하는 훈련을 많이 해야 효과가 있다. 첫 번째 단락의 키워드는 무엇이고, 이런 키워드를 바탕으로 첫 단락의 요지는 어떠한지를 파악하고, 이를 두 번째, 세 번째 단락까지 연결시키고, 이를 종합하면 글 전체의 요지를 구성할 수 있다. 처음에는 요약하는 훈련이 쉽지 않겠지만, 꾸준히 연습하다 보면 점점 핵심을 잡아내게 되고 전체를 압축적으로 바라볼 수 있는 눈이 생긴다. 그러기 위해서는 많은 글을 읽고 생각해야 하며, 평소에도 꾸준히 영어로 된 글을 자주 접해야 한다.

편입 시험 문제 중 자주 등장하는 '글의 제목'이란 글의 주제문을 압축적으로 표현한 것이다. 즉 지문에서 말하고 자 하는 중심 내용을 압축적으로 표현한 것으로, 대부분의 학교에서 출제되는 유형이다. 경우에 따라서는 한 학교 에서 제목을 묻는 문제가 3~4개 나올 정도로 출제 빈도가 높다.

01 질문 유형

What is the best title of the passage?
Choose the best title of the following passage.
Which is the best title for the following passage?
Which of the following is the most appropriate title of the passage?

02 문제 풀이 전략

❶ 중심 내용을 포섭하는 부분을 찾아야 한다.

설명이나 논증의 경우 나타내고자 하는 바가 있다. 저자가 정보를 제공하거나 자기의 주장을 밝혀 상대방을 설 득하고자 하는 의지가 드러나게 된다. 이러한 글에서는 중심 내용을 담고 있는 부분을 찾아야 하며, 주제문의 뒤에 뒷받침하는 문장들이 부연 설명이나 예증으로 붙는 경우가 많다. 특히 주제를 선명히 부각하기 위해 본문 에서 여러 번 제시되는 경우가 있으므로 반복되는 어휘나 표현에 유의하여야 한다.

❷ 주제문을 압축적으로 표현한 제목을 찾는다.

편입 시험에서는 특히 주제, 요지, 제목의 구분 없이 출제되는 경우가 종종 있다. 이 가운데 제목은 명사나 구 등으로 압축적으로 표현한 것이 많다. 너무 포괄적인 것, 너무 지엽적인 것은 제외해야 한다. 글 전체를 포괄하 는 타당한 보기를 골라야 한다는 뜻이다. 아무리 보기가 본문 내용에 합당하다 하여도, 그 범위를 너무 넓게 설 정하였거나 너무 좁게 설정하였다면 이는 제목이라 할 수 없다.

Even though you or your children do not smoke, your health may be endangered if you spend time with people who do. Smokers may choose to gamble with their health; passive smokers are involuntarily put at risk through environmental tobacco smoke that comes from the end of a burning cigarette or from smoke exhaled by a smoker. Active cigarette smoking is the most important cause of preventible death in the U.S. Despite the downward trend in the number of smokers, recent government statistics show that 25.7 percent of adult Americans still smoke, placing young children around them in danger. Youngsters exposed to environmental smoke miss more days in school, spend more time in emergency rooms in hospitals and run up bigger health-care bills than children living in smoke-free environments.

지문을 빠르게 읽고 중심 내용을 포함한 주제문을 찾는다. 보통 주제문은 설명 형식의 글은 앞부분에, 논증 구조의 글은 앞이나 혹은 접속사 뒤에 있는 경우가 대부분이다.

Q. Which is the best title for the passage?

① The Reasons to stop Smoking
② The Hazards of Secondary Smoke
③ The Ways to Stop Smoking Easily
④ The Danger of Youngster's Smoking

글의 핵심 내용을 담은 주제문을 압축적으로 나타낸 보기를 골라낸다.

정답   ②

해석   **다음 본문에 가장 알맞은 제목은 무엇인가?**

비록 여러분이나 여러분의 아이가 담배를 피우지 않더라도, 담배를 피우는 사람과 같이 시간을 보내면 여러분의 건강이 위협받을 수 있다. 흡연자는 자신의 건강을 놓고 도박을 하기로 한 것과 같다. 간접흡연자는 불붙은 담배 끝에서 나오는 연기나 흡연자가 내뿜는 연기로 인한 환경 흡연으로 인해 비자발적인 위험에 처하게 된다. 능동적인 흡연은 미국에서 예방 가능한 사망 원인 가운데 가장 중요한 원인이었다. 비록 흡연자의 수가 감소 추세에 있지만, 최근 정부 통계에 따르면 미국 성인 25.7퍼센트가 여전히 담배를 피우며, 그들 주위에 있는 어린이들을 위험에 빠뜨린다. 환경 흡연에 노출된 젊은이들은 담배가 없는 환경에서 산 아이들보다 학교를 더 많이 빠지고, 병원 응급실에 있는 시간이 더 많고, 더 많은 의료 비용을 지불한다.

① 금연의 이유   ② 간접흡연의 위험
③ 쉽게 금연하는 방법   ④ 젊은층의 흡연의 위험성

해설   본문 처음에서는 "your health may be endangered if you spend time with people who do.(담배를 피우는 사람과 같이 시간을 보내면 여러분의 건강이 위협받을 수 있다.)"는 문구와 함께 간접흡연의 위험성을 경고하며, 마지막에서는 "Youngsters exposed to environmental smoke miss more days in school, spend more time in emergency rooms in hospitals and run up bigger health-care bills than children living in smoke-free environments.(환경 흡연에 노출된 젊은이들은 담배가 없는 환경에서 산 아이들보다 학교를 더 많이 빠지고, 병원 응급실에 있는 시간이 더 많고, 더 많은 의료 비용을 지불한다.)"는 통계 수치를 들어 간접흡연이 아이들에게 끼치는 폐해를 말하고 있다. 따라서 답으로 가장 적절한 것은 ②이다. ① 과 ③은 본문과는 상관이 없고, ④의 경우는 비자발적인 경우가 아니라 능동적으로 담배를 피운 경우를 의미하는 것이므로 역시 답으로 볼 수 없다.

어휘   **endangered** ⓐ 위험에 처한
involuntarily ⓐⓓ 비자발적으로, 마지못해
environmental tobacco smoke 환경 흡연
preventable death 예방이 가능한 사망
place ⓥ ~을 …한 상황에 처하게 하다
hazard ⓝ 위험

gamble ⓥ 도박하다, (with) ~을 걸다
put ~ at risk ~을 위험에 처하게 하다
exhale ⓥ 숨을 내쉬다
downward trend 하락세
run up a bill 비용이 쌓이다

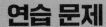

01 Which is the best title for the following passage?

Experiments have shown that relaxing before a learning session positively affects the results. When you take a few minutes to relax deeply, your brain waves slow down. When we experience alpha, or slower, waves, our mind is better able to focus because it's less distracted by muscle tension or irrelevant thoughts. Relaxation also appears to allow the two sides of our brain — the logical, linear left brain and the creative, holistic right brain — to work together. All in all, alpha waves seem to tune up our brains for increased mental performance.

① Brain Waves and Learning
② Relaxation and Brain Waves
③ Brain Waves and Mental Processes
④ Effects of Relaxing on Mental Performance

02 What is the best title of the passage? 인하대 2016

The diet industry's advertising and marketing strategy is based on the creation and perpetuation of fear, biases, and stereotypes. Fat people are portrayed as unhealthy, unattractive, weak-willed, and gluttonous. Weight loss or a thin figure is equated with virtue, health, and success. Failure to participate in dieting or lack of success in losing weight is blamed on a lack of willpower or determination. Fat people are taught to feel guilty and blame themselves for the failures of weight-loss programs, and to expect and accept rejection, mistreatment, and discrimination regarding their weight. This negative media campaign has a devastating impact on millions of fat people. These messages lower fat people's self-esteem and foster discontent, self-doubt, and self-hatred, especially during the weight regain state of the dieting "yo-yo" cycle.

① Diet Industry: Its Bad Effects on Fat People
② Success or Failure Depending on Dieters
③ Weight Loss as an Ultimate Goal of Dieters
④ Developing Strategies to Attract Dieters
⑤ Enhance Dieters' Mental State during the "yo-yo" Cycle

03 Which is the best title for the following passage?

Forty-one-year old Teresa Bell Kindred still wonders if she did everything she could when her mother became fatally ill with colon cancer. Throughout the ordeal Kindred kept thinking, maybe there's a new therapy we haven't heard about. Rationally, Kindred knew she had no control over her mother's illness. But an irrational part of her thought otherwise. "My mother was always able to fix everything in my life," Kindred says. "So when she needed me and I couldn't save her, it was a horrible feeling." We need to accept the fact that we aren't powerful enough to control everything that happens, says Herbert Strean, director emeritus of the New York Center for Psychoanalytic Training. Expecting perfection of yourself is a no-win situation. Guilt sufferers need to accept their basic human fallibility.

① Forgive Yourself
② Learn From Mistakes
③ Count Your Blessings
④ Accept Your Limitations

[01~03] 성균관대 2014

Longer battery life and miniaturization are making tracking cheaper and more practical. The easiest way is to use smartphones. Many mobile operators offer child-tracking at extra cost, but the number of free tracking applications is growing fast. These services and devices can provide children's location, or send alerts about their behaviour. Parents in Japan and America are the keenest on such gizmos. Europeans, seemingly more relaxed about child safety and with more complex privacy laws, are less enamoured. Enthusiasts say tracking means more freedom, not less. Parents who know they can easily find their children may be happier to let them roam. Teenagers are spared annoying phone calls. Critics say _____. Savvy kidnappers will dispose of phones or alert trackers. And strangers rarely attack children anyway: parents are the most likely murderers, and accidents are a far graver danger than assault. Location tracking won't stop children falling into a river. The same technology also enables snooping on adults. In America mobile subscribers can buy location-tracking services for all users of a family phone plan. Some survivors of domestic violence say this makes it harder to escape. Parents use webcams to keep an eye on their children's carers. A Saudi government agency that sends men text messages if their children leave the country also helps track wives.

01 **The best title of the passage would be** _____.

① New Families?: Change in Modern Relationships
② Positive Side for Technology and Children
③ Ethics of State Surveillance
④ Tracking Children: Nice for Parents, Not for Privacy
⑤ Technology: Unreliable Servant

02 Which of the following is most appropriate for the blank?

① tracking devices can also be used by kidnappers
② tracking does not really protect children
③ tracking devices are too expensive
④ teenagers do not like to carry tracking devices
⑤ smartphones are more efficient than tracking devices

03 According to the passage, which of the following is true?

① High cost of tracking applications deters wider use of tracking devices.
② Tracking devices may promote a dehumanizing tendency.
③ Europeans are not very keen on tracking devices because they trust each other more.
④ Mobile tracking services help prevent domestic violence in Saudi Arabia.
⑤ Children are more prone to surveillance than adults.

Solitude quietly eliminates all sorts of traits that were a part of you — among others, the desire to pose, to impress people as being something you would like to have them think you are even when you aren't. Some men I know are able to pose even in solitude; had they servants who help them dress, they no doubt would be heroes to them. But I find it the hardest kind of work myself, and as I am lazy I have stopped trying. To act without an audience is so wearisome and profitless that you gradually give it up and at last forget how to act at all. For you become more interested in making the acquaintance of yourself as you really are. Clothes, you learn, with something of a shock, have for you no interest whatsoever. You learn to regard dress merely as covering.

04 윗글의 제목으로 가장 알맞은 것은?

① Acting without an Audience in Fancy Clothes
② Being Heroes to Servants
③ Main Causes of Laziness
④ An Encounter with the Self through Solitude

05 윗글에 드러난 글쓴이의 입장에 가장 가까운 것은?

① A desire to appear at your best is a trait that goes with laziness.
② In solitude, the presence of servants becomes vital.
③ In solitude, clothes become a part of yourself.
④ A desire to appear well-dressed diminishes when you are alone.

[06~07]

Let's say you are offered a million dollars if you can win at least two consecutive games in a three-game chess match against a pair of adversaries, reigning world champion Vladimir Kramnik and an amateur player. You are also given the following option: You can choose to play either amateur — Kramnik — amateur or Kramnik — amateur — Kramnik. It might seem obvious that you should avoid playing Kramnik as much as possible, but in fact your chance of winning the purse is greater in the latter lineup, where you play him twice. The reason is that you can't win two consecutive games without winning the second one, so you're better off facing the weaker opponent in the middle and giving yourself two shots to topple the grandmaster.

06 **Which of the following is the best title of the passage?**

① Who Holds the Purse Rules the House
② If You Were Offered a Million Dollars
③ Strategies and Tactics Differ in Chess Games
④ Chess Players Do Not Yet Enjoy Prestige
⑤ Two Tough Challenges Can Be Better Than One

07 **Which of the following is stated about Vladimir Kramnik in the passage?**

① He often faces his kinsmen in consecutive chess games.
② He has never played against an amateur player in a chess game.
③ He will earn a million dollars by winning this year's chess match.
④ He usually prefers to play twice against the same player.
⑤ He is the internationally first-ranked chess player.

One afternoon, I noticed that my 15-month-old, Ben, had a brown line on one of ⓐ his top teeth that wouldn't come off. After it spread to another tooth, the dentist said ⓑ he had "baby-bottle tooth" (a rare diagnosis for a breastfed baby). He blamed it on my nursing and suggested I stop, but ⓒ he warned that the damage might be permanent. We went to another dentist, who believed the decay was more likely caused by Ben's weak enamel and predisposition to tooth decay, which my husband had as a baby. The good news: I wouldn't have to wean my son if we brushed his teeth after meals with a prescription fluoride toothpaste, offered water after snacks, wiped his teeth down after ⓓ he fell asleep, and went for monthly fluoride varnishes. The routine was tough, but it paid off: After a year, ⓔ his decay not only stopped, but it reversed. I learned the value of trusting my instincts, seeking second opinions, and working hard for my child's health.

08 Which is the best title of the passage?

① Danger in Doctor Shopping
② I Reversed My Son's Tooth Decay!
③ What Causes Baby's Tooth Decay?
④ Recent Increase in Tooth Problems in Babies
⑤ Importance of Breast-feeding to New-born Babies

09 Which of the following refers to a different person from the others?

① ⓐ   ② ⓑ
③ ⓒ   ④ ⓓ
⑤ ⓔ

Two features of the Singapore context are worth noting in this discussion of globalization and education. The first is that as a small island with no natural resources except a strategic location, Singapore's survival has always depended on its usefulness to major powers. It attracted colonial interest because it provided a well-placed base for economic penetration of the region; and the colonial experience, 1819 − 1963, served to deepen Singapore's integration into Britain's economic empire. Although there was political contestation in the 1950s over culture, languages and political issues, there was also early recognition of the value of English, the colonial language as an economic resource. Early planning for transforming Singapore's economy from an entrepot to an industrial economy in the late 1950s recognised the need for foreign capital, technology and markets. Singapore thus eschewed the ideology of economic nationalism that characterizes many postcolonial states. This clear grasp of the need for economic openness to global economic forces still characterizes planning in Singapore even though the country is now considered a developed economy with a per capita annual income of more than US $20,000. External trade is a major component of Singapore's economy, and Singapore's leaders are fond of making international comparisons as a way of benchmarking achievements. Singapore is perhaps unique in the world economy in that it relies very heavily on trade and therefore Ⓐ _____.

10 What is the best title of the passage?

① The colonial era of Singapore
② The importance of Singapore's strategic location
③ Singapore as the world's most globalized nation
④ The colonial language as an economic resource
⑤ Singapore's integration into Britain's economic empire

11 What is most appropriate for the blank Ⓐ?

① has to be dominated by external forces
② has had to have an open economy
③ has accelerated the resilience of education systems
④ has to emphasize the value of the civilization
⑤ has strengthened her cultural identity as an Asian state

12 Which one is NOT true of the above passage?

① Singapore's strategic location contributed to its economic growth.
② Singapore recognized the value of English for economic development.
③ Singapore relied on foreign capital as it has no natural resources.
④ Singapore maintains economic nationalism until present.
⑤ External trade is an important feature that describes Singapore's economy.

[13~15]

Work may be defined as carrying out tasks that require the expenditure of mental and physical effort, which has as its objective the production of goods and services that cater to human needs. An occupation, or job, is work that is done in exchange for a regular wage. A wage or salary is the main resource many people depend on to meet their needs. Without such an income, anxieties about coping with day-to-day life tend to multiply.

Work often provides a basis for the acquisition and exercise of skills and capacities. Even where work is routine, it offers a structured environment in which a person's energies may be absorbed. Without it, the opportunity to exercise such skills and capacities may be reduced. Work provides access to contexts that contrast with domestic surroundings. In the working environment, even when the tasks are relatively dull, individuals may enjoy doing something different from home chores.

The work environment often provides friendships and opportunities to participate in shared activities with others. Separated from the work setting, a person's circle of possible friends and acquaintances is likely to dwindle. Work is usually valued for the sense of stable social identity it offers. For men in particular, self-esteem is often bound up with the economic contribution they make to the maintenance of the household. Against the backdrop of this formidable list, it is not difficult to see why being without work may _____ individuals' confidence in their social value.

13 윗글의 제목으로 가장 적절한 것을 고르시오.

　① How to Increase the Number of Job Openings
　② The Social Organization of Work
　③ The Correlation between Work and Self-esteem
　④ The Social Significance of Work

14 윗글의 내용과 일치하는 것을 고르시오.

　① People often associate the notion of work with drudgery.
　② People would feel so disoriented when they become unemployed.
　③ People often tend to think of routine work as unpaid work.
　④ The work environment never provides a sense of rhythm in daily activities.

15 빈칸에 가장 알맞은 단어를 고르시오.

① develop   ② enhance   ③ undermine   ④ strengthen

The separation of space inside homes may vary from culture to culture. In most American homes the layout of rooms reveals the separateness and labeling of space according to function — bedroom, living room, dining room, playroom, and so on. This system is in sharp contrast to other cultures where one room in a house may serve several functions. In Japan, homes with sliding walls can change a large room into two small rooms so that a living room can also serve as a bedroom.

When a home or a city's design is influenced by another culture, the "native" architecture can be lost or disguised. For example, a French architect was asked to design Chadigarh, the capital city in Punjab, India. He decided to plan the city with centralized shopping centers which required public transportation and movement away from the village centers. Eventually, the Indians stopped meeting each other socially in their small neighborhoods. Apparently, the introduction of a non-Indian style of architecture affected some of the cultural and social patterns of those living in the city.

16 Why did the Indians' social patterns change after the foreign architect designed the capital city?

① Because public transportation destroyed social life in large cities.
② Because local neighborhoods were no longer the centers of social activities.
③ Because his non-Indian architecture encouraged local social interaction.
④ Because Indian architecture was introduced into the world.

17 What would be the best title of the passage?

① Cultural Variations in Architectural Design
② Influences of Architecture on the World History
③ The Layout of Spaces in Different Buildings
④ Shopping Centers and Urban Development

Millennials consist, depending on whom you ask, of people born from 1980 to 2000. To put it more simply, the group is made up of teens, 20s, and 30-somethings. At 80 million strong, they are the biggest age grouping in American history. Each country's millennials are different, but because of globalization, social media, the exporting of Western culture and the speed of change, millennials worldwide are more similar to one another than to older generations within their nations. Even in China, where family history is more important than any individual, the Internet, urbanization and the one-child policy have created a generation as overconfident and self-involved as the Western one.

They are the most threatening generation since the baby boomers brought about social revolution, not because they're trying to take over the Establishment but because they're growing up without one. The Industrial Revolution made individuals far more powerful — they could move to a city, start a business, and form organizations. The information revolution has further empowered the individuals by handing them the technology to compete against huge organizations: hackers vs. corporations, bloggers vs. newspapers, app-makers vs. entire industries. Millennials don't need us. That's why we're scared of them.

18 Choose the best title for the passage.

① Millennials, Beware of Yourselves
② Millennials: Emerging Hope and Promise
③ Millennials: A Lost Generation
④ Why Millennials Give Us a Scare

19 Choose the one that is not true according to the passage.

① Chinese millennials are more self-centered than the Western ones.
② Millennials are alike across countries due in part to globalization.
③ Millennials are growing up without the Establishment.
④ Millennials constitute the largest age group in the U.S. population.

Industrial growth has long been considered desirable, because of its contribution to health and happiness, for the creation of wealth, or simply for its own sake. Until recent times, progress was indeed identified with such quantitative growth. In contrast, modern societies have begun to question the desirability of certain innovations that are technologically feasible and economically profitable, but that have undesirable social aspects. The evaluation of potential long-range dangers for human beings and for the environment is becoming one of the crucial factors in the formulation of technological policies.

The partial banning of pesticides exemplifies a situation in which a technology that had first been accepted with enthusiasm was brought under strict control once its dangers had been recognized. Even more striking is the case of the fluorocarbons used in spray containers. There are some indications that these substances may be directly harmful to human beings, and also indirectly harmful through possible effects on the ozone layer of the atmosphere. With the information concerning the magnitude of these effects, there is new legislation controlling the use of fluorocarbons, and _____, the sale of spray has greatly decreased.

20 Which would the best title for the passage?

① Desirable Aspects of Technological Innovations
② Convenience That Industrial Growth Brings to Humans
③ Emergence of Policies on Technology Development
④ Harmful Effects of Industrial Products on Environment

21 Which of the following is most appropriate for the blank?

① in other words
② conversely
③ otherwise
④ consequently

22 Which of the following is true of modern societies?

① They are infatuated with industrial technologies as countries compete.
② They are more scrupulous so far as technological innovations are concerned.
③ They consider all innovations undesirable and perilous fallouts.
④ They formulate their technological policies on the basis of quantitative growth.

The growth of the Internet, social networking, and mobile technology have transformed how people communicate and exchange information, but Congress has lagged in updating federal privacy laws to safeguard digital communications from inappropriate prying. Late last month, the Senate Judiciary Committee made some serious progress in the right direction. By a voice vote, and with only one Senator asking to go on record in opposition, the committee approved a measure that would significantly enhance the privacy protection given to e-mails. The bill, an amendment to the outdated 1986 law that now governs e-mail access, would require law enforcement agents to get a search warrant from a judge in order to obtain e-mail content from a network service provider that holds private electronic messages, photos, and other personal records. This means having to show the court that there is probable cause to believe that the sought-after records may reveal evidence of wrongdoing.

23 Which of the following is the best title of the passage?

① Unanswered Questions on Privacy Concerns
② A Biased View of Online Privacy Policy
③ Effective Ways to Handle Privacy Issues
④ A Step Toward E-Mail Privacy Protection

24 Which of the following is stated in the passage?

① In 1986, federal privacy laws were abolished to encourage e-mail communications.
② Stricter federal laws have been enforced to promote the digital industry.
③ A search warrant was required to get access to e-mail contents in the past.
④ A Senate committee voted in favor of an amendment to the 1986 law.

Not only is aspirin a standard remedy for pain and fever, but it's also used to prevent serious illness. Millions of heart attack and stroke survivors pop a low-dose tablet every day to stop them having another event and, increasingly, healthy people are taking it daily to safeguard their cardiovascular health, too.

We've known for a long time that aspirin is very effective in preventing heart attacks and strokes in people with a cardiovascular problem. The drug works by thinning the blood to help prevent small blood clots. More recently, there's been evidence that low doses of daily aspirin can prevent gastro-intestinal cancers as well as breast and prostate cancer, and also slow mental decline.

But, because aspirin thins the blood, people taking it regularly may actually be at higher risk of a stroke because their brains bleed more. Its long-term use has also been linked to macular degeneration and increased risk of internal bleeding.

General practitioner Dr. Marles says those who can benefit from the drug include people who have had any sort of heart events, like a heart attack or a stroke. For everyone else, it's up to a doctor to carefully weigh up their risks of cardiovascular disease and bleeding.

25 Which is the best title of the passage?

① Widespread Use of Aspirin
② Aspirin, a Modern Panacea
③ How and When to Take Aspirin
④ Aspirin, What Is Good and Bad

26 Which is NOT a harmful side effect of aspirin?

① heart attack
② poorer eyesight
③ higher risk of a stroke
④ increased risk of internal bleeding

27 Which is NOT true according to the passage?

① Aspirin is effective in preventing certain cancers.
② One of the functions of aspirin is thinning the blood.
③ Aspirin is usually served as a pain and fever relief.
④ Doctors recommend people to take aspirin on a daily basis.

The school system is viewed by Bourdieu as an institution for the reproduction of legitimate culture through the hidden linkages between scholastic aptitude and cultural heritage. He believes that, despite ideologies of equal opportunity and meritocracy, few educational systems are called upon by the dominant classes to do anything other than reproduce the legitimate culture as it stands and produce agents capable of manipulating it legitimately.

Bourdieu has argued that it is the culture of the dominant group, which is embodied in schools. Educational differences are thus frequently misrecognized as resulting from individual giftedness, rather than from class-based differences, ignoring the fact that the abilities measured by scholastic criteria often stem not from natural "gifts" but from "the greater or lesser affinity between class cultural habits and the demands of the educational system or the criteria which define success within it."

The notion of cultural capital was proposed by Bourdieu in the early 1960s to describe familiarity with bourgeois culture, the unequal distribution of which helps to conserve social hierarchy under the cloak of individual talent and academic meritocracy. This notion includes such things as acquired knowledge (educational or otherwise), cultural codes, manner of speaking and so forth, which are embodied as a kind of "habitus" in the individual and are also objectified in cultural goods.

28 According to the passage, which of the following is NOT true?

① Working-class students may feel like outsiders in the middle-class habitus of higher education.

② Individuals tend to possess innate intelligence based on their social class.

③ Educational institutions ensure the profitability of the cultural capital of the dominant.

④ The dominant culture, by making itself recognized as universal, legitimizes the interests of the dominant group.

29 Which of the following statements can be inferred from the passage?

① According to Bourdieu, every culture is equally valued and equally legitimate.

② According to Bourdieu, schooling produces certain entrenched ways of recognizing that foster existing class stratification.

③ According to Bourdieu, individuals' efficacy is most strongly influenced by mastery experiences throughout all phases of their lives.

④ According to Bourdieu, cultural reproduction is a trivial mechanism through which socioeconomic polarization takes place.

30 What would be the best title of the passage above?

① The importance of individual giftedness in schooling

② The significance of students' achievement in schooling

③ The social responsibility of dominant culture in schooling

④ The reproduction of inequalities in schooling

At what point did it begin to matter what you wore? When, how and why did looks become deeply embedded in how people felt about themselves and others? The Renaissance was a turning point. I use the term in its widest sense to describe a long period, from ca.1300 to 1600. After 1300 a much greater variety and quantity of goods were produced and consumed across the globe. Textiles, furnishings and items of apparel formed a key part of this unprecedented diffusion of objects and increased interaction with overseas worlds. Tailoring was transformed by new materials and innovative techniques in cutting and sewing, as well as the desire for a tighter fit to emphasize bodily form, particularly of men's clothing. Merchants expanded markets in courts and cities by making chic accessories such as hats, bags, gloves or hairpieces, ranging from beards to long braids. At the same time, new media and the spread of mirrors led to more people becoming interested in their self-image and into trying to imagine how they appeared to others; artists were depicting humans on an unprecedented scale, in the form of medals, portraits, woodcuts and genre scenes, and print circulated more information about dress across the world, as the genre of 'costume books' was born. <u>These expanding consumer and visual worlds conditioned new ways of feeling.</u>

31 Which of the following would be the best title for the passage?

① Expansion of Global Trading in the Renaissance
② Birth of Fashion in the Renaissance
③ Consumer Culture and Clothing Industry
④ Luxury Goods in the Renaissance

32 Which of the following can be inferred from the underlined sentence?

① Clothing became a symbol of desire for stability and hierarchy to the nobility.
② Fine clothes were seen as a confirmation of one's virtue in the Renaissance.
③ The consumption of luxury goods lent itself to a moral and national matter.
④ The dynamics of sartorial customs changed people's sense of self and cultural sensitivity.

There are some research projects which demonstrate the positive aspects of incorporating cooperative discourse styles typical of women into public domain. Some scholars compare male and female interviewers and show how female interviewers encourage more open and more equal discussion through their interactive strategies. It has been pointed out that in professions such as psycho-therapy and counselling, where more "female" interactive patterns are highly valued, women are a significant presence. On the other hand, women attempting to pursue careers in the public domain will continue to encounter problems. If they adopt a more adversarial, more "male," interactive style, they are in danger of being labelled "unfeminine." If they attempt to retain a more cooperative style of interaction, they risk being viewed as ineffectual. As women enter the workforce in greater numbers and with higher expectations, it remains to be seen whether the more cooperative discourse style which women are skillful in will be welcomed in the public sphere as a new resource, or whether it will be challenged. More ⓐ _____ forms of discrimination against women are slowly being eradicated. But the continuing marginalization of women in the professions, and the fact that women are still having difficulty progressing in their chosen career, suggests that other ⓑ _____ means of discrimination are still at work.

33 윗글의 제목으로 가장 적절한 것은?

① Gender, Education, and Ethics
② Precious Resources for Women
③ Women, Language, and Career
④ Challenging Feminine Ideologies

34 윗글의 내용과 가장 가까운 것은?

① 여성이 직장에서 인정받기 위해서는 남성의 담화 스타일에 따라 대화하고 행동해야 한다.
② 여성은 담화 스타일로 인해서 직장에서 불이익을 받지 않는다.
③ 공공 분야에서 남성과 여성의 언어 차이는 점차적으로 사라져 가고 있다.
④ 상담이나 심리 치료 분야 직종에서 여성의 언어 스타일은 가치 있는 것으로 인정을 받고 있다.

35 윗글의 빈칸 ⓐ와 ⓑ에 들어갈 가장 적절한 표현은?

① overt – covert
② intense – relaxed
③ marginal – crucial
④ exclusive – inclusive

Although their resistance to antibiotics has been built up over a long period of time, bacteria actually replicate extraordinarily quickly, and any resistance developed is also duplicated as they divide. In addition, those bacteria carrying resistance genes happen to spread those genes further via 'horizontal gene transfer', a process whereby one bacterium passes on the resistance gene from another without even needing to be its parent. What makes the spread of these strains more difficult to control is that it occurs in a cyclical process. In the case of humans, when a person becomes infected and the resistant bacteria set up home in the gut, the ⓐ sufferer has two choices: look for help or stay at home. In seeking medical assistance, whether through an appointment to visit their local doctor, or taking themselves to hospital, they contaminate other patients, later to be discharged and sent home. The resistant bacteria then spread out into the local community. This is also the end result if the infected person decides not to seek any medical assistance at all: They keep the bacteria at home and allow them to breed without treatment.

36 Which of the following is a synonym for ⓐ sufferer in the text above?

① pesticide　　　　② defendant　　　　③ contagion

④ victim　　　　⑤ hospitalized

37 Which of the following is the most appropriate title for the text above?

① The Dangers of Antibiotic Resistance

② Should You Visit The Doctor?

③ How Are Bacteria Changing?

④ Cross-Contamination of Antibiotic Resistant Bacteria

⑤ How Does a Contamination Spread?

38 **What is the key argument made in the text above?**

① Bacteria change over time through 'horizontal gene transfer'.

② Bacteria are becoming more dangerous.

③ Sufferers are conflicted about seeking help.

④ It is better to remain home if you are infected.

⑤ Bacteria pass on resistance to each other.

In a fascinating experiment, researchers investigated the impact of photos on children's memories for events that had actually happened (true memories) and events that had never happened (false memories). In each of three interview sessions, 10-year-old children were shown a series of four photographs: three real photos provided by parents depicting events that occurred when the children were about 6 years old and one false photo (a photo of a hot air balloon). For half the children, the photo showed a group of unknown people in the balloon's basket (child-absent condition). For the other half, the photo had been doctored using Adobe Photoshop so that an image of the child along with some family members was inserted among other people in the basket (child-present condition). In reality, of course, none of the children had actually been in a hot air balloon. The researchers found that almost all of the children reported memories for the events pictured in the real photos. More importantly, many of the children also reported memories of riding in the hot air balloon, whether their picture appeared in the photo or not. False memories occurred significantly more often, however, when children had seen themselves in the photo (about 47%) than they had not (about 18%).

39 윗글의 제목으로 가장 적절한 것은?

① Riding in a Hot Air Balloon
② Memorizing Events in Photos
③ Interviewing Children with Photos
④ Creating False Memories in Children
⑤ Investigating Photos with Technologies

40 윗글의 내용과 일치하지 않는 것은?

① 실험에 참가한 아이들의 나이는 10세였다.
② 부모들은 아이들이 6세 즈음에 찍었던 사진들을 제공했다.
③ 아이들이 열기구를 타고 있는 사진들은 조작된 것이었다.
④ 모든 아이들은 실제로 열기구를 탄 적이 없었다고 보고했다.
⑤ 거의 모든 아이들은 진짜 사진들에 관한 사건들을 기억했다.

02 주제

글의 전체적인 이해 여부를 묻는 문제로 제목을 묻는 문제보다는 주제문을 중심으로 좀 더 자세히 주제를 형성할 수 있으며, 글의 핵심 내용을 요약한 부분으로 요지를 들 수 있다. 보통 설명과 논증의 글에서 주제나 요지를 묻는 문제가 많으며, 편입 시험에서는 주제와 요지가 큰 분별없이 혼용되고 있다.

01 질문 유형

What is the passage mainly about?

What is the most appropriate theme of the passage?

Which of the following is the main topic of the passage?

The main theme of the passage is _____.

02 문제 풀이 전략

❶ **주제문을 찾는다.**

설명이나 논증을 토대로 하는 경우, 설명의 경우에는 정보 제공의 목적으로, 논증의 경우에는 필자의 주장을 펼쳐서 상대방을 설득하려 하기에 주제문이 제시된다. 이러한 주제문은 중심 소재와도 밀접한 관련이 있으며, 반복되는 어구나 핵심 표현이 존재한다.

❷ **글 속에 주제를 뒷받침하는 문장이 존재한다.**

필자가 드러내고자 하는 내용의 정당성 내지는 타당성을 부여하기 위하여, 혹은 독자들의 이해를 증진시키기 위하여 주제문 뒤에 뒷받침해 주는 문장들이 나오게 된다. 즉 부연과 예시로 이루어진 문장들은 결국 주제를 선명히 부각시키기 위함이다.

❸ **글 전체의 논리에 근거하여 주제를 추론한다.**

주제를 고르는 문제는 필자의 의견이나 주장이 드러난 글 속의 중심 사상을 고르는 것으로, 글의 흐름을 파악하면 풀 수 있는 경우가 대부분이다. 주제문이 제시되어 있으면 주제문을, 주제문이 제시되어 있지 않다면 구체적인 진술이 아닌 일반적이고 추상적인 진술 가운데에서 정답을 고를 수 있다. 즉 필자의 주장이나 의견이 들어간 부분을 주의하면서 읽어 나가야 한다는 것이다. 답을 고른 이후에 주제를 뒷받침하는 구체적인 근거를 찾아보면서 정답을 잘 골랐는지 확인해 보는 것도 좋은 방법이다.

No wise person will marry for beauty mainly. It may exercise a powerful attraction in the first place, but it is found to be of comparatively little consequence afterwards. To marry a handsome figure without character, fine features unbeautified by sentiment or good nature, is the most deplorable of mistakes. As even the finest landscape, seen daily, becomes monotonous, so does the most beautiful face, unless a beautiful nature shines through it. The beauty of today becomes commonplace tomorrow. Whereas goodness displayed through the most ordinary feature is, perennially lovely.

→ 아름다움을 경치와 비교함으로써 무상함을 드러내고 있다.

→ 결국 아름다움이란 시간이 지나면 껍질에 불과할 뿐이며, 그 이상도 이하도 아니라는 핵심을 담은 주제문이다.

Q. Which of the following is the topic sentence of this passage?

① Goodness displayed through the most ordinary feature.
② It [beauty] may exercise a powerful attraction in the first place.
③ The beauty of today becomes commonplace tomorrow.
④ The finest landscape, seen daily, becomes monotonous.

→ 본문의 주제문을 그대로 인용한 핵심 문장이다. 이 문장이 주제문이 되어서 글의 핵심을 이끈다.

정답　③

해석　**다음 중 본문의 주제는 무엇인가?**

현명한 사람이라면 대개는 아름답다는 이유로 결혼하지는 않을 것이다. 처음에는 아름다움이 강한 매력을 발휘할 수 있을지 모르지만, 시간이 지나면 비교적 중요하지 않다는 것이 밝혀진다. 인품은 없고 단지 외양만 잘생긴 사람이나, 감성이나 온화한 성격을 통해 아름다워지지 않고 단지 이목구비만 뚜렷할 뿐인 사람과 결혼한다는 것은 실수 중에서도 가장 통탄할 실수이다. 심지어 아름다운 경치도 매일 보면 단조로워지듯이, 아주 아름다운 얼굴도, 그 속에 아름다운 품성이 빛을 발하지 않으면, 그와 같을(단조로워질) 뿐이다. 오늘의 아름다움이 내일에는 평범한 것으로 된다. 반면에 가장 평범한 이목구비에 드러나는 미덕은 해를 더할수록 사랑스럽다.
① 미덕은 가장 평범한 이목구비를 통해 드러난다.
② 그것[아름다움]은 우선은 강한 매력을 발휘할 수 있을지 모른다.
③ 오늘의 아름다움이 내일에는 평범한 것으로 된다.
④ 가장 아름다운 경치도 매일 보면 단조로워진다.

해설   본문의 주제는 아무리 외양이 아름다워도 내면의 아름다움이 없으면 소용이 없다는 것이다. 보기 중에서 이에 해당되는 것은 ③이다. 참고로 ④에서 언급된 경치는 본문에서 아름다움의 지속성에 관한 예로서 등장한 것일 뿐, 사람의 아름다움에 관해 말하는 본문의 주제와는 직접적 연관성이 떨어진다. 따라서 비록 아름다움에 관해 말하긴 해도 ④는 답이 될 수 없다.

어휘   **exercise** ⓥ 발휘하다   **of consequence** 중요한   **character** ⓝ 성격, 인품

figure ⓝ 인물, 외양   **feature** ⓝ 이목구비   **good nature** 온화함

deplorable ⓐ 개탄스러운, 통탄할 만한   **commonplace** ⓐ 평범한

perennially ⓐ 지속적으로, 영원히

01 What is the most appropriate theme of the passage?

People first traveled on their own two feet. Later, people tamed animals and rode them. They used many different kinds of animals, such as oxen, camels, and elephants. The animals people rode most often, however, belonged to the horse family, which includes horses, donkeys, and mules. Next, men and women built wagons that they attached to the animals, so more people could travel at one time. This was a big "step" forward. Why? Because it was the first time people used a wheel. The discovery of the wheel made traveling much easier and faster. Today our automobiles move along the highways with speed and comfort.

① The role of transportation in human history
② How people have utilized animals over the years
③ The development of transportation in human history
④ Diversity in traveling culture throughout the world

02 What is the main theme of the passage?

We have all experienced the frustration of forgetting a name or face, or not being able to remember what it was that we went into a shop to buy. Such incidents may be early warning signs that the brain's performance is declining, and that we need to exercise it more. Michael DeBakey, asked how he maintains the mental energy of a young man, said: "We say of muscles, 'Use them or lose them'. Well, the same applies to the mind: the more you use it, the better it functions." He believes the greatest threat to mental vigour is sitting mindlessly in front of the television. "There are so many better ways to stimulate the mind."

① Improving brain power
② Cherishing our memory
③ Evaluating mind control
④ Strengthening muscles

03 What is the main point of the passage?

Even if globalization is generating an increasing degree of homogenization, the world is still a highly diverse place. One still finds marked differences in culture, economy, and politics as well as in the natural environment. Such diversity is so vast that it cannot be readily extinguished even by the most powerful forces of globalization. In fact, globalization often provokes a strong reaction on the part of local people, making them all the more determined to maintain what is distinctive about their way of life. Thus, globalization is understandable only if one also examines the diversity that continues to characterize the world and perhaps most importantly, the tension between these two forces — the homogenization of globalization and the reaction against it in terms of protecting cultural and political diversity.

① Globalization is characterized by converging and homogenizing forces.
② Diversity and globalization should be understood as inseparable.
③ Local diversity is not always in conflict with global homogenization.
④ The trend of globalization is pervasive but its benefits are uneven.

[01~02]

Cultural differences in how children speak in the one-word stage bolster the idea that what children hear others say influences what they themselves say. Unlike American children, Korean toddlers show a "verb spurt" before a "noun spurt"; similarly, Mandarin-speaking toddlers utter more verbs than nouns as they and their mothers play with toys. Mothers from both Asian groups pepper their speech with many more verbs and action sequences saying such things as "what are you doing?" and "You put the car in the garage"; American mothers, _____, use far more nouns, e.g., "That's a ball," and ask questions that require a noun as an answer, e.g., "What is it?"

01 What is the most appropriate theme of the passage?

① How children's speech develops
② Nouns and verbs in child language
③ Cultural differences in language development
④ Effective question types for young children
⑤ Differences between American and Asian mothers

02 Which best fits in the blank?

① for example
② in addition
③ as a result
④ in short
⑤ in contrast

In different countries, colors other than white are worn by the bride or used as part of the wedding ceremony. In certain Asian countries and in the Middle East, red and orange are considered symbols of joy and happiness. In Chinese cultures, wedding invitations are usually red and gold as these are colors symbolic of wealth and happiness. Wedding guests give gifts of money to the newlyweds in small red envelopes. Not all cultures, however, consider money a suitable gift. In many Western countries, especially the U. K., wedding guests give the bride and groom household items that they may need for their new home. As part of many traditional wedding ceremonies, a bride wears a veil. Wearing a veil that covers the head and face is a tradition that is over 2,000 years old. Veils were originally worn as a sign of secrecy and modesty and could only be removed by the husband after the ceremony. Today, many brides wear a veil, but only for decoration. In some countries, a veil is placed between the bride and groom during the wedding ceremony so that they cannot see or touch each other until they are married.

03 윗글의 주제(topic)로 가장 적합한 것을 고르시오.

① the traditional significance of a veil
② various wedding ceremonies in different countries
③ colors and their different associations in various cultures
④ the symbolic meaning of various wedding gifts

04 다음 중 윗글의 내용과 일치하는 것을 고르시오.

① In the past, many brides wore a veil for the sake of decoration.
② In the U. K., wedding guests regard money as a suitable gift for newlyweds.
③ In Asia and the Middle East, it is not allowed to use red and orange in wedding ceremonies.
④ In some countries, the bride and groom are not supposed to see each other during the wedding ceremony

[05~07]

The number of people over 65 is going to increase greatly by the year 2100. Although demographers generally agree that population aging represents a "success story," with increasing numbers of people worldwide enjoying longer lives, they also note the sustained increase in the number of older people poses many challenges to their societies. In the United States, the government gives money to retired workers in the form of social security. However, this often isn't enough for retirees to live on; they must supplement it with their own investments and insurance. In China and most Asian countries, children bear the responsibility of caring for their elderly parents. As those societies change, _____, it is becoming more and more difficult for children to care for parents as well as their own families, especially since the implementation of the one-child policy in China. As people live longer lives than ever before, the entire world is affected.

05 What is the main theme of the passage?

① Only a few demographers agree that increased life expectancy is a sign of success.
② Societies with different cultures struggle in different ways to care for their elderly.
③ Population aging is a result of declining fertility rates and increasing longevity.
④ The world's population is aging fast, especially in China and most Asian countries.

06 Which best fits the blank?

① therefore
③ however
② furthermore
④ otherwise

07 Which is the least likely to be inferred from the passage?

① In the United States, a tax increase might be necessary to help support the aging population.
② The cost of caring for the elderly will increase because obesity is on the rise in many parts of the world.
③ In China, many people feel that it is their duty to take care of their aging parents.
④ As time goes on, the aging population has important implications for economic growth and well-being of all societies.

In 2017, the smartphone turned 10 years old; that means that gradually science is catching up, and new research is emerging about its world-changing impact. Having a computer in the palm of our hands has given us access to each other's lives — and an insight into our own lives — that was totally unprecedented before the internet. Many people may no longer even remember a time before social media. But is it making us any happier?

There's been a lot of talk recently that social media has a negative impact on our mental health, and you might be looking at the beginning of the new year as an opportunity for digital detoxing. The early studies suggest that, as well as making us more connected than ever before and giving us exhilarating hits of dopamine, social media usage is associated with symptoms of depression, anxiety and loneliness in some people.

Social networking giant Facebook responded to these concerns in a blogpost last month, claiming that it's down to how you use social media rather than social media itself being inherently bad. That's true — many technologies have the capacity to cause harm _____. But that doesn't mean that we shouldn't interrogate the design and impacts of social media in its current form. Indeed, Mark Zuckerberg has hinted that this will be a goal for Facebook in 2018: this week, he wrote that one of his challenges in the year ahead will be "making sure that time spent on Facebook is time well spent."

08 **Which of the following is most appropriate for the black?**

① by absorbing our concentration too much
② depending on the frequency of their use
③ if used improperly
④ for our ignorance of their intricacies
⑤ if managed strictly

09 **The best topic of the passage would be** _____.

① the most effective way to use social media
② the impact of social media on our mental well-being
③ the usefulness of social media
④ the radical innovation of the smartphone
⑤ the rapid change that social media brings to our life

Once the domain of childhood curiosity, the question of why we can't tickle ourselves is now exciting neuroscientists. To understand their interest, consider this: every time your body moves, it creates sensations that could potentially confuse you in all kinds of ways. Just imagine the chaos if every time one of your hands brushed your leg, you assumed that someone was fondling or attacking you. Being able to distinguish between your movement and the actions of others is a central part of our sense of self and agency. To find an answer to the question, Sarah-Jayne Blackemore scanned subjects' brains as her colleagues tickled the palms of their hands and as the participants attempted to do so themselves. From the resulting brain activity, she concluded that whenever we move our limbs, the brain's cerebellum produces precise predictions of the body's movements and then sends a second shadow signal that damps down activity in the somatosensory cortex where tactile feelings are processed. The Ⓐ _____ is that when we tickle ourselves, we don't feel the sensations with the same intensity as we would if they had come from someone else, and so we remain calm.

10 Which is the passage mainly about?

① the importance of childish curiosity
② the unreliability of human sensation
③ a recent advancement in brain scanning technology
④ a brain mechanism for distinguishing self and others

11 Which best fits into the blank Ⓐ?

① result   ② reason   ③ evidence   ④ prediction

12 Which is true according to the passage?

① People who are easy to tickle are intelligent.
② Palms are the most sensitive part of the human body.
③ People believe that they are attacked when tickled by themselves.
④ We cannot tickle ourselves because we predict that we will be tickled.

Whereas the discovery of the double-helical structure of DNA was originally revered, it is now thought to have opened a door to an uncertain future. The scientists were able to put new DNA parts into living cells; immediately, those activities were looked upon Ⓐ _____. It was considered that human civilization could be destroyed by some disease that could be engineered into cells. People realized that calls needed to be made for strict rules to control such research. Because of this, it took a while before scientists discovered recombinant-DNA technology. The controlling rules did not get put into action, fortunately, so when the fears about DNA technology went unfounded, all attempts at regulation, even moderate, dissipated.

13 Which of the following is most appropriate for the blank Ⓐ?

① suspiciously　　　　　　② favorably
③ impartially　　　　　　④ approvingly

14 Which of the following is best for the main idea of the passage?

① Successful attempts at regulations on DNA technology
② The unreliability of biology technology
③ Groundless fear of DNA technology
④ The potential of biological advances

I learned this, at least, by my experiment; that if one advances confidently in the direction of his dreams, and endeavors to live the life which he has imagined, he will meet with a success unexpected in common hours. He will put some things behind, will pass an invisible boundary; new, universal, and more liberal laws will begin to establish themselves around and within him; or the old laws be expanded, and interpreted in his favor in a more liberal sense, and he will live with the license of a higher order of beings. In proportion as he simplifies his life, the laws of the universe will appear less complex, and solitude will not be solitude, (A) _____ poverty poverty, (B) _____ weakness weakness. If you have built castles in the air, your work need not be lost; that is where they should be. Now put the foundations under them.

15 Which of the following is the main idea of the passage?

① Simplify your clutters in your life.
② Challenge your limits and hardships.
③ Have your dream and keep working on it.
④ Be more objective to yourself and the world.

16 Which of the following pairs completes the blanks (A) and (B)?

① and − and
② and − nor
③ nor − and
④ nor − nor

Do you want to successfully lead an organization? Then start mixing drinks rather than going to business school, writes Helen Rothberg in *The Perfect Mix*. Although Rothberg is now a management consultant and a professor of strategy at Marist College, she argues that she learned her most valuable leadership skills while she was tending bar during graduate school. Here are a few of them: reading body language to analyze interpersonal situations, which is useful in tamping down barroom brawls; managing charming but deadbeat workers, great for (A) _____ waiters who are more show than substance; and communicating key details. Communication of details is crucial because at her bar, sales started plummeting after a boss revamped the menu without explaining it to his waitstaff, who then couldn't explain it to their customers. Rothberg compares bartending to leading an organization, saying: "Sometimes you stir, sometimes you shake, and sometimes you blend. And sometimes you just serve it up neat, just as it is."

17 Which of the following is the main theme of the passage?

① Bartending is better than business school.
② Leadership skills come from interpersonal analysis.
③ Bartending can pay you through graduate school.
④ Going to graduate school is necessary for leaders.

18 Which of the following best fits into (A)?

① making out
② weeding out
③ branching out
④ selling out

We can sometimes observe people whose general intellectual abilities are much lower than average but whose talent in a certain area is extraordinary. They are often called "savants." One interesting example of savants is 'language savant.' Christopher had a lot of difficulties doing routine things due to his low general intelligence. He needed help even when he buttoned his shirt or vacuumed the carpet. However, there was one thing he could do extremely well; he was able to speak and write more than 10 languages. He had not been taught those languages by language teachers or any specialists. Rather, he acquired them in his own way, like reading grammar books by himself. How can we reconcile the conflict between his poor intelligence and superb linguistic ability? One possibility seems to be to propose that language faculty has little do to with general intelligence. In other words, linguistic ability neither reflects nor presupposes general intellectual ability. In fact, such a proposal has been made by some linguists and psychologist. _____ , little has been known so far about what makes it possible for language savants to have extraordinary talent. To know the truth, lots of research would be necessary on the ability of savants.

19 Fill in the blank.

① However   ② In addition

③ To sum up   ④ For instance

20 What is the passage about?

① The necessity of foreign language education for the disabled

② The definition of savants and their limitations in language learning

③ The importance of self-study in savants' language acquisition

④ The mystery of language savants' talent and low intelligence

21 Which of the following is correct about Christopher?

① He had an average nonverbal IQ while his language skills are unusual.

② He could do only simple jobs by himself such as vacuum cleaning

③ Grammar books were helpful for him to learn many languages by himself

④ He had a chance to learn more than 10 languages from language specialists.

The ultimate failure of Bohr and Einstein to continue their dialogues together symbolizes the degree of fragmentation that exists in the field of physics today. Despite their close friendship and the energy they brought to their encounters, the two men eventually reached the point where they had nothing more to say to each other. This break in communication was a result of the different and incompatible ways in which the informal language of physics was being used. Each protagonist was using certain terms in particular ways and laying stress on different aspects of the interpretation. A deeper analysis of this whole question shows that what was really at issue was the different notions of order involved. Bohr and Einstein both held to subtly different ideas of what the order of physics, and of nature, should be and this led to an essential break in their dialogue, a break which is reflected in the distance that lies between relativity and the quantum theory today. In particular, Bohr believed that the order of movement of a particle would admit ambiguity while Einstein felt that such a possibility was too absurd to contemplate. The source of this failure in communication between the two giants of modern physics therefore lay in their incompatible notions of order.

22 What is the passage mainly about?

① The cooperative measures that both Bohr and Einstein made
② The prospect of modern physics after Bohr and Einstein
③ The notions of order which Bohr and Einstein theorized differently
④ The way modern physics has eventually come to a dead end

23 What can be inferred from the passage?

① Einstein's relativity theory and Bohr's quantum theory can be seen as two different interpretations of order.
② The break in communication between the two scientists was due to the different orders contained in their theories.
③ Today it is generally acknowledged that science may not be the proper tool with which we can grasp reality.
④ Bohr and Einstein were fundamentally different in their methods of physics research.

If *2001: A Space Odyssey* was forcefully categorized into a single film type or genre, the answer would almost definitely be Science Fiction. Containing many Sci-Fi tropes, *2001* certainly uses several motifs of the genre. Travelling millions of miles through space, various different types of spacecraft, astronauts floating through space without the restraints of gravity—all of these images are perpetually attached to Science Fiction cinema, and rightly so. Why then, despite employing a range of classical genre elements, does *2001* feel like so much more than just a Science Fiction film? A possible explanation is the high-brow themes and ideologies that diverge themselves in *2001*, which, in the vast majority of other Science Fiction films, are largely avoided. Perhaps with the exception of Blade Runner, no other Sci-Fi blockbuster can claim to address existentialism, theology and the condition of the human purpose to such a complex, intellectual and elaborate degree; very few films at all can declare as much philosophical consciousness as 2001.

24 What is this passage mainly about?

① The ideological character of the Sci-Fi genre
② The philosophical aspects of 2001: A Space Odyssey
③ The motifs of the Sci-Fi genre found in 2001: A Space Odyssey
④ The special techniques with which 2001: A Space Odyssey was made

25 According to the passage, which of the following is true?

① Blade Runner shares essential themes with *2001: A Space Odyssey*.
② *2001: A Space Odyssey* cannot in fact be categorized into the Sci-Fi genre.
③ Sci-Fi films have only a few common features as the genre is relatively new.
④ The condition of the human purpose is one of the common motifs of Sci-Fi films.

CHAPTER 03

요지

편입 시험에서 요지는 주제, 제목과 더불어 전체적으로 글을 이해하였는지를 묻는 질문 유형이다. 최근에는 글의 요약을 묻는 문제 유형으로 출제되는 경우도 있다. 주의할 것은 글의 내용과 일치하며, 동시에 글의 범위와도 일치 하는 정답을 고르는 것이다. 본문의 핵심을 포섭하고 있는지를 주의해야 한다.

01 질문 유형

What is the main idea of the following passage?
What is the main idea expressed in the passage?
Which of the following best expresses the main idea of the passage?
Which of the following best states the main idea of the entire passage?
Choose the statement that best expresses the main idea of the paragraph.

02 문제 풀이 전략

❶ **문장의 핵심을 파악하라.**
글 전체의 흐름을 파악하고, 전체 줄거리를 요약한 것이 요지라고 보면 된다. 그러므로 이렇게 요지를 고르는 경우에는 첫 문장이 중요한 경우가 많다. 일반적으로 저자는 본인이 말하고 싶은 바를 처음에 제시하면서 글을 쓰는 경우가 많기 때문이며, 이는 영어가 기본적으로 두괄식 구조를 갖기 때문이기도 하다. 하지만 상대방의 주장을 먼저 명시하고 이에 대한 반박으로 글을 쓰는 경우도 있으므로 주의해야 한다.

❷ **전체를 포괄해야 한다.**
개별적인 내용은 답이 될 수 없으며, 전체의 범위와 일치하는 범위 내에서 저자가 글 속에서 나타내고자 하는 부분에 유념하면서 읽어 내려간다. 범위가 일치하지 않는다거나, 단락의 어느 일부만을 지칭하는 것은 전체 글의 주제나 요지가 될 수 없다. 범위 설정을 잘해서, 필자의 의견이나 주장이 들어 있는, 전체를 다 포괄하는 부분을 답으로 골라야 한다.

❸ **반복되는 idea를 중심으로 요약해 본다.**
단락의 핵심적인 내용을 설명하기 위하여 필자가 핵심적인 부분을 반복하는 경향이 있으므로, 중요한 idea가 여러 번 반복되는지를 눈여겨볼 필요가 있다. 필자의 주장도 역시 서론, 본론, 결론에서 골고루 자신이 말하고 자 하는 바를 제시하게 되므로 keyword를 중심으로 main idea를 골라 가야 한다. 요지를 파악하는 능력을 배양하기 위해서는 단락을 요약하는 연습을 하면 좋다. 처음에는 몇몇 단어를 중심으로 키워드를 찾는 연습부터 시작해서 단락의 핵심이 다 들어간 문장으로 요약하는 연습을 해야 한다.

전략의 적용

Communication scholar James McCroskey, who has studied communication apprehension for more than twenty years, defines it as "an individual's level of fear or anxiety associated with either real or anticipated communication with another person or persons." As this definition suggests, communication apprehension is not limited to public speaking situations. We may feel worried about almost any kind of communication encounter. If, for example, you are preparing to have a conversation with a romantic partner who, you think, is about to suggest ending the relationship, if your professor has called you into her office to discuss your poor attendance record, or if a police officer has motioned you to pull off the road for a "conversation," you know what communication apprehension is all about.

→ 의사소통의 불안감이 특정 인에게 한정된 것이 아니라 모두에게 공통적이라는 핵심 내용을 제공하고 있다.

Q. What is the main idea of the following passage?

① Communication apprehension is hard to define.
② Communication apprehension is hard to overcome while interaction with others.
③ Communication apprehension is closely related to the level of anxiety and fear.
④ Communication apprehension can occur in various kinds of situations.

→ 본문의 핵심적인 내용을 포섭 하고 있는 보기를 선택한다.

정답   ④

해석   **다음 본문의 요지는 무엇인가?**
의사소통 불안에 관해 20년 넘게 연구해 온 의사소통 분야의 학자인 Kames McCroskey는 의사소통 불안을 "다른 사람 또는 사람들과의 실제 또는 예측되는 의사소통과 관련된 공포 또는 불안의 개인별 수준"으로 정의한 다. 이 같은 정의에서 나타나듯이, 의사소통 불안은 사람들 앞에서 공개적으로 말하는 경우에만 국한되는 것은 아니다. 우리는 거의 모든 종류의 의사소통과 조우하면서 이에 불안감을 가질 수 있다. 예를 들어, 여러분이 이 제 그만 관계를 정리하자고 말할 것만 같다는 생각이 드는 애인과 대화를 해야 할 준비를 하는 경우, 교수님이 여러분의 저조한 출석률에 관해 이야기를 좀 하자고 교수실로 호출하는 경우, 경찰관에 여러분에게 차를 잠깐 대고 "대화를 나누자"고 몸짓으로 지시하는 경우 등에서 여러분은 의사소통 불안이 무엇에 관한 것인지 알 수 있을 것이다.

① 의사소통 불안은 정의하기 힘들다

② 의사소통 불안은 다른 사람과의 상호 작용에 있어 극복하기 힘들다.

③ 의사소통 불안은 불안과 공포의 정도와 밀접한 관계가 있다.

④ 의사소통 불안은 다양한 경우에서 발생할 수 있다.

해설 ④의 경우, "의사소통 불안은 사람들 앞에서 공개적으로 말하는 경우에만 국한되는 것은 아니다. 우리는 거의 모든 종류의 의사소통과 조우하면서 이에 불안감을 가질 수 있다."라는 문장이 암시하는 것과, 애인·교수님·경찰관 등의 예시를 통해 보여 준 것은, 의사소통 불안은 특정 상황에 국한되어 생겨나는 것이 아니라 여러 상황에서도 생겨날 수 있다는 것이다. 이를 통해 ④가 문장 전체의 주제임을 알 수 있으며, 따라서 답은 ④가 된다. ①의 경우, 본문에서 따옴표로 처리된 곳이 바로 의사소통 불안의 명확한 정의이다. 따라서 답이 될 수 없다. ②의 경우, 본문에는 극복에 관한 내용이 나와 있지 않기 때문에 답이 될 수 없다. ③의 경우, 본문의 따옴표 안에 제시된 의사소통 불안의 정의에서 "an individual's level of fear or anxiety(공포 또는 불안의 개인별 수준)"을 언급하고는 있지만, 그 개인별 수준과 의사소통 불안에 관한 관계가 어떠한지는 본문에 나와 있지 않다. 따라서 ③도 답이 될 수 없다.

어휘
communication apprehension 의사소통 불안
anticipated ⓐ 예상된
encounter ⓝ 마주침, 조우
attendance ⓝ 출석
pull off 차를 길 한쪽에 대다

be associated with ～와 관련 있는
be limited to ～에 국한된
is about to 막 ～하려고 하다
motion ⓥ 몸짓으로 지시하다
overcome ⓥ ～을 극복하다

01 What is the main idea of the passage?

Migration for better opportunity is as old as human history, but today it's likely that more people are living outside their countries of birth than ever before. Remittance is what economists call these person-to-family transfers, whisked home by electronic banking services or hand-delivered by couriers. Tiny in individual increments, aggregate remittances now constitute massive flows of capital into the world's developing countries. Of the many places from which the money is sent — the richest countries, where employers are willing to put needy foreigners to work — the United States tops the list.

① Migration causes massive flows of money into developing countries.
② International remittance occurs the most out of the United States.
③ Remittance is defined as a person-to-family transfer of money.
④ Migration is as complex and shifting as weather.
⑤ Migration has radically changed human history.

02 Which of the following best states the main idea of the paragraph?

Not all of the islands in the Caribbean Sea are the tops of a volcanic mountain range that begins under the sea. Some are the tops of older, nonvolcanic mountains, mountains that have been covered in coral. Coral is a hard, rocklike material that is made of the shells of sea animals called coral polyps. When coral polyps are alive, they attach to any base they can find, such as old mountaintops under the sea. When the polyps die, they leave their shells behind as rocky covering. Then, new polyps attach to this covering. The result is a coral island.

① All of the islands in the Caribbean Sea are the tops of old, underwater volcanoes.
② There are many small islands in the Caribbean Sea.
③ Coral is formed by sea animals called coral polyps.
④ Many of the Caribbean islands are the tops of old mountains that are covered with coral.

03 Which of the following best summarizes the passage? 덕성여대 2018

It is believed that the added stress causes people to partake in unhealthy behaviors, such as drinking, and instead of being motivational, friends' social media updates could actually be making things worse. In turn, this could raise the risk of dying over the next two decades by more than 70 percent, finds research. The expert's warning comes after two US studies revealed that worrying about exercise could be a health risk. Last year a study by Stanford University, which looked at more than 60,000 people, found those who thought they were more inactive than average for their age group were 71 percent more likely to die in the following 21 years than those who believed they were more active. It is thought that this could be because people who worry they are unfit are more negative, which in turn fuels feelings of stress and depression. The second study, by Harvard University in 2007, showed hotel workers who were told they met healthy exercise guidelines through cleaning actually lost weight. Researchers found these workers had lower blood pressure and body fat if they believed they were active — regardless of how much activity they actually did.

① Worrying about how much exercise you are getting could cause a premature death.
② Negative feelings such as stress and depression would lead to a serious health risk.
③ Inactive people are more likely to die much earlier than active people.
④ Physical exercises override psychological factors in controlling stress and weight.

[01~02]

The enormous and fascinating variety of clothing may express a person's status or social position. Several hundred years ago in Europe, Japan, and China, there were many highly detailed sumptuary laws — i.e., strict regulations concerning how each social class could dress. In Europe, for example, only royal families could wear fur, purple silk, or gold cloth. In Japan, a farmer could breed silkworms, but he couldn't wear silk. In many societies, a lack of clothing indicated an absence of status. In ancient Egypt, for instance, children who had no social status wore no clothes until they were about twelve. These days, in most societies (especially in the West), rank or status is exhibited through regulation of dress only in the military, where the appearance or absence of certain metal buttons or stars signifies the dividing line between ranks. With this exception of the military, the divisions between different classes of society are becoming less clear. The clientele of a Paris café, for example, might include both working-class people and members of the highest society, but how can one tell the difference when everyone is wearing denim jeans?

01 윗글의 대의(main idea)로 가장 적합한 것을 고르시오.

① A lack of clothing indicates an absence of status.
② Laws used to regulate how people could dress.
③ Clothing has usually indicated a social status, but this is less true in today's world.
④ Clothing has been worn for different reasons since the beginning of history.

02 윗글의 내용과 일치하지 <u>않는</u> 것으로 가장 적합한 것을 고르시오.

① Strict laws in some countries used to regulate what people of each social class could wear.
② Rich people wear more beautiful clothing than poor people do.
③ Even these days, rank or status can be seen through clothing among particular groups of people.
④ Today, the divisions between social classes are becoming less clear from the clothing that people wear.

Every winter, especially in cold climates, people sink into the familiar round of illness, with coughing and sore throat being two of the most common symptoms. Sometimes other conditions, such as fever, are also present and people wonder whether they have simply caught a cold or are suffering from the flu. Since the flu can be quite serious, it is wise to be aware of the differences. Coughing, blocked nose, and sore throat are the most common symptoms of colds, and they are often present with the flu as well. Chest pain may also accompany both illnesses, but with the flu it has a tendency to become severe. The symptoms particularly (A) the flu, which are rarely, if ever, present with the cold, are headache, high fever, and pains all over the body. Often the flu begins with vague body pains and headache, then quickly gets worse as the victim's body temperature rises. People with the flu may find themselves in bed for several days battling temperatures of 38 − 39 degrees, and may (B) pneumonia, which is serious. Waking moments may be spent coughing continuously. Though there is presently no cure for the common cold, antibiotics can help fight the flu. And getting a flu shot at the beginning of each season is a particularly good idea.

03 What is the main idea of the passage?

① There are several cold-weather illnesses.
② It is important to get a flu shot at the beginning of the winter.
③ Temperatures as high as 39 degrees are not uncommon with the flu.
④ Colds and the flu have many similarities but they also have some differences.

04 According to the passage, which of the following is true?

① There will soon be a cure for colds.
② Colds may lead to more serious illnesses.
③ The flu may lead to more complicated illnesses.
④ People can avoid catching colds if they are careful.

05 Which of the following best fits into (A) and (B)?

	(A)		(B)
①	concerning	–	cause
②	distinguishing	–	carry on
③	pertaining to	–	end up with
④	differentiating	–	become aware of

Some nineteen hundred years ago the Roman teacher Quintilian insisted that a good speaker must first of all be a good man. Listeners, he maintained, cannot separate what is said from the person who says it: they are influenced by their impression of the speaker as well as by the arguments he presents.

If a person is habitually devious or unreliable, speech training may give him skills, but it cannot make him effective as a speaker. His actions will contradict his words. He cannot convincingly urge honesty in government if he himself cheats in school or business; his appeal for an open mind in others will go unheeded if he himself is bigoted. Even a speaker's choice of words or arguments betrays his character, for he may habitually appear to dodge issues rather than face them or to say what is popular rather than say what is true or just. A speaker of poor character may succeed for a time, but in the long run he will be found out and his appeals will be (A) _____.

06 빈칸 (A) 에 들어갈 가장 적절한 단어를 고르시오.

① honored
② recognized
③ discounted
④ transformed

07 윗글의 요지로서 가장 적절한 것을 고르시오.

① As a general rule, a speaker can expect the best result of his speech when he acts just.
② Speech training is an essential part for someone who wants to be a good speaker.
③ If he is to influence people, a speaker should pay attention to his choice of words.
④ Even an unreliable person can be a good speaker when he masters some crucial skills.

[08~09]

During the American War of Independence, women were involved in the active fighting in three ways. First, as members of a distinct branch of the Army, referred to as "Women of the Army," women staffed field hospitals and acted as military support in such roles as water carriers. In an emergency, women-water-carriers, who had plenty of opportunity to observe the firing of cannons, could replace wounded comrades. The second way that women were involved in active fighting was as regular troop members who wore men's uniforms and fought side-by-side with their male counterparts. Theoretically, women were not supposed to be recruited into the Army. However, if a woman was a good soldier, no one made an issue of sex. The army was so short of soldiers that boys not yet in their teens were also recruited in violation of the rules. Third, women were occasional fighters affiliated with local military units of Committees of Safety formed to protect the local community.

08 **What is the main idea expressed in the passage?**

① Women were active in combat during the War.
② The Army was successful in teaching women to fire cannons.
③ Women played an important role in military hospitals during the War.
④ The services of women on Committees of Safety were crucial in winning the War.

09 **What is the main reason that women were permitted to fight in the war even if their formal participation was discouraged?**

① Only women were successful as water carriers.
② They were needed to make battle uniform.
③ Colonial women were particularly healthy and strong.
④ The army desperately needed combat soldiers.

[10~11]

Whereas family relationships usually constitute a child's first experience with group life, peer-group interactions soon begin to make their powerful socializing effects felt. From play group to teenage clique, the peer group affords young people many significant learning experiences — how to achieve status in a circle of friends. Peers are equals in a way parents and their children or teachers and their students are not. A parent or teacher sometimes can force young children to obey rules they neither understand nor like, but peers do not have formal authority to do this; thus the true meaning of exchange, cooperation, and equity can be learned more easily in the peer setting. Peer groups increase in importance as the child grows up and reaches maximum influence in adolescence, by which time they sometimes dictate much of a young person's behavior both in and out of school.

10 According to the passage, which of the following would feel the importance of a peer group the most?

① Toddlers
② Elementary school students
③ Kindergarteners
④ High school students
⑤ Adults

11 Which of the following best expresses the main idea of the passage?

① Children learn about cooperation in their peer groups.
② Peer groups are powerful influences in children's lives.
③ Parents can force children to do things that a peer group cannot.
④ Parents have greater influences on children than their teachers do.
⑤ Relationships in and out of school provide learning opportunities for children.

[12~13]

Exactly the same thing, however, is to be observed among men, except that women regard all other women as their competitors, whereas men as a rule only have this feeling towards other men in the same profession. Have you, reader, ever been so imprudent as to praise an artist to another artist? Have you ever praised a politician to another politician of the same party? Have you ever praised an Egyptologist to another Egyptologist? If you have, it is a hundred to one that you will have produced an explosion of jealousy. In the correspondence of Leibniz and Huygens there are a number of letters lamenting the supposed fact that Newton had become insane. "Is it not sad," they write to each other, "that the incomparable genius of Mr. Newton should have become clouded by the loss of reason?" And these two eminent men, in one letter after another, wept crocodile tears with obvious relish. As a matter of fact, the event which they were hypocritically lamenting had not taken place, though a few examples of eccentric behavior had given rise to the rumor.

12 What is the main thesis of this passage?

① Like women, men also experience jealousy, although somewhat differently.
② Newton was once thought to have become insane, but it turned out false.
③ It would be really sad if a genius like Newton lost his mind.
④ Women are more envious than men in that they envy all other women.
⑤ Such eminent persons as Leibniz and Huygens also harbored feelings of jealousy.

13 According to the author, what did Leibniz and Huygens really share in their letters about Newton's alleged loss of reason?

① Obvious sadness and sorrow
② Disguised envy and amusement
③ Criticism of Newton's eccentricity
④ Their wish for Newton's recovery
⑤ Admiration and sympathy

After I had gotten married and had lived in Japan for a while, my Japanese gradually improved to the point where I could take part in simple conversations with my Japanese husband and his family. I also began to notice that often, when I joined in, the others would look startled, and the conversational topic would suddenly (A) _____. After this happened several times, it became clear to me that I was doing something wrong.

Finally, I discovered what my problem was. Even though I was speaking Japanese, I was handling the conversations in a Western way. I realized I was trying to hold Western-style conversations while I was speaking Japanese. Similarly, students in my English classes kept trying to hold Japanese-style conversations even when they were speaking English.

A Western-style conversation between two people is like a game of (B) _____. If I introduce a topic, a conversational ball, I expect you to hit it back, and add something like a reason for agreeing or disagreeing. A Japanese-style conversation, however, is completely different. It's like (C) _____. You wait for your turn, and you always know your place in line.

14 Choose the best expression for (A)?

① burst out   ② commence

③ come to a halt   ④ resume

15 Choose the best word for (B) and (C).

① tennis — basketball   ② tennis — bowling

③ ice-hockey — bowling   ④ ice-hockey — basketball

16 Which one CANNOT be inferred from the passage?

① The author is not a Japanese native.

② The author has been a language teacher.

③ The author has always lived in Japan.

④ The author's Japanese improved enough for her to converse with others.

17 Which one is the best summary?

① People converse differently in Japan than in the West.

② It's important to join in conversations.

③ Getting married helps improve your Japanese.

④ People can converse better when they have an opportunity to live abroad.

Merriam-Webster announced that the personal pronoun *they* was its 2019 Word of the Year, noting that the tiny, unassuming word had undergone a rather radical transformation in usage in recent years, and found itself at the heart of some wide-ranging cultural conversations in the process. "English famously lacks a gender-neutral singular pronoun to correspond neatly with singular pronouns like *everyone* or *someone*, and as a consequence *they* has been used for this purpose for over 600 years," the dictionary publisher explained. "More recently, though, *they* has also been used to refer to one person whose gender identity is non-binary, a sense that is increasingly common in published, edited text, as well as social media and in daily personal interactions between English speakers." In other words, the usual singular pronouns *he* or *she*, rooted as they are in a male-female division of gender, can often prove misleading, inaccurate, or disrespectful when describing a person who doesn't identify strictly as a man or woman. Faced with a lack of satisfying singular options, folks have taken to doing what your high school English teacher might have red-penciled 10 years ago: using the typically plural pronoun *they* (A) _____.

18 **Which of the following is the passage mainly about?**

① Merriam-Webster's word of the year
② The etymology of the pronoun *they*
③ The predicament of *they* in English
④ Culture as a mirror of language

19 **Which of the following best fits into (A)?**

① to indicate plurality
② to describe one person
③ as a first-person pronoun
④ as a gender-specific pronoun

Every citizen has to be accountable for his or her deeds. We all have responsibilities to our peers. This responsibility weighs particularly heavily on scientists precisely because of the (Ⓐ) role played by science in modern society. Scientists understand technical problems and predictions better than the average politician or citizen, and knowledge brings responsibility. While their main purpose is to push forward the frontiers of knowledge, this pursuit should contain an element of pro-social utility, that is, (Ⓑ) to the human community. This means giving some precedence to projects likely to advance the welfare of humankind and the environment, and a total ban on those likely to do harm.

20 **What is the main idea of the above passage?**

① The average politician does not need to understand technical problems.
② All citizens have responsibilities to other members of society.
③ The scientist must recognize his or her social responsibility when pursuing knowledge.
④ Scientists have a better understanding of technical problems than most people.
⑤ Scientists must prioritize the pursuit of knowledge.

21 **Which of the following best fits into (Ⓐ) and (Ⓑ)?**

① surprising — harm
② insignificant — harm
③ dominant — harm
④ insignificant — benefit
⑤ dominant — benefit

The fundamental distinction between commitment and fanaticism is uncertainty. A fanatic is certain. A fanatic has the (A) _____. A fanatic knows what really is happening. A fanatic has the plan. When you understand this, you realize that fanaticism is not limited to just the extreme fringes of civilized society. Fanaticism is alive and well in mainstream society. It arises in all kinds of positions of authority. In fact, I would argue it is the first and most fundamental abuse of all positions of authority. From my standpoint, all true commitment lives in the domain of doubt. Anything less than that is calculation based on a belief that is held as absolute: "If this is the way it is, then this is what we must do." Without uncertainty or doubt, there is no foundation for tolerance. If there (B) _____, which we all generally see as our own, we have no space for the possibility that a different point of view may be valid. Because of that, of course, we have no humility. How can we have humility if we've got the answer?

22 **Which of the following is the most appropriate for the blank (A) and (B)?**

① question – is one right view

② answer – is one right view

③ answer – are multiple views

④ question – are multiple views

23 **According to the passage, which of the following is true?**

① Fanaticism is closely related to true commitment.

② Commitment cherishes the virtue of humbleness and doubt.

③ A meticulous calculation may distinguish fanaticism from commitment.

④ Mild fanaticism has a positive effect on human beings.

24 **Which of the following sentences best summarizes the passage above?**

① To get an ultimate answer, we need both fanaticism and commitment.

② Uncertainty is the cardinal prerequisite for doubt and humility.

③ Doubt distinguishes commitment from fanaticism.

④ The most critical abuse of commitment is fanaticism.

A baby develops the ability to hear by about 30 weeks' gestation, so he can make out his mother's voice for the last two months of pregnancy. Researchers tested 40 American and 40 Swedish newborns to see if they could distinguish between English and Swedish vowel sounds. The scientists gave the babies pacifiers fitted with sensors that counted the number of sucks they made. The researchers inferred the babies' interest in the sound by the amount of sucking they did. American babies consistently sucked more often when hearing Swedish vowel sounds, suggesting that the infants had not heard them before, and Swedish babies sucked more when hearing English vowels. Learning so quickly after birth was unlikely, the researchers concluded, so the babies' understanding the difference between native and nonnative sounds could be attributed only to prenatal learning.

25 Which of the following best expresses the main idea of the passage?

① Newborns react emotionally to native vowel sounds.
② Newborns can recognize their mothers' voices at birth.
③ Babies can learn native sounds even before their birth.
④ Babies learn their own native languages rapidly.

26 According to the passage, newborns suck more frequently when they hear _____.

① nonnative sounds
② their mother talk
③ English vowel sounds
④ new native vocabulary

A basic principle governing the status of older adults is the need to achieve a balance between their contributions to society and the costs of supporting them. The process of modernization and technological development often conflicts with traditions of _____. But the family continues to play an essential role in supporting its oldest members in most societies. The extent to which older citizens are engaged in society appears to vary with the nature of their power resources, such as their material possessions, knowledge, and social authority. In most of their exchanges, older people seek to maintain reciprocity and to be active, autonomous agents in the management of their own lives. That is, they prefer to give money, time, caregiving or other resources in exchange for services.

27 윗글의 빈칸에 들어갈 가장 알맞은 표현은?

① filial piety
② mutual help
③ family meeting
④ collective wisdom

28 윗글을 다음과 같이 요약했을 때 빈칸에 들어갈 가장 적절한 것은?

In general, old people who can no longer work but control resources essential to fulfill the needs of younger group members _____.

① are able to create rapid societal changes
② place unexpected burdens on younger people
③ are passive agents in the management of their lives
④ offset the societal costs incurred in maintaining them

To compare zombies to their rivals in the monster-movie pantheon,* vampires and werewolves symbolise the thrill and the romance of having superhuman strength and no conscience — hence the *Twilight* and *True Blood* franchises. But there's nothing glamorous about being a zombie. Unlike vampires and werewolves, they're not frightening because of how powerful they are. They're frightening because of how dismal it would be to become one yourself. Another difference is that werewolves and vampires are content to share the planet with the rest of us. They might tuck into the odd innocent bystander, but Dracula and the Wolfman don't threaten our way of life. In Romero's films and their many imitators, however, the monsters are either the cause or a symptom of a complete societal breakdown. When a botched* science experiment, a radiation leak, or a glowing meteorite begins zombifying the populace, the result is a pandemic which leaves the world in chaos.

*pantheon: all the gods of a nation, or a religious building built in honour of all gods
*botched: ruined, failed

29 What is the passage mainly about?

① Achievements of Romero in the history of monster films
② Differences between zombies and other monsters on screen
③ What zombies have in common with vampires and werewolves
④ Major filmic works representing zombies, vampires, and werewolves

30 Which of the following describes zombies, but not vampires or werewolves?

① They have amazing power and no conscience.
② They will tuck into the odd innocent bystander.
③ They are content to share the planet with the rest of us.
④ They are the cause or a symptom of a complete societal breakdown.

CHAPTER 04

글의 목적과 어조 등

글의 전체적인 이해를 바탕으로 푸는 문제들이다. 수능과는 다르게 편입에서는 출제가 빈번히 이루어지는 영역은 아니며, 출제되어도 쉽게 해결할 수 있는 부분이다. 다만 글의 목적을 묻는 부분은 자주 출제되며, 혼동 가능한 보기가 제시되므로 주의를 요한다.

01 질문 유형

Which of the following is the main purpose of the passage?
What is the general tone of the following passage?
What is the tone of the following passage?
What is the author's attitude toward the underlined ***?
Which of the following best describes ***'s reaction?

02 문제 풀이 전략

(1) 글의 목적

❶ 저자의 의도를 파악한다.

글의 목적이라 함은 저자가 글을 통해서 독자에게 전달하고자 하는 것이 무엇인가를 파악하는 것이다. 이러한 목적이 글 속에 나와 있는 경우도 있고, 글에는 나와 있지 않지만 당연히 전제되어 있는 경우도 있다. 글을 쓴 의도가 무엇인지를 고려하면 글을 쓴 목적을 파악할 수 있다.

❷ 제시된 보기를 본문과 맞춰 본다.

편입의 경우는 여타 시험과 다르게 목적을 좀 더 세부적으로 제시하기 때문에 제시된 보기를 꼼꼼히 살펴보면 저자가 글을 쓴 목적을 찾을 수 있다. 상황에 따라 쉽게 파악할 수 없는 경우에는 글의 서술 방식과 관련하여 설명의 경우에는 정보 제공으로, 논증의 경우에는 자신의 주장을 펼쳐 상대방을 설득하고자 한다는 대전제에서 접근하도록 한다.

(2) 글의 어조, 분위기

❶ 글의 정서적인 특성을 고려하도록 한다.

글을 통해 나타나는 정서적인 특성을 고려하도록 한다. 더불어 글을 쓴 의도가 무엇인지를 파악하고, 전반적으로 필자가 주장하는 부분이 있다면 그 부분을 유념해서 봐야 한다.

❷ 전체적인 흐름과 잘 맞는 형용사나 부사를 유의한다.

글에서 저자가 어떤 시각에서 써 내려갔는지를 고르라는 것으로 그 상황을 바라보는 작가의 입장을 고르면 된다. 글의 전체적인 흐름과 잘 맞는 형용사나 부사 등을 써서 필자의 감정을 드러내는 경우가 종종 있으므로 이에 유의하여 글을 보는 것도 하나의 요령이다. 결국 독자의 입장에서 글을 읽고 글에서 느껴지는 느낌을 파악해 보는 것이 중요하다.

전략의 적용

That's how this show works. In the dialogue between these two great artists, in their reciprocal affection, mutual treacheries and grudge matches on stretched canvas, lies a good part of the history of Modernism. So was Salmon right? Is it nearly impossible to admire both Picasso and Matisse? Don't believe it. No one will leave this show without loving them both. And the only people to be pitied are the ones who can't get it.

이 전시회를 보고 감탄하지 않을 수 없으며, 누구라도 만족할 수밖에 없다는 것을 강하게 주장하고 있다.

이러한 만족을 못 얻는다면 유감스럽다고 부연하여 자신의 주장을 강력하게 드러내고 있다.

Q. What is the author's attitude toward the underlined this show?

① negative
② sarcastic
③ indifferent
④ positive

전체적인 어조는 전시회에 대한 만족을 드러내는 보기를 골라야 하므로 ④를 쉽게 고를 수 있다.

정답 ④

해석 밑줄 친 '이번 전시회'에 대한 저자의 태도로 알맞은 것은?

여기서 이번 전시회가 위력을 발휘한다. 모더니즘 역사의 대부분은 이 두 위대한 예술가가 나눈 대화 속에서, 넓게 펼쳐진 캔버스 위에 그려진 서로에게 느낀 호의·상호 간의 배반 행위·숙명의 대결 속에 존재한다. 그렇다면 Salmon이 말한 것은 옳았는가? 피카소와 마티즈를 같이 동경하는 것은 거의 불가능할까? 그런 말은 믿지 말라. 이 두 거장을 사랑하지 않고서 이번 전시회를 떠나는 사람은 아무도 없을 것이다. 그리고 이것을 이해하지 못한 사람들은 동정받아야 할 것이다.

① 부정적인
② 비꼬는
③ 무관심한
④ 긍정적인

해설 본문의 마지막 부분을 보면 저자는 '이번 전시회'에 대해 "이 두 거장을 사랑하지 않고서 이번 전시회를 떠나는 사람은 아무도 없을 것이다. 그리고 오직 동정받을 이들은 이것을 이해하지 못한 사람들이다.(No one will leave this show without loving them both. And the only people to be pitied are the ones who can't get it.)"라고 말하고 있으므로, 저자의 태도가 '긍정적'인 것임은 쉽게 파악이 가능하다. 따라서 답은 ④가 된다.

어휘

work ⓥ (어떤 결실, 효과를) 낳다	**reciprocal** ⓐ 상호 간의, 서로의
affection ⓝ 애정, 호의	**mutual** ⓐ 상호 간의, 공통의
treachery ⓝ 배반	**grudge match** 숙명의 대결
stretch ⓥ 뻗다, 늘이다	**a good part of** ~의 대부분
pity ⓥ 동정하다	**sarcastic** ⓐ 비꼬는, 빈정대는

01 What is the tone of the following passage?

The idea that the number of people per square mile is a key determinant of population pressure is as widespread as it is wrong. The key issue in judging overpopulation is not how many people can fit into any given space but whether the Earth can supply the population's long-term requirement for food, water, and other resources. Most of the empty land in the United States, for example, either grows the food essential to our well-being or supplies us with raw materials. Densely populated countries and cities can be crowded only because the rest of the world is not.

① wistful   ② emphatic
③ dismayed   ④ ambivalent

02 다음 글의 목적으로 가장 적절한 것은? 건국대 2018

Demarketing in a tourism context is the process of discouraging all or certain tourists from visiting a particular destination. General demarketing occurs when all visitors are temporarily discouraged from visiting a location, usually due to perceived carrying capacity problems. A notable example is Venice, where intensive summer crowding occasionally prompts local authorities to run ads depicting unpleasant scenes of litter, polluted water, dead pigeons, and the like. The assumption is that the brand image of Venice is so strong that such imagery will not cause any permanent damage to the tourism industry. Most other destinations, however, do not have such a powerful brand and hence are generally reluctant to countermand brand-building efforts with demarketing.

① 역(逆)마케팅의 개념을 소개하려고
② 베니스라는 브랜드 이미지의 형성 과정을 소개하려고
③ 특정 여행지를 방문하려는 관광객들에게 정보를 제공하려고
④ 관광산업에서 역(逆)마케팅이 어떻게 활용되는지 설명하려고
⑤ 불쾌한 장면들을 묘사하는 광고를 만드는 방법을 소개하려고

03 Which best identifies the tone of the author?

When someone feels better after using a product or procedure, it is natural to credit whatever was done. However, this is unwise. Most ailments are self-limiting, and even incurable conditions can have sufficient day-to-day variation to enable quack methods to gain large followings. Taking action often produces temporary relief of symptoms (a placebo effect). In addition, many products and services exert physical or psychological effects that users misinterpret as evidence that their problem is being cured. Scientific experimentation is almost always necessary to establish whether health methods are really effective.

① ironic   ② skeptical
③ excited   ④ humorous

[01~02]

The role of second-hand smoke in causing disease has been under study for years. A mid-sized city in a western state unexpectedly added to our knowledge. Smoking in public and in workplaces was banned, and six months later the ban was lifted. During the time that smoking was prohibited in public places, the rate of hospital admissions for heart attacks was 24. During the typical six-month period, the rate is 40 admissions. Researchers believe that this drop shows the negative effects of second-hand smoke. It adds to the body of evidence that second-hand smoke contributes to heart attacks by elevating the heart rate and decreasing the ability of blood vessels to dilate.

01 **What is the tone of this passage?**

① elegiac
② repressive
③ challenging
④ informational

02 **What does the underlined part, typical six-month period, refer to?**

① the time of the study
② the six months after the study
③ the six months before the study
④ any time other than the six months during the ban

[03~05]

When you transport your goods internationally, several Ⓐ _____ must be taken to ensure proper shipment. Export shipments require greater handling than domestic transport and should be properly packaged and correctly documented so that they arrive safely and on time. You also need to make sure that breakable items are protected, and that other fragile goods will not be damaged by the stresses of air and ocean shipment, such as vibration and moisture.

You must first decide what mode of transport is best. When shipping within a continent, you may prefer land transportation. When shipping to another continent, the preferred method may be by sea or air. Although maritime shipping is generally less expensive than air, it can be much slower and thus less cost-effective. You should consider the additional costs of sea freight, such as surface transportation to and from the docks and port charges. Ocean freight can take longer than air freight and you may have to wait until the ship reaches its destination to receive payment.

03 빈칸 Ⓐ에 들어갈 가장 적절한 단어를 고르시오.

① predictions   ② procedures
③ precautions   ④ aids
⑤ announcements

04 윗글의 목적으로 가장 적절한 것을 고르시오.

① To inform freight forwarders about weight limitations
② To advise importers about insurance policies
③ To provide general information about shipping
④ To notify exporters about new safety measures
⑤ To help freight forwarders save money

05 다음 진술 중 해상 운송과 관련하여 윗글에서 진술된 내용을 고르시오.

① Shipping by sea is usually best.
② Shipping by sea usually costs more.
③ Shipping by sea is usually faster.
④ Shipping by sea usually costs less.
⑤ Shipping by sea is usually cost-effective.

One may object that I exaggerate the artificiality of our world. Man must obey the law of gravity as surely as does a stone, and as a living organism, man must depend for food, and in many other ways, on the world of biological phenomena. I shall plead guilty to overstatement, while protesting that the exaggeration is slight. To say that an astronaut, or even an airplane pilot, is obeying the law of gravity, hence is a perfectly natural phenomenon, is true, but its truth calls for some sophistication in what we mean by obeying a natural law. Aristotle did not think it natural for heavy things to rise or light ones to fall; but presumably, we have a deeper understanding of 'natural' than he did. So too must be careful about equating biological with natural. A forest may be a phenomenon of nature; a farm certainly is not. The very species upon which we depend for our food — our corn and our cattle — are artifacts of our ingenuity. A plowed field is no more part of nature than an asphalted street — and no less. These examples set the terms of our problem, for those things we call artifacts are not apart from nature. They have _____. At the same time, they are adapted to human goals and purposes. They are what they are in order to satisfy our desire to fly or to eat well.

06 **Which of the following is the most appropriate for the blank?**

① no dispensation to ignore or violate natural law
② dispensation to ignore or violate natural law
③ no dispensation to ignore or violate artificial law
④ dispensation to ignore or violate artificial law

07 **What would be the best title of the passage above?**

① The Complex Nature of the Natural Law
② The Complex Nature of the Artifact
③ The Pejorative Nature of Natural Science
④ The Pejorative Trait of the Artificiality

08 **How would you describe the author's attitude to artificiality?**

① surprised   ② ridiculous   ③ joyful   ④ inquisitive

[09~12]

To a man who expects a listener to be quietly attentive, a woman giving a stream of feedback and support will seem to be asking too much for a listener. To a woman who expects a listener to be active and enthusiastic in showing interest, attention, and support, a man who listens silently will seem not to be listening at all, but rather to have checked out of the conversation, taken marbles, and gone mentally home. But I have come to understand more recently, that it is also true that men listen to women less frequently than women listen to men, because the act of listening has different meanings for them. Some men really don't want to listen at length because they feel it frames them as subordinate. Many women do want to listen, but they expect it to be reciprocal.

09 **What is the main purpose of the passage?**

① to describe how reciprocal women are in conversation
② to show why men want to feel subordinate
③ to describe how differently men and women react as listeners
④ to show why women complain about men's attitudes in conversation

10 **How would a woman react to a man who listens silently?**

① She thinks that he wants to go home.
② She thinks that he is not listening at all.
③ She thinks that he is an enthusiastic listener.
④ She thinks that he does not want to be subordinate.

11 Why do some men hate to listen for a considerable time?

① Because it makes them feel bored.

② Because it makes them feel inferior.

③ Because it makes them feel obstinate.

④ Because it makes them feel arrogant.

12 What does it mean that many women want listening to be reciprocal?

① People can listen carefully.

② People should be cooperative in helping others.

③ People can understand each other.

④ People should take turns in listening.

[13~15]

Sometimes we are so busy that we feel we don't have time to plan, but in fact, no matter how busy we are, we should find it worthwhile to take time to plan our activities. Perhaps we don't have time to plan and do absolutely everything else we would like to get done. Yet, by neglecting to plan, we will free very little time; and by failing to plan, we shall probably not discriminate among the essential and nonessential activities. If we spend only ten minutes at the beginning or end of the day planning, our efforts will be repaid many times over. The less time we feel we have to spare, the more important it is to plan our time carefully.

Planning and making choices involve careful thinking and decision-making. In the process, we learn to recognize what criteria we use in setting priorities. In all types of planning, we make lists and set priorities. A most useful planning strategy is to make a daily "To do" list. Not all the items on the list are of equal value. Once we have made a list, we need to set priorities on the basis of what is important to us on this particular day.

13 Which of the following best expresses the main idea of the passage?

① Busy people need to plan their lives more.
② Prioritizing is not a difficult task to do.
③ Planning should be done on a daily basis.
④ Planning is essential in managing time and effort.

14 Which of the following cannot be inferred from the passage?

① Non-essential activities should be given low priority.
② The order of priorities of what to do should not be changed.
③ Things on a "To Do" list need not carry the same importance.
④ Planning for a short time can save much time later.

15 Which of the following best describes the author's attitude toward "planning"?

① bemused   ② favorable
③ skeptical   ④ malicious

History, at least in its state of ideal perfection, is a compound of poetry and philosophy. It impresses general truths on the mind by a vivid representation of particular characters and incidents. But, in fact, the two hostile elements of which it consists have never been known to form a perfect amalgamation; and at length, in our own time, they have been completely and professedly separated. Good histories, in the proper sense of the word, we have not. But we have good historical romances, and good historical essays. The imagination and the reason have made partition of a province of literature and now they hold their respective portions in severalty, instead of holding the whole in common.

To make the past present, to bring the distant near, to place us in the society of a great man or on the eminence which overlooks the field of a mighty battle, to invest with the reality of human flesh and blood beings whom we are too much inclined to consider as personified qualities in an allegory, to call up our ancestors before us with all their peculiarities of language, manners, and garb, to show us over their houses, these parts of the duty which properly belongs to the historian have been appropriated by the historical novelist. On the other hand, to extract the philosophy of history, to direct on judgement of events and men, to trace the connection of cause and effect, and to draw from the occurrences of former time general lessons of moral and political wisdom, has become the business of a distinct class of writers.

16 Which is the primary mode of composition of the passage?

① historical narration   ② process analysis

③ comparison and contrast   ④ cause and effect

17 In the first paragraph, which is NOT described as the two hostile pairs?

① severalty and history   ② imagination and reason

③ romances and essays   ④ poetry and philosophy

18 **Which is the purpose of the second paragraph?**

① To argue for the superiority of historical romances and what they can offer

② To describe what historical romances and historical essays each offer

③ To explain the process of making "the past present" and bringing "the distant near"

④ To evaluate which type of history is superior, leaving the answer up to the reader

01

When most people contemplate building a new home, they assume that the first order of business is to choose or design a plan to build. But, in fact, the first step is always to find the site that you want to build on. When you work with an architect, you'll find that the design for the house is as much influenced by the opportunities and constraints of the site as it is by your particular functional and aesthetic desires. This was eminently evident in one new house I saw a few years ago. The house was positioned on a hill, facing south overlooking a magnificent vista, but there was not a single window looking toward that extraordinary view. My guess is that the design had been picked out of a plan book long before the site had been chosen, and the original plan had been designed to be highly energy efficient with its (　A　) face oriented to the north. This new house had the (　B　) face oriented to the south just the direction one wants lots of glass in most climates.

19 **What is the purpose of the passage?**

① To explain the importance of aesthetic considerations in house construction
② To show the close connection between the design for a house and its site
③ To offer a step-by-step guide to the house building process
④ To illustrate how to build an energy-efficient house

20 **Which of the following is most appropriate for blanks (A) and (B)?**

① slim   ② round
③ blind   ④ glittering

The lore of the American Wild West has been familiar for generations. The brave lawmen, ruggedly individual cowboys, and rollicking frontier towns are well known around the world. In fact, the Wild West wasn't all that picturesque. America in the mid-nineteenth century was still forging a national identity. That identity did not yet include the grand heroes or elaborate mythology of other, older societies. Without being quite aware of it, the media of the time created those heroes and myths by giving the public a story it was ready to hear. The shootout towns of Tombstone and Dodge City had fewer killings in their entire heyday than nearly any modern US. city has in a year. Peacekeeper Wild Bill Hickok in Abilene shot only a pair of men while taming the town. One of the men was a fellow policeman. But facts like these are not the stuff of fables.

21 윗글의 목적으로 가장 적절한 것을 고르시오.

① To extol the Wild West

② To expound the lives in the Wild West

③ To introduce the heroes of the Wild West

④ To debunk the popular legend of the Wild West

All science is <u>subject</u> to human bias. This is especially true for social scientists. Since human behavior is their area of study, they are actually part of the subject matter. Furthermore, human behavior patterns vary from one place to another and from one group to another. This is in contrast to the subject matter of the natural sciences. When a chemist studies hydrogen, he can assume that one hydrogen atom is very much like another, wherever it is found, and that the conditions surrounding it can be quite accurately controlled. The same is true when a physicist measures a metal bar; he can be quite sure that it will not stretch or shrink in length as long as natural conditions are the same. This is why Earl Babbie quotes economist Daniel Suits, who calls the natural sciences the "easy sciences" because of the _____ nature of their subject matter.

22 **Select the best word that can replace the underlined subject.**

① reliable
② likely
③ susceptible
④ apathetic
⑤ immune

23 **Fill in the blank with a suitable word.**

① predictable
② versatile
③ flexible
④ formidable
⑤ whimsical

24 **The tone of the above passage can be described as _____.**

① critical
② objective
③ vindictive
④ cynical
⑤ ambivalent

25 What can be most likely inferred from the above passage?

① Human bias is the subject matter that social scientists mainly study.

② The conditions surrounding human behavior can be accurately controlled.

③ Social sciences may be called hard because of their stubborn subject matter.

④ Daniel Suits is quoted to support that natural sciences are subject to bias.

⑤ A metal bar may change in length according to natural conditions.

PART 02

세부적 이해

OVERVIEW 개관

CHAPTER 01 내용 일치

CHAPTER 02 특정 정보

CHAPTER 03 문법성 판단

CHAPTER 04 의미 파악

CHAPTER 05 재진술

CHAPTER 06 지시어구

CHAPTER 07 단어와 숙어

세부적인 내용을 이해해야 풀 수 있는 영역으로, 내용 일치, 특정 정보, 의미 파악, 지시어구, 문법성 판단과 본문에 사용된 어휘의 의미를 묻는 문제들이 여기에 해당한다. 요즘은 난이도가 높아지면서 본문의 내용을 알고 있는지, 알고 있다면 다른 말로 풀어쓸 수 있는지를 묻는 paraphrase의 문제도 점점 더 많이 선보이고 있다. 세부적인 사항을 묻는 문제는 주로 내용을 묻는 문제와 밑줄 친 부분에 대해 묻는 문제로 대별할 수 있다.

(1) 내용을 묻는 문제
(a) 내용 일치 판단
(b) 특정 정보 파악
(c) 문법성 판단

내용을 묻는 문제는 내용의 일치 여부의 판단, 특정 정보를 파악할 수 있는지의 문제 등이 주류를 이룬다. 더불어 본문에 사용된 문법적인 사항을 알고 있는지 묻는 것은 문법 사항을 독해에 적용할 수 있는지를 묻는 문제로 볼 수 있다.

(2) 밑줄 친 부분을 묻는 문제
(a) 의미 파악
(b) 지시어구
(c) 어휘

이에 비해 밑줄 친 부분의 내용을 묻는 문제는 그 부분이 의미하는 바가 뭔지를 아는지 묻는 의미 파악의 문제, 앞에 언급된 것을 뒤에 바꿔서 진술했을 경우 그 지시하는 바가 무엇인지를 알고 있는지를 묻는 지시어구의 문제, 본문에 사용된 어휘의 의미를 알고 있는지를 묻는 어휘 문제 등이 존재한다.

이렇게 글의 세부적인 부분을 이해하는지 묻는 문제들은 대부분 본문의 내용을 꼼꼼히 읽어 보면 본문 속에 답이 존재한다. 다만 시험에서는 시간이 부족하기 때문에 서두르다 보면 놓치는 경우가 있다. 세부적인 영역의 문제를 올바르게 해결하기 위해서 두 가지의 훈련이 필요하다. 먼저 모든 영어 학습의 핵심인 글을 많이 읽어 볼 것, 그리고 또 한 가지는 본문의 표현을 다른 방식으로 바꿔 보는 paraphrase 훈련을 해 보는 것이다. 쉽지는 않지만 처음에는 한국어로 나중에는 본문 속의 어휘를 사용하여 영어로, 마지막으로는 본문에 사용되지 않은 어휘를 사용하여 영어로 paraphrase를 연습해 보면 비약적인 발전이 있을 것이다.

CHAPTER 01

내용 일치

내용의 일치 여부를 묻는 문제는 전체적인 이해가 아닌 세부적인 이해를 요하는 문제 유형으로 본문에 근거해서 글의 내용과 일치하는지 아니면 글의 내용과 일치하지 않는지를 찾아내는 문제이다. 본문의 정확한 이해가 선행되어야 하는 문제이다. 이러한 점에서는 세부 내용을 묻는 문제와 공통되는 측면이 있다. 다만 이전보다 지문이 길어졌기 때문에 읽어야 하는 분량이 많으므로, 한 번 읽을 때 정확하게 읽어 내야 해서 이전보다 더 어려워졌다고 할 수 있다.

01 질문 유형

Which of following is true according to the passage?
According to the passage, which of the following is true?
According to the passage, which of the following is NOT true?
Which of the following is correct according to the passage?
Which of the following is true of ***?
According to the passage, which of the following statements is true regarding ***?

02 문제 풀이 전략

❶ **구체적인 사실에 근거를 두고 풀어라.**
전체적인 이해를 바탕으로 하는 주제나 요지를 찾는 문제와 달리 주어진 글에 나온 정보나 사실 관계를 바탕으로 점검해야 한다. 내용 일치 문제를 정확히 풀어내기 위해서는 독해를 해 나갈 때 keyword를 체크한 후에 문제에서 해당하는 영역이 나오면 그 부분을 다시 찾아서 빠르게 읽어 내려가면서 진위 여부를 판단하여야 한다.

❷ **주어진 정보 이외에는 고려하지 않는다.**
문제를 푸는 와중에 유추나 비약, 혹은 자신의 배경지식을 바탕으로 푸는 경우가 생긴다. 명심해야 할 것은 추론 문제가 아니고 본문에 근거한 내용과 일치하는지 불일치하는지를 묻는 문제이므로 글의 범위를 넘어서지 않도록 한다.

❸ **paraphrase로 변형된 선택지를 잘 골라야 한다.**
제시된 글과 선택지를 면밀히 비교하고 대조하여 답을 고르면 된다. 다만 최근의 경향은 본문의 표현 그대로가 아니라 본문의 내용과 일치하는 paraphrase된 문장을 선택지로 제시하는 경우가 많으므로 내용의 동일성을 유념하여 풀어 나가야 한다.

My present predicament is that I met a wonderful man who wants to marry me, but there's a problem: My fiance is a heavy smoker. He has asthma and bronchitis, and when he lights up he coughs, which makes me cringe. He keeps saying he's going to quit, but he's still smoking. He says that not everybody who smokes gets lung cancer. I feel as though he's killing himself, and there's nothing I can do about it. Should I go on like this and fall more deeply in love with him, only to watch him die an agonizing death from lung cancer? So far I'm distancing myself from him until I know what to do.

→ 남자 친구가 흡연자이다. 하지만 보기 ①에서는 주체를 여자로 바꿔 오답을 유도하고 있다.

→ 담배 피운다고 누구나 암에 걸리는 것은 아니라는 내용을 보기 ②에서 남자 친구가 암에 걸렸다는 오답으로 유도하고 있다.

→ 골초인 남자 친구와의 관계를 어떻게 유지해야 할지에 대해서 마음의 갈피를 잡지 못하는 상태를 적고 있다.

Q. According to the passage, which of the following is true?

① The woman is a heavy smoker.
② The woman's fiance was diagnosed with lung cancer.
③ The woman has moved in with a smoker.
④ The woman's fiance has just quit smoking.
⑤ The woman is reluctant to get closer to her fiance.

→ 본문의 마지막 문장을 근거로 답을 도출해 낼 수 있다.

정답   ⑤

해석   **윗글에 따르면 다음 중 올바른 것은?**

내가 현재 처한 곤경은 바로 나와 결혼하길 원하는 한 남자를 만나고 있는데 한 가지 문제가 있어요. 내 약혼자는 담배를 너무 많이 피우는 사람이에요. 그는 천식과 기관지염으로 고생하면서도, 또 담배에 불을 붙일 때 기침을 하는데, 이럴 때 나는 움찔하게 되지요. 그는 끊겠다고 약속했지만 여전히 담배를 피우고 있어요. 그는 언제나 담배 피우는 사람들 모두가 다 폐암에 걸리는 것은 아니라고 말해요. 나는 내 약혼자가 자신의 목숨을 단축시키는 것 같지만, 이에 대해 내가 할 수 있는 일이 없어요. 내가 지금처럼 계속 관계를 유지해서 그와 더욱더 사랑에 빠져 결국은 고통스럽게 그가 폐암으로 죽어 가는 것을 보아야 하나요? 지금까지 나는 내 자신이 어찌해야 할지를 알 때까지 그와의 거리를 두고 있는 중이에요.

① 그 여성은 골초이다.
② 그 여성의 약혼자는 폐암으로 진단받았다.
③ 그 여성은 흡연자와 함께 산다.
④ 그 여성의 약혼자는 막 담배를 끊었다.
⑤ 그 여성은 약혼자와 가까워지는 것을 꺼린다.

해설　　지금까지 나는 나 자신이 어찌해야 할지를 알 때까지 그와의 거리를 두고 있는 중이라는 것에서 ⑤가 정답임을 알 수 있다.

어휘　　**asthma** ⓝ 천식　　　　　　　　　　　**bronchitis** ⓝ 기관지염

　　　　cringe ⓥ 움찔하다, 움츠리다　　　　　**agonizing** ⓐ 고통스러운

　　　　distance oneself from 거리를 두다, ～에 관여하지 않다

01 다음 글의 내용과 가장 부합하지 <u>않는</u> 것은? 광운대 2015

> The lights stay on all night in Gangnam, where plastic surgery clinics line the streets. Signs in Chinese beckon visitors. Once they are inside, translators stand ready. Seizing an opportunity to tap the steady and ubiquitous flow of China's newly rich who are traveling overseas, Korea's government is promoting the country as a place to shop, eat, stay — and perhaps get a nip and a tuck. And the Chinese, mainly women, are visiting in droves for body modifications, from the minor, like double eyelid surgery, to the extreme, like facial restructuring. While plastic surgery is common in China, Korean hospitals are perceived to be safer and more hygienic, albeit pricier.

① Double eyelid surgery is considered a kind of minor plastic surgery.
② Plastic surgery is not expensive in Korea, compared with China.
③ Chinese men, as well as women, visit Korea for plastic surgery.
④ Some Chinese visitors even want a facial restructuring surgery.
⑤ Chinese visitors consider Korean hospitals cleaner than Chinese hospitals.

02 Which of the following is correct according to the passage?

> Golden beaches, fascinating cultures, and friendly people welcome visitors to Mozambique. Mozambique is on Africa's southeastern coast. The capital city, Maputo, is home to lively markets, sidewalk cafes, and wide tree-lined streets. Elephants, monkeys, and other animals can be found in the country's wildlife parks. Mozambicans are working to rebuild their poor nation. The country was ruled by Portugal for almost 500 years. Mozambique gained its independence in 1975. Later, about 15 years of civil war tore the country apart. Now many people are sick and can't afford medicine and doctors.

① Mozambique is an island country surrounded by beautiful beaches.
② You can see various wild animals on the streets of Maputo.
③ Mozambique used to be Portugal's colony before its independence.
④ Mozambique has remained a peaceful country throughout its history.

03 Which of the following is true according to the passage?

American surface informality often confuses the foreigner because he interprets it to mean no formality at all. He does not understand the point at which informality stops. A teacher, though friendly, pleasant, and informal in class, expects students to study hard, and he grades each student's work critically and carefully. He also expects to be treated with respect. Though students are free to ask questions about statements made by the teacher, they are not expected to contradict him.

① American students are free to contradict their teachers.
② American teachers are generous in grading their students' work.
③ American teachers are so strict that students often disobey them.
④ Americans, though apparently informal, know the limits of informality.

[01~02] 국민대 2021

In 1805, P. M. Roget, a British surgeon and inventor, took up a peculiar hobby: the classification of words according to ideas. His intention was to present those words in a kind of verbal catalogue that would assist writers and linguists in their search for the right manner of expressions. As he worked, he perhaps had in mind the ancient Sanskrit Amarakosha, arguably the first arrangement of words by subject, or the French Pasigraphie, published in 1797, which was an attempt to order words so they could be understood universally, without translation. Roget called his own work a "thesaurus" — a Latin word meaning 'treasury' or 'storehouse of knowledge'.

Roget's pastime became a lifelong passion and in 1852, at the age of seventy-three, Roget published his *Thesaurus of English Words and Phrases, Classified and Arranged so as to Facilitate the Expressions of Ideas and Assist in Literary Composition*. This new reference book became enormously popular and a second edition appeared only a year after the first. By the time of Roget's death in 1869, there had been over twenty-five editions and printings. Today, his name is synonymous with the thesaurus.

01 What is the passage mainly about?

① The Origin of English Thesaurus
② The First Thesaurus of the World
③ The Popularity of Roget's Thesaurus
④ The Relationship between Hobby and Profession

02 According to the passage, which is NOT true?

① Today the name Roget is closely associated with English thesaurus.
② The first edition of Roget's *Thesaurus* was in short supply in a year.
③ The first thesaurus was compiled by a surgeon-turned-linguist named Roget.
④ The popularity of Roget's *Thesaurus* seems to have never cooled down until he died.

An intelligence quotient, or IQ, is a score derived from one of several standardized tests designed to assess human intelligence. The abbreviation "IQ" was coined by the psychologist William Stern for the German term Intelligenz-Quotient, his term for a scoring method for intelligence tests he advocated in a 1912 book. When current IQ tests are developed, the median raw score of the norming sample is defined as IQ 100, and scores each standard deviation (SD) up or down are defined as 15 IQ points greater or less. By the definition, approximately two-thirds of the population scores an IQ between 85 and 115, and about 5 percent of the population scores above 125. IQ scores are used as predictors of educational achievement, special needs, and job performance. They are also used to study IQ distributions in populations and the correlations between IQ and other variables. Raw scores on IQ tests for many populations have been rising at an average rate that scales to three IQ points per decade since the early 20th century, a phenomenon called the Flynn Effect.

03 윗글의 내용과 가장 부합하지 <u>않는</u> 것은?

① IQ test was designed by the psychologist William Stern in his book.
② The majority of the population falls within one SD up or down in IQ scores.
③ About 5% of the population has an IQ score above 125 points.
④ IQ scores predict a person's capacity for education and work.
⑤ Populations have been distributed according to their IQ scores.

04 윗글에서 밑줄 친 **the Flynn Effect**에 대해 가장 옳게 나타낸 것은?

① It describes how IQ scores are spread in populations.
② It shows why raw scores are meaningful on the IQ test.
③ It indicates a steady growth of IQ points as to time.
④ It explains why IQ can predict many social phenomena.
⑤ It refers to the effect of the SD on the IQ score scales.

Impressive though the achievements of Western technological science are, there is no denying that they have been bought at a price which includes increased nervous strain and destruction of the Earth's natural riches. In the interests of progress, productivity, and the accumulation of wealth, we have exploited our fellow human beings, nature, and the environment for centuries. We are only just waking up to the fact that the exploited can kick back in (A   ) ways. Our reaction to the kick-back tends to (B   ) the problem because we always think in terms of more of the same. Our answers to the evils of technology is more and better technology. If rivers are becoming polluted, the solution is, we reason today, to develop (C   ) and therefore more expensive antipollutants.

05 (A), (B), (C)에 들어갈 말을 순서대로 바르게 짝지은 것은?

① expected – weaken – harmless
② expected – upgrade – more ecological
③ unexpected – solve – more harmful
④ unexpected – escalate – stronger

06 윗글의 내용과 일치하지 <u>않는</u> 것은?

① Western technologies have had both positive and negative effects on men's lives.
② We are now paying the price for the exploitation of nature by human beings.
③ One of the problems caused by Western technologies has been the exploitation of the environment.
④ Thanks to antipollutants the polluted rivers are recovering from pollution to their original state.

Terra-cotta, or "baked earth," was originally used in architecture during the height of the Roman Empire. During the Renaissance, however, terra-cotta became a much more artistic medium. Many sculptors, (A) _____, often used it to make *bozzetti*, or "rough drafts" of sculptures that would later be carved from stone or cast in bronze. Oddly enough, these *bozzetti* were often viewed as more interesting than the finished works, as art enthusiasts began collecting terra-cotta models for exhibition in their homes and in galleries. Collectors believed the models represented an artist's talent far more accurately. (B) _____, many of these "rough drafts" often commanded higher selling prices than the stone or bronze pieces on which they were based.

07 According to the passage, which is true?

① It was easy for sculptors to acquire *bozzetti*.
② Terra-cotta was just as sturdy as stone or bronze.
③ Bozzetti was more attractive to the collectors.
④ Terra-cotta was used more for architecture during the Renaissance than before.

08 Which is the most appropriate for the blanks (A) and (B)?

① nevertheless – However
② however – Therefore
③ thus – Moreover
④ for example – As a result

We live at a time when friendship has become both all and nothing at all. Already the characteristically modern relationship, it has in recent decades become the universal one: the form of connection in terms of which all others are understood, against which they are all measured, into which they have all dissolved. Romantic partners refer to each other as boyfriend and girlfriend. Spouses boast that they are each other's best friends. Parents urge their young children and beg their teenage ones to think of them as friends. Adult siblings, released from competition for parental resources that in traditional society made them anything but friends (think of Jacob and Esau), now treat one another in exactly those terms. Teachers, clergymen, and even bosses seek to mitigate and legitimate their authority by asking those they oversee to regard them as friends. We're all on a first-name basis, and when we vote for president, we ask ourselves whom we'd rather have a beer with. As the anthropologist Robert Brain has put it, _____.

09 Which of the following is correct according to the passage?

① Presidential election tends to be pushed aside for friendship.
② Friendship characterizes the modern relationship.
③ Homosexuality gets mixed up with friendship.
④ Siblings are now competing for friendship.

10 Which of the following is the most appropriate for the blank?

① we're concerned too much about the elected officials
② we're keen on friendship as much as freedom
③ we're ready to go abroad for friendship
④ we're friends with everyone now

[11~12]

One of the more important things that the Internet has fostered or strengthened has been freedom of speech and freedom of expression. The Internet is a very large common public area that is shared by people all around the world. Due to the diversity of the Internet's users, no one standard can be applied to govern speech on the Internet. (A) _____, the Internet's technology itself prevents complete blocking of access to information. In the late 1990s, (B) _____, many countries became alarmed at the freedom of speech accessible on the Internet and tried to restrict it. Singapore mandated that political and religious sites must register with the government. China ordered that all Internet users had to register with the police. And, Saudi Arabia restricted Internet use to only universities and hospitals. However, due to the nature of the Internet, none of these efforts has had much lasting effects.

11 밑줄 친 **(A)**, **(B)**에 들어가기에 가장 적합한 것을 고르시오.

① In addition – furthermore
② Furthermore – however
③ However – in addition
④ However – nevertheless

12 다음 중 윗글의 내용과 가장 일치하는 것을 고르시오.

① The Internet access to information can be completely prevented.
② Internet use is allowed in only universities and hospitals in China.
③ Many countries have tried to restrict Internet use and it is successful.
④ It is very difficult to make some criteria to control speech on the Internet.

Have you ever turned down your vacation days at work in an effort to impress your boss? If so, you've got it all wrong! Researchers recently determined that vacationing more is actually an overall positive career move.

The study found that more than half of the American workers surveyed intentionally left their vacation days unused. The study's author suspects workers worry that they'll look lazy or fall behind on the job, or they think that by leaving the days unused they'll impress the boss.

But the truth is, taking time off is far better for productivity than slaving away and putting your brain into overdrive. A day off here and a day off there from the office can improve your concentration, while long breaks boost your motivation. "The impact that taking a vacation has on one's mental health is profound," said Francine Lederer, a clinical psychologist. "Most people have better life perspective and are more motivated to achieve their goals after a vacation, even if it is a 24-hour time-out."

Giving up your vacation days might even be the reason you haven't been promoted. In the Project: Time Out study, one interesting realization was that employees who take 10 or less days of vacation time are less likely to have received a raise or bonus in the last three years than those who took 11 days or more. This is likely because your work performance suffers the fewer days off your take, and the more likely you have been noticeably burning out. Instead of skipping out on vacation days, try these smart strategies to build trust with your boss.

The takeaway here: Vacationing is not only great for your personal health and wellness, it also plays an important role in making you a better employee. And the great news is, you don't have to book a week off and worry about getting behind. Instead, take single days off throughout the year to go to your kid's recital, relax at home, or spend a day at the park. You'll quickly realize that taking time off makes all the difference.

13 What would be the main reason for employees not to use their vacation?

① to earn more money
② to please their supervisor
③ to make more products
④ to enjoy their job

14 Which of the following is true?

① Vacation is closely related with productivity.
② Vacationing less is better for promotion.
③ Vacation does not promote motivation.
④ Vacation is not important for mental health.

15 Which of the following is NOT true?

① Short vacation is still worthwhile.
② Vacationing is necessary for everybody.
③ The length of vacation is not crucial.
④ Long vacation hinders work performance.

In Kafka's time Prague was in the Austro-Hungarian empire: although the local population spoke largely Czech, ㉮ _____. In 1910, the population of Prague was 230,000, making it the third largest city in the Austro-Hungarian Empire. Including the suburbs, the population was about 600,000. 90.7% of the population spoke Czech and the rest spoke German. The social elite of business managers and entrepreneurs were largely German-speaking: there was essentially no German-speaking proletariat. According to a German tour book of the time, "In the best pubs and restaurants, and also in the biggest shops German is understood. Coachmen, people in the service industries and railway porters usually understand as much German as they need to deal with foreigners."

Today, English has taken the place of German as the main second language for international business in Prague while Czech is the official language. The population is about 1.3 million. The German minority has virtually disappeared: large numbers of German-speakers were forcibly removed from the country after the second world war, and most of the rest have assimilated.

16 빈칸 ㉮에 들어가기에 가장 적절한 것은?

① Kafka refused to write in Czech
② German was used for official business and by the upper classes
③ Czech pop culture was dominated by the Hungarian tradition
④ Early 20th century Czech began to be used as an official in tour books

17 윗글의 내용과 일치하는 것은?

① The German community has shrunk almost down to none in Prague these days.
② In 1910, German tourists were not allowed to enter the Czech border.
③ German minority of Prague in 1910 had little social and economical power at that time.
④ After World War II, English is also used for international business along with German in Prague.

[18~20]

In everyday life, we surround ourselves with an invisible "bubble" that constitutes what we consider our personal space, an area around our body that we reserve for ourselves, intimate acquaintances, and close friends. These personal spaces vary greatly from one culture to another and within cultures where people of different age, race, sex, and social class categories interact. Middle Easterners, for example, have much smaller distance requirements for casual interaction and men often embrace or kiss on the cheek when introduced for the first time — something that makes American men very uncomfortable. ⓐ _____ living in a very densely-populated country, the Japanese often maintain a larger social space when interacting with strangers. When two Japanese men are introduced, they bow toward one another, an act that requires a distance of about 180cm to prevent bumping heads. In the United States, women are generally ⓑ <u>far</u> more comfortable touching, hugging, or kissing one another than are men, and women generally will allow other women within their intimate distance, something a man rarely allows from another man, even if they are blood related.

18 **Which of the following best fits in blank ⓐ?**

① Because   ② Despite   ③ Since   ④ However

19 **According to the passage, which of the following statements is true?**

① American men may feel quite uneasy allowing people of the same gender within their "bubble."
② It would be offensive to kiss a man on the cheek in Iraq when introduced for the first time.
③ Japanese culture requires much smaller distance for casual interaction than American culture.
④ Members within the same cultural groups tend to keep the same amount of personal spaces when interacting with each other.

20 **Which of the following words CANNOT replace the underlined word ⓑ far?**

① way   ② away   ③ much   ④ considerably

How do you envisage the pursuit of happiness? For many, it is a relentless journey, and the more you put in, the more you get out. Just consider the following episode from Elizabeth Gilbert's best-selling inspirational memoir *Eat*, *Pray*, *Love*, in which she recounts some advice from her Guru. "Happiness is the consequence of personal effort. You fight for it, strive for it, insist upon it, and sometimes even travel around the world looking for it," she writes. "You have to participate relentlessly in the manifestations of your own blessings. And once you have achieved a state of happiness, you must make a mighty effort to keep swimming upward into that happiness forever, to stay afloat on top of it. If you don't, you will leak away your innate contentment." While this kind of attitude may work for some, the latest scientific research suggests that <u>it</u> can also seriously backfire for many people— leading, for instance, to feelings of stress, loneliness, and personal failure. According to this view, happiness is best seen as a timid bird: the harder you strive to catch it, the further it flies away.

21 **What does the underlined it refer to?**

① happiness
② a timid bird
③ a mighty effort to be happy
④ the latest scientific research

22 **According to the passage, which of the following is true?**

① The author regards happiness as a timid bird.
② The author recommends striving for happiness.
③ The author argues that happiness cannot be pursued.
④ The author thinks people have different attitudes to happiness.

Vitamin D is also known as the 'sunshine vitamin', as it is produced by our bodies when we are exposed to sunlight. It is vital to our health to consume a sufficient amount of Vitamin D. Vitamin D helps us maintain healthy bones and teeth, and also supports our immune system, brain, and nervous system. In addition, it also protects us against a wide range of diseases such as cancer, diabetes, and sclerosis. Though we may be fooled by the name, Vitamin D (A) _____ but a type of pro-hormone. Vitamins are defined as nutrients that cannot be produced by the body and must be obtained through our diet. However, our bodies are capable of creating 'Vitamin' D if exposed to direct sunlight for five to ten minutes, two or three times a week. Experts warn that in the winter, when we are generally exposed to less sunlight, Vitamin D can break down very quickly. They recommend that in order to prevent stores from running low, we should increase our intake of Vitamin D through food or nutritional supplements.

23 According to the passage, which of the following is NOT true of Vitamin D?

① A sufficient amount of Vitamin D is necessary for a healthy skeletal structure.
② Vitamin D is a type of pro-hormone that can be produced by our bodies.
③ Daily exposure to sunlight is necessary to produce enough Vitamin D.
④ Nutritional supplements of Vitamin D are recommended in the winter.

24 Which of the following best fits into (A)?

① is not only a vitamin
② is a rare type of vitamin
③ has several different forms
④ is actually not a vitamin

Every adult life could be said to be defined by two great love stories. The first — the story of our quest for sexual love — is well known, well charted, socially accepted, and celebrated in its vagaries of music and literature. The second — the story of our quest for love from the world — is a more secret and shameful tale. If mentioned, it tends to be in caustic, mocking terms, as something of interest chiefly to envious or deficient soul, or else the drive for status is interpreted in an economic sense alone. _____ this second love story is no less intense than the first, it is no less complicated, important or universal, and its setbacks are no less painful. There is heartbreak here too.

25 According to the passage, which is NOT true?

① The love from the world is one of the two important loves that are pursued in every adult life.

② The want for love from the world tends to be mocked at and is considered as something that interests envious people.

③ The quest for love from the world is less painful than the quest for sexual love.

④ The quest for sexual love is much more openly discussed and celebrated.

26 Which is the most appropriate for the blank?

① Accordingly
② Yet
③ Necessarily
④ By the way

To reduce youth violence, conflict-resolution skills should be taught to all children. In a dangerous society where guns are readily available, many youngsters feel they have no choice but to respond to an insult or an argument with violence. Many programs and courses around the country are teaching teens and preteens to work through disagreement without violence. Although conflict resolution is useful at any age, experts agree that students should first be exposed to conflict-resolution skills before they are hit by the double jolt of hormones and junior high school. Although opponents claim that this is a "Band-Aid" solution that does not address the root causes of teen violence — poverty, troubled families, and drugs to name a few — in fact, conflict-resolution training saves lives now. The larger social issues must be addressed, but they will take years to solve, whereas teaching students new attitudes and "people skills" will empower them immediately and serve them for a lifetime. One proven way to help youngsters protect themselves from violence is conflict-resolution training that begins early.

27 밑줄 친 "**a Band-Aid solution**"이 의미하는 것을 고르시오.

① a stand-in   ② a makeshift
③ a substitute   ④ an amendment

28 윗글의 내용과 일치하는 것을 고르시오.

① Poverty and drug-use have little to do with youth violence.
② Gun control is a more fundamental preventive measure of conflict resolution.
③ Conflict-resolution skills are not useful once children have arrived at adulthood.
④ The earlier students go into conflict-resolution training, the more effectively it serves them.

The first detective stories, written by Edgar Allan Poe and Sir Arthur Conan Doyle, emerged in the mid-nineteenth century, at a time when there was an enormous public interest in scientific progress. The newspapers of the day continually publicized the latest scientific discoveries, and scientists were acclaimed as the heroes of the age. Poe and Conan Doyle shared this fascination with the step-by-step, logical approach used by scientists in their experiments, and instilled in their detective heroes outstanding powers of scientific reasoning.

The character of Sherlock Holmes, for example, illustrates Conan Doyle's admiration for the scientific mind. In each case that Holmes investigates, he is able to use the most insubstantial evidence to track down his opponent. Using only his restless eye and ingenious reasoning powers, Holmes pieces together the identity of the villain from such unremarkable details as [A] _____. In fact, Holmes's painstaking attention to detail often reminds the reader of Charles Darwin's *On the Origin of the Species*, published some twenty years earlier.

29 **Which of the following is true about the passage above?**

① Holmes's enemies left no traces at the crime scene.
② The character of Holmes was based on Charles Darwin.
③ The emergence of detective stories is related with people's fascination with science.
④ No real detectives would have been capable of solving Holmes's cases.
⑤ Doyle's contemporaries were all familiar with Darwin's work.

30 **Which example would best fit [A]?**

① alibis of the suspects
② the blood type of the victim
③ the fingerprint on the doorknob
④ the kind of ink used in a handwritten letter
⑤ the testimony of an eyewitness

Pepper is the most widely traded spice in the world, and has been so for more than 3,000 years. It represents more than 25% of the world trade in spices and yet is produced in only a handful of countries within 15 degrees of the equator. India is the largest producer from the Malabar Coast of India, but Sri Lanka, Vietnam, Malaysia and Indonesia are also important producers. Pepper has also been cultivated in the New World and Brazil is a major exporter.

Pepper was used in ancient Egypt and in Roman times, supplied by Arab sea traders who kept the source secret. [A] Later it was supplied overland along the Silk Road. [B] At one point the Greeks, and later the Romans learned of the source of this valuable spice and the race was on. [C] The competition for this valuable spice has been fierce for over 2,000 years and spurred exploration and discovery of the New World by Christopher Columbus. [D] During the Middle Ages when the trade was monopolized by the Portuguese and later the Dutch, pepper was so valuable that it was worth more than gold by weight, and individual peppercorns were widely accepted as legal currency. [E]

31 Which is the best place in the passage for the sentence in the box?

Workers who handled pepper were issued clothes without pockets or cuffs to prevent theft.

① [A]   ② [B]   ③ [C]
④ [D]   ⑤ [E]

32 Which of the following is NOT true according to the passage?

① In ancient times, the source of pepper was kept secret by traders.
② Pepper accounts for more than 25% in the world spice trade market.
③ Arab traders supplied pepper to Egypt and Rome in ancient times.
④ Pepper was legal currency among the Portuguese traders 2000 years ago.
⑤ The discovery of the New World resulted from the competition for pepper.

A NASA study revealed that during twelve gravity-free weeks in space, astronauts grow an average of two inches. Why does rapid growth occur in a weightless environment? One way to answer the question is to observe _____. Between morning and night, everyday weight-bearing activities made possible by gravity such as sitting, standing, or walking cause compression in the spine. This compression squeezes fluid out of the spinal discs into nearby soft tissue. By the end of the day, the moisture gone from the disc causes a person to grow shorter by one-half to three-quarters of an inch. During sleep, where the body does not have to bear its own weight, the fluid soaks back into the spinal discs, lengthening the body to its former height.

In space, moisture from the bloodstream collects in the discs of the spine, just as it does on Earth, but because there is no gravitational pull, no compression occurs. Moisture is not squeezed out of the discs. It remains, making the discs plumper and consequently making a person taller. Most people probably wouldn't mind being an inch or two taller so that they could more easily reach things on high shelves. However, the height increase and spinal pull that occur in zero-gravity environments are frequently accompanied by concurrent negative effects, such as backaches and nerve irritation. In addition, on Earth the human skeleton and musculature must remain strong in order to do the work it takes to hold the body upright against the counterpull of gravity. In gravity-free environments, muscles and bones tend to weaken because they are not used. Astronauts combat this by maintaining a rigorous exercise routine while in space.

33 빈칸에 들어가기에 가장 적합한 것을 고르시오.

① the effect of gravity on the spine column
② the relationship between everyday activities and weight
③ how musculature works to counter the pull of gravity
④ how soft tissue surrounding the spinal disc develops to bear weight

34 윗글의 내용과 일치하지 <u>않는</u> 것으로 가장 적합한 것을 고르시오.

① A person is taller in the morning than in the evening on Earth.
② In space, astronauts turn back to their former heights after sleep.
③ Astronauts grow in height in space because their spinal discs retain moisture.
④ Zero-gravity environments often cause some negative effects on the human body.

Sports facilities built in the late 1970s, 80s, and early 90s were routinely designed to enhance in-facility experiences but routinely ignored the potential for (A) harnessing associated economic activity that could take place on adjacent real estate. Facilities built during this time period were constructed with substantial public investments. The failure to (B) diminish property values and capitalize on the economic activity taking place within the venue generated substantial levels of discontent with the decision to support a team's effort to secure a new venue. _____, all of the benefits from the building of venues (C) accrued to team owners and others linked to the sports industry. There was little if any financial return to the public sector partners. The situation was made worse when team owners were allowed to (D) retain most, if not all, of the revenue streams that were created in these new state-of-the-art facilities.

35 Which of the underlined words is NOT appropriate?

① (A)   ② (B)
③ (C)   ④ (D)

36 Which is the most appropriate for the blank?

① As a result   ② Nevertheless
③ Otherwise   ④ In contrast

37 According to the passage, which is true?

① The benefits from building new sports facilities are not fairly distributed.
② It is difficult for sports teams to find new facilities.
③ Financial management is the most significant in modern sports industry.
④ Team owners contributed to the development of public-invested sports industry.

A crime's been committed. The police are sure they have the right guy in custody. After all, they have an eyewitness. But should they be so sure? "No," claim psychologists who have studied eyewitness testimony.

Daniel Wright, a psychologist at Sussex University, has found that when witnesses are given misleading information after an incident, some will adapt their memories to accommodate this new information. In one experiment, 40 students looked at a picture book showing the story of two men meeting at a pool hall and of a woman later stealing one man's wallet. Each student studied the book on his or her own. Without any of the volunteers knowing, half of the group had slightly different information from the other half. Twenty students saw a picture book showing the women loitering outside the pool hall on her own before the crime. The other half saw a picture of her loitering with an accomplice. When questioned afterwards, on their own, about whether the woman had an accomplice, 39 of 40 students got it right.

Then the students were paired off so that, in each pair, only one had seen the picture book featuring the accomplice and one had viewed the picture book without the accomplice. Each pair was asked to discuss what they knew, and to answer the question jointly: Did the woman have an accomplice? Since the members of each pair had seen different scenarios, none of them should have reached agreement. In fact, fifteen pairs reached a compromise. In other words, 15 witnesses were _____ by what their partner had told them.

38 윗글의 빈칸에 들어갈 가장 알맞은 것을 고르시오.

① swayed ② ignored
③ defeated ④ obsessed

39 윗글의 내용과 맞지 않는 것을 고르시오.

① Psychologists have studied eyewitness testimony.
② Witnesses sometimes change their stories when they are given misleading information.
③ In the first experiment, only one of the 40 students who were questioned was wrong.
④ In the second experiment, virtually every pair reached agreement instantly.

'Text neck' refers to an overuse syndrome that triggers neck and shoulder pain. Simply put, text neck is the pain and injury one experiences from looking down to use a smartphone too much. The behavior can affect people at any age, but it is particularly dangerous for kids and teens. This is because not only do young people tend to use their handheld devices for longer periods, but developing necks and spines are more (A) _____ to abnormal forces. An obvious way to avoid developing text neck is to put down the smartphone. But since few people are willing to stop texting, a more realistic goal is to change the way you hold your phone. The more you can keep your neck in a(n) (B) _____ position, the less likely you are to develop text neck. Ideally, you would hold your head with your ears in line with your shoulders, holding your device at eye level. The more your neck is bent, the greater the forces on the neck. Text neck, though it may sound trendy, is most certainly a real issue. Posture issues from text neck can lead to conditions such as cracks in the discs, stenosis, pinched nerves, and more. An average head can weigh around 10 to 12 pounds in a neutral position, and looking down 15 degrees can increase the impact on the neck by 27 pounds.

40 Which one of the following ordered (A) and (B)?

① converted - neutral
② detrimental - vertical
③ susceptible - upright
④ vulnerable – sideways

41 According to the passage, which of the following is true?

① Text neck is a trendy, temporary problem.
② Medical conditions caused by text neck are incurable.
③ Handheld devices are more pain than they are worth.
④ Posture change will alleviate text neck.

42 According to the passage, which of the following is true?

① Adults use their smartphones longer than teens do.
② A head has less impact on the neck when it is bent.
③ Text neck can result in stenosis and pinched nerves.
④ A straightened neck increases the forces on the neck.

When faced with a decision to make, utilitarians prefer to create a list of pros and cons. One of the main ethical theories, utilitarianism (A) _____ that the key to determining what makes an act morally right or wrong is its consequences.

Whether people's intentions are good or bad is irrelevant; what matters is whether the result of their actions is good or bad. Happiness is the ultimate goal of human beings and the highest moral good. Thus, if there is great unhappiness because of an act, then that action can be said to be morally wrong. Utilitarians believe that people should carefully weigh the potential consequences of an action before they take it.

Another problematic aspect of utilitarianism is that it deems it acceptable to use another person as a means to an end and sacrifice the happiness of one or a few for the happiness of many.

43 **Choose the best word for (A).**

① denies   ② posits   ③ questions   ④ discredits

44 **Which one is TRUE?**

① Using utilitarianism to make a moral decision is not always easy.
② Utilitarians believe that consequences are irrelevant.
③ A pro/con list is the only way to make the right decision for utilitarians.
④ Utilitarians believe sacrifices are not necessary in life.

45 **Which one is NOT TRUE?**

① Utilitarians might use people as a means to an end.
② Utilitarians believe that actions that create a lot of unhappiness are morally wrong.
③ Utilitarians assert that having good or bad intentions is not important.
④ Utilitarians think that potential consequences should be weighed after the actions are taken.

CHAPTER 02

특정 정보

본문의 특정 내용을 묻는 문제는 본문의 내용을 정확하게 파악하고 이해하였는가를 확인하는 가장 대표적인 유형이다. 육하원칙에 근거하여 세부적인 내용을 묻는 문제는 주로 본문의 내용에 근거해서 묻는 것이므로 본문에 대한 정확한 이해가 선행되어야 한다. 즉 특정 정보를 글 속에서 제대로 찾아낼 수 있는지를 묻는 것이다. 글을 읽으면서 핵심 정보를 놓치지 않아야 한다.

01 질문 유형

Why does the author mention ***?
Which of the following was NOT a cause of ***?
According to the passage, what has changed ***?
Which of the following is NOT mentioned as an effect of ***?

02 문제 풀이 전략

❶ **본문의 해당 부분을 찾아낸다.**
세부적인 내용을 묻는 문제에 대처하기 위해서는 본문을 정확히 읽어 낼 수 있는 능력이 요구된다. 본문의 해당 부분만을 이해하면 풀리는 경우가 대부분이나, 다만 육하원칙에 근거하여 묻는 질문에 타당한 답변을 골라야지 대강의 뜻만으로 연결된 것을 막연히 정답으로 선택해서는 안 된다.

❷ **기본적인 내용의 변형 출제에 주의한다.**
쉬운 문제에 속하므로 출제자들이 내용을 약간 비틀어서 오답을 유인하는 경우가 종종 있다. 가령 주체의 혼동을 유발한다거나, 핵심 내용의 시제를 다르게 제시하는 등의 경우를 유의하여야 한다.

❸ **선택지를 본문과 대조하여 정답을 선택한다.**
문제가 요하는 특정 정보를 본문을 스캔하여 찾아냈다면, 선택지와 대조하여 올바른 정답을 골라낸다. 다만 paraphrase한 정답이 제시될 수 있으므로 본문에 나온 단어나 어구에만 집착할 필요는 없다. 즉 본문을 바탕으로 특정 정보를 정확하게 제시한 답을 선택한다.

The student of insects who does nothing but collect, kill, and mount these animals and study the dead specimens will miss the most interesting part of insect study. Anyone who takes time to study living insects will find that they are fascinating and often amazing little animals. They can be studied in the field or in captivity. Many are very easy to keep in captivity, where they can be studied more easily and at closer range than in the field. Some collectors try to catch an insect as soon as they see it. We suggest that you occasionally stop and watch an insect awhile before you try to collect it. You may learn things about its habits that you would not learn if you caught it immediately.

곤충을 바로 잡지 말고 지켜볼 것을 제안한다. 그래야만 얻을 수 있는 정보를 언급하기 위함이다.

포획 당시에는 놓칠 수 있는 곤충의 습성을 배울 수 있다고 언급되어 있다.

Q. What can be missed when you are observing insects in captivity?

① their colors
② their organs
③ their habits
④ their sizes

위의 두 문장을 근거로 곤충의 습성이 정답임을 알 수 있다.

정답 　 ③

해석 　 **채집된 곤충을 관찰할 때 놓칠 수 있는 것은 무엇인가?**

곤충을 잡아서, 죽이고, 고정시키기만 하고 죽은 표본만을 연구하는 학생들은 곤충 연구에서 가장 재미있는 부분을 놓치게 된다. 시간을 들여 살아 있는 곤충을 연구하는 사람은 누구나 곤충이 매혹적이고 종종 작지만 놀라운 존재임을 알게 될 것이다. 이러한 것들은 현장에서나 채집된 상태에서 연구될 수 있다. 많은 곤충들은 채집된 상태에서 보관하기 쉬우며, 채집된 상태에서는 현장에서보다도 더 가까운 거리에서 더 쉽게 연구될 수 있다. 일부 수집가들은 곤충을 보자마자 잡으려 한다. 우리는 여러분에게 곤충을 잡으려 하기 전에 가끔은 멈춘 다음 한 동안 지켜볼 것을 제안한다. 여러분은 곤충을 즉시 잡았을 때에는 배울 수 없을 곤충의 습성에 관해 배울 수 있을 것이다.

① 곤충의 빛깔　　　　② 곤충의 내장
③ 곤충의 습성　　　　④ 곤충의 크기

해설 　 본문의 가장 마지막에서 현장에서 곤충을 바로 사로잡는 대신 지켜보며 연구하면 "곤충을 즉시 잡았을 때에는 배울 수 없을 곤충의 습성에 관해 배울(may learn things about its habits that you would not learn)" 것이라고 명시되어 있다. 따라서 답은 ③이다.

어휘 　 **in captivity** 포로가 된, 사로잡힌, 채집된　　**mount** ⓥ 고정시키다
　　specimen ⓝ 표본　　　　　　　　　　　　**occasionally** ⓐ 가끔

01 What is the number of the combination lock?

Another man and I share a locker at work. Noticing that it needed a new combination lock, my partner who was thirty years old said he would pick one up on his way to work the next day. It occurred to me later that I might not see him in the morning. How would I find out the combination? I needn't have worried. When I arrived at work, I found that he had used the locker before me and had left a note reading: "To find the first number subtract 21 from my age. The second number is 6 less than that. To find the third number subtract 2 from the second."

① 860　　　　② 862　　　　③ 931　　　　④ 942

02 Which one is NOT the reason why fashions in our society change rapidly?

One reason that fashions soon become out-of-date is that our society values novelty; new things are considered desirable rather than a threat to established traditions. Another reason is that designers and apparel makers, who profit by producing popular new styles, encourage change. Finally, new fashions are a means of showing social status, as well as appearing attractive. The latest styles are adopted first by the wealthy who can afford them. Afterwards, inexpensive copies are made available to people of lower means. Sometimes, however, a reverse process takes place. Blue jeans were for many years the traditional clothes of the working class. Today they have become very popular with the middle and upper classes.

① Newness is valued.
② Wearing new fashions demonstrates social status.
③ Upper-class people get tired of their clothes more quickly than other social classes.
④ Clothing designers and manufacturers change style often in order to make more money.

03 Which of the following is not mentioned about vinegar? 명지대 2014

Vinegar can be produced from a range of products, including fruits, berries, potatoes, beets, malt, grains, and even coconuts. Vinegar is created when the natural sugars of the product ferment to form alcohol and then continue on to a secondary fermentation that changes them into an acid. Vinegar has been around for more than 10,000 years. It was originally discovered when a cask of wine had gone past its prime, turning into *vin aigre* ('sour wine' in French). Balsamic vinegar is a good choice for imparting flavor to recipes — even though it has a high acid level, it lends a somewhat mellow flavor because its sweetness balances the tartness. Balsamic vinegar is ideal to use with strawberries or mango. New spice-infused vinegars such as cinnamon, clove, and nutmeg can also lend an interesting flavor to recipes.

① how it is made
② how it was first made
③ what the word means in French
④ how it can be best preserved

[01~02]

The supercomputer has predicted a rise in temperature of 0.2°C each decade. This will be the fastest increase since the end of the last ice age, 10,000 years ago. Another supercomputer in Germany has made the same prediction. Changes in temperature, combined with even more important changes in rainfall, will be rapid enough to harm agriculture, forests, and natural ecosystems. The computer makes its prediction by showing how pollution is cooling, as well as warming, the planet. The temperature rise is caused by a buildup of heat-trapping greenhouse gases which are produced by burning fossil fuels and forests. But some kinds of pollution, like those that cause acid rain, also act to cool the planet by reflecting sunlight away before it has a chance to warm the earth. Sir John Houghton, a former Meteorological Office chief executive, has said, "We should take action now, that we can easily take, to limit emissions."

01 A new supercomputer simulation has shown that _____.

① the earth will get warmer
② the earth has a climate
③ the weather has become worse
④ the temperature will increase by 0.5°C

02 The temperature rise _____.

① was predicted by the new supercomputer a decade ago
② can be caused by acid rain
③ is mainly caused by reflecting sunlight away
④ can be prevented by limiting emissions

Early Victorian costume not only made women look weak and helpless, it made them weak and helpless. The main agent of this debility was the corset, which at the time was thought of not as a mere fashion item but as a medical necessity. Ladies' "frames," it was believed, were extremely delicate; their muscles could not hold them up without assistance. Well-brought-up little girls were laced into juvenile versions of the corset as early as three or four. Gradually their stays were lengthened, stiffened and tightened. By the time they reached late adolescence they were wearing cages of heavy canvas reinforced with steel, and their back muscles had often atrophied to the point where they could not sit or stand for long unsupported. The corset also deformed the internal organs and made it impossible to draw a deep breath. As a result fashionably dressed ladies fainted easily, suffered from digestive complaints, and felt weak and exhausted after any strenuous exertion.

03 According to the passage, why did people think that women needed corsets?

① Because they had to look beautiful.
② Because they wanted to look weak and helpless.
③ Because they needed to support their delicate bodies.
④ Because they were forced to wear them.
⑤ Because they had stiff backs.

04 Which of the following is NOT mentioned as an effect of wearing corsets?

① Weariness
② Indigestion
③ Poor appetite
④ Frequent fainting
⑤ Weak back muscles

[05~07]

The leading causes of amnesia are either physical or psychological. In antegrade amnesia, the subject is unable to recall the events that occur after a shock or an injury to the brain; however, past memories will not be lost. In retrograde amnesia, the patient is capable of recalling events that occur after the trauma. Interestingly enough, information stored before the shock is lost and cannot be retrieved. In para-amnesia, established memories are contorted. In psychogenic fugue, the subject may venture into a new lifestyle, trying to repress memories which lead to trepidation. The events happening during psychogenic fugue are non-retrievable. Nonetheless, the experiences that happened before the onset can be recovered. Among the most popular treatments for psychologically related amnesia are psychotherapy, the use of drugs, and hypnosis.

05 What is the main topic of the passage?

① The major causes of amnesia
② Popular treatments for amnesia
③ Interference of amnesia with our memory
④ Different types of amnesia

06 The underlined word trepidation could best be replaced by _____.

① anxiety   ② restraint
③ intimidation   ④ self-denial

07 Memories of patients' experiences while suffering psychogenic fugue are _____.

① distorted and unclear   ② lost
③ temporarily hidden   ④ quickly able to be recalled

Most of the Ⓐ _____ innovations developed during WWI were in response to equally advanced Ⓑ _____ innovations. One such weapon was poison gas, used for the first time in a large-scale assault by the Germans in 1915. While already considered a war crime — poison or poison weapons were forbidden under both the Hague Declaration of 1899 and the 1907 Hague Convention — the use of gas was also, in some ways, a predictable result of a type of warfare that confounded commanders with how to attack beyond an entrenched front line.

But when Germans first used chlorine gas against the Allies in spring 1915, British medical personnel weren't prepared to respond to the new weapon, which destroyed a victim's lungs and respiratory system over a matter of hours. Shortly after the first attacks, scientist John Scott Haldane travelled to the front to research what the gases were and how to prevent their worst effects.

One of his inventions was this oxygen apparatus, which was based on the finding that increasing the blood's concentration of oxygen was one of the best ways to work against the deadly gases as they damaged the lungs. It could treat four people simultaneously. The apparatus became a crucial innovation for the gas treatment units that were soon stationed near the front lines.

08 Choose one that is most appropriate for the blank Ⓐ and the blank Ⓑ.

① domestic — international
② chemical — industrial
③ medical — military
④ armed — military
⑤ civilian — martial

09 According to the passage, the best treatment for the gas-poisoned soldier is _____.

① to stop bleeding and perform blood transfusion
② to speed up the concentration ratio of oxygen in his blood
③ to open his respiratory system fully as soon as possible
④ to carry him to the nearest hospital as soon as possible
⑤ to provide a continuous, accurate flow of a mix of oxygen and ether

I'm not sure why, but startups are very counterintuitive. Maybe it's just because knowledge about them hasn't permeated our culture yet. But whatever the reason, starting a startup is a task where you can't always (A) _____. It's like skiing. When you first try skiing and you want to slow down, your instinct is to lean back. But if you lean back on skis, you fly down the hill out of control. So part of learning to ski is learning to suppress that impulse. Eventually you get new habits, but at first it takes a conscious effort. When you begin, there's a list of things you're trying to remember as you start down the hill. Startups are as unnatural as skiing, so there's a similar list for startups to remember. Startups are so weird that if you trust your instincts, you'll make a lot of mistakes. I often joke that my function is to tell founders things they would ignore. It's really true. Why do the founders not consider the advisor's advice seriously? Well, that's the thing about counterintuitive ideas: they are opposite to your instincts. You only need other people to give you advice that surprises you. That's why there are a lot of ski instructors and not many running instructors.

10 Startups are likened to skiing because they both _____.

① are easy to control
② contradict our intuitions
③ require intensive and extensive training
④ demand strategies like effective running

11 Which of the following best fits into (A)?

① get new habits
② rely on your experience
③ make use of your expertise
④ trust your instincts

12 Which of the following does the author suggest the startup founders do?

① Listen to their advisors
② Take in-depth courses
③ Make a list of creative ideas
④ Observe successful startups first

[13~15]

Homing pigeons are known for their uncanny internal compass, yet a new study reveals that sometimes the birds get home the same way we do: they follow the roads. Tim Guilford and Dora Biro at England's Oxford University followed pigeons over a three-year period, using tiny tracking devices equipped with global positioning system technology developed by Swiss and Italian colleagues. "We expected the birds to take the most energy-efficient route," says Guilford. "And we were interested in finding out what land features they used to do that."

What they discovered was surprising. Within ten kilometers of home, the pigeons relied less on their well-known talents for decoding the sun's position or deciphering the Earth's magnetic field to help them navigate. Instead they opted for a habitual route that followed the linear features in the landscape, such as roads, rivers, railways, and hedge lines — even when it wasn't the most direct way home.

13 The researchers at Oxford University were originally concerned with _____.

① whether pigeons could find out an efficient route to their way home
② how pigeons detected tracking devices attached to their body
③ what natural talents helped pigeons to navigate most efficiently in their flight
④ what land features pigeons used to take the most energy-efficient way

14 It was discovered that the way pigeons chose near home was _____.

① habitual   ② the most energy-efficient
③ the most direct   ④ indirect

15 Homing pigeons are similar to humans, in that _____.

① they often lose their way home
② they use global positioning technology to locate home
③ they sometimes stick to a linear route
④ they decode the sun's position or the magnetic field for navigation

In the spring of the year 399 B.C., a famous Greek philosopher was put on trial for having committed two crimes. One was impiety to the gods of the state; the other was the corruption of youth, by teaching them impiety. The penalty for a conviction on these charges was a severe one, possibly death. The prisoner's name was Socrates, and he was seventy years old at that time. There were other reasons, political reasons, for trying Socrates. He had been associated with the old aristocratic regime, now overthrown by the democracy, and he was held in suspicion as a critic of the democracy. Among other things, he became unpopular for his strange doctrine that even politicians ought to know ㉮ ＿＿＿＿＿＿＿ they are doing. Socrates was reputed to be the wisest man of his time. This reputation surprised him, he said, for he considered himself to be an ignorant man; ignorant of the answers to the supreme questions concerning human happiness and human destiny. But he was also sure that no one else knew the answers to these questions, and this furnished him with an explanation of his reputation as a wise man. ㉯ ＿＿＿＿＿＿＿ he was ignorant, he alone knew that he was ignorant, whereas other ignorant men did not know that they were, thinking they had all the answers.

16 Socrates was put on trial for impiety to the gods of the state and for ＿＿＿＿＿＿＿.

① rude conduct
② his writing against democracy
③ corruption of youth
④ theft
⑤ ignoring some supreme questions

17 Politically Socrates was _____.

   ① for the new democratic regime

   ② a revolutionary

   ③ a communist

   ④ a monarchist

   ⑤ against the new regime

18 Socrates held that he was _____.

   ① one of the wisest men of the time

   ② one of the most ignorant men of the time

   ③ an average thinker

   ④ ignorant because he could not answer certain supreme questions

   ⑤ unpopular because his doctrine was opposed by some politicians

19 What would be the most appropriate word pair to fill in ㉮ and ㉯?

   ① how − As

   ② that − If

   ③ what − Though

   ④ if − Despite

   ⑤ what − Whether

World War I, which began nearly 100 years ago, produced its own crop of bionic men. In previous wars, severely injured soldiers often succumbed to gangrene and infection. Thanks to better surgery, many now survived. On the German side alone, there were 2 million casualties, 64 percent of them with injured limbs. Some 67,000 were amputees. In all nations involved in the war an emerging generation of so-called "_____," loomed ominously over the pension and welfare system, and many government bureaucrats, military leaders and civilians worried about their long-term fate. One solution was returning mutilated soldiers to the workforce. At last various prostheses were designed to make that possible.

20 The best expression for the blank would be _____.

① war cripples   ② war veterans
③ the disabled   ④ the war neurotic
⑤ the insane

21 According to the passage, World War I led to _____.

① the medical advances in surgery
② a remarkable change in welfare policy
③ advances in the technology of prosthetic limbs
④ the long-term fate of war veterans
⑤ the women's revolt against the established social system

Coffee is best known as a powerful stimulant that helps people stay awake during night driving and cramming before final exams. Its caffeine is capable of boosting energy, increasing alertness, and quickening reaction time. It is also a mood elevator and may help mild depression. Recently, researchers from the University of Bristol reviewed a decade of research into caffeine's influence on cognition and mood. The survey revealed that a cup of coffee could help in the performance of tasks requiring sustained attention, even during low-alertness situations such as after lunch, at night, or when a person has a cold.

Coffee's health advantages are not confined to mood elevation and increased energy. Some over-the-counter cold formulas contain caffeine, partly to ⓐ _____ the sedative effects of the antihistamines they contain; and caffeine also helps open the bronchial tubes, relieving the congestion of colds and flu. Coffee's action as a bronchodilator can also help prevent asthma attacks. In addition, several studies show that, compared with plain aspirin, the combination of aspirin and caffeine relieves pain significantly better than aspirin alone. Finally, coffee may also improve physical stamina, according to a report published in the journal The Physician and Sports Medicine. Athletes who want coffee's benefits typically drink three or four cups during the hour or two before an event.

22 Which of the following best fits into ⓐ?

① gauge ② enhance
③ counteract ④ demonstrate
⑤ generate

23 Which of the following is NOT mentioned as a benefit of drinking coffee?

① speeding up metabolism
② shortening reaction time
③ enhancing alertness
④ boosting stamina
⑤ elevating mood

24 Which of the following is NOT stated in the passage?

① Research shows that coffee helps reduce depression.
② Caffeine helps relieve the congestion of colds and flu.
③ Coffee helps people perform better in tasks requiring sustained attention.
④ Some athletes drink coffee before an event takes place.
⑤ Coffee is a strong pain reliever by itself.

02

The traditional American Thanksgiving Day celebration goes back to 1621. In that year a special feast was prepared in Plymouth, Massachusetts. The colonists who had settled there had left England because they felt denied of religious _____. When they came to the new land, they faced many difficulties while sailing across the ocean. The ship which carried them was called the Mayflower. The North Atlantic which has bad storms made traveling difficult for them. They were assisted in learning to live in the new land by the Indians who inhabited the region. The Puritans, as they were called, had much to be thankful for. Their religious practices were no longer a source of criticism by the government. They learned to adjust their farming habits to the climate and soil. When they selected the fourth Thursday of November for their Thanksgiving celebration, they invited their neighbors, the Indians, to join them for dinner and prayer and to express gratitude to the Indians for helping them in their new life. They recalled the group of 102 men, women, and children who left England. They remembered the dead who did not live to see the shores of Massachusetts. They reflected on the 65 days' journey which tested their strength.

25 **Choose the one that best fills in the blank.**

① sacrifice   ② obligation   ③ freedom   ④ celebration

26 **They invited the Indians to dinner in order to _____.**

① teach them how to cook British dishes
② supply the hungry Indians with food
③ show their deepest gratitude to them
④ avoid war against them

27 **They gave thanks while remembering _____.**

① those who remained in England
② their friends who did not survive the journey
③ their former religious practices
④ to invite their Indian friends

"No one knows why we yawn," says Andrew Gallup, a psychology professor at the State University of New York at Albany. Now Gallup and fellow researchers have a new explanation: yawning, they said, is a way for the body to cool the brain. Writing in the May issue of Evolutionary Psychology, they reported that volunteers yawned more often in situations in which their brains were likely to be warmer. To prove their theory that yawning regulates brain temperature when other systems in the body are not doing enough, the researchers took advantage of the well-established tendency of people to yawn when those around them do. The volunteers were asked to step into a room by themselves and watch a video showing people behaving neutrally, laughing or yawning. Observers watching through a one-way mirror counted how many times the volunteers yawned. Some volunteers were asked to breathe only through their noses as they watched. Later, volunteers were asked to press warm or cold packs on their foreheads. "The two conditions (nasal breathing and forehead cooling) thought to promote brain cooling practically eliminated ⓐ _____," the researchers wrote. The study may also help explain why yawning spreads from person to person. A cooler brain, Gallup said, is a clearer brain. So yawning actually appears to be a way to stay more alert. And ⓑ _____, he said, may have evolved to help groups remain vigilant against danger.

28 다음 중 윗글에 나타난 **Gallup**과 그의 동료들의 연구 결과와 가장 일치하는 것을 고르시오.

① Yawning is associated with laughing.
② Yawning is associated with sleepiness.
③ Yawning is associated with nasal breathing.
④ Yawning is associated with oxygen levels in the blood.

29 밑줄 친 ⓐ와 ⓑ에 공통적으로 들어가기에 가장 적합한 것을 고르시오.

① high temperature　　　　② brain warming
③ brain alertness　　　　　④ contagious yawning

2020 has been a tumultuous year, and as we look forward to 2021, the 'K-shaped' economic recovery we're in cannot be ignored. This type of recovery isn't all that new — in fact, the world saw such a recovery in 2008. When an economy is bouncing back from a recession and starting to expand again, economists have an alphabet of the letter to describe said recession and recovery. The 'K-shaped' economic recovery is characterized by a stark split in the recovery pace of the economy — some sectors are bouncing back ahead of the rest at a much faster pace, while others are continuing a downward trajectory. The split in the recovery pace therefore resembles the letter 'K'. This begs the question, which industries are doing well, and which aren't? The industries that are on the upper curve are technology players, large corporations, governments, and public utilities. While these are industries that may bounce back faster than the rest, the industries on the lower curve, who are suffering the fallout from the pandemic, are the travel, entertainment, and food services industries. However, there is a way for businesses in most sectors, even those on the lower curve, to find a way to thrive.

30 According to the passage, which of the following represents the most likely economic activity for industries in the upper part of the 'K'?

① They are likely to recover quickly.
② Their recovery will continue to go downward.
③ Their economic activity is unaffected by a tumultuous economy.
④ Through government intervention their economic recovery is assured.

31 According to the passage, what is the most likely future for industries in the lower part of the 'K'?

① They can recover only with the help of industries in the upper part of the 'K'.
② They also have a way to survive, but the author of the passage doesn't mention what it is.
③ Industries such as the travel, entertainment, and food services industries can recover only with government assistance.
④ Many industries in the lower part of the 'K' will never recover.

Early one morning in August 1997, Korean Air Flight 801 was heading for a landing at Guam Airport. There was a spate of heavy weather — which wouldn't have been a problem in itself. But the airport's guidance system was down, and the pilot was dog-tired. Even though he'd landed at this airport many times in the past, he forgot that there was a big hill blocking the approach to the runway. He flew the plane right into it, killing 228 people. The consultant who came in to analyze the problem found a surprising reason for it: the Koreans' cultural tendency to be extremely deferential to their superiors. Both the first officer and the flight engineer had recognized the danger signs, but they couldn't bring themselves to confront the pilot directly or take control of the plane. The problem went away when the consultant required everyone in Korean Air's cockpits to speak English. Without the deferential forms of address used in Korean, the crew was able to speak more directly, and as a result, Korean Air went on to achieve one of the best safety records of any airline.

32 **Which of the following was NOT a cause of Korean Air Flight 801's accident?**

① Guam Airport's guidance system wasn't working.
② The pilot didn't know Guam Airport well.
③ Its first officer didn't confront the pilot directly.
④ The weather conditions were bad.

33 **According to the passage, what has changed Korean Air's safety record?**

① Making a huge investment in its safety equipment.
② Making its cockpit crew speak more directly to their superiors.
③ Making the flight crew more aware of potential hazards through increased training.
④ Making its employees attend safety workshops.

[34~36]

The word vitamin was originally derived from Funk's term "vital amine." In 1912, he was referring to Christian Eijkman's discovery of an amine extracted from rice polishings that could prevent beriberi. Funk's recognition of the antiberiberi factor as vital for life was indeed accurate. Researchers have since found that vitamins are essential organic compounds that the human body cannot synthesize. Two independent research teams, Osborne and Mendel at Yale University and McCollum and Davis at the University of Wisconsin, simultaneously discovered vitamin A in 1913.

Vitamin A is essential for vision (especially dark adaptation), immune response, bone growth, reproduction, the maintenance of the surface linings of the eyes, epithelial cell growth and repair, and the epithelial integrity of the respiratory, urinary, and intestinal tracts. Vitamin A is also important for embryonic development and the regulation of adult genes. Deficiency of vitamin A is found among malnourished, elderly, and chronically sick populations in the United States, but it is more ㉮ _____ in developing countries. Abnormal visual adaptation to darkness, dry skin, dry hair, broken fingernails, and decreased resistance to infections are among the first signs of vitamin A deficiency (VAD).

34 윗글의 제목으로 가장 적당한 것은?

① Vitamin a and Its Deficiency-related Symptoms
② The Origin of Vitamin a Research
③ Types of Vitamin a and Their Roles
④ Results of Vitamin a Deficiency

35 문맥상 빈칸 ㉮에 알맞은 것은?

① limited   ② uncommon   ③ prevalent   ④ isolated

36 윗글에서 **vitamin A deficiency**의 결과로 나타나는 증상으로 언급되지 <u>않은</u> 것은?

① abnormal dark adaptation   ② decreased immune response
③ broken finger nails   ④ epithelial cell growth

Tropical cyclones have officially been named since 1945 and are named for a variety of reasons, which include to facilitate communications between forecasters and the public when forecasts, watches, and warnings are issued. Names also reduce confusion about what storm is being described, as more than one can occur in the same region at the same time. The official practice of naming tropical cyclones started in 1945 within the Western Pacific and was gradually extended out until 2004, when the Indian Meteorological Department started to name cyclonic storms within the North Indian ocean.

Before the official practice of naming of tropical cyclones began, significant tropical cyclones were named after annoying politicians, mythological creatures, saints and place names. Names are drawn in order from predetermined lists and are usually assigned to tropical cyclones with one-, three-, or ten-minute sustained wind speeds of more than 65 km/h (40 mph) depending on which area it originates. However, standards vary from basin to basin with some tropical depressions named in the Western Pacific, while within the Southern Hemisphere tropical cyclones have to have a significant amount of gale-force winds occurring around the center before they are named.

37 **Which of the following is the best title of the passage?**

① Naming of Tropical Cyclones
② Diversity of Identifying Tropical Cyclones
③ Practice of Naming Tropical Cyclones in the Western Pacific
④ Names of Tropical Cyclones in the Southern Hemisphere

38 **The old method of naming tropical cyclones was _____.**

① to identify them by using numerical order
② to give them the names of politicians, saints, and places
③ to identify the according to their duration of time
④ to give them the names of areas they originate

39 **Which kind of quality is NOT mentioned in assigning the list to tropical cyclones?**

① duration of time   ② wind speed
③ amount of gale-force winds   ④ name of basin

The term "minority," at least as used to describe racial and ethnic groups in the United States, may need to be retired or rethought soon. By the end of this decade, according to Census Bureau projections released in 2012, no single racial or ethnic group will constitute a majority of children under 18. And in about three decades, the U.S. will have "a majority-minority population" as a whole. As the United States grows more diverse, the Census Bureau reported, it is becoming a "plurality nation." "The next half century marks key points in continuing trends — the U.S. will become a plurality nation, where the non-Hispanic white population remains the largest single group, but no group is in the majority," said the bureau's acting director. The diversity of the nation's children is increasing even faster than was previously expected. The Census Bureau expects that the demographic shift to a majority-minority child population will come in 2018, several years earlier than it previously predicted. The bureau predicts that by 2043 — which is a year later than it previously projected — there will be no single majority group in the country as a whole, as the share of non-Hispanic whites falls below 50 percent.

40 **Which of the following is the passage mainly about?**

① Demographic change
② Cultural diversity
③ Ethnic minority
④ Population growth

41 **Which of the following distributions would represent "a majority-minority population"?**

① Race A 23% Race B 55% Race C 14% Others 8%
② Race A 35% Race B 40% Race C 18% Others 7%
③ Race A 52% Race B 17% Race C 16% Others 15%
④ Race A 26% Race B 60% Race C 7% Others 7%

42 **Which of the following would be true of the U.S. population in 2020?**

① White Americans, including white Hispanic, will no longer be a majority.
② The Hispanic population is expected to exceed the population of whites.
③ Non-Hispanic whites will not be a majority among children under 18.
④ There will be no single majority among the entire population.

Depression is more than just feeling a bit down or overwhelmed; at its worst, it is a debilitating illness, leaving its sufferers unable to sleep or eat and filled with feelings of immense sadness and guilt. It is sometimes thought of as a modern affliction, a result of the rich world's leisurely preoccupation with the self. But that couldn't be Ⓐ _____ from the truth. Depression was once referred to as 'melancholia', a diagnosis recorded around the 5th century BC by philosophers like Hippocrates. Aretaeus described symptoms that sound all too familiar to modern clinicians: 'The patients become dull or stern, dejected or unreasonably torpid... they also become peevish, dispirited and start up from a disturbed sleep'. Depression is a reality for people in the developing world, too: one survey of Aids-stricken regions in Uganda showed that 21 percent of residents were clinically depressed, while studies in a Pakistani village showed that 44 percent of the population were suffering from some kind of depressive disorder.

43 Which of the following is most appropriate for blank Ⓐ?

① distracted   ② further
③ hidden   ④ saved

44 Which of the following is NOT mentioned as a symptom of depression in the passage?

① disappointment   ② suicide
③ inactivity   ④ irritation

45 According to the passage, which of the following is true?

① Depression was diagnosed recently in human history.
② People nowadays suffer more from depression than in the past.
③ The symptoms of depression seem similar both in the past and in the present.
④ Depression is more serious in developing countries than in the rich world.

03 문법성 판단

독해 속에서 문법적인 지식을 묻는 문제 유형이다. 글의 종합적인 이해를 평가하기 위해 독해 지문 내에서 문법이 어떻게 활용되고 있는지를 묻는다. 학교에 따라 다르기는 하지만 문법 문제의 비중이 낮은 학교들에서 문법의 보완으로 많이 묻고 있다.

01 질문 유형

Choose the one that is grammatically incorrect.
Choose the grammatically incorrect among ***.
Which of the following is best for the blank?
Which of the following is most appropriate for the blank?

02 문제 풀이 전략

❶ 독해 속에서 자주 선보이는 문법 사항을 철저히 숙지한다.

지문을 얼마나 이해했는지 평가하기 위한 문제 형식의 하나로, 독해 지문 내에서 문법이 어떻게 활용되고 있는지를 묻는 유형이다. 문제 형태는 일반적인 문법 문제와는 다르게 실제 글 속에서 많이 다루어지는 내용들, 예컨대 동사, 시제, 태, 가정법, 관계대명사, 분사구문, 일치 등을 묻는 문제들이 주류를 이루고 있다.

❷ 본문의 정확한 해석을 통하여 접근한다.

문법 문제라고 생각하지 말고, 글의 이해를 바탕으로 풀 수 있다는 생각으로 글의 흐름 속에서 판단해야 한다. 그러다 보면 어색한 부분이 생길 것이며, 그 부분을 집중적으로 아는 문법 지식을 동원해 본다. 이러한 문제 해결을 위해서 평소 해석해 나가다 어려운 부분은 문법적인 분석을 한두 문장씩 해 보는 게 도움이 된다. 그러다가 이해가 안 되면 문법책을 마치 사전처럼 참조하면 좋다. 그렇게 하면 글 속에서 문법을 바라볼 수 있는 능력이 생기게 된다.

Most smokers have basically the same habits and the same excuses for not quitting smoking. Generally nervous, these people are always searching in their pockets for a cigarette. How disappointed they are to discover ㉮ _____ they've just finished a pack! They must drop everything and run to store. It is ㉯ _____ smoking is an immediate demand. They shrug their shoulders ㉰ _____ reminded of the health hazards of smoking. Don't they realize the risks they're taking? Never. All of the smokers know smoking is a dangerous habit.

이유를 나타내는 접속사가 와야 한다. 만사를 제쳐 놓고 가게로 달려가는 것이 담배를 피워야 한다는 즉각적 요구 때문이다. 그러므로 빈칸에 that은 가능하지만 when은 적당하지 않다.

다음에 이어질 문장이 절이기 때문에 이유를 나타내는 접속사를 골라야 한다.

흡연의 위험을 상기하는 것과 어깨를 으쓱하는 것 사이의 시간적인 관계를 고려하면 관계부사인 when이 와야 한다.

02

Q. Choose the one that is arranged in the right order in the blanks.

① that − because − when   ② when − for − that
③ that − as if − that   ④ when − because − which

정답   ①

해석   **빈칸에 들어갈 말이 바르게 배열된 것을 고르시오.**

대개의 흡연자들은 기본적으로 똑같은 습관을 가지고 있고, 담배를 끊지 못하는 데 대한 변명도 똑같다. 대개 신경이 날카로운 흡연자들은 담배를 찾으려고 노상 주머니를 뒤지고 있다. 담배 한 갑을 방금 다 피운 것을 발견하는 것은 흡연자들에게 얼마나 실망스러울까? 흡연자들은 틀림없이 만사를 제쳐 놓고 가게로 달려간다. 그런 행동을 하는 이유는 흡연은 즉각 적인 요구 사항이기 때문이다. 흡연이 건강에 해롭다는 것을 상기시켜 줄 때에도 흡연자들은 어깨를 으쓱할 뿐이다. 흡연자들은 자신들이 처한 위험을 깨닫지 못하는 것일까? 전혀 그렇지 않다. 흡연자들 모두 흡연이 위험한 습관이라는 것은 알고 있다.

① that − because − when   ② when − for − that
③ that − as if − that   ④ when − because − which

해설   ㉮의 경우, 문맥상 흡연자가 "만사를 제쳐 놓고 가게로 달려가는(drop everything and run to store)" 것이 담배를 피워야 한다는 "즉각적 요구(an immediate demand)" 때문이라는 '이유'를 나타내는 접속사가 와야 한다. ㉯ 다음의 문장이 구가 아닌 절이므로 보기 중에서 because만 가능하다. 따라서 답은 ① 아니면 ④이다. ㉰의 경우, 빈칸에 들어갈 것은 which 아니면 when뿐인데, 문맥상 흡연자들은 위험을 상기시켜 줄 '때'마다 어깨를 으쓱하기만 한다는 의미의 when이 가장 적절하다. 이러한 모든 고려 요소를 결합하면 답으로 가장 적절한 것은 ①이다.

어휘   **excuse** ⓝ 변명, 핑계   **generally** ⓐⓓ 대개
      drop ⓥ (하던 일을) 그만두다, 중단하다   **shrug** ⓥ 어깨를 으쓱하다

[01~02]

All problem solving — whether personal or academic — involves decision-making. You have to make decisions to solve the problem. However, some problems occur because of the decisions you have made. In your school life, you ⓐ _____ decide not to study mathematics and science because you consider them too hard. Because of this decision, certain careers will be closed to you. You can see that many events in your life do not just happen; they are the result of your choices and decisions. Critical thinking and creativity can help you ⓑ _____ both personal and academic problems.

01 빈칸 ⓐ에 문맥상 가장 적합한 단어를 고르시오.

① shall   ② will   ③ may   ④ must

02 빈칸 ⓑ에 문맥상 가장 적합한 단어를 고르시오.

① to be solved   ② solve   ③ solving   ④ solved

03 **Choose the one that is grammatically incorrect.**

The clothes you wear while <u>working on</u> your car or painting your room would not be appropriate for a job interview. Nor would the expressions you use with your friends be appropriate when you <u>speak to</u> a police officer <u>whom</u> you are trying to impress. To be a good writer, therefore, you will be expected to follow the principles of standard written English — in other words, to use language that is right for the job. If your writing does not follow those principles — if it is <u>not</u> filled with errors in grammar, spelling, and punctuation — it will confuse and mislead your reader. It could even convince <u>him or her</u> that you and your ideas should not be taken seriously.

① working on   ② speak to
③ whom   ④ not
⑤ him or her

04 밑줄 친 ⓐ, ⓑ, ⓒ를 내용과 문법에 맞게 가장 정확히 배열한 것은?

Writing plain English is hard work. No one ever learned literature from a textbook. I have never taken a course in writing. I learned to write naturally and on my own. I did not succeed by accident: I succeeded by patient hard work. Verbal dexterity does not make a good book. Too many authors are more concerned with the style of their writing than with the characters they ⓐ write about. There are too many writers whose styles are often marred by verbosity and self-importance. Few great authors have a brilliant command of language. The indispensable characteristic of a good writer is a style ⓑ mark by lucidity.

A good writer is wise in his choice of subjects, and exhaustive in his accumulation of materials. A good writer must have an irrepressible confidence in himself and in his ideas. Good writers know how to excavate significant facts from masses of information. The toughest thing for a writer is ⓒ maintain the vigor and fertility of his imagination. Most writers fail simply because they lack the indispensable qualification of the genuine writer. They are intensely prejudiced. Their horizon, in spite of their education, is a narrow one.

	ⓐ	ⓑ	ⓒ
①	are writing	to mark	maintaining
②	wrote	marked	to maintain
③	wrote	to mark	maintaining
④	are writing	marked	to maintain

[01~02]

New technology enables monitoring of doctor's prescriptions, with both good and bad consequences: Some medical overseers use it to make sure that doctors choose the medicine that best treats patients' ailments, while others use it to pressure doctors to prescribe not the most effective drug but the cheapest one. Similarly, the existence of digital records tracking patients' medical histories can enhance treatment and promote epidemiological research, but it can also lead to invasion of patients' privacy. Computers can bring new realms into the classroom, but they may divert precious funds _____ more solely needed educational tools and deepen the divide between rich and poor classrooms. The list of good news-bad news effects goes on and on.

01 **Which would be the best title of the passage?**

① The dilemmas in the information age
② The effective use of computers in modern education
③ How to distinguish good news and bad news
④ The impact of public policy on individual privacy
⑤ How modern technology promotes human rights

02 **Which of the following is best for the blank?**

① by   ② without
③ with   ④ at
⑤ from

People who eat more protein — especially from seafood — may be less likely to have a stroke, according to survey analysis conducted by the Nanjing University School of Medicine in China. The study, Ⓐ <u>publishing</u> in *Neurology*, the medical journal of the American Academy of Neurology, involved seven separate studies Ⓑ <u>totalling</u> 254,489 people and found that Ⓒ <u>eating</u> just 20 additional grams of protein every day lowered the risk of stroke by 26%.

Overall, the participants with the highest protein intake were 20% less likely to develop a stroke than those with the lowest amount of protein in their diets. The link was strongest for people Ⓓ <u>getting</u> their protein from seafood rather than from grains or red meat. Protein and the fatty acids in fish lower blood pressure, which may help protect against stroke.

03 Which is grammatically INCORRECT?

① Ⓐ

② Ⓑ

③ Ⓒ

④ Ⓓ

04 Which is the best title of the passage?

① How to Increase Fish Consumption

② How to Avoid Red Meat and Grains

③ A Way to Reduce the Risk of Stroke

④ Check Your Blood Pressure Regularly

Rodrigo Bonilla turns off the motor of the boat. We get off the boat and follow him along the path into the rain forest. Above us, a monkey with a baby hangs from a tree. On this hot January day, Rodrigo is not looking for wild animals, but for medicinal plants — plants that can cure or treat illnesses. Medicinal plants grow in rain forests around the world. Rodrigo is Costa Rican. He learned about jungle medicine from his grandmother. He shows us many different plants, such as the broom tree. He tells us that parts of the broom tree can _____. People have always used natural products as medicine. In fact, about 50 percent of Western medicines, such as aspirin, come from natural sources. And some animals eat certain kinds of plants when they are sick. This is why medical researchers are so interested in plants. Many companies are now working with local governments and searching the rain forests for medicinal plants. So far, the search has not produced any new medicines. But it's a good idea to keep looking. That's why we are now here in the Costa Rican rain forest.

05 빈칸에 들어갈 가장 알맞은 것을 고르시오.

① help stop bleed
② help to stop bleed
③ help stop to bleeding
④ help stop bleeding

06 윗글의 내용과 맞지 <u>않는</u> 것을 고르시오.

① It's not easy to find out new medicinal plants.
② Rodrigo leads the expedition to find medicinal plants.
③ Medicines are entirely produced from natural sources.
④ Some animals use medicinal plants to cure themselves.

A novel storm formula is shedding new light on lightning. While researching cloud behavior, David Romps and colleagues devised ⓐ what they say is the most accurate model yet for predicting lightning strikes. Then they used that model to project how strikes will multiply — and how that could lead to more wildfires — if the planet continues to warm Ⓐ For a storm to produce the sudden electric discharge known as lightning, liquid water and ice, plus updrafts fast enough ⓑ to keep both suspended, must be present. Ⓑ He multiplied the measured precipitation by the convective available potential energy, or ⓒ how fast can a storm cloud rise. His calculations using 2011 data matched recorded lightning strikes 77 percent of the time. The conventional model was only 39 percent accurate. Ⓒ The warmer the air is, the more storm-fueling water vapor it can hold. For every degree Celsius that the world warms, lightning strikes may ㉠ _____ about 12 percent in the U.S., Romps says. d. Ⓓ If carbon dioxide emissions continue at the current rate, that could mean ⓓ 50 percent more lightning strikes by 2100.

07 Which is the best place for the following sentence?

> Romps theorized that by putting those factors into an equation, he could calculate how often lightning would strike.

① Ⓐ   ② Ⓑ
③ Ⓒ   ④ Ⓓ

08 Which is grammatically INCORRECT?

① ⓐ   ② ⓑ
③ ⓒ   ④ ⓓ

09 Which best fits into the blank ㉠?

① hit   ② take
③ plunge   ④ increase

Some museums refuse to accept any objects that have a questionable provenance because they might have been stolen from archaeological sites or looted from other museums. It is not unusual during times of war or political upheaval, as recent wars in Afghanistan and Iraq have illustrated, for artifacts to be stolen and offered for sale to the highest bidder. However, some other museum directors insist that there are good reasons for accepting artifacts of unknown origin. Curators are, for example, reluctant to turn down artifacts that have been in private collections for several generations. They argue that a lack of paper documentation does not necessarily mean that those donating the artifacts got them by illegal means since it's difficult to hold on to paperwork for several generations. Curators willing to display artifacts of uncertain provenance also insist that _____, they wouldn't be fulfilling their function of providing the public with historical information about ancient cultures. The Metropolitan Museum of Art, for example, displayed artifacts of unknown origin during an exhibit of art objects from Bactria, an ancient country once located in what is now Afghanistan.

10 What would be the best title for the passage?

① Curators' Roles
② Unknown Provenance
③ Museums' Dilemma
④ Exhibition of Artifacts

11 Which of the following is most appropriate for the blank?

① although they didn't do so
② when they didn't do so
③ if they didn't do so
④ as they didn't do so

[12~14]

In the beginning there was a debate as to whether the global warming was real or not, but (가) <u>today we know it is happening</u>. Today the debate lies in whether or not it is we humans that are causing it. Generally, when (나) <u>people say they do not believe in global warming</u>, what they really mean is that (다) <u>they don't believe that driving cars, clearing forests and draining marshes are responsible for it</u>, or that even if that is the case, it isn't as much of a threat as certain people make it out to be. Alas, they are in denial; they just want to say:

(A) _____.

To state today that one does not believe in global warming at all is not really a reasonable statement to make. Certainly it can be made, but like saying that the earth is the centre of universe, it goes against everything we know. Almost the same can be said for those who do not believe humans are the prime factor in global warming. Yes, nature is hardy and can adapt to amazing situations, the world is not going to crumble due to global warming, but (라) <u>never before such huge a new factor like humans have been introduced into the system</u>. We are now geological agents, capable of affecting the processes that determine climate. And when you think how many of us there are, that should hardly be surprising.

12 빈칸 (A)에 가장 알맞은 것은?

① We are not to blame　　　　　② The buck stops here
③ Don't be so precious　　　　　④ Waste not, want not

13 밑줄 친 부분 (가)~(라) 중 문법적으로 <u>틀린</u> 것은?

① (가)　　　　② (나)　　　　③ (다)　　　　④ (라)

14 윗글의 제목으로 가장 알맞은 것은?

① Denial: A Dangerous State of Mind
② Global Warming: Real or Malarkey?
③ The Human Factor in Global Warming
④ Population Explosion: A Global Disaster

Up to the early 1990s the cell phone was a rare luxury, but since the late 1990s, it has outsold almost every other electrical gadget — as a professional tool, domestic convenience, and even a fashion accessory. The typical cell phone has also ⓐ shrunk in size, due to improvements in rechargeable batteries, which now store more electricity for longer in a smaller package, and to smaller, more efficient electronics that use less electricity. A cell phone is basically a low-power radio receiver- transmitter, plus a tiny microphone to convert sounds into electrical signals, and a small speaker ⓑ that does the reverse. A liquid crystal display(LCD) shows numbers, letters, and symbols. Newer models have a larger screen for more complex images in color, and ⓒ some incorporates other functions such as internet access, radio, and an audio player. When the cell phone is activated, it sends out a radio pulse that is answered by nearby mast transmitter-receivers. The phone locks onto the clearest signal and uses this ⓓ while within range (the range of each transmitter is known as a cell). The phone continuously monitors signal strength and switches to an ⓔ _____ transmitter when necessary.

15 밑줄 친 ⓐ~ⓓ 중 어법상 잘못된 것은?

① ⓐ   ② ⓑ   ③ ⓒ   ④ ⓓ

16 빈칸 ⓔ에 가장 알맞은 것은?

① irrelevant   ② equivocal   ③ ambivalent   ④ alternative

17 윗글의 내용과 가장 일치하지 않는 것은?

① The cell phone always tries to find the clearest, strongest signal.
② The 1990s saw the cell phone sold more than almost any other electrical product.
③ The size of the cell phone got smaller as the capacity of rechargeable batteries increased.
④ Newer models have many additional functions such as internet access, an audio player and a camera.

The American Revolution symbolized the connection between the rights of the citizen and the rights of the state. The free citizen had a right to govern himself; therefore the whole community of the free citizens had a right to govern itself. This was not yet modern nationalism. The American people did not see themselves as a national group but as a community of free men dedicated to a proposition. But within two decades, the identification had been made.

The French Revolution, proclaiming the Rights of Man, formed the new style of nation. The levée-en-masse which defeated the old dynastic armies of Europe was the first expression of total nation unity as the basis of the sovereign state. Men and nations had equally the right to self-determination. Men could not be free if their national community was not.

The same revolution quickly proved that (A) _____. The nation could become completely unfettered in its dealings with other states while enslaving its own citizens. In fact, over-glorification of the nation might lead inevitably to the extinction of individual rights. The citizen could become just a tool of the national will. But in the first explosion of revolutionary ardour, the idea of the Rights of Man and of the Rights of the Nation went together. And, formally, that is (B) _____ they have remained.

18 Which of the following best fills in the parenthesis (A)?

① both might be mutually complementary   ② the reverse might be also true

③ both might be completely contradictory   ④ the reverse might not be true

19 Which of the following can be the key words of the passage?

① Individualism and nationalism

② Individual rights and national prosperity

③ Revolution and free citizens

④ Sovereign states and nationalism

20 Which of the following best fills in the parenthesis (B)?

① where   ② what

③ which   ④ that

CHAPTER 04

의미 파악

밑줄 친 부분에 내포된 의미를 묻거나 그 부분이 의도하는 바를 묻는 문제로 본문과의 관련성을 묻는 문제 유형이다. 관용어의 의미를 안다고 해서, 더불어 본문 내용을 해석만 한다고 해서 풀 수 있는 유형은 아니다. 내포된 의미를 찾을 수 있는 힘을 키워야 하는데, 결국 이해력을 상승시키는 것이 관건이다.

01 질문 유형

The underlined sentence means that _____.
Find the sentence that is implied in ***.
What does the underlined *** mean?
Which of the following is implied in the underlined term ***?

02 문제 풀이 전략

❶ 밑줄 친 부분의 정확한 의미를 파악해야 한다.

글을 읽으면서 특정 부분이 무엇을 의미하는지를 안다는 것은 글을 이해하는 데 있어서 상당히 중요하다. 이러한 점을 묻기 위한 의미를 파악하는 문제는 글의 특정 부분에 밑줄 등을 쳐 놓고, 그 부분의 뜻은 무엇인지, 또 무엇을 의미하는지를 묻는 유형이다. 본문에 대한 정확한 이해와 글의 흐름 이외에도 세부 내용을 파악하고 있는가를 묻기에 적합한 유형이기 때문이다.

❷ 전후 관계를 고려해 의미하는 바를 문맥에서 파악한다.

밑줄 친 부분에 내포된 의미를 묻거나 그 부분이 의도하는 바를 묻는 문제에 대해서, 실제 시험에서 밑줄 친 부분의 내용이 파악이 안 되는 경우의 대응책은 앞뒤의 문맥을 파악하면서 글의 흐름을 보고 답을 찾는 것이다. 만약 여의치 않으면 소거법을 이용하여 가장 적당하지 않은 순서로 오답을 제거해 나가야 한다.

A cowboy rode into town and stopped at a saloon for a drink. Unfortunately, the locals always had a habit of picking on strangers. When he finished his drink, he found his horse had been stolen. He went back into the bar, handily flipped his gun into the air, caught it above his head without even looking and fired a shot into the ceiling. "Which one of you sidewinders stole my horse?", he yelled with surprising forcefulness. No one answered. "Alright, I'm gonna have another beer, and if my horse ain't back outside by the time I finish, I'm gonna do what I did in Texas! And I don't like to have to do what I did in Texas!" Some of the locals shifted restlessly. The man, true to his word, had another beer, walked outside, and his horse had been returned to the post. He saddled up and started to ride out of town. The bartender wandered out of the bar and asked, "Say partner, before you go … what happened in Texas?" The cowboy turned back and said, "I had to walk home."

밑줄 친 부분이 의미하는 것을 글의 문맥을 고려하여 찾아내야 하는데, 이 글에서는 뒷부분에 구체적인 내용이 나온다. 상황에 따라서는 앞부분에 근거가 제시되는 경우도 있다.

답의 명확한 정보가 바로 이 부분에서 제시되어 있다.

Q. What did the cowboy mean by the underlined part?

① He killed many people.
② He stole another horse.
③ He robbed a bank.
④ He walked home.

본문의 마지막 문장을 근거로 정답을 찾아낼 수 있다.

정답   ④

해석   **밑줄 친 부분에서 카우보이가 의도한 것은 무엇인가?**

한 카우보이가 마을로 말을 타고 와서는 한잔하기 위해 술집에서 멈춰 섰다. 불행히도 그 마을 사람들에게는 낯선 사람을 괴롭히는 관습이 항상 있었다. 카우보이는 술을 다 마시고 보니 자신의 말을 도둑맞은 것을 발견했다. 그는 술집으로 다시 들어가서는 솜씨 있게 권총을 공중으로 툭 던진 다음 쳐다보지도 않고서 머리 위에서 잡은 다음에 천정에 한 방 쐈다. 그는 놀랄 만큼 단호하게 "여기 중에서 어떤 도둑놈이 내 말을 훔쳤지?"라고 소리쳤다. 아무도 대답하지 않았다. "좋았어. 나 이제부터 맥주 한 잔 더 할 건데, 다 마실 때까지도 내 말이 밖에 돌아와 있지 않으면 내가 텍사스에서 했던 짓을 그대로 하겠어! 그리고 난 내가 텍사스에서 했던 짓을 해야 하는 게 싫다고!" 마을 사람 몇몇이 불안해하면서 자리를 옮겼다. 카우보이는 말한 그대로 맥주를 한 잔 더 한 다음에 밖으로 돌아왔고, 그의 말은 말뚝에 다시 돌아와 있었다. 그는 안장을 얹고선 말을 타고 마을 밖으로

가기 시작했다. 바텐더는 술집 밖으로 걸어와서는 "이봐 친구, 가기 전에 말이야 텍사스에서 무슨 일이 있었는지 말해 주겠나?"라고 물었다. 카우보이는 뒤돌아보면서 "난 집으로 걸어가야 했지"라고 말했다.

① 그는 많은 사람을 죽였다. ② 그는 다른 말을 훔쳤다.
③ 그는 은행을 털었다. ④ 그는 집으로 걸어갔다.

해설 본문의 마지막에 바텐더가 텍사스에서 있었던 일을 물으니 카우보이는 말이 없어서 "집으로 걸어가야 했다.(I had to walk home.)"라고 말했다. 따라서 밑줄 친 것은 ④를 의미한다.

어휘
saloon ⓝ 술집	pick on 괴롭히다
handily ⓐ 솜씨 있게	flip ⓥ 툭 던지다, 휙 젖히다
sidewinder ⓝ 믿을 수 없는 사람, 뒤통수를 치는 사람	forcefulness ⓝ 단호함, 강압적임
restlessly ⓐ 불안하게	true to one's word 말한 그대로, 약속을 지켜서
post ⓝ 말뚝	saddle up 안장을 얹다

의미 파악 (paraphrase 포함)

01 개념 정의

글을 읽으면서 특정 부분이 무엇을 의미하는지를 아는 것을 글을 이해하는 데 있어서 상당히 중요하다. 이러한 점을 묻기 위한 의미를 파악하는 문제는 글의 특정 부분에 밑줄 등을 쳐 놓고, 그 부분의 뜻은 무엇인지, 또 무엇을 의미하는지를 묻는 유형이다. 이러한 의미를 파악하는 문제는 빈번하게 출제하는 유형으로, 본문의 정확한 이해와 그 부분의 이해를 측정하여 글의 흐름 이외에 세부 내용을 파악하고 있는가를 묻기에 적합한 유형이기 때문이다. 이에 더불어 최근의 문제를 살펴보면 단순히 의미를 파악하고 있는지를 넘어서 다른 문장으로 대체한 경우를 찾아낼 수 있는지도 묻고 있다. 이를 도식화하면 다음과 같다.

의미 파악 문제 유형	1차적 의미 파악 – 단순한 해석, 관용어의 의미 등을 묻는 문제
	2차적 의미 파악 – 내포된 의미 파악, 본문과의 관련성 묻는 문제
	PARAPHRASE – 다른 문장으로 바꿔놓은 것을 고르는 문제

02 경향 분석

(1) 동의어나 관용어의 의미 등을 묻는 문제

단순한 해석만을 묻기도 하고, 관용어의 의미를 묻기도 한다. 이러한 단어나 숙어의 의미 파악인 경우는 내용 파악이 되고도 특정 내용을 몰라서 틀리기도 하고, 내용 파악이 안 된 경우에도 그 부분만의 이해만으로도 풀 수 있는 영역이기도 하다. 그 이야기는 부분의 글을 이해할 수 있는 다의어 등 어휘와 관용어구 등을 많이 익혀야 한다.

(2) 내포된 의미를 묻거나 본문과의 관련성을 묻는 문제

밑줄 친 부분의 내포된 의미를 묻거나 그 부분의 의도하는 바를 묻는 이차적인 문제 형태를 뜻하며, 본문과의 관련성을 묻는 문제들이다. 이러한 의미를 파악하는 문제는 세부 내용을 묻는 문제이지만 문제의 형식이 다르고, 관용어의 의미를 안다고 해서, 더불어 본문 내용을 해석만 한다고 풀 수 있는 유형은 아니다. 내포된 의미를 찾을 수 있는 힘을 키워야 하는데, 결국 이해력을 상승시키는 것이 관건이다.

(3) PARAPHRASE 형식의 문제

고려대를 중심으로 점점 더 많은 상위권 대학에서 본문을 다르게 표현한 paraphrase의 문제를 묻고 있다. 밑줄 친 내용을 정확히 이해하고 있다면 다른 문장으로 바꿔 쓴다 하더라도 이해할 수 있는지를 묻는 것이다. 이에 대하여는 아래에서 자세히 살펴보겠다.

03 학습 전략

(1) 동의어나 관용어의 의미 등을 묻는 문제

일단 동의어나 관용어에 대한 충분한 학습이 그 해답이 된다. 그 이유는 내용 파악이 되고도 특정 표현을 몰라서 틀리기도 하고, 상황에 따라서는 내용 파악이 안 된 경우에도 그 부분만의 이해만으로도 풀 수 있기 때문이다. 하지만 시험에서는 모르는 표현이 문제화되어도 당황하지 말고 글의 전후 관계를 파악하면서 오답을 제거해 나가야 한다.

(2) 내포된 의미를 묻거나 본문과의 관련성을 묻는 문제

내포된 의미를 찾을 수 있는 힘을 키워야 하는데, 결국 이해력을 상승시키는 것이 관건이다. 글의 숨은 속뜻을 파악해야 하기 때문이다. 하지만 실제 시험에서 밑줄 친 부분의 내용이 파악이 안 되는 경우의 대응책으로는 앞뒤의 문맥을 파악하면서 글의 흐름을 보고 오답을 제거해 나가야 한다.

(3) PARAPHRASE 형식의 문제

paraphrase 문제는 내용의 동일성을 바탕으로 구조나 표현의 변화를 동반하는 것이다. 이런 문제는 본문 속의 표현을 그대로 쓰지 않고, 표현을 다양화하여 상황에 맞게 적절히 변형할 수 있는 능력, 이를 바탕으로 실제 글에서도 인용하면서 자신의 생각으로 글을 풀어가며 바꿔 줄 수 있는 능력을 측정하고자 하는 것이다. 그러므로 핵심 키워드를 중심으로 본문에 나온 내용을 바꿔 쓴 표현을 정확하게 파악해 가는 것이 중요하다.

01 What is the reason for the underlined part?

Two elderly couples were enjoying friendly conversation   when   one of the men asked the other, "Fred, how was the memory clinic you went to last month?" "Outstanding," Fred replied. "They taught us all the latest psychological techniques — visualization, association — it has made a big difference for me." "That's great! What was the name of that clinic?" Fred went blank. He thought and thought but couldn't remember. Then a smile broke across his face and he asked, "What do you call that flower with the long stem and thorns?" "You mean a rose?" "Yes, that's it!" Then he turned to his wife and asked, "Rose, what was the name of that clinic?"

① He was going to ask the name of the clinic of his wife.
② He realized that the name of the clinic was associated with a flower.
③ He was going to ask for help from the memory clinic.
④ He found out that Rose was the name of the clinic.

02 Which does "what was underneath" correspond to in the passage? 인하대 2016

Rhetoric made speech persuasive. It was sometimes used as a bag of tricks which got others to agree and to admire, whatever you said. You won power by using words. It became a diet rather like the old-fashioned cooking which heaped sauce and spice on food, concealing what was underneath. People enjoyed it because they enjoyed being charmed, and they became the slaves of what they thought was beauty. Winning an argument became a substitute for discovering the truth. Forcing others to agree became the source of self-esteem. Rhetoric became a weapon of war, subjugating millions.

① truth
② speech
③ beauty
④ rhetoric
⑤ a bag of tricks

다음 글에서 밑줄 친 문장이 뜻하는 것을 고르시오.

While the population of the world is growing rapidly, it is not growing at the same rate in all regions. Wealthier, more developed countries tend to have declining birth rate, while the populations of poorer, still developing countries tend to be growing exponentially. The reason for the difference is that educated women in developed countries no longer want to have as many children as before. They also want to work instead of staying at home to raise children. In developing countries, lack of education and inadequate knowledge of birth control means people continue to have many children. The resulting problem is that more people are competing for fewer resources. In developed countries, the declining birth rate is also an issue; with an aging population and a declining labor force, economists predict there will not be enough young workers to care for the aged in the long run. <u>The U.S. is the only exception to this trend.</u>

① The population in the U.S. is not growing rapidly, but at the same rate as developing countries.
② The population in the U.S. tends to have a decreasing birth rate unlike other developed countries.
③ The educated women in the U.S. want to raise many children while keeping a job for themselves.
④ The U.S. will have a sufficient number of young workers who can care for the senior citizens.
⑤ The U.S. will not compete for fewer resources with other developed and developing countries.

[01~03] 한국외대 2021

The famous French philosopher Denis Diderot lived nearly his entire life in poverty, but that all changed in 1765. Diderot was 52 years old and his daughter was about to be married, but he could not afford to provide a dowry. When Catherine the Great, the Empress of Russia, heard of Diderot's financial troubles she offered to buy his library from him for a huge amount of money. Suddenly, Diderot had money to spare. Shortly after this lucky sale, Diderot acquired a new scarlet robe. Diderot's scarlet robe was so beautiful that he immediately noticed how Ⓐ _____ it seemed when surrounded by the rest of his common possessions. He soon felt the urge to buy some new things to match the beauty of his robe. He replaced his old rug with a new one from Damascus. He decorated his home with beautiful sculptures and a better kitchen table. These reactive purchases have become known as the Diderot Effect. It states that obtaining a new possession often creates a spiral of consumption leading you to acquire more new things. As a result, we Ⓑ end up buying things that our previous selves never needed to feel happy or fulfilled.

01 Which of the following is the best title for the passage?

① The Diderot Effect: Why We Buy Things We Don't Need
② The Ingenuity of Diderot: How He Overcame Poverty
③ The Privacy of Diderot: What Is Not Known
④ The Double Life of Diderot: Man of Poverty and Luxury

02 Which of the following best fits into Ⓐ?

① out of focus
③ out of place
② out of season
④ out of the question

03 Which of the following is closest in meaning to ⓑ?

① Eventually come to buy things
② Decisively stop buying things
③ Unconsciously suspend buying things
④ Constantly hesitate to buy things

There's a widespread perception that everything cats do is just a little self-serving, a touch self-centered. But not content with idle stereotypes, we put this little question — are cats selfish? — to the audience forum.

Some of you didn't like the question at all. "Selfish is a human trait," argued Ann Halim. "'Selfish' is hard to apply to any animal other than humans," agreed Kevin Bonin. It certainly is hard, but that has never stopped us trying. In his 1871 book *The Descent of Man*, Charles Darwin argued that animal minds are similar to ours in many ways. "The difference in mind between man and the higher animals is certainly one of degree and not kind," he wrote. If that's true, then surely a cat — or any other higher animal — might _____.

Many of you identified with the idea that cats are out for themselves. "Are cats selfish? That's like asking has the pope got a balcony?!" says Jane Ramsden. "Let's just say, there is an I in kitty," says Dan Oken.

04 **Which of the following is most appropriate for the blank?**

① evolve its temperament into a better state
② deny the general concept of the stereotype
③ meet the definition of selfish
④ not be confirmed to the category of a human trait
⑤ do altruistic acts to others

05 **The underlined "That's like asking has the pope got a balcony?!" implies that** _____.

① It is absolutely nonsense!
② It's none of my business!
③ Who knows?
④ Obviously, yes!
⑤ Who did it?

During the final days at Denver's Stapleton airport, a crowded United flight was cancelled. A single agent was rebooking a long line of inconvenienced travellers. Suddenly an angry passenger pushed his way to the desk and slapped his ticket down on the counter saying, "I HAVE to be on this flight, and it HAS to be first class." The agent replied "I'm sorry, sir. I'll be happy to try to help you, but I've got to help these folks first, and I'm sure we'll be able to work something out." The passenger was unimpressed. He asked loudly, so that the passengers behind him could hear, ㉮ "Do you have any idea who I am?" Without hesitating, the gate agent smiled and grabbed the public address microphone. "May I have your attention, please?" she began, her voice bellowing through the terminal. ㉯ "We have a passenger here at the gate WHO DOES NOT KNOW WHO HE IS. If anyone can help him find his identity, please come to the gate." The folks behind him in line laughed hysterically.

06 What is the most likely reason that the angry passenger uttered ㉮?

① Because he wanted to know his identity.
② Because he wanted to entertain the passengers behind him.
③ Because he hoped to intimidate the gate agent.
④ Because he hoped to anger the passengers behind him.

07 What is the most likely reason that the gate agent uttered ㉯?

① Because she wanted to make the angry passenger laugh.
② Because she wanted to know the angry passenger's name.
③ Because she wanted to help the angry passenger find his identity.
④ Because she wanted to make fun of the angry passenger.

08 Which of the following best characterizes the passage?

① Humorous
② Sad
③ Informative
④ Monotonous

Automation keeps getting more and more capable. Automatic systems can take over tasks that used to be done by people, whether it is maintaining the proper temperature, automatically keeping an automobile within its assigned lane at the correct distance from the car in front, enabling airplanes to fly by themselves from takeoff to landing, or allowing ships to navigate by themselves. When the automation works, the tasks are usually done as well as or better than by people. Moreover, it saves people from the dull, dreary routine tasks, allowing more useful, productive use of time, reducing fatigue and error. But when the task gets too complex, automation tends to give up. The paradox is that automation can take over the dull, dreary tasks, but fail with the complex ones. When automation fails, it often does so without warning. When failure occurs, "the human is out of the loop." This means that the person has not been paying much attention to the operation, and it takes time for the failure to be noticed and evaluated, and then to decide how to respond.

09 What would be the best title of the passage above?

① The Paradox of Automation
② The Increased Efficiency of Automation
③ The Sequence of Automation
④ How to Cope with the Automation Failure

10 The passage, "the human is out of the loop" may mean _____ when the automation fails.

① even the most expert driver may have only a fraction of a second to avoid an accident
② a well-trained pilot can notice the automation failure immediately and cope with the situation
③ without the help of GPS (Global Positioning Systems), manual checking of location can be done in a cruise ship
④ we can notice ship's location by estimating speed and directions of travel, though the measurement is not accurate in navigation

11 What can be inferred from the given passage?

① When you have substantial amount of highly complex problems, you may find the necessity of the increased networked electrical generation systems with automatized machines.

② Small tests and simulations can reduce the complexity and unexpected events that characterize real system failure.

③ Major automobile providers need to make intentional errors in their final products to test how well the driver can respond.

④ Automation in factories and aviation have increased efficiency while lowering the rate of error when the task is simple.

One of the few pieces of positive news concerning America's crisis-plagued airline industry is that Washington has finally raised the mandatory retirement age for commercial pilots to 65 from 60. Virtually every other nation in the world beat us to the punch on this. In fact, if Congress hadn't enacted special legislation, which the President signed last month, the retirement age ⓐ _____ at 60 for the foreseeable future.

This move is right, morally and practically. Pilots are in short supply, and to keep forcing these experienced hands to retire was harmfully capricious. Some 3,000 pilots reach the age of 60 each year; more than half are now expected to stay on, as long as they continue to pass their frequent physicals and regular piloting exams. There is, however, one more thing Congress could do on this front: work out a deal for those pilots who turned 60 before this legislation was enacted and are not yet 65. As things stand, they cannot reclaim their jobs or seniority if they want to go back to work. Under current rules ⓑ <u>these individuals</u> would be treated as spanking-new hires instead of the seasoned veterans they are. It's no surprise that a number of them are signing up for ⓒ _____ airlines instead of ⓓ _____ ones. Why not let them work for our carriers, with their seniority intact, as long as they pass those vital exams?

12 빈칸 ⓐ에 가장 알맞은 것은?

① remained
② have remained
③ will remain
④ would have remained

13 밑줄 친 ⓑ **these individuals**가 가리키는 것은?

① pilots who retired at the age of 60, now training new hires
② pilots who have passed physicals and piloting exams and are over 65
③ pilots who turned 60 before this legislation was enacted and are not yet 65
④ pilots who reach the age of 60 and do not want to sign up the retirement regulations

14 빈칸 ⓒ와 ⓓ에 가장 알맞은 것은?

	ⓒ		ⓓ
①	local	—	federal
②	rural	—	urban
③	newborn	—	experienced
④	foreign	—	domestic

15 윗글의 내용과 일치하는 것은?

① Pilots retire at the age of 60 in all nations except America in the world.

② Pilots who are over 60 will have to retire if they do not pass regular piloting exams.

③ The special legislation on the mandatory retirement age is still under discussion.

④ About 3,000 senior pilots are expected to go back to work as new hires every year.

According to a new paper by Paola Acevedo of Tilburg University and Steven Ongena of the University of Zurich, the trauma affects how bankers subsequently do business. The authors look at bank lending after heists in Colombia, a country where 835 bank robberies took place between 2003 and 2011. They find that loan officers treat would-be borrowers differently in the aftermath of an armed robbery. Loan volumes did not change, but the duration of loans issued in the first 90 days after a stickup is 70% longer. The average Colombian loan matures in 5.4 months, but a newly burgled branch typically lends for 8.7 months. The traumatized loan officers also demand collateral more of the time, and more of it, but offer slightly lower interest rates than normal. All of these changes reduce the need to deal with new customers in person. Lending for longer periods pushes repayment meetings further into the future. Taking more collateral reduces the need to vet customers thoroughly. And the lower interest rates suggest that loan officers spend less time haggling. This behaviour is a classic symptom of post-traumatic stress disorder.

16 After armed robberies, bankers _____.

① give out loans on better terms
② tend to reduce the duration of loans
③ would not give out loans to new customers
④ do not require any collateral
⑤ charge their clients very high interest rates

17 The underlined expression, 'This behaviour,' means the _____.

① aggressive attitude towards clients
② ambiguous attitude towards clients
③ tendency to please customers
④ tendency to avoid customers
⑤ tendency to distrust customers

Email is the most common form of written communication in the business world. Although emails are often seen as less formal than business letters, they still need to be professional in tone and structure, and are quite different from the casual messages you send to friends and family. However, business emails are not just letters sent via a computer — they have a style of their own which is important to understand. One of the most important things to remember when emailing to business colleagues is to be concise. Many professionals receive a multitude of emails throughout the day and often don't have the time to read thoroughly each piece of correspondence. Because the recipient may have to evaluate which incoming messages have the greatest priority, choose the contents of the subject line carefully and use it to give a clear summary of the email's purpose. Email messages being sent outside of the company should end with a closing signature that includes the sender's full name and business affiliation. Most email programs provide an option whereby a closing signature may be created and automatically appended to all outgoing messages. It is good business practice to use the 'reply' option to an existing message rather than opening a 'new message' page. The 'reply' gives the recipient a link, commonly called a thread, to the original message, and a path to follow if several replies to one message pile up. Or, if the incoming message is lengthy and only certain items require a response, the sender can copy only those relevant parts and paste them into a 'new message', then key in the appropriate responses.

18 글의 내용에 의하면, 업무상 이메일이 간결해야 하는 이유는?

① Because email is the most common form of written communication in the business world.
② Because email is still considered a professional way of communication in the business world.
③ Because computers can process more efficiently when email follows a certain style of its own.
④ Because many professionals are usually too busy to read all the emails that they receive each day.
⑤ Because it is not polite and also ineffective to write lengthy emails to business colleagues.

19 밑줄 친 the 'reply' option과 가장 잘 부합하는 것은?

① It is recommended to make a reply with a new message page instead of an existing message page.

② It is recommended to make a reply to every message showing a link or a thread to the original message.

③ It is recommended to include the original message and to show a path to guide previous messages in the reply.

④ It is recommended to make just one reply to the recipient although he has sent several messages.

⑤ It is recommended to include all the original messages with appropriate responses although they may be lengthy.

20 윗글의 내용과 부합하지 <u>않는</u> 것은?

① Business emails should be written more professionally compared with casual emails to friends and family.

② Brief business emails are preferred to lengthy business emails among many professionals.

③ The contents of the subject line should indicate the priority level of the message.

④ When enclosing a closing Signature, the sender's full name and company name should be stated.

⑤ When incoming email is lengthy. only the relevant parts of the message can be replied in a new page.

지문 속의 내용을 paraphrase한 것을 고르라는 문제로, 의미 파악 유형의 발전된 단계이다. 제일 먼저 밑줄 친 부분이 뜻하는 바를 묻고, 그 다음으로 본문과의 관련성이나 내포된 의미를 물은 후, 마지막으로 바꿔 쓴 표현을 찾아낼 수 있는지 묻는 유형이다. paraphrase까지 완전히 발전하지는 않았지만, 발전 중에 있는 문제도 범위에 넣었다.

01 질문 유형

The underlined expression suggests that _____.
What does the underlined *** mean?
Which of the following best explains the meaning of the underlined ***?
Choose the one that best expresses the implied meaning of the underlined part.

02 문제 풀이 전략

❶ 밑줄 친 부분의 내용을 정확하게 이해한다.
고려대를 중심으로 점점 더 많은 상위권 대학에서 본문을 다르게 표현한 paraphrase의 문제를 묻고 있다. 밑줄 친 내용을 정확히 이해하고 있다면 다른 문장으로 바꿔 쓴다 하더라도 이해할 수 있는지를 묻는 것이다. 그러므로 이런 문제 유형의 경우 본문의 이해가 가장 중요하다.

❷ 내용의 동일성을 바탕으로 구조와 표현의 변화에 유의한다.
paraphrase 문제는 내용의 동일성을 바탕으로 구조나 표현의 변화를 동반하는 것이다. 이런 문제는 본문 속의 표현을 그대로 쓰지 않고, 표현을 다양화하여 상황에 맞게 적절히 변형할 수 있는 능력, 이를 바탕으로 실제 글에도 인용하면서 자신의 생각으로 글을 풀어 가며 바꿔 줄 수 있는 능력을 측정하고자 하는 것이다. 그러므로 핵심 키워드를 중심으로 본문에 나온 내용을 바꿔 쓴 표현을 정확하게 파악해 가는 것이 중요하다.

We live in a nation where states have enacted legislation permitting asthmatic children to carry their inhalers to school (one in 13 must do so). A federal labeling law mandates manufacturers clearly state in plain English whether major allergens — peanuts, soy, shellfish, eggs, wheat, milk, fish, and tree nuts — are ingredients in any product. And Americans spend billions to treat the symptoms of allergies. <u>Those of us over 40 don't remember having so much as a conversation about food allergies in school.</u> Today 6 percent of young children have food allergies — and the number of those with potentially fatal peanut allergy doubled between 1997 and 2002.

Q. Choose the one that best expresses the implied meaning of the underlined part.

① People over 40 don't have food allergies.
② People over 40 don't like to talk about food allergies.
③ In the past we didn't have much food to cause allergies.
④ People over 40 didn't suffer from food allergies as much as students today.

40대가 넘은 사람들은 (과거 학창 시절에) 식품 알레르기에 대해 그렇게 많은 대화를 나눈 것을 기억하지 못한다는 의미는, 그러한 문제로 그렇게 큰 고통을 받지는 않았었다는 의미로 이해할 수 있다.

본문의 내용을 바꿔 쓴다면, 40대 이상은 식품 알레르기에 대해 대화를 나눈 것을 기억하지 못한다는 것은 결국 식품 알레르기로 크게 고생하지는 않았다는 것이다. 여기에서 핵심 정보를 추리면 40대 이상은 식품 알레르기와 다소 무관한 삶을 살았다는 핵심 내용을 담은 ④가 정답이다.

정답　④

해석　**밑줄 친 부분의 의미를 암시하는 가장 적절한 표현을 찾으시오.**

우리는 주들이 천식으로 고생하는 아이들에게 학교에 흡입기를 가져오게 하는 입법을 실행하는 국가에서 산다.(13명 중의 한 명이 그러하다) 연방 상표법은 제조자들이 쉬운 영어로 알레르기 유발 요인 — 땅콩, 콩, 조개, 계란, 밀, 우유, 생선, 나무 열매 등 — 이 성분 속에 포함되어 있는지를 분명히 적시할 것을 명령한다. 그리고 미국인들은 이러한 알레르기 증상을 치료하는 데 수십억 달러를 쓴다. 우리들 중 40세가 넘는 사람들은 학교에서 식품 알레르기에 관해 그렇게 많은 대화를 나눈 것을 기억하지 못한다. 오늘날 6퍼센트의 아이들이 식품에 대한 알레르기가 있다. 그리고 잠재적으로 치명적 인 땅콩 알레르기가 있는 아이들의 숫자는 1997년에서 2002년 사이에 두 배가 되었다.

① 40세가 넘는 사람들은 음식에 대한 알레르기가 없다.
② 40세가 넘는 사람들은 음식 알레르기에 대한 이야기를 하는 것을 좋아하지 않는다.
③ 과거에 우리는 알레르기를 일으키는 음식이 많지 않았다.
④ 40세가 넘는 사람들은 오늘날의 학생들만큼 음식 알레르기로 고생하지 않았다.

해설　우리들 중 40세가 넘는 사람들은 학교에서 식품 알레르기에 관해 그렇게 많은 대화를 나눈 것을 기억하지 못한다는 것은 40세가 넘는 사람들은 오늘날의 학생들만큼 음식 알레르기로 고생하지 않았다는 의미이다.

01 The underlined expression suggests that _____.

The best neighbour I ever had was an Italian restaurant. Emergency lasagna available night and day, change for the launderette on Sundays, a permanent door-keeper against gatecrashers and policemen with parking tickets. Even if our fourth floor bath water did run dry every time they filled up the Expresso machine, I miss them still. Bad neighbours can blight a house worse than dry rot but there is no insurance against them, no effective barricades in the compulsory intimacy except a decent caution and conversation ruthlessly restricted to matters of meteorology. And it only takes a tiny breach in the wall of platitudes to unleash appalling dramas of persecution and passion.

① showing no response makes the neighbour happy
② getting violent is not helpful in improving the hostile relationship
③ watching a film together might be a good way to sort out a problem
④ the person who takes the extreme action will succeed
⑤ trivial things could escalate to the terrible rows

02 What does the underlined "received just a few sentences" mean?

Last summer, Martin Torres was working as a cook in Austin, Texas, when, on the morning of Aug. 23, he received a call from a relative. His 17-year-old nephew, Emilio, had been murdered. According to the police, Emilio was walking down a street on Chicago's South Side when someone shot him in the chest, possibly the culmination of an ongoing dispute. Like many killings, Emilio's received just a few sentences in the local newspapers. Torres, who was especially close to his nephew, got on the first Greyhound bus to Chicago. He was grieving and plotting retribution. "I thought, Man, I'm going to take care of business," he told me recently. "That's how I live. I was going hunting. This is my own blood, my nephew."

① received a short letter
② got a few words of consolation
③ got little attention
④ was sentenced to a couple of days
⑤ was asked to write a few letters

Choose the number with a correct set of statements that can be restated or inferred from the original sentence.

03 Although a human infant is ill-equipped for independent survival in the first years of its life compared to lower order life forms, as it grows it will become far more adept at survival than other organisms thanks to its brain with an astonishing memory capacity.

Ⓐ Human infants are largely helpless when first born.
Ⓑ Lower order life forms are to be born ready-made.
Ⓒ Human beings are the products of better evolutionary processes.
Ⓓ Human infants are better prepared to participate in life with a minimum of learning.

① Ⓐ & Ⓑ　　　② Ⓐ & Ⓓ　　　③ Ⓑ & Ⓒ
④ Ⓑ & Ⓓ　　　⑤ Ⓐ, Ⓑ & Ⓒ

04 Research has shown that aggressive behavior can be acquired through a combination of modeling and positive reinforcement of the aggressive behavior; children are influenced by the combined forces of observing aggressive behavior in live or fictional role models and of noting either positive reinforcement for the aggressive behavior, or a lack of negative reinforcement for the aggressive behavior.

Ⓐ Aggression can be viewed as a learned behavior.
Ⓑ Children will learn aggression even when the aggression is negatively reinforced.
Ⓒ Aggression of a fictional role model can be more influential than that of a live role model.
Ⓓ Children can learn aggressive behavior by seeing aggressive behavior that is rewarded or is not punished.

① Ⓐ & Ⓑ　　　② Ⓐ & Ⓓ　　　③ Ⓑ & Ⓒ
④ Ⓑ & Ⓓ　　　⑤ Ⓐ, Ⓒ & Ⓓ

[01~02] 아주대 2016

Choose the number with a correct set of statements that can be restated or inferred from the original sentence.

01 Such serious mental disorders as mania, schizophrenia, and severe depression are two to three times more common among men in jails than among men in the general population.

> Ⓐ Most of men in jails are vulnerable to serious mental disorders.
> Ⓑ Individuals with serious mental disorders are more frequently placed in jail than people in the general population.
> Ⓒ There are more men in jails who have certain mental disorders than there are men in the general population with those disorders.
> Ⓓ There is a direct relationship between individuals' mental disorders and the antisocial behaviors that may have caused imprisonment.

① Ⓐ & Ⓑ   ② Ⓐ & Ⓒ   ③ Ⓑ & Ⓒ
④ Ⓑ & Ⓓ   ⑤ Ⓑ, Ⓒ & Ⓓ

02 Imagine the worst time with lack of sleep you have ever had after staying up all night to study for an exam; then imagine your worst-ever case of flu; that combination and then some is what chronic fatigue syndrome (CFS) feels like on a "normal" day.

> Ⓐ Patients with CFS suffer from sleeplessness.
> Ⓑ Suffering from CFS is by far worse than having the flu.
> Ⓒ CFS is typically accompanied by characteristic symptoms of a flu.
> Ⓓ If you have a severe case of flu, you have a higher risk of having CFS.

① Ⓐ & Ⓒ   ② Ⓐ & Ⓓ   ③ Ⓑ & Ⓒ
④ Ⓑ & Ⓓ   ⑤ Ⓐ, Ⓑ & Ⓒ

Mathematics departments around the world regularly receive letters from amateur mathematicians who claim to have solved famous problems, and virtually without exception these 'solutions' are not merely wrong, but laughably so. Some, while not exactly mistaken, are so unlike a correct proof of anything that they are not really attempted solutions at all. Those that follow at least some of the normal conventions of mathematical presentation use very elementary arguments that would, had they been correct, have been discovered centuries ago. The people who write these letters have no conception of how difficult mathematical research is, of the years of effort needed to develop enough knowledge and expertise to do significant original work, or of the extent to which Ⓐ mathematics is a collective activity.

03 Which is NOT suitable for a paraphrase of the underlined Ⓐ mathematics is a collective activity?

① Combined efforts of mathematicians usually lead the development of mathematics.
② Many mathematicians are simultaneously engaged in tackling mathematical questions.
③ A genius of mathematics is required to solve particularly difficult mathematical questions.
④ A lot of mathematicians contributed to the development of mathematics over a long period of time.

04 Which is true according to the passage?

① It is virtually impossible for amateurs to solve famous mathematical problems.
② Originality is not valued so much in mathematical researches as consistent efforts.
③ Amateurs are often equipped with enough knowledge and expertise to do original work.
④ Even amateurs often make significant breakthroughs in solving difficult mathematics problems.

In nature, animals use many different techniques to ensure their survival and the survival of their species. One of the most common survival adaptations is natural camouflage, which many animals use to hide from predators. Camouflage develops differently according to the animals' environment, physiology, and behavior. The simplest camouflage technique is for the animal to blend in with its surroundings. <u>In such cases, elements from the animals' natural habitat are the models for its camouflage.</u> _____, a frog's skin is a similar color and texture to the leaves in its environment. In terms of physiology and behavior, the lifestyle and physical features of an animal also determine what types of camouflage are possible. An animal with fur will develop a different sort of camouflage from an animal with scales. Some animals also change their fur coloring from season to season through molting.

05 What is the meaning of the underlined part?

① Animals change their surroundings to hide from predators.
② Animals' appearances resemble their environments or some items commonly found in their surroundings.
③ Animals behave like some other animals in their environment.
④ Animals cover themselves with items from their environment to blend in with the surrounding vegetation.

06 Which is the most appropriate for the blank?

① As a result
② Otherwise
③ Nevertheless
④ For example

[07~10]

It's the height of summer in Mongolia, and the nation is set to celebrate Eriin Gurvan Naadam, an Olympic-like festival where the so-called three manly sports of wrestling, horse racing, and archery take center stage. Naadam is held annually from July 11 to July 13. ⓐ The timing coincides with the anniversary of the 1921 Mongolian Revolution, in which the nation gained independence from competing Chinese and Russian forces. The festival traces its roots to the 12th century, when the Mongols, led by Genghis Khan, established an empire that at its height stretched across nearly all of Eurasia. Wrestling, horse racing, and archery were necessary skills for success on the battlefield. ⓑ Making them into sports-trained warriors to be better warriors. Naadam traditionally was a time for men who had trained all year to ⓒ _____ that they have mastered these skills. Often described as the "manly sports," the festival's events were originally limited to men. Today women participate in both the horse racing and archery competitions, and young boys and girls in particular take to the horse racing. The country celebrations attract scattered nomadic herders who gather to take part in friendly competition, to drink a fermented mare's milk, and to feast on a variety of dairy products. Today, the skills are mostly reserved for athletic competition and camaraderie. But the luster and nationalistic pride surrounding Naadam still shines as bright as ever.

07 What can be inferred from the passage about Eriin Gurvan Naadam?

① It has been held annually since the days of Genghis Khan.
② It was originally aimed at bringing together scattered Mongols all over Eurasia.
③ Women and children are now allowed to compete in some of the events.
④ In the past, it was held in the military camps where professional athletes were trained.

08 Which of the following best fills in the blank ⓒ?

① remember
② show off
③ hold fast
④ assume

09 The underlined clause ⓐ relates the Naadam festival to _____ .

① the nationalistic pride

② nomadic cultural heritage

③ the tradition of the "manly sports"

④ athletic competition and camaraderie

10 The underlined sentence ⓑ means that _____ .

① warriors were shaped into athletes

② the military enjoyed spectator sports

③ ancient Mongols loved sport and recreation

④ sports were used as a course for military training

According to researchers, gossip has some benefits. Exchanging information can create a healthy connection. It can build rules for acceptable and unacceptable behavior. It can improve society. (A) _____, gossip is useful in the business world. Gossip researcher Professor Frank McAndrew says, "If people are talking about good things others do, we want to emulate that good behavior. It is a nice way of socially controlling people." When a company faces bad times, gossip about the future of the employees can reduce fear and uncertainty. It can also create a feeling of fellowship.

(B) _____, bad gossip, the negative talk about other people's lives, can be destructive. Disappointingly enough, the researchers spend little time on this form of malice. People engage in negative gossip for several reasons. They may do it to bond with another person. They may do it to pass the time or to deny problems. They may gossip to build themselves up through comparisons with others, or they may want to hurt others.

11 Which is the most appropriate for the blanks (A) and (B)?

① Nevertheless — However
② However — Similarly
③ However — Nevertheless
④ Similarly — However

12 Which is the meaning of the underlined part?

① to imitate that good behavior
② to criticize that good behavior
③ to civilize that good behavior
④ to notice that good behavior

13 Which is the main idea of the passage?

① People don't realize how destructive gossip can be.
② Gossip can be beneficial or negative for society and people's lives.
③ Gossip is needed because employees may be able to create a feeling of fellowship.
④ People may be involved in negative gossip for various reasons.

[14~15]

Since 1992, Sarah Gordon, an expert in computer viruses and security technology, has studied the psychology of virus writers. "A hacker or a virus writer is just as likely to be the guy next door to you." she says, "or the kid at the checkout line bagging your groceries. Your average hacker is not necessarily some Goth type dressed entirely in black and sporting a nose ring." The virus writers Gordon has come to know have varied backgrounds. Some are solidly academic, while others are athletic. Many have good relationships with their parents and families; most are popular with their peers. They don't spend all their time in the basement. One virus writer volunteers in his local library, working with elderly people. One of them is a poet and a musician and another in an electrical engineer. ㉮ You wouldn't pick them out of a lineup as being the perpetrator.

14 밑줄 친 ㉮를 가장 잘 설명한 것은?

① Usually hackers or virus writers look normal, which renders it hard to judge them by their appearances.

② We might be easily deceived by most hackers and virus writers since they hide themselves in the image of good guys.

③ Most hackers or virus writers are so brilliant and intelligent but from time to time suffer from frustrations.

④ Since hackers or virus writers have similar jobs, it is easy to define their job-based common character.

15 윗글에서 <u>다른</u> 의미로 쓰인 구절은?

① "the kid at the checkout line bagging your groceries"

② "the guy next door to you"

③ "some Goth type dressed entirely in black"

④ "a poet and a musician"

㉮ _____ He practiced pseudo-delegation. Thus most people thought he left domestic matters largely to his chief of staff, the former governor of New Hampshire, Sherman Adams. Adams himself seems to have shared ㉯ <u>this illusion</u>. He said that Eisenhower was the last major figure who actively disliked and avoided using the phone. But the logs show he made multitudes of calls about which Adams knew nothing. On foreign policy, he used sources of advice and information about which, equally, Dulles was unaware. He used the industrious Dulles as a superior servant; and Dulles complained that, though he often worked late into the night with the President at the White House, he had 'never been asked to a family dinner.' The notion that ㉰ <u>Adams and Dulles were prima donnas</u> was deliberately promoted by Eisenhower, since they could be blamed when mistakes were uncovered, ㉱ _____ .

16 Which of the following is most suitable as the topic of the passage for the blank ㉮?

① Eisenhower's delegates had excessive powers.
② Eisenhower was a very humane politician.
③ Eisenhower left everything to his staff.
④ Eisenhower was in charge throughout.

17 What does the underlined phrase ㉯ refer to?

① that Eisenhower practiced pseudo-delegation
② that most people were interested in politics
③ that Adams was in charge of domestic matters
④ that Adams was the former governor of New Hampshire

18 What does the underlined sentence ㉯ mean?

① Adams and Dulles liked opera very much.

② Adams and Dulles were treated as servants.

③ Adams and Dulles played major roles.

④ Adams and Dulles made a lot of mistakes.

19 Which of the following would be most suitable for the blank ㉱?

① only to incur a great damage to his honor

② but he helped them maintain their political career

③ contrary to what he intended

④ thus protecting the office of the presidency

[20~23]

Research in the United Kingdom has shown that among men there is a significant increase in heart attack deaths over Christmas and the New Year holidays. This may be attributed to people ignoring symptoms and delaying seeking help because of the inconvenience of getting to a hospital during the holidays. Others who are traveling may take longer to find the right medical help. Ellen Mason, a nurse at the British Heart Foundation, said: "It is well known that in cold weather the blood is thicker, which increases the risk of a heart attack, but it is likely that the delay in seeking medical assistance over the holidays may lead to more deaths." Men's health expert Dr. Mike Ingram warns that, for men in particular, the festive period can be a dangerous one, with the risk of heart attack significantly increased. And he blames that on increased seasonal colds and flus causing increased breathing problems, excessive physical exertion, overeating, cold weather, lack of sleep, emotional stress, excess salt and alcohol. "The biggest killer of men is heart disease and too many men are dying from this condition by failing to tackle their risks," said Dr. Ingram. He said men could be their own worst enemies, adding, "If a man wants to enjoy a long and active life he needs to focus more on reducing his heart attack risk factors. He should stop smoking, drink in moderation, cut out the heavy fatty food, exercise regularly and watch the blood pressure. Too challenging? Then start by cutting out salt."

20 The passage clearly states that _____.

① far more men than women die in winter
② salt is particularly bad for your health
③ multiple factors contribute to increased male mortality in winter
④ a heart attack in cold weather is almost invariably fatal

21 The passage clearly suggests that _____.

① a heart attack must be treated without delay as soon as it occurs

② hospitals in the United Kingdom are often shut at Christmas

③ it is unwise to travel while having a heart attack

④ some people avoid going to hospital in winter

22 The underlined passage "men could be their own worst enemies" suggests that _____.

① men blame each other bitterly for what happens to them

② we are all responsible for our own health care provision

③ hating other people is bad for your health

④ if a man persists in a risky lifestyle, he only has himself to blame for the consequences

23 The passage does NOT say or suggest that _____.

① the largest single cause of male deaths is heart problems

② breathing difficulties can bring about heart trouble

③ people often drink too much at Christmastime

④ it is impossible for older men to avoid heart attacks

24 That last sentence suggests starting by cutting out salt probably because _____.

① salt is especially dangerous

② that is an easy first step

③ that is a particularly difficult thing to do

④ food without salt tastes better

Some facts contradict the central dogma's cardinal maxim: that a DNA gene exclusively governs the molecular processes that give rise to a particular inherited trait. Because of their commitment to an obsolete theory, most molecular biologists operate under the assumption that DNA is the secret of life, whereas the careful observation of the hierarchy of living processes strongly suggest that it is the other way around. Why, then, has the central dogma continued to stand? To some degree the theory has been protected from criticism by a device more common to religion than science; dissent, or merely the discovery of a ⓐ _____ fact, is a punishable offense, a heresy that might easily lead to professional ostracism. Much of this bias can be attributed to institutional inertia, a failure of rigor, but there are other, more insidious, reasons why molecular geneticists might be satisfied with ⓑ the status quo; the central dogma has given them such a satisfying, seductively simplistic explanation of heredity.

25 윗글의 내용과 일치하지 <u>않는</u> 것은?

① The theory of DNA governing molecular processes has proved valid.
② Genetic engineering is based upon spurious foundation.
③ Exclusive tenets are entrenched in science just like in religion.
④ Reductionism is at the heart of the myth of DNA dogma.

26 윗글의 문맥상 빈칸 ⓐ에 가장 알맞은 단어는?

① discordant
② impartial
③ refutable
④ annoying

27 다음 중 밑줄 친 ⓑ가 의미하지 <u>않는</u> 것은?

① new facts into the governing theory by redefining its meaning
② conveniently devoid of more recent observations
③ the traditional scientific economy of prestige
④ immune to divergent facts for the governing theory

Future pandemics will happen more often, kill more people, and wreak even worse damage to the global economy than Covid-19 without a fundamental shift in how humans treat nature. Warning that there are up to 850,000 viruses which, like the novel-coronavirus, exist in animals and may be able to infect people, the panel known as IPBES said pandemics represented <u>an existential threat to humanity</u>.

Authors of the 'special report on biodiversity and pandemics' said that habitat destruction and insatiable consumption made animal-borne diseases far more likely to make the jump to people in the future. There is no great mystery about the cause of the Covid-19 pandemic. The same human activities that drive climate change and biodiversity loss also drive pandemic risk through their impacts on our agriculture.

Covid-19 was the sixth pandemic since the influenza outbreak of 1918. All of these pandemics have been entirely driven by human activities. These include unsustainable exploitation of the environment through deforestation, agricultural expansion, wildlife trade, and consumption. All of this exploitation puts humans in increasingly close contact with wild and farmed animals and the diseases they harbor.

Seventy percent of emerging diseases such as Ebola, Zika, and HIV/AIDS are zoonotic in origin, meaning they circulate in animals before jumping to humans. Around five new diseases break out among humans every single year, anyone of which has the potential to become a pandemic.

28 **Which is the best paraphrase to represent "an existential threat to humanity" in the second sentence of this passage?**

① hypothetical danger to human beings
② actual danger to human survival
③ imminent danger to living things but probably not human beings
④ danger which existed previously to human beings

29 According to the passage, which of the following is true about the COVID-19 pandemic?

① Its cause and origin are not zoonotic unlike other diseases such as Ebola, Zika, and HIV/AIDS.
② It is rather unique so future pandemics similar to COVID-19 are unlikely.
③ The cause of COVID-19 is still unknown to scientists.
④ Its underlying causes are habitat destruction and insatiable consumption.

30 According to the passage, what do climate change, biodiversity loss, and pandemics all have in common?

① Their cause is a great mystery to scientists at the present time.
② They are all caused by human activities.
③ Their danger has been understood only recently.
④ The author doesn't mention the commonality of these phenomena.

CHAPTER 06

지시어구

지시어구로 처리된 부분이 대신 받고 있는 원래의 단어나 어구는 무엇인지를 아는 것은 글을 이해하는 데 있어서 상당히 중요하다. 즉 지시어구란 앞에서 언급된 단어나 어구를 다시 쓰지 않고, 다른 어구로 바꿔 쓴 지칭어를 말한다. 이런 유형을 출제하는 이유는 글을 바르게 이해하기 위해선 지시어구가 무엇을 가리키는지 아는 게 중요하기 때문이다.

01 질문 유형

What does the underlined *** refer to?

The underlined *** refers to _____.

Among ⓐ, ⓑ, ⓒ, and ⓓ, which one differs from the others in what it refers to?

02 문제 풀이 전략

❶ **앞뒤 관계에 유의하면서 핵심 내용을 정확하게 파악한다.**

최근 지시어구를 묻는 문제들의 추세는 점점 더 어려워지고 있다. 단순히 대명사를 확인하거나 지시하는 바를 고르라는 정도를 넘어서 본문의 핵심적인 내용을 지칭하고 있으며, 이제는 의미 파악에 근접한 수준으로 넘어가고 있다. 그러므로 의미 파악과 지시어구의 경계를 허무는 문제들이 출제되고 있으므로, 글을 읽을 때 앞뒤 관계에 유의하여 뜻하는 바를 명확히 해 놓아야 한다.

❷ **지시하는 바를 찾을 때 수의 일치나 반복되는 표현에 유의한다.**

지시어구를 고르라는 문제를 풀 때는 다음의 것들을 염두에 두면서 풀어 나가야 한다. 핵심어구나 관련된 표현을 반복하고 있는지, 아니면 대명사의 형태를 띠는지를 먼저 확인하고 이에 따라 대처해야 한다. 물론 단수와 복수의 확인 역시 중요하다. 이러한 문제들이 어렵게 출제되면 그 지시하는 어구를 찾기 어렵기 때문에 가능한 모든 단서를 이용하여 범위를 압축하고 글로부터 추론하여 풀어 나가야 하는 경우도 있다. 더불어 글의 의미를 파악하여 지시어구와 연결시키는 연습도 중요하다.

To individuals, ⓐ their decisions are very important. Decisions indicate how well individuals are integrated with society and its development. We should not be as concerned with how individuals mold society but rather with how well ⓑ they adapt to society and to the variables that determine its development. Unless individuals successfully relate to society, ⓒ they cannot fully use what society provides nor be psychologically at peace with ⓓ themselves. Why should we bother with issues and problems today that have little direct bearing on our lives? We bother with them because we want to be an integral part of society. Unless we relate to ⓔ them today, we cannot relate to others in our society. In fact. one of the most important burdens we have is showing how well integrated we are. We feel a constant need to prove we belong to a group, be it a social organization with its own patterns of behavior or our own families.

their는 앞에 나온 individuals를 받는다.

how individuals mold에서 individuals를 뜻함을 알 수 있다.

they는 종속절에서 주어가 되는 individuals임을 문장에서 파악할 수 있다.

cannot A nor B의 구조에서 볼 때 여기의 themselves는 역시 종속절의 주어인 individuals를 뜻함을 알 수 있다.

them이 지칭하는 것을 찾기 위해 앞 문장으로 가도 역시 them이 나올 뿐이므로 다시 그 앞의 문장으로 이동하여 살펴보면 them은 issues and problems를 뜻하는 것을 찾을 수 있다.

Q. Among ⓐ, ⓑ, ⓒ, ⓓ, and ⓔ which one differs from the others in what it refers to?

① ⓐ   ② ⓑ   ③ ⓒ   ④ ⓓ   ⑤ ⓔ

02

정답　⑤

해석　ⓐ, ⓑ, ⓒ, ⓓ, ⓔ 중에서 가리키는 것이 다른 하나는?

개개인에게는 자신들이 내리는 결정은 매우 중요하다. 결정은 개개인이 얼마만큼 사회와 사회 발전에 융합되었는지 나타낸다. 우리는 어떻게 개개인이 사회를 형성하는 것에 관심을 쏟기보다는 어떻게 개개인이 사회와 사회 발전을 결정짓는 여러 변수들에 잘 순응하는지에 더 관심을 쏟아야 한다. 개개인이 사회에 성공적으로 공감하지 못한다면, 그들은 사회가 제공하는 것을 제대로 사용할 수 없고 스스로도 심리적으로 편안하게 지낼 수 없다. 왜 우리는 우리의 삶과 직접적으로 별 관계도 없는 사건이나 문제에 신경을 써야 할까? 우리가 신경을 쓰는 이유는 사회의 필수적인 한 부분이 되고 싶기 때문이다. 우리가 이러한 사건과 문제에 지금 공감하지 못하면, 우리는 사회의 다른 사람들에게 공감하지 못한다. 사실 우리가 지니고 있는 중요한 부담 중 하나는 우리가 얼마나 잘 융합되었는지 보여 주는 것이다. 우리는 독자적인 행동 양태를 지닌 사회적 조직에 속하였거나 아니면 자신의 가족에 속하였든 간에 어느 단체에 속해 있음을 증명할 필요가 항상 있음을 자각한다.

① ⓐ   ② ⓑ   ③ ⓒ   ④ ⓓ   ⑤ ⓔ

해설 ⓔ를 제외하면 모두 '개개인'을 가리키며, ⓔ는 문맥상 '이러한 사건과 문제(issues and problems)'를 가리킨다. 따라서 답은 ⓔ이다.

어휘 **integrated** ⓐ 통합된, 융합된   **mold** ⓥ 형성하다

adapt to 적응하다, 순응하다, ~에 적응하다, 순응하다

variable ⓝ 변수   **relate to** ~와 관련되다, ~에 공감하다

at peace 평화롭게, 안심하고   **bearing on** ~에의 관련, 영향

integral ⓐ 필수적인   **constant** ⓐ 끊임없는

integration ⓝ 통합   **individuality** ⓝ 개성

resolution ⓝ 해결   **make best use of** ~을 최대한 활용하다

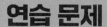
01 What does the underlined Three refer to?

As a high school soccer coach, I'm aware that student athletes tend to focus too much on sports. A fellow coach, Bob, was talking about one such player, who called him at home one night. When his wife informed the kid that Bob wasn't home, he became frantic and said he had to speak to the coach right away. "Just calm down, and I'll have him call you as soon as he gets home," the coach's wife told him. "What's your number?" The flustered kid replied, "Three."

① his phone number
② his uniform number
③ his room number
④ the number of his team members

02 Which of the following does the underlined Ⓐ silent heroes refer to? 가천대 2019

Since the advent of the automobile, over 20 million fatalities have been recorded. Even as late as the 1950's, car manufacturers stood by the claim that it was impossible to make vehicles any safer than they were because the physical forces of a crash were too great to overcome. At the same time, after testing with cadavers, the first crash test dummy was unveiled. A crash test dummy is a full-scale anthropomorphic test device (ATD) that resembles the body in weight, proportions, and movement. Today's dummies are equipped with sensitive high-tech sensors that provide vital crash test data. Thanks to these Ⓐ silent heroes, humans have the greatest chances of surviving fatal accidents than they have ever had.

① fatalities
② manufacturers
③ cadavers
④ dummies

밑줄 친 ⓐ~ⓓ 중 가리키는 대상이 나머지 셋과 <u>다른</u> 것은?

Today even the most incorrigible junk food addicts know that fats in any form are bad for their health and girth, but ⓐ <u>trans fats</u> are doubly bad for the heart. Formed when ⓑ <u>liquid oils</u> are solidified by adding hydrogen, trans fats boost bad-cholesterol (LDL) and depress good-cholesterol (HDL) levels in the blood. A recent study estimates that processed food and oils account for 80% of Americans' intake of trans fats. Researchers recommend people cut down as much as possible on ⓒ <u>the fats</u>. Another study concluded that eliminating ⓓ <u>hydrogenated oils</u> could prevent up to 100,000 premature coronary deaths a year.

① ⓐ   ② ⓑ

③ ⓒ   ④ ⓓ

[01~02]

Matthew is the only Gospel that mentions 'the three wise men' at all, and there is no mention in any of the Gospels of the number of wise men who brought gifts to the infant Jesus. ㉮ It says simply that "there came wise men from the east to Jerusalem." The idea that there were only three wise men crept in no doubt because the gifts included three types of treasures: gold, frankincense, and myrrh. When the Bible story was translated into stone in the churches, it was most natural to portray one wise man for each of the three kinds of gift. There could have been many men and many gifts.

01 윗글의 내용과 일치하지 않는 것은?

① The wise men were not native to Jerusalem.
② It was assumed that each wise man brought a different gift.
③ Many Gospels in the Bible claim that there were three wise men.
④ It is possible that there were more than three wise men.

02 밑줄 친 ㉮가 지칭하는 것은?

① the journey of the wise men
② the life of Jesus
③ the Church
④ the Gospel of Matthew

A century ago, we had essentially no way to start to explain how thinking works. Then psychologists like Sigmund Freud and Jean Piaget produced their theories about child development. Somewhat later, on the mechanical side, mathematicians like Kurt Gödel and Alan Turing began to reveal the hitherto unknown range of what machines could be made to do. These two streams of thought began to merge only in the 1940s when Warren McCulloch and Walter Pitts began to show how ⓐ _____ might be made to see, reason, and remember. Research in the modern science of Artificial Intelligence started only in the 1950s, stimulated by the invention of modern computers. ⓑ This inspired a flood of new ideas about how machines could do what only minds had done ⓒ _____ .

03 빈칸 ⓐ에 문맥상 가장 적합한 단어를 고르시오.

① computers
② minds
③ machines
④ Artificial Intelligence

04 밑줄 친 ⓑ가 지시하는 핵심 단어를 고르시오.

① research
② computer
③ invention
④ none of them

05 빈칸 ⓒ에 문맥상 가장 적합한 단어를 고르시오.

① seemingly
② exceedingly
③ previously
④ rapidly

An argument often advanced for the encouragement of religion is that, to paraphrase St. Mathew's report of Jesus's words, it leads people to love their neighbors as themselves. That would be a powerful point were it true. But is it? This was the question Jean Decety, a developmental neuroscientist at the University of Chicago, asked in a study just published in *Current Biology*.

Dr. Decety is not the first to wonder, in a scientific way, about the connection between religion and _____. He is, though, one of the first to do it without recourse to that standard but peculiar laboratory animal beloved by psychologists, the undergraduate student. Instead, he collaborated with researchers in Canada, China, Jordan, South Africa and Turkey, as well as with fellow Americans, to look at children aged between 5 and 12 and their families.

06 **What does the underlined 'it' mean?**

① Most people are religious.
② The object of belief is not important.
③ Jesus emphasized the love of people.
④ Science and religion are not different.
⑤ Religion makes people help others.

07 **Choose one that is most appropriate for the blank.**

① altruism   ② individualism
③ egoism   ④ capitalism
⑤ narcissism

08 **According to the passage, psychologists' favorite subject of experiment is** _____.

① children   ② college students
③ Americans   ④ animals
⑤ researchers

Prague castle is not only a beautiful complex of historical monuments, but also a place that is closely connected with the political and legal developments of our country. Within these walls are reflected both great and tragic events. Since (A) it was built, the castle has fulfilled a number of functions — (B) it was the monarch's residence, a military fortification, a tribal sanctuary, a centre of Christianity, the seat of provincial councils and the hub of courts and administrative offices. Not least is (C) its function as the burial place of Czech kings and the repository of the Czech Crown Jewels, which are still a symbol of Czech statehood. Since 1918, (D) it has been the seat of the President of the Republic, together with his office, and continues the tradition of Prague Castle as the seat of the head of the country, which has lasted for more than 1,000 years. The symbol of the presidential seat is the flag of the President of the Republic flying over Prague Castle, one of the state symbols of the Czech Republic with a great state coat of arms in (E) its centre and the motto *Pravda vitezi*, which means "Truth prevails."

09 밑줄 친 (A)~(E) 가운데 가리키는 것이 <u>다른</u> 하나는?

① (A) ② (B) ③ (C) ④ (D) ⑤ (E)

10 밑줄 친 **a number of functions**의 예로 언급되지 <u>않은</u> 것은?

① 최고 통치자의 거소(居所) ② 국가적 상징물의 보관소
③ 왕실의 무덤 ④ 문화예술 공연장
⑤ 군사 요새

ⓐ <u>Television</u> is the most effective marketing tool ever created. Many advertisements apply basic psychology by sort of appealing to our insecurities and desires. Ads convince us that the things we once thought were luxuries are now necessities. Television is highly skilled at creating images of affluence, not just in the ads, but in the programs as well. Using sophisticated market research, programmers and advertisers sort of paint a picture of life centered on material possessions. This kind of life may look glamorous and desirable, but ⓑ <u>it</u> is all at the expense of personal relationships. As you probably can tell, I tend to agree with critics of ⓒ <u>the media</u>. (가) _____, and products we really need don't require advertising. Television promotes consumerism. ⓓ <u>It</u> shows us things, things, and more things. It encourages greed and envy. Television helps create a(n) (나) _____ society, where things are thrown out long before they are worn out.

11 밑줄 친 ⓐ, ⓑ, ⓒ, ⓓ 중에서 가리키는 바가 <u>다른</u> 것은?

① ⓐ   ② ⓑ   ③ ⓒ   ④ ⓓ

12 빈칸 (가)에 들어갈 가장 적절한 것은?

① Advertising disregards our securities
② Advertising conceals our inner desires
③ Advertising creates false needs
④ Advertising reveals personal relationships

13 빈칸 (나)에 들어가기에 적절하지 <u>않은</u> 것은?

① extravagant   ② frugal   ③ uneconomic   ④ wasteful

14 윗글의 내용과 일치하지 <u>않는</u> 것은?

① Television may be an obstacle to the sound consumption climate.
② Television fosters a culture of consumerism.
③ Television has a negative effect on advertising industries.
④ Television shows us images of an affluent society.

[15~16]

ⓐ The drug wasn't always so controversial in the scientific establishment. The U.S. Pharmacopeia, a doctors' listing of remedies begun in 1820, first included cannabis in 1870. The pharmacopeia didn't drop pot until its 1942 edition, the first published after cannabis was outlawed in 1937. Eventually most physicians began to view the drug as little more than a crude intoxicant. They tended to favor new-fashioned drugs that were refined by pharmaceutical firms into pure chemicals. Raw marijuana contains some 400 compounds. It wasn't until the '70s that modern methods were applied to test the medical effects of cannabis. As Earleywine recounts, a UCLA study designed to confirm police reports that pot dilates pupils found instead a slight constriction. That's how doctors discovered the drug could help glaucoma sufferers by reducing intraocular pressure.

15 밑줄 친 ⓐ The drug이 가리키지 않는 것은?

① pot
② cannabis
③ marijuana
④ intoxicant

16 윗글의 내용에서 추론할 수 없는 것은?

① The use of pot was not illegal in the past.
② Pot dilates pupils.
③ Glaucoma patients have higher intraocular pressure.
④ Marijuana can help glaucoma patients.

Professor Westbury has been doing important work, exploring the connections between language difficulties and brain function. As part of his inquiry, Westbury presents patients suffering from aphasia — whose comprehension of words and speech is often impaired — with a string of letters and asks whether or not it constitutes a real English word. One day, a graduate student pointed out something curious: certain nonsense words consistently made patients smile and sometimes even laugh out loud. "Particularly," Westbury says, "'snunkoople'." He started checking with friends and colleagues to see whether they had the same reaction, and the response was nearly unanimous. Snunkoople was funny. But why? Westbury presents what he believes could be the answer: the inherent funniness of a word, or at least of context-free non-words, can be quantified — and not a nonsense is created equal. According to Westbury, the less statistically likely it is for a certain collection of letters to form a real word in English, the funnier it is. The playwright Neil Simon seemed to grasp this implicitly in his 1972 work *The Sunshine Boys*, in which an old character tells his nephew, "If it doesn't have a 'k' in it, it's not funny!" — 'k' being one of the least frequently used letters in the alphabet.

17 윗글의 제목으로 가장 적절한 것은?

① Aphasia: The Way We Laugh
② Why Certain Words Are Funny
③ Humor as an Art of Equivocation
④ "Snunkoople," an Unusual Cluster of Letters

18 밑줄 친 "this"가 의미하는 것으로 적절하지 <u>않은</u> 것은?

① Laughter is the by-product of a kind of incongruity.
② The less plausible a word sounds, the funnier we deem it to be.
③ Laughter arises from the sudden violation of an expectation.
④ Humor works when a word squares intuitively with our expectations.

Contrary to conventional wisdom, the combination of exercise and cold exposure does not act synergistically to enhance metabolism of fats, according to a study published in 1991 in the journal *Sports Medicine*. The study, done at the Hyperbaric Environmental Adaptation Program of the Naval Medical Research Institute in Bethesda, Md., found that some of the bodily processes involved in fat metabolism were actually slowed down by the effects of relatively cold temperatures on human tissue. The researchers suggested that the slowdown in metabolic processes might be linked to the constriction of blood vessels in the peripheral fatty tissues when exercise is done in the cold. The study found that the volume of air inhaled and exhaled in one minute increases upon initial exposure to the cold but may return to rates comparable to those in warm-air exercise upon prolonged exertion. The heart rate is often, but not always, lower during cold-weather exercise, the study found, while oxygen uptake may increase, something the researchers suggested could be at least in part the result of shivering.

19 **What can you learn from the study in the passage?**

① People burn more fat exercising in cold weather than in hot weather.
② Exercising in warm weather increases the volume of air inhaled.
③ Cold weather can bring about the slowdown in some metabolic processes.
④ The oxygen uptake increased by shivering makes the heart rate higher.

20 **What does the underlined those refer to?**

① rates
② metabolic processes
③ increases
④ fatty tissues

Noise is among the most pervasive but Ⓐ transient pollutants today. Noise pollution can broadly be defined as unwanted or offensive sounds that unreasonably intrude into our daily activities. We experience noise in a number of ways. On some occasions, we can be both the cause and victim of noise, such as when we are operating noisy appliances or equipment. There are also instances when we experience noise generated by others, just as people experience secondhand smoke. In both instances, noise is equally damaging physically. Secondhand noise is generally more troubling, however, because it is put into the environment by others, without our consent.

The air into which secondhand noise is emitted and on which Ⓑ it travels is "a commons." Ⓒ It belongs not to an individual person or a group, but to everyone. People, businesses, and organizations, therefore, do not have unlimited rights to broadcast noise as they please. Ⓓ _____ they have an obligation to use the commons in ways that are compatible with other uses. Those that disregard the obligation to "not interfere" with others' use of the commons by producing noise pollution are acting like a bully in a school yard. Although they may do so unknowingly, they disregard the rights of others and claim for themselves rights that are not theirs.

21 밑줄 친 Ⓐ **transient**와 의미가 가장 비슷한 것은?

① transparent   ② transferable
③ transitory   ④ transcendent

22 밑줄 친 Ⓑ와 Ⓒ의 **it**이 각각 지칭하는 것은?

① the air, secondhand noise
② the air, the air
③ secondhand noise, the air
④ secondhand noise, secondhand noise

23 빈칸 ⓓ에 가장 적합한 것은?

① In addition

② On the contrary

③ Nevertheless

④ Therefore

24 윗글의 내용과 일치하지 <u>않는</u> 것은?

① Secondhand noise can be extremely annoying because it is out of control.

② Secondhand noise can be harmful as much as noise generated by us.

③ We may interfere with others' use of the commons unintentionally.

④ We are not so much the victim as the cause of noise pollution.

The Norman kings were often totally ignorant of the English, although Henry I, who had an English wife, was an ⓐ _____ and could speak some English. No doubt in upper-class circles it was the fashionable thing to speak French. To this day the use of French words in conversation is thought to show sophistication, or savoir fair. Though French had the social and cultural prestige, Latin remained the principal language of religion and learning. The English vernacular survived as the common speech. The mingling of these three powerful traditions can be seen in the case of a word like kingly. The Anglo-Saxons had only one word to express this concept, which, with typical simplicity, they made up from the word king. After the Normans, three synonyms enter ⓑ the language: royal, regal, and sovereign. The capacity to express three or four different shades of meaning and to make fine distinctions is one of the hallmarks of ⓒ the language after the Conquest, as word groups such as rise-mount-ascend, ask-question-interrogate, or time-age-epoch suggest.

25 ⓐ에 들어갈 가장 적절한 표현을 고르시오.

① example   ② expert
③ expertise   ④ exception

26 밑줄 친 ⓑ와 ⓒ의 **the language**가 구체적으로 지시하는 쌍을 고르시오.

① English – Latin   ② English – French
③ Latin – French   ④ English – English

27 윗글의 내용에 가장 잘 부합하는 것을 고르시오.

① Henry I could not speak English like other Norman kings.
② To speak French in public was thought to be a shame.
③ Latin was the most prestigious language in churches and schools at that time.
④ The word king has a French origin.

A cottage industry has sprung up facilitating the sale and donation of human breast milk on the Internet, but a study published Monday confirms the concerns of health professionals over this unregulated marketplace. The report found that breast milk bought from websites was contaminated with high levels of bacteria, including salmonella. The amounts detected were sufficient to sicken a child. "The study makes you worry," said Dr. Richard of Columbia University. "This is a potential cause of disease. Even with a relative, it's probably not a good idea to share." After a spate of research showing that breast milk protects infants from infections and other ailments, health care providers have strongly encouraged new mothers to abandon formula and to breast-feed. But ⓐ this can be a difficult challenge. Parents who have adopted, for instance, or have had mastectomies often rely on donated or purchased breast milk.

28 Which does the underlined ⓐ this refer to?

① To regulate marketplace
② To adopt or to have mastectomies
③ To prevent potential causes of disease
④ To abandon formula and to breast-feed

29 Which is NOT true according to the passage?

① Recent study findings unnerve some parents.
② Human breast milk can guard babies against illnesses.
③ Research has demonstrated the benefits of donated milk.
④ Some samples from milk-sharing sites contain dangerous levels of bacteria.

30 Which is the best title of the passage?

① Looking for Breast Milk? Be Cautious.
② Having an Oversupply? Sell Online.
③ Take Risks. It's for Your Child.
④ Don't Breast-feed. It Is Tainted.

CHAPTER 07

단어와 숙어

단어와 숙어, 이디엄을 묻는 문제들이 종종 선보이고 있다. 단어는 막연한 동의어뿐 아니라 다의어를 묻는 문제들도 출제된다. 숙어와 이디엄은 정확히 알지 못하면 시험에서 활용할 수 없으므로 시험 전에 중요 숙어나 관용어구들은 꼭 암기하여야 한다.

01 질문 유형

What does the underlined word *** mean?
Which of the following can best replace the underlined ***?
The underlined word *** most closely means _____.
The underlined word *** is closest in meaning to _____.

02 문제 풀이 전략

❶ 단어와 숙어의 뜻을 문맥상에서 어떻게든 판단한다.
단어와 숙어의 문제는 그러한 단어나 숙어를 암기하고 있는지를 묻는 것이다. 만약 모르는 단어라면 그 단어가 빈칸의 형태인 문장 완성 문제로 보고 그 단어 없이 앞뒤 관계를 추측하여 문제를 풀어 나간다. 의외로 동의어보다 문장 완성의 원리로 푸는 것이 쉬운 문제들이 있기 때문이다.

❷ 만약 단어나 숙어의 뜻을 모르면 소거법을 활용한다.
문제를 푸는 도중에 단어나 숙어의 뜻이 기억나지 않거나, 혹은 전혀 모르는 것들이라면 가장 관련성이 떨어지는 보기부터 차례차례 소거해 나가야 한다. 그렇게 해서 하나 내지 두 개의 보기를 제거하면 정답으로 갈 확률이 훨씬 높아지기 때문이다. 하지만 가장 중요한 것은 평소 많은 어휘를 폭넓게 익혀 두는 것이 가장 바람직하다.

Since time immemorial, people have worried about the earth's future. We once believed that the sky would fall. More recently we worried that technology would grind to a halt because of a computer bug that was supposed to be unleashed at the turn of the millenium. Those fears melted away, but today the world has many real, pressing problems. Think about the environment, economics, health, or population, ⓐ _____ you'll find plenty of reasons to worry. Unfortunately, however, we tend to focus on just some of the planet's biggest issues, and we get a distorted view of the world as a result. Deforestation is a challenge that has attracted widespread anxiety. It is, to be blunt, a popular cause. It seems surprising, then, to learn that deforestation is a diminishing problem. The solution wasn't found in condemnation from the west of developing country practices, but in economic growth. Developed countries generally increase their forested areas, because they can afford to do so. Developing countries can't.

'서서히 멈추다(stop slowly)'의 뜻을 나타내는 표현이다. 본문에서는 과학 발전이 서서히 멈출 수 있다는 의미로 사용되었다.

to be blunt은 '솔직하게 말하면, 쉽게 설명하면'이란 의미이다. 앞부분에 대한 부연 설명으로 볼 수 있다.

삼림 파괴 행위를 '비난'하려는 게 아니라는 뜻으로 쓰였다.

Q1. What is the phrase that is closest in meaning to the underlined phrase "grind to a halt"?

① aggravate gradually   ② stop laboriously
③ lose vitality   ④ throw into confusion

Q2. Fill in the blank ⓐ with a suitable word.

① and   ② but
③ though   ④ because

Q3. Choose one that is closest in meaning to the underlined phrase "to be blunt".

① however   ② naturally enough
③ willy-nilly   ④ roughly speaking

'대략적으로 말하자면, 대충 말하자면'의 뜻이지만, 앞의 내용에 대해서 간략하게 전반적인 얘기를 하므로 부연의 성질을 띤 것으로 볼 수 있다.

Q4. What would be the closest in meaning to condemnation?

① conviction

② denunciation

③ approbation

④ introspection

해석　태곳적부터 인간은 지구의 미래를 걱정해 왔다. 하늘이 무너질 것이라고 믿은 적도 있었다. 더 최근에는 새천년의 전환기에 나타날 컴퓨터 버그로 인해 과학 기술 발전이 서서히 멈출 것을 우려하기도 했다. 물론 이제 그런 두려움은 사라졌지만 오늘날의 세계는 많은 현실적이고 절박한 문제들을 안고 있다. 환경, 경제, 의료, 인구 문제를 생각해 보라. 걱정할 만한 이유는 수없이 많다. 그러나 안타깝게도 우리는 지구가 당면한 몇 가지 큰 문제에만 초점을 맞추는 경향이 있고, 그 결과 왜곡된 세계관을 갖게 되었다. 삼림 파괴는 광범위한 불안을 일으킨 문제이다. 쉽게 말하자면, 그것은 잘 알려진 문제이다. 따라서 삼림 파괴는 점차 줄어들고 있는 문제라는 것을 알면 놀랄 것이다. 이 문제의 해결책은 선진국들이 개발 도상국의 삼림 파괴 행위를 비난하는 데 있는 것이 아니라 경제 성장에 있다. 선진국들은 일반적으로 삼림 면적을 늘리고 있다. 그럴 만한 경제적 여유가 있기 때문이다. 그러나 개발 도상국들은 그렇지 못하다.

Q1. 다음 중 밑줄 친 "grind to a halt"와 의미가 가장 비슷한 것은?

① 점차 악화시키다

② 애써서 멈추다

③ 활기를 잃다

④ 혼란스럽게 하다

정답　②

해설　문장 속의 인과 관계를 이용해 표현의 의미를 유추한다. 컴퓨터 버그가 원인이므로 과학 기술 발전의 중단이 결과로서 자연스럽다. 과학 기술 발전이 불가능해지는 결과는 과학 기술의 악화라기보다는 중단이 더 적절한 표현이므로 ①이 아니라 ②가 적절하다.

Q2. 빈칸 ⓐ를 적절한 단어로 채우시오.

① 그리고

② 그러나

③ 그렇기는 하지만

④ 왜냐하면

정답　①

해설　앞 절과 뒤 절이 "명령문 + and" 구조로 이루어진 문장이다. "~해라. 그러면 ~할 것이다"라는 의미이다.

Q3. 밑줄 친 "to be blunt"와 의미가 가장 비슷한 것은?

① 그러나

② 매우 당연히

③ 싫든 좋든

④ 간단히 말하자면

정답　④

해설　to be blunt은 "솔직하게 말하면, 쉽게 설명하면"이란 의미이다. 문맥상 앞 문장의 내용을 간단하게 요약하는 부연 문장에서 쓰였으므로 ④가 적절하다. ②, ③은 앞 문장과의 논리 관계를 정확히 밝혀 주는 표현이 아니므로 선택하지 않도록 주의한다.

Q4. 밑줄 친 <u>condemnation</u>과 의미가 가장 비슷한 것은?

① 확신 　　　　　　　② 비난

③ 인가, 승인 　　　　④ 성찰

정답　②

해설　condemnation은 비난을 뜻하므로 ② denunciation이 동의어이다.

어휘

immemorial ⓐ 기억할 수 없는

unleash ⓥ 풀어 주다, 해방시키다

pressing ⓐ 시급한, 절박한

reason ⓝ 이유

distorted ⓐ 왜곡된

widespread ⓐ 광범위한

to be blunt 솔직히 말하면

diminishing ⓐ 줄어드는

practice ⓝ 행위, 관행

aggravate ⓥ 악화시키다

laboriously ⓐⓓ 힘들게, 애써서

approbation ⓝ 허가, 인가, 찬동

throw in confusion 혼란에 빠지게 하다

grind to a halt 서서히 멈추다(중단하다)

grind to a halt 서서히 멈추다

melt away 차츰 사라지다

plenty of 많은

focus on ~에 집중하다

deforestation ⓝ 삼림 파괴

anxiety ⓝ 불안, 우려

cause ⓝ (대화 등의) 주제, 원인, 명분

condemnation ⓝ 비난, 유죄 선고

afford ⓥ ~할 능력이 있다

denunciation ⓝ 맹렬한 비난

vitality ⓝ 활기, 생명력

introspection ⓝ 성찰, 자기반성

01 밑줄 친 **celibate**와 의미가 가장 가까운 것을 고르시오.

For years, scholars and researchers tried to study geniuses by analyzing statistics, as if piles of data somehow illuminate genius. In his 1904 study of genius, Haverlock Ellis noted that most geniuses were fathered by men older than 30, had mothers younger than 25, and usually were sickly as children. Other scholars reported that many were celibate (Descartes), others were fatherless (Dickens) or motherless (Darwin). In the end, the piles of data illuminated nothing.

① abstinent   ② parentless
③ promiscuous   ④ affluent

02 Which of the following uses of 'charge' is closest in meaning to the underlined ㉮?

People in Asia use gestures far more frequently and productively than do people in the West. This is particularly noticeable in dance and drama, which, in many Far Eastern countries are highly complex, with hundreds of formal gestures of both hand and body. Most of these gestures are like a foreign language to the uninformed Westerner. Much of Asian dance and drama has a religious background, with the result that the gestures of the performers are ㉮ charged both with information and with emotional power that is communicated to the audience.

① With unparalleled bravery the cavalry charged the enemy.
② With the festival approaching, the air was charged with excitement.
③ A whistle-blower's information led him to be charged with embezzlement.
④ The director charged his secretary with the management of his correspondence.
⑤ I was not charged for the repair because the TV was defective.

Modern Greece is the sum of extraordinary diversity of influences. Romans, Arabs, French, Venetians, Slavs, Albanians, Turks, Italians, ⓐ to say nothing of the great Byzantine empire, have all been here and gone since the time of Alexander the Great. All have left their marks: the Byzantines in countless churches and monasteries; the Venetians in impregnable fortifications in the Peloponnese; the Franks in crag-top castles, again on the Peloponnese but also in the east Aegean. Most obvious, perhaps, is the heritage of 400 years of Ottoman Turkish rule which exercised an inestimable influence on music, cuisine, language and the way of life. The contributions, and continued existence, of substantial minorities — Vlachs, Muslims, Jew, Gypsies — ⓑ round out the list of those who have helped to make up the Hellenic identity.

03 밑줄 친 ⓐ와 의미가 가장 가까운 것은?

① to speak ill of ② not to mention

③ to set at nought ④ to make light of

04 밑줄 친 ⓑ와 의미가 가장 가까운 것은?

① rule ② circle ③ complete ④ circumvent

[01~02] 항공대 2015

Once it established that basic method of buying directly from manufacturers to get the deepest discounts possible, Wal-Mart focused (A) <u>relentlessly</u> on three things. The first was working with the manufacturers to get them to cut their costs as much as possible. The second was working on its supply chain from those manufacturers, wherever they were in the world, to Wal-Mart's distribution centers, to make it as low-cost and frictionless as possible. The third was constantly improving Wal-Mart's information systems, so it knew exactly what its customers were buying and could feed that information to all the manufacturers, so the shelves would always be stocked with the right items at the right time.

Wal-Mart quickly realized that if it could save money by buying directly from the manufacturers, by constantly innovating to cut the cost of running its supply chain, and by keeping its inventories low by learning more about its customers, it could beat its competitors on price every time. Sitting in Bentonville, Arkansas, it didn't have much choice.

01 According to the passage, which of the following does Wal-Mart need to do to increase the chance to beat its competitors on price?

① lowering the customers' information levels on its information system
② purchasing directly from manufacturers
③ elevating inventory levels on warehouse
④ making its supply chain as complicated as possible

02 What would be the closest in meaning to (A)?

① harmoniously   ② flexibly
③ compliantly   ④ persistently

Most schools and institutions of education in contemporary English-speaking countries such as the UK, USA, Ireland, Australia and New Zealand use English as the medium of instruction. Because a working knowledge of English is perceived as being required in many fields, professions, and occupations, many countries throughout the world ⓐ mandate the teaching of English, at least a basic level, in an effort to increase the competitiveness of their economies. The language researcher David Graddol, however, predicts that the global spread of English, will lead to serious economic and political disadvantages in the future in the UK unless plans are put in place immediately to ⓑ redress the situation. Graddol concludes that monolingual English graduates face a ⓒ bleak economic future as qualified multilingual young people from other countries are proving to have a competitive advantage over their British counterparts in global companies and organizations.

03 Which of the following can best replace the underlined ⓑ?

① require   ② remedy
③ reduce   ④ realize
⑤ relate

04 Which title does best describe the passage above?

① Competitiveness of English language
② Importance of English language education
③ Power of English in economic and political sectors in UK
④ Future of English in the era of globalization
⑤ Monolingual power of English

05 Choose the most appropriate pair of the words to replace the underlined ⓐ – ⓒ above.

① require – dismal   ② inundate – unsure
③ cancel – grim   ④ oppose – unfair
⑤ choose – advantageous

The universe is a tough place these days for creators of new books on astronomy. Faster than writers and editors can go to press, their efforts are overtaken by far-out discoveries and eyepopping photos of things no one on Earth has ever seen before. As unwinnable as the race may be, Mary K. Baumann and her coauthors have given it a run in What's Out There, a collection of some of the most memorable and interesting celestial images from the past few years. The pictures, accompanied by short bits of text in plain English, juxtapose relatively familiar views of space with sights that may surprise even veteran space watchers. Topics are presented in alphabetical order instead of thematically, effectively shuffling them like a deck of cards. Venus, the second planet from the sun, follows the seventh — Uranus — which appears right behind the Hubble Space Telescope's dazzling "ultra deep field" shot of the most distant galaxies ever photographed at visible wavelengths.

06 밑줄 친 **juxtapose**에 가장 가까운 의미는?

① act or speak officially for
② put side by side or close together
③ make something bad slightly less bad
④ find a satisfactory way of dealing with

07 윗글의 내용과 일치하지 <u>않는</u> 것은?

① 메리 바우만의 책의 순서는 주제별로 나열되어 있다.
② 우주 관련 분야에서 새 천문학책을 펴내기는 매우 어렵다.
③ 메리 바우만은 동료들과 함께 "저 먼 곳에 무엇이 있나"라는 제목의 책을 출판했다.
④ 메리 바우만의 책에는 태양에서 두 번째 행성인 금성이 천왕성 뒤에 소개된다.

Since the early 1900s, Hollywood has been synonymous with the film industry. Today, it is the mecca for film producers, would-be movie stars, and other Californian dreamers of cinematic careers. The blend of two features first attracted film makers to Hollywood in the early 1910s. One was the sunny and mild climate of its southern California location. The other was the diverse landscape and geography. Television and record companies followed suit in the 1950s. By this time, Hollywood was already the center of the entertainment business. The real estate market and cost of living have been skyrocketing in the Los Angeles area, which has made many film companies move to more economical suburbs. Nevertheless, Hollywood still remains the symbolic epicenter of the entertainment industry. Tourism now accounts for a major portion of the city's income. Studio tours, landmarks, and celebrity homes continue to attract visitors from around the world.

08 Which of the following is closest in meaning to the underlined followed suit?

① rode for a fall
② stood in others' shoes
③ had a free ride
④ got on the bandwagon

09 Which of the following is true of the passage?

① Many television companies left Hollywood in the 1950s.
② Hollywood is losing its dominance in the film business.
③ Weather contributed to the success of Hollywood as a place for the film industry.
④ A number of moviemakers moved to downtown due to high living costs.

Like many other parts of the media industry, publishing is being Ⓐ radically reshaped by the growth of the internet. Online retailers are already among the biggest distributors of books. Now e-books threaten to Ⓑ boost sales of the old-fashioned kind. In response, publishers are trying to ⓐ shore up their conventional business while preparing for a future in which e-books will represent a much bigger chunk of sales. Publishers fret that online shopping has conditioned consumers to expect lower prices for all kinds of books. And they worry that the downward spiral will further Ⓒ erode their already thin margins as well as bring further dismay to struggling ⓑ brick-and-mortar booksellers. Ⓓ Unless things change, some in the industry predict that publishers will suffer a similar fate to that of music companies, whose fortunes faded when Apple turned the industry upside down by selling individual songs cheaply online.

10 Which is NOT properly used in the context of the passage?

① Ⓐ
② Ⓑ
③ Ⓒ
④ Ⓓ

11 Which is closest in meaning to the underlined ⓐ shore up?

① shovel
② sustain
③ eradicate
④ liquidate

12 Which is closest in meaning to the underlined ⓑ brick-and-mortar?

① factory
② wholesale
③ off-line
④ large-scaled

Jetmakers are equipping planes with the latest generations of information technology. The goal is to let busy executives be in touch with their far-flung offices at all times. One of the most popular items these days is a high-speed Internet connection that works at 35,000 feet. Gulfstream's Broadband MultiLink, for instance, delivers up to 3.5 megabits a second of raw data to the plane for Web browsing, e-mail, and watching stock prices. The _____ is that it's likely to be faster than the connections most have at their homes.

So is anything really out of bound for high-flying road warriors? Well, due to the requirement of flight, hanging chandeliers are out of the question — especially in a cabin that's only six feet tall. A marble bathroom with a shower may be an enviable addition to an aircraft, but on the downside, the extra plumbing, water, and stone will add hundreds of pounds to a plane's takeoff weight, restricting its range and performance. Like any construction project, ultimately, it's a design tradeoff.

13 The most appropriate word for the blank would be _____.

① paradox   ② hyperbole

③ contradiction   ④ irony

⑤ dilemma

14 What does the underlined "out of bound" mean?

① luxurious   ② impossible

③ essential   ④ threatening

⑤ rewarding

Success is boring. Success is proving that you can do something that you already know you can do, or doing something correctly the first time, which can often be a problematical victory. First-time ⓐ _____ is usually a ⓑ _____. First-time ⓒ _____, by contrast, is ⓓ _____; it is the natural order of things. Failure is how we learn. I have been told of an African phrase describing a good cook as "she who has broken many pots." If you've spent enough time in the kitchen to have broken a lot of pots, probably you know a fair amount about cooking. I once had a late dinner with a group of chefs, and they spent time comparing knife wounds and burn scars. They knew how much credibility their failures gave them. I earn my living by writing a daily newspaper column. Each week I am aware that one column is going to be the worst column of the week. I don't set out to write it; I try my best every day. Still, every week, one column is inferior to the others, sometimes spectacularly so. I have learned to cherish that column. A successful column usually means that I am treading on familiar ground, going with the tricks that work, preaching to the choir or dressing up popular sentiments in fancy words. Often in my inferior columns, I am trying to ⓔ <u>pull off</u> something I've never done before, something I'm not even sure can be done.

15 ⓐ, ⓑ, ⓒ, ⓓ에 각각 들어갈 적절한 표현을 고르시오.

① victory – defeat – victory – foreseen
② success – fluke – failure – expected
③ achievement – problem – mistake – pardoned
④ recognition – fake – ignorance – endured

16 ⓔ를 적합하게 풀어 쓴 표현을 고르시오.

① carry out despite difficulties   ② postpone
③ accept   ④ put aside

17 윗글의 내용과 잘 부합하는 표현을 고르시오.

① The chefs were ashamed of their job.
② I want to be a columnist winning the praise of my readers.
③ Usually first-time success is an accidental advantage.
④ I am a failure as a columnist.

On top of the high demand, there is a pressure on employers to increase gender diversity in their workforce. "All the top companies are absolutely committed to increasing diversity and inclusion," Wing said. Some, of course, may just be spurred <u>by optics</u>. "Companies know they need women because otherwise they will be shamed by the press and outspoken advocates," said Ingersoll, who previously led efforts to create Google Fiber.

The smart ones, however, also realize it can be a huge asset to <u>their bottom line</u>. Take gaming. Women make up only 22% of game developers yet represent 50% of people who play video games, said Elizabeth Brown, the chief people officer of Unity Technologies. So it makes good business sense to want to hire more women developers because the people who create the games should represent an industry's customer base, Brown said.

18 The underlined "by optics" means _____.

① without false pretension
② in general appearance
③ by mutual consent
④ by the public's perception
⑤ in genuine attention

19 The underlined "their bottom line" means _____.

① their ethical criterion
② their labor cost
③ their company reputation
④ their human resource
⑤ their net profit

There are several myths on weight-lifting. One myth about building muscles is that it's good to (A) _____ protein. Protein is necessary, but your body can absorb only so much, then it eliminates the rest. Another myth about weight training is that you have to work out every day. Muscle tissue needs at least 48 hours to recover from hard exercise, so working the same muscle two days in a row is overtraining and provides no benefit. Weight-lifting (B) takes commitment and determination. You should be consistent and not give up if you don't see results right away. Your body will develop muscles in its own time. There are several common misconceptions about the relationship between weight-lifting, cardiovascular fitness and weight loss. Weight-lifting can increase muscle endurance, but it's not the best way to improve cardiovascular fitness or to lose weight. So, it's best to combine weight training with a cardio program.

20 Choose the best expression for (A)?

① overload on   ② log on
③ work out   ④ spread out

21 Which one can replace (B) takes?

① improves   ② requires
③ estimates   ④ accompanies

22 Which one is NOT TRUE?

① There is a limit to the amount of protein our body can absorb.
② Muscles need at least two days to recover from exhausting exercises.
③ Weight-lifting is the best way to lose weight.
④ It's beneficial to combine weight training with a cardio program.

Experts say that if you feel drowsy during the day, even during boring activities, you haven't had enough sleep. If you routinely fall asleep within five minutes of lying down, you probably have severe sleep deprivation. The widespread practice of "burning the candle at both ends" in Western industrialized societies has created so much sleep deprivation that what is really abnormal sleepiness is now almost the norm. Many studies make it clear that sleep deprivation is dangerous. Sleep-deprived people who are tested by using a driving simulator perform as badly as or worse than those who are intoxicated. Sleep deprivation also _____ alcohol's effects on the body, so a fatigued person who drinks will become much more impaired than someone who is well-rested. Since drowsiness is the brain's last step before falling asleep, driving while drowsy can lead to disaster. Caffeine and other stimulants cannot overcome the effects of severe sleep deprivation. The National Sleep Foundation says that if you have trouble keeping your eyes focused, if you can't stop yawning, or if you can't remember driving the last few miles, you are probably too drowsy to drive safely.

23 According to the passage, what does the underlined part mean?

① an ardent desire to achieve goals
② a state of extreme agitation
③ a latent period before a conflict has created
④ an unrelenting schedule that affords little rest

24 Which is the most appropriate for the blank?

① shutters
② hampers
③ magnifies
④ partitions

25 What is the main purpose of the passage?

① To offer preventive measures for sleep deprivation
② To alert the signs and risks of not getting enough sleep
③ To discuss the effects of alcohol on a sleep-deprived person
④ To explain why sleeplessness is common in Western societies

PART 03

논리적 이해

OVERVIEW　　　개관

CHAPTER 01　순서 연결

CHAPTER 02　연결 구조

CHAPTER 03　문맥과 흐름

CHAPTER 04　전후 관계

CHAPTER 05　추론

CHAPTER 06　유사 추론

CHAPTER 07　어휘형 논리

CHAPTER 08　독해형 논리

논리적 이해를 요하는 경우는 크게 두 가지 경우로 대별할 수 있는데, 문장과 단락의 관계에 대한 이해 여부를 묻는 경우와 본문에 언급되지 않은 사항을 추론하여 끌어낼 수 있는지를 묻는 문제 등이다. 문장과 단락의 관계에 대한 부분은 역시 둘로 나누어 보면, 문장 간의 관계 파악의 문제와 단락 간의 관계에 대한 파악 문제로 나눌 수 있다. 편입 시험은 그 특성상 대학생들을 대상으로 하기 때문에 논리적인 이해를 요하는 문제들의 출제 빈도가 높다.

(1) 문장 간의 관계에 대한 이해 문제
(a) 순서 연결
(b) 문장 삽입
(c) 문장 삭제

문장 간의 관계에 대한 부분을 살펴보면 글의 흐름을 이해하여 문장의 순서를 제대로 판단할 수 있는지, 또 문장 간의 유기적 관계로 볼 때 더해져야 할 부분, 빼야 할 부분을 판단할 수 있는지를 묻는다. 그 이유는 문법을 공부하면서 문장은 해석을 잘하지만, 문장 간의 유기적 관계를 모르는 경우가 많기 때문에 이를 확인하는 문제들이다.

(2) 단락 간의 관계에 대한 이해 문제
(a) 연결 구조
(b) 문맥과 흐름
(c) 전후 관계

문장이 더해져 이루어진 단락과 단락 간의 관계를 파악하고 있는지를 묻는 문제들로, 전환어구는 문장 간의 관계에서도 물을 수 있는 유형이지만, 그 특성상 단락 간의 관계로 본다. 문맥과 흐름은 글의 흐름상 맞지 않는 단어를 고르는 형태이다. 전후 관계를 판단하는 문제는 글의 흐름을 이해하고 앞뒤에 어떤 식으로 글이 전개될지를 파악할 수 있는지를 묻는 문제이며, 단락 간의 관계를 제대로 나눌 수 있는지 묻는 것이 단락 구분의 문제이다.

(3) 추론을 요하는 문제
(a) 추론
(b) 빈칸 추론 (문장 완성)

추론을 요하는 문제는 본문 속에 나온 내용을 바탕으로 글에서 명시적으로 언급하진 않았지만, 100% 타당한 내용을 끌어낼 수 있는가를 묻는 유형이다. 이에 비해 빈칸 추론은 독해 지문 내에서의 문장 완성 문제이며 출제 빈도가 상당히 높다. 이러한 논리적인 문제들을 해결하기 위해서는 글의 흐름을 정확히 이해하며, 생각하며 글을 읽어 나가야 한다.

01 순서 연결

지문으로 제시된 문장 간의 유기적 관계를 제대로 이해하는지 묻는 문제들이다. 순서를 연결하는 문제 유형으로는 문장의 삽입 및 삭제, 올바른 순서대로 배열하는 문제 등이 있다. 이 가운데 문장의 삽입 문제의 출제 확률이 제일 높으며, 순서 배열 문제는 가끔씩 선보이지만, 삭제 문제는 드물게 출제된다.

01 질문 유형

Choose the best order of the paragraphs [Ⅰ], [Ⅱ] and [Ⅲ].

Where does the following sentence fit the best in the passage?

Choose the most appropriate place to insert the sentence in the box below.

The following sentence could be added to the passage. Where would the sentence best fit?

02 문제 풀이 전략

❶ 문제의 핵이 되는 단서를 찾아라.

단지 몇 문장만을 주고 연결시키라거나, 주어진 글의 해당 부분에 문장을 넣으라고 한다면 분명히 단서가 있을 것이다. 이를 파악하는 것이 핵심이다. 이렇게 글의 전후 관계를 묻는 문제는 글의 구조를 이용하여 풀 수도 있으며, 어휘를 이용한 단서를 파악하여 풀 수도 있다.

❷ 논리적 연결 고리를 생각하라.

가령 시간의 흐름순으로 나열되어 있는 글이라면 이를 파악함으로써 쉽게 풀릴 것이고, 글이 일반적인 진술이라면 뒤에 나올 얘기는 예시나 일화와 같은 구체적인 글로 이어질 것이다. 예가 여러 개 나온다면 그것들 사이에는 순서가 없겠지만, 어느 하나에 for example이 붙어 있다면 그 문장이 먼저 온다는 것이다.

This holiday season, online sales are zooming, even as online retailers offer fewer discounts and turn picky about who shops at their sites. After two years of relative malaise, online sales grew 12 percent in the first 47 days of the holiday season, according to comScore, to $27.5 billion.

판매가 12% 급증했다는 진술과 이어지는 문장을 골라야 한다.

㉮ Instead, offers go to selected customers, and are specialized: a discount on wool jackets, free hoop earrings when people spend $100, a "mystery" discount amount that is revealed only at checkout.

쿠폰 대신에 선택적으로 제공하는 얘기로 현실 상황을 드러낸다.

㉯ That significantly outpaces the growth rate of retail sales overall, which analysts expect to rise 3 to 4 percent this holiday season.

그 수치(제시문의 12퍼센트)는 성장률을 압도한다는 내용으로 주어진 문장과 연결시킬 수 있다.

㉰ But online retailers are now protecting their margins with careful offers, dispensing with the promotions of the last two holiday seasons that were meant to drive sales and get rid of extra inventory.

긍정적인 것만은 아니라는 얘기를 이어 가려고 한다. 그러므로 긍정적인 진술인 ㉯ 뒤에 이어질 수 있다.

㉱ Gone are the coupons that give shoppers 40 percent off all purchases.

쿠폰을 주던 시절은 이미 지나갔다는 사실을 전한다. 그러면 현재는 어떠한지에 대한 진술이 따라와야 한다.

Q. Choose the best order from ㉮ through ㉱ for a passage starting with the paragraph in the box.

① ㉮ – ㉯ – ㉱ – ㉰
② ㉯ – ㉰ – ㉱ – ㉮
③ ㉰ – ㉮ – ㉱ – ㉯
④ ㉱ – ㉯ – ㉮ – ㉰

정답   ②

해석   상자 안의 문장 다음에 오는 ㉮에서 ㉱의 순서가 올바른 것을 고르시오.
비록 온라인 소매업자들이 (고객들에게) 할인 혜택을 덜 제공하고 자신들의 사이트에서 쇼핑하는 사람이 누구인지 까다롭게 따지게 되긴 했지만, 올해 홀리데이 시즌에 온라인 판매는 급증하고 있다. 대략 2년간의 상대적 불안감이 가시면서, 온라인 판매가 홀리데이 시즌 최초 47일 동안 12퍼센트 증가했고, comScore에 따르면 판매 총액은 275억 달러에 달한다.

㉮ 대신, 할인 혜택은 선별된 고객에게만 제공되고, 그것도 한정적이 되었다. 예를 들면 양모 재킷에만 적용되는 할인, 고객이 100달러를 썼을 때만 제공되는 무료 후프 이어링, 계산할 때만 드러나는 "미지의" 할인액 등이 있다.

㉯ 이는 분석가들이 대략 올해 홀리데이 시즌에 3에서 4퍼센트 증가할 것으로 예상한 전반적인 소매 판매의 성장률을 크게 뛰어넘는 수치이다.

㉰ 하지만 온라인 소매업자들은 이제는 할인 혜택을 신중하게 제시하여 자신들의 마진을 보호하고 있으며, 판매 촉진과 여분의 제고를 없애기 위해 지난 2년간의 홀리데이 시즌 동안 해 온 판촉 활동을 생략하고 있다.

㉱ 쇼핑객들에게 모든 구매에 40퍼센트 할인을 제공하던 쿠폰은 옛날이야기이다.

① ㉮ - ㉯ - ㉱ - ㉰   ② ㉯ - ㉰ - ㉱ - ㉮   ③ ㉰ - ㉮ - ㉱ - ㉯   ④ ㉱ - ㉯ - ㉮ - ㉰

해설   ㉮에서 ㉱의 내용을 간단히 요약하면 다음과 같다. ㉮ 할인 혜택이 보편적이기보다는 선별적으로 주어진다. ㉯ that이 전반적인 소매 판매 성장률을 뛰어넘는 수치를 보였다. ㉰ 그러나 온라인 소매업자들은 마진 때문에 할인 혜택을 줄이고 연휴 판촉도 없애고 있다. ㉱ 모든 이에게 40퍼센트 쿠폰을 제공하던 것은 과거의 일이다. 상자 안의 내용은 온라인 판매가 연휴 동안 급증했다는 내용이다. 총액은 275억 달러임을 알 수 있는데, 문맥상 ㉯에서 that이 가리키는 것이 이 275억 달러이다. 전반적인 소비 판매를 that이 뛰어넘었다고 했으므로, that이 수치와 관련된 것임을 알 수 있고, 상자 안의 문장이 수치와 관련된 내용으로 끝나므로 상자 다음에 ㉯가 와야 한다. 남아 있는 ㉮, ㉰, ㉱ 중에서 잘 살펴보면 ㉱ 다음에 ㉮가 옴을 알 수 있는데, "모든 구매(all purchases)"에 따른 것이 아니라 "선별된 고객(selected customers)"에게만 할인 혜택이 주어지기 때문이다. 그리고 ㉰는 ㉯ 다음에 와야 흐름이 이어지는데, 왜냐하면 ㉯에서 수치가 높아졌음에도, '그러나' 온라인 소매업자들은 혜택을 줄이고 있기 때문이다. 따라서 답은 ②가 된다.

어휘   **holiday season** 연휴, 휴가철   **zoom** ⓥ 급등하다
        picky ⓐ 까다로운   **malaise** ⓝ 불안, 문제들
        outpace ⓥ 앞지르다   **offer** ⓝ 할인 혜택
        dispense with ~을 없애다

01 Choose the best place for the sentence in the box. 명지대 2014

> Elvis was such a favorite with the fans that many refused to accept he had died.

> When the undisputed king of rock 'n' roll, Elvis Presley, died on August 16, 1977, the whole world was all shook up. A 20th-century superstar, the US singer was a musical legend and a major heartthrob, with his sparkly jumpsuits and swiveling hips. (㉮) Some believe he went into hiding to escape the spotlight, while others argue he was abducted by aliens. (㉯) Interest and intrigue surround the death of Elvis, with hundreds of "sightings" reported since his untimely death. (㉰) Shortly after news broke of Elvis's death, a man calling himself Jon Burrows, which happened to be the name Elvis often used to travel under, bought a one-way ticket to Buenos Aires, Argentina. (㉱) This has fueled the rumors that Elvis faked his own death to end the fame game.

① ㉮   ② ㉯   ③ ㉰   ④ ㉱

02 Which is the proper order of the sentences Ⓐ~Ⓓ?

> That genius is unusual goes without saying. Ⓐ However another link, between savant syndrome and autism, is well established. Ⓑ A link between artistic genius on the one hand and schizophrenia and manic-depression on the other is widely debated. Ⓒ But is it so unusual that it requires the brains of those that possess it to be unusual in other ways, too? Ⓓ It is, for example, the subject of films such as "Rain Man," in which the autistic brother shows an extraordinary talent of memorizing figures.

① Ⓐ – Ⓑ – Ⓒ – Ⓓ   ② Ⓐ – Ⓓ – Ⓒ – Ⓑ
③ Ⓒ – Ⓑ – Ⓓ – Ⓐ   ④ Ⓒ – Ⓑ – Ⓐ – Ⓓ

03 Which of the following does NOT fit in the passage? 가톨릭대 2016

[A] Teotihuacan was one of the first true urban centers in the Western Hemisphere, covering nearly eight square miles at its heyday. [B] Precious artifacts recovered from the Pyramid of the Moon and other structures reveal that this was a wealthy trade metropolis with far-reaching connections. [C] Inexplicably, the city suffered sudden and violent collapse in about A.D. 600. and many people fled. [D] Assuming that some of the buildings were tombs, they called the boulevard Street of the Dead. [E] They left few written records, just the ruins of their city and intriguing clues about a once-powerful culture.

① [A]
② [B]
③ [C]
④ [D]
⑤ [E]

04 Choose the best place in the passage for the sentence in the box.

In doing so, they are reacting to the static electricity that enters the air before a thunderstorm.

Creatures that are very sensitive to the changes in the air before a storm can predict a change in the weather. [A] Birds, for example, sense the pressure change and fly lower. [B] Similarly, houseflies detect this change and move indoors to avoid the downpour. [C] And cats are known to groom themselves just before a storm. [D] The electricity separates their fur and makes them feel dirty, so they lick themselves to make the fur smooth and clean again.

① [A]
② [B]
③ [C]
④ [D]

[01] 서강대 2020

Ⓐ It may be difficult to judge when the leap from talented but derivative work to major innovation has occurred. What distinguishes a creative assimilation, a deep intertwining of appropriation and experience, from mere mimicry?

Ⓑ For most people the period of imitation and apprenticeship lasts a long time.

Ⓒ Some people, having undergone such an apprenticeship, may remain at the level of technical mastery without ever ascending to major creativity.

Ⓓ It is a time when one struggles to find one's own powers, one's own voice. It is a time of practice, repetition, and mastering of skills.

01 Reorder the following sentences in the BEST way to form a coherent passage for each question.

① Ⓑ – Ⓓ – Ⓒ – Ⓐ
② Ⓐ – Ⓑ – Ⓒ – Ⓓ
③ Ⓓ – Ⓒ – Ⓐ – Ⓑ
④ Ⓒ – Ⓐ – Ⓓ – Ⓑ

Virtual reality provides an open field for various and even multiple identities and identifications. In virtual environments, people are not confined to any one stable unifying subject position, but can adopt multiple identities (either serially or simultaneously). ① From the graphical avatars adopted to represent users in virtual environments, to the handles used in chatrooms, to something as simple as multiple e-mail accounts, all of these can be used to produce and maintain virtual identities. Identity in virtual reality becomes even more malleable than in real life, and can be as genuine and constitutive of the self as the latter. ② Whether Platonist, Cartesian, or Kantian in orientation, in all of these systems there is a shared notion of a unified and unifying subject whose existence provides a ground for knowledge, action, and personal identity. ③ Ongoing or adopted temporarily, identities can be altered, edited, fabricated, or set aside entirely. ④ Thus, virtual reality opens the possibility not only of recreating space and time, but the self as well. The subject is produced anew as it comes to occupy this new space.

02 문맥상 글의 전체 흐름과 <u>관계없는</u> 문장을 고르시오.

    ①   ②   ③   ④

Abraham Lincoln's election to the presidency in 1860 brought to a climax the long festering debate about the relative powers of the federal and the state governments. (A) By the time of his inauguration, six Southern states had seceded from the Union and formed the Confederate States of America, soon to be followed by five more. (B) The war that followed between North and South put constitutional government to its severest test. (C) After four bloody years of war, the Union was preserved, four million African American slaves were freed, and an entire nation was released from the oppressive weight of slavery. (D) The war can be viewed in several different ways: as the final, violent phase in a conflict of two regional subcultures; as the breakdown of a democratic political system; as the climax of several decades of social reform; or as a pivotal chapter in American racial history. (E) As important as the war itself was the tangled problem of how to reconstruct the defeated South. However interpreted, the Civil War stands as a story of great heroism, sacrifice, triumph, and tragedy.

03 글의 흐름으로 보아, **(A)**~**(E)** 가운데 어색한 것은?

① (A)   ② (B)   ③ (C)   ④ (D)   ⑤ (E)

Years from now, historians will likely look back at this period in American history as one of heightened prejudice amongst a significant portion of the public and shortsightedness amongst many political leaders. [A] The consensus among serious observers of the Middle East is that the reasons for Ⓐ _____ in the region towards the United States are multifold, having to do with: the United States' unconditional support of Israel and its expansionary and oppressive policies against the Palestinians; propping up of a host of unrepresentative, corrupt and repressive dictatorships throughout the Middle East and North Africa; and widespread military intervention in the Muslim world, from drone attacks that have claimed tens of thousands of civilian lives to whole-scale invasions that have cost the lives of hundreds of thousands of Muslims. [B] Nearly 80 percent of the people living under the Palestinian Authority and Hamas qualify America as an "enemy." [C] Polls show that 7 of the top 10 countries that view the United States most unfavorably are Muslim countries, while only 1 of the top 10 countries that view America most favorably is Muslim. [D]

04 **Choose the best word for blank Ⓐ above.**

① redolence　　　　　　　② comity

③ animosity　　　　　　　④ rapprochement

05 **Choose the best location for the following statement.**

"About 85 percent of Egyptians and Jordanians and 73 percent of Turks, all key U.S. allies in the Middle East, have an analogous opinion."

① [A]　　　　　　　② [B]

③ [C]　　　　　　　④ [D]

06 Select the statement most consistent with the passage.

① The antipathy between the U.S. and the Middle East is expected to decrease in the near future.

② Muslim countries have a pejorative feeling towards the U.S.

③ The U.S. lacks a strong confederate in the Middle East.

④ America's asymmetrical interference in the Middle East is one of the causes of stridency in the region.

There has never been a period in medicine when the future has looked so bright. The scientists who do research on the cardiovascular system are entirely confident that they will soon be working close to the center of things, and they no longer regard the mechanisms of ㉠ _____ disease as impenetrable mysteries. The cancer scientists, for all their public disagreements about how best to organize their research, are in possession of insights into the intimate functioning of normal and neoplastic cells that were unimaginable a few years back. The neurobiologists can do all sorts of things in their investigation, and ㉡ the brain is an organ different from what it seemed 25 years ago.

In short, I believe that the major diseases of human beings have become approachable biological puzzles, ultimately solvable. ㉮ It follows from this that it is now possible to begin thinking about a human society relatively free of disease. ㉯ This would surely have been an unthinkable notion a half century ago. ㉰ What will we do about dying, and about all that population, if such things were to come about? ㉱ What can we die of, if not disease?

07 빈칸 ㉠에 가장 적절한 것은?

① heart   ② lung   ③ liver   ④ kidney

08 밑줄 친 ㉡에서 추론할 수 있는 것은?

① The neurobiologists have carefully investigated the shape of the brain.
② The brain study has drastically been developed for two and a half decades.
③ It is not always possible to diagnose the brain more accurately than ever.
④ The brain is a special organ distinguished from all the other organs in the human body.

09 다음 문장이 들어갈 가장 적절한 곳은?

Oddly enough, it has an apocalyptic sound today.

① ㉮   ② ㉯   ③ ㉰   ④ ㉱

Some years ago I went to my 25th high school reunion. I had not seen most of my classmates since our graduation in 1959. A few were just as I remembered them, hardly changed at all. Others looked so aged that I could barely find points of coincidence with the pictures of them I had in my head. (A) Why the difference? Why are some individuals so outwardly altered by time and others not? In other words, why is there often a discrepancy between ⓐ _____ age and biological age? I believe the answer has to do with complex interactions of genetics and environment. I also believe, on the basis of evidence I have reviewed, we actually have control over some of those factors. (B) I do not subscribe to the view that aging suddenly overtakes us at some point in life, whether at 60 or some other milestone. (C) Some physicians say that we are born, grow rapidly to maturity, and then coast along on a more or less comfortable plateau until we begin to decline. (D) But I find it more useful to think of aging as a continuous and necessary process of change that begins at conception. Wherever you are on the continuum, it is important to learn how to live in appropriate ways in order to maximize health and happiness.

10 Which best fits into the blank ⓐ?

① virtual
② chronological
③ juvenile
④ environmental

11 Which is the best place for the following sentence?

They call this period of decline 'senescence' and consider it distinct and apart from what came before.

① (A)　　　　　　　　　　　② (B)
③ (C)　　　　　　　　　　　④ (D)

12 Which is true according to the passage?

① The author could recognize few of his classmates in his high school reunion.

② The author suggests that we should not control hereditary factors without clear evidence.

③ The author assumes that the decline of our body does not start until a certain milestone of age.

④ The author thinks that aging is part of a continuous changing process that starts when we are conceived.

03

A study of people's ability to translate training that involves clicking and twiddling a computer mouse reveals that the brain can apply that expertise to other fine-motor tasks requiring the hands. A research team led by Kording and Wei recruited three groups of people: Chinese migrant workers with no computer experience, workers who were matched by age and education but did have computer experience through a job, and (A) a control group of college students who were computer proficient. All the subjects went through a 2-week training period during which they had to use a computer mouse to play games. The researchers ran each group through a battery of standard motor control tests before and after the training. The test that Kording and Wei were most interested in gauged (B) generalizability. If you learn how to use a computer mouse, is that skill applied to similar motor tasks? To measure the subjects' ability to perform unfamiliar tasks, the researchers tested motor skills that involved no mouse at all, such as controlling the position of a finger when the hand is hidden beneath a cover. Before the training period, migrant workers who already had computer experience performed better than their (C) computer-naive peers on all the tests. Individuals without computer experience found it far more difficult to make finely controlled adjustments of the hand, especially when the hand was hidden. But after just 2 weeks of training, migrant workers with no previous computer experience performed (D) worse than college students at using a computer mouse and applying that skill to other fine-motor hand skills.

13 윗글의 주제로 가장 적합한 것을 고르시오.

① The transferability of motor skills to unfamiliar tasks
② The importance of motor skills in using the computer
③ Difficulty of assessing motor skills in science research
④ The brain structure for handling motor skills

14 윗글의 흐름상 가장 적합하지 <u>않은</u> 것을 고르시오.

① (A)   ② (B)   ③ (C)   ④ (D)

People have known about the benefits of vitamin C — ascorbic acid — for a long time. (A) <u>Sailors used to pack their ships with citrus and other vitamin C-rich foods to prevent scurvy.</u> People have been downing their vitamin C to supplement their daily diets for many years. For as long as people have been taking it as a supplement, however, scientists have been debating just how good for us vitamin C really is. (B) <u>Some believe that vitamin C taken in large doses can cure the common cold. Others think it can cure cancer.</u> What scientists do agree about is what vitamin C does inside our bodies. Ascorbic acid is needed for the body to produce collagen, which is the substance that binds cells to one another. (C) <u>Another way to get it is from processed foods that have been vitamin-enriched.</u> In addition, because vitamin C dissolves in water, it, like other water-soluble vitamins, helps to prevent vitamins that are gas-dissolving from oxidizing in our bodies. Because our bodies do not make ascorbic acid, we have to add it from the outside. You can get it from fresh fruits, green leafy vegetables, cooked vegetables (the less cooked, the more vitamin C), and nightshades (that is, tomatoes, potatoes, and eggplant). (D) <u>The question is: How much do we need on a daily basis?</u> It probably won't surprise you to learn that scientists are debating about that too.

15 윗글의 흐름상 가장 적합하지 <u>않은</u> 것을 고르시오.

① (A)   ② (B)

③ (C)   ④ (D)

(a) Tomorrow, the Book of Genesis will be rewritten. In the unlikely setting of the European Patent Office in Munich, a group of international civil servants will decide whether living animals are part of the natural world or whether they can be artifacts — inventions — created by human ingenuity.

(b) And it is unlikely to stop there. 'Oncodogs' or 'Oncorabbits' or 'Oncomonkeys' are likely to follow, designed to be used in cancer research.

(c) At issue is a mouse. Not an ordinary mouse, though. This is the first animal not to have been invented by God, but by humans. In 1984, genetic engineers at Harvard University manipulated the biological instructions encoded in the genes of a laboratory mouse. The engineers, Timothy Stewart, Paul Patterngale and Philip Leder, unzipped the double helix of the mouse's DNA and stitched in a gene that fatally dooms the animals to the development of cancer.

(d) Now the president and fellows of Harvard University want to patent the animal as their 'invention', because it has, in the language of patent law, 'utility' in research into how tumors form. The university has even coined a trademark for its product, the Harvard Oncomouse, and wants to profit from the exclusive right to sell these animals.

(e) Patents are immensely important in the global biotechnology industry that has developed over the past 20 years. The industry spends more than $100 million a year just to protect its intellectual property, which of course ranges far more widely than patents on living animals.

16 Put the above story into a logical order.

① (a) — (c) — (d) — (b) — (e)
② (d) — (a) — (b) — (c) — (e)
③ (e) — (a) — (c) — (b) — (d)
④ (b) — (a) — (d) — (e) — (c)

I believe it took me a day to copy into my tablet everything printed on that first page of the dictionary, down to the punctuation marks. Then, aloud, I read back, to myself, everything I'd written on the tablet. Over and over, aloud, to myself, I read my own handwriting.

㉮ I suppose it was inevitable that as my word-base broadened, I could for the first time pick up a book and read and now begin to understand what the book was saying. Anyone who has read a great deal can imagine the new world that opened. Let me tell you something: from then until I left that prison, in every free moment I had, if I was not reading in the library, I was reading on my bunk. You couldn't have gotten me out of ㉠ _____ with a wedge. Between my correspondence, my visitors and my reading of books, months passed without my even thinking about being imprisoned. In fact, up to then, I never had been so truly free in my life.

㉯ I woke up the next morning, thinking about those words — immensely proud to realize that not only had I written so much at one time, but I'd written words that I never knew were in the world. Moreover, with a little effort, I also could remember what many of these words meant. I reviewed the words whose meanings I didn't remember. Funny thing, from the dictionary's first page right now, that "aardvark" springs to my mind. The dictionary had a picture of it, a long-tailed, long-eared, burrowing African mammal, which lives off termites caught by sticking out its tongue as an anteater does for ants.

㉰ I was so fascinated that I went on — I copied the dictionary's next page. And the same experience came when I studied that. With every succeeding page, I also learned of people and places and events from history. Actually, the dictionary is like a miniature encyclopedia. Finally the dictionary's A section had filled a whole tablet — and I went on into the B's. That was the very way I started copying what eventually became the entire dictionary. ㉡ It went a lot faster after so much practice helped me to pick up handwriting speed. Between what I wrote in my tablet, and writing letters, during the rest of my time in prison I would guess I wrote a million words.

17 첫 문단 이후에 이어질 글의 순서로 가장 적절한 것은?

① ㉮ – ㉯ – ㉰ 　　　　② ㉯ – ㉰ – ㉮

③ ㉯ – ㉮ – ㉰ 　　　　④ ㉰ – ㉮ – ㉯

18 윗글의 제목으로 가장 적절한 것은?

① Why I Started to Copy the Dictionary
② Aardvark. My One Millionth Word
③ Freedom of Speech in the U.S. Prisons
④ ABC's of Improving One's Handwriting

19 빈칸 ㉠에 가장 적절한 것은?

① jail 　　　　② dictionary

③ ants 　　　　④ books

20 밑줄 친 ㉡이 의미하는 바는?

① having the same experience
② taking a tablet as prescribed
③ copying the dictionary
④ learning about people, places and events

21 Choose the best order from [A] to [C] for a passage starting with the sentence(s) in the box. 인하대 2016

> The mouse was invented by Douglas Engelbart in 1964 and consisted of a wooden shell, circuit board and two metal wheels that came into contact with the surface it was being used on.

[A] This mouse was produced for $17 and sold for $35. Despite this, it wasn't until 10 years later around 1998 that optical mice became a commercially viable alternative to the ball mouse and infiltrated the mass consumer market.

[B] An optical mouse was developed 8 years later in 1980, eliminating the ball which often became dirty from rolling round the desktop, negatively affecting its operation. In another 8 years, US patent no. 4751505 was issued for an optical mouse invented by Lisa M. Williams and Robert S. Cherry.

[C] Bill English developed the design further 8 years later by inventing what is known as the "Ball Mouse." The ball replaced the wheels and was capable of monitoring movement in any direction. It came into contact with two rollers that in turn spun wheels with graduations on them that could be turned into electrical pulses representing direction and speed.

① [A] − [B] − [C]
② [B] − [A] − [C]
③ [C] − [B] − [A]
④ [B] − [C] − [A]
⑤ [C] − [A] − [B]

Since the dawn of Western civilization, music has been a source of profound anxiety because of its ability to inspire subversive thought and action. (A) The ancient Greeks attributed to music the capacity to strengthen or degrade people's character. They went so far as to assign different moral values to each musical scale, so that some tones were believed to cause aggression and violence, while others encouraged noble conduct. Plato posited a correlation between the movements of the soul and the rhythms of music. He maintained that music was not a superficial means of amusement, but rather, a key component in education, the aim of which was to achieve self-mastery over the passions and strengthen moral character. (B) Thus, music was not a private matter, but a public one. The cultivation of "good" music led to a more ordered soul in the listener, and therefore a more ethical and disciplined citizenry, whereas "bad" music dangerously enflamed individual passions, and thus fostered discord in the community. (C) Plato claimed that the introduction of a new kind of music must be shunned as imperiling the whole state; since styles of music are never disturbed without affecting the most important political institutions. (D) We may perceive traces of it in widespread beliefs that hip hop music, rather than outrage over police brutality and systemic racism, compels young men to commit acts of violence against law enforcement officers.

22 아래의 문장이 들어갈 가장 알맞은 곳을 고르시오.

> While Plato wrote this in 360 BC, his basic premise still resonates in the contemporary world.

① (A) ② (B)
③ (C) ④ (D)

The importance of _____ cannot be stressed enough. It can help ward off fatigue, keep hunger at bay, and boost metabolism. Also consider the calorie savings: If you replace every 150-calorie can of soda consumed daily with a glass of water, you save more than 1,000 calories per week, which translates to 15 pounds lost over a year. Drinking a glass of water before a meal can help fill you up and eat fewer food calories. In the same way you plan meals, you can plan your water intake. This is especially important for older individuals, for whom thirst can be a poor indicator of one's fluid needs. Additionally, since thirst can be mistaken for hunger, planning to drink throughout the day can help you avoid unnecessary snacking. Finally, some people simply don't feel like drinking plain water. Ⓐ Altogether, you can select ones that are naturally appealing to you. Ⓑ If plain water is unappealing, try adding fruit or vegetable slices such as oranges, lemons, or cucumbers to boost flavor. Ⓒ And carbonated water seems to be another option. Ⓓ There are countless options of flavored sparkling water on the store shelves these days.

23 What is the best expression for the blank?

① being adequately hydrated
② reducing fat intake
③ planning your meals
④ eating a healthy snack

24 Which of the following is the best order?

① Ⓐ – Ⓑ – Ⓒ – Ⓓ
② Ⓑ – Ⓒ – Ⓓ – Ⓐ
③ Ⓒ – Ⓓ – Ⓐ – Ⓑ
④ Ⓓ – Ⓑ – Ⓐ – Ⓒ

The words "friend" and "friendship" are used to describe a wide range of human relationships. Further complicating matters, friendship is unique in its capacity to arise as a free-standing relationship on its own terms between two persons, or as a sincerely lived dimension of other relationships, such as the friendship developed between siblings, spouses, parents and children, or coworkers. ① <u>In these instances friendship is not a necessary part of the relationship; countless such bonds exist devoid of friendship.</u> ② <u>It is a negotiated attachment between persons that always reflects shared personal dispositions and material sociocultural possibilities.</u> ③ <u>Despite and perhaps because of its pervasive presence in human life, the necessity of "friendship" itself intellectually captivates a number of researchers.</u> ④ <u>You cannot force or require friendship of any genuine emotional validity between people; and friendship may be restricted, prohibited, or even unthinkable in certain circumstances.</u>

25 문맥상 글의 전체 흐름과 <u>관계없는</u> 문장을 고르시오.

    ①   ②   ③   ④

From the brain's complexity, it naturally follows that a genetic marker that predicts behavior will not Ⓐ <u>necessarily</u> be explanatory. In other words, it does not follow that linkage between a DNA marker and a psychiatric disease leads to an understanding of how the genetic variation alters behavior; or if the understanding of the intervening steps is achieved, comprehension may arrive years after the discovery and long after the genetic marker is used as a predictor. We may be able to predict whose brain works Ⓑ <u>differently</u>, but not be able to explain why. It's a little as if a policeman noticed that red cars are faster than blue cars. Perhaps the policeman begins to pay more attention to the red cars but what he hasn't figured out is that, for example, ⓐ _____. Although the brain's complexity is beginning to be unraveled, it is Ⓒ <u>likely</u> that the mechanism of action of a genetic variant predicting brain function will remain Ⓓ <u>mysteriously</u> long after we understand why some cars are faster than others.

26 Which is NOT properly used in the context of the passage?

① Ⓐ   ② Ⓑ   ③ Ⓒ   ④ Ⓓ

27 What is the passage mainly about?

① The complexity of the human DNA
② How to predict human behavior based on genetic variation
③ Difficulty of explaining associations between behavior and genetic markers
④ The possibility of using genetic information to predict violation of traffic rules

28 Which best fits into the blank ⓐ?

① the speeds of the cars are over the limit
② the blue cars are slower than the red cars
③ the cars that look red actually are pinkish yellow
④ the red cars have a better engine than the blue cars

One phase of the business cycle is the expansion phase. This phase is a twofold one, including recovery and prosperity. (A) It is not prosperity itself but expectation of prosperity that triggers the expansion phase. During the recovery period there is ever-growing expansion of existing facilities, and new facilities for production are created. More businesses are created and older ones expanded. Improvements of various kinds are made. There is an ever-increasing optimism about the future of economic growth. Much capital is invested in machinery or heavy industry. More labor is employed. More materials are required. As one part of the economy develops, other parts are affected. (B) For example, a great expansion in automobiles results in an expansion of the steel, glass, and rubber industries. Roads are required; thus the cement and machinery industries are stimulated. (C) Demand for labor and materials results in greater prosperity for workers and suppliers of raw materials, including farmers. This increases purchasing power and the volume of goods bought and sold. Thus, prosperity is diffused among the various segments of the population. (D) This prosperity period may continue to rise and rise without an apparent end. However, a time comes when this phase reaches a peak and stops spiraling upwards. This is the end of the expansion phase.

29 윗글의 흐름상 가장 적합하지 <u>않은</u> 것을 고르시오.

① (A) ② (B)
③ (C) ④ (D)

30 윗글을 통해 추론할 수 있는 것으로 가장 적합한 것을 고르시오.

① When consumers lose their confidence in the market, a recession follows.
② In the expansion phase, many parts of the economy are mutually benefited.
③ Luxury goods such as jewelry are unaffected by industrial expansion.
④ The creation of new products is crucial in the prosperity period.

CHAPTER 02 연결 구조

문장의 결합으로 이루어진 단락의 특성을 이해해야 풀 수 있는 문제 유형이다. 주로 빈칸에 들어갈 적당한 지시어구를 찾는 유형의 문제로, 문장의 연결 고리를 파악하고 있는지를 묻는 문제와, 단락의 구분을 이해하고 있는지를 묻는 단락 구분 문제로 크게 대비할 수 있는데, 단락의 구분에 대한 문제는 주로 성균관대에서 많이 나오는 유형이다.

01 질문 유형

Which of the following best fits into blank ⓐ?
Which one transitional phrase may fit ⓐ best?
Which of the following sequences fits best in blanks ⓐ, ⓑ, and ⓒ?
When the above passage can be divided into three paragraphs, which would be the best boundaries?

02 문제 풀이 전략

❶ **논리적인 흐름에 따라 글을 문장이나 단락 단위로 구별해 본다.**
글을 읽으면서 논리적 흐름에 따라 구분하기 위해서는 연결사나 혹은 전환어구의 파악이 중요한 경우가 많다. 글의 흐름에 따라 글의 방향성이 순접으로 진행되는 경우도 있으며, 방향이 바뀌며 역접으로 진행되는 경우도 있는데, 이를 나타내는 대표적인 것이 연결사이다. 즉 연결사는 글의 흐름을 이어 주거나 전환시키는 장치로서 논리적인 글의 이해에 필수적인 요소이므로 문장이나 단락의 전후 관계를 바탕으로 연결사를 파악한다.

❷ **구조적인 흐름 속에서 핵심을 요약하여 답을 도출해 낸다.**
연결사를 묻는 문제는 글의 구조적인 흐름을 파악하는 연습으로 대비하는 것이 좋다. 즉 다시 말해서 서술 형태가 인과적 진행인지, 추상적인 진술에 뒤이어 오는 구체적인 예증을 나타내는 것인지, 정의를 내리고 이를 부연하여 설명하는 것인지를 살펴보면서 읽는 습관을 들여야 한다. 단락의 구분에 관해서는 한 단락씩 읽고 요약하는 습관을 들이며 연결사의 사용에 유의하면서 읽는 것이 좋은 훈련이 된다.

Should a child who is short but otherwise perfectly healthy be given growth hormones to make him or her taller? That's the question facing thousands of U.S. parents in the wake of the Food and Drug Administration's decision last month to approve the use of human growth hormone for children whose predicted adult height is less than 150 cm for boys and 140 cm for girls. That is a really tough call. It's not easy being short in a world filled with tall people. You get teased. You're picked last in gym class. When you get older, you have trouble making dates and finding mates. _____, parents don't want to send their children the message that they're somehow deficient because they're not NBA material.

부모의 입장에서 아이에게 성장 호르몬을 주입할지를 결정하는 판단을 내리기가 쉽지 않음을 얘기하고 있다.

키가 작은 경우의 여러 가지 문제로 인해 아이가 받을 고통에 대해서 언급하고 있다.

하지만 이러한 결정으로 인해 아이가 받게 될 상처에 대해서 염려하지 않을 수가 없는 부모의 심경이 잘 드러나 있다.

Q. Choose the one that is most appropriate for each blank.

① As a result
② In conclusion
③ In other words
④ On the other hand

결국 빈칸을 중심으로 위의 두 문장은 작은 키로 인해 생기는 문제에 대해 상반되는 입장에서 서술하였으므로 정답은 대조를 드러내는 ④가 타당하다.

정답　④

해석　**빈칸에 들어갈 적절한 것을 고르시오.**

키는 작지만 다른 면에서는 완벽한 아이에게 키를 크게 해 주려고 성장 호르몬을 주입해야만 하는가? 이것이 바로 지난달 식약청의 결정이 있은 직후 수천의 미국인 부모들이 직면한 문제이다. 식약청은 성인이 되었을 때의 신장이 남아는 150cm, 여아는 140cm 미만이라 예상되는 경우에는 성장 호르몬 주입을 허용한다는 결정을 내렸었다. 이 문제에 대하여 는 판단하기가 쉽지 않다. 키 큰 사람들 사이에서 작은 키로 살아간다는 것은 쉬운 일이 아니다. 놀림을 받게 되고, 체육 시간에도 제일 마지막에 호명되며, 심지어 나이가 들어서는 데이트도 쉽지 않고 짝을 구하기도 어렵다. 반면에 부모들은 아이들이 키가 크지 않다고 해서(NBA에 뛸 만큼 키가 크지 않다는 것은 비유적인 표현) 아이들이 무언가 부족하다는 것을 아이들에게 알려 주고 싶지는 않은 게 부모의 마음이다.

① 결과적으로　　② 결론적으로　　③ 다시 말하자면　　④ 반면에

해설　성장 호르몬을 사용해야 할 근거를 대고 아이들이 받게 될 심리적인 상처를 고려하면 마땅히 주입하는 게 옳겠지만, 이로 인해 아이들이 받게 될 상처를 생각해서 성장 호르몬 주입에 대해 쉽게 결정을 내리지 못하는 부모들의 심적인 고통을 말하고 있다. 그러므로 이를 이어 주는 데는 앞뒤가 상반되는 표현이 들어가야 한다.

어휘　**in the wake of** ～에 뒤이어, ～를 본떠서, ～의 결과로서
　　　tough call 어려운 결정　　　　　　　**deficient** ⓐ 불충분한, 부족한

01 밑줄 친 ㉮와 ㉯에 들어가기에 가장 적합한 것을 고르시오.

> While empiricism, or "positivism" as it was also called, was somewhat in retreat throughout the nineteenth century, it enjoyed a rebirth in the early twentieth as a result of work on the foundations of logic. Many philosophers believed that mathematical logic would give them the apparatus they lacked to formalize the distinction between mathematical truth, synthetic statements, and metaphysical nonsense. ㉮ _____, logic promised to provide a formalism to make explicit the relation between a statement and the observations and procedures which could lead to its verification. ㉯ _____, twentieth- century empiricism is often called "logical empiricism" or "logical positivism." The wide appeal empiricist philosophy enjoyed in the intellectual community at this time is undoubtedly related to the fact that there was no period in American history in which there was greater respect for the methods and results of science.

① However – Accordingly   ② Therefore – Nonetheless

③ Furthermore – Hence   ④ Moreover – On the contrary

02 다음 글을 두 단락으로 나누고자 할 때 가장 적절한 곳은?

In the UK there is a National Health Service, the NHS, which is paid for by taxes and National Insurance, and in general people do not have to pay for medical treatment. Every person has a General Practitioner(GP), a doctor who is trained in general medicine and who treats people in their local area. If they are ill they can make an appointment to see their GP, or they can call their GP to visit them at home. ㉮ People have to pay part of the cost of the medicines that the doctor prescribes, unless they are children, unemployed, or over 60 years old. ㉯ If a GP decides that it is necessary, he or she will make an appointment for the patient to see a specialist doctor at a hospital. Anyone who is very ill can call an ambulance and get taken to hospital for free urgent medical treatment. ㉰ Although medical treatment is free in the NHS, people often have to wait for a long time before they are treated. The problem of NHS waiting lists is discussed by a lot of politicians and ordinary people. ㉱ A small number of people choose to 'go private,' which means paying to have treatment done privately, and they get treated more quickly. People who do this usually have private health insurance. As the average age of the population gets older and older, the NHS is becoming more and more expensive to run, and people are worried that medical care will not be free in the future.

① ㉮　　　　　　　　　　　② ㉯

③ ㉰　　　　　　　　　　　④ ㉱

[01~02] 이화여대 2016

One theory that integrates diverse findings on hunger, eating, and weight argues that body weight is governed by a set-point, a homeostatic mechanism that keeps people at roughly the weight they are genetically designed to be. Set-point theorists claim that everyone has a genetically programmed basal metabolism rate, the rate at which the body burns calories for energy, and a fixed number of fat cells, which are cells that store fat for energy. These cells may change in size (the amount of fat they contain), but never in number. After weight loss, they just lurk around the body, waiting for the chance to puff up again. According to set-point theory, there is no single area in the brain that keeps track of weight. [A] _____, an interaction of metabolism, fat cells, and hormones keeps people at the weight their bodies are designed to be. When a heavy person diets, the body slows down to conserve energy (and its fat reserves). When a thin person overeats, the body speeds up to burn energy.

01 Which expression best fits [A]?

① In addition
② Likewise
③ Rather
④ Therefore
⑤ Specifically

02 Which statement can be best inferred from the passage above?

① A genetically thin person can easily gain weight.
② How to keep fat cells from enlarging remains a mystery.
③ Humans are genetically designed to be obese.
④ People don't have as much control over their body weight as they might think.
⑤ It is impossible for genetically predisposed overweight people to lose weight.

Language frequently serves as an ethnic boundary marker. The native language of an individual is the primary indicator of ethnic group identity in many areas of the world. In the south-western United States, Hopi and Navajo members are readily distinguished by their language alone. However, just because two populations share a common language, it does not mean they share a common identity, any more than the fact that two populations speak different languages means that they have two distinct identities. For example, the Serbs and Croats of what was Yugoslavia speak Serbo-Croatian. They are, however, distinct and historically antagonistic ethnic groups. Ⓐ _____, a person may be Irish and speak either Gaelic or English as his or her native language. The German government grants automatic citizenship to all ethnic German refugees from Eastern Europe. A difficulty in Ⓑ _____ these refugees is that many speak only Polish or Russian. Thus, one does not have to speak German to be an ethnic German.

03 According to the passage, which is true?

① Hopi and Navajo members do not share a common language.
② German Citizenship is automatically granted to a person who can speak German.
③ The Serbs and Croats share a common identity because they speak the same language.
④ The native language is the most essential single indicator of ethnic group identity in every country.

04 Which is the most appropriate for the blank Ⓐ?

① Therefore   ② Conversely
③ As a result   ④ To begin with

05 Which is the most appropriate for the blank Ⓑ?

① lauding   ② secluding
③ assimilating   ④ calumniating

ⓐ _____ the smoke from a cigar or pipe contains higher concentration of both tar and nicotine than does cigarette smoke, even a few cigarettes a day poses a greater risk to health than a number of cigars or pipes of tobacco would. This may be because, while it is extremely difficult to smoke cigarettes without inhaling, it is more difficult to inhale cigar or pipe smoke voluntarily. Cigarette smokers tend to inhale actively, deeply and constantly. ⓑ _____ because the smoke from burning cigar or pipe tobacco is very harsh, it is more difficult to breathe it directly into healthy lungs. ⓒ _____, simply switching to a pipe or cigars from cigarettes is likely to increase your risk instead of lessening it. This is because you have probably become accustomed to inhaling. You may find yourself retaining <u>the habit</u>, and you will then be inhaling even more harmful smoke than before.

06 **Which of the following sequences fits best in blanks ⓐ, ⓑ, and ⓒ?**

	ⓐ	ⓑ	ⓒ
①	But	— Although	— However
②	But	— However	— Although
③	Although	— However	— But
④	Although	— But	— However

07 **What is the meaning of <u>the habit</u>?**

① smoking cigars 　　　　　② smoking cigarettes
③ actively inhaling when smoking 　　　　　④ smoking both cigars and cigarettes

08 **According to the passage, which of the following is the most harmful?**

① smoking cigars 　　　　　② smoking cigarettes
③ exhaling cigar smoke voluntarily 　　　　　④ switching from cigarettes to cigars

Freud became interested in how people think and dream while he was studying to be a doctor. He tried to help by letting them talk about their past. Through his work, Freud realized that unconscious thoughts from a person's past could affect the person's actions. These unconscious thoughts could also show up in a person's dreams. The images in a person's dream might be real images from the person's past. Or the image might be a symbol of a person or thing from the person's life.

_____, the findings of modern analysis of dreams in a study of dreams done by researchers in California in 1996, might seem to point to the fact that dreams have no function in the brain. The researchers had people record the dreams that they remembered each night in journals along with their normal daily activities. Through the journals, the researchers reported that dreams usually had stories related to them, and these stories included important parts of the person's day or life. Over time, these dreams could show a lot about a person's personality or the concerns in a person's life, but no real psychological function had been found for dreams yet for sure.

09 Which of the following is most appropriate for the blank?

① However
② For example
③ As a result
④ Furthermore

10 Which of the following is the most appropriate title for the passage?

① Talking Cure
② Freud's Blunders
③ Meaning of Dreams
④ Unconsciousness in Sleeping

There was a time when Bernie, 19, doubted that she could even finish high school, _____ go to college. As a sophomore, she became pregnant and briefly thought about dropping out. (A) But since transferring to the Academy of Urban Planning, she has passed all five of the required state exams for graduation. (B) She is retaking one exam in the hopes of getting a diploma with the state's highest distinction. (C) Her personal turnaround mirrors that of the school she now attends. (D) The academy is housed in the same building that five years ago was known as Bushwick High School. Bushwick had one of the lowest four-year graduation rates of any school in New York — a dismal 23 percent. And violence plagued the school's hallways. (E) Then five years ago, New York Mayor Michael Bloomberg took control of the city's school districts, launching a flurry of reforms that led to Buchwick's division into four smaller schools.

11 **Which is most appropriate for the blank?**

① much less   ② much more

③ far more   ④ more or less

⑤ even less

12 **When the above passage can be divided into two which of the following would be the best boundary between them?**

① (A)   ② (B)   ③ (C)   ④ (D)   ⑤ (E)

13 **According to the passage, Bernie _____.**

① passed the college entrance examination

② gave up the high school diploma

③ is thinking of transferring to another school

④ is retaking one exam to get a better score

⑤ learned a lot from Bushwick High School

The nation has lived with TV for more than 50 years now. We are not, as it was once predicted we would be, fantastically well-informed about other cultures or about the origins of life on earths. (A) People do not remember much from television documentary beyond how good it was. Only those who knew something about the subject in the first place retain the information. (B) Documentaries are not what most people want to watch anyway. Television is at its most popular when it celebrates its own present. Its ideal subjects are those that need not be remembered and can be instantly replaced, where what matters most is what is happening now and what is going to happen next. (C) Sports, news, panel games, cop show, long-running soap operas, situation comedies — these occupy us only for as long as they are on. (D) However good or bad it is, a night's viewing is wonderfully forgettable. It's a little sleep, it's Entertainment; our morals remain intact. (E) The box is further neutralized by the sheer quantity people watch. Of course, some programs are infinitely better than others. (F) There are gifted people working in television. But seen from a remoter perspective — say, four hours a night viewing for three months — the quality of individual programs means as much as the quality of each car in the rush-hour traffic.

14 When the above passage can be divided into three paragraphs, which would be the best boundaries?

① (A) and (C)
② (B) and (C)
③ (B) and (E)
④ (C) and (E)
⑤ (D) and (F)

15 The underlined expression implies that the longer you watch TV, _____.

① the more informed you become
② the less moral you become
③ the more excited you become
④ the more of its content matters
⑤ the less of its content matters

16 According to the passage, the author argues that _____.

① TV industry needs more intelligent program makers

② many people avoid TV documentaries because they do not contain any moral messages

③ TV turns out to be no transformer of our minds and societies

④ TV will have greater impact on human civilization in the future

⑤ TV is getting more and more successful as a moral educator

03

Gettysburg is considered by most historians to be the turning point of the American Civil War. Before Gettysburg, Confederate forces under General Robert E. Lee had defeated their Union counterparts — sometimes by considerable margins — in a string of major battles. In this engagement, (A) _____, the Confederate army was defeated and driven back. Even more important than their material losses, though, was the Confederacy's loss of momentum. Union forces took the initiative, finally defeating the Confederacy less than two years later. By invading Union territory, the Confederate leadership had sought to shatter the Union's will to continue the war and to convince European nations to recognize the Confederacy as an independent nation. (B) _____, the Union's willingness to fight was strengthened and the Confederacy squandered its last chance for foreign support.

17 빈칸에 들어갈 가장 알맞은 것을 고르시오.

	(A)		(B)
①	however	—	Instead
②	however	—	In addition
③	moreover	—	Instead
④	moreover	—	In addition

18 윗글의 내용과 맞는 것을 고르시오.

① The Confederate forces had completely defeated the Union counterparts before the Gettysburg engagement.

② European nations were finally convinced to recognize the Confederate as an independent nation.

③ Due to the victory in the Gettysburg engagement, Union forces took the lead.

④ The Confederate forces' invasion into Union territory shattered the Union's will to continue to fight.

Every year about 120,000 organs, mostly kidneys, are transplanted from one human being to another. Sometimes the donor is a living volunteer. Usually, though, he or she is the victim of an accident, stroke, heart attack, or similar sudden event that has terminated the life of an otherwise healthy individual. But a lack of suitable donors, particularly as cars get safer and first aid becomes more effective, means the supply of such organs is limited. Many people therefore die waiting for a transplant. That has led researchers to study the question of how to build organs from scratch. One promising approach is to print them. Lots of things are made these days by three-dimensional printing, and there seems no reason why body parts should not be among them. _____, such "bioprinting" remains largely experimental. But bioprinted tissue is already being sold for drug testing, and the first transplantable tissues are expected to be ready for use in a few years' time.

19 빈칸에 들어갈 가장 알맞은 것을 고르시오.

① As yet
② Instead
③ Nevertheless
④ As a result

20 윗글의 내용과 맞는 것을 고르시오.

① Only organs from living volunteers can be transplanted.
② Bioprinted organs are being transplanted to human beings these days.
③ Improvements in technology regarding safety have decreased the supply of organs for transplant.
④ 3D printing technology is the main factor leading researchers to explore the possibility of bioprinting transplantable tissues.

글을 읽고, 그 흐름 속에서 올바른 단어를 선택하는 유형이다. 주어진 두 개의 단어 가운데 문맥에 맞게 올바른 단어를 선택하는 문제와, 어휘의 적절성을 판단하는 문제로 구성된다. 후자는 지문 가운데 어휘를 흐름과 전혀 다른 것으로 바꿔 놓은 후 문장이나 문맥상 근거를 파악하여 밑줄 친 단어의 적정성을 판단하는 문제를 뜻한다.

01 질문 유형

(A), (B), (C)에 들어갈 말로 바르게 짝지어진 것은?

(A), (B), (C)의 각 네모 안에서 문맥에 맞는 낱말로 가장 적절한 것은?

Which is LEAST consistent with the context?

Which of the following underlined (A), (B), (C), and (D) is NOT appropriately used?

02 문제 풀이 전략

❶ **글을 구성하는 중심 개념을 파악한다.**

글 속에서 흐름상 어색한 어휘를 고르는 문제는 맥락과 관련하여 판단할 수 있다. 결국 글의 흐름을 제대로 파악하고 있는지를 보는 것이다. 그러므로 무엇에 대한 글인지를 판단하고, 그 흐름에 맞춰서 논지의 흐름이 모순이 없는가를 판단해야 한다.

❷ **근거를 파악하여 문맥의 흐름상 어색한 부분을 찾는다.**

어휘가 맥락에 어긋나는 경우는 글의 흐름상 앞뒤 관계가 전혀 다르거나 모순적인 상황이 된다. 이를 파악하는 것이 필요하다. 상황에 따라서는 글의 순서를 연결시키는 방식을 덧붙여서 풀어나가야 한다. 그러면서 순서상 너무 동떨어진 것을 고르는 방식으로 해결해 간다.

It is clear from a world-wide opinion survey that young people today are very much concerned about their (A) physical / psychological appearance. This issue appears to be even more important to them than health. Results show that the perception of health has gradually moved away from the traditional concept of (B) absence / presence of major illnesses. Now health is perceived in terms of fitness or slimness. According to the opinions of the respondents in the survey, a new definition of health should include physical appearance, a positive state of wellbeing (feeling well and healthy) and improved endurance and energy. However, the findings of the survey and the concern for physical appearance and skin care over exercise and eating habits among young people have many (C) amplifications / implications for health-care education

젊은이들이 신경 쓰는 외모는 밖으로 드러나는 모습이므로, 심리적 외형이 아닌 신체적 외형. 즉 외모라는 뜻에서 physical이 되어야 한다.

건강에 대한 전통적인 인식을 나타내며, 질병이 없는 상태여야 건강한 것이므로 absence가 되어야 한다.

조사의 결과가 건강관리 교육이 함축하는 바를 나타낼지 아니면 그 영향의 확대를 나타낼지 고려해 보면, 조사의 결과에 대한 판단이므로 그 교육이 드러내는 현상에 주목해야 한다. 그러므로 implications가 정답이다.

Q. (A), (B), (C)의 각 네모 안에서 문맥에 맞는 낱말로 가장 적절한 것은?

	(A)	(B)	(C)
①	physical	··· absence	··· amplifications
②	physical	··· presence	··· amplifications
③	physical	··· absence	··· implications
④	psychological	··· absence	··· amplifications
⑤	psychological	··· presence	··· implications

정답 ③

해석 **(A), (B), (C)의 각 네모 안에서 문맥에 맞는 낱말로 가장 적절한 것은?**

요즘 젊은이들은 자신의 신체적 외모에 무척 신경을 많이 쓴다는 것이 전 세계 여론조사에서 뚜렷하게 나타난다. 젊은이들에게 이 문제는 건강보다 더 중요한 것처럼 보인다. 조사 결과들에서는 건강에 대한 인식이 심각한 질병이 없는 상태라는 전통적 인식에서 점차 멀어지고 있음을 보여준다. 이제 건강은 몸매 가꾸기 혹은 날씬함이라는 관점에서 인식되고 있다. 조사에 참여한 응답자들의 견해에 따르면, 건강에 대한 새로운 정의에는 신체적 외모, 긍정적 웰빙 상태(행복하고 건강하다는 느낌), 그리고 지구력과 기운의 증가 등이 내포되어야 한다고 말한다. 하지만 조사의 결과 및 운동과 식습관보다는 신체적 외모와 피부 관리에 더 신경 쓰는 젊은이들의 관심은 건강관리 교육에 많은 영향을 미치고 있다.

해설　기존에는 건강하다는 것이 특정 질병이 없다는 것이었지만 이제는 건강하다는 것에 신체적 외모, 웰빙 등이 포함된 것으로 인식된다는 내용이다. 따라서 첫 번째 빈칸에는 심리적 외형이 아닌 신체적 외형, 즉 외모라는 뜻에서 physical이 되어야 하며, 두 번째 빈칸에는 주요한 질병의 부재를 의미하는 absence가 와야 한다. 그리고 이런 모든 현상들이 건강 관련 교육에 많은 영향이나 파장을 미치고 있다는 내용이므로, implications가 와야 한다.

어휘　**opinion survey** 여론조사

be concerned about ～을 걱정하다; ～에 관심을 가지다

physical ⓐ 신체의, 물리적인   **psychological** ⓐ 심리학적인

perception ⓝ 인지, 인식; 지각, 이해   **gradually** ⓓ 서서히, 점차

absence ⓝ 부재, 결석, 결여   **presence** ⓝ 존재, 참석

fitness ⓝ 신체 단련, (신체적인) 건강   **definition** ⓝ 정의

endurance ⓝ 인내, 지구력   **amplification** ⓝ 확대, 확장

implication ⓝ 영향[결과]; 함축, 암시

01 밑줄 친 (A)~(E) 가운데, 문맥상 적절하지 <u>않은</u> 것은? 건국대 2018

For government policy to assume that young women can (A) <u>rely on</u> others for financial support is dangerous. Firstly, some young women do not receive support from their families, either because they are not in contact with them or because their families cannot, or do not want to, (B) <u>support</u> them financially. Secondly, living in the same house as a partner or family member does not mean that a young woman is receiving her fair share of the household's resources. Women's (C) <u>lower</u> contribution to the household's income can mean that they receive less money for themselves and consume fewer household resources, which can lead to poverty. Thirdly, financial dependence means a young woman is always at risk of experiencing (D) <u>wealth</u> if support is withdrawn or a relationship ends. Young women need an adequate (E) <u>income</u> of their own from work or the social security system. Many of the most vulnerable young women are not in work or able to access work easily.

① (A)　　　　② (B)　　　　③ (C)　　　　④ (D)　　　　⑤ (E)

02 (A), (B), (C)의 각 네모 안에서 문맥에 맞는 낱말로 가장 적절한 것은?

"Symptoms and signs" in Oriental Medicine have a rather different meaning than in Western Medicine. They are different from the relatively (A) wide / narrow area explored by Western Medicine despite its battery of clinical tests. Instead, the doctor of Oriental Medicine widens his or her view to assess changes in a broad range of common (B) emotional / bodily functions such as urination, sweating, thirst and so on. Furthermore, the doctor of Oriental Medicine takes into account many clinical manifestations ranging from certain facial and bodily signs to psychological and emotional traits which are not really "symptoms" or "signs" as such, but rather expressions of a certain (C) harmony / disharmony .

	(A)		(B)		(C)
①	wide	–	bodily	–	harmony
②	wide	–	emotional	–	disharmony
③	narrow	–	emotional	–	disharmony
④	narrow	–	bodily	–	harmony
⑤	narrow	–	bodily	–	disharmony

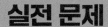

[01] 가천대 2020

Nowadays seeing a person walking down the street talking on a cell phone has become such a (A) <u>ubiquitous</u> sight that a picture of modern man with one hand next to his ear should be painted next to the ape-like Cro-Magnon to (B) <u>distort</u> the evolution of humans. According to recent press reports, American doctors are now warning of so-called "cell phone elbow" syndrome. It seems (C) <u>farcical</u> that medical professionals are making such a fuss about this. Just like people who suffer daily from the constant pain of tennis elbow after playing tennis, cell phone gabbers (D) <u>grumble</u> about pain or numbness in the hand — especially the pinky and ring fingers.

01 **Which of the following underlined (A), (B), (C), and (D) is NOT appropriately used?**

① (A) ② (B) ③ (C) ④ (D)

Philip Guston's artistic language and poetic motives seek to better understand and apprehend the illogical and paradoxical realities of human existence. The task of the painter is not "how to represent" but "how to know." Guston, having abandoned (A) abstraction / concretion , returned to figurative painting, to a simple and direct figuration. What appears at first glance to be a difficult iconography often refers back to the pictures of his youth — light bulbs, shoe soles, and trash can lids — as if they were elements taken from the frescos of Piero della Francesca. Guston's iconography is not a simple representation that can be interpreted through a (B) descriptive / prescriptive logic. It relates back to a more profound knowledge, to the *anima* of Carl Jung. Guston's illogical iconography does not speak of a descriptive figuration, but of an underlying figuration in the mythical subconscious, an epiphany or something that manifests itself as something (C) logically / illogically received — a divination.

02 윗글의 주제로 가장 적절한 것은?

① Philip Guston 시(詩)의 언어적 특징
② Philip Guston의 그림에 나타난 논리성
③ 추상예술과 구상예술의 철학적 배경
④ Carl Jung이 현대 예술에 미친 영향
⑤ Philip Guston 회화의 양식적 특징

03 (A), (B), (C)에 들어갈 말로 바르게 짝지어진 것은?

	(A)	(B)	(C)
①	abstraction	— descriptive	— logically
②	abstraction	— descriptive	— illogically
③	abstraction	— prescriptive	— logically
④	concretion	— prescriptive	— illogically
⑤	concretion	— descriptive	— logically

The current academic system has fudged the distinctions between training and education. Administrations of most colleges and universities have responded to the economic and cultural uncertainties provoked by budget constraints and Ⓐ a volatile job market by constructing their institutions on the model of the modern corporation. Consequently, many have thrust training to the fore and called it education. Lacking a unified national culture into which to socialize students and in any case lacking Ⓑ an educational philosophy capable of steering an independent course, the academic system as a whole is caught in Ⓒ a market logic that demands students be job-ready upon graduation. Under these imperatives colleges and universities are unable to implement an educational program that prepares students for Ⓓ the competitive job market. ⓐ _____, academic leaders chant the mantra of "excellence," which means that all of the parts of the university "perform" and are judged according to how well they deliver knowledge and qualified labor to the corporate economy and how well the administration fulfills the recruitment and funding goals needed to maintain the institution.

04 **Which is LEAST consistent with the context?**

① Ⓐ   ② Ⓑ

③ Ⓒ   ④ Ⓓ

05 **Which best fits in the blank ⓐ?**

① Instead   ② Proactively

③ Fortunately   ④ Nevertheless

It is a common saying that thought is free. A man can never be hindered from thinking whatever he chooses so long as he conceals what he thinks. The working of his mind is limited only by the bounds of his experience and the power of his imagination. But this natural liberty of private thinking is ⓐ of great value. It is unsatisfactory, to the thinker himself if he is not permitted to communicate his thoughts to others, and it is obviously of no value to this neighbours. Moreover, it is extremely ⓑ difficult to hide thoughts that have any power over the mind. If a man's thinking leads him to call in question ideas and customs which regulate the behaviour of those about him, to reject beliefs which they hold, to see better ways of life than those they follow, it is almost ⓒ impossible for him, if he is convinced of the truth of his own reasoning, not to betray by silence, chance words or general attitude that he is different from them and does not ⓓ share their opinions. Some have preferred, like Socrates, some would prefer to-day, to face death rather than ⓔ conceal their thoughts. Thus freedom of thought, in any valuable sense, includes freedom of _____.

06 Which is NOT appropriate in the context?

① ⓐ   ② ⓑ
③ ⓒ   ④ ⓓ
⑤ ⓔ

07 Which best fits in the blank?

① assembly   ② religion
③ speech   ④ criticism
⑤ movement

Artificial intelligence technology restores the voices of deceased musicians to sing contemporary songs. A game company airs a song competition show for the soundtrack of its title game. The local music scene Ⓐ underline{continues to evolve}, with the convergence of media, technology and industries.

South Korean game company Nexon adopted a TV competition show format to best fit Dungeon and Fighter, an arcade-style action game. The five-episode series, available on YouTube channel Dingo Music, has garnered more than 2 million views as of Thursday, the company said. It is not the first time that Nexon has sought Ⓑ a conventional collaboration with the music industry. The company has previously collaborated with a wide range of musicians, from the Czech National Symphony Orchestra to popular singer-songwriter Yozoh. The company has also been arranging concerts featuring both classical and popular music.

The increased use of artificial intelligence is Ⓒ invigorating the local popular music scene. Music channel Mnet recently presented AI music project "Once More Time," featuring deceased artists through holograms and AI voice covers. South Korean broadcaster SBS also aired a competition between AI and human experts in which they sought to re-create legendary singer Kim Kwang-suk, who died in 1996 at the age of 31. "If the previous music competition programs focused on the contest, recent music programs are taking more diverse approaches Ⓓ by applying new technologies and Ⓔ introducing different types of music, like game soundtracks. Such novel attempts are expected to continue making an impact," said a local music critic.

08 What is NOT appropriate for the whole context?

① Ⓐ   ② Ⓑ   ③ Ⓒ   ④ Ⓓ   ⑤ Ⓔ

09 **What is the author's view on artificial intelligence technology?**

① ambiguous ② suspicious ③ hostile
④ uncertain ⑤ promising

10 **What is the main idea of the passage?**

① Collaboration of AI and music industry
② Revival of the voices of deceased musicians
③ Combination of classical and popular music
④ Recreation of old popular songs
⑤ Competition between AI and human experts

CHAPTER 04

전후 관계

전후 내용 추론이란 글의 앞과 뒤에 나올 내용을 본문에 나와 있는 단서를 이용하여 찾아내는 문제 유형을 말한다. 넓게 보면 본문에 나오지 않은 부분을 찾아내는 것이므로 추론의 영역이고, 글의 흐름으로 보면 파악되는 측면이므로 글의 전체적 흐름과도 무관하지 않은 부분이다.

01 질문 유형

Which of the following would be most likely to precede the passage?

The paragraph immediately preceding this passage is most likely to be concerned with _____.

Which of the following is most likely to follow the above passage?

Which of the following is NOT likely to be discussed right after the passage?

02 문제 풀이 전략

❶ 전후 관계를 판단하는 문제는 첫 문장과 마지막 문장에 유의한다.

글의 앞부분에 나올 내용을 고르는 문제를 풀 때에는 첫 문장에서 제시하는 내용을 유심히 보고 단서를 찾아야 한다. 뒷부분에 나올 내용과는 다르게 앞부분의 얘기는 대부분 단서가 처음에 명확히 제시되어 있다. 반면에 뒷부분에 나오는 내용을 고르는 문제는 글 중간에 단서가 있기도 하고 마지막에 연결될 수도 있다. 그러므로 글의 흐름에 따라 찾아가는 것이 올바른 방법이다.

❷ 뒤에 이어지는 내용을 고를 때 본문에서 이어지는지를 판단한다.

뒤에 나올 내용을 고르라는 문제에서는 본문에 제시한 내용 중에 미처 소개하지 못한 내용이 이어지는지 혹은 마지막 문장에서 계속해서 연결되는 내용인지를 판단하여야 한다. 즉 본문에서 핵심적인 정보의 나열 중에 글이 끊긴 것인지, 마지막 문장의 부연 설명으로 이어지면 되는지를 글의 흐름으로 판단하여야 한다.

It's a parent's worst nightmare. You're sitting down to dinner when, all of a sudden, your 9-month-old starts having difficulty breathing and begins swelling up around the mouth. Your child just consumed soy and is experiencing anaphylactic shock, an allergic reaction. What most people can eat freely might be fatal to someone with an allergy to that food. An allergic reaction occurs when the immune system mistakes a perfectly harmless substance for a dangerous one. In response, the system launches a full-scale attack, all the while wreaking havoc on your body. If you're raising a child or even just like giving dinner parties, you should be familiar with some of the most prominent allergenic foods. Catering to someone's special dietary needs could save his or her life.

> 당위를 나타내는 should라는 조동사를 이용하여 부모에게 알레르기를 유발하는 음식에 대한 주의를 환기시키고 있다.

> 제대로 된 음식의 선택이 건강에 영향을 끼칠 뿐만 아니라 생명에도 영향을 준다고 적고 있다.

Q. Which of the following is most likely to follow the above passage?

① a list of food to cause food allergy
② how to treat an allergic reaction
③ causes of soy allergy
④ how to strengthen your immune system

> 그렇다면 이렇게 중요한 알레르기를 유발하는 음식에 대하여 부모 등 아이를 돌보는 사람들이 알아야 할 음식의 목록이 나올 수 있을 것이다.

정답   ①

해석   **윗글에 이어질 내용으로 가장 적절한 것은?**

이것은 부모에게는 최악의 악몽과도 같다. 식사를 하려고 앉았을 때 갑자기 9개월 된 아기가 숨을 잘 못 쉬며 입 주위가 부어오른다. 아이가 콩을 먹은 후 과민성 알레르기 쇼크를 겪고 있는 것이다. 대부분의 사람들은 아무렇지 않게 먹을 수 있는 것이 그 음식에 알레르기가 있는 사람에게는 치명적일 수 있다. 알레르기 반응은 면역 체계가 아무런 문제가 없는 물질을 위험한 것으로 오인할 때 발생하는 것이다. 이에 대한 반응으로, 면역 체계는 전면적인 공격을 감행하고 그러는 한편 신체에 큰 피해를 가한다. 만약 당신이 아이를 키우거나 디너파티를 준비 중이라면 이러한 알레르기를 유발하는 음식 중 몇몇 음식에 대해서는 잘 알고 있어야 한다. 누군가의 특별한 음식 요구에 맞추는 것이 그 사람의 목숨도 구할 수 있기 때문이다.

① 음식물 알레르기를 일으킬 수 있는 음식 목록　　　② 어떻게 알레르기 반응을 치료할 것인가
③ 콩 알레르기의 원인　　　④ 어떻게 면역 체계를 강화시킬 것인가

해설   본문의 마지막 줄에 보면 "알레르기를 일으키는 몇몇 음식에 대해서는 잘 알고 있어야 한다.(you should be familiar with some of the most prominent allergenic foods.)"고 말하면서, 각 개인에 맞는 음식을 주는

것이 목숨을 좌지우지 할 정도로 중요하다는 말을 후반부에 하고 있으므로 다음 이어질 내용은 ①이 적당하다.

어휘   **swell up** 부어오르다

be fatal to ~에 치명적인

mistake A for B A를 B로 오인하다

all the while 그동안 내내

havoc ⓝ 파괴, 황폐

prominent ⓐ 현저한, 두드러진

cater to ~의 요구를 만족시키다, ~의 취향을 만족시키다

dietary ⓐ 음식물의

anaphylactic ⓐ 과민증의

immune system 면역 체계

launch ⓥ 시작하다, 일으키다

wreak ⓥ 가하다

wreak havoc on 피해를 주다

01 Which of the following is most likely to be discussed right before the passage?

The other memorable double dip was in the early 1980s. After the election of Ronald Reagan in 1980, the economy recovered from a recession but was still hobbled by double-digit interest rates and inflation. Then Federal Reserve Chairman Paul Volcker waged a relentless assault against inflation by keeping rates sky-high, which dampened consumer spending and curtailed investment. As a result, inflation ebbed, but the economy was plunged into recession once again before rebounding after 1982.

① Definition of double dip
② Causes of double dip
③ One example of double dip
④ Problems of double dip

02 다음 글에 이어질 문장으로 가장 알맞은 것은? 국민대 2011

The "Spanish Prisoner," a scam dating back to 1588, is alive and well on the Internet. In its original form, the con artist tells the victim that he is in touch with an aristocrat who has been imprisoned in Spain under a false identity. The alleged prisoner cannot reveal his identity without serious repercussions, and is relying on the con artist to raise the money needed to secure his release. The con artist offers to let the victim supply some of the money, with a promise that he will be rewarded generously when the prisoner is freed. However, once the victim has turned over his money, he is informed by the con man that further difficulties have arisen, and that more money is required. This will continue until he is cleaned out.

① The promised fortune will be a means of stoking his greed.
② The Internet is indeed a hotbed of freeloaders.
③ He will pocket the promised fortune, to boot.
④ Similar frauds are played out throughout the Internet.

03 Which of the following is most likely to be mentioned right after the passage?

Each year around 50,000 people die in this city, and each year the mortality rate seems to graze a new low, with people living healthier and longer. A great majority of the deceased have relatives and friends who soon learn of their passing and tearfully assemble at their funeral. A reverent death notice appears. Sympathy cards accumulate. When the celebrated die or there is some heart-rending killing of the innocent, the entire city might weep. Yet a much tinier number die alone in unwatched struggles. Death even in such forlorn form can cause a surprising amount of activity. Sometimes, along the way, a life's secrets are revealed. Here's a story.

① Life secrets of celebrities
② Detailed procedures of a funeral
③ A story of a person who died alone
④ Causes of the decreasing death rate
⑤ Sorrows from losing friends or relatives

[01~02] 항공대 2017

The pervasiveness of the belief in a just world, called in social psychology the just-world hypothesis, was first described by Melvin Lerner decades ago. Lerner argued that people wanted to think that the world was predictable and comprehensible and, therefore, potentially controllable. Or, as another psychologist described it, from early childhood "we learn to be 'good and in control' people." How else could we navigate a world that is random and can't be controlled without feeling thwarted and frustrated much of the time? The desire for control and predictability results in a tendency to see the world as a just place because a just world is one that is also understandable and predictable. Behave by the rules and you will be all right; fail to follow the rules and bad things will happen. The just-world hypothesis holds that most people believe that people get what they deserve; that is, that the good people are likely to be rewarded and the bad to be punished. Most important, the phenomenon works in reverse: if someone is seen to prosper, there is a social psychological tendency for observers to decide that the lucky person must have done something to deserve his good fortune.

01 What would be the best title of the passage above?

① psychological mechanism of just-world hypothesis
② insignificance of predictability and comprehensiveness
③ redundancy of a predictable behaviour
④ irreversible desire for reward

02 Which of the following statements is likely to follow the final sentence?

① Moreover, victims of random bad luck must have done something worthwhile to deserve their big success.
② Believing that world is fair, people note the various possibilities in the environment.
③ Success will promote efforts to find the many negative attributes in those who are successful.
④ He or she becomes a better person simply by virtue of the observed rewards.

Bradley Wilson believes that studying small movements in all kinds of animals could give scientists new insights into their emotional states. To show how this might work, Wilson and his colleagues put pocket-sized accelerometers on two very different animals: elephants and humans. It's popular for scientists to track animals' large-scale movements — GPS and motion detectors have followed the migrations of birds and giant crabs, for example. But Wilson wasn't interested in where animals were going. Instead, he wanted to know how their small-scale movements revealed their emotions or other internal states.

First, the researchers looked at elephants, using accelerometers on neck collars to measure the movements of the animals. As the elephants walked around, an observer noted whether they were moving for a "positive" or "negative" reason. Positive movement meant walking toward something desirable — maybe some food or a nice pile of mud to wallow in. Being chased away by a dominant herd member, on the other hand, was negative movement. When the researchers combined this information with the 3D accelerometer data, they found a significant difference in how elephants moved their bodies during positive and negative states.

03 **Which of the following is most likely to be the purpose of Wilson's experiments?**

① To observe animals' movements to learn how they feel
② To test new devices developed for spying on animals' movements
③ To distinguish positive and negative movements of large animals
④ To compare different animals in their ways of using intellect

04 **Which of the following is the author most likely to write about immediately after this passage?**

① How far elephants can move a day
② How the researchers tracked the elephants
③ Results of Wilson's experiment with humans
④ Usefulness of accelerometers in the experiments

There are a number of common misconceptions about digital and analog signals. One is that analog means continuous, whereas digital means discrete. Although this is often the case, it is not the basis for the distinction. Think of analog as meaning analogous: analogous to the real world. If the real world event is discrete, so too will be the analog one. If the physical process is continuous, then so too will be the analog one. Digital, however, is always discrete: one of a limited number of values, usually one of two, but occasionally one of three, four, or ten. A widespread misconception is that digital is somehow good, analog bad. This just isn't so. Yes, digital is good for our contemporary machine, but analog might be better for future machine. And analog is certainly far better for people mainly because of the impact of noise. We have evolved to match the world. If you want to understand how human perception works, it helps to start off by understanding how the world of light and sound works, because the eyes and ears have evolved to fit the nature of these physical signals.

05 What would be the best title of the passage above?

① the benefit of digital
② the malfunction of analog
③ the horror of analog
④ the misconception about analog

06 Which of the following is NOT true?

① When the real world event is discrete, the analog is discrete.
② When the real world event is continuous, the analog is continuous.
③ When the real world event is continuous, the digital is continuous.
④ When the real world event is discrete, the digital is discrete.

07 Which of the following statements is likely to follow the final sentence?

① What this means is that we interact best with systems that are either part of the real world or analogous to them.

② The ever-increasing complexity of everyday life brings with it both great opportunities and grief.

③ Note that some deception is essential for the smooth pursuit of digital interactions.

④ The real problem with being digital is that it implies a kind of slavery to accuracy, a requirement that is most unlike the natural workings of the person.

It was Herbert Spencer who invented the poisoned phrase "survival of the fittest." He became one of the band of philosophers known as social Darwinists. The social Darwinists thought that measures to help the poor were wasted, since people were obviously unfit and thus doomed to sink. For 100 years Darwinism was associated with a particularly harsh and unpleasant view of the world and, worse, one that was clearly not true — at least not the whole truth. People certainly compete, but they collaborate, too. They also have compassion for the fallen and frequently try to help them, rather than treading on them. Humanity relies not on Spencer's idea of individual competition, but on social interaction. That interaction is sometimes confrontational and occasionally bloody. But it is frequently collaborative, and even when it is not, it is more often manipulative than violent. This is a comforting view because it suggests the possibility of the reconciliation of competition and collaboration. Human nature is not, to use another of Spencer's phrases, red in tooth and claw.

08 Which of the following would the social Darwinists NOT argue?

① People get what they deserve.
② The fittest not only survive, but prosper.
③ The ranking by wealth is genetically determined.
④ Society is the natural environment in which humanity is evolving.

09 Which of the following is most likely to follow the above passage?

① Social Darwinism has to figure out how society and human behavior have evolved.
② Herbert Spencer is the very one that is responsible for the evil of social Darwinism.
③ As a result, the practical application of social Darwinism has been even more promising.
④ Societies built around the idea that human nature is only competitive are doomed to early failure.

When it comes to New Year's resolutions, year after year the No. 1 spot is most likely occupied by "lose weight." Its persistence probably has something to do with the fact that most people have trouble actually succeeding. There is a simple reason for this. Everyone understands they have to burn more calories than they take in, said Professor Jakicic. But "most people don't know how many calories they burn a day," he said. "They have no clue." Getting a clue — or at least an accurate estimate — used to require a visit to a laboratory or the use of complex scientific equipment. Guess how often people took that approach?

Now though, there are simplified electronic monitors that are designed to accurately gauge physical activity and the calories burned, which is the silver bullet for weight loss. "There is a lot of evidence that shows they work," Professor Jakicic said. How well a monitor works depends on how much it is used, which boils down to personal taste. Are you more likely to use one that offers games and challenges, one that just reports the numbers, or one that is inconspicuous? We tried four of the more common products.

10 **According to the passage, why do many people fail to lose weight?**

① They do not understand the mechanism of losing weight.
② They do not know how many calories they use a day.
③ They do not consume as many calories as they need.
④ They do not pay attention to the weight issue.

11 **Which of the following is stated or implied in the passage?**

① Advances in medical technology help diagnose what problems people have who fail to lose weight.
② The effectiveness of a monitor gauging the calories burned depends on the frequency of its use.
③ The first thing people decide to do at the beginning of a year is to lose weight.
④ People prefer challenging machines for weight loss to simple ones.

12 Which of the following is most likely to follow the passage?

① An introduction of the best weight gain methods
② An explanation of the weight loss mechanism
③ An elaboration of the reasons many people fail to lose weight
④ A description of some electronic monitors for weight loss

Though the South is politically a part of America, the problem that faced her was peculiar and the struggle between the whites and the blacks after the Civil War was in essence a struggle for power, ranging over thirteen states and involving the lives of tens of millions of people. But keeping the ballot from the Negro was not enough to hold him in check; disfranchisement had to be supplemented by a whole panoply of rules, taboos, and penalties designed not only to insure peace (complete submission), but to guarantee that no real threat would ever arise. Had the Negro lived upon a common territory, separate from the bulk of the white population, this program of oppression might not have assumed such a brutal and violent form. But this war took place between people who were neighbors, whose homes adjoined, whose farms had common boundaries. Guns and disfranchisement, therefore, were not enough to make the black neighbor keep his distance.

13 **What is the main idea of the passage?**

① The blacks and the whites lived together after the Civil War.

② Many measures had been taken to keep the blacks in distance.

③ Guns should be eliminated for the peace of the blacks and the whites.

④ Disfranchisement had been a good way to defend white dominance over the blacks.

14 **Which of the following is NOT likely to be discussed right after the passage?**

① Threatening the blacks violently with weapons.

② Segregating the blacks residentially from the whites.

③ Limiting the amount of education that the blacks could receive.

④ Restricting the black's participation in the professions and jobs.

[15~16]

Forty years ago a young, radical journalist helped ignite the "War on Poverty" with his pioneering book *The Other America*. In its pages, Michael Harrington warned that the recently proclaimed age of affluence was a mirage, that beneath the surface of U.S. prosperity lay tens of millions of people stuck in hopeless poverty that only massive government intervention could help. Today, a new generation of journalists is straining to duplicate Harrington's feat — to convince contemporary America that its economic system doesn't work for millions and that only government can lift them out of poverty. These new journalists face a tougher task than Harrington's, though, because all levels of government have spent about $10 trillion on poverty programs since his book appeared, with disappointing, even counterproductive, results. And over the last four decades, millions of poor people, immigrants and native-born alike, have risen from poverty, without recourse to the government programs that Harrington inspired.

15 Which of the following is NOT true according to the passage?

① Michael Harrington was a journalist who called for governmental intervention in poverty.
② According to *The Other America*, many Americans suffered from poverty.
③ The contemporary journalists have been influenced by Harrington's claim.
④ Governmental poverty programs have helped millions of poor people escape from poverty.

16 Which of the following is most likely to follow the passage?

① The achievements of Harrington's strong conviction
② The re-evaluation of Harrington's argument
③ Successful examples of the U.S. governmental efforts to help the poor
④ The positive effects of the U.S. governmental efforts on economy

Another way to manipulate the results is through the questions asked. Words can have positive, negative, or neutral connotations. If I were to ask you, "Who do you prefer, beautiful Miss Piggy or ugly Oscar?" The words 'beautiful' and 'ugly' would invariably influence your answer.

The appearance of the interviewer can also affect the respondent's answer. The Caucasian in a business suit will elicit different answers than the informally dressed African-American when asking the same questions of persons in an African- American inner city ghetto, or of Caucasian professionals in an advertising agency. Another factor is the mood of the respondent. Mood influences opinion. To obtain negative answers from respondents about an incumbent politician or an existing policy, interviewers conduct polls on cloudy, rainy days, especially if they fall on a Monday. Generally people feel more depressed on these days and therefore are less inclined to be satisfied with the way things are.

If the public were not so easily manipulated, candidates, governments and other public and private institutions would not be spending billions of dollars each year to do so. Polling would not be such a large industry. But then you and I, as part of the public, want to show how well integrated into society we are. We are uncomfortable being misfits. Therefore, if 80% of the people support X, you and I will most likely (A) _____.

17 Which of the following best fits into (A)?

① feel comfortable
② support X, too
③ feel uncomfortable
④ manipulate the poll
⑤ refuse to vote

18 Which of the following is NOT stated or implied in the passage?

① Private institutions do not spend much money on public polls.
② Interviewers may gain more favorable answers from respondents on sunny days.
③ Government officials manipulate polls to get favorable results.
④ Words used in interviews can influence respondents' answers.
⑤ Respondents can be affected by interviewers' clothes.

19 The paragraph immediately preceding this passage is most likely to be concerned with _____.

① how to apply the technology of public opinion polls
② how to do sampling
③ how important public opinion polls are
④ how to manipulate polls
⑤ how to interpret polls

Post-secondary institutions serve students beyond the age of compulsory attendance. In the United States, post secondary students are an extremely diverse lot of traditional- and nontraditional-age students whose goals range from very specific occupational training to more general aims such as acquiring a liberal education to highly specialized preparations for further professional study. The role and extent of bilingual approaches observed for each such student group vary considerably. Some bilingual programs for adults in the United States have been developed to provide short-term, highly focused vocational training for special populations, such as refugees who qualify for special government support. Where there are large numbers of English learners who share the same home language, native language instruction may be included as a part of relatively short programs aimed at helping participants find employment as soon as possible.

20 **Which of the following best continues the paragraph?**

① However, the institutions are indeed bilingual in that full degree programs are offered using both English and Spanish.

② These bilingual programs including native language instruction tend to be found in areas with the largest settlement of recent immigrants.

③ A recent study indicates that most of English learners see their school as the one place of regular access to English language development.

④ Post-secondary students enrolled in degree programs may have access to academic instruction in a second language.

05 추론

추론은 편입 시험에서 단골로 출제되는 영역으로 상위권 대학에서는 비중이 상당히 높은 편에 속하는 유형이다. 본문에 나와 있는 진술이 아닌, 본문으로부터 끌어낼 수 있는 진술을 고르는 문제로 논리적인 판단을 요하는 문제에 속한다.

01 질문 유형

What can be inferred from the following passage?
Which of the following can be inferred from ***?
Which statement can NOT be inferred from the passage?
Which of the following is NOT stated or implied in the passage?

02 문제 풀이 전략

❶ **본문 전체를 빠르게 읽어야 하며, 내용의 일치를 추론으로 혼동하면 안 된다.**
추론 문제는 본문에 나와 있는 내용을 바탕으로 끌어낼 수 있는 정보를 찾도록 구성된 문제이므로 본문에 대한 이해가 선행되어야 한다. 다만 본문의 내용과 일치한다는 것은 재진술의 경우도 마찬가지이므로 내용 일치만으로 정답을 선택하는 우를 범해서는 안 된다.

❷ **본문에 명시적으로 드러나지 않지만, 본문에 근거를 둔 진술을 찾아낸다.**
추론이란 글에 나와 있는 정보를 바탕으로 해서, 이로부터 글에 언급되지 않은 확실한 진술을 끌어내는 것을 의미한다. 즉 본문에 없지만, 그 전제가 되는 이야기이거나 너무나 당연한 것이기에 언급하지 않았을 수도 있는 진술을 골라내는 것이다. 본문과의 관련성이 많이 떨어지는 추상적인 진술보다는 구체적으로 연결될 수 있는 진술이 추론에 더 적당하다.

The rattlesnake has a reputation as a dangerous and deadly snake with a fierce hatred for mankind. Although the rattlesnake is indeed a venomous snake capable of killing a human, its nature has perhaps been somewhat exaggerated in myth and folklore. The rattlesnake is not inherently aggressive and generally strikes only when it has been put on the defensive. In its defensive posture the rattlesnake raises the front part of its body off the ground and assumes as S-shaped form in preparation for a lunge forward. At the end of a forward thrust, the rattlesnake pushes its fangs into the victim, thereby injecting its venom. There are more than thirty species of rattlesnakes, varying in length from 20 inches to six feet and also varying in toxicity of venom. In the United States there are only a few deaths annually from rattlesnakes, with a mortality rate of less than 2 percent of those attacked.

→ 방울뱀의 길이도, 독성도 다양하다는 진술로 미루어 볼 때 모든 방울뱀의 독성이 동일하지 않다는 것을 알 수 있다.

Q. It can be inferred from this passage that _____.

① all rattlesnake bites kill people
② the venom of all rattlesnakes is equally toxic
③ all rattlesnake bites are not equally harmful
④ the number of fatalities from rattlesnake bites has been increasing

→ 방울뱀의 독성이 다양하다는 본문의 문장으로부터 정답을 끌어낼 수 있다.

정답   ③

해석   **다음 중 지문에서 유추할 수 있는 것은 _____.**

방울뱀은 인간을 맹렬히 증오하는 위험하고 치명적인 뱀으로 알려져 있다. 방울뱀이 인간을 죽일 수 있는 독사이기는 하지만 방울뱀의 본성은 신화와 전설에서 어느 정도는 과장된 면도 있다. 방울뱀은 본성적으로 공격적이지 않고 수세에 몰렸을 때만 문다. 수세에 몰렸을 때, 방울뱀은 땅 위로 몸 앞부분을 곧추세우고, S자 모양으로 도사린 채 앞으로 공격할 태세를 갖춘다. 방울뱀은 앞으로 빠르게 돌진해서 송곳니로 상대를 물고, 독을 내뿜는다. 방울뱀은 길이가 20인치부터 6피트에 이르기까지 다양한 종류가 있고, 독성의 정도도 다양하다. 미국에서는, 방울뱀에게 물려서 사망하는 경우는 드문데, 희생자의 사망률은 2% 미만이다.
① 방울뱀이 물면 인간은 죽는다.   ② 모든 방울뱀의 독성은 동일하다.
③ 모든 방울뱀 상처가 똑같이 위험하지는 않다.   ④ 방울뱀에 의한 사망률은 증가하고 있다.

해설   밑에서 두 번째 문장에 "방울뱀은 길이도, 독성도 다양하다."는 언급이 있으므로 ③이 적절한 추론이다.
"varying in toxicity of venom" 부분 참조.

어휘
rattlesnake ⓝ 방울뱀

deadly ⓐ 치명적인

hatred ⓝ 증오

nature ⓝ 본성, 본질

myth ⓝ 신화

inherently ⓐ 원래, 본질적으로

on the defensive 수세에 몰린, 궁지에 몰린

thrust ⓝ 돌진

injection ⓝ 주입

toxicity ⓝ 독성

mortality rate 사망률

reputation ⓝ 명성

fierce ⓐ 맹렬한, 치열한

venomous snake 독사

exaggerate ⓥ 과장하다

folklore ⓝ 전설

aggressive ⓐ 공격적인

lunge ⓝ 공격

fang ⓝ 송곳니

vary ⓥ 다양하다

annually ⓐ 매년

01 추론의 개념

추론이란 글에 나와 있는 정보를 바탕으로 해서, 이로부터 글에 언급되지 않은 확실한 진술을 끌어내는 것을 의미한다. 즉 본문에 없지만, 그 전제가 되는 이야기이거나 글로부터 너무나 당연한 것이기에 언급하지 않았을 수도 있는 진술을 골라내는 것이다. 유의할 점은 본문에 언급되어 있다면, 옳고 그름의 문제는 될지언정 추론의 문제는 아니다. 반면에 유사 추론이란 본문의 내용에는 언급하고 있진 않지만, 글로부터 타당하게 이끌어 낼 수 있는 답변의 문제를 의미하는 것으로 보면 추론의 문제와 유사하다. 그러므로 넓은 의미에서 본다면 추론의 범주 안에 들어간다고 할 수 있겠지만, 다만 문제의 형태를 추론과는 약간 달리한다.

02 경향 분석

추론 문제는 서강대를 비롯하여 대부분의 대학에서 출제하는 대표적인 문제이다. 다만 학교에 따라서 추론의 문제 수에서 차이가 나며, 일반적으로 상위권 대학에서 출제 빈도가 높다. 현재 우리의 편입 시험에서는 추론을 묻는 경우는 강한 의미의 추론 문제보다는 약한 의미의 추론 문제가 더 보편적이기는 하나, 강한 의미의 추론 또한 가끔 등장하고 있다. 그러므로 우리는 이에 두 가지 모든 경우에 대비해야 한다. 한 가지 주의할 점은, imply와 infer는 동의어가 아니라는 것이다. 우리는 흔히 암시와 추론을 같이 다루는 경우를 종종 보는데, 이는 잘못된 것이다. imply의 영역은 글을 쓰는 사람이나 말을 하는 사람이 할 수 있는 영역이고, 독자나 듣는 청자의 입장에서는 오직 추론할 수 있을 뿐이다. 개념의 혼동이 있어서는 안 된다. 더불어 추론은 단순한 가능성을 요하는 것이 아니라, 확실성을 요하는 것임을 명심해야 한다. 즉 본문에서 끌어낼 수 있는 100% 타당한 진술이라는 것을 인식하고 문제를 풀어야 한다.

유사 추론 문제의 개별적인 문제 형태를 보면 (1) "다음 중 어떤 경우라면 저자가 동의하겠는가"라는 유형이 대표적으로 여기에 속한다. 저자가 동의하는 것이 무엇인지는 본문에 밝혀져 있지는 않다. (2) 결론을 묻는 문제의 유형 역시 여기에 속한다. 그 이유는 주어진 글의 결론을 묻는다는 것도 결국은 본문에 제시되지는 않았지만, 본문으로부터 끌어낼 수 있는 것이 되므로, 역시 추론의 일부로 볼 수 있다. 또 어떤 면에서 보면 글을 요약하라는 것 역시 일종의 유사 추론 문제로 볼 수 있다. (3) 저자가 전하려는 메시지는 무엇인가 (4) 윗글에 대한 답변으로 알맞은 것은 무엇인가 등의 문제 역시 유사 추론의 문제 유형에 속한다.

03 학습 전략

추론의 문제를 푸는 요령이라면 먼저 글 안의 단서를 찾는 것이 중요하다. 지문에 나와 있지는 않지만, 당연히 100% 확실히 글을 통해서 알 수 있는 것을 고르는 것 그것이 바로 추론 문제에 접근하는 방법이다. 다음과 같은 문장을 예로 들어 보면, The Mayer admitted owning the gun that killed his wife. 이 문장을 보면, 어떤 식의 추론이 가능할까? '시장은 결혼을 했었고, 그의 아내는 지금 죽었다'는 것이 너무나도 당연한 추론일 것이다. 이 문장에서 '시장은 그의 아내를 죽인 총을 소지하는 것을 허락받았다'라고 되어 있지만, 이것만으로도 시장이 결혼했었다는 것은 추론이 가능하다. 그 이유는 그의 아내라는 부분이 있으므로 가능하며, 그의 아내를 살해한 총이란 부분에서 아내는 죽었다는 것 역시 100% 확실한 이야기이다. 이 글 어디에서도 아내가 죽었다거나 시장이 결혼했다는 이야기는 없지만, 우리는 글을 읽고 미루어 100% 확실한 것을 끄집어낼 수 있고, 이것이 바로 진정한 의미의 추론인 것이다. 하지만 '시장이 아내를 죽였다'라는 추론은 가능하지 않다. 그 이유는 시장이 죽었는지, 자살을 했는지는 알 수가 없고 단지 알 수 있는 사실은 그 총에 맞아 시장의 아내가 죽었다는 사실뿐이다. 그러므로 결론적으로 '100% 확실하지만 지문에 안 나와 있다'의 의미를 위의 각도에서 생각해 보면 충분히 이해할 수 있을 것이다.

위의 이야기를 바탕으로 해서 추론의 의미에 대해서 감이 잡혔다면, 이제 추론을 세부적으로 분류해 보기로 한다. 강한 의미의 추론이라 하면, 글을 읽고 글에서 언급되지 않은 내용이지만, 글을 통해서 그 글이 당연히 전제하고 있는 내용이라든가 그 글의 매듭이나 연결 고리로서 글에 숨어 있는 것을 찾는 것이다. 위에 든 예에서 살펴본 바와 같다. 반면에 약한 의미의 추론이란 사실에 근거하여 옳고 그름의 문제로 되는 경우를 말한다. 바꿔 말하기(paraphrasing)의 형태로 동의어 등을 활용하여 약간의 변형을 주기는 하나 옳은 것을 고르라거나 틀린 것을 고르라는 식의 문제처럼 느껴질 수도 있다.

더하여 유사 추론 문제 전반을 검토해 보면 저자가 동의하는 것이 무엇인지, 저자의 메시지는 무엇인지 본문에 명시적으로 밝혀져 있지는 않다. 하지만 글을 읽으면서 저자의 의도나 주장을 종합해 보면 저자가 동의할 만한 부분은 무엇인지, 저자의 메시지는 무엇인지를 파악할 수 있다. 그리고 어떠한 글이며, 이 글의 결론은 어떠한지, 어떤 식의 답변을 하면 논리적으로 연결이 될 수 있는지를 파악할 수 있다. 글의 흐름을 꿰뚫어 보고, 저자가 숨겨 놓은 정보 이면의 내용을 파악해 놓으면 문제를 푸는 것 자체는 어렵지는 않을 것이다

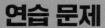

01 What can be inferred from the passage? 가톨릭대 2019

Effective decision makers do not rely on careful analysis alone. Instead, they also use their intuition, a method of arriving at a conclusion by a quick judgment or gut feeling. Relying on intuition is like relying on your instincts when faced with a decision. Intuition takes place when the brain gathers information stored in memory and packages it as a new insight or solution. Intuitions, therefore, can be regarded as stored information that is reorganized or repackaged. Developing good intuition may take a long time because so much information has to be stored.

① Intuition can be cultivated as knowledge accumulates over time.
② Intuition is an essentially inborn, or genetically determined trait.
③ In making decisions, intuition is a more important factor than reasoning.
④ The concept of intuition is something that is difficult to understand and explain.

02 Which of the following CANNOT be inferred from the passage?

The guard's reluctance to let the foreigner continue on is understandable. Other than a handful of scientists bound for the government-run observatory in Hanle, most Westerners have been denied access since the end of the Chinese-Indian war of 1962. Fearing that spies from China might slip over the border into Hanle, which sits just 12 miles from the disputed frontier, the Indian government declared the area off-limits.

① Hanle belongs to the Indian territory.
② Hanle is located near the borderline.
③ People in Hanle do not like Chinese people.
④ There are a lot of Westerners staying in Hanle.
⑤ There is a government-run observatory in Hanle.

03 According to the following passage, which can be inferred as an example of an adaptation to desert life?

Desert life is interesting and varied. Though the desert is a punishing place — it is difficult to find food and water — many animals live there. Because there is so little water, desert animals have adapted. Camels can survive for days without drinking. Other animals get their water from the insects and plants they eat. The extreme temperatures of the desert can make life difficult as well. Many desert mammals have thick fur to keep out the heat and the cold. Some desert animals are nocturnal, sleeping by day and hunting by night, when the air is cooler. It may seem that all deserts are the same, but they are as different as the animals that inhabit them.

① The heavy outer shell of the beetle.
② The large hood of the cobra that scares off predators.
③ The quick speed of the mongoose so that it may catch its prey.
④ The long ears of the hedgehog that give off heat to cool the animal.

Nobody believes that media by themselves cause aggression. But Leonardo Eron and Rowell Huesmann of the University of Michigan found in a 22-year study following kids from third grade through adulthood that the single best predictor of later aggression — better than poverty, grades, a single-parent home or exposure to real violence — is a heavy childhood diet of TV carnage. "Of course not every youngster is affected," says Eron. "Not everyone who gets lung cancer smoked cigarettes. And not everyone who smokes cigarettes gets lung cancer. But nobody outside the tobacco industry denies that smoking causes lung cancer." Much of the most effective research has been done on children because they are considered most _____. As Centerwall puts it, "Later variations in exposure, in adolescence and adulthood, do not exert any additional effect." In the early '60s, Albert Bandura at Stanford was the first to show that kids learned behavior from TV, not just from their parents. Psychologists have used four theories of learning to describe how TV violence may influence kids: they learn to imitate what they see on TV, especially when the behavior is rewarded; from the frequency of violence on TV they learn that violence is normal; they become desensitized to real people's suffering; and they become aroused by images on television, triggering violent responses.

01 Which of the following is inferred from the above passage?

① Media can cause copycat crimes.
② Smoking always gives rise to lung cancer.
③ The poverty in childhood plays the most important role in later violence.
④ Exposure to violence on TV leads kids to be sensitive to people's suffering.
⑤ Bandura believes that kids do not learn violent behavior from their parents.

02 Which best fits in the blank?

① susceptible   ② immature
③ rebellious   ④ influential
⑤ aggressive

In medical usage, a "placebo" is a treatment that has no specific physical or chemical action on the condition being treated, but is given to affect symptoms by a psychologic mechanism, rather than a purely physical one. Ethicists believe that placebos necessarily involve a partial or complete deception by the doctor, _____ the patient is allowed to believe that the treatment has a specific effect. They seem unaware that placebos, far from being <u>inert</u> (except in the rigid pharmacological sense), are among the most powerful agents known to medicine. It can strengthen the weak or paralyze the strong, transform sleeping, feeding, or sexual patterns, remove or induce a vast array of symptoms, mimic or abolish the effect of very powerful drugs. It can even alter the functions of most organs.

03 Which of the following CANNOT be inferred from the above passage?

① "Placebo" is a medical treatment based on the patient's psychology.
② Some people believe that "placebo" is wrong because it is a lie.
③ "Placebo" is actually an effective method to some patients.
④ "Placebo" has no effect on the patient's physical conditions.
⑤ The writer of the passage supports the use of "placebo."

04 Which can best replace the underlined <u>inert</u>?

① indolent   ② affective
③ rejuvenated   ④ detrimental
⑤ optimistic

05 What would be the best expression for the blank?

① but   ② and
③ since   ④ despite
⑤ as long as

The oral-tradition narratives, as well as everyday speech in oral societies, tend to use rhymes and rhythms, which appeal to the psychology of memory. The rhymes and rhythms of poetry are remembered more easily than non-rhythmic prose. Likely, you can remember simple childhood poetry or rhymes, things you neither have heard nor said for years. Just as likely, you have forgotten much of what you read in an earlier textbooks, particularly the specific language used to express the ideas. Song lyrics also are remembered and recalled ㉮ _____. Since rhythmic, rhyming patterns are recalled more easily, oral-tradition narratives not surprisingly employ ㉯ both devices.

06 Which of the following can be inferred from the passage?

① All the people could recollect the books that they had read.
② Reading books increases the ability of memory rapidly.
③ Audio-tradition should be regarded more important than oral-tradition.
④ Song lyrics can be remembered effectively.

07 Which of the following is the most appropriate for blank ㉮?

① with great difficulty
② with amazing ease
③ for a very short time
④ for their own good

08 Which of the following to the closest meaning of ㉯ both devices?

① high school and university
② novels and poetry
③ rhymes and rhythms
④ oral-tradition and audio-tradition

The tendency of Americans to overestimate what they have accomplished on their own and deny how much they owe to others has been codified in the myth that the colonists came on an "errand into the wilderness" and built a land of plenty out of nothing. In reality, however, the abundant concentrations of game, plants, and berries that so astonished Eastern colonists were not "(A) _____"; they had been produced by the cooperative husbandry and collective land-use patterns of Native Americans. In the Northwest, the valuable Douglas fir forests and plentiful herds of deer and elk found by early settlers existed only because Native American burning practices had created sustained-yield succession forests that (B) _____ use of these resources without exhausting them.

09 Which of the following best fills in the blank (A)?

① helpful
② civilized
③ aggressive
④ natural

10 Which of the following best fills in the blank (B)?

① maximized
② devastated
③ exacerbated
④ demolished

11 Which of the following can be inferred from the passage?

① Eastern colonists brought deer and elk from Europe.
② Native Americans used burning as a means of cultivating.
③ Native Americans preferred to cultivate the land individually.
④ Americans strongly believe that they could achieve a lot with the help of others.

[12~13]

Sleep could have more effect on your health than you think. The less sleep you get, the higher your body mass index tends to be. [I] Research showed that people who sleep five hours a night were found to have 15 percent more ghrelin(a hormone that boosts hunger) in their bodies and 15 percent less leptin(a hormone that suppresses hunger) than those sleeping eight hours. Furthermore, sleep plays a key role in making new memories stick in the brain. An experiment showed that subjects taught complex finger movements such as a piano scale recalled them better after 12 hours' sleep than 12 hours' wakefulness. [II] Good sleep also boosts the immune system. Melatonin, produced when you sleep, is a cancer-fighting antioxidant. Night-shift workers may have up to 70 times greater risk of breast cancer. [III] Last, if you're a child, you'd better sleep more. [IV] The depression and low self-esteem often associated with just being a teenager actually correlate with sleep shortage. Young kids who sleep poorly are more than twice as likely to take to drink and drugs in adolescence. [V]

12 Which of the following is NOT stated in the passage as a reason to get more sleep?

① More sleep could make you weigh less.
② More sleep could boost your memory.
③ More sleep can fight cancer.
④ More sleep can slow down aging.
⑤ More sleep could keep your mental health.

13 Which letter [I], [II], [III], [IV], or [V] can be best replaced by the following sentence?

> In addition to preventive chemicals, the chemical to repair damage to the stomach lining is secreted during sleep.

① [I]   ② [II]
③ [III]   ④ [IV]
⑤ [V]

The dictionary defines winning as "achieving victory over others in a competition, receiving a prize or reward for achievement." Yet some of the most meaningful wins of my life were victories over no other person, and I can remember winning when there was no prize for performance.

My first experience of winning occurred in elementary school gym. Nearly every day, after the preparatory push-ups and squat-thrusts, we had to run relays. Although I had asthma as a child, I won many races. My chest would burn terribly for a few minutes, but it was worth it to feel so proud, not because I had beaten others or won a prize, but because I had overcome a handicap.

I consider the fact that I am now attending college winning. To get here, I had to surmount many obstacles, both outside and inside myself. College costs money, and I don't have much of it. College takes time, and I don't have much of that either with a little son to care for. But I overcame these obstacles and a bigger one — lack of confidence in myself. I had to keep saying, "I won't give up." And here I am, winning.

14 윗글의 제목으로 가장 알맞은 것을 고르시오.

① How to Overcome Asthma
② What It Really Means to Win
③ The Magical Power of Winning
④ Juggling Several Things at College

15 글쓴이의 발언이라고 추론할 수 없는 것을 고르시오.

① I don't trust anything that comes too easily.
② Never give up and you can have self-reliance.
③ I will follow the road not taken rather than a trodden one.
④ I appreciate a win more when there is a strong contender in a competition.

Humans are classed anatomically among the primates, the order of which includes apes, monkeys, and lemurs. Among the hundreds of living primate species, only humans are naked. Two kinds of habitat are known to give rise to naked mammals — a (A) _____ one or (B) _____ one. There is a naked Somalian mole rat which never ventures above ground. All other nonhuman mammals which have lost all or most of their fur are either swimmers like whales and dolphins, or wallowers like hippopotamuses and pigs and tapirs. The rhinoceros and the elephant, though found on land since Africa became drier, bear traces of a more watery past and seize every opportunity of wallowing in the mud or water.

It has been suggested that humans became hairless to prevent overheating in the savannah. But no other mammal has ever resorted to this strategy. A covering of hair acts as a defense against the heat of the sun: that is why even the desert-dwelling camel retains its fur. Another version is to facilitate sweat-cooling. But again many species resort to sweatcooling quite effectively without needing to lose their hair. One general conclusion seems undeniable from an overall survey of mammalian species: that while a coat of fur provides the best insulation for land mammals, the best insulation in water is not fur, but a layer of fat.

16 Which is the most appropriate for blank (A) and (B)?

① subterranean − wet ② icy − humid
③ tropical − frigid ④ sandy − grassy

17 It can be inferred from the passage that the reason why humans are less hairy than other primates is because

① they are descended from forest-dwelling apes.
② their earliest ancestors lived in watery places.
③ they had to adapt to the hot savannah environment.
④ their ancestors had to keep their body dry.

More than anything, it's Chua's maternal confidence — her striking lack of ambivalence about her choices as a parent — that has inspired both ire and awe among the many who have read her words. Since her book's publication, she says, email messages have poured in from around the globe, some of them angry and even threatening but many of them wistful or grateful. "A lot of people have written to say that they wished their parents had pushed them when they were younger, that they think they could have done more with their lives," Chua recounts. "Other people have said that after reading my book they finally understand their parents and why they did what they did. One man wrote that he sent his mother flowers and a note of thanks, and she called him up, weeping."

For though Chua hails the virtues of "the Chinese way," the story she tells is quintessentially American. It's the tale of an immigrant striver, determined to make a better life for himself and his family in a nation where such dreams are still possible. "I remember my father working every night until 3 in the morning; I remember his wearing the same pair of shoes for eight years," Chua says. "Knowing the sacrifices he and my mother made for us made me want to uphold the family name, to make my parents proud."

Hard work, persistence, no patience for excuses: whether Chinese or American, that sounds like a prescription for success with which it's very difficult to argue.

18 Which of the following can NOT be inferred from the above?

① Chua talks about the readers' responses to her book.
② Chua's book addresses various issues about the parent-child relationship.
③ Chua compares aspects of "Chinese parenting" with those of Western parenting in her book.
④ Chua's book has received a unanimous acclamation.

19 The author concludes that Chua's tiger-mother approach to raising her children isn't an ethnicity but a philosophy because _____.

① to push ourselves forward is the way America often have in the past
② Chinese mothers don't have to be Chinese
③ to expect the best from one's children is a common impetus found in any accomplished ethnic groups
④ Chua now understands the difference between working hard on something and dashing something off

On September 11, 2001, at 8:46 a.m., a hijacked airliner crashed into the North Tower of the World Trade Center in New York. At 9:03 a.m. a second plane crashed into the South Tower. The resulting infernos caused the buildings to collapse, the South Tower after burning for an hour and two minutes, the North Tower twenty-three minutes after that. The attacks were masterminded by Osama bin Laden, who hoped to intimidate the United States into ending its military presence in Saudi Arabia and its support for Israel and to unite Muslims in preparation for a restoration of the caliphate.

9/11, as the happenings of that day are now called, has set off debates on a vast array of topics. Exactly how many events took place in New York on that morning in September? It could be argued that the answer is one. The attacks on the buildings were part of a single plan conceived in the mind of one man in service of a single agenda.

Or it could be argued that the answer is two. Three and a half billion dollars were the sum in dispute in a set of trials determining the insurance payout to Larry Silverstein, the leaseholder of the World Trade Center site. Silverstein held insurance policies that stipulated a maximum reimbursement for each destructive "event." If 9/11 comprised a single event, he stood to receive three and a half billion dollars. If it comprised two events, he stood to receive seven billion.

20 According to the passage, which of the following was NOT true one of Osama bin Laden's aims in 9/11 attacks?

① To change the U.S. policy toward Israel
② To terminate the American military presence in Saudi Arabia
③ To bring Muslims together again in one political system
④ To support the activities of Al Qaeda terrorists

21 **Which of the following is most likely to have been claimed by Silverstein's lawyers?**

① Osama bin Laden should be punished.
② 9/11 consisted of two events.
③ Silverstein was not involved in the 9/11 plot.
④ The American legal system is too lenient with terrorists.

22 **Which of the following is NOT stated or implied in the passage?**

① Through the 9/11 attacks, Osama bin Laden was supported by the majority of Muslims.
② 9/11 has caused people to debate on a wide range of topics.
③ Larry Silverstein was the leaseholder of the World Trade Center buildings.
④ What fell down first on 9/11 was the North Tower of the World Trade Center.

What is likely to be the development of the family during the next two centuries? We cannot tell, but we can note certain forces at work which are likely, if unchecked, to have certain results. There are certain things in modern civilised communities which are tending to weaken the family; the chief of them is humanitarian sentiment toward children. More and more people come to feel that children should not suffer more than can be helped through their parents' misfortunes or even sins. In the Bible the lot of the orphan is always spoken of as very sad, and so no doubt it was; nowadays he suffers little more than other children. There will be a growing tendency for the state or charitable institutions to give fairly adequate care to neglected children, and consequently children will be more and more neglected by unconscientious parents or guardians. Gradually the expense of caring for neglected children out of public funds will become so great that there will be a very strong inducement for all who are not well off to avail themselves of the opportunities for giving their children over to the state; probably this will be done, in the end, as now with schooling, by practically all who are below a certain economic level.

23 According to the passage, humanitarian sentiment toward children _____.

① will weaken the family by making parents spend too much money on their children
② will eventually make children more and more neglected by parents or guardians
③ will lead the state to take children away forcefully from their poor or sinful parents
④ will cause a state financial crisis and even state bankruptcy

24 The writer mentions the Bible to show _____.

① the similarity of the living conditions of orphans and of other children in the past
② the difference of the living conditions of orphans and of other children in the present
③ the similarity of the living conditions of orphans in the past and in the present
④ the difference of the living conditions of orphans in the past and in the present

25 Which of the following is implied in the passage?

① At present, the burden of child-caring is entirely borne by the state and public institutions.

② In the future, most parents will be so well educated as to give adequate care to their children.

③ At present, the state takes responsibility for the schooling of the children from families below a certain economic level.

④ In the future, practically all parents will give their children over to the state for their care as well as for their schooling.

A big-data revolution is underway in health care. Start with the vastly increased supply of information. Over the last decade, pharmaceutical companies have been aggregating years of research and development data into medical databases, while payers and providers have digitized their patient records. Meanwhile, the US federal government and other public stakeholders have been opening their vast stores of health-care knowledge, including data from clinical trials and information on patients covered under public insurance programs. In parallel, recent technical advances have made it easier to collect and analyze information from multiple sources — a major benefit in health care, since data for a single patient may come from various payers, hospitals, laboratories, and physician offices.

Health-care stakeholders are well versed in capturing value and have developed many levers to assist with this goal. But traditional tools do not always take complete advantage of the insights that big data can provide. Unit-price discounts, for instance, are based primarily on contracting and negotiating leverage. And like most other well-established health-care value levers, they focus solely on reducing costs rather than improving patient outcomes. Although these tools will continue to play an important role, stakeholders will only benefit from big data if they take a more holistic, patient-centered approach to value, one that focuses equally on health-care spending and treatment outcomes.

26 According to the author of this passage, who will be able to benefit the most from this great store of data being gathered?

① pharmaceutical companies
② individual patients and their health care providers
③ the US federal government
④ physicians and other hospital staff

27 Who has the biggest source of data mentioned in this passage?

① the US federal government and other public stakeholders

② the pharmaceutical companies

③ the public insurance authority

④ the health-care stakeholders

28 Which of the following can be inferred from this passage?

① The big data revolution will enable patients to have available to them more holistic, alternative health options such as acupuncture.

② It has always been easy to collect and analyze information from multiple sources.

③ The big-data revolution will make possible a more patient-centered approach to health care focusing on both reducing costs and improving patient care.

④ It will no longer be necessary to use traditional tools such as unit-price discounts.

The use of credit continued throughout history, as merchants utilized a variety of methods to keep track of their customers' debts. For example, during the eighteenth century in Great Britain, tallymen would sell clothes to customers in exchange for small, weekly payments. In order to keep track of the shoppers' debts, the tallymen kept long wooden sticks with notches on one side representing the payments made and notches on the other side representing the amount of money still owed. Other types of credit measures, such as metal plates and coins, were also used to keep track of debt in ancient and early modern times.

The first credit cards originated in the United States during the 1920s. Enjoying the booming economy of the era and hoping to attract more customers, individual companies began to issue cards to their customers that would allow them to make purchases at the store or company and pay the money back at a later date. While these cards could be used only at the store that issued them, some companies began to accept each other's credit cards during the late 1930s. This was the first use of thirdparty payment, where the company that issued the card would pay the merchant that accepted the card. The customer would then pay back the card-issuing company. Third-party payment would later become the primary operating method of bank credit cards.

29 Which of the following is the best title of the passage?

① Types of Institutions Issuing Credit Cards
② History of Credit Transactions
③ Different Shapes of Credit Cards
④ Alternatives for Credit Transactions

30 According to the passage, which of the following is NOT mentioned as credit measures in the early period of credit use?

① metal plates
② wooden sticks
③ coins
④ gold

31 Which of the following is stated or implied in the passage?

① Tallymen were an important part of early credit history.

② The British bankers first invented the credit card.

③ Banks issued credit cards earlier than individual companies.

④ Third-party payment was available from the early history of credit.

It is important to distinguish between being legally allowed to do something, and actually being able to go and do it. A law could be passed allowing everyone, if they so wish, to run a mile in two minutes. That would not, however, increase their effective freedom, because, although allowed to do so, they are physically incapable of it. Having a minimum of restrictions and a maximum of possibilities is fine, but in the real world most people will never have the opportunity either to become all that they are allowed to become, or to need to be restrained from doing everything that is possible for them to do. Their effective freedom depends on actually having _____.

This idea of effective freedom relates back to the consideration of fairness. The quest for a fair society — whether through the sort of agreements suggested by Rawls, or through a utilitarian assessment of benefits — is at the same time a quest for a society in which effective freedom is maximized. To be treated unfairly is to have one's potential limited, and therefore to be denied things that would be possible if one had a fairer share of resources. Poverty is not just a matter of having insufficient money or resources, it is also about not being free to do the things that people with more money are freely able to choose to do.

32 윗글에서 빈칸에 들어가기에 가장 적합한 것을 고르시오.

① he social agreement on utilitarian views
② legal regulations which defend their rights
③ maximum benefits from minimum restrictions
④ the means and ability to do what they choose

33 윗글을 통해 추론할 수 있는 것으로 가장 적합한 것을 고르시오.

① Assuring a maximum of possibilities by law contributes to more effective freedom.
② Effective freedom can be enhanced by increasing fairness of a society.
③ Law often fails to reflect reality and thus needs to be amended.
④ Poverty cannot be reduced even with the increase of effective freedom.

The New York Times has featured a story of a man who lives in a glass house. His home is filled with transparent walls. He has chosen to live without any physical privacy in a home that allows every action to be seen. He has created his own panopticon, a place in which everything is in full view of others. Jeremy Bentham first coined the term panopticon in the late eighteenth century when he was describing his idea of how prisons should be designed. The prisoner's cells would be placed in a circle with a guard tower in the middle. All walls facing the center of the circle would be glass. In that way, every prisoner's cell would be in full view of the guards. The prisoners could do nothing unobserved, but the prisoners would not be able to see the guard tower. They would know they were being watched, but they would never know when the guard was actually monitoring their actions because they could not see the observer. People behave (A) _____ when they know they are being watched. In these situations, people are (B) _____ to be themselves; instead, they will act the way they think they should act when they are being observed by others.

34 Choose the best word for (A) and (B).

	(A)		(B)
①	actively	—	more likely
②	differently	—	more likely
③	actively	—	less likely
④	differently	—	less likely

35 Which one can be inferred about panopticons?

① They are not applicable outside of the prison dynamic.
② They can be an effective tool for social control.
③ They should be used regularly in public places.
④ They will expand privacy in the future.

36 Which one is TRUE?

① A man in New York built a glass house to watch others.
② The term panopticon was first made by Jeremy Bentham decades ago.
③ The original panopticon was composed of a tower and surrounding cells.
④ The prisoners in the panopticon were able to observe the guards.

The Ⓐ _____ of humanitarianism is nowhere clearer than in the enthusiastic re-invigoration of UN celebrity advocacy — a humanitarian genre with a history of success associated with major Hollywood icons, such as Audrey Hepburn and, more recently, Angelina Jolie. The advocacy of such star figures has always relied upon a(n) Ⓑ _____ performativity of humanitarian discourse, which combines "impersonation," the celebrity's testimony of the suffering of others, with "personification," the infusion of such testimony with the celebrity's own distinct star aura. What differentiates contemporary from past articulations of advocacy, however, is the tendency of the former to privilege a "confessional" communicative structure of celebrity. Unlike the strict formality of earlier forms of celebrity advocacy, confessional performativity rests upon "intimacy at a distance" — a key feature of today's popular culture that refers to our Ⓒ _____ access to the intimate sphere of celebrity lives, rendering this sphere an inherent aspect of their public personae.

37 Which of the following can LEAST be inferred from the passage?

① Celebrities share the suffering of others with a popular audience.
② Celebrity humanitarianism was more formal in the past.
③ Celebrities today use their public personae to confess their guilt.
④ Hollywood icons today infuse their testimony with their star power.

38 Choose the BEST set of words for blanks Ⓐ, Ⓑ, and Ⓒ.

① Ⓐ spread — Ⓑ opaque — Ⓒ open
② Ⓐ proliferation — Ⓑ abstruse — Ⓒ free
③ Ⓐ conglomeration — Ⓑ decadent — Ⓒ minute
④ Ⓐ commodification — Ⓑ ambivalent — Ⓒ mediated

"However we analyse the difference between the regular and the irregular, we must ultimately be able to account for the most basic fact of aesthetic experience, the fact that delight lies somewhere between boredom and confusion." declares Ernst Gombrich in *A Sense of Order*. We have already seen how the human being is locked into a perpetual conflict between the need to maintain a sense of order and predictability on the one hand, whilst on the other being aware that such stability is vulnerable to dissolution and collapse. Hence, the compulsive need to draw together threads of meaning by which to maintain the wholeness of the being, to reassure oneself of one's existence. However, it is also true that to be in a constantly predictable state can lead to boredom and restlessness — even worse is experienced in the total absence of stimulation, or what might be called 'super-continuity' as in the case of sensory deprivation.

39 **What would be the best title of the passage above?**

① The value of moderation
② How to prevent perceptual and conceptual errors
③ Automated creativity
④ The compulsive requirement for continuity

40 **What can be inferred from the passage above?**

① In the turbulent times, people often ignore rich experience of delight.
② Accommodating the necessary degrees of simultaneous coherence and confusion is necessary.
③ Diverse juxtaposition leads to incoherence and disorder.
④ More common fragmentary experience contributes to super-continuity.

In 1937, the ABC (Atanasoff-Berry Computer) began to be developed by Professor John Vincent Atanasoff and graduate student Cliff Berry. Its development continued until 1942 at Iowa State University. The ABC was an electrical computer that used vacuum tubes for digital computation. including binary math and Boolean logic, and had no CPU. On October 19th. 1973. U.S federal judge Earl R. Larson ruled that the ENIAC (electronic numerical integrator and computer) patent by J. Presper Eckert and John Mauchly was invalid. He additionally named Atanasoff the inventor of the electronic digital computer.

The ENIAC began to be constructed in 1943, which was not completed until 1946. It occupied about 1,800 square feet and used about 18,000 vacuum tubes, weighing almost 50 tons. Although the judge ruled that the ABC computer was the first digital computer, many still consider the ENIAC to be the first digital computer because it was fully functional. The ENIAC was used by the military to compute the trajectories of projectiles.

Nowadays, computers are all around us. Your cell phone has a computer inside, as do many credit cards and farecards for public transit. A modern car has several computers to control the engine, brakes, lights, and the radio.

The (A) _____ of ubiquitous computing changed many aspects of our lives. While factories used to employ people to do repetitive assembly tasks, those tasks are today carried out by computer-controlled robots, operated by a few people who know how to work with computers. Books, music, and movies are often consumed on computers, and computers are almost always involved in their production.

41 What is the author's main purpose in writing this passage?

① To introduce a brief history of computers
② To criticize certain uses of computers
③ To underestimate the importance of computers
④ To define the functions of digital computers

42 Which of the following is most suitable for the blank (A)?

① contagion   ② advent

③ exodus   ④ divergence

43 According to the passage, where was the ENIAC used?

① cell phones   ② army

③ cars   ④ public transit

44 According to the passage, which of the following is true?

① The ABC was not completed until the ENIAC was invented.

② Nowadays factories dramatically reduce repetitive assembly tasks.

③ The ABC lacked the full functionality of the ENIAC.

④ Only few would mention that the ENIAC is the first digital computer.

45 Which of the following can be inferred from the passage?

① The ABC was developed at Iowa State University between 1937 and 1946.

② The ENIAC occupied huge buildings called date centers.

③ John Vincent Atanasoff did not file for a patent on a digital computing device.

④ According to the court, many ideas of the ENIAC were derived from the ABC.

06 유사 추론

유사 추론이란 본문의 내용에는 언급하고 있진 않지만, 글로부터 타당하게 이끌어 낼 수 있는 답변의 문제를 의미하는 것으로 추론 문제와 유사하다. 그러므로 넓은 의미에서 본다면 추론의 범주 안에 들어간다고 할 수 있겠지만, 문제의 형태에 있어서 추론과는 약간 다르다.

01 질문 유형

Which question is NOT answered directly by the given passage?
What would be the most logical conclusion to the passage above?
Which of the following are the researchers most likely to agree with?
Which of the following can be supported by the passage?

02 문제 풀이 전략

❶ **본문에 나와 있지 않지만, 본문으로부터 끌어낸다.**

본문에 나와 있지 않은 예로는 "다음 중 어떤 경우라면 저자가 동의하겠는가?"라는 유형이 대표적인데, 저자가 동의하는 것이 무엇인지 본문에 밝혀져 있지는 않다. 결론을 묻는 문제의 유형 역시 여기에 속하며, 그 이유는 주어진 글의 결론을 묻는다는 것도 결국은 본문에 제시되지는 않았지만, 본문으로부터 끌어낼 수 있는 것이 되므로, 역시 추론의 일부로 볼 수 있다. "윗글에 대한 답변으로 알맞은 것은 무엇인가" 등의 문제도 유사 추론의 문제 유형에 속한다.

❷ **본문에서 찾을 수 있는 내용이 아니라 본문에서 끌어낼 수 있는 내용이어야 한다.**

막연히 본문과 관련성이 있다는 게 아니라 실제 본문으로부터 끌어낼 수 있는 경우이지만, 문제의 표현을 추론이라 칭하는 것이 아닌 결론을 도출하라든지 저자가 동의할 수 있는 상황은 어떠한지 등을 묻는다. 즉 본문으로부터 특정한 사항에 대하여 판단하고 자신만의 의견을 정립할 수 있는지를 묻는다. 그러므로 본문의 단순한 내용이 아닌 본문으로부터 끌어낼 수 있는 내용이어야 한다. 추론이란 단어를 사용하진 않았지만 추론과 유사한 원리가 적용된다.

Scientists disagree about the place of instinct in human behavior. Sociologists argue that even complicated forms of human behavior can have an instinctive basis. They believe we have an inborn urge to propagate our own genes and those of our biological relatives. Social customs that enhance the odds of such transmission survive in the form of kinship bonds, courtship rituals, altruism, taboos against female adultery, and many aspects of social life. Other social scientists have argued that human behavior can be explained solely by learning. Psychologists today generally take a middle path. They acknowledge that human behavior is influenced by our biological heritage, but most doubt that either imprinting or true instincts occur in human beings.

과학자들 사이에서도 의견이 분분하다는 것을 밝히고 있다.

본능에 기반을 둔다는 주장도 있다.

학습에 의하여 설명할 수 있다는 견해도 있다.

생물학적 요인에 의해서 영향을 받는다.

Q. After reading this passage readers would probably conclude that _____.

① several factors have an impact on human behavior
② the desire to procreate is behavior which we learn
③ exploring human behavior is not a great concern to psychologists of today
④ there is a single theory of human behavior on which social scientists agree

결국 인간의 행동은 본능, 학습, 욕구 등 여러 가지 다양한 요인들에 의해서 영향을 받는다.

정답 ①

해석 **윗글을 읽은 후에 독자들은 _____.라고 결론지을 것이다.**

과학자들은 인간 행동에 있어서 본능의 역할에 대해서 의견이 일치하지 않는다. 사회학자들은 아무리 복잡한 인간의 행동 이라도 본능적인 토대를 기반으로 하고 있다고 주장한다. 그들은 우리가 우리 자신의 유전자와 우리의 생물학적 친지들의 유전자를 퍼뜨리고자 하는 타고난 욕구가 있다고 생각한다. 이러한 전달[계승]의 가능성을 높여 주는 사회적 관습들은 친족 간의 유대, 구애 의식, 이타주의, 여성의 간통에 대한 금기와 많은 것들이 사회적 삶의 형태로 남아 있다. 다른 사회 과학자들은 인간의 행동은 단지 학습에 의해서만 설명될 수 있다고 주장한다. 오늘날의 심리학자들은 일반적으로 중도적인 입장을 취한다. 그들은 인간의 행동이 우리의 생물학적 유전에 의해 영향을 받는다는 것은 인정하지만, 대부분의 심리학자들은 인간의 행동에서 발생한 것이 각인된 것인지 혹은 진정한 본능인지에 대해 의구심을 가지고 있다.

① 많은 요소가 인간 행동에 영향을 끼친다.

② 자손을 퍼뜨리고자 하는 욕구는 후천적 행동이다.

③ 인간 행동을 탐구하는 것은 오늘날의 심리학자들에게 주요한 관심사는 아니다.

④ 인간 행동에 대한 사회 과학자들이 동의할 수 있는 하나의 이론이 있다.

해설   전문가들의 의견을 종합해 볼 때 본능, 욕구, 학습 등 여러 가지 요소가 인간 행동에 영향을 미쳤다는 결론을 내릴 수 있다.

어휘
instinct ⓝ 본능

inborn ⓐ 타고난

urge ⓝ 욕구

propagate ⓥ 널리 퍼뜨리다, 선전하다, 보급하다

transmission ⓝ 전달, 전송

kinship ⓝ 혈족 관계, 친척 관계

courtship ⓝ 구애, 구혼

imprinting ⓝ 각인

condescending ⓐ 겸손한, 공손한, 저자세의

01 What can be concluded from the passage?

As Israel marks its 60th birthday, its citizens would seem to have plenty to celebrate. Situated on a patch of stony land, democratic Israel has endured the ravages of war and terrorism and an assortment of enemies sworn to destroy it. But the mood in Israel today is more pensive than jubilant. Israelis worry about the threat of a nuclear attack from Iran. They worry that Hizballah will pepper them with more missiles launched from southern Lebanon. And they worry that Palestinian suicide bombers will once again explode in the buses and cafes of Tel Aviv and Jerusalem.

① Israel still lives in peril and without peace.
② Israel more resembles a mosaic than a real country.
③ For Israelis, religion is more important than national identity.
④ Israelis think they must give the Palestinians their own state.

02 What is the major assumption of the following passage?

Recently excavated artifacts from Pakistan have inspired a reevaluation of one of the great early urban cultures — the enigmatic Indus Valley civilization, one of the four great early Old World states — along with Mesopotamia, Egypt, and China's Yellow River civilization. Much less is known about the Indus civilization than about these other states because linguists have yet to decipher the Harappan script found on recovered objects. Attempting to understand these vanished people and their social structures, my colleagues and I have drawn clues from the miscellaneous objects we had uncovered and sites we had excavated. In this effort, the Harappan writings have not been totally useless; we have gleaned insights by examining the context of the writing's use.

① The spot within an excavated site where an object is found is a clue to its social significance.
② It is a great help in understanding a civilization to be able to decode its language.
③ There are similarities among the social structures of ancient urban civilizations.
④ An effective archaeologist should learn the language of the civilization being studied.

03 다음 우화가 시사하는 것으로 가장 알맞은 것은?

One winter a farmer found a snake stiff and frozen with cold. The snake said to the farmer; "If you pick me up and hold me to your stomach, your body will make me warm." The farmer said; "If I do that you will bite me." The snake answered: "Why would I do that if you save me?" The farmer had compassion on the snake, and taking it up, placed it in his bosom. The snake was quickly revived by the warmth, and resuming its natural instincts, bit its benefactor, inflicting on him a mortal wound. "Oh," cried the farmer, "Why did you bite me after I saved you?" "You knew I was a snake when you picked me up," answered the snake. With his last breath the farmer said: "I am rightly served for pitying a scoundrel."

① Some things are easier said than done.
② A wise man learns from the misfortunes of others.
③ The greatest kindness cannot change natural instincts.
④ Do not play tricks on others that you do not want to be played on you.

[01~02] 한국외대 2018

Invasive species are a scientific puzzle. Humans transport animals and plants thousands of miles from where they first evolved. Many of those species die off in their new homes. Some barely eke out an existence. But some become ecological nightmares, outcompeting natives. Scientists aren't certain why species like these are proving superior so far from home, and ask: (A) "If natives are adapted to their environment and exotics are from somewhere else, why are they able to invade?" Ecologists have observed that many alien species in the northeastern United States invaded from East Asia. But the opposite is not true. This is not a coincidence. It has to do with the habitats in which invasive species evolve. There is evidence that some parts of the world have been evolutionary incubators, producing superior competitors primed to thrive in other environments. Invasive plants are more likely to have evolved in habitats with a great diversity of competing species. These species continue to grow more diverse, to evolve, and eventually to become (B) _____ — ready to invade.

01 According to the passage, which of the following could be the answer to (A)?

① It depends on where the exotics evolved.
② It has to do with the natural enemies in the habitat.
③ Exotics tend to be mutations with superior genetic makeup.
④ Exotics fast evolve on the way to a new environment.

02 Which of the following best fits into (B)?

① extinct in no time
② evolutionary niches
③ superior competitors
④ too complicated to survive

"Paint me as I am." said Oliver Cromwell to the artist Lely. "If you leave out the scars and wrinkles, I will not pay you a shilling." Even in such a trifle, Cromwell showed good sense, he did not wish all that was characteristic in his countenance to be lost, in a vain attempt to give him regular features and smooth cheeks. He was content that his face should show all the blemishes put on it by time, by war, by sleepless night, by anxiety, perhaps by remorse; but with valor, policy, authority, and public care written on it as well. If great men knew what was in their best interests, it is thus that they would wish their minds to be portrayed.

03 The author views Cromwell's choice about the way in which he wanted to be painted with _____.

① disengagement
② cynicism
③ approval
④ distaste

04 The passage suggests that painters who conceal their subjects' blemishes and imperfections _____.

① are better paid than those who paint more realistically
② are doing their subjects no real favor
③ reveal their subjects' inner beauty
④ expose their own aesthetic preferences

While one purpose of folk tales may have been to entertain, that was not their only function. The reason they have survived for so long and are so (A) _____ in all human societies is that they educate their audiences. They seek to instill values that the society may consider imperative for its survival, such as a sense of right and wrong or the need for self-reliance. In addition to providing models for appropriate behavior, they give explanations, often derived from folklore, of the origin and meaning of the natural world.

Scholars have been struck by how frequently the same situations recur in folk tales from many different places. [1] Perhaps the same stories appeared spontaneously in many distant societies, or perhaps they were spread by travelers and adapted to fit the needs of their listeners. In addition to the same stories, the same themes are also found again and again. One of the commonest is the use of guile as a weapon of the helpless against the powerful. [2] There are no better examples of this than the *Uncle Remus* stories of Joel Chandler Harris, based on African-American folk tales of the American South.

One of the funniest of the *Uncle Remus* stories tells of Brer Rabbit, who falls into the clutches of Brer Fox. He begs his captor not to throw him into the brier patch, saying he would rather be hanged, drowned, or even skinned alive. [3] Brer Fox, being of a mean disposition, promptly does what his victim has begged him not to do. Brer Rabbit, of course, extricates himself with ease from the brier patch, mocking Brer Fox as he scampers away by calling out that he was "bred and born in a brier patch." [4]

05 Which of the following is most suitable for the blank (A)?

① contingent   ② nominal   ③ prevalent   ④ anonymous

06 Which is the most appropriate place for the sentence below?

> Over three hundred versions of the Cinderella story have been identified.

① [1]   ② [2]   ③ [3]   ④ [4]

07 The author uses the story of Brer Rabbit to exemplify _____.

① a recurrence of situations from folk tales of other cultures
② trickery as a theme to survive and outlast an opponent
③ how folk tales survived through entertainment
④ to show the origin of the natural world for African-Americans

08 According to the passage, which of the following is true?

① The theme of a folk tale is never repeated in any others.
② To entertain the audience is the primary purpose of folk tales.
③ Folk tales are useful to educate their audiences.
④ No folk tales try to provide moral guidelines.

[09~11]

Back in my early twenties I tried a diet that was limited to just a few healthy foods. Three weeks into it, I had nearly reached my goal of losing eight pounds. But my progress wasn't as sweet as I had expected. One night I abandoned the diet and gorged on every food I'd been missing. Over the next two weeks, I ate more than ever. No surprise that I quickly regained eight pounds, and put on two more. It sounds like the old diet-binge cycle that we've all heard about so often. My brazen act of indulgence was the direct effect of a boring, restrictive diet. "If you tell someone they cannot have, say, a piece of cheesecake, then that is the first thing they want to have," says Dr. Hubbert. And then when they eat that piece of cheesecake, they say, "Oh, now I've blown it, so I might as well blow it every day." At Tufts University in Boston, researchers studied 71 healthy men and women aged 20 to 80 years who provided detailed reports of everything they ate for six months. People who routinely ate a variety of nutrient-dense foods such as vegetables, fruits, and whole grains tended to be lean. The researchers found that when people eat a variety of desirable foods, especially vegetables, they eat fewer nutrient-poor, calorie-dense foods such as cookies, candy, and chips. Overall, they consume fewer calories without consciously restricting their intake.

09 Which of the following is the main topic of the passage?

① Importance of a restrictive diet
② Dangers of calorie-dense foods
③ Effects of long-term weight training
④ Advantages of long-term weight control
⑤ Importance of eating nutrient-dense foods

10 Which of the following are the researchers most likely to agree with?

① Exercise after eating.
② Go on a restrictive diet continually.
③ Eat lots of calorie-dense foods.
④ Resist the temptation of foods.
⑤ Eat a variety of nutrient-rich foods.

11 Which of the following best describes the organization of the passage?

① Several different opinions on a theory are presented.

② A problem is described, and possible solutions are discussed.

③ Two solutions for a problem are suggested and both are accepted.

④ A general idea is introduced, and several specific examples are given.

⑤ A recommendation is analyzed and rejected.

Most of us are aware that a positive attitude can improve health and speed recovery from illness, but does this also work the other way around? 'Embodied cognition' is a term used by psychologists to describe how the way we move affects the way we think and feel. An early study in this fascinating field demonstrated that holding a pencil horizontally between your teeth activates the same muscles used for smiling, thus sending pleasure signals to our brain, while people who have Botox injected to reduce laughter lines are less happy afterwards. If you've ever cried during a massage you will know that muscles are not simply an amalgamation of tissue and fibers. They contain delicate traces of our emotional lives and have the capacity to engender feelings without the executive influence of the mind. Our body can be _____ of feeling and a powerful co-creator of our emotional experience and there's research to prove it.

12 **Which of the following is most appropriate for the blank?**

① a mirror
② a master
③ a reservoir
④ an originator

13 **Which of the following is NOT a proper example for the main idea of the passage?**

① Open your arms when you feel timid.
② Recall happy memories when you feel bad.
③ Have a hot bath when you're feeling lonely.
④ Take a dance lesson when you need to be creative.

Another critical factor that plays a part in susceptibility to colds is age. Research done by the Indiana University School of Public Health revealed <u>particulars</u> that seem to hold true for the general population. Infants are the most cold-ridden group, averaging more than six colds in their first year. Boys have more colds than girls up to age three. After the age of three, girls are more susceptible than boys, and teenage girls average three colds a year to boys' two.

The general incidence of colds continues to decline into maturity. Elderly people who are in good health have as few as one or two colds annually. One exception is found among people in their twenties, especially women, who show a rise in cold infections, because people in this age group are most likely to have young children. Adults who delay having children until their thirties and forties experience the same sudden increase in cold infections.

The study also revealed that economics plays an important role. As income increases, the frequency at which colds are reported in the family decreases. Families with the lowest income suffer about a third more colds than families at the upper end. Lower income generally forces people to live in more <u>cramped</u> quarters than those typically occupied by wealthier people, and crowding increases the opportunities for the cold virus to travel from person to person. Low income may also adversely influence diet. The degree to which poor nutrition affects susceptibility to colds is not yet clearly established, but an inadequate diet is suspected of lowering resistance generally.

14 Which of the following is closest in meaning to the word 'particulars' in paragraph 1?

① Minor problems
② Specific facts
③ Small distinctions
④ Individuals

15 What does the author claim about the research discussed in the passage?

① It contains many inconsistencies.
② It specializes in children.
③ It contradicts the results of earlier research in the field.
④ Its results apparently are relevant for the population as a whole.

16 There is information in the second paragraph of the passage to support that _____.

① men are more susceptible to colds than women
② children infect their parents with colds
③ people who live in a cold climate have more colds than those who live in a warm one
④ people who don't have children are more susceptible to colds than those who do

17 The author's main purpose in writing the last paragraph of the passage was to _____.

① explain how cold viruses are transmitted
② prove that a poor diet causes colds
③ discuss the relationship between income and frequency of colds
④ discuss the distribution of income among the people in the study

18 The word 'cramped' is closest in meaning to _____.

① cheap   ② crowded
③ depressing   ④ simple

If you have ever made a list of pros and cons to help you make a decision, you have used the utilitarian method of moral reasoning. One of the main ethical theories, utilitarianism posits that the key to deciding what makes an act morally right or wrong is its consequence. Whether our intentions are good or bad is irrelevant; what matters is whether the result of our actions is good or bad. To utilitarians, happiness is the ultimate goal of human beings and the highest moral good. Thus, if there is great unhappiness because of an act, then that action can be said to be morally wrong. If, on the other hand, there is great happiness because of an act, then that act can be said to be morally right. Utilitarians believe that we should carefully weigh the potential consequences of an action before we take it. Will the act lead to things that will make us, or others, happy? Will it make us, or others, unhappy? According to utilitarians, we should choose to do that which creates the greatest amount of happiness for the greatest number of people. This can be difficult to determine, though, because sometimes an act can create short-term happiness but misery in the long term. Another problematic aspect of utilitarianism is that it deems it acceptable — indeed, even necessary — to use another person as a means to an end and sacrifice the happiness of one or a few for the happiness of many.

19 **According to the definition of utilitarianism in the passage, which of the following is true about "stealing bread to feed hungry children"?**

① It is morally right because it has good intentions.
② It is morally wrong because it violates other's rights.
③ It is morally right because it has positive consequences.
④ It is morally wrong because stealing is illegal.

20 Which of the following best describes the utilitarian principles according to the passage?

① We should always think of others first.
② We should make our intentions clear to others.
③ We should do what will make most people happy.
④ We should do what will bring us the most happiness.

21 What is the main idea of the passage?

① Sacrifice is necessary in life.
② Using utilitarianism to make a moral decision is not always easy.
③ Long-term consequences are more important than short-term consequences.
④ A pro/con list is the most effective technique for making an important decision.

[22~26]

Sir Nicholas Stern, a distinguished development economist and former chief economist at the World Bank, is not a man given to hyperbole. Yet he says, "Our actions over the coming few decades could create risks of major disruption to economic and social activity, later in this century and in the next, on a scale similar to those associated with the great wars and the economic depression of the first half of the 20th Century." His recently published "Stern Report" gives prescriptions for how to minimize this economic and social disruption. His central argument is that spending large sums of money now on measures to reduce carbon emissions will bring dividends on a colossal scale. However, he warns that we are too late to prevent any deleterious consequences from climate change (commonly known as "global warming"). He believes it is practical to aim for a stabilization of greenhouse gas levels in the atmosphere of 500 to 550 ppm (parts per million) by 2050 — which is double pre-industrial levels and compares with 430 ppm today. Even to stabilize at that level, every country's emissions per unit of gross domestic product would need to be cut by an average of three-quarters by 2050. The costs of these changes should be around 1% of global GDP by 2050. The way to look at this 1% is as an investment, because the costs of not taking this action are unimaginably large.

22 The underlined words given to hyperbole could be replaced without change of meaning by _____.

① fond of flattery
② inclined to mendacity
③ accustomed to exaggeration
④ liking ambiguity

23 The "Stern Report" says that the steady increase of greenhouse gases in the atmosphere must be _____.

① augmented
② stopped
③ contradicted
④ denied

24 One of the principal arguments in the "Stern Report" is that money spent on this issue now will later bring _____.

① imminent disaster   ② unacceptable debts

③ immense profits   ④ unforeseeable problems

25 The text tells you clearly that the level of greenhouse gases in the atmosphere today _____.

① is virtually the same as several centuries ago

② has become disastrously high

③ has already been stabilized

④ will continue to increase for some time whatever is done

26 The last sentence in the text suggests that _____.

① uncontrolled global warming will bring untold disaster

② carbon emissions cannot be restricted by any means

③ no one is prepared to accept this proposition

④ the cost of cutting carbon emissions is negligible

From Ben Franklin to Horatio Alger to Oprah Winfrey, American heroes seem always to be the self-made men or women who strode into the world all on their own. It's almost a source of shame to follow in a parent's footsteps. But, actually, it's a great idea to study the example of your ancestors, as revealed in the stories of how they spent their lives. You may find clues to what to do based on shared talents, dispositions, or interests. There may be a compelling reason beyond good connections why so many medical school students have a parent who's a doctor or why farmers or firefighters run in some families. But you may find signs that are just as strong about _____. If your mother despised sitting in an office all day, you might think twice about business school. On the other hand, if Uncle Louie wore out early as a construction worker, a desk job might not look too bad.

27 Which of the following is most likely to be suggested by the writer?

① To follow your parents' footsteps
② To think twice about your work
③ To pursue the lives of self-made men or women
④ To study how your ancestors spent their lives

28 Which of the following best fits in the blank?

① what not to do   ② what not to share
③ what you are good at   ④ what you want to do

"If it were totally up to me, I would raise the cigarette tax so high the revenues from it would go to zero," thundered Michael Bloomberg back in 2002. New York city' combative mayor has since raised cigarette taxes several times. The effect has been limited, so he wants to try something new. He recently proposed to outlaw discounting cigarettes and displaying them openly in stores. Whether these measures will be approved and help remains to be seen. But Mr Bloomberg may well be right to push for more bans. A new paper by Abel Brodeur of the Paris School of Economics, based on extensive surveys in America, suggests that bans on smoking are not just effective but actually make smokers happier. By not allowing them to light up in restaurants and bars, governments give weaker-willed individuals an excuse to do what they otherwise cannot: stop smoking. As an additional benefit, bans also seem to make spouses of smokers happier.

29 According to the passage, the mayor _____.

① has tried to tighten smoking laws
② is still skeptical of high cigarette taxes
③ has proposed the bill outlawing smoking on the street
④ has reversed his position on cigarette tax because of his political ambition
⑤ gave in to pressure from tobacco companies

30 Mr Brodeur's research suggests that _____.

① bans do not much to stop smoking
② bans may work as a way of discouraging smoking
③ American smokers do not mind the price rise of cigarettes
④ smokers are happier than non-smokers
⑤ the spouses of smokers believe that drinking is less harmful than smoking

편입 시험에서는 빈칸에 단어를 넣어 문장을 완성시키라는 문제가 많이 출제된다. 출제하기는 간단하지만 문제를 푸는 학생들의 입장에서는 어려운 문제이므로 자주 등장하는 문제 유형이다. 요즘은 난도를 높이기 위해 복수의 빈칸을 채우는 문제가 주류이다.

01 질문 유형

Which of the following is most appropriate for the blank?
Choose the one that is most appropriate for each blank.
Which of the following best fits the blank?
Which of the following best fits into (A) and (B)?

02 문제 풀이 전략

❶ 시험에 나올 만한 어휘들을 철저히 숙지한다.

보통 독해에서 빈칸을 완성시키기 위해 출제되는 단어들은 편입 어휘의 범위에 포섭되는 어휘들인 동시에, 단어를 위한 단어가 아닌 글 속에 살아 있는 어휘로 이루어져 있다. 그러므로 핵심적인 어휘 학습의 토대 위에서 빈칸을 채울 수 있다. 문제를 해결할 수 있을 만큼의 충분한 어휘력이 요구된다.

❷ 어휘를 모르겠으면 추측과 소거법을 이용한다.

어휘 형식의 문장 완성의 경우에는 글의 구조와 방향성을 따져서 들어갈 어구를 추측해 내야 한다. 그러므로 단서를 찾는 능력이 필요한데, 이것은 아무리 열심히 단서를 발견해 내더라도 보기의 어휘를 모르면 풀 수 없으므로 어휘가 문장 완성에서는 상당히 중요한 부분이다. 혹시 상황에 따라서는 앞뒤 관계를 추측해 봐도 적당하지 않다면 전혀 타당하지 않은 보기를 걸러 내는 소거법을 사용해 보도록 한다.

In the year 1665, when Newton was twenty-two, the plague broke out in southern England, and the University of Cambridge was closed. Newton therefore spent the next eighteen months at home, removed from traditional learning, at a time when he was impatient for knowledge. In an eager boyish mood, sitting one day in the garden of his widowed mother, he saw an apple fall. So far the books have the story right. But now they miss the _____ of the story. For what struck the young Newton at the sight was not the thought that the apple must be drawn to the earth by gravity; that conception was older than Newton. What struck him was the _____ that the same force of gravity, which reaches to the top of the tree, might go on reaching out beyond the earth and its air, endlessly into space. Gravity might reach the moon: this was Newton's new thought.

Q. 빈칸에 가장 적합한 단어 또는 어구를 고르시오.

① origin – hearsay
② moral – fallacy
③ rhetoric – dictum
④ crux – conjecture

기존의 내용들은 어느 정도까지는 맞지만 그 후 일화의 무언가를 놓치고 있다고 하면서, 그 일화의 중요 부분에 대한 설명이 따른다. 즉 여기에서는 '핵심'이나 '정수'를 뜻하는 단어가 와야 논리의 흐름이 이어진다.

뉴턴 사상의 핵심이라 할 수 있다. 기존의 사고 체계와는 다른 생각이었다. 처음에는 입증할 수 없었으므로 일종의 가설이나 추측이었어야 함을 알 수 있다.

정답   ④

해석   **빈칸에 가장 적합한 단어 또는 어구를 고르시오.**

뉴턴이 22세가 되던 1665년, 전염병이 영국 남부를 휩쓸었고 캠브리지대학은 휴교에 들어갔다. 뉴턴은 이후 18개월을 기존의 대학 교육을 받지 못한 채 집에서 보내게 된다. 이때 그는 지식에 매우 목말랐다. 그러던 어느 날, 배움에 열정적인 소년이었던 그는 미망인이 된 어머니의 정원에 앉아 있다가 사과가 떨어지는 것을 봤다. 여기까지는 책들이 전하는 일화가 맞다. 그러나 바로 여기서부터 책들은 이 일화의 핵심을 놓친다. 그 광경을 본 소년 뉴턴이 떠올린 것은 사과가 틀림없이 중력 때문에 땅에 떨어졌다는 생각이 아니기 때문이다. 그런 생각은 뉴턴 이전에 이미 알려져 있었다. 그 순간 그를 스친 것은 나무 꼭대기에 미치는 바로 그 중력이 지표면과 대기를 벗어나 우주 공간으로 끝없이 미칠지도 모른다는 추측이었다. 중력은 달까지 도달할 수도 있다. 이것이야말로 뉴턴의 새로운 생각이었다.

① 기원 – 전해 들은 말   ② 도덕 – 오류   ③ 수사 – 격언   ④ 핵심 – 추측

지문의 주제는 뉴턴의 사과 일화에서 발견할 수 있는 핵심, 즉 중력의 법칙이 지구뿐 아니라 우주에까지 적용될 수 있다는 아이디어이다. 빈칸 ①에는 핵심, 요즘을 뜻하는 "crux"가, 빈칸 ②에는 추측을 뜻하는 "conjecture"가 적절하다.

어휘   **plague** ⓝ 전염병   **break out** 발발하다

be removed from ～을 박탈당하다   **be impatient for** ～을 초조하게 기다리다

eager ⓐ 열정적인   **widowed** ⓐ 미망인이 된

miss ⓥ 놓치다   **crux** ⓝ 요점, 가장 중요한[곤란한] 부분

strike ⓥ (생각 등이) 떠오르다   **sight** ⓝ 광경

gravity ⓝ 중력   **conception** ⓝ 개념

conjecture ⓝ 추측   **reach** ⓥ 도달하다

go on 계속하다   **space** ⓝ 우주, 공간

thought ⓝ 생각, 사고

빈칸 추론 문제 해결의 원리

01 문장 완성 단서의 발견

문장 완성은 어휘와 독해의 중간 영역으로 볼 수 있다. 즉 기초적인 문법과 구문의 기반하에 어휘와 논리를 바탕으로 분석하고 추리하는 능력을 필요로 하는 문제이다. 그러므로 단서를 찾는 능력이 필요하지만, 아무리 열심히 단서를 발견해 내더라도 보기의 어휘를 모르면 풀 수 없으므로 어휘의 숙지 여부가 문장 완성에서는 상당히 중요한 부분이다. 그러므로 어휘를 충분히 학습한 후라는 전제에서 어떤 식으로 문장 완성 문제를 접근하여야 하는지를 살펴보기로 한다.

단서를 발견하는 것에 관해서 보면, 글의 방향성을 따져 보아야 한다. 글의 전개가 순차적 흐름이거나 인과 관계와 같은 한 방향의 글의 흐름인지 아니면 역접이나 대조를 사용해서 다른 방향으로 글이 진행되는지를 검토해 보고 이에 알맞은 어휘를 선택하면 된다. 이러한 단서를 찾기 위해서는 접속사나 전치사 등의 활용을 이해하는 것이 중요하다. 더불어 글의 흐름으로 나올만한 내용을 예측하면서 문장을 살펴보는 추론의 기술이 필요하기도 하다. 문장 완성에서는 정답 이외에는 제거할 만한 충분한 이유가 있는 경우가 대부분이지만, 미묘한 차이로 오답이 되는 경우도 종종 있기 때문에 성급하게 전체 보기를 다 읽지도 않고 답을 선택하는 우(愚)를 범해서는 안 된다.

문장 완성에서는 글의 방향성을 파악하여 논리적인 연관성을 따져 보는 훈련이 중요하다. 그러기 위해서는 담화의 표지(Discourse markers)를 알아두는 것이 중요하다. 아래에서는 방향성과 함께 담화의 표지를 살펴보고, 방향성이 두드러지지 않은 경우의 해결 원리 등에 대해 검토해 보기로 한다. 여기서 제기한 것은 전반적인 틀에 해당하며 이 이외에도 다른 단서나 지표가 있을 수 있지만, 글이란 일정한 방향성이 있기 때문에 대략 다음과 같은 틀을 알고 있으면 충분히 응용이 가능할 것이다. 그러므로 아래에 나오는 표지를 정확히 숙지하는 활용하는 연습을 충분히 하기 바란다.

다만 주의할 것은 하나의 단락에서도, 심지어 문장에서도 단 하나의 지표만 있는 것은 아니고 여러 가지 사항들이 존재할 수 있다. 그렇지만 논리의 유형을 학습하기 위하여 하나의 틀에 묶은 것이고, 여러 가지에 포섭될 수 있는 경우도 존재한다. 예를 들어서 하나의 연구 과정을 나타내는 경우는 인과 관계로도, 시간적 구성으로도 볼 수 있고, 이전의 성과를 반박한다면 반박이나 일축으로, 연구의 결과를 드러낸다면 결론으로 볼 여지가 있는 것이다. 그러므로 어느 하나의 담화표지만으로 글을 파악하는 것이 아니라, 글은 글 자체로 판단하되 문제를 푸는 단서에서 여러 가지 지표를 활용하면 좀 더 유리하다는 뜻으로 이해하면 된다.

02 순방향으로의 진행

전환어구를 중심으로 문장완성의 원리를 파악하는 것이 가장 보편적인 해법이다. 글이 한 방향으로 진행된다는 것은 글의 논리적인 흐름상 역전되거나 반대되는 이야기가 나오는 것이 아니라 무리 없는 순차적인 흐름의 글이 이어진다는 것이다. 앞에 추상적인 진술이 나오고, 이에 대해 구체적인 진술이 나오는 경우와 같이 글의 흐름이 무리 없이 순차적으로 진행되는 경우를 뜻하며, 시험에서도 출제 빈도가 높은 유형이다. 여기에 해당하는 부분은 상당히 많으며, 이해의 편의를 위하여 8가지 유형으로 나누어서 살펴보겠지만, 더 큰 틀로 나눈다면 아래와 같이 네 개로 묶을 수 있다.

먼저 개념을 바탕으로 하는 경우이다. 정의와 동격은 개념을 바탕으로 글을 전개하고 이어가는 방식이며, 예시와 부연은 추상적이거나 복잡한 내용을 예를 들거나 다시 한번 설명해서 독자의 이해를 돕는 측면이다.

원인과 결과는 인과 관계를 이루고 있으며, 시간적인 측면과도 관련이 된다. 여기에 이유를 넣어서 설명하기도 한다. 시간적 구성이나 과정을 나타내는 표현들 역시 인과 관계와 어느 정도의 연관성을 띠고 있다. 시간과 조건 역시 인과적 구성을 띠고 있으며, 순차적 구성이므로 한 방향의 진행으로 볼 수 있다. 목적과 수단이란 문장이 달성하고자 하는 바를 위하여 어떠한 목적을 어떠한 수단을 통하여 달성하고자 하는지를 제시하는 것이다.

비교와 유사는 유사점을 바탕으로 비교하여 이해를 도모하는 경우이다. 물론 대조를 넣어서 비교는 유사함을, 대조는 차이점을 바탕으로 글을 이끌어 가지만, 여기에서는 편의상 비교는 순방향에서, 대조는 역방향에서 다루기로 한다. 편의상 이렇게 나누지만, 일반적으로 글 속에서는 양자의 관계가 설정되기 때문에 비교와 대조가 혼재되어 나오는 경우가 많다.

병렬과 상관관계의 표현은 양자나 혹은 이상의 사이에서의 관계 설정이다. 글은 자신이 드러내고자 하는 바가 있으며, 그 부분이 여럿이라면 병렬적 구성을, 추가 역시 병렬과 같은 측면을 지닌다. 반면에 둘을 대비하여 어느 쪽을 두드러지게 부각시키려면 상관관계의 표현을 이용할 수 있다. 결론이나 강조의 경우도 역시 글 속에서 어느 부분을 부각시키는 면이 있으며, 핵심적인 부분이 결론적으로 제시되거나 강조를 통해서 나타날 수 있다.

03 역방향으로의 진행

글의 흐름이 전환되거나, 앞의 진술과 다르게 진행되는 경우이다. 글의 전환어구를 중심으로 전개되는 내용이 앞과 뒤의 흐름이 전환되는 것을 파악할 수 있다. 크게 네 부분으로 나눠서 살펴보면, 대조나 반대와 같이 글의 흐름으로 역전되는 현상도 그러하며, 하나의 사실을 인정하면서 다른 사실을 제시하는 양보의 경우 역시 다른 방향의 진행으로 볼 수 있다. 더불어 반박이나 일축, 부정과 대체의 경우도 역방향에 함께 넣어서 판단할 수 있다.

우선 대조나 반대의 표현들은 글 속에서 전환어구를 사용하여 이미 진행되어 오던 글의 흐름과 대비되거나 반대되는 흐름으로 진행하는 경우이다. 글에 적당한 전환어구를 두어 단서를 주기 때문에, 이를 중심으로 판단하여 빈칸에 들어갈 적합한 것을 고르면 된다.

양보의 경우는 양보, 용인 등으로 나타낼 수 있는데, 일부의 사실을 인정하면서 새로운 사실을 제시하는 경우이다. 일부의 사실을 부정하지 않는 데서 '부정' 표현과는 다르고, 동등하게 양측을 인정하지는 않는다는 점에서 '병렬'과는 차이가 있다. 문장의 무게중심이 양보의 전환어구가 아닌 주절에 실린다는 점을 염두에 두고 있어야 한다.

반박이나 반론을 제기하는 경우, 어떤 주장을 묵살하거나 일축해 버리는 경우 등도 역시 역방향으로의 진행으로 볼 수 있다. 이러한 관련 지표가 나오는 경우는 상대방의 주장을 무시하면서 결국 자신의 이야기, 앞으로 진행될 이야기에 귀를 기울이라는 신호이기 때문이다.

마지막으로 부정 표현이나 대체 표현이 있는데, 결국 이러한 표현의 핵심은 하나를 부정하거나, 대체해서 원하는 다른 하나에 초점을 맞추게 되는 것이다. 영어에서는 양자 간의 관계 설정에 대한 표현들이 상당수 존재하는데, 그런 경우에 부정과 대체는 역방향의 진행으로 볼 수 있다.

04 방향성 이외의 단서

앞서 언급한 글의 방향성으로 문장 완성을 해결하는 방식 이외의 문제가 많이 출제된다. 그 이유는 편입시험의 문장 완성 문제들이 단지 논리력만을 묻는 것이 아니라 독해력도 또한 묻고자 하기 때문이다. 그러므로 방향성 이외의 단서를 파악해 보는 연습이 필요하다. 여기에서는 크게 문법적인 부분, 어휘(표현 포함)적인 부분, 그리고 문맥을 활용하여 푸는 방식으로 구별하였다.

먼저 문법 지식을 필요로 하는 부분은 문장부호(구두점)와 문법을 활용한 문제들이다. 일반적으로 구두점은 그 하나하나가 자신의 독특한 기능을 수행하므로 이를 충분히 숙지한다면, 구두점을 단서로 부연이나 인과적인 흐름을 판단하여 단서로 사용할 수 있다. 문법의 경우에도 관계대명사를 이용한 부연, 분사구문을 이용한 인과 관계, 비교를 이용하여 문제를 해결해 갈 수 있다.

두 번째로 어휘와 관련되는 부분을 들 수 있다. 시험에서는 단순한 단어, 숙어, 관용어의 의미를 묻는 지식적 측면과 이러한 것들을 글을 활용하여 유추해 낼 수 있는지를 묻는 유추 문제로 크게 나눌 수 있다. 지식적인 측면은 암기가 동반되지 않으면 풀 수 없도록 짧은 문장으로 구성되어 있으면서 별도의 단서가 없거나 아주 약하다. 반면에 유추 능력을 묻는 문제들은 문장 뒤에 뒷받침하는 문장이 존재하거나, 물어보고자 하는 어휘나 표현의 paraphrase된 형태가 제시되기도 한다. 그러므로 지식적인 측면을 위해서 어휘 등도 열심히 외우고, 유추 능력을 위해서 글을 이해하고 논리적인 사고력도 충분히 갖춰 나가야 한다.

마지막으로 문맥을 이용해서 푸는 경우이다. 요즘은 논리 문제의 지문도 길어지고, 여러 문장으로 구성되는 문제들이 많아지면서 더욱 중요성이 커지는 부분이다. 글의 흐름에 따라 유추하면서 나올 내용에 대해 예측하면서 찾아가야 한다. 글의 앞뒤 흐름에 유의하면서 논리적인 판단을 해 나가야 하지만, 상황에 따라서 단서가 약한 경우는 보기 중 오답의 확률이 높은 것부터 소개해 나가야 한다. 즉 글의 일부를 발췌해서 출제하는 경우 그 단락만의 완결성이 떨어지는 경우가 있기 때문에, 문맥을 파악하면서 풀어가는 경우는 상황에 따라 답이 확정적이라기보다 소거에 의해 고르는 경우가 존재할 수 있다.

01 Which of the following is most appropriate for the blank?

As the nonstop TV commercials have made clear, the U.S. Census Bureau really hopes you've sent back your questionnaire by now. But in reality, we don't have to wait for the census results to get a basic picture of America's demographic future. The operative word is "more": by 2050, about 100 million more people will inhabit this vast country, bringing the total U.S. population to more than 400 million. With a fertility rate 50 percent higher than Russia, Germany, or Japan, and well above that of China, Italy, Singapore, South Korea, and virtually all of Eastern Europe, the United States has become a(n) _____ among its traditional competitors, all of whose populations are stagnant and seem destined to eventually decline.

① aging society　　　　　　　　② global adviser
③ outlier　　　　　　　　　　　④ failure

02 Which of the following is most appropriate for the blank (A)? 가천대 2020

Piazza di Spagna in Rome has long been a place for young Italians to meet and rest. It also provided the romantic setting for the classic Audrey Hepburn and Gregory Peck film "Roman Holiday." In contrast, the Bebelplatz in central Berlin embraces the wounds of history. In 1933, the Nazi burned more than 20,000 books there that had been (A) _____ under the regime. German poet Heinrich Heine wrote in the memorial engraving at the square: "Where they burn books, they ultimately burn people."

① propagated　　　　　　　　② sanctified
③ banned　　　　　　　　　　④ alloyed

03 Choose the one that is most appropriate for each blank.

The expansion of our digital universe — Second Life, Facebook, MySpace, Twitter — has shifted not only how we spend our time but also how we construct identity. For her coming book, "Alone Together," Sherry Turkle, a professor at M.I.T., interviewed more than 400 children and parents about their use of social media and cellphones. Among young people especially she found that the self was increasingly becoming _____ manufactured rather than _____ developed: a series of profiles to be sculptured and refined in response to public opinion. "On Twitter or Facebook you're trying to express something real about who you are," she explained. "But because you're also creating something for others' consumption, you find yourself imagining and playing to your audience more and more. So those moments in which you're supposed to be showing your true self become a performance. Your psychology becomes a performance."

① negatively — positively
② positively — negatively
③ internally — externally
④ externally — internally

[01~02] 가천대 2018

There is no completely clean vehicle. An American automobile magazine featured a confession from a former Volkswagen executive that a clean diesel engine at a reasonable price was an unrealistic goal. When there is no fuel-powered vehicle that Ⓐ _____ the environment, the company fabricated that it could be overcome by technology to mitigate the guilt of pollution, and consumers and the carmakers spread the myth of a clean car. Perhaps, we had reasonable doubts that clean diesel didn't make sense. But we may have turned a(n) Ⓑ _____ eye to drive a powerful, efficient and brand-name German car and claim to be environmentally friendly at the same time. As we condemn Volkswagen's dishonesty, we also need to reflect on our consumer awareness.

01 which of the following is most appropriate for the blank Ⓐ?

① abuses
② benefits
③ contaminates
④ cultivates

02 which of the following is most appropriate for the blank Ⓑ?

① blind
② keen
③ impartial
④ penetrating

Although it's been a long time, I vividly recall my reaction when I learned that I had been admitted to Amherst College: the admissions office must have made a terrible mistake. I had graduated from a Long Island high school where most students didn't go to college, so I was convinced that at Amherst I would be overmatched by my better-educated, more sophisticated classmates and sliced to ribbons by my brilliant professors. To my surprise, I fared well academically, but I never entirely got over the feeling of <u>being an impostor</u>. Only decades later, at a class reunion, did I discover that many of my peers had felt exactly the same way.

Regardless of their credentials, many freshmen doubt that they have the necessary brainpower or social adeptness to succeed in college. This fear of failing hits poor, minority and first-generation college students especially hard. If they flunk an exam, or a professor doesn't call on them, their fears about whether they belong may well be confirmed. The cycle of doubt becomes self-reinforcing, and students are more likely to _____.

03 What does the underlined <u>being an impostor</u> imply?
① Receiving terrible grades
② Setting an unrealistic goal
③ Being admitted due to luck
④ Having disadvantaged backgrounds

04 Which of the following best fits in the blank?
① drop out
② reach out for help
③ feel privileged
④ challenge their professors

A stubborn old lady was walking down the middle of a street to the great confusion of the traffic and with no small danger to herself. It was pointed out to her that the sidewalk was the place for pedestrians, but she replied: "I'm going to walk where I like. We've got liberty." It did not occur to the old lady that if liberty entitled the pedestrian to walk down the middle of the road, then the end of such liberty would be universal chaos. There is a danger of the world getting liberty-drunk these days like the old lady, and it is just as well to remind ourselves of what the rules of the road mean. They mean that in order for the liberties of all to be preserved, the liberties of everybody must be (A) _____. When a policeman at a busy intersection steps into the middle of the road and puts out his hand, he is the symbol not of tyranny, but of liberty. You may, being in a hurry, feel that your liberty has been outraged. Then, if you are a reasonable person, you will reflect that if he did not interfere with you, he would interfere with no one, and the result would be a frenzied intersection you could never cross at all. You have submitted to a (B) _____ of private liberty in order to enjoy a social order which makes your liberty a reality.

05 Which of the following is the main theme of the passage?

① The world is too liberty-drunk these days.
② Individual liberty always leads to social chaos.
③ Policemen are necessary for unreasonable drivers.
④ You should compromise private liberty for social order.

06 Which of the following ordered pairs best fits into (A) and (B)?

① denied – denial
② allotted – allotment
③ secured – security
④ curtailed – curtailment

We know that Darwin's uniqueness does not reside in his support for the idea of evolution — scores of scientists had preceded him in this. His special ㉮ _____ rests upon his documentation and upon the novel character of his theory about how evolution operates. Previous evolutionist had proposed unworkable schemes based on internal perfecting tendencies and inherent directions. Darwin advocated a natural and testable theory based on immediate interaction among individuals. The theory of natural selection is a creative ㉯ _____ to biology of Adam Smith's basic argument for a rational economy: the balance and order of nature does not arise from a higher, external (divine) control, or from the existence of laws operating directly upon the whole, but from struggle among individuals for their own benefits.

07 빈칸 ㉮에 들어갈 가장 알맞은 것은?

① charity
③ donation

② contrivance
④ contribution

08 빈칸 ㉯에 들어갈 가장 알맞은 것은?

① transfer
③ transaction

② movement
④ alteration

09 윗글의 다윈에 대한 설명으로 가장 알맞은 것은?

① His theory of immediate interaction among individuals is unworkable and untestable.
② He is very unique and creative in his idea of evolution.
③ His theory of natural selection is formulated by analogy with Adam Smith's rational economy.
④ He thought the order of nature did arise from the existence of laws operating directly upon the whole.

The impact of human pollutants on nature can be vastly amplified by food chains, the serial process by which weak creatures are typically eaten by stronger ones in ascending order. The most closely studied example is the effect of pesticides, which have sharply improved farm crops but also caused (A) spectacular kills of fish and wildlife. In the Canadian province of New Brunswick, for example, the application of only one-half pound of DDT per acre of forest to control the spruce budworm has twice (B) _____ almost an entire year's production of young salmon in the Miramichi River. In this process, rain washes the DDT off the ground and into the plankton of lakes and streams. Fish eat the DDT-tainted plankton; the pesticide becomes (C) _____ in their bodies, and the original dose ultimately reaches multifold strength in fish-eating birds, which then often die or stop reproducing.

10 Which word is the closest in meaning to (A)?

① trenchant ② concomitant
③ pliable ④ conspicuous

11 Which word is not suitable in (B)?

① annihilated ② eradicated
③ disclaimed ④ obliterated

12 Which of the following best fits (C)?

① insuperable ② concentrated
③ widened ④ turbid

Whereas the scientific and technical nature of decision-making and a focus on security oriented and medical responses imply a narrowing of the potential for political-democratic contestation, the growing role of the EU (and wider transnationalisation) increases the distance between governance and the governed. In short, the democratic legitimacy and accountability of decision-making in public health clearly seems a lot more difficult, particularly in terms of _____. What makes this even more problematic is that it is happening at a time when scientific and technical knowledge and expertise in this context and others remain dominant even as uncertainty and non-knowing about the scale and nature of risk mean that they are increasingly undermined. Despite being key addressees of public health regulation, and being implicated in its implementation, the role of the EU's citizenry or indeed those who are not formally speaking citizens but are nevertheless affected by EU governance is rather opaque.

13 빈칸에 들어갈 가장 적절한 것은?

① political legislation
② citizen participation in governing
③ security issues in EU governance
④ the transnational dimension of the EU
⑤ the legitimation of centralized governance

14 윗글의 내용과 가장 거리가 먼 것은?

① Public health has key implications for democracy.
② It is unclear how citizens are animated by and through governance.
③ The EU's regulatory power sharpens the political sensitivity of the public.
④ It is not easy to relate public health interventions to the EU's citizenry.
⑤ The knowledge citizens have is hardly implicated in shaping boundaries of governance.

A misuse of statistics occurs when a statistical argument asserts a falsehood. In the period since statistics began to play a significant role in society, they have often been misused. In some cases, the misuse was accidental. In others, it was purposeful and for the gain of the perpetrator. When the statistical reason involved is false or misapplied, this constitutes a statistical fallacy. The false statistics trap can be quite damaging to the quest for knowledge. For example, in medical science, correcting a falsehood may (A) _____ decades and (B) _____ lives. Misuses can be easy to fall into. Professional scientists, even mathematicians and professional statisticians, can be fooled by even some simple methods, even if they are careful to check everything.

15 **Identify the (A) − (B) pair of the words to fill in the blanks above.**

① bring − take   ② give − take

③ take − cost   ④ make − do

⑤ cost − make

16 **Which title does best describe the passage above?**

① Purpose of the Misuse of Statistics

② Beginning of Statistical Fallacy

③ Temptation of the Misuse of Statistics

④ Knowledge of Statistical Argument

⑤ Danger of the Misuse of Statistics

The dead were believed to have great power over daily events. Unhappy ancestors could cause illness or disaster among the living, and many oracle bones refer to human sacrifices meant to _____ these spirits. At one complex of tombs in Henan Province, excavations have uncovered more than 1,200 sacrificial pits, most of which contain human victims. An archaeologist once told me that he had counted 60 different ways a person could be killed during a Shang ceremony. But he also reminded me that they were rituals, not murder and mayhem. From the Shang perspective, human sacrifice was simply part of a remarkably well organized system. The Shang kept a strict calendar, with certain sacrificial days devoted to certain ancestors. They were meticulous almost to the point of scientific inquiry. In one instance, a diviner patiently made 70 individual oracle-bone cracks in order to determine which ancestor was responsible for a living king's toothache.

17 **Which is most appropriate for the blank?**

① feed
③ worship
⑤ appease

② protect
④ stir

18 **According to the passage, it was believed that** _____.

① afterlife is more important than the present one
② people's current lives were up to their ancestors
③ death could bring people happiness
④ people could live forever
⑤ ancestors were always there to help us

Evolutionary biology has always been controversial. This is largely because Darwin's theory directly contradicted the supernatural accounts of human origins rooted in religious tradition and replaced them with fully natural ones. The philosopher Daniel Dennett has described evolution as a sort of "universal acid" that "eats through just about every traditional concept, and leaves in its wake a revolutionized world-view, with most of the old landmarks still recognizable, but transformed in fundamental ways." Fearing this _____ idea, opposition in the U.S. to evolution mainly came from Right-wing evangelical Christians who believed God created life in its present form, as described in Genesis.

19 내용상 빈칸에 들어가기에 가장 적절한 것은?

① corrosive   ② constructivist

③ collaborative   ④ contemporary

⑤ contemptuous

20 윗글의 내용과 가장 잘 부합하는 것은?

① Christians in the U.S. no longer believe that Darwin is right.

② Darwin was praised by Right-wing evangelists for some time.

③ Dennett accounted for the origin of human beings via chemistry.

④ Darwin's theory turned out to support the supernatural accounts of human origins.

⑤ According to Dennett, "universal acid" transforms old concepts to a completely new world-view.

The notion that geniuses such as Shakespeare, Mozart, and Picasso were "gifted" or possessed innate talents is a (A) _____, according to a study by a British psychologist. After examining outstanding performances in the arts and sports, Professor Michael Howe and colleagues at Exeter University concluded that excellence is determined by opportunities, encouragement, training, motivation, self-confidence, and — most of all — practice. The theory — a radical (B) _____ with traditional beliefs — has been applauded by academics worldwide. It has significant implications for teachers and parents, not least because children who are not thought to be gifted are being denied the encouragement they need to succeed. The authors took as their starting point the "widespread belief that to reach high levels of ability a person must possess an innate potential called talent." They said it was important to establish whether the belief was correct because it had social and educational consequences affecting selection procedures and training. However, studies of accomplished artists and mathematicians, top tennis players and swimmers reported few early signs of promise prior to parental encouragement. No case was found of anyone reaching the highest levels of achievement without devoting thousands of hours to serious training. Even those who were believed to be exceptionally talented — whether in music, mathematics, chess, or sports — required lengthy periods of instruction and practice.

21 **Which of the following is the best title for the passage?**

① Parents Make Genius
② Genius Needs Talent
③ Practice Produces Genius
④ Motivation Promises Genius

22 **Which of the following pairs is most appropriate for the blanks (A) and (B)?**

① myth – break
② truth – principle
③ conception – confirmation
④ presumption – proof

23 Which of the following is NOT true according to the passage?

① Prof. Howe suggested several factors accounting for excellent performances in the arts and sports.

② Many scholars around the world welcomed the pedagogical implications that Howe's theory brought.

③ Howe's theory emphasizes the importance of parental encouragement in raising children.

④ There were many exceptionally talented people who did not need instruction and practice.

The average Swiss watch costs $685. A Chinese one costs around $2 and tells the time just as well. So how on earth can the Swiss watch industry survive? Exports of watches made in Switzerland have grown by 32% by value over the past two years. Demand in the biggest markets (China, America and Singapore) dipped recently, but some of the Ⓐ slack was picked up by watch-loving Arabs and Europeans. No one buys a Swiss watch to find out what time it is. The allure is ⓐ _____: precise engineering, beautifully displayed. The art of fine watchmaking has all but died out elsewhere, but it thrives in Switzerland. "Swiss-made" has become one of the world's most valuable brands. Recently, the Swiss government seems about to ⓑ _____ the definition of "Swiss-made". Currently, a watch may not claim to be Swiss unless 50% of its components, by value, were crafted in the cantons. Swiss watchmakers are trying to get the threshold raised to 60%.

24 Which is closest in meaning to the underlined Ⓐ slack?

① boom
② recess
③ supply
④ demand

25 Which best fits into the blank ⓐ?

① intangible
② improbable
③ inexorable
④ insufferable

26 Which best fits into the blank ⓑ?

① clarify
② tighten
③ stipulate
④ proclaim

Girls generally speak sooner, learn to read faster and have fewer learning disorders. The reason, according to Yale University professors of neurology, may be that they use neural regions on both sides of brain when they read or engage in other verbal exercise. In contrast, males draw only on neural regions in the left hemisphere.

This approach may give women an advantage by allowing them to draw on the emotions and experiences of the right brain as well as the reasoning powers of the logical left brain. As adults, women tend to be more verbally _____ than men: in timed tests, women think of more words that start with the same letter, list more synonyms and come up with names for colors or shapes more quickly than men. Women even memorize letters of the alphabet faster.

But female brain's dual-hemisphere language processing provides far more significant benefit: It helps women who suffer stroke or brain injury recover more easily. "Because women activate a larger number of neurons than men when they speak or read, they're less vulnerable if part of the brain is damaged," says a neurologist. "In medicine, we've observed that women who have strokes tend to regain more of their verbal abilities than men do, and their use of neurons in both hemispheres may be why."

27 윗글의 빈칸에 들어갈 말로 가장 적절한 것은?

① normal   ② concise   ③ sluggish
④ adept   ⑤ instructive

28 윗글의 내용과 일치하지 <u>않는</u> 것은?

① 언어 활동을 할 때 여성들은 뇌의 양 측면을 사용한다.
② 여성들은 남성들보다 알파벳 글자들을 더 빨리 암기한다.
③ 여자아이들은 남자아이들보다 일반적으로 더 일찍 말을 시작한다.
④ 남성들은 말할 때 여성들보다 더 많은 수의 뉴런이 활성화된다.
⑤ 여성들은 뇌가 손상되더라도 남성들보다 회복이 용이하다.

When people feel truly heard, they are more likely to return that favour by thinking highly of you, entertaining your points of view and cooperating with you. However, active listening requires effort. First of all, you have to stay in the moment, focusing fully on what the speaker is saying, both verbally and physically. If your mind wanders, ⓐ _____ as soon as you notice. Most importantly, don't assume you know where the other person is going: be open to hearing something you may not have expected. Next, you should demonstrate to the speaker that you're listening. You can do this by making eye contact, nodding, inserting short acknowledgements such as 'Uh-huh' or 'Yeah', paraphrasing their comments or asking questions. It's true that some of these signals can be fudged, but watch out: many speakers can sense the difference between an active listener and a ⓑ _____ listener.

03

29 **Which best fits in the blank ⓐ?**

① own up
③ snap back

② get away
④ come forward

30 **Which best fits in the blank ⓑ?**

① phony
③ positive

② prudent
④ penitent

08 독해형 논리

독해 형식의 논리 문제란 본문 속에서 빈칸을 구, 절, 혹은 문장의 형태로 채우라는 문제이다. 과거에 비해 편입 시험에서 단순한 어휘만이 아니라 이러한 문장 단위의 빈칸을 채우라는 문제가 늘고 있다. 이런 문제는 글의 흐름을 이해해야 풀 수 있으며, 글 전체 맥락을 유의해서 읽어야 한다.

01 질문 유형

Which of the following is most appropriate for the blank?

Choose the one that is most appropriate for each blank.

Which of the following best fits the blank?

Which of the following best fits into ***?

02 문제 풀이 전략

❶ 글을 천천히 읽으면서 빠진 부분을 추측해 본다.

글의 정상적인 흐름에서 일부 표현을 빼놓고 채워 넣으라는 문제이므로, 빈칸 없이는 흐름이 어색하기가 쉽다. 분명히 빈칸 전후에 단서가 존재하며 그 부분을 꼼꼼히 읽어 보는 게 좋다. 더불어 유사한 보기가 있으면 그 보기와 본문 사이에 필연적인 연관이 있는가를 따져 보아야 한다.

❷ 빈칸의 위치에 따라 전략이 다르다.

독해 형식의 문장 완성에서 글의 마지막에 나오는 경우에는 글의 흐름대로 읽어 보면 들어갈 어구를 찾기가 어렵지 않은 데 비해서, 글의 처음에 빈칸이 나오는 경우에는 글의 주제나 요지 등 전개해 나가고자 하는 바를 미리 피력한 것인지 살펴보아야 한다. 즉 작가가 글을 전개하는 방식으로 도대체 어떤 사실을 말하고 이에 대해서 풀어 간 것인지를 역으로 추적하는 과정이 필요하다.

Less than 10 percent of U.S. high school students are eating the combined recommended daily amount of fruits and vegetables, according to a report by the U.S. Centers for Disease Control and Prevention (CDC). The report based on 2007 data found that only 13 percent of U.S. high school students get at least three servings of vegetables a day and just 32 percent get two servings of fruit. Less than 1 in 10 get enough of both combined.

The CDC said the report was the first to give such detailed information on adolescents' fruit and vegetable consumption. The information comes from a national survey of about 100,000 high school students in 2007. CDC officials said the findings indicate a disheartening gap between _____ and what they're actually doing in an era of rampant obesity. Federal nutrition goals for 2010 call for at least 75 percent of Americans to eat two servings of fruit each day and at least 50 percent to eat three vegetable servings.

Q. Which of the following is most appropriate for the blank?

① how students behave themselves
② what market surveys reveal
③ how people should be eating
④ what adolescents believe

권장량만큼 과일과 야채를 섭취하는 학생들이 별로 없다는 것이 바로 what they're actually doing을 뜻한다.

_____와 실제 하고 있는 일 사이에 낙담시킨 만큼의 격차가 있다고 하였다. 그렇다면 이런 차이를 판단하기 위해서 what they're actually doing이 무엇을 뜻하는지를 판단해야 한다.

그러므로 앞으로 나가야 할 방향과 실제로 벌어지는 현실 사이에는 격차가 있다는 것을 밝혀 주어야 글의 흐름이 올바르게 이어질 수 있다.

03

정답 ③

해석 **다음 중 빈칸에 가장 알맞은 것은 무엇인가?**

미국 질병 통제 예방 센터(CDC)의 한 보고서에 따르면 미국 고등학생 중 야채와 과일을 다 합해 1일 권장량 만큼 먹는 수는 10%도 안 된다고 한다. 이 보고서는 2007년도의 데이터에 기반을 두고 있는데, 여기에 따르면 하루에 야채를 최소 세 번 섭취하는 미국 고등학생은 13%에 불과했고 과일을 두 번 먹는 고등학생은 32% 밖에 없었다. 야채와 과일을 다 합해 충분히 먹는 고등학생은 열 명 중 하나뿐이었다.

CDC는 이 보고서가 청소년들의 과일 및 야채 섭취에 관해 매우 자세한 정보를 제공해 준다고 말했다. 이 정보는 2007년 10만 명가량의 고등학생을 대상으로 실시된 전국 단위 조사에서 나온 것이다. CDC 직원들은 이 결과는 지금같이 걷잡을 수 없이 비만이 확산되는 시기에 사람들은 음식을 어떻게 먹어야 할지와 실제 사람들이 하고 있는 행동 간에 낙담시킬 만큼의 격차가 벌어졌음을 나타낸다고 말했다. 2010년의 연방 정부의 영양 목표는 최소 75%의 미국인들이 매일 과일을 두 번을 먹어야 하고 50%의 미국인들이 야채를 세 번을 먹어야 할 것을 요구한다.

① 학생들은 어떻게 예의 바르게 행동해야 하는가　　② 시장 조사가 나타내는 것은 무엇인가

③ 사람들은 음식을 어떻게 먹어야 하는가　　④ 청소년들이 믿는 것은 무엇인가

해설　CDC의 조사 결과는 빈칸의 어떤 행동과 "실제 사람들이 하고 있는 행동(what they're actually doing)" 간에 "낙담시킬 만큼의 격차(disheartening gap)"가 벌어졌음을 의미하고 있다. 그리고 본문의 내용으로 미루어 보면 "실제 사람들이 하고 있는 행동"은 권장량에 미치지 못하는 야채와 과일의 섭취를 의미하고, "격차"는 권장량과 실제 섭취 현황과의 차이를 의미한다. 따라서 보기 중에서 빈칸에 가장 적합한 것은 권장량을 의미하는 ③의 "how people should be eating(사람들은 음식을 어떻게 먹어야 하는가)"이며, 답은 ③이 된다.

어휘　combined ⓐ 종합된, 결합된　　recommended ⓐ 권장된

serving ⓝ (음식의) 1인분　　detailed ⓐ 자세한

adolescent ⓝ 청소년　　disheartening ⓐ 낙담시킬 만한

gap between A and B A와 B 사이의 격차　　rampant ⓐ 걷잡을 수 없는, 횡행하는

obesity ⓝ 비만　　behave oneself 예의 바르게 행동하다

01 Which of the following is most appropriate for the blank?

An increasing number of studies suggest that the main danger of television may not be the message, but the medium itself, just looking at TV. In Bedford, Mass., Psycho-physiologist Thomas Mulholland and Peter Crown, a professor of television and psychology at Hampshire College, have attached electrodes to the heads of children and adults as they watched TV. Mulholland thought that kids watching exciting shows would show high attention. To his surprise, the reverse proved true. While viewing TV, the subjects' output of alpha waves increased, indicating they were in a passive state, as if they were "just sitting quietly in the dark." The implication: TV may be _____.

① a training course in art of inattention
② an efficient medium to improve kids' attention
③ a useful machine when kids watch it moderately
④ an important medium to send the message correctly to kids

02 Which of the following is most appropriate for the blank?

The neuro-economists are using a new technology that allows them to trace the activity of neurons inside the brain and thereby study how emotions influence our purchase choices. For instance, when humans are in positive arousal state, they think about prospective benefits and enjoy the feeling of risk. But when people think about costs, they use different brain modules and become more anxious. If one truth shines through, it is that people are not consistent or fully rational decision makers. This fact was corroborated with the help of the medical devices such as MRI and CT, which clearly showed how people _____. From this empirical evidence, neuro-economists concluded that brains assess risk and return separately, rather than making a single calculation of what economists call expected utility.

① compartmentalized their choices into different parts of their brains
② integrated the existing resources into the specific hemisphere of the brain
③ miscalculated the weight of potential risks and benefits of purchase choices
④ exhibited centralized command and control to allocate the neurons properly

03 Which of the following is most appropriate for the blank?

Differences in genes make a difference in mind and behavior, and the most dramatic demonstrations come from studies of twins. Identical twins (who share all their genes) are far more similar than fraternal twins (who share just half their genes). This is as true when the twins are separated at birth and raised apart as when they are raised in the same home by the same parents. Moreover, biological siblings, who also share half their genes, are far more similar than adoptive siblings, who share no more genes than strangers. Indeed, adoptive siblings are barely similar at all. Alternative positions that _____ have been tested and rejected.

① everything is determined by heredity
② we are born with innate mental faculties
③ the effects of the genes are reduced to zero
④ we are products of both nature and nurture

[01~02] 한국외대 2020

Science is hard enough to understand, especially when there are so many "facts" floating around that aren't actually true. You've probably heard that the Great Wall of China is the only man-made structure you can see from the moon. Interestingly, this myth has been around at least since 1932, when a *Ripley's Believe it or Not!* cartoon deemed the Great Wall of China is "the mightiest work of man, the only one that would be visible to the human eye from the moon." Of course, that was almost 30 years before a machine would touch down on the moon, so the claim was ridiculous. Astronauts have now confirmed that even the Great Wall actually can't be seen from space, except at low altitudes. Even at those relatively low heights, it's actually easier to see roads and plane runways, whose colors don't blend into the ground like the Great Wall's do. However, it does not mean that (A) _____, because it is the largest wall ever made.

01 According to the passage, which of the following is true of the Great Wall of China?

① It was mentioned in a cartoon.
② In 1962, the astronauts saw it from the moon.
③ It can be seen from high altitudes in space.
④ It is easily distinguished from the ground.

02 Which of the following best fits into (A)?

① you should disbelieve a widely shared myth
② no one has figured out how it was built
③ this weird fact is scientifically true
④ the landmark isn't impressive

People who repeatedly gain and lose weight acquire a permanent, long-term change in their metabolism. Their metabolism slows down, so that they consume less food energy than others. The result is that the excess energy in their food becomes stored as fat. This means that crash dieting is self-defeating. Experiments on rats have shown that alternating underfeeding with overfeeding results in a lower metabolic rate. The lower rate enabled the rats to gain weight more easily, with less food than they would ordinarily need. Further, a study of high school wrestlers found that some of them lost and regained weight as often as 10 times during the wrestling season. In the off-season, they were no fatter than those whose weight did not vary, but their metabolic rate was substantially lower. The implication is that people who crash-diet and then regain weight are likely to _____.

03 빈칸에 들어갈 가장 알맞은 것을 고르시오.

① crash-diet again and again
② control their weight fairly easily
③ be eager to keep their metabolic rate low
④ experience more and more difficulty in losing it

04 윗글의 내용과 맞는 것을 고르시오.

① Human beings and rats repeatedly gain and lose weight.
② High school wrestlers are recommended to crash-diet in the off-season.
③ The metabolic rate has a lot to do with the ability to lose weight.
④ Alternating underfeeding with overfeeding does not affect rat's metabolism.

[05~07]

Fluff up the pillows and pull up the covers. Preventing the common cold may be as easy as getting more sleep. Researchers paid healthy adults $800 to have cold viruses sprayed up their noses, then wait five days in a hotel to see if they got sick. Habitual eight-hour sleepers were much less likely to get sick than those who slept less than seven hours or slept fitfully. "The longer you sleep, the better off you are, the less susceptible you are to colds," said lead author Sheldon Cohen, who studies the effects of stress on health at Pittsburgh's Carnegie Mellon University. Prior research has suggested that sleep boosts the immune system at the cell level. This is the first study to show small sleep disturbances increasing the risk of getting sick, said Dr. Michael Irwin, who researches immune response at the University of California, Los Angeles, and was not involved in the study. "The message is to maintain regular sleep habits because those are really critical for health," Irwin said. During cold season, staying out of range of sneezing relatives and co-workers may be impossible. The study, appearing Monday in *The Archives of Internal Medicine*, mimicked those conditions by exposing participants to a common cold virus — rhinovirus — and most became infected with it.

_____.

05 **What is the main idea of the passage above?**

① The flu can be conquered in the near future.
② Sleep may change the body's immune response.
③ Sleep is instrumental in preventing the common cold.
④ It is most important to work out longer hours in a cold season.

06 **The term "slept fitfully" most likely means "_____."**

① had a sound sleep
② fell asleep instantly
③ slept in a drunken state
④ tossed and turned in sleep

07 **Which of the following best fills in the blank at the end of the passage above?**

① But not everyone suffered cold symptoms.
② Everyone indeed caught a cold.
③ Most of them then slept less hours.
④ But their acquaintances are to blame for a cold.

Ⓐ _____. While attractive men may be considered better leaders, for instance, implicit sexist prejudices can work against attractive women, making them Ⓑ _____ likely to be hired for high-level jobs that require authority. And as you might expect, good-looking people of both genders run into jealousy — one study found that if you are interviewed by someone of the same sex, they may be less likely to recruit you if they judge that you are more attractive than they are. More worryingly, being beautiful or handsome could harm your medical care. We tend to link good looks to health, meaning that illnesses are often taken less seriously when they affect the good-looking. When treating people for pain, for instance, doctors tend to take Ⓒ _____ care over the more attractive people.

---

08 **Which of the following is most appropriate for the blank Ⓐ?**

① Good looks get you far in life
② A pleasing appearance can work its magic
③ There are pitfalls for the beautiful
④ No amount of beauty can make up for a bad personality
⑤ Beauty is only skin deep

09 **Choose one that is most appropriate for the blanks Ⓑ and Ⓒ.**

① less — less
② less — more
③ more — less
④ most — more
⑤ more — most

For the first time in history, across much of the world, to be foreign is a perfectly normal condition. It is no more ⓐ _____ than being tall, fat, or left-handed. Nobody raises an eyebrow at a Frenchman in Berlin, a Zimbabwean in London, a Russian in Paris, a Korean in New York. The desire of so many people, given the chance, to live in countries other than their own makes nonsense of a long-established consensus in politics and philosophy that ⓑ _____. The error of philosophy has been to assume that man, because he is a social animal, should belong to some particular society. No doubt many people do feel most at ease with a home and a homeland. But what about the others, who find home ⓒ _____ and foreignness ⓓ _____?

Theirs is a choice that gets both easier and more difficult to exercise with every passing year. Easier, because the globalisation of industry and education tramples national borders. More difficult, because there are ever fewer places left in this globalised world where you can go and feel utterly foreign when you get there.

10 Which best fits into the blank ⓐ?

① positive   ② ludicrous
③ distinctive   ④ vulnerable

11 Which best fits into the blank ⓑ?

① the human animal is best off at home
② nonsense can sometimes make consensus
③ the human desire is always self-contradictory
④ it is good to human nature to live in foreign countries

12 Which best fits into the blanks ⓒ and ⓓ?

	ⓒ		ⓓ
①	comfortable	—	disconcerting
②	agreeable	—	disagreeable
③	unsatisfactory	—	unpleasant
④	oppressive	—	liberating

Much of what we do as adults is based on imitative absorption during our childhood years. Frequently we imagine that we are behaving in a particular way because such behaviour accords with some abstract, lofty code of moral principles, when in reality all we are doing is obeying a deeply ingrained and long 'forgotten' set of purely imitative impressions. (A) This is the cross we have to bear if we are going to sail through our vital juvenile 'blotting paper' phase of rapidly mopping up the accumulated experiences of previous generations. (B) Even when faced with exciting, brilliantly rational new ideas, based on the application of pure, objective intelligence, the community will still cling to its old home-based habits and prejudices. (C) It is the unmodifiable obedience to these impressions that makes it so hard for societies to change their customs and their beliefs. We are forced to take the biased opinions along with the valuable facts.

Luckily we have evolved a powerful antidote to this weakness which is inherent in the imitative learning process. We have a sharpened curiosity, an intensified urge to explore which work against the other tendency and produce a balance that has the potential of fantastic success. Only if a culture becomes too rigid as a result of its slavery to imitative repetition, or _____, will it flounder. Those with a good balance between the two urges will thrive. Lucky is the society that enjoys the gradual acquisition of a perfect balance between imitation and curiosity, between slavish, unthinking copying and progressive, rational experimentation.

13 Which of the following is the best order?

① (A) − (B) − (C)
② (B) − (A) − (C)
③ (C) − (A) − (B)
④ (C) − (B) − (A)

14 What is the best expression for the blank?

① is reluctant to disobey authority
② too daring and rashly exploratory
③ is dominated by its heavy burden of taboos
④ too democratized to serve its original function

It is easier to establish what Expressionism was not, than what it was. Certainly Expressionism was not a coherent, singular entity. There was no such thing as a unified band of "Expressionists" on the march. Yet unlike the small groups of painters dubbed "Fauves" and "Cubists" in France, consequently, ⓐ _____. The era of German Expressionism was finally extinguished by the Nazi dictatorship in 1933. But its most incandescent phase of 1910−20 left a legacy that has caused ⓑ _____ ever since. As some artists recognised the political danger of Expressionism's characteristic inwardness, they became more committed to exploring its potential for political engagement or wider social reform. But utopian aspirations and the high stakes involved in ascribing a redemptive function to art, meant that Expressionism also bore an immense potential for despair, disillusionment and atrophy.

15 윗글의 내용과 일치하지 않는 것은?

① The unified identity of a group of painters called "Fauves"
② Spiritual inwardness as an artistic facet of Expressionism
③ Expressionists' artistic implication for social reform
④ Expressionists' artistic styles in affinity with Fauves and Cubists

16 다음 중 문맥상 빈칸 ⓐ에 들어갈 가장 알맞은 어구는?

① Expressionists' longing for spiritual idealism, beyond their purposes, were so great
② Expressionists of one hue or another, across the arts, were so numerous
③ Expressionists strove to be united under the same flag beyond their artistic interests
④ Expressionists' artistic style was rarely distinguished from other groups artistic style

17 다음 중 빈칸 ⓑ에 들어갈 가장 알맞은 단어는?

① intellectualism
② malaise
③ insecurities
④ reverberations

The history of cosmetics spans at least 6,000 years and is present in almost every society on Earth. Archaeological evidence of cosmetics dates from ancient Egypt and Greece. It is known that some women in ancient Rome invented makeup formulas to whiten the skin. During the 1900s, makeup was not popular because it was still mostly used by the 'ladies of the night'. Around 1910, makeup became fashionable in the United States and Europe owing to the influence of ballet and theater stars. During World War II, cosmetics were in short supply because their basic ingredients were diverted into war supply. (A) _____, at this time when they were restricted, lipstick, powder, and face cream were most desired, and most experimentation was carried out for the postwar period. This is because cosmetics developers rightly predicted that the war would result in a phenomenal boom afterwards. During the 1960s and 1970s, many women influenced by feminism (B) _____ to cosmetics' role in the second-class status of women, making them mere sex objects. Although modern makeup has been used mainly by women, an increasing number of men are using cosmetics to enhance their own facial features. Cosmetics brands are releasing products such as concealers especially created for men. There is some controversy over this, however, as many feel that men who wear makeup are neglecting traditional gender roles. But others view this as a sign of ongoing gender equality since they feel that (C) _____.

18 Which one of the following ordered pairs best fits into (A) and (B)?

① Ironically – objected
② In fact – adhered
③ Sadly – yielded
④ Naturally – corresponded

19 Which of the following best fits into (C)?

① men should purchase cosmetics for women
② men are free to buy cosmetics as long as they remain masculine
③ men have long purchased their own cosmetics
④ men also have the right to use cosmetics if women do

20 According to the passage, which of the following is NOT true?

① Actors contributed to the popularity of makeup in the 1910s.
② Formulas to whiten the skin first appeared in Greece.
③ There are concealers exclusively produced for men.
④ There came a boom in cosmetics after World War II.

Most visitors to Easter Island come specifically to see the 887 moai, enormous statues carved out of volcanic rock, ⓐ <u>scattered</u> around the island. Moai were regarded by the native people ⓑ <u>as</u> representations of their ancestors and powerful chiefs, living and dead. However, after a devastating civil war, only a fraction of them remain intact, and many lie half-buried in the ground. The question remains: with the average statue ⓒ <u>weighing</u> more than an elephant, _____ Writer Eric von Däniken claimed that the statues must have been built by aliens using materials from outer space. Unsurprisingly, historians are skeptical about this claim. It is more conceivable that the moai were simply dragged to their sites — an immense task, which accounts for many of them ⓓ <u>being</u> left at their quarry. Not all historians agree, however, and the riddle of the statues remains ⓔ <u>unsolving</u>.

21 Which is the best title for the passage?

① the Mysterious Moai
② the Biggest Statues
③ Beautiful Easter Island
④ Excellent Architecture
⑤ the Identities of Moai

22 Which is the most suitable expression for the blank?

① how old were the gigantic statues?
② who carved 887 statues out of volcanic rock?
③ how was it feasible to transport them?
④ why do many of them remain half-buried?
⑤ why did the native people make huge statues?

23 Select the part grammatically wrong.

① ⓐ   ② ⓑ   ③ ⓒ   ④ ⓓ   ⑤ ⓔ

Child care is still a two-class system in the United States. Those with adequate income can generally purchase first-rate care for their preschool children; those without adequate income are left at the mercy of the political and economic forces that determine social policy. While the poor, the near poor, and the working class sometimes have access to good care, more often than not they are faced with long waiting lists, inadequate teacher-child ratios, and a rapid [A] _____ of caregivers. Statistics from the National Center of Education show that 53 percent of children ages three to four whose families had incomes of $25,000 and above attended a preschool program in 1982, while less than 29 percent of children whose families had incomes below $25,000 were in preschool. In addition, approximately half of the three-year-olds and 72 percent of the four-year-olds whose mothers were college graduates were in such programs in 1982. For child care, as for other human services, [B] _____.

24 Which expression best fits [A]?

① increase
② influx
③ pullout
④ turnout
⑤ turnover

25 Which expression best completes [B]?

① affordability and accessibility have become key issues
② many people are still ambivalent about its importance
③ its treatment varies a great deal from society to society
④ the government is not responsible for financially supporting working-class parents
⑤ the government and the family form a partnership

여러분의 작은 소리
에듀윌은 크게 듣겠습니다.

본 교재에 대한 여러분의 목소리를 들려주세요.
공부하시면서 어려웠던 점, 궁금한 점,
칭찬하고 싶은 점, 개선할 점, 어떤 것이라도 좋습니다.

에듀윌은 여러분께서 나누어 주신 의견을
통해 끊임없이 발전하고 있습니다.

에듀윌 도서몰 book.eduwill.net
• 부가학습자료 및 정오표: 에듀윌 도서몰 → 도서자료실
• 교재 문의: 에듀윌 도서몰 → 문의하기 → 교재(내용, 출간) / 주문 및 배송

에듀윌 편입영어 핵심유형 완성 독해

발 행 일	2022년 10월 19일 초판
편 저 자	홍준기
펴 낸 이	권대호
펴 낸 곳	(주)에듀윌
등록번호	제25100–2002–000052호
주 소	08378 서울특별시 구로구 디지털로34길 55
	코오롱싸이언스밸리 2차 3층

www.eduwill.net
대표전화 1600-6700

취업, 공무원, 자격증 시험준비의 흐름을 바꾼 화제작!

에듀윌 히트교재 시리즈

에듀윌 교육출판연구소가 만든 히트교재 시리즈!
YES24, 교보문고, 알라딘, 인터파크, 영풍문고 등 전국 유명 온/오프라인 서점에서 절찬 판매 중!

공인중개사 기초입문서/기본서/핵심요약집/문제집/기출문제집/실전모의고사 외 12종

주택관리사 기초서/기본서/핵심요약집/문제집/기출문제집/실전모의고사

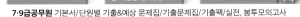

7·9급공무원 기본서/단원별 기출&예상 문제집/기출문제집/기출팩/실전, 봉투모의고사

공무원 국어 한자·문법·독해/영어 단어·문법·독해/한국사·행정학·행정법 노트/행정법·헌법 판례집/면접

7급공무원 PSAT 기본서/기출문제집   **계리직공무원** 기본서/문제집/기출문제집   **군무원** 기출문제집/봉투모의고사   **경찰공무원** 기본서/기출문제집/모의고사/판례집/면접   **소방공무원** 기본서/기출문제집/실전, 봉투모의고사   **뷰티** 미용사/맞춤형화장품

검정고시 고졸/중졸 기본서/기출문제집/실전모의고사/총정리   **사회복지사(1급)** 기본서/문제집/핵심요약   **직업상담사(2급)** 기본서/기출문제집   **경비** 기본서/기출/1차 한권끝장/2차 모의고사   **전기기사** 필기/실기/기출문제집   **전기기능사** 필기/실기

한국사능력검정시험 기본서/2주끝장/기출/우선순위50/초등

조리기능사 필기/실기

제과제빵기능사 필기/실기

SMAT 모듈A/B/C

ERP정보관리사 회계/인사/물류/생산(1, 2급)

전산세무회계 기초서/기본서/기출문제집

무역영어 1급 | 국제무역사 1급

KBS한국어능력시험 | ToKL

한국실용글쓰기

매경TEST 기본서/문제집/2주끝장

TESAT 기본서/문제집/기출문제집

운전면허 1종·2종

스포츠지도사 필기/실기구술 한권끝장

산업안전기사 | 산업안전산업기사

위험물산업기사 | 위험물기능사

토익 입문서 | 실전서 | 종합서

컴퓨터활용능력 | 워드프로세서

정보처리기사

월간시사상식 | 일반상식

월간NCS | 매1N

NCS 통합 | 모듈형 | 피듈형

PSAT형 NCS 수문풀

PSAT 기출완성 | 6대 출제사 | 10개 영역 찐기출

한국철도공사 | 서울교통공사 | 부산교통공사

국민건강보험공단 | 한국전력공사

한수원 | 수자원 | 토지주택공사

행과연형 | 휴노형 | 기업은행 | 인국공

대기업 인적성 통합 | GSAT

LG | SKCT | CJ | L-TAB

ROTC·학사장교 | 부사관

꿈을 현실로 만드는
에듀윌

DREAM

공무원 교육
- 선호도 1위, 인지도 1위!
  브랜드만족도 1위!
- 합격자 수 1,800% 폭등시킨
  독한 커리큘럼

자격증 교육
- 6년간 아무도 깨지 못한 기록
  합격자 수 1위
- 가장 많은 합격자를 배출한
  최고의 합격 시스템

직영학원
- 직영학원 수 1위, 수강생 규모 1위!
- 표준화된 커리큘럼과 호텔급 시설
  자랑하는 전국 53개 학원

종합출판
- 4대 온라인서점 베스트셀러 1위!
- 출제위원급 전문 교수진이
  직접 집필한 합격 교재

어학 교육
- 토익 베스트셀러 1위
- 토익 동영상 강의 무료 제공
- 업계 최초 '토익 공식' 추천 AI 앱 서비스

콘텐츠 제휴 · B2B 교육
- 고객 맞춤형 위탁 교육 서비스 제공
- 기업, 기관, 대학 등 각 단체에 최적화된
  고객 맞춤형 교육 및 제휴 서비스

부동산 아카데미
- 부동산 실무 교육 1위!
- 상위 1% 고소득 창업/취업 비법
- 부동산 실전 재테크 성공 비법

공기업 · 대기업 취업 교육
- 취업 교육 1위!
- 공기업 NCS, 대기업 직무적성,
  자소서, 면접

학점은행제
- 97.6%의 과목이수율
- 14년 연속 교육부 평가 인정 기관 선정

대학 편입
- 편입 교육 1위!
- 업계 유일 500% 환급 상품 서비스

국비무료 교육
- 자격증 취득 및 취업 실무 교육
- 4차 산업, 뉴딜 맞춤형 훈련과정

IT 아카데미
- 1:1 밀착형 실전/실무 교육
- 화이트 해커/코딩 개발자 양성 과정

에듀윌 교육서비스 **공무원 교육** 9급공무원/7급공무원/경찰공무원/소방공무원/계리직공무원/기술직공무원/군무원 **자격증 교육** 공인중개사/주택관리사/전기기사/세무사/전산세무회계/경비지도사/검정고시/소방설비기사/소방시설관리사/사회복지사1급/건축기사/토목기사/직업상담사/전기기능사/산업안전기사/위험물산업기사/위험물기능사/ERP정보관리사/재경관리사/도로교통사고감정사/유통관리사/물류관리사/행정사/한국사능력검정/한경TESAT/매경TEST/KBS한국어능력시험/실용글쓰기/IT자격증/국제무역사/무역영어 **어학 교육** 토익 교재/토익 동영상 강의/인공지능 토익 앱 **대학 편입** 편입 교재/편입 영어·수학/경찰대/의치대/편입 컨설팅/면접 **공기업·대기업 취업 교육** 공기업 NCS·전공·상식/대기업 직무적성/자소서·면접 **직영학원** 공무원 학원/기술직공무원 학원/군무원학원/경찰학원/소방학원/공무원 면접학원/공인중개사 학원/주택관리사 학원/전기기사학원/취업아카데미/경영아카데미 **종합출판** 공무원·자격증 수험교재 및 단행본/월간지(시사상식) **학점은행제** 교육부 평가인정기관 원격평생교육원(사회복지사2급/경영학/CPA)/교육부 평가인정기관 원격사회교육원(사회복지사2급/심리학) **콘텐츠 제휴·B2B 교육** 교육 콘텐츠 제휴/기업 교육·대학 취업역량 강화 교육 **부동산 아카데미** 부동산 창업CEO과정/실전 경매 과정/디벨로퍼 과정 **국비무료 교육(국비교육원)** 전기기능사/ 전기(산업)기사/소방설비 (산업)기사/IT(빅데이터/자바프로그램/파이썬)/게임그래픽/3D프린터/실내건축디자인/웹퍼블리셔/그래픽디자인/영상편집(유튜브) 디자인/온라인 쇼핑몰광고 및 제작(쿠팡, 스마트스토어)/전산세무회계/컴퓨터활용능력/ITQ/GTQ/직업상담사 **IT 아카데미** 화이트 해커/코딩

교육
문의 **1600-6700** www.eduwill.net

eduwill

업계 최초 대통령상 3관왕,
정부기관상 18관왕 달성!

2010 대통령상

2019 대통령상

2019 대통령상

대한민국 브랜드대상
국무총리상

서울특별시장상

과학기술부장관상

정보통신부장관상

산업자원부장관상

고용노동부장관상

미래창조과학부장관상

법무부장관상

여성가족부장관상

과학기술정보통신부
장관상

문화체육관광부
장관상

농림축산식품부
장관상

2004
서울특별시장상 우수벤처기업 대상

2006
산업자원부장관상 대한민국 e비즈니스대상

2007
정보통신부장관상 디지털콘텐츠 대상
산업자원부장관 표창 대한민국 e비즈니스대상

2010
대통령 표창 대한민국 IT 이노베이션 대상

2013
고용노동부장관 표창 일자리 창출 공로

2014
미래창조과학부장관 표창 ICT Innovation 대상

2015
법무부장관 표창 사회공헌 유공

2017
여성가족부장관상 사회공헌 유공
2016 합격자 수 최고 기록 KRI 한국기록원 공식 인증

2018
2017 합격자 수 최고 기록 KRI 한국기록원 공식 인증

2019
대통령 표창 범죄예방대상
대통령 표창 일자리 창출 유공
과학기술정보통신부장관상 대한민국 ICT 대상

2020
국무총리상 대한민국 브랜드대상
2019 합격자 수 최고 기록 KRI 한국기록원 공식 인증

2021
고용노동부장관상 일·생활 균형 우수 기업 공모전 대상
문화체육관광부장관 표창 근로자휴가지원사업 우수 참여 기업
농림축산식품부장관상 대한민국 사회공헌 대상
문화체육관광부장관 표창 여가친화기업 인증 우수 기업

2022
농림축산식품부장관상 대한민국 ESG 대상

에듀윌 편입영어

핵심유형 완성 독해

전과정 학습로드맵 제공

월별 학습계획 및
학습방법 제공

무료 진단고사

나의 위치에 맞는
전문 학습매니저의 1:1 학습설계

실시간 알림 서비스

최신 편입정보
알림 서비스

강의용 PDF 제공

편입 스타터팩을 위한
강의용 PDF 제공

고객의 꿈, 직원의 꿈, 지역사회의 꿈을 실현한다

펴낸곳 (주)에듀윌   **펴낸이** 권대호   **출판총괄** 김형석
개발책임 우지형, 윤대권   **개발** 윤관식
주소 서울시 구로구 디지털로34길 55 코오롱싸이언스밸리 2차 3층
대표번호 1600-6700   **등록번호** 제25100-2002-000052호
협의 없는 무단 복제는 법으로 금지되어 있습니다.

에듀윌 도서몰 book.eduwill.net
• 부가학습자료 및 정오표: 에듀윌 도서몰 → 도서자료실
• 교재 문의: 에듀윌 도서몰 → 문의하기 → 교재(내용, 출간) / 주문 및 배송

에듀윌
편입영어

핵심유형 완성
독해 정답과 해설

홍준기 편저

eduwill

3년 연속 100% 합격자 배출
교수진이 만든 교재

에듀윌
편입영어

핵심유형 완성

독해

정답과 해설

PART 01

전체적 이해

CHAPTER 01 제목

CHAPTER 02 주제

CHAPTER 03 요지

CHAPTER 04 글의 목적과 어조 등

01 다음 글에 가장 적절한 제목은 무엇인가?

실험에 따르면 수업 시간에 들어가기 전에 긴장을 푸는 것이 결과에 긍정적 영향을 미친다고 한다. 깊이 긴장을 풀 수 있도록 몇 분 정도 활용하면, 여러분의 뇌파는 늦춰진다. 우리가 알파파 또는 느린 뇌파를 체험할 때 우리의 마음은 더욱 집중하기가 쉬워지며 이는 근육의 긴장이나 불필요한 생각으로 정신이 덜 산만해지기 때문이다. 긴장을 풀면 또한 우리 뇌의 논리적이고 직선적인 좌뇌와 창조적이고 전체적인 우뇌 둘 다 같이 협력할 수 있게 하는 것으로 보인다. 전체적으로 알파파는 정신적인 성과를 증대시킬 수 있도록 우리의 뇌를 조율하는 것으로 보인다.

① 뇌파의 학습
② 긴장을 푸는 것과 뇌파
③ 뇌파와 정신적 과정
④ 긴장을 푸는 것이 정신적 성과에 미치는 영향

| 정답 | ④

| 해설 | 전반부에서는 잠시나마 "relaxing before a learning session(수업 시간에 들어가기 전에 긴장을 풀면)" 느린 뇌파인 알파파가 나타나면서 더욱 집중하기 쉬워진다고 주장한다. 여기서 "relaxing(긴장을 푸는 것)"이라는 단어가 전반부의 핵심어임을 유추할 수 있다. 따라서 보기 중에서는 ②나 ④가 답이 된다. 후반부에서는 여기에 더해 긴장을 푸는 행위가 "allow the two sides of our brain ... to work together(뇌의 양 부분을 같이 활용할 수 있게 한다)"고 말한다. 따라서 긴장을 풀면 생성되는 알파파는 "tune up our brains for increased mental performance(정신적인 성과를 증대시킬 수 있도록 우리의 뇌를 조율)"하는 역할을 한다. 따라서 종합해 보면 긴장을 푸는 행위를 통해 정신적 성과가 증대됨을 알 수 있다. 따라서 답은 ④가 된다.

| 어휘 | **experiment** ⓝ 실험   **learning session** 수업 시간
distract ⓥ (마음 · 주의를) 흐트러뜨리다; (마음을) 어지럽히다
irrelevant ⓐ 관계없는, 무관계한   **linear** ⓐ 선의; 직선적인
holistic ⓐ 전체적인   **tune up** ~을 조율하다, 맞추다

02 가장 적절한 제목은 무엇인가? 인하대 2016

다이어트 업계의 광고 및 마케팅 전략은 공포 · 편견 · 고정관념을 창조한 다음 이를 영속시키는 것에 기반을 둔다. 뚱뚱한 사람은 건강이 좋지 않고, 매력이 없고, 의지가 박약하고, 탐욕스러운 사람으로 묘사된 다. 체중 감소나 날씬한 몸매는 미덕 · 건강 · 성공과 동일시된다. 다이어트에 돌입하지 않거나 체중 감소에 실패한 것은 의지 부족이나 투지 부족으로 비난받는다. 뚱뚱한 사람들은 체중 감소 프로그램에 실패한 것이 자기 탓이라고 죄의식을 갖고 스스로를 비난하도록, 그리고 자신의 체중과 관련하여 배제당하고 학대받고 차별받는 상황을 예측하고 수용하도록 가르침을 받는다. 매체를 통해 벌어지는 이러한 부정적인 캠페인은 수많은 뚱뚱한 사람들에게 대단히 파괴적인 충격을 가한다. 이러한 메시지는 뚱뚱한 사람들의 자부심을 낮추

고 불만과 자기 회의 및 자기 증오를 조장하며, 특히 다이어트 중 "요요" 순환 과정을 겪으면서 체중이 다시 불어나는 상태엔 더욱 그러하다.

① 다이어트 업계 : 뚱뚱한 사람들에게 미치는 나쁜 영향
② 다이어트를 하는 사람들에게 달린 다이어트의 성공과 실패
③ 다이어트를 하는 사람들의 궁극적 목표로서의 체중 감소
④ 다이어트를 하는 사람들을 끌어들이기 위한 전략 개발
⑤ "요요" 순환 과정을 겪는 중인 다이어트를 하는 사람들의 정신 상태를 강화하기

| 정답 | ①

| 해설 | 본문은 다이어트 업계의 광고 및 마케팅 전략이 뚱뚱한 사람들에게 어떤 악영향을 미치는지를 말하고 있다. 따라서 답은 ①이다.

| 어휘 |
perpetuation ⓝ 영구[영속, 불후]화
gluttonous ⓐ 많이 먹는, 탐욕스러운
equate ⓥ 동일시하다
be blamed on ~로 비난받다
rejection ⓝ 배제, 거절
devastating ⓐ 대단히 파괴적인, 엄청난 손상을 가하는
self-esteem ⓝ 자부심
discontent ⓝ 불만

portray ⓥ 묘사하다
figure ⓝ 몸매
virtue ⓝ 미덕, 덕목
determination ⓝ 투지
mistreatment ⓝ 학대, 혹사
foster ⓥ 조장하다
self-doubt ⓝ 자기 회의

03 이 글의 제목으로 적당한 것은?

Teresa Bell Kindred(41세)는 그녀의 어머니가 결장암으로 고통스러워하실 때 자신이 할 수 있는 일을 다 했는지에 대해서 여전히 의문스럽다. 이런 시련 내내 그녀는 계속 아마도 자신이 모르는 새로운 치료법이 있을 거라고 생각했다. 이성적으로는 어머니의 병에 대해 자신이 통제할 수 있는 것은 없다는 것을 알고 있다. 그렇지만 비이성적인 생각은 이와 다르다. "내 어머니는 내 인생의 모든 문제를 해결해 주셨어요." 그녀는 "어머니가 나를 필요로 하는데 내가 아무것도 할 수 없다는 게 너무도 괴로워요."라고 얘기한다. 우리는 우리 인생에서 발생하는 모든 것을 통제할 수 있는 능력이 없다는 것을 받아들일 필요가 있다고 뉴욕심리분석센터의 명예 소장인 Herbert Stean은 말한다. 스스로에게 완벽한 것을 기대하는 것은 승산이 없는 일이다. 죄책감으로 괴로워하는 사람은 인간이 한계가 있다는 것을 받아들여야 필요가 있다.

① 스스로를 용서하라
② 실수로부터 배워라
③ 당신이 받은 축복을 생각하라
④ 당신의 한계를 받아들여라

| 정답 | ④

| 해설 | 우리 인생에서 발생하는 모든 것을 통제할 수 있는 능력이 없다는 것을 받아들일 필요가 있다는 전문가의 얘기를 인용한 후 결론적으로 스스로에게 완벽한 것을 기대하는 것은 승산이 없는 일이며, 죄책감으로 괴로워하는 사람은 인간이 한계가 있다는 것을 받아들여야 필요가 있다고 적고 있다. 그러므로 정답은 ④이다.

| 어휘 |
colon cancer 결장암
otherwise ⓐⓓ 이와 다르게
no-win situation 승산이 없는 상황

ordeal ⓝ 시련, 고통
director emeritus 명예 소장
fallibility ⓝ 오류를 범하기 쉬움

01	④	02	②	03	②	04	④	05	④	06	⑤	07	⑤	08	②	09	③	10	③
11	②	12	④	13	④	14	②	15	③	16	②	17	①	18	④	19	①	20	④
21	④	22	②	23	④	24	④	25	④	26	①	27	④	28	②	29	②	30	③
31	②	32	④	33	③	34	④	35	①	36	③	37	①	38	②	39	④	40	④

[01~03] 성균관대 2014

해석

더 길어진 배터리 수명과 기기 소형화는 위치 추적의 비용을 낮추고 위치 추적을 더 실용적인 것으로 변모시키고 있다. 위치 추적을 위한 가장 간단한 방법은 스마트폰을 사용하는 것이다. 많은 이동 통신 사업자들은 추가 요금을 받고 자녀 위치 추적 기능을 제공하지만, 무료 위치 추적 앱의 수도 빠르게 증가하고 있다. 이들 위치 추적 서비스 및 기기는 자녀의 위치를 제공하거나 자녀의 행동에 관해 경보를 발한다. 일본 및 미국의 부모는 이러한 기기에 가장 큰 관심을 보이고 있다. 자녀 안전 문제에 관해서는 더 여유 있는 태도를 보이는 듯하며 다른 곳보다 더 까다로운 개인 정보 보호법을 갖고 있는 유럽인들의 경우는 좋아함의 정도가 좀 덜한 듯하다. 위치 추적 분야의 열렬한 지지자들은 위치 추적은 자유를 감소시키는 것이 아니라 더 늘려 준다고 본다. 자녀의 위치를 쉽게 찾을 수 있는 부모는 자녀가 돌아다니도록 더 기꺼이 내버려 둔다. 10대 청소년들은 짜증 나는 전화를 굳이 받지 않아도 된다. 비판론자들은 위치 추적이 정말로 자녀를 보호한다고만은 할 수 없다고 한다. 영리한 납치범들은 휴대 전화나 경보 추적 장치를 없애 버릴 것이다. 그리고 낯선 사람이 아동을 공격하는 경우는 거의 없다. 자녀를 살해할 가능성이 가장 높은 사람은 부모이고 폭행보다 사고가 훨씬 더 큰 위험이다. 위치 추적으로 자녀가 강에 빠지는 것을 막지는 못한다. 이와 동일한 기술이 성인을 염탐하는 것도 가능케 해 준다. 미국의 경우 이동 통신 가입자들은 가족 약정 상품을 구매했을 경우 해당되는 모든 이용자를 대상으로 하는 위치 추적 서비스를 구매할 수 있다. 가정 폭력의 일부 생존자들은 이 서비스로 인해 폭력 가정으로부터의 탈출이 더욱 힘들어졌다고 말한다. 부모는 웹캠을 활용해 자녀 돌보미들을 감시한다. 자녀가 출국할 경우 부모에게 문자 메시지를 보내는 사우디 정부의 한 기구는 부인의 위치 추적도 돕고 있다.

---

01 본문의 제목으로 가장 알맞은 것은 무엇인가?

① 새로운 가족?: 현대의 관계 변화
② 기술과 자녀의 긍정적 측면
③ 국가 감시 윤리
④ 자녀 위치 추적 : 부모에게는 좋은 일이지만 사생활 문제에는 좋은 일이 아니다.
⑤ 기술: 신뢰할 수 없는 하인

| 정답 | ④

| 해설 | 본문은 위치 추적 기술의 장점과 단점을 말하면서 특히 사생활 차원에서 악용될 소지가 있음을 폭력 가정이나 사우디아라비아의 사례를 통해 들고 있다. 따라서 답은 ④이다.

02 다음 중 빈칸에 가장 알맞은 것은 무엇인가?

① 위치 추적 기기를 납치범이 사용할 수도 있다

② 위치 추적이 정말로 자녀를 보호한다고만은 할 수 없다고 한다

③ 위치 추적 기기는 너무 비싸다

④ 10대 청소년들은 위치 추적 기기를 들고 다니기를 좋아하지 않는다

⑤ 스마트폰은 위치 추적 기기에 비에 더 효율적이다

| 정답 | ②

| 해설 | 빈칸 뒤 내용은 납치범이 위치 추적 장치를 없애 버리거나, 위치 추적 장치가 사고를 예방하는 것은 아니라는 사실 등 위치 추적 장치만으로 자녀의 보호가 완벽하게 이루어지는 것은 아님을 말하고 있다. 따라서 답은 ②이다.

03 본문에 따르면 다음 중 사실인 것은 무엇인가?

① 위치 추적 앱이 고가인 관계로 위치 추적 장비가 널리 쓰이지 못하고 있다.

② 위치 추적 장비는 인간성의 말살 경향을 촉진시킬지도 모른다.

③ 유럽인들은 서로를 더 많이 신뢰하고 있으므로 위치 추적 장비에 관심을 많이 보이지는 않는다.

④ 휴대 전화 위치 추적 서비스는 사우디아라비아에서 가정 폭력을 예방하는 데 도움이 된다.

⑤ 자녀는 어른에 비해 더 감시를 받기 쉽다.

| 정답 | ②

| 해설 | "가정 폭력의 일부 생존자들은 이 서비스로 인해 폭력 가정으로부터의 탈출이 더욱 힘들어졌다고 말한다. 부모는 웹캠을 활용해 자녀 돌보미들을 감시한다. 자녀가 출국할 경우 부모에게 문자 메시지를 보내는 사우디 정부의 한 기구는 부인의 위치 추적도 돕고 있다(Some survivors of domestic violence say this makes it harder to escape. Parents use webcams to keep an eye on their children's carers. A Saudi government agency that sends men text messages if their children leave the country also helps track wives)." 이 세 가지 모두 위치 추적 기술로 인해 인간이 감시받고 결국에는 인간성이 말살되는 사례라 할 수 있다. 따라서 답은 ②이다.

| 어휘 | keen ⓐ 열렬히 원하는, ~에 대단히 관심이 많은

gizmo ⓝ 장치, 기기

enamoured ⓐ ~을 좋아하는, ~이 마음에 드는

roam ⓥ 돌아다니다, 배회하다

spare ⓥ ~을 겪지 않아도 되게 하다

savvy ⓐ 요령 있는, 영리한

assault ⓝ 폭행

snoop ⓥ 염탐하다, 기웃거리다

surveillance ⓝ 감시

deter ⓥ 막다, 그만두게 하다

dehumanize ⓥ 인간성을 말살하다, 비인간적으로 만들다

prone to ~하기[당하기] 쉬운

해석

홀로 있으면 우리 자신의 일부인 온갖 특성들이 소리 없이 사라진다. 그런 특성 중에서도 남들 앞에서 폼 잡고 싶은 욕망을 들 수 있는데, 사실은 그렇지 않은데도 남들이 그렇게 생각해 주었으면 하는 사람이 마치 자신인 것처럼 남들에게 인상 남기길 원하는 그런 마음도 사라진다. 물론 내가 아는 어떤 이들은 홀로 있을 때조차도 폼을 잡을 수 있다. 만일 그들에게 옷 입는 것을 도와주는 하인들이 있다면, 그들은 틀림없이 하인들에게 영웅처럼 비칠 것이다. 하지만 이는 내게 가장 힘든 일임을 잘 알고 있고, 또한 나는 게으른 사람이기에 그런 시도는 그만두었다. 바라봐 줄 사람 없이 연기하는 것은 매우 피곤하고 무익하기 때문에 누구든지 그런 행동을 차츰 포기하고 마침내는 아예 연기하는 법조차 잊어버린다. 있는 그대로의 자기 자신을 만나는 데 더 관심을 갖게 되기 때문이다. 옷이 우리에게 아무런 관심거리가 되지 못한다는 것을 다소 충격을 받으며 알게 된다. 옷은 단지 가리개 정도로 여기게 된다.

04 윗글의 제목으로 가장 알맞은 것은?

① 화려한 의상을 입고 관객 없이 행하는 연기
② 하인들에게 영웅 되기
③ 게으름의 주요 원인들
④ 고독을 통한 자아와의 조우

| 정답 | ④

| 해설 | 본문에 나오는 solitude는 외롭고 쓸쓸함을 내포하고 있는 '고독'의 의미보다는 다른 이들과 함께 있지 않고 '홀로 있음'을 뜻하는 말이다. 다른 이들과 함께 있을 때는 폼 잡기 급급하지만, 홀로 있으면 그럴 필요가 없어지며, 남들을 위해 꾸미지 않는 있는 그대로의 자기 자신을 만나게 된다고 설명하고 있다. 따라서 이런 의미를 함축적으로 담고 있는 제목으로는 ④가 적절하다.

05 윗글에 드러난 글쓴이의 입장에 가장 가까운 것은?

① 최상의 모습만 보여 주고 싶은 욕망은 게으름과 함께 어울리는 특징이다.
② 홀로 있을 때, 하인들의 존재는 필수적이다.
③ 홀로 있을 때, 의복은 자신의 일부분이 된다.
④ 잘 차려입은 모습을 보여 주고 싶은 욕망은 홀로 있을 때는 약해진다.

| 정답 | ④

| 해설 | 저자는 폼 잡는 것도 게으르지 않아야 할 수 있는 일이라고 에둘러 표현하고 있으므로 ①은 정답이 될 수 없으며, ②는 단어만 일부 같고 내용은 본문과 무관하다. ③은 본문과 반대로 말하고 있으므로 답이 될 수 없다. 정답은 ④로 홀로 있을 경우에는 좋은 모습을 보이고 싶은 욕망이 사라진다는 내용에 부합된다.

| 어휘 | **solitude** ⓝ (특히 즐거운) 고독, 홀로 있음   **trait** ⓝ 특성
pose ⓥ 뻐기다, 으스대다, 폼 잡다   **wearisome** ⓐ (아주) 지루한, 싫증나는
profitless ⓐ 수익성이 없는; 무익한   **merely** ⓐ 한낱, 그저, 단지
laziness ⓝ 게으름, 나태함   **encounter** ⓝ 조우, 만남
vital ⓐ 필수적인   **diminish** ⓥ 줄어들다, 약해지다; 줄이다, 약화시키다

무적의 체스 세계 챔피언 Vladimir Kramnik과 아마추어를 상대로 세 번 대결하는 체스 게임에서 연속 두 번 이기면 백만 달러를 받는다고 해 보자. 선택할 수 있는 대진표는 다음과 같다. "아마추어—Kramnik—아마추어" 혹은 "Kramnik—아마추어—Kramnik". 당연히 당신은 Kramnik과의 대결을 최대한 피해야 할 것이다. 그러나 당신이 상금을 탈 가능성이 더 높은 대진표는 Kramnik과 두 번 대결해야 하는 후자이다. 두 번째 게임에서 이기지 못하면 연속 두 게임을 이길 수 없으므로, 더 약한 상대는 중간에 만나고 그랜드 마스터(최고 수준의 체스 선수)를 이길 기회를 두 번 갖는 것이 더 유리하기 때문이다.

06 다음 중 가장 적절한 제목은 무엇인가?

① 지갑을 쥔 사람이 가정을 지배한다
② 백만 달러를 받는다면
③ 체스 게임마다 다른 전략과 전술
④ 아직 인정받지 못하는 체스 선수들
⑤ 강자와의 대결 두 번이 한 번보다 낫다

| 정답 | ⑤

| 해설 | 지문의 주제는 "but in fact your chance of winning the purse is greater in the latter lineup, where you play him twice."에 담겨 있다. 이 부분을 가장 잘 전달하는 것은 ⑤이다. 체스 게임의 전략과 전술을 예시하는 글이 아니므로 ③을 선택하지 않도록 주의한다.

07 다음 중 Vladimir Kramnik에 대해 사실인 것은?

① 그는 연속 두 게임에서 친척과 대결했다.
② 그는 체스 게임에서 아마추어와 대결한 적이 없었다.
③ 그는 올해 체스 게임에서 우승해 백만 달러 상금을 받을 것이다.
④ 그는 주로 같은 선수와 두 번 대결하는 것을 선호한다.
⑤ 그는 세계 최고 수준의 체스 선수이다.

| 정답 | ⑤

| 해설 | "reigning world champion Vladimir Kramnik", "grandmaster"에서 그가 세계적인 최고 수준의 체스 선수임을 알 수 있다.

| 어휘 | **consecutive** ⓐ 연속적인   **reigning** ⓐ 지배적인
obvious ⓐ 명백한   **lineup** ⓝ 라인업, 시합 등의 순서
better off ⓐ 더 나은, 더 유리한   **opponent** ⓝ 상대, 적
give a shot 시도하다   **topple** ⓥ 넘어뜨리다, 실각시키다
grand-master 그랜드 마스터, 최고 수준의 체스 선수

해석

어느 날 오후 나는 15개월 된 벤(Ben)의 윗니 하나에 사라지지 않는 갈색 선이 하나 나 있는 것을 발견했다. 그것이 다른 치아로 퍼진 후, 치과 의사는 아기가 "우유병 치아 우식증(baby-bottle tooth)"이 있다고 말했는데, 모유 수유를 하고 있는 아기에게는 매우 드문 진단이었다. 그는 아기의 충치를 나의 (우유병) 수유 탓으로 돌렸고, 당장 중단할 것을 제안했지만, (중단한다고 해서 아이의 치아에 발생한) 손상이 사라지지는 않을 것이라고 경고했다. 우리는 다른 치과 의사를 찾아갔는데, 그 치과 의사는 아기의 치아 에나멜이 취약하고 (그로 인해) 충치를 가질 경향이 큰 것 때문에 충치가 발생했을 가능성이 크다고 생각했다. 남편도 어린 시절 아기와 비슷했다. 한 가지 다행인 점은 아기의 모유 수유를 중단하지 않아도 된다는 점이었다. 대신 식사를 한 후 처방받은 불소치약을 사용해 아기의 이를 닦아 주고, 간식을 먹인 후에는 물을 주고, 아기가 잠이 들면 이를 (천으로) 닦아 주고, 한 달에 한 번 불소 바니쉬(도포)를 해야 한다고 했다. 그런 과정을 유지하는 것은 어려운 일이었지만, 효과는 대단했다. 일 년이 지난 후 아기의 충치가 멈추었을 뿐만 아니라 원래의 상태로 돌아갔다. 나는 나의 본능을 믿고, 다른 의사의 진단을 구하고, 내 아이의 건강을 위해 열심히 노력하는 것이 가치 있다는 사실을 배웠다.

08 다음 중 본문의 제목으로 가장 적합한 것은?

① 의사 쇼핑의 위험
② 나는 내 아들의 충치를 되돌렸다!
③ 아기의 충치를 유발하는 것은 무엇일까?
④ 최근 아기들의 치아 문제의 증가
⑤ 신생아에게 모유 수유의 중요성

| 정답 | ②

| 해설 | 아기에게 충치가 발생했고, 처음 찾아간 치과 의사의 소견이 잘못된 것이라는 생각으로 두 번째 치과 의사를 찾아 갔고, 결국 의사의 처방을 따라 아기의 충치를 막고 원래의 상태로 되돌렸다는 개인의 성공담을 말하고 있다. 따라서 본문의 제목으로 "나는 내 아들의 충치를 되돌렸다!"라는 ②가 적합하다.

09 다음 중 밑줄 친 대상이 다른 하나는?

① ⓐ
② ⓑ
③ ⓒ
④ ⓓ
⑤ ⓔ

| 정답 | ③

| 해설 | 모두 충치를 갖게 된 Ben이라는 아기를 지칭하지만, ③은 첫 번째 찾아갔던 치과 의사를 지칭하고 있다.

| 어휘 | **come off** (얼룩이) 빠지다, (칠이) 벗겨지다
baby-bottle tooth (decay) 우유병 치아 우식증(우유병을 이에 물고 잠이 드는 습관으로 인해 생기는 충치)
diagnosis ⓝ 진단   **breastfeed** ⓥ 모유를 먹이다
blame A on B A를 B의 탓으로 돌리다, A의 책임을 B에게 묻다
nursing ⓝ 수유, 양육   **permanent** ⓐ 영구적인
tooth decay 충치   **enamel** ⓝ (치아의) 에나멜질
predisposition ⓝ 기질, 성향   **wean** ⓥ (아기의) 젖을 떼다, 이유를 시작하다
prescription ⓝ 처방; 명령, 규정   **fluoride toothpaste** 불소치약
varnish ⓝ 니스, 광택제   **pay off** 성과를 거두다; ~을 다 갚다, 청산하다

instinct ⓝ 본능

doctor shopping 사실 doctor shopping은 Konglish(broken English)이고, 다른 의사의 진단을 경청한다는 의미로 second opinion이 올바른 영어 표현이다.

[10~12]

해석

세계화와 교육에 대한 이번 논의에 있어 싱가포르의 사정과 관련된 두 가지 특성을 주목해 볼 만 하다. 첫 번째 특징으로는, 전략적 위치를 제외하고 천연자원을 찾을 수 없는 작은 섬인 싱가포르의 생존은 싱가포르가 강대국에게 있어 유용성을 갖췄는지 여부에 항상 좌우되었다는 점이다. 싱가포르는 그 지역의 경제적 침투를 위한 기지로서 좋은 위치에 자리 잡았기 때문에 식민지로서 관심을 끌었다. 싱가포르는 1819년에서 1963년까지 식민지였고, 그 때의 경험은 싱가포르가 영국의 경제 제국의 일원으로 깊이 융합되는데 기여했다. 1950년대에는 문화와 언어 및 정치적 문제를 둘러싸고 정치적인 논쟁이 있었지만, 식민지의 언어인 영어가 경제적 자원으로서 지닌 가치에 대해서는 일찌감치 인식하고 있었다. 1950년 말 싱가포르의 경제를 수출입항에서 산업 경제로 전환시키려는 초창기 계획은 해외 자본과 기술 및 시장의 필요성을 인식한 것이다. 따라서 싱가포르는 식민지로부터 독립한 여러 국가의 특징인 경제적 민족주의 이념을 멀리했다. 싱가포르는 현재 1인당 연간 소득이 미화 2만 달러가 넘는 선진국으로 간주되지만, 그럼에도 전 세계의 경제 세력을 상대로 개방성을 유지해야 한다는 필요성을 이처럼 분명하게 인식하고 있는 점을 싱가포르의 계획 수립의 특징으로 볼 수 있다. 대외 무역은 싱가포르 경제의 주요 구성요소이며, 싱가포르의 지도자들은 업적을 벤치마킹하기 위한 하나의 방법으로서 국제적 기준에 따라 비교하기를 좋아한다. 싱가포르는 무역에 상당히 크게 의존하고 있으며 이에 따라 개방 경제를 보유할 수 밖에 없다는 점에서 어쩌면 세계 경제에서 특별한 위치를 점할 것이다.

10 본문의 제목으로 가장 알맞은 것은 무엇인가?

① 싱가포르의 식민지 시대
② 싱가포르의 전략적 위치의 중요성
③ 세계에서 가장 세계화된 나라로서의 싱가포르
④ 경제적 자원으로서의 식민지 시대의 언어
⑤ 싱가포르가 영국의 경제 제국의 일원으로서 융합됨

| 정답 | ③

| 해설 | 본문은 세계화 및 교육과 관련하여 싱가포르의 사례를 들고 있으며, 특히 싱가포르가 국가 발전을 위해 세계화 측면에서 어떤 노력을 해 왔는지를 말하고 있다. 본문에 따르면 싱가포르는 세계에서 가장 세계화된 나라라 할 수 있으며, 따라서 답은 ③이다.

11 빈칸 Ⓐ에 가장 알맞은 것은 무엇인가?

① 외부 세력의 지배를 받아야 한다
② 개방 경제를 보유할 수밖에 없다
③ 교육제도의 회복력을 가속화하다
④ 문명의 가치를 강조해야 한다
⑤ 아시아 국가로서의 문화적 정체성을 강화하다

| 정답 | ②

| 해설 | 빈칸 앞을 보면 싱가포르가 무역에 크게 의존하고 있음을 알 수 있다. 무역의 속성을 생각하면 싱가포르가 "개방 경제를 보유할 수밖에 없음"으로 빈칸의 내용을 유추할 수 있다. 따라서 답은 ②이다.

12 다음 중 사실이 **아닌** 것은 무엇인가?

① 싱가포르의 전략적 위치가 경제 성장에 기여했다.
② 싱가포르는 경제 발전에 있어 영어의 가치를 인식했다.
③ 싱가포르는 천연자원이 없었기 때문에 외국 자본에 의존했다.
④ 싱가포르는 현재까지 경제적 민족주의를 유지한다.
⑤ 대외무역은 싱가포르 경제를 설명하는 주요 특징 중 하나이다.

| 정답 | ④

| 해설 | "따라서 싱가포르는 식민지로부터 독립한 여러 국가의 특징인 경제적 민족주의 이념을 멀리했다"를 보면 ④의 내용은 본문과 거리가 멀다는 것을 알 수 있으며, 따라서 답은 ④이다.

"싱가포르는 그 지역의 경제적 침투를 위한 기지로서 좋은 위치에 자리 잡았기 때문에 식민지로서 관심을 끌었다"는 ①의 근거가 된다. "식민지의 언어인 영어가 경제적 자원으로서 지닌 가치에 대해서는 일찌감치 인식하고 있었다"는 ②의 근거가 된다. "전략적 위치를 제외하고 천연자원을 찾을 수 없는 작은 섬인 싱가포르의 생존은 싱가포르가 강대국에게 있어 유용성을 갖췄는지 여부에 항상 좌우되었다는 점이다"는 ③의 근거가 된다. "대외 무역은 싱가포르 경제의 주요 구성요소이며"는 ⑤의 근거가 된다.

| 어휘 |
context ⓝ 맥락, 전후 사정 　　**penetration** ⓝ 침투 　　**integration** ⓝ 통합, 융합
contestation ⓝ 논쟁, 쟁점 　　**recognition** ⓝ 인식, 인정 　　**entrepot** ⓝ 수출입항
eschew ⓥ 피하다, 멀리하다 　　**characterize** ⓥ ~의 특징이 되다
postcolonial ⓐ 식민지로부터 독립한, 식민지로부터 독립 후의 　　**grasp** ⓝ 이해, 파악
per capita 1인당 　　**component** ⓝ (구성)요소 　　**globalized** ⓐ 세계화된
accelerate ⓥ 가속화하다 　　**resilience** ⓝ 회복력, 탄성

[13~15]

해석

일이란 정신적이고 육체적인 노력을 소모해야 할 업무를 수행하는 것으로 정의되며, 인간의 필요에 부합하는 물품과 서비스를 제공하는 것을 목표로 삼는다. 직업이나 일자리는 정기적으로 받는 임금을 대가로 수행되는 일이다. 임금 또는 봉급은 많은 사람들의 자신의 필요를 충족시키기 위해 의존하는 주요 재원이다. 이러한 소득이 없다면 매일의 삶에 대처하는 과정에서 발생하는 괴로움은 증대되는 경향이 있다.

일은 종종 능력 및 역량을 획득하고 발휘할 수 있는 기반이 된다. 일은 반복적이더라도 사람의 에너지가 흡수될 수 있는 조직화된 환경을 제공한다. 일이 없다면, 이러한 기술과 역량을 발휘할 수 있는 기회는 줄 것이다. 일은 가정 환경과는 대조되는 정황에 접할 수 있도록 해 준다. 직장 환경하에서는 임무가 비교적 재미없는 것이더라도, 사람들은 집에서 하는 허드렛일과는 다른 것을 하며 즐길 수 있다.

직장 환경은 종종 우정 및 다른 사람들과 공유하는 활동에 참가할 수 있는 기회 등을 제공하곤 한다. 작업 환경과는 별개로, 한 사람이 보유한 친구 및 지인의 범위는 줄어들기 쉽다. 일은 안정적인 사회적 정체성을 일이 제공해 준다는 의미에서 가치 있게 여겨진다. 특히 남자의 경우, 자부심은 종종 자신이 가정의 생계유지를 위해 제공하는 경제적 기여도와 밀접한 관계가 있다. 이와 같은 어마어마한 목록을 배경으로 놓고 봤을 때, 왜 일자리가 없는 것이 스스로의 사회적인 가치에 관한 개인의 자신감을 약화시키는지 아는 것은 어렵지 않다.

13 윗글의 제목으로 가장 적절한 것을 고르시오.

① 일자리의 수를 늘리는 방법
② 일의 사회 조직
③ 일과 자부심 간의 상호 관계
④ 일의 사회적 중요성

| 정답 | ④

| 해설 | 본문은 일이란 무엇인지 설명한 다음 일이 사람에게 있어 사회적으로 왜 중요한 의미를 갖는지 설명하고 있다. 따라서 답은 ④ 이다.

14 윗글의 내용과 일치하는 것을 고르시오.

① 사람들은 종종 일 하면 힘들고 단조로운 것으로 연상한다.
② 사람들은 실직하면 큰 혼란에 빠진다.
③ 사람들은 종종 반복적인 일을 무보수로 생각하는 경향이 있다.
④ 업무 환경은 일상적 활동 속에서 리듬감을 제공하지 못한다.

| 정답 | ②

| 해설 | "이러한 소득이 없다면 매일의 삶에 대처하는 과정에서 발생하는 괴로움은 증대되는 경향이 있다(Without such as income, anxieties about coping with day-to-day life tend to multiply)." 즉 직업이 없어 소득을 얻지 못한다면 괴로움이 더 커지는 것이다. 덧붙여 사람은 직업을 잃게 되면 자신감을 잃고 위축된다. 이러한 점 등을 미루어 봤을 때 답으로 가장 적절한 것은 ②이다.

15 빈칸에 가장 알맞은 단어를 고르시오.

① 발전시키다   ② 증진시키다   ③ 약화시키다   ④ 강화시키다

| 정답 | ③

| 해설 | "일은 안정적인 사회적 정체성을 제공해 준다는 의미에서 가치 있게 여겨진다. 특히 남자의 경우, 자부심은 종종 자신이 가정의 생계유지를 위해 제공하는 경제적 기여도와 밀접한 관계가 있다.(Work is usually valued for the sense of stable social identity it offers. For men in particular, self-esteem is often bound up with the economic contribution they make to the maintenance of the household)" 따라서 "일자리가 없는 것(being without work)"은 "스스로의 사회적인 가치에 관한 개인의 자신감(individuals' confidence in their social value)"을 강화시키는 것이 아니라 "약화시킬(undermine)" 것이다. 그러므로 답은 ③이다.

| 어휘 | **expenditure** ⓝ 지출, 소모
cater to ~을 충족시키다, ~에 부합하다
in exchange for ~을 대가로, ~와 교환하여
multiply ⓥ 증대하다; 곱하다
context ⓝ 정황, 배경
circle ⓝ 계, 범위

objective ⓝ 목적, 목표
occupation ⓝ 직업, 일자리
cope with 대처하다, 대응하다
structured ⓐ 구조가 있는, 조직화된
chores ⓝ 잡일, 허드렛일
dwindle ⓥ 줄어들다

self-esteem ⑪ 자부심	**be bound up with** ~와 밀접한 관계가 있다
against the backdrop of ~을 배경으로	**formidable** ⓐ 가공할, 어마어마한
confidence ⑪ 자신감	**undermine** ⓥ 약화시키다
significance ⑪ 중요성, 중대성	**associate A with B** A와 B를 서로 연관 짓다
drudgery ⑪ 고된 일, 힘들고 단조로운 일	**disoriented** ⓐ 혼란에 빠진

[16~17] 서울여대 2014

해석

집 안에서 공간의 분할은 문화마다 차이를 보이기도 한다. 대부분의 미국 가정에서는 방의 배치는 침실, 거실, 식당, 놀이방 등으로 기능에 따라 공간을 분리시키고 각기 명명하는 모습을 드러낸다. 이러한 체계는 집에서 방 하나가 다양한 기능을 수행하기도 하는 다른 문화권과는 극명한 대조를 이룬다. 일본에서는 이동식 벽이 달린 집의 경우 큰 방을 두 개의 작은 방으로 변환시킬 수 있으며 따라서 거실이 침실 역할을 하기도 한다.

집이나 도시의 디자인이 다른 문화의 영향을 받을 경우, "본래의" 건축 양식이 사라지거나 모습을 감출 수 있다. 예를 들어, 한 프랑스 건축가가 인도 펀자브 지역의 수도인 찬디가르를 설계해 달라는 요청을 받았다. 그는 대중교통과 마을 중심부로부터의 이동을 요하는 중앙 집중식 쇼핑센터를 갖춘 형태로 도시를 설계하기로 결정했다. 결국 인도인들은 자신들이 사는 작은 지역 내에서 서로 사교적인 만남을 갖지 않게 되었다. 분명하게도 인도식 건축 양식이 아닌 것을 도입한 것이 도시 내에 거주하는 사람들의 문화 및 사회적 패턴에 영향을 미치게 된 것이었다.

---

16 외국인 건축가가 수도를 설계한 이후 인도인들의 사회적 패턴에 변화가 생긴 이유는 무엇인가?

① 대중교통이 대도시의 사회적 삶을 파괴했기 때문이다.
② 지방 지역이 더 이상 사회적 활동의 중심이 되지 못했기 때문이다.
③ 그 건축가가 내놓은 인도식과 거리가 먼 건축 양식이 지방의 사회적 교류를 촉진시켰기 때문이다.
④ 인도식 건축 양식이 전 세계에 소개되었기 때문이다.

| 정답 | ②

| 해설 | "그는 대중교통과 마을 중심부로부터의 이동을 요하는 중앙 집중식 쇼핑센터를 갖춘 형태로 도시를 설계하기로 결정했다. 결국 인도인들은 자신들이 사는 작은 지역 내에서 서로 사교적인 만남을 갖지 않게 되었다. 분명하게도 인도식 건축 양식이 아닌 것을 도입한 것이 도시 내에 거주하는 사람들의 문화 및 사회적 패턴에 영향을 미치게 된 것이었다(He decided to plan the city with centralized shopping centers which required public transportation and movement away from the village centers. Eventually the Indians stopped meeting each other socially in their small neighborhood. Apparently, the introduction of a non-Indian style of architecture affected some of the cultural and social patterns of those living in the city)." 이 말은 쇼핑센터로 인해 사람들이 중앙으로 몰리게 되면서 정작 말단부에서는 사회적 교류가 벌어지지 않게 되었고 그 결과 과거 지방 중심의 사회적 활동이 중앙에 집중되면서 변화를 겪게 되었음을 의미한다. 따라서 답은 ②이다.

본문의 제목으로 가장 알맞은 것은 무엇인가?

① 건축 설계에 있어서의 문화적 변화
② 세계사에 있어 건축이 미친 영향
③ 다양한 건물의 공간 배치
④ 쇼핑센터와 도시 개발

| 정답 |　①

| 해설 |　본문의 전반부는 집의 공간 활용에 있어 문화적인 차이가 드러남을 말하고 있으며 후반부는 도시 공간의 활용에 있어 다른 문화의 영향을 통해 기존의 문화가 변모하는 사례에 관해 말하고 있다. 즉 본문은 문화에 따른 건축 양식의 변화에 관해 그리고 건축 설계로 인한 문화적 변화에 관해 말하고 있다. 보기 중에서 이를 포괄하는 답은 ①이다.

| 어휘 |　**separation** ⓝ 구분, 분할
layout ⓝ 지면 구획, 배치, 설계
separateness ⓝ 분리, 단독
in sharp contrast to ~와 극명한 대조를 이룬다
native ⓐ (사물에) 고유한, 본래 갖추어져 있는
disguise ⓥ 변장하다, 감추다
public transportation 대중교통
apparently ⓐⓓ 분명하게
variation ⓝ 변화, 차이

vary ⓥ 다르다, 차이가 있다
reveal ⓥ 드러내다, 보이다
label ⓥ 라벨을 붙여 분류[명시]하다, 이름을 붙이다, 명명하다
sliding ⓐ 이동하는, 변화하는
architecture ⓝ 건축, 건축 양식, 건축물
centralized ⓐ 집중화된, 중앙 집권화된
neighborhood ⓝ 이웃, 지역
interaction ⓝ 상호 작용[영향]

[18~19] 명지대 2015

해석

밀레니엄 세대는 여러분이 묻는 사람이 누군지에 따라 1980년에서 2000년 사이에 태어난 사람들로 구성된다. 더 간단히 말하자면, 밀레니엄 세대는 10대, 20대, 30대로 구성된 사람들이다. 8천만 명에 달하는 밀레니엄 세대는 미국 역사상 가장 큰 연령 집단이다. 세계 각국의 밀레니엄 세대는 서로 차이가 있지만, 세계화ㆍ소셜 미디어ㆍ서양 문화의 수출ㆍ변화의 속도 등으로 인해 전 세계적으로 밀레니엄 세대끼리는 오히려 고국의 구세대에 비해 더 큰 유사성을 보이고 있다. 개인보다 가문의 역사를 더 중요시하는 중국에서조차도 인터넷과 도시화 그리고 한 자녀 정책으로 인해 서양만큼 지나치게 자신만만하고 자신에게만 관심을 보이는 세대가 등장하게 되었다.

밀레니엄 세대는 베이비 붐 세대가 사회 변혁을 야기한 이후 등장한 가장 위협적인 세대이며, 그 이유는 이들이 기성세대를 장악하려고 하기 때문이 아니라 기성세대 없이 성장하고 있기 때문이다. 산업 혁명은 개인에게 훨씬 큰 힘을 부여했다. 이제 개인은 도시로 이동하여 사업을 개시하고 조직을 구축할 수 있다. 정보 혁명은 개인에게 거대한 조직과 맞서 경쟁할 수 있는 기술을 제공하여 개인에게 더 큰 힘을 실어 주었다. 그 결과 해커 대 기업, 블로거 대 신문, 애플리케이션 개발자 대 산업 전체 등의 구도가 형성되었다. 밀레니엄 세대는 우리를 필요로 하지 않는다. 때문에 우리는 밀레니엄 세대가 두렵다.

18 본문의 제목으로 알맞은 것을 고르시오.

① 밀레니엄 세대, 여러분 자신에 경계하라
② 밀레니엄 세대 : 부각되는 희망과 약속
③ 밀레니엄 세대 : 잃어버린 세대
④ 왜 밀레니엄 세대는 우리에게 두려움을 주는가

| 정답 | ④

| 해설 | 본문 첫 단락이 밀레니엄 세대가 무엇인지 운을 띄우고 있다면, 두 번째 단락은 왜 밀레니엄 세대가 위협적인 세대이고 저자의 세대에게 두려움을 주는지 말하고 있다. 즉 본문의 핵심은 두 번째 단락인 것이다. 따라서 답은 ④이다.

19 본문에 따르면 사실이 <u>아닌</u> 것은 무엇인가?

① 중국의 밀레니엄 세대는 서양의 밀레니엄 세대에 비해 더 자기중심적이다.
② 각국의 밀레니엄 세대는 서로 비슷하며 이는 어느 정도 세계화 때문이다.
③ 밀레니엄 세대는 기성세대 없이 성장하고 있다.
④ 밀레니엄 세대는 미국 인구 가운데 최대 연령 집단을 이룬다.

| 정답 | ①

| 해설 | "개인보다 가문의 역사를 더 중요시하는 중국에서조차도 인터넷과 도시화 그리고 한 자녀 정책으로 인해 서양만큼 지나치게 자신만만하고 자신에게만 관심을 보이는 세대가 등장하게 되었다(Even in China, where family history is more important than any individual, the Internet, urbanization and the one-child policy have created a generation as overconfident and self-involved as the Western one)." 여기서 중국의 밀레니엄 세대는 '서양에 비해 더 자기중심적인' 세대가 아니라 '서양만큼 자기중심적인' 세대임을 알 수 있다. 따라서 답은 ①이다.

| 어휘 | **millennials** ⓝ 밀레니엄 세대
be made up of ~로 구성되다
strong ⓐ (집단의 수를 나타내는 명사 뒤에 쓰여) ~ 명의[~에 달하는]
age grouping 연령 집단
self-involved ⓐ 자신에게만 몰두한[관심이 있는]
the Establishment 기성세대
self-centered ⓐ 자기중심[본위]의, 이기적인

consist of ~로 구성되다

overconfident ⓐ 지나치게 자신만만한
take over 장악하다, 대체하다
empower ⓥ 권한을 주다, 힘을 실어 주다
constitute ⓥ ~을 구성하다[이루다]

해석

산업 성장이 건강과 행복에 기여하고, 부를 창조하며, 그리고 단순히 산업 성장 그 자체를 위해서도, 산업 성장은 오래도록 바람직한 것으로 간주되었다. 최근까지만 하더라도 진보는 사실 이와 같은 양적인 성장과 동일시되었다. 이와는 대조적으로, 현대 사회는 기술적으로 실현 가능하고 경제적으로 이득이 되지만, 바람직하지 못한 사회적 요소를 지니는 이와 같은 혁신이 과연 바람직한가에 대해 의문을 품기 시작했다. 인간과 환경에 대한 광범위한 잠재적 위협들에 대한 평가는 기술 정책 수립 시 고려해야만 하는 주요 요소 중 하나가 되어 가고 있다. 농약 사용에 대한 부분적 금지는, 처음에는 열렬한 환영을 받으며 수용되었던 기술이 이에 대한 위험이 알려진 이후 엄격한 통제 아래 놓이게 되었다는 사실에 대한 좋은 예이다. 보다 더 충격적인 예가 바로 스프레이 용기에 사용되는 프레온 가스이다. 이 물질은 인체에 직접적으로 유해하며, 대기 오존층에 미치는 영향을 통해 간접적으로 유해하다는 보고들이 나오고 있다. 이런 영향의 정도에 관한 정보를 토대로, 프레온 가스 사용을 규제하는 새로운 법안이 나왔으며, <u>결과적으로</u> 스프레이 제품 판매가 크게 줄었다.

---

20 본문의 제목으로 가장 적절한 것은?

① 기술 혁신의 바람직한 측면들   ② 산업 성장이 인류에게 가져온 편리함

③ 기술 개발에 대한 정책의 출현   ④ 산업 제품이 환경에 미치는 유해한 영향들

| 정답 | ④

| 해설 | 본문은 일단 산업 성장에 대해 부정적인 시각으로 바라보고 있다. 두 번째 문단에서 농약이나 프레온 가스 등의 예를 들고 있기 때문이다. 따라서 ①과 ②는 제목으로 적당하지 않으며, ③에 대해서도 본문 후반부에 언급되고 있기는 하지만 정책이나 법안은 결과적인 측면으로 나온 것이기 때문에 정답은 ④가 된다.

---

21 다음 중 빈칸에 들어갈 가장 적절한 것은?

① 다시 말하면   ② 반대로

③ 만약 그렇지 않다면   ④ 결과적으로

| 정답 | ④

| 해설 | 빈칸 바로 앞부분을 보면, 프레온 가스가 유해한 영향을 준다는 정보로 인해 이를 규제하는 법안이 나왔다는 내용이다. 그리고 뒷부분은 프레온 가스를 담고 있는 스프레이 용기 제품 판매가 크게 줄었다는 내용이다. 따라서 앞부분이 원인, 뒷부분이 결과의 내용이기 때문에 정답은 ④ consequently가 된다.

---

22 다음 중 현대 사회에 관해 바르게 서술한 것은?

① 국가들 간의 경쟁이 치열해지면서 현대 사회는 산업 기술에 심취해 있다.

② 기술 혁신에 관한 한 현대 사회는 보다 세심한 주의를 기울이고 있다.

③ 현대 사회는 모든 혁신을 바람직하지 않고 위험한 부산물로 간주하고 있다.

④ 현대 사회는 양적 성장에 기초해 기술 정책을 생성하고 있다.

| 정답 | ②

| 해설 | 농약이나 프레온 가스 경우처럼, 처음에는 좋아 보였던 기술도 나중에는 그렇지 않다는 사실이 드러난 이후 기술을 통제하고, 이에 대한 법안을 만들고 있다는 내용을 고려하면, 정답은 기술 혁신에 대해 보다 주의(scrupulous)해야 한다는 ②가 된다. ①은 본문과 무관하고, ③은 본문의 사실에 대해 너무 비약된 내용이며, ④의 경우 본문에서 인간과 환경에 대한 장기적 위험 요소를 평가해서 기술 정책을 만들고 있다고 했으므로 이를 양적 성장(quantitative growth)이라고 보는 것은 맞지 않다.

| 어휘 | desirable ⓐ 바람직한, 가치 있는   for its own sake 그것 자체를 위해

be identified with ~과 동일시되다, ~과 밀접한 관계를 맺다

innovation ⓝ 혁신   feasible ⓐ 실현 가능한

evaluation ⓝ 평가   pesticide ⓝ 살충제, 농약

ban ⓥ 금지하다   enthusiasm ⓝ 열광, 열의

exemplify ⓥ 전형적인 예가 되다   recognize ⓥ 인지하다, 인정하다

striking ⓐ 현저한, 이목을 끄는, 충격적인   fluorocarbon ⓝ 프레온 가스, 탄화 플루오르

substance ⓝ 물질   concerning ⓟⓡⓔⓟ ~에 관하여

legislation ⓝ 법안   conversely ⓐⓓ 거꾸로, 반대로

consequently ⓐⓓ 그 결과, 결과적으로   be infatuated with ~에 심취한

scrupulous ⓐ 양심적인, 꼼꼼한, 세심한, 용의주도한   as far as A is concerned A에 관한 한

perilous ⓐ 위험한   fallout ⓝ 좋지 못한 결과; 낙진

[23~24] 한국외대 2014

해석

인터넷, 소셜 네트워킹, 이동 통신 기술 등의 성장은 사람들의 의사소통 및 정보 교환 방식에 변화를 가져왔지만 의회는 디지털 통신이 부적절한 사생활 감청으로 피해를 입지 않도록 보호하기 위한 연방 정부 차원의 사생활 보호법을 제때 갱신하지 못하고 뒤쳐지고 있어 왔다. 지난달 말 상원 법사위가 이 문제에 있어 제대로 방향을 잡고 중대한 진전을 이루었다. 오직 한 명의 상원 의원만이 반대 의견을 공식적으로 표명한 구두 투표를 통해 법사위는 이메일에 주어지는 사생활 보호 수단을 대폭 강화하는 조치를 승인했다. 이 법안은 1986년에 제정되어 이미 구식이 되었지만 현재의 이메일 접속 관련 사항을 규제하는 법안을 개정한 것으로, 개인의 전자 메시지, 사진, 그 외 개인 신상 기록을 보유한 네트워크 서비스 제공 업체로부터 이메일 내용을 수집하려면 법 집행 담당관이 판사로부터 수색 영장을 받을 것을 요구하는 법이다. 즉 수색 대상이 되는 기록으로 불법 행위의 증거가 드러난다고 믿을 수 있을 만큼 상당한 근거가 존재함을 법원에 제시해야 한다는 의미이다.

23 다음 중 본문의 제목으로 가장 알맞은 것은 무엇인가?

① 개인 사생활 침해 우려에 관해 답이 나오지 않은 문제
② 온라인 사생활 보호 정책에 관한 편향된 시각
③ 사생활 관련 문제에 있어 효과적인 방안
④ 이메일 관련 사생활 보호를 위한 한 단계 전진

| 정답 | ④

| 해설 | 본문은 상원에서 통과된 새로운 법이 이메일상의 사생활 보호를 위한 하나의 중대한 진전을 이루었음을 말하고 있다. 따라서 답은 ④이다.

24 다음 중 본문에서 언급된 것은 무엇인가?

① 1986년 연방 정부의 사생활 보호 관련 법안은 이메일 통신의 활성화를 위해 폐지되었다.
② 디지털 산업의 부흥을 위해 연방 정부의 더 엄격한 법이 집행되고 있었다.
③ 과거에는 이메일 내용을 접하려면 수색 영장이 필요했다.
④ 상원 위원회는 1986년 법의 개정에 찬성표를 던졌다.

| 정답 | ④

| 해설 | 이번에 상원에서 통과된 법은 "1986년에 제정되어 이미 구식이 되었지만 현재의 이메일 접속 관련 사항을 규제하는 법안을 개정한 것(an amendment to the outdated 1986 law that now governs e-mail access)"이다. 따라서 답은 ④이다.

| 어휘 | **lag in** ~에서 뒤떨어지다
voice vote 구두[호명] 투표
probable cause 상당한 근거[이유]
abolish ⓥ 폐지하다

pry ⓥ (남의 사생활을) 캐묻다[캐다]
go on record 공식적으로 표명하다
biased ⓐ 편향된

[25~27] 국민대 2015

`해석`

아스피린은 통증과 열을 치료하기 위해 표준적으로 쓰이는 약품일 뿐만 아니라 심각한 질병을 예방하기 위해서도 쓰인다. 심장 발작 및 뇌졸중에 시달렸던 경험이 있는 수백만의 사람들은 재발을 막기 위해 매일 소량의 아스피린 정제를 상용하고 있으며, 건강한 사람도 점차 많은 수가 심혈관 건강을 지키기 위해 매일 아스피린을 복용하고 있다.
우리는 아스피린이 심혈관계에 문제가 있는 사람들이 심장 발작이나 뇌졸중에 걸리지 않도록 예방하는 데 매우 효과적이라는 사실을 오래전부터 잘 알고 있다. 아스피린은 혈액을 묽게 만들어서 작은 크기의 혈전이 생성되지 않게 막아 준다. 보다 최근에 보면 매일 소량의 아스피린을 섭취할 경우 유방암과 전립선암뿐만 아니라 위암과 장암을 예방하며 정신적 능력의 감퇴를 늦춰 준다.
하지만 아스피린은 혈액을 묽게 만들기 때문에 규칙적으로 아스피린을 섭취하는 사람들은 어쩌면 뇌졸중에 걸릴 위험성이 더 클 수 있으며 그 이유는 출혈을 더 많이 하기 때문이다. 아스피린의 장기간 섭취는 또한 시력 감퇴 및 내출혈 위험성의 증가와 연관이 있다.
일반의인 닥터 말스(Marles)는 아스피린으로 혜택을 보는 사람들은 심장 발작이나 뇌졸중 같이 모종의 심장 관련 문제를 겪은 사람들이다. 그 외 다른 사람들의 경우 심혈관 질환과 내출혈의 위험성을 신중하게 가늠하는 일은 의사의 몫이다.

25 다음 중 본문의 제목으로 가장 알맞은 것은 무엇인가?

① 아스피린의 폭넓은 사용
③ 아스피린 섭취 방법 및 시기

② 현대의 만병통치약 아스피린
④ 아스피린의 장점과 단점

| 정답 | ④

| 해설 | 본문은 아스피린을 정기적으로 섭취하는 것에 어떤 장점이 있고(첫 번째 및 두 번째 단락), 어떤 단점이 있는지(세 번째 단락) 설명하고 있다. 따라서 답은 ④이다.

26 아스피린의 해로운 부작용이 <u>아닌</u> 것은 무엇인가?

① 심장 발작　　　② 시력 감퇴　　　③ 뇌졸중 위험 증가　　　④ 내출혈 위험 증가

| 정답 | ①

| 해설 | 아스피린은 심장 발작과 뇌졸중이 발생하지 않게 예방한다고 나와 있으며 세 번째 단락에 제시된 부작용 가운데 심장 발작은 언급되지 않았다. 따라서 답은 ①이다.

---

27 본문에 따르면 사실이 <u>아닌</u> 것은 무엇인가?

① 심장 아스피린은 특정 암의 예방에 효과적이다.
② 아스피린의 여러 기능 중 하나는 혈액을 묽게 하는 것이다.
③ 아스피린은 보통은 진통제와 해열제로 쓰인다.
④ 의사들은 사람들에게 매일 아스피린을 섭취하라고 권장한다.

| 정답 | ④

| 해설 | 아스피린을 정기적으로 섭취할 것을 권장받은 사람들은 어디까지나 모종의 심장 관련 문제를 겪은 사람들만이며, 그 외 사람들은 의사의 신중한 판단을 따를 것을 권장하고 있다. 따라서 답은 ④이다.

| 어휘 | **remedy** ⓝ 치료(약), 요법
low-dose ⓐ 소량의, 투여량이 낮은
cardiovascular ⓐ 심혈관의
blood clot 혈전
prostate ⓝ 전립선
internal bleeding 내출혈
weigh up 가늠하다, 저울질하다
fever relief 해열제

pop ⓥ (알약을) 상용하다
tablet ⓝ 정제
thin ⓥ (액체를) 묽게 만들다
gastro-intestinal ⓐ 위장의
macular degeneration 시력 감퇴
general practitioner 일반의(전문의가 아닌)
panacea ⓝ 만병통치약

[28~30] 홍익대 2020

해석

부르디외(Bourdieu)는 교육제도를 학업적 적성과 문화적 유산 사이의 감춰진 연계를 통해 합법적 문화를 재생산해 내기 위한 기관으로 간주한다. 평등한 기회와 성과주의 이념에도 불구하고, 지배 계층이 교육제도에 요구하는 것은 합법적 문화를 현재의 상태 그대로 재현하고 합법적으로 이를 조작할 수 있는 대리인을 배출하는 것 이외의 다른 것은 없다고 그는 믿는다.

부르디외는 그것이 학교를 통해 구체화된 지배그룹의 문화라고 주장했다. 따라서 학업적 기준에 의해 측정된 능력은 선천적 '재능'이 아니라 "계층의 문화적 습관과 교육제도의 요구 혹은 교육제도 내에서 성공을 정의하는 기준들 사이의 다소간의 연관성"에 기인한다는 사실을 무시하면서, 교육적 차이가 계급에 기초한 차이가 아니라 개인의 재능에서 비롯되는 것으로 잘못 인식되는 경우가 많다.

문화자본(cultural capital)에 대한 개념은 부르디외가 1960년대 초 부르주아 문화에 대한 친숙함을 기술하기 위해 제안했으며, 이때 부르주아 문화의 불평등한 분배가 개인의 재능과 학문적 성과주의를 빙자하여 사회의 계층 구조를 보존하는 데 도움을 준다. 이 개념은 지식의 습득(교육에 의한 것이든 아니면 그 외의 것이든), 문화적 코드, 화법 등을 포함하며, 이는 개인에게 일종의 '아비튀스(habitus)'로 체화되고, 문화적 상품으로 객관화된다.

28 다음 중 본문의 내용과 일치하지 <u>않는</u> 것은?

① 노동자 계층 학생들은 고등교육의 중산층 아비튀스 속에서 외부인처럼 느낄 수 있다.

② 개인은 사회 계층에 따라 선천적 지능을 갖는 경향이 있다.

③ 교육기관은 지배 계층의 문화자본의 수익성을 보장해 준다.

④ 지배 문화는 스스로를 보편적으로 인식되도록 만들어서 지배 집단의 이익을 합법화한다.

| 정답 | ②

| 해설 | ① 교육기관은 지배 계층의 문화를 재생산하는 곳이라고 했으므로, 노동자 계층의 학생은 그곳에서 이질감을 느낄 수 있다. ③ 본문의 "it is the culture of the dominant group, which is embodied in schools."에서 교육 제도는 지배 계층의 문화의 재생산 역할을 담당한다고 했으므로, 이는 지배 계층의 문화자본의 수익성을 지켜준다는 것을 의미한다. ④ 부르디외가 말한 '습관'에 해당하는 '아비튀스(habitus)'에 대한 설명이다. 정답은 ④로, 본문의 두 번째 문단에서 "학업적 기준에 의해 측정된 능력은 선천적 '재능'이 아니라 "계층의 문화적 습관과 교육제도의 요구 혹은 교육제도 내에서 성공을 정의하는 기준들 사이의 다소간의 연관성"에 기인한다"고 했으므로, 본문에서는 개인의 선천적 지능에 대해 언급하고 있지 않다.

29 다음 중 본문을 통해 추론할 수 있는 것은?

① 부르디외에 따르면, 모든 문화는 동등하게 가치 있고, 동등하게 정당하다.

② 부르디외에 따르면, 학교 교육은 기존의 계급 계층화를 촉진하는 뿌리 깊게 자리 잡은 인식의 방식을 만들어 낸다.

③ 부르디외에 따르면, 개인의 효능은 삶의 모든 단계에 걸쳐 마스터한 경험에 의해 가장 큰 영향을 받는다.

④ 부르디외에 따르면, 문화적 재생산은 사소한 매커니즘으로 이를 통해 사회경제적 양극화가 발생한다.

| 정답 | ②

| 해설 | 부르디외는 학교 교육을 통해 기존의 계급의 계층 구조가 보존된다고 했다. 즉 학교 교육은 이러한 계층 구조를 촉진하기 위한 인식의 틀을 제공해 주는 기관이므로 정답은 ②가 된다.

30 다음 중 본문의 제목으로 가장 적합한 것은?

① 학교 교육에서 개인의 재능이 갖는 중요성

② 학교 교육에서 학생의 성취가 갖는 중요성

③ 학교 교육에서 지배적 문화의 사회적 책임

④ 학교 교육에서 일어나는 불평등의 재생산

| 정답 | ④

| 해설 | 본문의 첫 번째 문단에서 학교 교육이란 지배 계층의 문화를 재생산(an institution for the reproduction of legitimate culture)하기 위한 제도이며, 학교 교육을 통해 합법적 문화를 재생산하고 그러한 문화를 관리할 수 있는 대리인을 만들어 내는 것(reproduce the legitimate culture as it stands and produce agents capable of manipulating it legitimately)이라고 설명하고 있다. 그리고 이를 통해 사회적 계층구조를 보존한다(conserve social hierarchy)고 설명하고 있으므로, 교육은 계층 간의 불평등을 고착시키기 위한 도구인 것이다. 따라서 정답은 ④가 된다.

| 어휘 | **Bourdieu** 부르디외(프랑스의 사회학자)　　**institution** ⓝ 제도, 기관

reproduction ⓝ 재현, 재생　　**legitimate** ⓐ 합법적인, 정당한

linkage ⓝ 연결, 결합

scholastic ⓐ 학업의

aptitude ⓝ 소질, 적성

heritage ⓝ 유산

meritocracy ⓝ 성과주의, 실력주의

call upon 요청하다, 부탁하다

dominant ⓐ 지배적인

other than ~외에, ~이 아닌

reproduce ⓥ 번식하다; (그림, 글) 복사[복제]하다; 재생[재현]하다

as it stands 현재 상태 그대로

agent ⓝ 대리인

manipulate ⓥ 조종하다, 조작하다

embody ⓥ (사상·특질을) 상징[구현]하다, 포함하다, 담다

criterion ⓝ (pl. criteria) (판단이나 결정을 위한) 기준

stem from ~에서 생겨나다, 유래하다

affinity ⓝ 친밀감; 관련성

notion ⓝ 생각, 관념

cultural capital 문화자본, 문화적 자본(한 개인이 자신의 가정이 계급적으로 위치한 범주에 따라 전수받는 일련의 다양한 언어적, 문화적 능력을 말함)

bourgeois ⓝ 자본가 계급, 부르주아

conserve ⓥ 보존하다, 보호하다

hierarchy ⓝ (특히 사회나 조직 내의) 계급, 계층

under the cloak of ~을 핑계로, ~의 구실 아래

and so forth ~ 등등

habitus ⓝ 습관, 버릇, 아비튀스(인간 행위를 생산하는 무의식적 성향)

objectify ⓥ ~을 객관화하다

[31~32] 서강대 2011

> 해석

어느 시점부터 우리가 입는 것이 중요해지기 시작했을까? 언제, 어떻게, 왜 외모가 사람들이 자신이나 다른 이들에 대해 느끼는 방식에 깊게 자리 잡게 되었을까? 르네상스 시대가 전환점이었다. 나는 르네상스라는 용어를 매우 넓게 잡고 있는데, 대략 1,300년부터 1,600년의 긴 기간을 의미한다. 1,300년 이후 매우 다양한 제품들이 전 세계적으로 생산되고 소비되었다. 직물과 가구, 의상 장식품들이 물품들의 유례없는 확산에 주요 부분을 차지했으며 전 세계와의 상호 작용을 늘어나게 했다. 새로운 재료 및 절단·재봉 분야에서의 혁신적인 기술, 그리고 특히 남성복에서 몸의 외관을 강조하고자 보다 더 조이게 입으려는 욕망 등이 어우러져 재단 분야는 급격한 변화를 보였다. 상인들은 모자, 지갑, 장갑, 그리고 턱수염에서 긴 땋은 머리에 이르는 헤어피스 등과 같은 세련된 장식품들을 만들어 궁정이나 도시에서 시장을 넓혀 갔다. 이와 동시에, 새로운 미디어와 거울의 확산으로 인해 보다 더 많은 이들이 자신의 외모에 관심을 갖게 되었으며, 남들에게 자신이 어떻게 보일지 상상해 보게 되었다. 예술가들은 메달이나 초상화, 목판이나 풍속화에서 인간을 전례 없던 규모로 묘사하기 시작했으며, 의상 전문 서적(costume books)이라는 새로운 장르도 생겨났다. <u>이런 소비자 및 시각적 세상이 확장되면서, 느낌의 새로운 방식이 생겨날 수 있는 조건을 형성했다.</u>

---

31 다음 중 본문의 제목으로 가장 적절한 것은?

① 르네상스 시대의 세계 무역의 확장

② 르네상스 시대의 패션의 탄생

③ 소비자 문화 및 의복 산업

④ 르네상스 시대의 사치품

| 정답 | ②

| 해설 | 본문에서는 언제부터 우리가 입는 것이 중요해졌는지, 그리고 어떻게 이런 현상이 생겨났는지에 대해 서술하고 있다. 따라서 보기 ②의 '르네상스 시대의 패션의 탄생'이 제목으로 적절하다. ③의 경우는 소비자(consumer)나 의복(clothing) 등이 본문

에 등장하지만, 본문에서 이를 문화(culture)나 산업(industry)의 개념으로 확장하고 있지는 않으므로 정답이 될 수 없다.

---

32 다음 중 밑줄 친 문장에서 유추할 수 있는 것은?

① 의상은 안정을 위한 욕망과 귀족적 계층 구조를 나타내는 상징이 되었다.
② 르네상스 시대에는 좋은 의상이 자신의 미덕을 확인시켜 주는 것으로 생각되었다.
③ 사치품의 소비는 그 자체로 도의적이며 국가적인 문제가 되었다.
④ 의복 관습의 변화로 사람들의 스스로에 대한 인식 및 문화적 민감도에 변화가 생겼다.

| 정답 | ④

| 해설 | 밑줄의 내용을 다시 정리하자면, 의상과 관련된 물품들을 소비할 수 있는 소비자(consumer)들이 늘어나고, 외형의 모습을 보다 더 시각화(visual)하는 세상이 되면서, 감정의 새로운 방식(패션)이 생겨날 조건이 갖추어졌다는 내용이다. 보기에서 ①과 ③은 본문의 내용과 전혀 상관이 없으며, ②의 경우 약간의 유추는 가능하나 미덕을 확인시켜 주는 도구로서의 의상에 대한 내용은 본문과 무관하다. 답은 ④로 옷을 입는 방식(customs)에 대한 변화(dynamics)가 자신의 지각과 문화적 민감도에 영향을 주었으며, 이로 인해 패션이 생겨날 수 있었다고 유추할 수 있다.

| 어휘 |

be embedded in ~에 박히다, 자리잡다
goods ⓝ 상품
furnishing ⓝ 가구, 비품
unprecedented ⓐ 전례 없는, 미증유의
tailoring ⓝ 재단
emphasize ⓥ (중요성을) 강조하다
braid ⓝ 땋은 머리
depict ⓥ 묘사하다
circulate ⓥ 순환하다, 퍼뜨리다
luxury goods 사치품
nobility ⓝ 귀족

circa(= c., ca.) ⓟⓡⓔⓟ (연대·날짜 앞에서) 약, …경
textile ⓝ 직물
apparel ⓝ 의류
diffusion ⓝ 보급, 유포
sewing ⓝ 재봉, 바느질감
court ⓝ 궁정, 대궐, 궁궐
A lead to B A가 B를 이끌어 내다, 도출해 내다
genre scene 풍속화
condition ⓥ 요건[조건]을 이루다
hierarchy ⓝ 계층, 계급 제도, 체계
virtue ⓝ 미덕

[33~35]

해석

여성의 전형적 특징인 협동적 대화 스타일을 공공의 영역으로 포함시킬 경우 나타나는 긍정적 요소를 입증하는 연구 프로젝트가 존재한다. 일부 학자들은 남성 및 여성 면접관을 비교한 다음, 여성 면접관들이 상호 작용을 이 끌어내기 위한 전략을 통해 (남성에 비해) 더욱 공개적이면서 평등한 논의를 한다는 점을 제시했다. 더욱 "여성스러운" 대화 양식을 매우 귀중하게 취급하는 정신 치료 및 상담 등의 직업에서도 여성의 비중이 상당하다는 점이 제시된 바 있다. 반면에 공공 영역에서 경력을 추구하고자 하는 여성들은 지속적으로 문제와 맞닥뜨리게 된다. 만약 여성들이 더욱 적대적이고 더욱 "남성적"인 대화 양식을 도입할 경우, 이들은 "여성스럽지 않다"는 꼬리표가 붙을 위험에 처한다. 엄청난 수의 여성들이 점차 높은 기대를 품고 직업 시장에 뛰어드는 상황에서, 여성들이 더 뛰어난 모습을 보이는 협력적 대화 유형이 새로운 자원으로서 공공 영역에서 환영받을 것인지 아니면 도전을 받게 될 것인지는 더 두고 볼 필요가 있다. 여성을 대상으로 한 더 명시적인 형태의 차별은 서서히 근절되고 있다. 하지만 직장에서 여성을 소외시키는 행위는 지속되고 있으며, 여성이 자신이 선택한 직업에서 더욱 발전하는 데 여전히 어려움을 겪고 있다는 점에서 기타 <u>은밀한</u> 형태의 차별 수단은 여전히 작동 중에 있다는 점이 드러난다.

33 윗글의 제목으로 가장 적절한 것은?

① 성, 교육, 윤리
② 여성을 위한 귀중한 자원
③ 여성, 언어, 직업
④ 여성적 이념에 대한 도전

| 정답 | ③

| 해설 | 본문은 여성, 여성의 대화 양식, 여성의 직업 추구와 대화 양식 간의 관계, 직장 내 여성 차별 등에 관한 내용을 담고 있다. 따라서 답은 ③이 된다.

34 윗글의 내용과 가장 가까운 것은?

① 여성이 직장에서 인정받기 위해서는 남성의 담화 스타일에 따라 대화하고 행동해야 한다.
② 여성은 담화 스타일로 인해서 직장에서 불이익을 받지 않는다.
③ 공공 분야에서 남성과 여성의 언어 차이는 점차적으로 사라져 가고 있다.
④ 상담이나 심리 치료 분야 직종에서 여성의 언어 스타일은 가치 있는 것으로 인정을 받고 있다.

| 정답 | ④

| 해설 | "더욱 '여성스러운' 대화 양식을 매우 귀중하게 취급하는 정신 치료 및 상담 등의 직업에서도 여성의 비중이 상당하다는 점이 제시된 바 있다(It has been pointed out that in professions such as psycho-therapy and counselling, where more "female" interactive patterns are highly valued, women are a significant presence)."는 보기 ④의 근거로 볼 수 있다. 따라서 답은 ④이다.

35 윗글의 빈칸 ⓐ와 ⓑ에 들어갈 가장 적절한 표현은?

① 명시적인 – 은밀한
② 격렬한 – 느긋한
③ 미미한 – 중대한
④ 독점적인 – 포괄적인

| 정답 | ①

| 해설 | 문맥상 빈칸 ⓐ가 들어 있는 문장과 빈칸 ⓑ가 들어 있는 문장은 서로 대조되기 때문에 빈칸 역시 이를 기준으로 유추해야 한다. 빈칸 ⓐ와 ⓑ 모두 여성에 대한 차별의 성격을 말하고 있다. 그리고 빈칸 ⓐ로 묘사되는 여성을 향한 차별이 "서서히 근절되고 있다(are slowly being eradicated)"면 빈칸 ⓐ로 묘사되는 여성을 향한 차별은 "여전히 작동 중에 있다(are still at work)." 빈칸 ⓑ가 들어간 문장에서 "직장에서 여성을 소외시키는 행위는 지속되고 있으며, 여성이 자신이 선택한 직업에서 더욱 발전하는 데 여전히 어려움을 겪고 있다는 점(the continuing marginalization of women in the professions, and the fact that women are still having difficulty progressing in their chosen career)"을 통해 미루어 보건데, ⓐ에 들어갈 것은 '드러내 놓고 하는 차별은 근절되고 있다'는 의미에서 "명시적인(overt)"이고 ⓑ에 들어갈 것은 '아직도 여성에 대한 차별은 은밀히 진행 중에 있다'는 의미에서 "은밀한(covert)"이다. 따라서 답은 ①이다.

| 어휘 | demonstrate ⓥ 입증하다
cooperative ⓐ 협력하는, 협동적인
interviewer ⓝ 면접관
interactive ⓐ 상호 작용을 하는, 대화식의
label ⓥ (부당한) 꼬리표를 붙이다
incorporate ⓥ 포함하다
discourse ⓝ 담론, 담화
psycho-therapy ⓝ 심리 치료
adversarial ⓐ 대립적인, 적대적인
unfeminine ⓐ 여자답지 못한, 여성스럽지 않은

overt ⓐ 명시적인, 공공연한

marginalization ⓝ 소외

covert ⓐ 은밀한

marginal ⓐ 미미한, 중요하지 않은

inclusive ⓐ 포괄적인

eradicate ⓥ 근절하다

profession ⓝ 직업, 직장

ideology ⓝ 이념, 관념

exclusive ⓐ 독점적인

[36~38] 상명대 2019

해석

박테리아의 항생제 내성은 오랜 기간 축적된 것이지만, 실제 박테리아는 엄청나게 빠른 속도로 복제하며, 형성된 내성도 분열 시 복제된다. 뿐만 아니라 내성 유전자를 보유한 박테리아는 '수평적 유전자 전이(horizontal gene transfer)'를 통해 내성 유전자를 전파한다. 이런 과정을 통해 모체가 되지 않고서도 다른 박테리아로부터 받은 내성 유전자를 전달할 수 있다. 이러한 변종의 확산을 통제하기 한층 어렵게 만드는 것은 그것이 순환 과정에서 발생하기 때문이다. 사람의 경우, 사람이 감염되고 내성 박테리아가 내장에 자리를 잡게 되면 <u>고통을 당하는 측</u>은 둘 중 하나를 선택하게 되는데, 도움을 구하거나 아니면 집에 머무른다. 의학적 도움을 구할 때, 지역 의사를 방문하기로 예약을 하든 아니면 직접 대형 병원에 가는 것이든, 그들은 다른 환자들을 감염시키고, 나중에 퇴원해서 집으로 돌려보내진다. 그러면 내성 박테리아는 지역 사회로 퍼져나가게 된다. 감염자가 의료 치료를 전혀 받지 않기로 결정한 경우 그것이 최종 결과가 된다. 그들은 박테리아를 집에 두고 치료 없이 번식하도록 허용한다.

---

36 다음 중 밑줄 친 ⓐ sufferer의 동의어로 적합한 것은?

① 살충제 ② 피고 ③ 전염 ④ 희생자 ⑤ 입원한

| 정답 | ④

| 해설 | ⓐ의 'sufferer'는 내성 박테리아에 감염된 사람을 뜻하므로, '희생자'를 뜻하는 ④ victim이 동의어가 된다.

---

37 다음 중 본문의 제목으로 가장 적합한 것은?

① 항생제 내성의 위험

② 의사를 방문해야 하는가?

③ 박테리아는 어떻게 변화하고 있는가?

④ 항생제 내성 박테리아의 교차 감염

⑤ 감염은 어떻게 확산되는가?

| 정답 | ①

| 해설 | 본문에서는 항생제에 내성을 가진 박테리아가 자신이 획득한 내성을 어떻게 복제하고 전달하는지 설명하고 있고, 항생제 내성 박테리아의 확산을 통제하기 어려운 점에 대해 말하고 있다. 따라서 '항생제 내성 박테리아가 지닌 위험성'에 대해 말하고 있으므로, 제목으로 ①이 적합하다. ③과 ⑤는 키워드인 '항생제 내성'이 빠져있어 의미가 포괄적이므로 정답이 될 수 없다.

38 다음 중 본문의 핵심 논점은 무엇인가?

① 박테리아는 시간이 지남에 따라 '수평적 유전자 전이'를 통해 변한다.

② 박테리아가 점점 위험해지고 있다.

③ 감염자들은 도움을 구하는 것에 대해 갈등을 겪고 있다.

④ 감염되면 집에 있는 것이 좋다.

⑤ 박테리아는 서로 내성을 전달한다.

| 정답 | ②

| 해설 | 본문은 항생제 내성을 가진 박테리아가 통제하기 어렵다는 것이 핵심 논점이다. 따라서 이와 유사한 ②가 정답이 된다.

| 어휘 |

resistance ⓝ 내성, 저항	antibiotic ⓝ 항생제
build up 축적되다	replicate ⓥ 재현하다, 복제하다
extraordinarily ⓐ 비상하게, 엄청나게	duplicate ⓥ 복사하다, 복제하다
gene ⓝ 유전자	happen to 우연히 ~하다
via ⓟ (어떤 장소를) 경유하여[거쳐]	horizontal ⓐ 수평의; 수평선
bacterium ⓝ 박테리아(bacteria)의 단수	pass on 넘겨주다, 전달하다
strain ⓝ (세균의) 변종, 균주	cyclical ⓐ 순환하는, 주기적인
gut ⓝ 내장	contaminate ⓥ 오염시키다, 더럽히다
discharge ⓥ 퇴원시키다, 방출하다, 해고하다	breed ⓥ 기르다
pesticide ⓝ 살충제	defendant ⓝ 피고
contagion ⓝ 전염	victim ⓝ 희생자
hospitalized ⓐ 입원한	cross-contamination ⓝ 교차 감염, 교차 오염

[39~40] 건국대 2017

해석

한 흥미로운 실험에서 연구자들은 실제로 일어난 사건(참된 기억)과 실제 일어나지 않은 사건(거짓 기억)에 대해 사진이 아이들의 기억에 미치는 영향을 조사했다. 세 차례 진행한 면담에서 매번 10세 아이들에게 네 장의 사진을 보여 줬다. 세 장의 사진은 부모가 제공한 것으로 아이가 6세 때 겪었던 일이 담겨 있고, 한 장의 사진은 열기구가 찍힌 가짜 사진이었다. 절반의 아이들에게는 열기구에 알지 못하는 사람들이 타고 있는 사진(아이가 없는 상태)을 보여 주었고, 나머지 절반의 아이들에게는 포토샵을 이용해 사진을 편집해서 일부의 가족들과 아이가 다른 사람들과 함께 타고 있는 사진(아이가 있는 상태)을 보여 주었다. 당연한 말이지만, 실제 아이들은 그 누구도 열기구에 탄 적이 없었다. 연구원들은 거의 모든 아이들이 실제 사진에 있는 사건에 대해 추억을 떠올렸다. 더 중요한 것은, 많은 어린이들이 사진에 자신이 등장하든 아니든 열기구를 탔던 추억도 떠올렸다는 것이다. 하지만 아이들이 자신을 사진에서 볼 수 있었을 때(약 47퍼센트) 그렇지 않은 경우(약 18퍼센트)보다 가짜 기억이 훨씬 더 빈번하게 발생했다.

39 윗글의 제목으로 가장 적절한 것은?

① 열기구 타기

② 사진에 있는 사건을 기억하기

③ 사진을 가지고 아이들과 인터뷰하기

④ 아이들에게 거짓 기억을 생성

⑤ 기술을 이용한 사진 조사

| 정답 | ④

| 해설 | 본문은 "사진이 아이들의 기억에 미치는 영향(the impact of photos on children's memories for events)"에 대한 연구를 보여 주고 있다. 실제로 경험하지 않은 일이라도 사진을 가공해 실제로 경험한 일처럼 제시할 경우 아이들이 가짜 기억을 빈번하게 떠올린다는 실험이다. 따라서 조작된 사진이 기억에 영향을 미치는 '아이들에게 거짓 기억을 생성'이라는 ④가 정답이 된다.

---

40 윗글의 내용과 일치하지 <u>않는</u> 것은?

① 실험에 참가한 아이들의 나이는 10세였다.
② 부모들은 아이들이 6세 즈음에 찍었던 사진들을 제공했다.
③ 아이들이 열기구를 타고 있는 사진들은 조작된 것이었다.
④ 모든 아이들은 실제로 열기구를 탄 적이 없었다고 보고했다.
⑤ 거의 모든 아이들은 진짜 사진들에 관한 사건들을 기억했다.

| 정답 | ④

| 해설 | 본문 후반부의 "many of the children also reported memories of riding in the hot air balloon"을 통해, 많은 아이들이 자신이 그런 경험을 한 적이 없음에도 불구하고 실제 열기구를 탄 적이 있다고 거짓 기억을 떠올렸다고 했으므로 ④가 본문과 일치하지 않고 있다.

| 어휘 | **fascinating** ⓐ 흥미로운, 매력적인   **depict** ⓥ 묘사하다
doctor ⓥ 조작[변조]하다   **a hot air balloon** 열기구

연습 문제   01   ③   02   ①   03   ②

01 다음 글의 주제로 가장 적절한 것은?

사람들은 처음 두 발로 이동했다. 이후 동물들을 길들여 타고 다녔다. 사람들은 황소나 낙타, 코끼리 같은 다양한 동물들을 이용했다. 하지만 사람들이 가장 많이 탄 동물들은 말과에 속하는 동물로 말이나 당나귀, 노새 등이 포함된다. 이후 사람들은 마차를 제작해 동물들에 연결시켜서 보다 많은 사람들이 한시에 이동했다. 이것은 커다란 진전이었다. 왜일까? 이는 사람들이 처음으로 바퀴를 사용한 것이기 때문이다. 바퀴의 발명으로 이동이 훨씬 더 쉬워지고 빨라졌다. 오늘날 자동차를 이용해 빠르고 안락하게 이동한다.

① 인류 역사에서 운송의 역할
② 수년간 인류가 동물을 이용한 방식
③ 인류 역사에서 운송의 발전 과정
④ 전 세계적으로 이동 문화의 다양성

| 정답 | ③

| 해설 | 본문은 인류가 어떻게 이동을 발전시켜 나갔는가에 대해 서술하고 있다. 처음에는 발로, 나중에는 동물을 이용해서, 이후에는 바퀴를 사용해 자동차까지 발명하게 되었다는 내용이므로 정답은 ③이 된다.

| 어휘 | **belong to** ～에 속하다   **mule** ⑩ 노새
　　　　transportation ⑩ 운송, 수송, 교통   **diversity** ⑩ 다양성

02 다음 글의 주제로 가장 적절한 것은?

우리는 모두 사람의 이름이나 얼굴을 기억하지 못하거나 가게에 들어갔는데 무엇을 사려고 했는지 기억하지 못해 당황했던 경험이 있다. 이런 일들은 뇌의 실행 능력이 감소하고 있으며, 좀 더 뇌를 쓰는 연습을 해야 한다는 것을 알려 주는 조기 경보일 수 있다. 젊은 사람의 정신력을 어떻게 유지하고 있는지 질문을 받은 Michael DeBakey는 "우리들이 근육을 예로 들면, 근육은 사용하면 튼튼해지고 사용하지 않으면 쇠약해지는데요, 이와 같은 예가 정신에도 적용될 수 있습니다. 정신을 더 사용하면 할수록 정신은 더 잘 작동하지요"라고 밝혔다. 정신적 활력의 가장 큰 위협은 TV 앞에서 아무런 생각 없이 앉아 있는 것이라고 믿는 그는 "정신을 자극하는 데 더 좋은 방법들이 매우 많다"고 말한다.

① 지력을 향상시키기
② 추억을 소중히 간직하기
③ 마인드 컨트롤 평가하기
④ 근육을 강화시키기

| 정답 | ①

| 해설 | 본문의 내용은 근육 강화와는 무관한다. 근육은 예로 든 것으로 근육이 사용하면 강해지듯이 정신(mind)도 그러하다는 것을 강조하고 있으므로, 정신력이나 지력과 관계된 ①이 주제로 적당하다.

| 어휘 | **frustration** ⑩ 좌절   **early warning** 조기 경고
　　　　decline ⓥ 감소하다, 기울다   **muscle** ⑩ 근육
　　　　the same apply to A 같은 내용이 A에도 적용되다

function ⓥ 작동하다
mindlessly 匎 무관심하게, 아무 생각 없이
threat ⓝ 위협
cherish ⓥ 간직하다
strengthen ⓥ 강화하다

vigour ⓝ 활력, 정력
stimulate ⓥ 자극하다
encouragement ⓝ 격려
evaluate ⓥ 평가하다

03 본문의 핵심은 무엇인가?

비록 세계화가 동질화의 수준을 높이긴 하지만 세계는 여전히 매우 다채로운 곳이다. 사람들은 자연환경뿐만 아니라 문화 · 경제 · 정치 등에서 여전히 뚜렷한 차이를 발견할 수 있다. 이러한 다양성은 너무나 광범위하기 때문에 심지어 세계화의 힘이 가장 강력하게 발휘되는 경우라도 쉽사리 없어지지 않는다. 사실 세계화는 종종 현지인들에게 강렬한 반응을 불러일으키며, 그 결과 현지인들은 자신들의 삶의 방식에 있어 다른 이들과 구별되는 독특한 요소를 지속적으로 단호히 유지하겠다는 결심을 하게 되었다. 따라서 세계화는 세계가 지속적으로 특징을 갖게끔 기여하는 다양성 또한 고찰하고, 어쩌면 가장 중요한 요소인, 세계화를 통한 동질화와 문화적 다양성과 정치적 다양성의 보호 차원에서의 세계화에 대한 반응, 이 두 종류의 힘 사이에 존재하는 긴장을 고찰할 경우에만 이해가 가능해진다.

① 세계화는 하나로 수렴되는 힘과 동질화를 야기하는 힘을 특징으로 한다.
② 다양성과 세계화는 서로 떼어놓을 수 없는 것으로 이해되어야 한다.
③ 지역적 다양성은 세계의 동질화와 항상 갈등 관계에 있지 않다.
④ 세계화의 추세는 널리 퍼져 있지만 그로 인한 혜택은 균등하지 않다.

| 정답 | ②

| 해설 | "세계화는 종종 현지인들에게 강렬한 반응을 불러일으키며, 그 결과 현지인들은 자신들의 삶의 방식에 있어 다른 이들과 구별되는 독특한 요소를 지속적으로 단호히 유지하겠다는 결심을 하게 되었다(globalization often provokes a strong reaction on the part of local people, making them all the more determined to maintain what is distinctive about their way of life)." 즉 세계화는 동질성을 높일 뿐만 아니라 각자 만의 독특한 요소 즉 다양성 또한 높인다. 따라서 답은 ②이다.

| 어휘 | globalization ⓝ 세계화
marked 匎 뚜렷한
readily 손쉽게, 순조롭게
provoke ⓥ 불러일으키다, 선동하다
all the more 더욱, 오히려
distinctive 匎 특유의, 독특한
characterize ⓥ 특징을 나타내다, 특징짓다
protect ⓥ 보호하다
inseparable 匎 불가분의, 떼어놓을 수 없는
trend ⓝ 성향, 유행, 추세
uneven 匎 고르지 않은, 균등하지 않은

homogenization ⓝ 동질화, 균질화
diversity ⓝ 다양성
extinguish ⓥ 끝내다, 없애다
reaction ⓝ 반응, 반작용, 반향, 반발
determined 匎 단단히 결심한, 단호한
understandable 匎 이해 가능한, 당연한
tension ⓝ 긴장(감)
converge ⓥ 모여들다, 집중하다; 수렴되다
conflict ⓝ 갈등, 논쟁
pervasive 匎 스며드는, 널리 퍼진, 만연하는

01	③	02	⑤	03	②	04	④	05	②	06	③	07	②	08	③	09	②	10	④
11	①	12	④	13	①	14	③	15	③	16	④	17	②	18	②	19	①	20	④
21	③	22	③	23	①	24	②	25	①										

[01~02]

해석

아이들이 한 단어로 말을 하는 단계에서 어떻게 말하는지에 대한 문화적인 차이는 아이들이 남이 말하는 것을 듣는 것이 아이들이 말하는 것에 영향을 끼친다는 것을 보여 준다. 미국의 아이들과 다르게 한국의 유아들은 명사보다 동사가 먼저 터져 나온다. 이와 유사하게 중국어를 사용하는 유아들은 그 어머니들과 장난감을 가지고 놀 때 명사보다 동사를 더 많이 말한다. 양 아시아 그룹의 어머니들은 그들의 말에 훨씬 더 많은 동사를 사용하고 이어서 동작이 따라 나오는 말을 한다. 예를 들어 "너 뭐 하니?"라고 말하든지 "자동차를 차고에 넣어."라고 한다. 반면에 미국의 어머니들은 <u>이와는 대조적으로</u> 명사를 훨씬 더 많이 사용한다. 예를 들어 "그건 공이다."처럼 명사를 더 많이 말한 뒤 이어서 "그게 뭐지?"라고 명사를 답으로 요하는 질문을 한다.

01 윗글의 적절한 주제는 무엇인가?
① 아이들의 언어가 발달하는 방법
② 아이들의 언어에 있어 명사와 동사
③ 언어 발달에 있어 문화적 차이
④ 어린이들에게 효과적인 질문 형태
⑤ 미국과 아시아 부모 사이의 차이

| 정답 | ③

| 해설 | 아이들이 말을 하는 단계에서 어떻게 말하는지에 대한 문화적인 차이에 대하여 설명하고 이에 대한 예시를 들고 있으므로, 정답은 ③이다.

02 빈칸에 들어갈 적당한 것은?
① 예를 들어
② 이에 더하여, 게다가
③ 결과적으로
④ 요약하면, 짧게 말하면
⑤ ~와 대조적으로

| 정답 | ⑤

| 해설 | 양 아시아 그룹의 어머니들은 그들의 말에 훨씬 더 많은 동사를 사용한다고 한 후, 미국의 어머니들은 명사를 훨씬 더 많이 사용한다고 하였다. 그렇다면 한국과 중국의 어머니들과 미국의 어머니들은 서로 대조되는 관계이므로 정답은 ⑤가 된다.

| 어휘 | **bolster** ⓥ 지지하다, 강화하다 **spurt** ⓝ 용솟음, 분출
pepper ⓥ 후추를 치다, 퍼붓다 **in short** 요약해서
in contrast ~와 대조적으로

여러 나라에서, 신부의 옷이나 결혼식에는 흰색을 제외한 다른 색이 사용되었다. 일부 아시아 국가들과 중동에서는, 붉은색과 주황색이 기쁨과 행복의 상징으로 간주되었다. 중국 문화권에서는, 청첩장에 부와 행복을 상징하는 붉은색과 황금색이 사용되었다. 하객들은 작은 붉은 봉투에 축의금을 넣어서 신혼부부에게 주었다. 그러나 모든 문화권에서 돈이 적절한 결혼 선물로 생각된 것은 아니다. 많은 서구권 국가들, 특히 영국에서 하객들은 신랑 신부의 신혼집에 필요한 생활용품을 선물한다. 전통적 결혼식에서는 신부가 베일을 쓴다. 머리와 얼굴을 가리는 베일을 쓰는 것은 2,000년 이상 된 전통이다. 베일은 원래 비밀과 정숙함의 상징이었기 때문에, 식이 끝난 후 신랑만이 벗길 수 있었다. 오늘날에도 많은 신부들이 베일을 쓰지만 장식용일 뿐이다. 몇몇 국가에서는, 부부가 되기 전까지 서로를 보거나 만질 수 없도록 결혼식 내내 신랑 신부의 사이에 베일을 드리우기도 한다.

03 윗글의 주제(topic)로 가장 적합한 것을 고르시오.

① 베일의 전통적 의미 　　　　　　　 ② 여러 나라의 다양한 결혼 의식
③ 색과 문화마다 다른 색의 상징 　　 ④ 다양한 결혼 선물들의 상징적 의미

| 정답 | ②

| 해설 | 중국, 중동, 영국 등 '문화권마다 다른 결혼 의식'을 소개하는 글이므로 ②가 정답이다. 결혼 의식에 사용되는 베일, 색, 선물 등은 의식의 다양성을 보여 주는 예시에 불과하므로 나머지 보기들은 적당하지 않다.

04 다음 중 윗글의 내용과 일치하는 것을 고르시오.

① 과거에는, 많은 신부들이 장식을 위해 베일을 썼다.
② 영국에서는, 결혼식 하객들이 돈을 신혼부부를 위한 적절한 선물로 여긴다.
③ 아시아와 중동에서는, 결혼식에 붉은색과 주황색을 사용하지 못한다.
④ 일부 국가에서는, 신랑과 신부가 결혼식 중 서로를 봐서는 안 된다.

| 정답 | ④

| 해설 | 마지막 문장 "In some countries, a veil is placed between the bride and groom during the wedding ceremony so that they cannot see or touch each other until they are married."에서, 일부 국가에서 신랑과 신부가 결혼식 중 서로를 보는 것이 금지되어 있다는 것을 알 수 있다.

| 어휘 | **wedding invitation** 청첩장　　　**newlywed** ⓝ 신혼부부　　　**envelope** ⓝ 봉투
　　　 suitable ⓐ 적절한　　　　　　 **bride** ⓝ 신부　　　　　　　　 **groom** ⓝ 신랑
　　　 household item 생활용품　　　 **secrecy** ⓝ 비밀, 신비　　　　 **modesty** ⓝ 정숙함(단정함), 겸손

[05~07]

해석

65세 이상 인구는 2100년까지 크게 증가할 것이다. 인구학자들은 전 세계적으로 장수하는 인구가 늘고 있다는 점에서 인구 고령화가 일종의 "성공 사례"라는 데는 동의하지만, 고령 인구의 지속적 증가는 사회에 많은 문제를 일으킬 것이라는 점도 지적한다. 미국에서는 정부가 은퇴자들에게 사회 보장 연금을 지급한다. 그러나 이것만으로는 은퇴자들이 생계를 유지할 수 없기 때문에, 개인 투자나 보험으로 보완해야 한다. 중국을 위시한 대부분의 아시아 국가에서는, 자녀들에게 연로한 부모를 부양할 책임이 있다. 그러나 이러한 사회가 변화하면서, 특히 중국의 한 자녀 정책 이후, 자녀들이 자신의 가정은 물론이고 부모를 부양하기가 점차 어려워지고 있다. 사람들이 그 어느 때보다 장수하게 되면서 전 세계가 영향을 받고 있다.

05 윗글의 주제는 무엇인가?

① 오직 소수의 인구학자들만이 늘어난 수명이 성공의 증거라는 데 동의한다.
② 문화가 다른 사회들은 서로 다른 방식으로 노인 부양책을 모색한다.
③ 인구 고령화는 사망률은 감소하고 장수는 증가한 결과이다.
④ 세계 인구는 특히 중국과 대부분의 아시아국에서 빠르게 고령화되고 있다.

| 정답 | ②

| 해설 | 이 글의 소재는 '인구 고령화'이고 주제는 '문화권마다 다른 인구 고령화 대책'이므로 정답은 ②이다. 미국과 중국이 문화가 다른 사회의 예시로 제시되었다. ①은 지문의 내용과 일치하지 않고, ③, ④는 지문에 언급되지 않았다.

06 다음 중 빈칸에 가장 적절한 것은?

① 그래서   ② 게다가
③ 그러나   ④ 그렇지 않다면

| 정답 | ③

| 해설 | 빈칸을 전후로 대조적 내용이므로 역접의 연결어 however가 필요하다. "children bear the responsibility of caring for their elderly parents.(자녀가 연로한 부모를 부양해야 한다.) ↔ however, it is becoming more and more difficult for children to care for parents…(그러나 자녀가 부모를 부양하기가 점점 더 어려워지고 있다…)"

07 다음 중 지문에서 추론할 수 없는 것은?

① 미국에서는, 고령 인구를 부양하기 위해 세금을 인상해야 할 것이다.
② 고령 인구 부양 비용은 증가할 것이다. 전 세계에서 비만이 증가하고 있기 때문이다.
③ 중국에서는, 많은 사람들이 연로한 부모를 부양할 의무가 자신에게 있다고 생각한다.
④ 시간이 지날수록, 고령 인구는 경제 성장과 사회의 안녕에 중요한 영향을 미치게 된다.

| 정답 | ②

| 해설 | 추론은 주제에서 벗어나지 않는 범위까지만 가능하다. 지문의 주제는 '인구 고령화 문제와 그 대책'이고 ①, ③은 대책, ④는 문제이므로 모두 주제와 관련 있다. 비만은 주제와 무관하므로 ②는 추론 불가능하다.

| 어휘 | **demographer** ⑪ 인구학자

note ⑰ 주목하다, 언급하다

pose ⑰ 제기하다, 드러내다

social security 사회 보장

insurance ⑪ 보험

as well as ~는 물론이고

affect ⑰ 영향을 미치다, (정서적 충격, 연민 등을) 유발하다

represent ⑰ 표현하다, 대표하다

sustained ⓐ 지속적인

retired worker ⑪ 은퇴자, 퇴직자

supplement ⑰ 보완[보충]하다

bear a responsibility 책임을 지다

ever before 예전보다, 그 어느 때보다

[08~09] 성균관대 2018

해석

2017년 스마트폰이 출시된 지 10년이 됐다. 이것이 의미하는 것은 점차 과학이 따라잡고 있고, 세상을 바꾸는 스마트폰의 영향에 대한 새로운 연구가 등장하고 있다는 것이다. 손안에 스마트폰이라는 컴퓨터를 가지고 있는 것은 우리에게 인터넷 이전에는 전례가 없던 서로의 삶에 접근하는 것을 가능하게 했고, 우리 자신의 삶에 대한 통찰력 또한 제공해 주었다. 많은 사람들은 소셜 미디어 이전의 시기를 더 이상 기억하지 못할 수 있다. 하지만 그것이 우리를 더 행복하게 하고 있을까?

최근 소셜 미디어가 우리의 정신 건강에 부정적인 영향을 미친다고 많은 사람들이 말하고 있다. 그런 의미에서 새해 초반을 디지털 해독의 기회로 삼는 것도 나쁘지 않을 것이다. 초기 연구들을 보면, 소셜 미디어가 우리를 이전보다 더 밀접하게 서로를 이어 주고 있고, 우리에게 환상적인 도파민 자극을 제공해 주고 있지만, 이와 동시에 소셜 미디어의 사용이 일부 사람들에게는 우울증과 불안, 외로움 등의 증상과 관련이 있다고 말한다.

소셜 미디어 업계의 거인 페이스북은 지난달 블로그 포스트를 통해 이러한 우려에 대응하면서, 소셜 미디어 자체가 본질적으로 나쁜 것이라기보다는 소셜 미디어를 어떻게 사용하는가에 달려 있다고 주장했다. 그렇다. 많은 기술들이 부적절하게 사용될 경우 피해를 입힐 수 있는 능력을 가지고 있다. 그렇다고 해서 우리가 현재 형태에 대한 소셜 미디어의 디자인과 영향에 대해 심문해서는 안 된다는 것을 의미하는 것은 아니다. 실제로 마크 주커버그는 이것이 2018년 페이스북의 목표가 될 것이라고 암시했다. 그는 이번 주에 쓴 글을 통해, 올해 자신의 목표 중 하나는 "페이스북에 사용된 시간이 잘 사용된 시간이 되도록 하는 것"이라고 밝힌 바 있다.

---

08 다음 중 빈칸에 들어갈 가장 적합한 것은?

① 우리의 집중력을 지나치게 많이 흡수함으로써

② 그것들을 사용하는 빈도에 따라

③ 부적절하게 사용될 경우

④ 그것들의 복잡성에 대한 우리의 무지를 위해

⑤ 엄격하게 관리될 경우

| 정답 | ③

| 해설 | 빈칸 바로 앞에서 소셜 미디어가 태생적으로 나쁜 것이 아니라 소셜 미디어를 사용하는 방법에 따라 잘못이 발생할 수 있다는 내용이므로, 많은 기술이 잘못 사용할 경우 피해를 유발할 수 있다는 내용이 이어져야 한다. 따라서 '부적절하게 사용될 경우'라고 한 ③이 정답이 된다.

09 다음 중 본문의 주제로 가장 적합한 것은?

① 소셜 미디어 활용을 위한 가장 효과적인 방법 ② 소셜 미디어가 우리의 정신적 건강에 미치는 영향

③ 소셜 미디어의 유용성 ④ 스마트폰의 과감한 혁신

⑤ 소셜 미디어가 우리의 삶에 가져온 급격한 변화

| 정답 | ②

| 해설 | 본문의 키워드는 스마트폰이 아닌 '소셜 미디어'로, 소셜 미디어가 가져오는 정신 건강에 대한 부정적인 영향에 대해 말하고 있으며, 그래서 두 번째 문단에서 '디지털 해독'을 권하고 있다. 따라서 정답은 ②가 된다.

| 어휘 |
turn ⓥ (어떤 나이 · 시기가) 되다

catch up 따라잡다, 따라가다

insight ⓝ 이해, 간파, 통찰력

have a negative impact on ~에 나쁜 영향을 주다

exhilarating ⓐ 아주 신나는[즐거운], 유쾌한, 상쾌한

dopamine ⓝ 도파민(신경 전달 물질 등의 기능을 하는 체내 유기 화합물)

be associated with ~와 연관된

depression ⓝ 우울증

inherently ⓐⓓ 본질적으로, 선천적으로

gradually ad 서서히, 점차

palm ⓝ 손바닥

unprecedented ⓐ 전례가 없는, 공전의

detox ⓥ 해독하다 ⓝ 해독

symptom ⓝ 징후, 증상

blogpost ⓝ 블로그 포스트, 블로그에 올린 글

interrogate ⓥ 심문하다

[10~12] 국민대 2016

해석

어린 시절 호기심의 영역이었던 우리는 왜 우리 자신을 간지럽힐 수 없는지에 대한 의문이 이제 신경과학자들을 흥분시키고 있다. 그들의 관심을 이해하려면 다음과 같은 사실을 고려해야 한다. 신체가 움직일 때마다 모든 종류의 방법으로 당신을 혼란스럽게 할 수 있는 감각이 만들어진다는 사실이다. 당신의 양손 중 하나가 당신의 다리를 스칠 때마다 누군가가 당신을 성희롱하거나 공격한다고 가정할 때 발생할 수 있는 엄청난 혼란을 상상해 보라. 당신의 행위와 다른 사람들의 행위를 구별할 수 있다는 것이 주체 의식과 대행자 의식의 핵심 부분이다. 이 질문에 대한 답을 찾기 위해, 사라 제인 블랙모어(Sarah-Jayne Blackmore)는 그녀의 동료들이 실험 참가자들의 손바닥을 간지럽게 했을 때와 실험 참가자들이 스스로 간지럽게 했을 때 각각 실험 참가자들의 두뇌를 단층 촬영했다. 실험 결과 나타난 두뇌 활동을 통해 그녀는 다음과 같은 결론을 내렸다. 즉 우리가 팔다리를 움직일 때마다 소뇌가 신체의 움직임에 대한 정확한 예측을 산출한 다음, 촉각이 처리되는 체감각 피질에서 활동을 감소시키는 또 다른 그림자 신호를 내보낸다는 것이다. 그 결과 우리가 스스로를 간지럽힐 경우 다른 누군가가 우리를 간지럽힐 때와 동일한 강도를 느끼지 못하며, 그래서 우리는 차분한 상태를 유지할 수 있게 된다.

10 다음 중 본문의 주제에 해당하는 것은?

① 어린아이와 같은 호기심의 중요성

② 신뢰할 수 없는 인간의 감각

③ 뇌의 단층 촬영 기술의 최근 발전상

④ 자신과 타인을 구별하는 뇌의 메커니즘

| 정답 | ④

| 해설 | 윗글은 '우리는 왜 스스로를 간지럽힐 수 없는가?'에 대한 질문에 답하고 있는 내용으로, 우리가 자극을 했을 때와 타인이 자극을 했을 경우 감각이 처리되는 신호 과정이 각각 다르다는 것이 질문에 대한 답변이 된다. 따라서 자신과 타인을 구별하는 뇌의 메커니즘이라는 ④가 글의 주된 내용을 설명하는 보기가 된다.

11 다음 중 빈칸 ⓐ에 들어갈 가장 적합한 것은?

① 결과　　　　　　　　　　　② 이유
③ 증거　　　　　　　　　　　④ 예측

| 정답 | ①

| 해설 | 빈칸 ⓐ 이후 that절의 내용은 바로 앞 문장에 대한 '결과'에 해당한다.

12 다음 중 본문의 내용과 일치하는 것은?

① 쉽게 간지럼을 타는 사람들은 똑똑한 사람들이다.
② 손바닥은 인간의 신체 중 가장 예민한 부분이다.
③ 사람들은 자기 자신을 간지럽힐 때 공격을 당한다고 생각한다.
④ 우리는 우리가 간지럽게 할 것이라는 것을 예측할 수 있기 때문에 우리는 자기 자신을 간지럽힐 수 없다.

| 정답 | ④

| 해설 | 본문 후반의 "whenever we move our limbs, the brain's cerebellum produces precise predictions of the body's movements and then sends a second shadow signal that damps down activity in the somatosensory cortex where tactile feelings are processed" 부분을 통해, 왜 우리는 스스로를 간지럽힐 수 없는지에 대해 설명하고 있다. 우리가 스스로를 간지럽게 할 경우, 우리의 뇌는 이를 예측해서 강도를 약화시키는 'a second shadow signal'을 내보내기 때문이라고 했으므로, 이 내용이 보기 ④와 일치하게 된다.

| 어휘 |

domain ⓝ 영역	**tickle** ⓥ 간지럼을 태우다	**neuroscientist** ⓝ 신경 과학자
fondle ⓥ 애무하다, 희롱하다	**agency** ⓝ 힘, 작용	**sense of self** 주체 의식
sense of agency 대행자 의식	**subject** ⓝ 실험 대상	**palm** ⓝ 손바닥
limb ⓝ 팔, 다리, 사지	**cerebellum** ⓝ 소뇌	**damp down** 둔화시키다
somatosensory ⓐ 체감각의	**cortex** ⓝ 피질	**tactile** ⓐ 촉각의

[13~14] 가천대 2019

해석

DNA의 이중 나선 구조의 발견은 처음에는 숭배의 대상이었지만, 지금은 불확실한 미래의 문을 연 것으로 여겨진다. 과학자들은 새로운 DNA의 일부를 살아있는 세포에 삽입할 수 있었고, 즉각적으로, 이러한 활동은 꺼림칙한 시선을 받게 되었다. 유전 조작을 통해 세포로 삽입될 수 있는 일부 질병으로 인해 인간 문명이 파괴될 수 있다고 여겨진 것이다. 사람들은 이러한 연구를 통제할 수 있도록 엄격한 규칙에 대한 요구가 이루어져야 함을 깨달았다. 이러한 점 때문에 과학자들이 재조합-DNA 기술을 발견하기까지 시간이 꽤 걸렸다. 다행스럽게도 통제 규정은 실행되지 않았고, 따라서 DNA 기술에 대한 공포가 근거 없는 것임이 드러났을 때, 규제 시도는 온건한 규제일지라도 모두 소멸했다.

> **13** 빈칸 Ⓐ에 가장 알맞은 것은 무엇인가?
>
> ① 꺼림칙한   ② 호의적으로
>
> ③ 공명정대하게   ④ 찬성하여

| 정답 | ①

| 해설 | 빈칸 뒤를 보면 유전 조작을 통해 세포로 일부 질병이 삽입되면 인간 문명이 파괴될 수 있다고 여겨졌다는 말에서, DNA 및 유전 조작과 관련된 연구가 사람들의 "꺼림칙한" 시선을 받게 되었음을 유추할 수 있다. 따라서 답은 ①이다.

> **14** 다음 중 본문의 주제로 가장 적합한 것은 무엇인가?
>
> ① DNA 기술에 대한 성공적인 규제 시도
>
> ② 신뢰할 수 없는 생물학 기술
>
> ③ DNA 기술에 대한 근거 없는 두려움
>
> ④ 생물학적 발전의 가능성

| 정답 | ③

| 해설 | 본문은 DNA 기술에 대해 사람들이 처음에는 근거 없는 두려움을 가졌지만 이후 재조합-DNA 기술의 발견과 함께 두려움을 가질 필요가 없음을 깨닫게 되면서 규제 시도 또한 사라지게 되었음을 말하고 있다. 따라서 답은 ③이다. 참고로 이 글은 시사 독해 실렉션 (홍준기 저 종합출판 발간)에서 인용한 지문이다.

| 어휘 | **double-helical** ⓐ 이중 나선의   **revere** ⓥ 숭배하다, 존경하다

suspiciously ⓐⓓ 수상쩍게[의심스럽게], 꺼림칙하게   **engineer** ⓥ 유전자를 조작하다

call (for) ⓝ ~에 대한 요청[요구]   **recombinant** ⓐ (유전자 간의) 재조합형(의)

unfounded ⓐ 근거 없는, 사실무근의   **dissipate** ⓥ 소멸하다, 소멸되다

favorably ⓐⓓ 호의적으로   **impartially** ⓐⓓ 편견 없이, 공명정대하게

approvingly ⓐⓓ 찬성하여, 만족스러운 듯이   **unreliability** ⓝ 신뢰할 수 없음, 믿을 수 없음

groundless ⓐ 근거 없는   **potential** ⓝ 가능성, 잠재력

[15~16] 단국대 2014

해석

> 나는 최소한 실험을 통해 다음의 사실을 배웠다. 만일 누군가가 자신의 꿈을 향해 자신 있게 나아가고 자신이 꿈꾸었던 인생을 살기 위해 노력한다면, 그 사람은 평범한 상황에서는 예상할 수 없었던 성공을 맛보게 될 것이다. 그 사람은 몇 가지 일들은 과거로 남겨 두고, 보이지 않는 한계를 뛰어넘는다. 이렇게 되면 새로우면서 보편적인 그러면서 더욱 자유로운 법칙이 그 사람의 주변에서 그리고 그 사람의 안에서 자리 잡기 시작한다. 아니면 오래 된 법칙이 확장되면서 좀 더 자유로운 의미로 자신에게 편리한 방향으로 해석되며, 더욱 높은 단계에 속한 존재라는 허가를 받아 살아가게 될 것이다. 그 사람이 자신의 삶을 간소화하는 데 비례하여 세상의 법칙은 점차 덜 복잡해 보일 것이며, 고독은 더 이상 고독이 아니게 될 것이며, 가난은 더 이상 가난이 아니게 될 것이고, 약점은 더 이상 약점이 아니게 될 것이다. 만일 허황된 꿈을 품고 있다 하더라도, 여기서 노력을 잃지 말았으면 한다. 꿈에서 출발하여 노력을 지속해 나가는 것이다. 이제 꿈을 기반으로 삼는 것이다.

15 다음 중 본문의 주제로 가장 적합한 것은 무엇인가?

① 인생의 온갖 잡동사니를 간소화하라.

② 자신의 한계와 곤란에 도전하라.

③ 꿈을 갖고 이를 달성하기 위해 지속적으로 노력하다.

④ 자신과 세상을 향해 더욱 객관적이 되라.

| 정답 | ③

| 해설 | "만일 누군가가 자신의 꿈을 향해 자신 있게 나아가고 자신이 꿈꾸었던 인생을 살기 위해 노력한다면, 그 사람은 평범한 상황에서는 예상할 수 없었던 성공을 맛보게 될 것이다(if one advances confidently in the direction of his dreams, and endeavors to live the life which he has imagined, he will meet with a success unexpected in common hours)" 및 "만일 허황된 꿈을 품고 있다 하더라도, 여기서 노력을 잃지 말았으면 한다. 꿈에서 출발하여 노력을 지속해 나가는 것이다. 이제 꿈을 기반으로 삼는 것이다(If you have built castles in the air, your work need not be lost; that is where they should be. Now put the foundations under them)" 를 보면 저자는 꿈을 갖고 이를 달성하기 위해 노력할 것을 주장하고 있음을 알 수 있다. 따라서 답은 ③이다.

16 다음 중 빈칸 (A)와 (B)에 가장 적합한 것은 무엇인가?

① 그리고 – 그리고

② 그리고 – ~도 아닌

③ ~도 아닌 – 그리고

④ ~도 아닌 – ~도 아닌

| 정답 | ④

| 해설 | 빈칸 앞 문장이 부정문이며, 같은 단어(solitude)를 반복하여 강조하고 있으므로, 빈칸에도 부정을 나타내는 의미의 단어가 와야 한다. 즉, poverty 및 weakness가 들어간 두 문장도 solitude와 같은 구성하에서 부정을 나타내는 단어가 와야 한다. 따라서 '~은 더 이상 ~이 아니다'라는 의미에서 nor가 와야 하며, 그러므로 답은 ④이다.

| 어휘 | **advance** ⓥ 전진하다, 나아가다

endeavor ⓥ 노력하다, 시도하다

boundary ⓝ 경계, 한계

establish oneself 자리 잡다, 들어앉았다

license ⓝ 허가, 인가, (행동의) 자유, 방종

in proportion as ~하는 데 비례하여

solitude ⓝ 고독, 쓸쓸한 곳

build castles in the air 공중누각을 세우다, 공상에 잠기다, 허황된 꿈[계획]을 세우다[품다]

foundation ⓝ 기초, 토대, 기반

confidently ⓐ 자신 있게, 확신을 가지고

put behind (불쾌한 일 따위를) 잊어버리다

universal ⓐ 보편적인, 일반적인, 전 세계의

in one's favor ~에게 편리하게, ~에게 좋게

order ⓝ 계층, 서열, 단계

simplify ⓥ 간소화하다, 단순화하다

clutter ⓝ 잡동사니, 혼란, 어수선함

해석

조직을 성공적으로 이끌기를 원하는가? 헬렌 로스버그(Helen Rothberg)는 자신의 저서 "The Perfect Mix"에서 만일 그렇다면 비즈니스 스쿨에 진학하는 대신에 술을 섞기 시작하라고 썼다. 로스버그는 현재 경영 컨설턴트이자 마리스트 컬리지(Marist College)에서 전략학 교수직을 맡고 있지만, 대학원 시절 바텐더로 일하면서 가장 귀중한 리더십 기술을 익혔다고 주장한다. 그중 몇 가지 예를 들면, 대인 관계와 관련 있는 상황을 분석하기 위해 신체 언어를 판독하는 기술은 바에서 벌어지는 싸움을 억누르는 데 도움이 되며, 매력은 넘치지만 술값은 떼어먹으려는 노동자들을 상대하는 기술은 알맹이는 없고 보여 주기 식인 웨이터들을 <u>솎아 내는</u> 데 매우 유용하고, 여기에 핵심적인 주요 사항에 대해 의사소통하는 기술 또한 익힐 수 있었다. 세부적인 사항에 관해 의사소통을 하는 것은 매우 중요한 일이며, 그 이유는 바에서는 사장이 웨이터 일을 하는 직원들에게 설명하지 않고 메뉴를 개량할 경우 직원들이 고객들에게 메뉴에 관해 설명을 할 수 없어서 매출이 뚝 떨어지기 때문이다. 로스버그는 바텐더 일과 조직을 이끄는 일을 서로 비교하면서 다음과 같이 말했다. "술을 섞을(조직 내에서 어떤 분위기를 유발할) 때도 있고, 술을 흔들(조직 내에서 충격을 야기할) 때도 있고, 술을 혼합할(조직 내에서 융합을 이끌) 때도 있습니다. 그리고 있는 그대로 깔끔하게 내놓을 때도 있습니다."

17 다음 중 본문의 주제는 무엇인가?

① 바텐더 일이 비즈니스 스쿨보다 더 낫다.
② 리더십 기술은 대인 관계 분석에서 유래한다.
③ 바텐더 일을 하면 대학원 학비를 벌 수 있다.
④ 리더가 되려면 대학원에 진학할 필요가 있다.

| 정답 | ②

| 해설 | 로스버그가 바텐더 일을 강조한 이유는 바텐더로 일하면서 귀중한 리더십 기술을 익혔기 때문이다. 본문에서 바텐더 일을 하면서 배운 리더십 기술의 예로 제시된 것들은 모두 사람을 상대하는 방법과 관련이 있고 여기에 더해 의사소통 기술 또한 포함된다. 사람을 상대하는 것과 의사소통 기술 모두 대인 관계 분석과 관련이 있다. 즉 리더십 기술은 대인 관계 분석과 깊은 관련이 있다. 따라서 답은 ②이다.

18 (A)에 가장 알맞은 것은 무엇인가?

① 파악하다   ② 솎아 내다
③ 진출하다   ④ 매진되다

| 정답 | ②

| 해설 | 바가 성공하려면 웨이터 가운데 알맹이는 없고 보여 주기 식으로 행동하는 사람들은 단순히 파악하는 데 그치지 않고 "솎아 내야" 할 것이다. 따라서 답은 ②이다.

| 어휘 | **interpersonal** ⓐ 대인 관계에 관련된   **tamp down** 틀어막다, 억누르다
brawl ⓝ 싸움, 소동   **deadbeat** ⓝ 돈을 떼어먹으려는 사람[회사]
weed out (불필요하거나 부족한 대상 등을) 제거하다[솎아 내다]
substance ⓝ 실체, 알맹이   **plummet** ⓥ 급락하다, 뚝 떨어지다
revamp ⓥ 개량하다, 개조하다
stir ⓥ 섞다, 휘젓다; (감정·분위기를) 유발하다[불러일으키다]

shake ⓥ 흔들다; 충격을 주다, 동요시키다　　　　blend ⓥ 섞다, 혼합하다; 융합하다

make out ~을 알아보다[파악하다]

branch out (새로운 사업을) 시작하다[(새로운 분야로) 진출하다]

sell out 매진되다, 다 팔리다

[19~21] 가톨릭대 2015

해석

우리는 전반적인 지적 능력은 평균에 훨씬 미치지 못하지만 특정 분야에 비범한 재능을 보이는 사람들을 때때로 보곤 한다. 이들은 종종 "서번트"라 불린다. 흥미로운 서번트의 사례 중 하나는 바로 "언어 서번트"이다. 크리스토퍼는 전반적으로 지능이 낮기 때문에 일상적인 일들을 하는 데 많은 어려움을 겪었다. 셔츠의 단추를 잠그거나 카페트를 진공청소기로 청소하는 등의 일에도 도움을 필요로 했다. 하지만 크리스토퍼가 아주 잘하는 한 가지가 있으니, 바로 10개 이상의 언어를 읽고 쓸 줄 안다는 것이다. 크리스토퍼는 이들 언어를 언어 교사나 전문가를 통해 배운 적이 없다. 그보다는 혼자 문법책을 읽는 등의 방법을 통해 알아서 언어를 습득했다. 지능은 낮은데 언어 능력은 뛰어난 이렇게 상충되는 상황을 우리는 어떻게 받아들여야 할까. 한 가지 가능성으로 제시할 만한 것은 언어 능력이 전반적인 지능과는 별 관계가 없다는 의견이다. 다시 말하면, 언어 능력은 전반적인 지적 능력을 반영하는 것도 아니고 이를 추정하도록 돕지도 않는다. 사실 이러한 의견은 일부 언어학자 및 심리학자들이 제의한 것이다. 하지만 현재까지 언어 서번트 들이 무엇을 통해 비범한 재능을 보이게 되었는지에 관해 알려진 바는 거의 없다. 진실을 알기 위해서는 서번트의 능력에 관해 많은 연구가 필요할 것이다.

---

19 빈칸을 채우시오.

① 하지만　　　　　　　　　　　　② 게다가

③ 요약하자면　　　　　　　　　　④ 예를 들어

| 정답 | ①

| 해설 | 빈칸 앞 내용과 빈칸 뒤 내용을 비교해 보면, '일부 언어학자 및 심리학자가 의견을 제시했지만 이에 대해 알려진 바가 없으므로 연구가 필요하다'로 간단히 요약이 가능하다. 즉 빈칸을 기점으로 서로 역접의 관계가 형성된다. 따라서 답은 ①이다.

---

20 본문의 주제는 무엇인가?

① 장애인을 대상으로 한 외국어 교육의 필요성

② 서번트의 정의 및 언어 학습에 있어 이들이 겪는 한계

③ 서번트의 언어 습득과 관련하여 독학의 중요성

④ 언어 서번트의 재능과 낮은 지능 간의 수수께끼

| 정답 | ④

| 해설 | 본문은 언어 재능은 매우 뛰어난 데 반해 일반 지능은 매우 뒤떨어지는 언어 서번트에 관해 말하고 있다. 본문 마지막 부분을 보면 이들이 언어 능력은 뛰어난데 지능이 낮은 이유에 관해 아직 확실히 밝혀진 바가 없음을 알 수 있다. 따라서 답은 ④이다.

다음 중 크리스토퍼에 관해 맞은 무엇인가?

① 크리스토퍼는 언어 능력이 뛰어나지만 언어와 관련 없는 분야의 IQ는 평균이다.

② 크리스토퍼는 진공청소기 청소 같은 간단한 일만 혼자 할 수 있다.

③ 크리스토퍼가 혼자 많은 언어를 배우는 데에는 문법책이 도움이 되었다.

④ 크리스토퍼에게는 언어 전문가들을 통해 10개가 넘는 언어를 배울 수 있는 기회가 있었다.

| 정답 | ③

| 해설 | "크리스토퍼는 이들 언어를 언어 교사나 전문가를 통해 배운 적이 없다. 그보다는 혼자 문법책을 읽는 등의 방법을 통해 알아서 언어를 습득했다(He had not been taught those languages by language teachers or any specialists. Rather, he acquired them in his own way, like reading grammar books by himself)." 따라서 답은 ③이다.

| 어휘 | **savant** ⓝ 서번트; 자폐증 등의 장애를 앓고 있는 사람들 가운데 특정 분야에 놀라운 천재성을 보이는 극히 소수의 사람들

reconcile ⓥ 조화시키다, 받아들이다   **linguistic** ⓐ 언어의

faculty ⓝ 능력; 교수진   **presuppose** ⓥ 예상하다, 추정하다

to sum up 요약하자면, 요약컨대   **nonverbal** ⓐ 말로 할 수 없는, 비언어적인

[22~23] 가톨릭대 2016

해석

보어(Bohr)와 아인슈타인(Einstein)이 결국 함께 대화를 지속하지 못하게 된 것은 현재 물리학계에 존재하는 분열상이 어느 정도인가를 상징적으로 보여 준다. 보어와 아인슈타인은 친분을 유지했고 서로의 만남은 에너지가 넘쳤지만, 결국 두 사람은 서로 할 말이 아무것도 없는 지경에 이르렀다. 이와 같은 소통의 단절은 일상적인 물리학 언어가 사용되는 방식에 서로 공존할 수 없는 차이점이 존재했던 결과로 인한 것이었다. 두 주인공은 각자 특정한 용어를 특정한 방식에 따라 사용했고 해석에 있어 각기 다른 측면을 강조했다. 이러한 전체적 문제를 좀 더 깊이 분석해 보면 위와 관련하여 질서에 대한 견해차가 실제 쟁점이었던 것임이 나타난다. 보어와 아인슈타인 모두 물리학적 법칙과 자연의 법칙이 어떠해야만 하는지에 관해 미묘하게 다른 견해를 고수했었는데, 이것이 서로 간의 대화가 근본적으로 단절되는 결과를 낳았고, 둘 사이의 대화 단절은 오늘날 상대성 이론과 양자론 간에 놓인 거리를 통해 반영된다. 특히 보어는 입자 운동의 질서를 살펴보면 모호함이 존재함을 인정하게 될 것으로 믿었지만 아인슈타인은 그런 모호함이 존재한다는 가능성은 고려의 대상으로 삼기엔 너무나 터무니없는 것이라고 생각했다. 질서에 대한 서로 양립할 수 없는 견해가 바로 현대 물리학계의 두 거두 간의 이와 같은 소통의 실패의 근원인 것이다.

22 **본문의 주제는 무엇인가?**

① 보어와 아인슈타인이 구축했던 협력 수단

② 보어와 아인슈타인 이후 현대 물리학의 전망

③ 보어와 아인슈타인이 각기 다르게 학설을 세운 질서에 대한 견해

④ 현대 물리학이 결국에는 막다른 길에 도달한 상황

| 정답 | ③

| 해설 | "이러한 전체적 문제를 좀 더 깊이 분석해 보면 위와 관련하여 질서에 대한 견해차가 실제 쟁점이었던 것임이 나타난다. 보어와 아인슈타인 모두 물리학적 법칙과 자연의 법칙이 어떠해야만 하는지에 관해 미묘하게 다른 견해를 고수했었는데, 이것이 서

로 간의 대화가 근본적으로 단절되는 결과를 낳았고, 둘 사이의 대화 단절은 오늘날 상대성 이론과 양자론 간에 놓인 거리를 통해 반영된다(A deeper analysis of this whole question shows that what was really at issue was the different notions of order involved. Bohr and Einstein both held to subtly different ideas of what the order of physics, and of nature, should be and this led to an essential break in their dialogue, a break which is reflected in the distance that lies between relativity and the quantum theory today)." 즉 본문은 우선 보어와 아인슈타인이 서로 좁힐 수 없는 입장 차를 보였고, 그 원인은 인용된 문장을 통해 알 수 있듯이 두 사람이 질서에 대해 서로 다른 견해를 지녔던 데 있다. 따라서 답은 ③이다.

---

23 본문에서 유추할 수 있는 것은 무엇인가?

① 아인슈타인의 상대성 이론과 보어의 양자론은 질서에 대한 서로 다른 해석으로 볼 수 있다.
② 두 과학자 간의 소통의 단절은 각자의 이론에 담긴 서로 다른 질서 때문이다.
③ 오늘날 대체로 과학은 우리가 현실을 파악하기 위한 올바른 도구가 아닐지도 모른다고 인정된다.
④ 보어와 아인슈타인은 물리학 연구 방법에 있어 근본적으로 차이를 보였다.

| 정답 | ①

| 해설 | 앞 문제의 해설에서도 언급되었다시피 질서에 대한 서로 다른 해석이 상대성 이론과 양자론이란 형태로 반영된 것을 알 수 있다. 따라서 답은 ①이다. 본문에서 말하는 질서는 같은 질서를 두고 서로 해석이 갈리는 경우의 질서이므로 ②에서 말하는 '서로 다른 질서'와는 거리가 있다.

| 어휘 |

symbolize ⓥ 상징하다	fragmentation ⓝ 분열
encounter ⓝ 만남, 접촉	eventually ⓐⓓ 결국
incompatible ⓐ 양립할 수 없는, 공존할 수 없는	protagonist ⓝ 주인공
lay stress on ~을 중요시하다, ~을 강조하다	at issue 쟁점인, 문제가 되는
subtly ⓐⓓ 미묘하게	hold to 고수하다, 고집하다
quantum theory 양자론	particle ⓝ 입자, 미립자
admit ⓥ 인정하다, 승인하다	ambiguity ⓝ 애매성, (애매)모호함
contemplate ⓥ 고려하다, 생각하다	cooperative ⓐ 협력하는, 협조하는
prospect ⓝ 전망	theorize ⓥ 이론을 제시하다[세우다], 학설을 세우다

[24~25]

해석

만일 "2001: 스페이스 오디세이(2001: A Space Odyssey)"를 강제로 하나의 영화 유형이나 장르로 분류했을 경우, 그 답은 '공상과학'이었을 것임이 거의 분명하다. 공상과학 장르에서 볼 수 있는 비유적 표현을 다수 담고 있는 "2001: 스페이스 오디세이"는 분명히 해당 장르의 모티프를 여럿 활용한다. 수백만 마일의 우주공간을 이동하고, 여러 다양한 유형의 우주선이 등장하며, 중력의 제약 없이 우주인들이 우주공간에 떠다니는 등, (영화 속) 이 모든 이미지는 공상과학 영화에서 영구히 떠올리게 될 것이 되었고, 그렇게 되는 것이 맞다. 그렇다면, 왜 "2001: 스페이스 오디세이"는 공상과학 장르의 고전적인 요소를 다양하게 활용하고 있음에도 불구하고 단순한 공상과학 영화에 그치지 않고 그 이상의 작품으로 느껴지는 걸까? "2001: 스페이스 오디세이"의 고상한 주제와 관념이 작품 속에서 각기 분기해 나간다는 것을 하나의 설명으로 제시할 수 있는데, 이는 다른 대다수의 공상과학 영화에서는 대체로 피하는 사항이다. 아마도 "블레이드 러너(Blade Runner)"를 제외하면, 실존주의와 신학 및 인간 목적의 조건을 그처럼 복잡하면서도 지적이고 정교한 수준으로 다루고 있다고 주장할 수 있는 공상과학 블록버스터는 없을 것이다. "2001: 스페이스 오디세이"만큼 철학적 의식을 드러낼 만한 영화는 거의 존재하지 않는다.

24 본문의 주제는 무엇인가?

① 공상과학 장르의 이념적 성격

② "2001: 스페이스 오디세이"의 철학적 양상

③ "2001: 스페이스 오디세이"에서 발견할 수 있는 공상과학 장르의 모티프

④ "2001: 스페이스 오디세이"를 만들 때 사용된 특수기술

| 정답 | ②

| 해설 | 본문은 "2001: 스페이스 오디세이"가 공상과학 영화로 분류되긴 하지만, "단순한 공상과학 영화에 그치지 않고 그 이상의 작품"으로 간주될 뿐만 아니라 "실존주의와 신학 및 인간 목적의 조건을 그처럼 복잡하면서도 지적이고 정교한 수준으로 다루"고 "철학적 의식을 드러내"는 작품이라 강조한다. 따라서 답은 ②이다.

25 본문에 따르면 다음 중 사실인 것은 무엇인가?

① "블레이드 러너"는 "2001: 스페이스 오디세이"와 핵심적인 주제를 공유한다.

② "2001: 스페이스 오디세이"는 실제로는 공상과학 장르로 분류할 수 없다.

③ 공상과학 영화는 비교적 새로운 장르이기 때문에 공통된 특징이 얼마 안 된다.

④ 인간 목적의 조건은 공상과학 영화의 공통된 모티프 중 하나이다.

| 정답 | ①

| 해설 | "아마도 "블레이드 러너(Blade Runner)"를 제외하면, 실존주의와 신학 및 인간 목적의 조건을 그처럼 복잡하면서도 지적이고 정교한 수준으로 다루고 있다고 주장할 수 있는 공상과학 블록버스터는 없을 것이다"를 보면, "2001: 스페이스 오디세이"와 "블레이드 러너"가 서로 핵심적인 주제를 공유하는 영화임을 쉽게 알 수 있다. 따라서 답은 ①이다.

| 어휘 | **forcefully** ⓐ 억지로

definitely ⓐ 확실히, 분명히

motif ⓝ 모티프

perpetually ⓐ 영구히, 영속적으로

employ ⓥ 이용하다, 활용하다

high-brow ⓐ 고상한

ideology ⓝ 이념, 관념

address ⓥ 다루다, 고심하다

theology ⓝ 신학

consciousness ⓝ 자각, 의식

essential ⓐ 핵심적인, 필수적인

categorize ⓥ 분류하다

trope ⓝ 비유, 비유적 표현

restraint ⓝ 통제, 제약

attach ⓥ 연관되다; 연관짓다, 부여하다

a range of 다양한

diverge ⓥ 분기하다, 나뉘다

exception ⓝ 예외

existentialism ⓝ 실존주의

elaborate ⓐ 정교한, 정성들인

aspect ⓝ 측면, 양상

연습 문제   01 ①   02 ④   03 ②

01 다음 중 글의 요지를 가장 잘 나타낸 것은?

더 나은 기회를 찾아 이민을 떠나는 행위는 인간의 역사만큼이나 오래되었지만, 오늘날은 어느 때보다도 더 많은 이들이 자신이 태어난 고국을 떠나 해외에서 거주하는 것 같다. 경제학자들은 이처럼 한 개인이 가족에게 돈을 부치는 행위를 송금이라 칭하며, 송금은 전자 은행 서비스를 통해서나 배달부가 인편으로 전달하는 방식으로 재빨리 이루어진다. 개별 송금액의 증가분은 극히 미약하지만, 이를 종합한 총 송금액의 규모를 보면 현재 전 세계의 개도국에 흘러들어 가고 있는 자본의 규모는 엄청난 것으로 여겨진다. 송금액이 발송되는 여러 장소들 중에서, 즉 형편이 어려운 외국인들에게 고용주들이 일을 기꺼이 시키려 하는 부유한 국가들 중에서, 미국이 선두를 달린다.

① 이민으로 인해 엄청난 규모의 돈이 개도국으로 흘러들어 가게 되었다.
② 국제 송금의 대부분은 미국 밖에서 이루어진다.
③ 송금은 개인이 가족에게 돈을 부치는 것으로 정의된다.
④ 이주는 날씨만큼이나 복잡하고 유동적이다.
⑤ 이주가 인간의 역사를 근본적으로 바꿨다.

| 정답 | ①

| 해설 | 점차 많은 개도국 국민들은 고국을 떠나 선진국으로 이주한 후, 그곳에서 일을 하며 벌어들인 돈을 고국으로 송금하고 있다. "개별 송금액의 증가분은 극히 미약하지만, 이를 종합한 총 송금액의 규모를 보면 현재 전 세계의 개도국에 흘러들어 가고 있는 자본의 규모는 엄청난 것으로 여겨진다(Tiny in individual increments, aggregate remittances now constitute massive flows of capital into the world's developing countries)." 여기서 답은 ①이 됨을 유추할 수 있다. 참고로 ③은 맞는 말이지만 글의 전반적인 내용을 포괄한다기보다는 단순한 하나의 사실일 뿐이다.

| 어휘 | **migration** ⓝ 이주, 이민
  whisk ⓥ 재빨리[휙] 가져가다[데려가다]
  aggregate ⓐ 종합한, ~총
  needy ⓐ 어려운, 궁핍한
  radically ⓐⓓ 근본적으로, 급진적으로

  remittance ⓝ 송금액, 송금
  increment ⓝ (수·양의) 증가
  constitute ⓥ ~이 되는 것으로 여겨지다, ~이 되다
  shifting ⓐ 바뀌는, 변하기 쉬운

02 다음 중 본문의 요지를 가장 잘 언급한 것은 무엇인가?

카리브해의 섬들 모두가 해저에서 솟아오른 화산 산맥의 꼭대기로 구성된 것은 아니다. 일부는 화산이 아니면서 오래된 산, 즉 산호로 덮인 산들의 정상부로 구성되었다. 산호는 딱딱하고 바위 같은 물질로 산호충이라 불리는 바다 동물의 껍질로 이루어졌다. 산호충은 살아 있을 때 해저의 오래된 산꼭대기 같이 발견 가능한 모든 기반부에 부착된다. 산호충은 죽으면서 바위 같은 층을 형성하는 껍질을 남긴다. 그 이후 새로운 산호충이 층 위에 덧붙여진다. 그 결과로 산호섬이 형성된다.

① 카리브해의 모든 섬은 오래된 해저 화산의 꼭대기이다.
② 카리브해에는 작은 섬이 많이 있다.
③ 산호는 산호충이라 불리는 바다 동물에 의해 형성되었다.
④ 카리브해 섬 중 많은 수는 오래된 산의 산호로 뒤덮인 꼭대기이다.

| 정답 | ④

| 해설 | 본문은 서두에 카리브해의 섬들로는 화산 산맥이 물 위로 돌출된 것뿐만 아니라 산호로 만들어진 섬도 있음을 언급하고 있으며, 그 다음부터는 산호섬이 어떻게 형성되는지를 말하고 있다. 따라서 본문의 주제문은 '카리브해의 섬은 크게 화산 산맥이 물 밖으로 돌출된 것과 산호가 쌓여 형성된 것으로 구성된다'이다. ①의 경우는 '모두 ~인 것은 아니다… (Not all…)'라고 명시되어 있으므로 답이 될 수 없다. ②는 본문에 언급된 바가 없다. ③의 경우는 사실이긴 하지만 본문 전체를 포괄하는 주제문으로 보기엔 부족하다. 이러한 모든 사항을 고려해 보면 답으로 가장 적절한 것은 ④이다.

| 어휘 | **mountain range** 산맥   **nonvolcanic** ⓐ 화산이 아닌   **coral** ⓝ 산호
coral polyp 산호충   **base** ⓝ 기반, 토대   **mountaintop** ⓝ 산꼭대기
covering ⓝ 막, 층; 덮개

03 다음 중 본문을 가장 잘 요약한 것은 무엇인가? 덕성여대 2018

스트레스를 받으면 사람들은 음주처럼 건강에 좋지 않은 행위에 참여하게 되며, 친구의 SNS 업데이트는 동기를 부여하기보다 실제로는 오히려 상황을 더욱 악화시킬 수도 있다고 여겨진다. 연구 결과에 따르면 이러한 상황은 결과적으로 앞으로 20년 내에 사망할 위험을 70퍼센트 높인다. 미국에서 운동에 대한 걱정이 건강상의 위험이 될 수 있다는 것을 밝힌 두 건의 연구가 발표된 이후 이러한 전문가의 경고가 등장했다. 작년 스탠퍼드 대학(Stanford University)에서 실시한 한 연구에서는 6만 명이 넘는 사람들을 관찰했으며 연구 결과 자신이 속한 연령대 집단을 기준으로 평균보다 자신이 더 활동적이지 않다고 생각하는 사람들은 더 활동적이라고 생각하는 사람에 비해 향후 21년 내에 사망할 가능성이 71퍼센트 더 높다고 나왔다. 이는 아마도 몸 상태가 좋지 않다고 생각하는 사람들은 더 부정적이며 이는 결과적으로 스트레스와 우울함을 느끼게 하기 때문일 것이다. 2007년 하버드 대학(Harvard University)에서 실시한 두 번째 연구에 따르면 청소를 통해 건강에 좋은 운동 지침을 준수했다는 말을 들은 호텔 근로자들은 실제로 살이 빠졌다. 연구진은 해당 근로자들은 실제 얼마나 많은 행동을 했는지와는 관계없이 스스로가 활동적이라고 믿을 경우 혈압과 체지방이 낮게 나왔음을 발견했다.

① 운동을 얼마나 해야 할지를 걱정하면 이른 죽음을 맞이할 수 있다.
② 스트레스와 우울함 같은 부정적 감정이 심각한 건강상의 위험으로 이어질 수 있다.
③ 활동적이지 않은 사람은 활동적인 사람에 비해 훨씬 일찍 죽을 가능성이 높다.
④ 신체적 운동은 스트레스와 체중을 관리하는 데 있어 심리적 요소보다 더 중요하다.

| 정답 | ②

| 해설 | 친구가 SNS 업데이트를 한 이유는 뭔가 남들에게 자랑해도 괜찮은 일이 있기 때문일 것이며, 이를 바라보는 나는 부러움과 함께 스트레스를 받을 것이다. 운동을 하면 건강에 좋지만, 운동을 해야 한다는 걱정 또한 스트레스이다. 자신

이 활동적이지 않다고 생각하는 사람은 자신의 몸 상태가 좋지 않다고 생각하기 때문에 신체적 활동에 대해 부정적이고 이는 결과적으로 스트레스와 우울함을 유발한다. 활동적이지 않다고 생각하는 사람의 사망률이 높다는 점에서 스트레스와 우울함 같은 부정적 감정이 건강에 좋지 않음을 짐작할 수 있다. 따라서 답은 ②이다. ①과 ③은 본문에 언급은 되어 있지만 본문 전체를 포괄하는 것으로 보기는 힘들다. ④는 본문의 내용과 별 관련이 없다.

| 어휘 | **partake in** ~에 참가하다[참여하다] **motivational** ⓐ 동기를 부여하는
in turn 결국 **unfit** ⓐ 건강하지 않은, 몸 상태가 안 좋은
premature death 이른 죽음, 조기 사망 **override** ⓥ ~보다 더 중요하다[우선하다]

실전 문제

01	③	02	②	03	④	04	③	05	③	06	③	07	①	08	①	09	④	10	④
11	②	12	①	13	②	14	①	15	②	16	③	17	①	18	②	19	②	20	③
21	⑤	22	②	23	②	24	③	25	③	26	①	27	①	28	④	29	②	30	④

[01~02]

해석

의복에는 엄청나고 매혹적인 다양성이 존재하고 이를 통해 한 개인의 신분이나 사회적 지위를 표현할 수 있다. 수백 년 전의 유럽·일본·중국에는 매우 상세한 사치 금지법, 즉 각 사회 계급별로 옷을 어떻게 입어야 할지 엄격하게 규제하는 법이 있었다. 예를 들어 유럽에서는 왕족만이 모피, 자주색 비단, 또는 황금색 옷 등을 입을 수 있었다. 일본에서는 농부는 누에를 키울 수 있었지만, 정작 (양잠을 통해 얻은) 비단을 입을 수는 없었다. 많은 사회에서 옷이 없는 것은 신분이 없음을 나타냈다. 예를 들어 고대 이집트에서는 (특정한) 사회적 신분에 속하지 못한 아이들은 12세가 되기 전까지는 옷을 입지 않았다. 오늘날에는 대부분의 국가(특히 서구)에서는 오직 군대에서만 계급이나 신분이 복장 규정을 통해 드러나는데, 군대에서는 특정 금속 휘장이나 별의 유무가 계급 간의 경계선을 나타낸다. 군대의 경우를 제외하면, 사회에서 계급 간 구분은 점차 모호해지고 있다. 예를 들어 파리에 위치한 한 카페의 고객으로는 노동자 계급 사람도 있을 수 있고 최상류 사회 구성원도 있을 수 있지만, 모두가 청바지를 입고 있는 상황에서는 계급의 차이를 어떻게 구분할 수 있을까?

01 윗글의 대의(main idea)로 가장 적합한 것을 고르시오.
① 옷이 없는 것은 신분이 없음을 나타낸다.
② 과거 법은 사람들이 어떻게 옷을 입을지 규제했다.
③ 옷은 보통 사회적 지위를 나타내지만, 오늘날 세상에서는 꼭 그렇지만은 않다.
④ 옷은 역사가 시작될 때부터 여러 다양한 이유로 입혀졌다.

| 정답 | ③

| 해설 | 본문의 대의는 과거에는 옷을 통해 신분 구별을 하였지만 현대는 군을 제외하고 옷을 통해 신분이 드러나지는 않는다는 것이다. 따라서 답은 ③이다.

02 윗글의 내용과 일치하지 <u>않는</u> 것으로 가장 적합한 것을 고르시오.

① 몇몇 국가에선 각 사회 계층마다 어떤 옷을 입을 수 있는지 규제하는 엄격한 법이 있었다.
② 부유한 사람들은 가난한 사람들보다 더 아름다운 옷을 입는다.
③ 오늘날에도 특정한 집단 속에서는 계급이나 신분이 옷을 통해 드러난다.
④ 오늘날에는 사회 계급 간의 구분은 사람들이 입는 옷을 통해서는 덜 분명해졌다.

| 정답 | ②

| 해설 | ②의 경우 본문 어디에도 부유한 사람들이 가난한 사람들보다 더 아름다운 옷을 입고 있다는 언급은 없다. 따라서 답은 ②이다. ①의 경우는 본문의 "사치 금지법(sumptuary law)"을 통해 답이 아님을 알 수 있다. ③의 경우를 보면 ③에서 말하는 '특정한 집단'은 본문에 따르면 '군대'를 의미하며, 여전히 군대에서는 '계급이나 신분이 복장 규정을 통해 드러나(rank or status is exhibited through regulation of dress)'기 때문에 ③ 또한 답이 될 수 없다. ④의 경우를 보면, 본문 마지막의 "예를 들어 파리에 위치한 한 카페의 고객으로는 노동자 계급 사람도 있을 수 있고 최상류 사회 구성원도 있을 수 있지만, 모두가 청바지를 입고 있는 상황에서는 계급의 차이를 구분할 수 있는 사람이 과연 얼마나 있을까?(The clientele of a Paris café, for example, might include both working-class people and members of the highest society, but how can one tell the difference when everyone is wearing denim jeans?)"라는 문장을 통해 오늘날에는 옷을 통해서 착용자의 신분을 파악하기가 힘들어졌음을 알 수 있고 따라서 ④ 역시 답으로 볼 수 없다.

| 어휘 |

enormous ⓐ 엄청난
detailed ⓐ 상세한
i.e. 다시 말하면, 즉
silkworm ⓝ 누에
clientele ⓝ 고객, 손님
denim ⓝ 데님, 데님으로 만든 옷

fascinating ⓐ 대단히 흥미로운, 매력적인
sumptuary law (개인 소비를 금지하는) 사치 금지법
royal ⓐ 왕족의
rank ⓝ 계급
working-class ⓐ 노동자 계급의

[03~05]

해석

매년 겨울, 특히 기후가 추운 지역에서는, 사람들은 기침을 하고 목이 아프다는 일반적인 증상을 보이며 앓아 눕는 일이 흔하다. 가끔은 발열 같은 다른 증상도 나타나기 때문에 사람들은 자신이 단순히 감기에 걸린 것인지 아니면 독감에 걸린 것인지 궁금해한다. 독감은 매우 위험할 수 있기 때문에, 감기와의 차이를 알아 두는 것이 좋다. 재채기, 코 막힘, 목의 통증은 감기의 가장 흔한 증상이지만 독감에서도 자주 나타난다. 감기와 독감 모두 가슴 통증을 동반하지만 독감의 경우에는 그 정도가 심하다. 감기에서도 나타나긴 하지만 거의 드문 독감 관련 증상은 두통, 고열, 몸살이다. 일반적으로 독감은 약한 몸살과 두통으로 시작되지만, 갑자기 악화되며 체온이 오른다. 독감 환자들은 며칠 동안 앓아 누운 채 38~39도의 고열에 시달리다가 결국 폐렴으로 악화되어 위험할 수도 있다. 환자는 깨어 있는 동안 계속 기침을 할 것이다. 현재로서는 감기의 치료제는 없지만, 독감은 항생제로 치료할 수 있다. 매년 초겨울에 독감 주사를 맞는 것도 좋은 생각이다.

03 지문의 요지는 무엇인가?

① 추운 계절에 유행하는 몇 가지 질병들이 있다.　② 초겨울의 독감 예방 주사 접종이 중요하다.

③ 39도까지 올라가는 고열은 독감에서는 일반적이다.　④ 감기와 독감은 유사점도 많지만 차이점도 있다.

| 정답 | ④

| 해설 | 지문에는 감기와 독감의 유사점과 차이점이 상술되어 있으므로 "감기와 독감은 유사점도 있지만 중요한 차이점도 있다."는 요지를 확인할 수 있다. "Since the flu can be quite serious, it is wise to be aware of the differences."가 주제문이다. 독감을 예방하기 위해 독감 주사를 맞으라는 권고는 있지만 주제가 아닌 지엽적인 사실이므로 ②를 선택하지 않도록 주의한다.

04 지문에 따르면 다음 중 사실인 것은?

① 감기 치료제가 곧 나올 것이다.　② 감기는 더 심각한 병으로 악화될 수도 있다.

③ 독감은 합병증으로 발전할 수도 있다.　④ 주의하면 감기에 걸리지 않을 수 있다.

| 정답 | ③

| 해설 | 독감이 위험한 이유는 폐렴 등의 합병증으로 전이되기 때문이다. "People with the flu may find themselves in bed for several days battling temperatures of 38~39 degrees, and may end up with pneumonia, which is serious." 참조. ①은 비약이고, ②는 지문의 내용과 일치하지 않고, ④는 지문의 내용만으로는 알 수 없다.

05 다음 중 빈칸 (A)와 (B)에 가장 적절한 것은?

	(A)	(B)
①	~와 관계된	유발하다
②	~의 특징인	지니다
③	~와 관계된	결국 ~하고 말다
④	~의 특징인	알게 되다

| 정답 | ③

| 해설 | 빈칸이 위치한 문장은 감기와 독감의 차이를 상술한다. 따라서 빈칸 (A)는 독감과 "관련된" 혹은 독감의 "특징인"이란 표현으로 완성해야 한다. "concerning", "distinguishing (to)", "pertaining to", "differentiating" 모두 빈칸에 적합하다.

빈칸 (B)는 독감이 악화된 결과가 폐렴이라는 내용을 완성해야 하므로 결과를 표현하는 "end up with(결국 ~하고 말다)"가 적합하다. 독감에 걸린 사람들(People with the flu)이 폐렴에 걸릴 수 있는 것이지 폐렴을 유발(cause)하는 것은 아니므로 "cause"는 적절하지 않다.

ex. Infected patients end up with respiratory paralysis. (○)

cf. Infected patients cause respiratory paralysis. (×)

| 어휘 |

climate ⓝ 기후	**sink into** ~한 상태에 빠져들다	**familiar** ⓐ 친숙한, 익숙한
round ⓝ 한 차례	**coughing** ⓝ 기침	**sore throat** 목이 아픔, 후두염
common ⓐ 흔한, 공통적인	**symptom** ⓝ 증상	**condition** ⓝ 병, 병세
fever ⓝ 열	**present** ⓐ 나타나는, 존재하는	**wonder** ⓥ 궁금해하다
catch a cold 감기에 걸리다	**suffer from** ~을 앓다	**serious** ⓐ 심각한, 정도가 심한

be aware of ~을 알고 있다	**blocked nose** 코 막힘	**as well** 또한
chest ⓝ 가슴	**pain** ⓝ 통증, 고통	**accompany** ⓥ 동반하다
tendency ⓝ 경향	**severe** ⓐ 심각한, 가혹한	**pertain to** ~와 관련되다
rarely ⓐ 거의 ~하지 않다	**headache** ⓝ 두통	**vague** ⓐ 희미한, 모호한
victim ⓝ 환자, 희생자	**body temperature** 체온	**degree** ⓝ 도, 정도
battle ⓥ 싸우다	**end up with** ~로 끝나다	**pneumonia** ⓝ 폐렴
waking ⓐ 깨어 있는	**continuously** ⓐ 계속	**presently** ⓐ 현재는
cure ⓝ 치료제, 치료법	**antibiotic** ⓝ 항생제	**get a shot** 주사를 맞다
season ⓝ 계절	**particularly** ⓐ 특히	

[06~07]

해석

대략 1,900년 전에 로마의 교사 퀸틸리안은 뛰어난 연설가는 우선 뛰어난 인물이라고 주장했다. 청자들은 화자가 얘기하는 것과 그 얘기를 하는 화자를 구별하지 못한다는 게 그의 주장이었다. 청중들은 화자가 제시하는 주장뿐 아니라 화자의 인상에 의해서도 영향을 받는다.

만약 연설자가 습관적으로 솔직하지 못하거나 기만적이라면, 연설의 훈련은 그에게 기술을 줄지는 몰라도 그를 효과적인 연사로 만들지는 못한다. 그의 행동은 그의 말과 모순될 것이다. 그는 만약 자신이 학교나 회사에서 속인다면, 그는 정부의 정직성을 설득력 있게 주장할 수 없다. 그가 남들에게 마음을 열라고 호소할 때 그 자신이 고집불통이라면 그 얘기는 무시될 것이다. 심지어 웅변가의 단어의 선택이나 주장이 그의 인격을 드러낸다. 왜냐하면 그는 습관적으로 문제를 정면으로 맞서기보다는 피하려고 하기 때문이며, 또 진실하고 정당한 말보다는 인기 있는 말을 하는 것처럼 보이기 때문이다. 인격이 받쳐 주지 않는 화자는 한동안 성공할 수 있어도 결국 장기적으로는 그의 인격이 드러나게 될 것이고 그의 호소는 무가치해질 것이다.

---

06 빈칸 (A)에 들어갈 가장 적절한 단어를 고르시오.

① 존경받다

② 인식되다

③ 무시되다

④ 전환되다

| 정답 | ③

| 해설 | 인격이 받쳐 주지 않는 화자는 한동안 성공할 수는 있어도 결국 장기적으로는 그의 실체는 드러나게 될 것이고 그렇다면 그의 호소는 그의 인격과 비례하여 무가치해질 것이다.

---

07 윗글의 요지로서 가장 적절한 것을 고르시오.

① 일반적으로 화자는 자신이 정당하게 행동할 때 연설의 최고의 결과를 예상할 수 있다.

② 연설 훈련은 화자가 되기 위하여 필수적인 부분이다.

③ 만약 그가 사람들에게 영향을 끼치고자 한다면 그는 단어의 선택에 주의를 기울여야 한다.

④ 심지어 믿을 수 없는 사람이라도 몇 가지 중요한 기술을 습득하면 좋은 연설자가 될 수 있다.

| 정답 | ①

| 해설 | 뛰어난 웅변가는 결국 뛰어난 인격을 지닌 사람인 것이며, 인격과 그의 연설은 분리할 수 없다는 것이 이 글의 요지이다.

| 어휘 | **separate** ⓥ 분리시키다   **impression** ⓝ 인상, 영향   **devious** ⓐ 솔직하지 않은, 비뚤어진

    unreliable ⓐ 믿을 수 없는   **contradict** ⓥ 모순되다   **convincingly** ⓓ 설득력 있게

    urge ⓥ 강요하다, 주장하다   **unheeded** ⓐ 고려되지 않는, 무시된   **bigoted** ⓐ 고집불통의

    betray ⓥ 배반하다, 누설하다, 드러내다   **dodge** ⓥ 교묘히 회피하다   **for a time** 한동안, 얼마간은

    in the long run 결국   **discount** ⓥ 무시하다   **transform** ⓥ 변형시키다

    as a general rule 일반적으로   **pay attention to** ~에 주의를 기울이다

    crucial ⓐ 결정적인, 중대한

[08~09]

해석

미국의 독립 전쟁 동안에 여성들은 세 가지 방법으로 전투에 참여했다. 첫 번째로 '군대의 여성(여군)'이라고 불리는 군대의 별개 분과의 구성원으로, 여성들은 야전 병원의 직원으로 일하거나 수로 운송자(물을 운반하는 사람)와 같은 역할로 참여하였다. 비상시에는 수로 운송자의 역할을 하면서 대포의 발포를 근처에서 관찰했던 여성들이 부상당한 동료들을 대신하는 경우도 있었다. 여성이 전투에 적극적으로 참여했던 두 번째 방법은 남성들의 군복을 입고 남성 동료들과 함께 정규군으로 활약하는 것이다. 이론적으로는 여성들은 군대에 징병되지 않도록 되어 있었다. 하지만 만약 여성이 훌륭한 군인이라면 아무도 성을 문제 삼지 않았다. 군대는 군인들이 너무나 부족해서 아직 10대의 티를 벗지 못한 소년들도 규칙을 어기고 징병하고 있었다. 세 번째로는 여성들은 지역을 방어하기 위하여 때때로 지역의 군인들 혹은 안전 위원회와 연대하여 함께 싸웠다.

08 본문의 요지는 무엇인가?

① 전쟁 중에 여성들은 전투에 적극적으로 참여하였다.

② 군은 여성들에게 대포를 발포하는 방법을 가르치는 데 성공적이었다.

③ 전쟁 중에 여성들은 야전 병원에서 중요한 역할을 담당하였다.

④ 여성들이 안전 위원회에 참여한 것은 전쟁에서 승리하는 데 결정적이었다.

| 정답 | ①

| 해설 | 미국의 독립 전쟁 동안에 여성들은 세 가지 방법으로 전투에 참여한 것에 대해 하나씩 차례로 서술하는 나열식의 글이다. 그러므로 여성들의 전쟁 참여를 언급하고 있는 ①이 정답이다.

09 정식으로는 군대에 복무할 수 없음에도 여성들이 전투에 참여하도록 허용된 주된 이유는 무엇인가?

① 오직 여성들만이 수로 운송자로서 성공적이어서   ② 여성들이 전투에서 착용하는 군복을 만들 수 있어서

③ 식민지의 여성들이 특히 건강하고 튼튼해서   ④ 군대에서 군인들이 절대적으로 필요해서

| 정답 | ④

| 해설 | 군대는 군인들이 너무나 부족해서 아직 10대의 티를 벗지 못한 소년들 역시 징집하고 있는 시기였고, 그러므로 만약 여성이 훌륭한 군인이라면 아무도 성을 문제 삼지 않았다. 결국 군인들의 수가 절대적으로 부족하기 때문에 여성들이 전투에 참여할 수 있었다.

| 어휘 | **involve** ⓥ 참여하다   **field hospital** ⓝ 야전 병원   **fire** ⓥ 발포하다

cannon ⓝ 대포   **wounded** ⓐ 부상당한   **comrade** ⓝ 동료, 동지

be short of ~이 부족하다   **affiliate** ⓥ 제휴하다, 연대하다

[10~11]

해석

보통 가족 관계가 아이들의 집단생활에 있어서의 첫 번째 경험을 이루지만 또래 집단과의 상호 관계 또한 곧 그들의 사회화 과정에 강력한 영향을 끼치는 것이 느껴지게 한다. 놀이 집단에서 10대의 파벌에 이르기까지 또래 집단은 젊은이들에게 집단 내에서 자기 자리를 어떻게 확보해 가는지에 대하여 많은 중요한 학습 기회를 제공한다. 부모와 아이들, 교사와 학생들은 평등하지 않지만, 또래 집단은 평등하다. 부모나 교사들은 때때로 학생들에게 이해할 수도 없고 좋아하지도 않는 규율에 복종하라고 강제하지만, 또래 집 단은 이렇게 할 만한 공식적인 권위가 없다. 그리하여 상호 교류, 협력, 평등의 진정한 의미를 또래 집단에서 배울 수 있는 것이다. 또래 집단은 아이들이 성장해 가면서 점점 중요성이 증가하여 청소년기에 절정에 달하는데, 이때는 또래 집단이 때때로 학교 안팎 에서 학생들의 행동의 많은 부분을 규율한다.

10 다음 중 또래 집단이 가장 중요하다고 느끼는 때는?

① 아장아장 걷는 아기들   ② 초등학교 학생들

③ 유치원 원아들   ④ 고등학교 학생들

⑤ 성인들

| 정답 | ④

| 해설 | 또래 집단은 아이들이 성장해 가면서 증가하여 청소년기에 절정에 달한다. 그러므로 정답은 ④의 '고등학교 학생들'이다.

11 윗글의 요지로 적당한 것은?

① 아이들은 또래 집단으로부터 협력에 관해 배운다.

② 또래 집단은 아이들의 삶에 강력한 영향을 미친다.

③ 부모들은 아이들로 하여금 또래 집단이 하지 못하는 일을 하도록 강제할 수 있다.

④ 부모들은 교사들보다 아이들에게 강력한 영향력을 행사한다.

⑤ 학교 안팎의 관계는 아이들에게 학습 기회를 제공한다.

| 정답 | ②

| 해설 | 또래 집단이 다른 어떤 집단보다도 평등을 바탕으로 상호 교류, 협력, 평등의 진정한 의미를 배우고, 또 아이들이 성장해 가면 서 중요성이 증가하여 청소년기에 절정에 달하는 인간관계를 형성하기도 한다. 즉 아이들의 사회생활에서는 또래 집단이 너무 도 중요한 기능을 수행한다는 것을 밝히는 것이 이 글의 요지이다.

| 어휘 | **interaction** ⓝ 상호 작용   **clique** ⓝ 파벌

status ⓝ 지위, 상태, 자격   **dictate** ⓥ 명령하다, 구술하다

해석

여성들은 다른 모든 여성들을 자신의 경쟁자로 여기는 반면 남성들은 대체로 이런 느낌은 같은 직종에 종사하는 남성들에게서만 느낀다는 점을 제외하고는 정확하게 똑같은 것이 남성에서도 관찰된다. 당신은 경솔하게 예술가에게 다른 예술가를 칭찬해 본 적이 있는가? 정치가에게 같은 당의 다른 정치가를 칭찬해 본 적이 있는가? 이집트학자에게 다른 이집트학자를 칭찬해 본 적이 있는가? 그렇다면 분명히 당신은 질투심을 유발시켰을 것이다. 라이프니츠와 호이겐스의 서신 교환에서, 뉴턴이 미쳤다고 추정되는 사실을 슬퍼하는 수많은 편지가 오고 갔다. 그들은 "뉴턴과 같은 뛰어난 천재가 이성의 상실에 의해 판단력이 흐려져야 한다는 게 너무 슬프지 않은가?"라고 서로에게 편지를 썼다. 그리고 이 두 저명한 과학자들은 명백히 즐거워하면서 편지에서는 거짓 눈물을 흘렸다. 사실 루머를 불러일으킬 만한 몇 가지 예가 있긴 했지만, 이들이 가정적으로 슬퍼했던 뉴턴이 미쳤다는 사실은 발생하지 않았다.

12 윗글의 주제는 무엇인가?

① 여성처럼 남성들도 조금 다르게 느끼긴 하지만 질투심을 느낀다.
② 뉴턴은 한때 미쳤다고 생각됐었지만 사실이 아니었다.
③ 뉴턴 같은 천재가 미친다면 너무나 슬플 것이다.
④ 여성은 다른 모든 여성들을 부러워한다는 점에서 남성보다 더 부러움을 느낀다.
⑤ 라이프니츠와 호이겐스 같이 저명한 사람들 또한 질투심을 느꼈다.

| 정답 | ①

| 해설 | 남성도 차이는 있지만 여성처럼 질투를 한다는 것이 이 글의 주제이다.

13 작가에 따르면 라이프니츠와 호이겐스는 뉴턴이 이성을 잃었다는 주장에 대해 편지에서 어떤 것들을 주고받았는가?

① 명백한 슬픔과 유감   ② 가식적인 부러움과 놀라움
③ 뉴턴의 기행에 대한 비판   ④ 뉴턴이 회복하기를 바라는 소망
⑤ 감탄과 동정

| 정답 | ②

| 해설 | 본문의 wept crocodile tears with obvious relish를 근거로 보면 그들은 슬픔을 비춰 보였지만, 사실 속마음은 즐거워했다는 것을 알 수 있다. 그러므로 ②가 정답이다.

| 어휘 | **as a rule** 일반적으로, 대체로   **explosion** ⓝ (감정의) 폭발, (물질적) 폭발
        incomparable ⓐ 비교할 수 없는, 독보적인   **cloud** ⓥ 시야를 흐리게 하다
        relish ⓝ 즐거움, 흥분   **eccentric** ⓐ 괴상한, 비정상적인
        disguise ⓥ 가장하다, 위장하다   **reason** ⓝ 이유, 이성, 판단력
        crocodile tears 거짓된 눈물

> 해석

결혼하고 한동안 일본에서 산 이후, 나의 일본어 실력은 점점 향상되었고 일본인 남편과 그의 가족들과 간단한 대화에 참여할 수 있는 수준까지 향상됐다. 나는 내가 대화에 참여할 때 다른 사람들이 종종 놀라는 표정을 짓고 대화의 주제가 갑자기 멈춘다는 사실을 알아채기 시작했다. 이런 상황이 몇 번에 걸쳐 일어난 이후, 내가 무엇인가 잘못하고 있다는 생각이 분명해졌다.

마침내 나는 나의 문제가 무엇이었는지 발견했다. 나는 일본어로 말하고 있지만, 대화를 서양식으로 처리하고 있었던 것이다. 나는 일본어를 말하면서도 서양의 대화 방식을 고수하려 한다는 사실을 깨달았다. 비슷하게 내 영어 수업을 듣는 학생들도 영어로 말하는 순간에도 일본의 대화 방식을 고수하려는 노력을 지속했다.

두 사람 간의 서양식 대화는 마치 테니스 경기와 같다. 내가 대화의 볼이라고 할 수 있는 주제를 꺼내면, 나는 상대가 그것을 맞받아칠 것이고, 찬성 혹은 반대에 대한 이유와 같은 무언가를 첨가할 것이라고 기대한다. 하지만 일본식 대화는 완전히 다르다. 그것은 마치 볼링 경기와 같다. 그들은 자신의 차례를 기다리며, 기다리는 줄에서 자신의 위치가 어디인지 항상 잘 알고 있다.

---

14 다음 중 빈칸 (A)에 올 수 있는 가장 적합한 것을 고르시오.

① 갑자기 ~하기 시작하다

② 시작하다

③ 멈추다

④ 다시 시작하다

| 정답 | ③

| 해설 | 필자가 대화에 참여할 때마다 사람들이 놀라며 대화가 멈추는 것을 통해 자신에게 문제가 있음을 깨달았다는 내용이므로, '멈추다'에 해당하는 ③이 정답으로 적합하다. 나머지 보기는 모두 그 반대인 '시작하다'의 뜻을 담고 있다.

---

15 다음 중 빈칸 (B)와 (C)에 올 수 있는 가장 적합한 것을 고르시오.

	(B)	(C)
①	테니스	– 농구
②	테니스	– 볼링
③	아이스하키	– 볼링
④	아이스하키	– 농구

| 정답 | ②

| 해설 | 서양식 대화와 일본식 대화의 차이점을 스포츠 경기에 비유해 설명하고 있다. 중간의 however를 통해 대조의 모습을 보인다. 서양식 대화인 (B)의 경우 서로 주고받으며(introduce a ball ... hit it back) 경기를 치르는 것을 알 수 있다. 따라서 '테니스'가 정답으로 적합하다. (C)의 경기는 자신의 차례를 기다려 플레이하는 것이므로 '볼링'이 된다.

16 다음 중 본문을 통해 추론할 수 있는 것이 <u>아닌</u> 것은?

① 저자는 토종 일본인이 아니다.

② 저자는 언어를 가르치는 교사이다.

③ 저자는 항상 일본에서 살았다.

④ 저자의 일본어는 다른 사람과 대화하기에 충분한 정도까지 향상됐다.

| 정답 | ③

| 해설 | 결혼 후 한동안 일본에서 생활했다는 내용과 일본어를 배우는 과정이라는 사실을 통해 ③이 본문과 다르다는 것을 알 수 있다.

17 다음 중 본문의 요약으로 가장 알맞은 것은?

① 일본에서 사람들이 대화하는 방식은 서구의 대화 방식과 다르다.

② 대화에 참여하는 것이 중요하다.

③ 결혼은 당신의 일본어 향상에 도움을 준다.

④ 외국에 살 기회를 얻게 되면 사람들은 대화를 더 잘할 수 있다.

| 정답 | ①

| 해설 | 본문은 일본의 대화 방식과 서구의 대화 방식이 매우 다르다는 내용이므로 정답은 ①이 된다.

| 어휘 | **for a while** 잠시 동안

to the point ~라고 할 (수 있을) 정도로

notice ⓥ 알아차리다, 주목하다 ⓝ 공지, 목록

similarly 囵 비슷하게, 유사하게

wait for one's turn 자신의 차례[순서]를 기다리다

commence ⓥ 시작하다(되다)

resume ⓥ 재개하다

gradually 囵 점차

take part in 참여하다

startled ⓐ 놀란

conversational ⓐ 대화의

burst out 갑자기 ~하기 시작하다; 버럭 소리를 지르다

come to a halt 멈추다, 서다, 정지하다

[18~19] 한국외대 2020

해석

메리엄 웹스터(Merriam-Webster)는 인칭대명사 'they'를 2019년 올해의 단어(Word of the Year)로 선언했는데, 이 짧고 암전한 느낌의 단어가 용례에 있어 최근 수년간 다소 급격한 변화를 겪었고, 이 과정에서 광범위한 문화적 대화의 중심에 있게 되었다고 언급했다. 메리엄 웹스터 사전의 출판사인 메리엄 웹스터에서는 다음과 같이 말했다. "영어는 'everyone'이나 'someone'처럼 단수대명사와 깔끔하게 들어맞는 성 중립적 단수대명사가 없는 것으로 유명하며, 그 결과 'they'가 600년이 넘도록 성 중립적 단수대명사를 나타내는 목적으로 사용되었습니다. 하지만 보다 최근에 'they'는 성 정체성이 논바이너리인 사람들을 가리키는 용도로도 사용되는데, 이러한 의미로는 SNS와 영어권 화자 간의 일상적인 대인간 상호작용에서뿐만 아니라 편집을 마치고 출간된 텍스트에서도 점차 흔하게 쓰이고 있습니다." 달리 보면, 일반적인 단수대명사인 'he'나 'she'는 성별의 남녀 구분에 근간을 둔 단어인데, 성 정체성을 남성이나 여성으로 엄격하게 확인할 수 없는 사람을 묘사할 경우에는 오해를 유발하거나 부정확하거나 무례한 단어임이 드러날 수 있다. 단수대명사 가운데 만족할 만한 선택지가 없다는 상황에 직면한 사람들은 10년 전이었다면 고등학교 영어 선생님이 빨간 펜으로 수정했을 행동을 자주 하게 되었는데, 바로 일반적으로는 복수대명사로 사용되는 'they'를 <u>한 사람을 묘사</u>하는 데 사용하는 것이다.

18 다음 중 본문의 주제는 무엇인가?

    ① 메리엄 웹스터의 올해의 단어
    ② 대명사 'they'의 어원
    ③ 영어에서 'they'를 둘러싼 고충
    ④ 언어를 비추는 거울로서의 문화

| 정답 | ①

| 해설 | 본문은 사전의 출판사인 메리엄 웹스터에서 they를 올해의 단어로 선정했는데, 왜 선정이 되었는지를 최근의 they 용법 변화와 연결 지어 설명하고 있다. 여기서 본문의 주제가 ①임을 알 수 있다.

---

19 (A)에 가장 알맞은 것은 무엇인가?

    ① 복수임을 나타냄
    ② 한 사람을 묘사함
    ③ 1인칭 대명사로서
    ④ 한쪽 성만을 가리키는 데 쓰이는 대명사로서

| 정답 | ②

| 해설 | 우선 빈칸이 삽입된 문장에서 콜론 앞 문장을 보면 "10년 전이었다면 고등학교 영어 선생님이 빨간 펜으로 수정했을 행동"이 언급되는데, 이 행동이 무엇인지가 콜론 뒤에 제시되고 있다. 콜론 뒤를 보면 복수대명사 they를 "빈칸"의 용법으로 사용하는 경우가 "10년 전이었다면 고등학교 영어 선생님이 빨간 펜으로 수정했을 행동"임을 알 수 있다. 여기서 "빈칸"은 보통의 문법이라면 금지했을 행위임을 알 수 있다. 그리고 본문에서 they가 "성 정체성이 논바이너리인" 사람의 단수형을 나타내는 용도로 쓰임을 알 수 있다. 즉 복수대명사인 they로 단수 즉 "한 사람을 묘사"하는 행위가 옛날이었으면 금지된 행위인 것이다. 따라서 답은 ②이다.

| 어휘 |

personal pronoun 인칭대명사

undergo ⓥ (특히 변화 · 안 좋은 일 등을) 겪다[받다]

find oneself (깨닫고 보니) …에 있다

singular ⓐ 단수의

as a consequence 결과적으로, ~의 결과

non-binary ⓐ 논바이너리의, 여성도 남성도 아닌 성별로 이분법적인 성별에 속하지 아니하고 트렌스젠더나 젠더퀴어에 속하는 사람인

interaction ⓝ 상호작용

misleading ⓐ 호도하는, 오해의 소지가 있는

take to -ing ~을 자주 하게 되다

plural ⓐ 복수의

predicament ⓝ 고충, 곤경

gender-specific ⓐ 한쪽 성에 국한된

unassuming ⓐ 얌전한, 겸손한

transformation ⓝ 변신, 탈바꿈

gender-neutral (낱말 등이) 성중립적인

correspond with ~에 상응하다, ~에 부합하다

gender identity 성 정체성, 성별 인식

rooted (in) ⓐ ~에 뿌리를 둔[근간을 둔]

disrespectful ⓐ 무례한, 실례하는

red-pencil ⓥ (빨간 펜으로) 수정하다[정정하다]

etymology ⓝ 어원

plurality ⓝ 복수(인 상태)

해석

모든 시민은 자신의 행동에 책임을 져야 한다. 우리는 모두 서로에 대한 책임을 갖는다. 이러한 책임은 과학자들에게 특히 더 무겁게 지워지는데, 엄밀히 말하자면 이는 현대 사회에서 과학이 수행하는 <u>지배적</u> 역할 때문이다. 과학자들은 일반 정치인이나 시민보다 기술적인 문제나 향후 예측을 더 잘 이해하고 있으며, 지식은 책임을 동반한다. 그들의 주된 목적이 지식의 지평을 넓히는 것이지만, 이러한 일은 친사회적 효용, 즉 인간 공동체에 대한 <u>이익</u>에 대한 요소를 포함해야 한다. 이것은 인류의 안녕과 환경을 증진시킬 가능성이 있는 사업에 일정 부분 우선권을 주고 해를 끼칠 가능성이 있는 사업들을 전면적으로 금지하는 것을 의미한다.

20 다음 중 글의 요지에 해당하는 것은?
① 보통 정치인은 기술적 문제를 이해할 필요가 없다.
② 모든 시민은 다른 사회 구성원에 대한 책임이 있다.
③ 과학자는 지식을 추구할 때 자신의 사회적 책임을 인식해야 한다.
④ 과학자들은 대부분의 일반인들보다 기술적 문제에 대해 더 잘 이해하고 있다.
⑤ 과학자들은 지식 추구를 우선시해야 한다.

| 정답 | ③

| 해설 | 모든 사람들이 자신의 행동에 책임을 져야 하지만, 과학자의 책임은 더 막중하다고 말한다. 그 이유로 기술적 문제나 향후 예측을 일반 사람들보다 더 잘할 수 있기 때문이라고 밝히고 있다. 따라서 글의 요지는 '과학자는 지식을 추구할 때 자신의 사회적 책임을 인식해야 한다'는 ③이 적합하다.

21 다음 중 빈칸 (Ⓐ) 와 (Ⓑ)에 들어갈 가장 적합한 것은?
	Ⓐ	Ⓑ
① 놀라운	– 피해
② 하찮은	– 피해
③ 지배적인	– 피해
④ 하찮은	– 이익
⑤ 지배적인	– 이익

| 정답 | ⑤

| 해설 | Ⓐ의 경우, 과학자들의 책임이 더 막중한 이유를 설명하고 있는 대목이다. 이러한 이유는 현대사회에서 과학이 수행하는 역할이 '크기' 때문이어야 하므로, 앞의 빈칸에는 dominant가 적합하다. Ⓑ의 경우, 바로 앞에 위치한 '즉'이라는 의미의 'that is'를 통해 'pro-social utility'와 뒤에 이어지는 표현이 동격임을 알 수 있다. 여기서 utility는 경제학에서 말하는 효용을 의미하며, 친사회적 효용이란 사회 전반에 유용한 것을 의미해야 하므로, harm이 아닌 benefit가 와야 한다. 따라서 정답은 ⑤가 된다.

| 어휘 | **be accountable for** ~에 책임을 지는
peer ⓝ 동료, 또래
prediction ⓝ 예측
pursuit ⓝ 추구
utility ⓝ 효용

deed ⓝ 행동
precisely ⓐⓓ 정밀하게, 엄밀히
frontier ⓝ 경계 지역
pro-social ⓐ 친사회적인, 사회에 이로운
precedence ⓝ 우선권

give precedence to ~에게 우선권을 주다
be likely to ~할 가능성이 있다, ~하기 쉽다
prioritize ⓥ 우선순위를 매기다
dominant ⓐ 지배적인, 우세한

ban ⓝ 금지
pursue ⓥ 추구하다
insignificant ⓐ 하찮은, 무의미한

[22~24] 항공대 2015

해석

헌신과 광신 간의 근본적인 차이점은 불확실성에 있다. 광신도는 확신에 가득 차 있다. 광신도는 답을 알고 있다. 광신도는 실제로 무슨 일이 벌어지고 있는지를 알고 있다. 광신도에게는 계획이 있다. 여러분은 이 점을 이해하고 있다면 광신이 문명사회의 극단적 비주류의 전유물이 아님을 깨달을 것이다. 광신은 주류 사회 속에서 건재하다. 광신은 권력을 지닌 온갖 종류의 지위로부터 발생된다. 사실 나는 광신이 권력을 지닌 모든 지위를 가장 근본적으로 남용한 것이라고 주장한다. 내 관점에서 보면 진정한 헌신은 모두 의심의 영역 내에 속해 있다. 이에 미치지 못하는 모든 것은 절대적인 것으로 간주되는 믿음에 근거한 계산이다. "만일 이것이 원래 그런 것이라면, 이것이야말로 우리가 해야 할 것이다." 불확실성이나 의심이 없다면 관용의 근거는 존재하지 않는다. 만일 하나의 올바른 견해가 존재하며, 우리 모두가 전반적으로 스스로의 견해를 올바른 견해로 여기고 있다면, 다른 관점이 유효할 것이라는 가능성이 존재할 여지가 없게 된다. 물론 이 때문에 우리는 겸손할 수 없게 된다. 우리에게 답이 존재하는 상황에서 어떻게 겸손할 수 있겠는가.

---

22 다음 중 빈칸 (A)와 (B)에 가장 적절한 것은 무엇인가?

① 의문 – 하나의 올바른 견해
② 답 – 하나의 올바른 견해
③ 답 – 다수의 견해
④ 의문 – 다수의 견해

| 정답 | ②

| 해설 | (A): 빈칸 앞뒤 문장을 보면 광신도는 확신에 가득 찬 사람이며, 어떤 일이 벌어질지를 알고 있는 사람이다. 따라서 광신자는 "답"을 알고 있는 사람으로 보는 것이 타당하다.

(B): "불확실성이나 의심이 없다면(without uncertainty or doubt)", 그리고 "오로지 하나의 올바른 견해만" 존재한다면 "다른 관점이 유효할 것이라는 가능성이 존재할 여지가 없게 된다(we have no space for the possibility that a different point of view may be valid)."

이러한 점들을 감안했을 때 답으로 가장 적합한 것은 ②이다.

---

23 본문에 따르면 다음 중 사실인 것은 무엇인가?

① 광신은 진정한 헌신과 긴밀한 관계가 있다.
② 헌신은 겸손함과 의심의 미덕을 소중하게 여긴다.
③ 세심한 계산을 통해 광신과 헌신을 구분할 수 있다.
④ 약한 수준의 광신은 인간에게 긍정적 영향을 미친다.

| 정답 | ②

| 해설 | 본문은 우선 헌신과 광신의 차이가 불확실성에 있음을 말하고 있으며, 진정한 헌신은 모두 의심의 영역 내에 속해 있고, 확신에

가득 찬 광신 상태에서는 겸손할 수 없음을 말하고 있다. 즉 광신이 아닌 헌신에서는 불확실성, 즉 의심과 겸손을 중하게 여긴다. 따라서 답은 ②이다.

---

24 다음 중 위 본문을 가장 잘 요약한 것은 무엇인가?
  ① 궁극적인 답을 얻기 위해서는 광신과 헌신 모두가 필요하다.
  ② 불확실성은 의심과 겸손을 위한 기본적 전제 조건이다.
  ③ 의심이 헌신과 광신을 구분시켜 준다.
  ④ 헌신을 가장 결정적으로 남용하는 것이 광신이다.

| 정답 | ③

| 해설 | 본문의 핵심은 첫 문장인 "헌신과 광신 간의 근본적인 차이점은 불확실성에 있다(The fundamental distinction between commitment and fanaticism is uncertainty)"이다. 불확실성이란 의심을 의미하며, 따라서 답은 ③이다.

| 어휘 |
distinction ⓝ 차이[대조] commitment ⓝ 헌신 fanaticism ⓝ 광신
uncertainty ⓝ 불확실성, 반신반의 fanatic ⓝ 광신도 fringe ⓝ 주변부, 비주류
alive and well 남아서, 건재하여 standpoint ⓝ 견지, 관점 domain ⓝ 영역, 범위
calculation ⓝ 계산 hold ⓥ ~하다고 여기다, 간주하다 tolerance ⓝ 용인, 관용
valid ⓐ 유효한, 타당한 humility ⓝ 겸손 cherish ⓥ 소중히 여기다
humbleness ⓝ 겸손함 meticulous ⓐ 꼼꼼한, 세심한 cardinal ⓐ 가장 중요한, 기본적인
prerequisite ⓝ 전제 조건

[25~26] 한국외대 2014

> 해석

아이의 청력은 대략 임신 30주부터 발달하므로, 임신 마지막 두 달 동안은 아이는 어머니의 목소리를 알아들을 수 있다. 연구진은 갓 태어난 마흔 명의 미국 및 스웨덴 아이를 대상으로 아이들이 영어의 모음과 스웨덴어의 모음을 분간할 수 있는지 시험했다. 과학자들은 아이들이 빠는 횟수를 세는 센서가 달린 노리개 젖꼭지를 아이들에게 줬다. 연구진은 아이들이 노리개 젖꼭지를 빨아들이는 총 횟수를 보고 아이가 소리에 얼마만큼의 관심을 보이는지 유추했다. 미국 아이들은 스웨덴어의 모음을 들었을 때 노리개 젖꼭지를 더 자주 빨았고 이는, 즉 아이들이 이 소리를 이전에 들어본 적이 없음을 나타낸다. 그리고 스웨덴 아이들은 영어의 모음을 들었을 때 노리개 젖꼭지를 더 자주 빨았다. 연구진은 출생 이후에 (영어와 스웨덴어의 모음 차이를) 그렇게 빨리 배울 가능성은 없으므로 아이가 모국어의 소리와 모국어가 아닌 언어의 소리 간의 차이를 이해하는 것은 부모로부터 (태어나기 전부터) 배운 덕분이라 할 수 있다.

---

25 다음 중 본문의 주제를 가장 잘 표현한 것은 무엇인가?
  ① 신생아는 모국어의 모음에 감정적으로 반응한다.
  ② 신생아는 태어날 때 어머니의 목소리를 인식할 수 있다.
  ③ 아기는 태어나기 전부터 모국어의 소리를 배우게 된다.
  ④ 아기는 빠르게 모국어를 습득한다.

| 정답 | ③

| 해설 | 본문의 핵심은 마지막 문장의 "아이가 모국어의 소리와 모국어가 아닌 언어의 소리 간의 차이를 이해하는 것은 부모로부터 (태

어나기 전부터) 배운 덕분이라 할 수 있다(the babies' understanding the difference between native and nonnative sounds could be attributed only to prenatal learning)"이다. 따라서 답은 ③이다.

26 본문에 따르면 신생아는 _____를 들었을 때 더 자주 노리개 젖꼭지를 빤다.

① 모국어가 아닌 언어의 소리   ② 어머니가 말하는 소리

③ 영어의 모음   ④ 모국어의 새로운 어휘

| 정답 | ①

| 해설 | 본문을 보면 미국 아이들도 스웨덴 아이들도 자신의 모국어가 아닌 소리를 들었을 때 노리개 젖꼭지를 더 자주 빨았음을 알 수 있다. 따라서 답은 ①이다.

| 어휘 | **gestation** ⓝ 임신   **make out** 알아듣다, 알아보다

newborn ⓝ 갓난아이, 신생아   **pacifier** ⓝ 노리개 젖꼭지

consistently 끊임없이, 항상   **attribute A to B** A는 B 덕분으로 보다

[27~28] 한양대 2017

해석

노년층의 지위를 좌우하는 기본 원칙은 그들의 사회에 대한 기여와 그들을 부양하는 데 드는 비용의 균형을 유지할 필요가 있다는 것이다. 근대화와 기술 발전의 과정은 종종 과거의 효도의 전통과 상충된다. 그러나 가족이 대부분의 사회에서 가장 나이가 많은 고령자를 부양하는 데 필수적인 역할을 계속하고 있다. 노인들의 사회 참여 정도는 그들의 물질적 소유, 지식 및 사회적 권위와 같은 권력 자원의 성격에 따라 달라지는 것으로 보인다. 그들이 사회에서 서비스를 주고받는 대부분의 과정에서, 노인들은 호혜성을 유지하길 추구하며, 자신의 삶을 관리하는 데 있어 능동적이고 자율적인 행위자가 되기를 추구한다. 즉, 노인들은 서비스를 교환하는 과정에서 돈, 시간, 보살핌 또는 다른 자원을 주는 것을 선호한다.

27 윗글의 빈칸에 들어갈 가장 알맞은 표현은?

① 효도   ② 상호 도움

③ 가족 모임   ④ 공동 지혜

| 정답 | ①

| 해설 | 빈칸 뒤 but을 이용한 역접의 내용을 보면 가족이 "노인들을 부양(supporting its oldest members)"하는 역할을 계속하고 있다고 설명한다. 앞의 내용은 그런 기존의 전통과 과학 기술의 발전이 서로 상충한다는 설명이므로, 빈칸에는 노인들을 부양하는 것과 가장 밀접한 ①이 정답이 된다.

28 윗글을 다음과 같이 요약했을 때 빈칸에 들어갈 가장 적절한 것은?

일반적으로 더 이상 일할 수 없지만 젊은 그룹 구성원의 필요를 충족시키는 데 필수적인 자원을 통제할 수 있는 노년층은 _____.

① 급속한 사회 변화를 일으킬 수 있다
② 젊은 사람들에게 예기치 않은 짐을 부과한다
③ 그들의 삶을 관리하는 수동적인 행위자이다
④ 그들을 부양하는 데 소요된 사회적 비용을 상쇄시킨다

| 정답 | ④

| 해설 | 본문에서 "a balance between their contributions to society and the costs of supporting them"과 "reciprocity" 등의 단어를 통해 노년층을 부양하는 데 들어가는 비용과 노년층이 사회에 기여할 수 있는 일에 대한 균형, 혹은 서로 주고받는 다는 의미의 '호혜'에 대해서 설명하고 있으므로, 이런 균형과 호혜에 대한 ④가 정답으로 적합하다.

| 어휘 | **modernization** ⓝ 현대화, 근대화 **conflict** ⓥ 충돌하다

play an essential role in -ing ~하는 데 중요한 역할을 수행하다

authority ⓝ 권위 **reciprocity** ⓝ 호혜, 상호 관계

autonomous ⓐ 자주적인, 자율적인 **agent** ⓝ 행위자, 대리인

filial piety 효도 **offset** ⓥ 상쇄하다

incur ⓥ 초래하다, 발생시키다

[29~30] 서울여대 2017

해석

괴물 영화의 신전에서 좀비와 라이벌을 비교해 본다면, 뱀파이어와 늑대 인간은 스릴과 로맨스를 상징하며, 초인간적인 힘을 가지고 있고 양심을 가지고 있지 않은 존재로 그려진다. 이런 이유로 〈트와일라잇(Twilight)〉과 〈트루 블러드(True Blood)〉와 같은 시리즈가 존재한다. 하지만 좀비가 되는 것에는 매력적인 요소가 없다. 뱀파이어와 늑대 인간과는 달리, 그들은 얼마나 강력한지의 이유가 사람들에게 두려움을 주지 않는다. 그들이 두려운 이유는 우리 자신이 좀비가 되었을 때 얼마나 암울한가에 있다. 또 다른 점은 늑대 인간과 뱀파이어는 우리와 함께 지구를 공유하는 데 만족한다는 것이다. 뱀파이어와 늑대 인간은 무고한 행인들을 덮쳐서 잡아먹지만, 뱀파이어와 늑대 인간은 우리의 생활 방식을 위협하지 않는다. 그러나 로메로(Romero, 미국의 영화감독이자 현대 좀비 영화의 아버지)의 영화와 그 이후 나타난 모방 작품에서는 좀비를 사회가 완전히 붕괴하는 원인이나 증상으로 묘사한다. 실패로 끝난 과학 실험이나, 방사능 누출이나, 혹은 작열하는 운석 등이 사람들을 좀비로 만들기 시작하고, 그 결과 세상을 대혼란에 빠트리는 전 세계적 유행병이 나타난다.

* pantheon: 한 국가의 모든 신들, 혹은 모든 신들을 모시기 위해 지어진 신전
* botched: 망가진, 실패한

29 다음 중 글의 주제로 적합한 것은?

① 괴물 영화의 역사에서 로메로 감독이 세운 업적

② 영화에 나타난 좀비와 다른 괴물과의 차이점

③ 좀비가 뱀파이어와 늑대 인간과 공유하는 공통점

④ 좀비, 뱀파이어, 늑대 인간이 나오는 주요 영화 작품들

| 정답 | ②

| 해설 | 본문에서는 좀비를 뱀파이어와 늑대 인간과 비교하면서 차이점을 서술하고 있으므로 정답은 ②가 된다.

---

30 다음 중 뱀파이어나 늑대 인간이 <u>아닌</u> 좀비를 묘사하고 있는 것은?

① 좀비는 놀라운 힘을 가졌고, 양심을 가지고 있지 않다.

② 좀비는 무고한 행인을 덮쳐서 잡아먹는다.

③ 좀비는 우리와 지구를 공유하는 데 만족한다.

④ 좀비는 사회의 완전한 붕괴의 원인이거나 증상에 해당한다.

| 정답 | ④

| 해설 | 정답은 ④로, 나머지는 모두 뱀파이어와 늑대 인간의 특징으로 설명된 내용이다.

| 어휘 | **pantheon** ⓝ (한 국가·민족의 모든) 신들, (한 국가의 모든 신들을 모신) 만신전; (국가의 위인들을 모신) 사원[사당]

werewolf ⓝ 늑대 인간

franchise ⓝ 선거권, 특권

dismal ⓐ 슬픈, 우울한, 황량한, 비참한

tuck into 게걸스럽게 먹다(eat something eagerly), 밀어 넣다

bystander ⓝ 구경꾼, 행인

imitator ⓝ ~을 모방하는 사람[모방한 것]

botched ⓐ 잘못하거나 잘못 계획되어 실패한, 망가진

leak ⓝ 유출, 누설 ⓥ 새다

meteorite ⓝ 운석

pandemic ⓝ 전국[전 세계]적인 유행병 ⓐ 전국적으로 유행하는

conscience ⓝ 양심

glamorous ⓐ 매혹적인, 매력적인

content ⓐ 만족한 ⓝ 만족감, 내용

threaten ⓥ 위협하다, 협박하다

societal breakdown 사회의 붕괴

radiation ⓝ 방사선 치료; 방사, 복사

glowing ⓐ 작열하는, 열렬한, 극찬하는

populace ⓝ 대중, 민중

연습 문제   01 ②   02 ④   03 ②

01 다음 문장의 어조는 어떠한가?

> 평방 마일당 사람의 수가 인구 과잉 여부의 주요 결정 요인이라는 생각은 잘못된 만큼 널리 퍼져 있다. 인구 과밀을 판단하는 주요 쟁점은 어떤 주어진 공간에 얼마나 많은 사람들이 들어가 있는지 여부가 아니라 지구에게 인류가 오랜 기간 필요로 하는 음식, 물 및 기타 자원들을 공급할 여력이 있는지의 여부이다. 예를 들어 미국의 사람이 살고 있지 않은 빈 땅의 대부분은 우리의 건강과 행복을 위해 꼭 필요한 식품이 자라는 곳이거나 우리에게 원자재를 제공한다. 인구 밀도가 높은 국가나 도시에 사람이 붐비는 이유는 단지 세계의 다른 곳이 붐비지 않기 때문이다.

① 애석해하는   ② 단호한

③ 낭패한   ④ 상반된 감정이 공존하는

| 정답 | ②

| 해설 | 저자는 첫 문장부터 딱 잘라서 '~라는 생각은 …… 잘못되었다(The idea …… is wrong)'라고 말하고 있으며, 이후에도 이유를 들어 가면서 단호한 어조로 자신의 주장을 이끌어 나가고 있다. 그러므로 답은 ②이다. ①의 경우, 본문 어디에서 애석해하는 부분을 찾을 수 없기 때문에 답으로 보기 힘들다. 마찬가지 이유로 ③이나 ④의 경우도, 본문 어디에도 실망하거나 갈피를 못 잡거나 상반된 감정을 드러내는 부분을 찾을 수 없기 때문에 답으로 볼 수 없다.

| 어휘 | **determinant** ⓝ 결정 요인   **population pressure** 인구압

ㅤㅤㅤㅤㅤ**overpopulation** ⓝ 인구 과잉, 인구 과밀   **well-being** ⓝ (건강과) 행복, 웰빙

ㅤㅤㅤㅤㅤ**wistful** ⓐ 애석해하는   **emphatic** ⓐ 단호한

ㅤㅤㅤㅤㅤ**dismayed** ⓐ 낭패한   **ambivalent** ⓐ 상반된 감정이 공존하는

02 다음 글의 목적으로 가장 적절한 것은? 건국대 2018

관광의 상황에서 역마케팅(demarketing)은 모든 혹은 일부 관광객들이 특정 여행지를 방문하려는 의욕을 꺾는 과정이다. 보통 수용력 문제에 대한 인식으로 인해, 일반적인 역마케팅은 일시적으로 어떤 지역을 방문하고자 하는 모든 방문객들을 단념시킬 때 발생한다. 주목할 만한 예는 베니스인데, 이곳에서는 여름철 집중적인 인파가 종종 지방자치 단체들로 하여금 쓰레기, 오염된 물, 죽은 비둘기 등과 같이 불쾌한 장면들을 묘사하는 광고를 하도록 한다. 그들은 베니스라는 브랜드 이미지가 매우 강해서 그러한 묘사가 관광산업에 영구적 손상을 끼치지 않을 것이라고 생각한다. 하지만, 대부분의 다른 관광지는 그런 강력한 브랜드를 갖고 있지 않고, 따라서 일반적으로 역마케팅으로 브랜드 형성 노력을 철회하는 걸 주저한다.

① 역(逆)마케팅의 개념을 소개하려고
② 베니스라는 브랜드 이미지의 형성 과정을 소개하려고
③ 특정 여행지를 방문하려는 관광객들에게 정보를 제공하려고
④ 관광산업에서 역(逆)마케팅이 어떻게 활용되는지 설명하려고
⑤ 불쾌한 장면들을 묘사하는 광고를 만드는 방법을 소개하려고

| 정답 | ④

| 해설 | 역마케팅의 개념을 소개하고 있지만, 관광산업 분야에서 실제 역마케팅이 어떻게 사용되는지 베니스의 사례를 통해 제시하고 있으므로, 정답은 ④가 적합하다.

| 어휘 | **demarketing** ⓝ 역(逆)마케팅(기업이 자사 상품을 구입하는 고객의 구매를 의도적으로 줄여 적정 수요를 형성하고 관리해 제품을 합리적으로 판매하는 기법)

discourage ⓥ 낙담시키다, 단념시키다	**tourist** ⓝ 관광객
destination ⓝ 목적지, 도착지	**temporarily** ⓐⓓ 일시적으로, 임시로
carrying capacity (여행) 관광지의 수용력	**notable** ⓐ 주목할 만한, 저명한
intensive ⓐ 집중적인, 철저한	**prompt** ⓥ 자극하다, 촉구하다 ⓐ 신속한, 시간을 엄수하는
local authorities 지방(자치 단체) 당국	**run ads** 광고를 싣다
depict ⓥ 설명하다, 묘사하다	**and the like** 기타 등등
permanent ⓐ 영구적인	**be reluctant to** ~을 주저하다, 망설이다
countermand ⓥ 취소하다, 철회하다	

03 저자의 논조를 가장 잘 나타낸 것은 무엇인가?

어떤 제품을 활용하거나 처치를 받은 후에 몸 상태가 더욱 나아졌다는 기분이 들 경우, 자신에게 시술된 것이 무엇이든 이를 신뢰하게 되는 것은 자연스러운 결과이다. 하지만 이런 믿음은 현명한 행위가 아니다. 대부분의 질병은 자체적으로 더 이상 진행되지 않도록 제약이 이루어지며, 심지어 불치의 질환이라도 돌팔이들이나 사용하는 방법이 엄청난 수의 추종자를 확보할 수 있을 정도로 하루 단위로 (긍정적인) 변화를 이끌어 낼 수 있다. 조치를 취할 경우 종종 증상이 일시적으로 완화되기도 한다(위약 효과). 더군다나 여러 제품 및 서비스는 사용자로 하여금 자신의 질병이 치유되고 있다는 증거로 오해할 수 있는 신체적 효과나 정신적 효과를 발휘한다. 건강을 위한 여러 방법이 실제 효과가 있는지를 밝히기 위해서는 거의 항상 과학적 실험이 필요하다.

① 반어적인　　　　② 회의적인　　　　③ 신이 난　　　　④ 익살스러운

| 정답 | ②

| 해설 | 저자는 질병의 치료와 증상 완화를 주장하는 각종 의약품은 주장과는 달리 실제로는 별 효능이 없는 것일 수도 있으므로 항상

과학적 실험을 통해 확실히 검증해야 한다는 주장을 말하고 있다. 이로 미루어 봤을 때 저자는 시중에 판매되는 온갖 의약품에 대해 "회의적인" 태도를 갖고 있는 것으로 유추가 가능하다. 따라서 답은 ②이다.

| 어휘 |

tone ⓝ 어조, 논조
credit ⓥ 신뢰하다, 믿다
self-limiting ⓐ 스스로 제한[제약]하는
condition ⓝ 질환
quack ⓐ 사기꾼의[이 쓰는], 가짜의, 돌팔이의
placebo ⓝ 플라세보, 위약
misinterpret ⓥ 잘못 해석[이해]하다, 오해하다
ironic ⓐ 반어적인, 비꼬는

procedure ⓝ 처치, 순서, 절차
ailment ⓝ 병, 질병
incurable ⓐ 불치의, 치유할 수 없는
variation ⓝ 변화, 차이
following ⓝ 추종자, 지지자
exert ⓥ 발휘하다, 내다
establish ⓥ (사실을) 규명하다[밝히다]
skeptical ⓐ 의심 많은, 회의적인

실전 문제

01	④	02	④	03	③	04	③	05	④	06	①	07	②	08	④	09	③	10	②
11	②	12	④	13	④	14	②	15	②	16	③	17	①	18	②	19	②	20	③
21	④	22	③	23	①	24	②	25	⑤												

[01~02]

해석

간접흡연의 질병 유발 기능은 수년간 연구 대상이었다. 서쪽에 위치한 주의 어느 중형 도시의 사례가 예상치 못하게 우리의 (간접흡연 관련) 지식을 늘려 줬다. (그 도시에서는) 공공장소와 직장에서 흡연이 금지되었다가 6개월 후 그 금지 조치가 해제되었다. 공공장소에서 흡연이 금지되었던 기간 중에 심장병으로 인한 입원 비율이 24였다. (1년 중 금지 조치가 내려지지 않은) 보통의 6개월 동안에는 입원 비율은 40이었다. 연구진들은 이 같은 하락이 간접흡연의 해로운 영향을 보여 주고 있다고 본다. 또한 이 사례는 간접흡연이 심박동 수를 증가시키고 혈관의 팽창력을 떨어뜨려 심장 마비의 원인이 된다는 수많은 증거에 또 하나를 더한 것이다.

01 본문의 논조는 어떠한가?

① 구슬픈
② 억압적인
③ 도전적인
④ 정보 제공의

| 정답 | ④

| 해설 | 간접흡연의 해로움을 실제 사례를 들어 설명하는 글이다. 따라서 답은 ④이다.

02 밑줄 친 보통의 6개월은 무엇을 나타내는가?

① 연구 기간
② 연구 이후 6개월
③ 연구 이전 6개월
④ 금지 기간인 6개월 이외의 때

| 정답 | ④

| 해설 | 공공장소에서 흡연을 금지시킨 6개월 동안의 심장병으로 인한 입원 비율이 24였는데, '보통의 6개월간' 다시 40으로 올라갔다는 점에서 이 '보통의 6개월'이 바로 흡연 금지 조치가 내려지지 않았던 기간임을 알 수 있다.

| 어휘 |

second-hand smoke 간접흡연

ban ⓥ 금지하다

prohibit ⓥ 금지하다

admission ⓝ 입원

contribute to ~에 기여하다, ~의 원인이 되다

dilate ⓥ 팽창하다

elegiac ⓐ 구슬픈

informational ⓐ 정보 제공의

unexpectedly ⓐⓓ 예상치 못하게

lift ⓥ (금지를) 해제하다

typical ⓐ 전형적인, 보통의, 일반적인

body of 수많은

blood vessel 혈관

tone ⓝ 어조, 논조

repressive ⓐ 억압적인

[03~05] 상명대 2017

해석

해외로 물품을 운송할 때는, 운송이 제대로 되기 위해 몇 가지 예방 조치를 취해야 한다. 국제 운송은 국내 운송보다 더 많은 취급 주의를 요구하며, 포장을 적절하게 잘 하고 서류도 정확하게 작성해야 물건이 안전하게 그리고 제시간에 도착할 수 있다. 또한 깨지기 쉬운 물건을 잘 보호해야 하며, 그 밖의 취약한 물건도 진동이나 습기와 같은 지상 및 해상 운송의 충격에 손상되지 않도록 주의해야 한다.

먼저 가장 적합한 운송 방법을 결정해야 한다. 대륙 내에서 운송될 경우, 지상 운송이 더 적합하다. 다른 대륙으로 운송될 경우는 해상 운송이나 항공 운송이 더 적합하다. 해상 운송은 일반적으로 항공 운송보다 더 저렴하지만 훨씬 느리고 이에 따라 비용 대비 효율성이 떨어질 수 있다. 부두까지 오고 가는 지상 교통 및 항만 요금 등 해상 운송에 들어가는 추가적인 비용도 고려해야 한다. 해상 운송은 항공 운송보다 오래 걸릴 수 있으며, 결제 대금을 받기 위해서는 선박이 목적지에 도착할 때까지 기다려야 할 수도 있다.

03 빈칸 Ⓐ에 들어갈 가장 적절한 단어를 고르시오.

① 예측   ② 절차   ③ 예방 조치

④ 도움   ⑤ 발표

| 정답 | ③

| 해설 | 두 번째 문장 이후로 국제 운송에 필요한 주의 사항에 대해 서술하고 있으므로, 국제 배송에 취해야 할 '예방 조치'에 해당하는 ③ precautions가 정답으로 적합하다.

04 윗글의 목적으로 가장 적절한 것을 고르시오.

① 화물 운송업자들에게 허용되는 화물 중량 기준치를 알려 주기 위해
② 수입업자들에게 보험 증서에 대해 조언하기 위해
③ 운송에 대한 일반적인 정보를 제공하기 위해
④ 수출업자들에게 새로운 안전 조치를 통지하기 위해
⑤ 화물 운송업자들이 비용을 절감할 수 있도록 도와주기 위해

| 정답 | ③

| 해설 | 국제 운송에 필요한 주의 사항에 대해 서술하고 있다. 취약한 제품은 포장을 잘 해야 하고, 서류도 정확히 작성해야 하는 등 많은 취급 주의가 요구된다고 설명하고 있다. 또한 대륙 안에서 이뤄지는 배송인지 아니면 대륙 밖으로 넘어가는 배송인지에 따라 운송의 방법 또한 결정되어야 하며, 그 과정에서 고려해야 할 요소들을 설명하고 있다. 즉, 이 글은 이와 같은 운송에 대한 일반적인 정보를 제공하는 내용을 담고 있으므로, 정답은 ③이 적합하다.

05 다음 진술 중 해상 운송과 관련하여 윗글에서 진술된 내용을 고르시오.

① 해상 운송이 일반적으로 가장 좋다.
② 해상 운송이 일반적으로 비용이 더 많이 든다.
③ 해상 운송이 일반적으로 더 빠르다.
④ 해상 운송이 일반적으로 비용이 더 적게 든다.
⑤ 해상 운송이 일반적으로 비용 대비 효율이 좋다.

| 정답 | ④

| 해설 | 배로 가면 비용은 저렴하지만 시간이 오래 걸려서 비용 대비 효율이 떨어진다고 설명한다. 따라서 올바른 진술은 '해상 운송이 일반적으로 비용이 더 적게 든다'는 ④가 된다.

| 어휘 | transport ⓥ 수송하다
shipment ⓝ 수송, 선적
on time 시간을 어기지 않고, 정각에
fragile ⓐ 부서지기[손상되기] 쉬운; 허약한
moisture ⓝ 습기, 수분
continent ⓝ 대륙 ⓐ 자제하는, 절제하는
maritime ⓐ 바다의, 해상의
freight ⓝ 화물, 화물 운송
to and from ~로부터 오고 가는
precaution ⓝ 예방책, 예방 조치
insurance ⓝ 보험

ensure ⓥ ~을 보장하다, 확실하게 하다
domestic ⓐ 가정의; 국내의; 길들여진, 애완용의
make sure 반드시 (~하도록) 하다
vibration ⓝ 진동
mode ⓝ 방법, 방식, 유형
transportation ⓝ 수송, 운송; (과거의) 귀양, 유배
cost-effective ⓐ 비용 효율적인
surface transportation 지상 교통
destination ⓝ 목적지, 도착지
freight forwarder 화물 운송업자

해석

어떤 이는 내가 우리가 사는 세상의 인공적 면을 과장하고 있다고 항의할지도 모른다. 인간은 돌과 마찬가지로 중력 법칙을 확실히 따라야 하고, 인간은 생명체로서 식량을 얻기 위해 그리고 다른 여러 방식을 통해 생물학적 현상이란 세계에 의존해야 한다. 나는 과장에 대해서는 죄를 인정하지만, (내 과장은 어디까지나) 사소한 과장에 불과하다고 이의를 제기하고자 한다. 우주인이나 심지어 비행기 조종사도 중력 법칙을 따르며 따라서 중력 법칙이 완벽하게 자연스러운 현상이라고 하는 것은 맞는 말이다. 하지만 이러한 진실은 자연의 법칙을 따른다는 것이 우리에게 어떤 의미를 갖는지에 관해 정교한 설명을 요한다. 아리스토텔레스(Aristotle)는 무거운 물체가 올라가거나 가벼운 물체가 떨어지는 것을 자연스러운 현상으로 보지 않았다. 하지만 아마도 우리는 아리스토텔레스에 비해 '자연적인 것'에 관해 더 깊이 이해하고 있을지도 모른다. 따라서 마찬가지 이유로 우리는 '생물학적인 것'과 '자연적인 것'을 서로 동일시하는 데 있어 조심할 필요가 있다. 숲은 자연 현상일 수 있지만 농장은 분명히 말해 그렇지 않다. 옥수수와 소 같이 우리가 식량을 얻기 위해 의존하는 바로 그 생물 종들은 우리가 재주를 부려 창안한 인공물이다. 경작된 밭은 아스팔트가 깔린 도로와 마찬가지로 더 이상 자연의 일부라 할 수 없고, 아스팔트가 깔린 도로나 경작된 밭이나 다 마찬가지이다. 이러한 사례는 우리가 직면하고 있는 문제에 있어 조건을 부여하는 역할을 하며, 그 이유는 우리가 인공물이라 부르는 것들은 자연과 별개의 존재가 아니기 때문이다. 인공물은 자연의 법칙을 무시하거나 위반해도 좋다는 특별한 허가를 받은 존재가 아니다. 동시에 인공물은 인간의 목표와 목적에 맞게 되어 있다. 인공물은 하늘을 날거나 잘 먹고자 하는 우리 인간의 욕구를 만족시키기 위해 현재의 모습으로 존재한다.

06 다음 중 빈칸에 가장 알맞은 것은 무엇인가?

① 자연의 법칙을 무시하거나 위반해도 좋다는 특별한 허가를 받은 존재가 아님
② 자연의 법칙을 무시하거나 위반해도 좋다는 특별한 허가를 받은 존재임
③ 인공적 법칙을 무시하거나 위반해도 좋다는 특별한 허가를 받은 존재가 아님
④ 인공적 법칙을 무시하거나 위반해도 좋다는 특별한 허가를 받은 존재임

| 정답 | ①

| 해설 | 빈칸 앞을 보면 "우리가 인공물이라 부르는 것들은 자연과 별개의 존재가 아니다(those things we call artifacts are not apart from nature)"라고 나와 있다. 즉 인공물은 자연의 법칙을 무시하거나 위반할 수 있는 존재가 아니다. 따라서 답은 ① 이다.

07 윗글의 제목으로 가장 알맞은 것은 무엇인가?

① 자연법의 복잡한 성격
② 인공물의 복잡한 성격
③ 자연 과학의 경멸적 성격
④ 인공적인 면의 경멸적 특성

| 정답 | ②

| 해설 | 본문은 인공물이 어떤 존재인지에 관해 그리고 인공적 특성에 관해 말하고 있다. 따라서 보기 중에서는 인공물의 성격에 관해 말하는 ②를 답으로 볼 수 있다.

08 인공적인 면에 대한 저자의 태도는 무엇으로 묘사할 수 있는가?

① 놀란

② 터무니없는

③ 즐거운

④ 탐구심이 많은

| 정답 | ④

| 해설 | 본문은 인공적인 특성에 관해 심도 깊게 탐구하고 있는 글이다. 보기 중에서 이러한 글의 성격과 가장 잘 맞는 것은 ④이다.

| 어휘 | **object** ⓥ 반대하다, 항의하다

artificiality ⓝ 인위적임, 인공적임

plead guilty 유죄를 인정하다

sophistication ⓝ 세련됨, 정교함

equate ⓥ 동일시하다

artifact ⓝ 인공물

plowed ⓐ 경작된

no more A than B A가 아닌 것은 B가 아닌 것과 같다. B가 아닌 것과 같이 A도 아니다

no less A than B A 못지않게 B한, B만큼이나 A한

pejorative ⓐ 경멸적인

inquisitive ⓐ 꼬치꼬치 캐묻는, 탐구심[호기심]이 많은

exaggerate ⓥ 과장하다

biological ⓐ 생물학의

overstatement ⓝ 과장

presumably ⓐⓓ 아마, 짐작건대

biological ⓐ 생물학의

ingenuity ⓝ 기발한 재주, 재간, 창의력

dispensation ⓝ 특별 허가, (신의) 섭리

trait ⓝ 특성

[09~12]

해석

상대방이 조용히 관심을 기울이며 들어 주기를 바라는 남성에게 엄청난 피드백과 지원을 해 주는 여성은 청자의 역할로는 지나치다는 생각이 든다. 남자가 적극적이며 열정적으로 흥미, 관심을 보여 주고 자기편을 들어 주길 바라는 여성에게 조용히 듣기만 하는 남성은 듣는 데 전혀 흥미가 없어 보이며, 오히려 대화에서 빠져나가고 싶어 하고, 그만두고 싶어 하고, 머리는 딴 데 가 있는 것으로 보인다. 그러나 나는 최근에 그 이유를 이해하게 되었다. 즉 남자는 여자보다 상대방의 얘기를 덜 듣는데, 왜냐하면 경청하는 행위는 그들에게 각각 다른 의미를 주기 때문이다. 일부 남성들은 그들이 종속된다는 느낌을 받기 때문에 자세히 얘기를 듣는 것을 원치 않는다. 많은 여성들은 듣는 것을 원하지만, 이것이 서로 상호적이길 바란다.

09 윗글의 목적은 무엇인가?

① 여성들이 대화에서 얼마나 상호적인지 설명하기 위해

② 왜 남성들은 종속적인 느낌을 원하는지 보여 주기 위해

③ 남자와 여자가 청자로서 얼마나 다르게 반응하는지 설명하려고

④ 왜 여성들이 대화 시 남성들의 태도에 대하여 불평하는지를 보이기 위해

| 정답 | ③

| 해설 | 남성들과 여성들이 상대방의 대화를 듣는 입장에서 어떻게 성별에 따라 차이가 있는지를 설명한 글이므로 정답은 ③이다.

10 여성들은 조용히 얘기만 듣고 있는 남성들에 대해 어떤 반응을 보이는가?

   ① 여성은 남성이 집에 가길 원한다고 생각한다.

   ② 여성은 남성이 전혀 (자기 얘기를) 듣지 않는다고 생각한다.

   ③ 여성은 남성이 열정적으로 얘기를 들어 준다고 생각한다.

   ④ 여성은 남성이 종속적이길 원치 않는다고 생각한다.

| 정답 | ②

| 해설 | 남자가 적극적이며 열정적으로 흥미, 관심과 지원을 보이길 바라는 여성에게 조용히 듣기만 하는 남성은 듣는 데 전혀 흥미가 없어 보이며, 오히려 대화에서 빠져나가고 싶어 하고, 그만두고 싶어 하고, 머리는 딴 데 가 있는 것으로 보인다.

11 왜 일부 남성들은 상당한 시간 동안 얘기를 들어 주는 것을 싫어하는가?

   ① 왜냐하면 그들이 지루하게 느끼도록 하기 때문이다.

   ② 왜냐하면 그들이 열등하게 느끼도록 하기 때문이다.

   ③ 왜냐하면 그들이 고집 세게 느끼도록 하기 때문이다.

   ④ 왜냐하면 그들이 거만하게 느끼도록 하기 때문이다.

| 정답 | ②

| 해설 | 일부 남성들은 그들이 종속된다는 느낌을 받기 때문에 자세히 얘기를 듣는 것을 원치 않는다.

12 많은 여성들이 경청하는 행위가 상호적이라는 것은 무슨 뜻인가?

   ① 사람들은 주의 깊게 들을 수 있다.

   ② 사람들은 남을 돕는 데 협력해야 한다.

   ③ 사람들은 서로를 이해할 수 있다.

   ④ 사람들은 들을 때 교대로 들어야 한다.

| 정답 | ④

| 해설 | 여성들이 대화가 상호적이길 바란다는 것은 자신도 상대방의 얘기를 들어 주고, 상대방도 자신의 얘기를 경청해 주길 바란다는 뜻이다.

| 어휘 |
stream ⓝ 경향, 흐름, 연속, 시내
enthusiastic ⓐ 열정적인
at length 오랫동안, 마침내
subordinate ⓝ 하위의 사람, 부하
inferior ⓝ 하급자, 부하
arrogant ⓐ 오만한, 거만한

feedback ⓝ 반응, 의견
take one's marbles 포기하다, 그만두다
frame ⓥ 만들다, 짜 맞추다
reciprocal ⓐ 상호의, 답례의
obstinate ⓐ 완고한, 고집 센

[13~15]

우리는 종종 너무 바빠서 계획을 세울 시간이 없다고 생각한다. 하지만 실제로는, 우리가 아무리 바쁘다고 해도, 해야 할 일들을 미리 계획하는 데 들이는 시간은 그만한 가치가 있다는 사실을 깨달아야 한다. 우리가 끝마치고자 하는 모든 것을 완벽히 계획하고 실행할 시간은 아마도 없을 것이다. 하지만 계획 세우는 것을 등한시하면, 여유 시간이 거의 남지 않게 될 것이다. 계획을 세우지 않으면, 정말 중요한 일과 별로 중요하지 않은 일을 서로 구분하지 못하게 될 가능성이 크다. 우리가 하루의 시작이나 끝에 단 10분만이라도 계획을 세우는 데 시간을 보낸다면, 그 노력은 몇 번이고 다시 보상받게 될 것이다. 계획을 세울 만한 시간이 부족하다고 느끼면 느낄수록, 시간을 어떻게 사용할지 신중히 계획하는 것은 더더욱 중요해진다.

계획과 선택은 신중한 사고와 의사 결정을 수반한다. 그런 과정에서 우리는 우선순위를 정하는 데 어떤 기준을 사용해야 할지 자각하게 된다. 어떠한 종류의 계획 수립에서도 우리는 해야 할 일의 목록을 작성하고 우선순위를 정하게 된다. 계획을 수립하는 데 있어 매우 유용한 전략 하나는 매일매일 해야 "할 일"의 목록을 작성하는 것이다. 목록에 기재된 모든 항목이 모두 동일한 가치를 지니는 것은 아니다. 일단 우리가 목록을 작성했다면 그날의 중요한 것을 중심으로 항목별 우선순위를 결정해야 한다.

13 다음 중 본문의 요지를 가장 잘 표현한 것은?

① 바쁜 사람들일수록 더 많은 계획을 세워야 한다.
② 우선순위를 정하는 것은 어려운 일이 아니다.
③ 계획은 매일 세워야 한다.
④ 시간과 노력을 관리하는 데 있어 계획은 필수적이다.

| 정답 | ④

| 해설 | 본문에서는 어떤 일을 하기 전에 계획을 세우는 것이 중요하며, 바쁠수록 더 중요하다고 강조하고 있다. 그러면서 계획을 세우려면 매일 목록을 작성해 우선순위를 정하는 것이 큰 도움이 된다고 보충하고 있다. 이런 관점에서 ①은 바쁠수록 더 많은 계획을 세우라는 의미이기 때문에, 바쁠수록 계획이 더 중요해진다는 본문과 내용이 맞지 않아서 답이 될 수 없다. ②는 본문과 무관하며, ③의 경우 본문에 나오는 내용이지만 지엽적인 내용이다. 따라서 정답은 계획의 중요성을 강조한 ④가 된다.

14 다음 중 본문을 통해 유추할 수 있는 것이 <u>아닌</u> 것은?

① 별로 중요하지 않은 일은 우선순위가 낮게 배정되어야 한다.
② 해야 할 일에 대한 우선순위의 순서는 바뀌어서는 안 된다.
③ 해야 할 일의 목록에 들어 있는 일들은 동일한 중요도를 갖지 않아도 된다.
④ 잠시 동안이라도 계획하면 이후 많은 시간을 절약할 수 있다.

| 정답 | ②

| 해설 | 본문의 마지막 문장에서 해당 일을 기준으로 중요한 일에 따라 우선순위는 달라져야 한다고 했으므로 ②는 사실이 아님을 유추할 수 있다. ①과 ③은 본문 중 "Not all the items on the list are of equal value" 부분을 통해 유추할 수 있으며, ④는 첫 번째 문단의 "If we spend only ten minutes at the beginning or end of the day planning, our efforts will be repaid many times over." 부분을 통해 유추할 수 있다.

15 다음 중 계획에 대한 저자의 태도를 가장 잘 묘사한 것은?

① 어리벙벙한

② 호의적인, 찬성하는

③ 회의적인

④ 악의적인

| 정답 | ②

| 해설 | 저자는 어떤 일을 하기 전 계획을 세우는 것이 가치 있고 중요하다고 했으므로 긍정적으로 생각하고 있음을 알 수 있다. 따라서 정답은 찬성하다는 뜻의 ② favorable이 된다.

| 어휘 | **no matter how busy we are** 우리가 아무리 바쁘다고 하더라도

worthwhile ⓐ ~할 가치가 있는   **discriminate** ⓥ 식별하다, 구별하다

many times over 몇 번이고 다시   **spare** ⓥ 할애하다

criterion ⓝ 기준 (pl. criteria)   **priority** ⓝ 우선순위

to-do list 해야 할 일을 적은 목록   **of equal value** 같은 가치를 지니는

bemused ⓐ 어리벙벙한   **favorable** ⓐ 호의적인, 찬성하는

skeptical ⓐ 회의적인   **malicious** ⓐ 악의적인

[16~18] 단국대 2021

해석

역사는 적어도 이상적으로 완전한 상태에서는, 시와 철학이 합성된 것이다. 역사는 특정 인물 및 사건을 생생하게 묘사함으로써 사람들의 마음속에 일반적인 사실에 관해 인상을 남긴다. 하지만 실제로는 역사를 구성하는 이 두 가지 적대적인 요소(시와 철학)는 완벽한 융합을 이루고 있는 것으로 알려진 경우가 없고, 오랜 시간이 흘러 지금 우리 시대가 돼서야 이 두 요소는 완전히 그리고 공공연히 분리되었다. 우리에게는 훌륭한 역사란 것은, 이 '훌륭한 역사'란 용어의 진정한 뜻을 살펴봤을 때, 존재하지 않았다. 하지만 우리에게는 훌륭한 역사 소설과 훌륭한 역사 에세이가 존재한다. 상상력과 이성이 문학이란 분야와 분리되었고, 이제는 공통된 전체 영역을 보유하는 대신에 각기 개별성 측면에서 자신만의 분야를 보유하고 있다.

과거를 현재로 만드는 것, 먼 곳의 것을 가까이로 끌고 오는 것, 우리를 위대한 인물의 집단에 속하게 하거나 대규모 전투가 벌어지는 현장을 내려다보는 고지에 올려놓는 것, 우화에서 우리가 의인화된 자질로 간주하려는 경향이 매우 크게 드러나는 인간의 살과 피라는 현실을 띠게 하는 것, 언어와 예의 및 의복 상의 특성을 갖춘 우리의 조상을 우리 앞에 불러내는 것, 우리에게 조상의 집을 안내해 보이는 것 등은 역사가가 마땅히 해야 할 의무의 일부로, 역사 소설가가 자기 것으로 전용해 온 것들이다. 반면에 역사에서 철학을 추출하는 것, 사건과 인물에 대한 판단에 대해 지시하는 것, 인과관계를 추정하는 것, 과거에 있었던 일로부터 도덕적 지혜 및 정치적 지혜라는 일반적인 교훈을 이끌어 내는 것 등은 뚜렷이 다른 부류의 작가(역사 에세이 작가)의 일이 되었다.

16 본문의 주된 구성 방식은 무엇인가?

① 역사 서술   ② 과정 분석

③ 비교와 대조   ④ 원인과 결과

| 정답 | ③

| 해설 | 본문은 역사를 구성하는 요소인 시와 철학을 비교 및 대조하고 있으며, 이뿐만 아니라 역사 소설과 역사 에세이, 상상력과 이성, 역사가와 역사 에세이 작가를 마찬가지로 비교 및 대조하고 있다. 여기서 본문의 구성 방식이 비교 및 대조임을 유추할 수 있다. 따라서 답은 ③이다.

---

17 첫 번째 단락에서 두 개의 적대적인 한 쌍으로 묘사되지 않은 것은 무엇인가?

① 개별성과 역사

② 상상력과 이성

③ 소설과 에세이

④ 시와 철학

| 정답 | ①

| 해설 | 본문에서 "두 가지 적대적인 요소(시와 철학)", "훌륭한 역사 소설과 훌륭한 역사 에세이", "상상력과 이성"은 적대적인 한 쌍으로 언급된다. 하지만 ①에서 "개별성"은, 앞서 언급된 여러 요소가 공통된 영역이 아니라 각기 "개별성"을 갖고 있음을 나타내기 위해 사용한 단어이지 역사와 적대적인 한 쌍으로 사용된 단어는 아니다. "개별성"과 적대적인 한 쌍에 해당하는 것은 "공통된"이다. 따라서 답은 ①이다.

---

18 두 번째 단락의 목적은 무엇인가?

① 역사 소설의 우월성과 역사 소설이 제공할 수 있는 것을 주장하기

② 역사 소설과 역사 에세이 각각이 제공할 수 있는 것을 묘사하기

③ "과거를 현재로" 만들고 "먼 곳의 것을 가까이로" 끌고 오는 과정을 설명하기

④ 어떤 유형의 역사가 우월한지 평가하고, 답은 독자의 몫으로 남겨 놓기

| 정답 | ②

| 해설 | 두 번째 단락은 역사 소설과 역사 에세이가 각기 어떤 역할을 하는지 설명하고 있으며, 따라서 답은 ②이다.

| 어휘 |

perfection ⓝ 완벽, 완전

impress on one's mind ~의 마음에 인상을 남기다

representation ⓝ 묘사, 표현

amalgamation ⓝ 융합

professedly ⓐ 공공연히, 외양으로는

in the proper sense of the word 그 말의 본래의[진정한] 뜻에 있어서

romance ⓝ 전기(傳奇) 소설, 공상[모험, 연애] 소설

province ⓝ (개인의 특정 지식·관심·책임) 분야

severalty ⓝ 각자(임), 개별성

eminence ⓝ 명성; 고지, 언덕

inclined ⓐ ~하는 경향이 있는, ~할 것 같은

quality ⓝ 자질, 특성

peculiarity ⓝ 특성

show A over B A에게 B를 안내해 보이다

appropriate ⓥ 전용하다, 제 것으로 삼다

trace ⓥ (기원·원인을) 추적하다[(추적하여) 밝혀내다]

occurrence ⓝ 발생하는[존재하는/나타나는] 것

compound ⓝ 혼합물, 합성물

vivid ⓐ 생생한, 선명한

consist of ~로 이루어지다[구성되다]

at length 오랜 시간이 흘러, 상세히

separate ⓥ 분리하다, 나누다

partition ⓝ 분할, 나눔

respective ⓐ 각자의, 각각의

society ⓝ 집단, 단체

invest with (특정한 자질·특징 등을) 띠게 하다

personify ⓥ 의인화하다

allegory ⓝ 우화, 풍자

garb ⓝ (특이한 또는 특정 유형의 사람이 입는) 의복

properly ⓐ 당연히, 마땅히

direct ⓥ 지휘하다, 지시하다

cause and effect 인과, 인과관계

distinct ⓐ 뚜렷이 다른, 별개의

composition ⓝ 구성 요소, 구성
superiority ⓝ 우월성, 우세

narration ⓝ 서술, 내레이션

[19~20] 경기대 2018

| 해석 |

대부분의 사람들이 새로 집을 짓겠다고 생각할 때, 최우선적으로 해야 하는 일은 건축 도면을 선택하거나 설계하는 것이라고 가정한다. 하지만 사실 가장 먼저 해야 하는 일은 항상 그렇듯 집 지을 부지를 먼저 찾아보는 것이어야 한다. 당신이 건축가와 함께 작업할 경우, 주택 설계라는 것이 당신이 생각하는 특정한 기능적·심미적 욕망에 영향을 받는 것만큼이나 집 지을 부지가 제공하는 기회나 제약에도 마찬가지로 영향을 받는다는 것을 깨닫게 될 것이다. 이런 사실은 몇 년 전 내가 봤던 한 새로 지은 집에서 분명하게 드러났다. 그 집은 언덕에 위치해 있었고, 남쪽이 멋진 풍경을 내려다보는 집이었다. 하지만 그런 멋진 풍경을 향해 있는 창문은 하나도 없었다. 추측해 보건대 부지가 선정되기 훨씬 전에 건축 책자에서 설계도를 선정했을 것으로 생각되며, 원래 설계 도면은 북향 면에 출입구나 창문이 없는 에너지 효율이 매우 우수하도록 설계된 집이었을 것이다. 하지만 새로 지은 그 집은 <u>출입구나 창문이 없는</u> 면이 남쪽을 향해 있었다. 남향은 대부분의 기후에서 사람들이 많은 창문을 설치하기 원하는 방향인데도 말이다.

19 다음 중 본문을 쓴 목적으로 적합한 것은?

① 주택 건축에서 심미적 고려가 갖는 중요성을 설명하기 위해서
② 주택 설계와 주택 위치 사이의 긴밀한 연관성을 보여 주기 위해서
③ 주택이 건설되는 프로세스를 단계별로 안내해 주기 위해서
④ 에너지 효율이 좋은 집을 어떻게 지을 수 있는지 보여 주기 위해서

| 정답 | ②

| 해설 | 본문의 전반부에 저자의 주장이 제기되어 있고, 후반부에는 왜 그래야 하는지에 대한 예시가 등장하고 있다. 집을 새로 지을 때 부지를 먼저 확인하는 것이 중요하다는 내용이므로, 주택 설계와 주택 위치(부지) 사이에 긴밀한 연관성이 있다고 말한 ②가 글의 목적으로 적합하다.

20 다음 중 빈칸 (A)와 (B)에 가장 적합한 것은?

① 날씬한, 호리호리한
② 둥근
③ 창문이 없는, 앞이 막힌
④ 눈부신, 화려한

| 정답 | ③

| 해설 | 후반부에 예시로 등장한 집은 남쪽 면에 창문이 하나도 없는 집이었다. 따라서 이러한 '출구[창문]가 없는, 앞이 막힌, 막다른' 등의 의미를 지니는 ③ blind가 빈칸에 공통으로 적합하다.

| 어휘 | contemplate ⓥ 심사숙고하다
the first order of business 최우선 과제
functional ⓐ 기능 위주의, 실용적인

assume ⓥ 추정하다; (태도를) 취하다; (책임을) 떠맡다
constraint ⓝ 제약; 강제, 압박, 속박
aesthetic ⓐ 미적인

eminently ⓐ 대단히, 탁월하게　　　　　　　　　evident ⓐ 분명한

face south 남향이다　　　　　　　　　　　　　overlook ⓥ 내려다보다; 감시하다; 간과하다; 눈감아 주다

vista ⓝ (아름다운) 경치, 풍경　　　　　　　　　extraordinary ⓐ 비범한, 기이한, 놀라운

energy efficient 에너지 효율적인　　　　　　　　blind ⓐ 출구[창문]가 없는, 앞이 막힌, 막다른

glittering ⓐ 눈부신, 성공적인, 화려한

[21] 한양대 2014

해석

미국 서부 시대의 구비 설화는 여러 세대에 걸쳐 익숙한 이야기이다. 용감한 보안관, 다부지고 개성 있는 카우보이, 신나는 변경의 마을 등이 전 세계에 잘 알려져 있다. 실제로는 미국 서부는 그렇게 그림 같은 곳이 아니었다. 19세기 중반의 미국은 아직도 국가적 정체성을 형성하던 중이었다. 이러한 국가적 정체성에는 다른 사회에서 볼 수 있는 위대한 영웅이나 정교한 신화가 포함되지 않았다. 이에 관해 잘 알고 있지는 않았지만 당시 언론은 대중을 대상으로 이들이 기꺼이 듣고 싶어 하는 이야기를 제공하는 식으로 이들 영웅과 신화를 창조했다. 툼스톤과 다지 시티 같이 총격전이 벌어진 마을에서 한창때 사망한 사람 전체보다 현대의 거의 모든 미국 도시에서 1년에 사망하는 사람 수가 더 많다. 평화를 유지하기 위해 힘쓴 애빌린의 와일드 빌히콕은 애빌린을 다스리던 동안 오직 두 명에게만 총을 쐈다. 둘 중 한 사람은 동료 경찰이었다. 하지만 이런 사실은 서부 시대 이야기의 소재로 쓰이지 않는다.

21　윗글의 목적으로 가장 적절한 것을 고르시오.

① 미국 서부를 극찬하기

② 미국 서부 시대에 관해 자세히 설명하기

③ 미국 서부의 영웅에 관해 소개하기

④ 미국 서부의 잘 알려진 전설이 틀렸음을 드러내다

| 정답 |　④

| 해설 |　본문은 미국 서부에 관한 이야기가 실제와는 거리가 있음을 말하고 있다. 따라서 답은 ④이다.

| 어휘 |　lore ⓝ 구비 설화　　　　　　　　　　　　Wild West (미국 개척 시대의) 황량한[거친] 서부

lawman ⓝ 법 집행관, 보안관　　　　　　　　ruggedly 강인하게, 다부지게

individual ⓐ 개성 있는　　　　　　　　　　rollicking ⓐ 신나는, 흥겨운

picturesque ⓐ 그림 같은　　　　　　　　　heyday ⓝ 한창때

tame ⓥ 다스리다, 길들이다　　　　　　　　extol ⓥ 극찬하다, 격찬하다

expound ⓥ 자세히 설명하다　　　　　　　　debunk ⓥ 틀렸음을 드러내다

해석

모든 과학은 인간의 편견에 <u>좌우되기</u> 마련이다. 특히 이는 사회 과학자들에게 있어 더욱 그러하다. 사회 과학자들은 인간의 행동을 연구 분야로 삼기 때문에 실제로는 자신들도 연구 대상이 된다. 게다가 인간의 행동 패턴은 지역마다 다르고 집단마다 다르다. 이는 자연 과학의 연구 대상과 대조를 이룬다. 화학자가 수소를 연구할 경우, 이 화학자는 하나의 수소 원자는 어디서 발견한 것이든 관계없이 다른 수소 원자와 거의 동일하다고 추정할 수 있으며, 수소 원자를 둘러싼 환경 또한 꽤 정확히 통제할 수 있을 것으로 추정할 수 있다. 이는 물리학자가 금속 막대를 측정하는 경우에도 마찬가지이다. 물리학자는 자연 환경이 동일하게 유지되는 한 길이가 늘어나거나 줄어들 일은 없을 것으로 확신한다. 이 때문에 얼 배비(Earl Babbie)는 연구 대상이 <u>예측 가능한</u> 속성을 지녔다는 이유로 자연 과학을 "쉬운 과학"으로 부른 경제학자 다니엘 수츠(Daniel Suits)의 말을 인용했다.

---

22 밑줄 친 subject를 가장 잘 대체할 수 있는 것은 무엇인가?

① 믿을 수 있는   ② 가능성이 높은
③ 영향을 받기 쉬운   ④ 무관심한
⑤ 영향을 받지 않는

| 정답 | ③

| 해설 | be subject to는 '~에 좌우되다, ~에 영향을 받다'는 의미를 지니며, 보기 중에서 이와 의미상 가장 가까운 것은 ③이다.

---

23 빈칸에 가장 적합한 것은 무엇인가?

① 예측 가능한   ② 다재다능한
③ 유연한   ④ 어마어마한
⑤ 기발한

| 정답 | ①

| 해설 | 사회 과학과 자연 과학을 비교해 봤을 때, 사회 과학은 인간의 행동을 연구 대상으로 삼기 때문에 예측을 한다는 것이 쉽지 않음이 자명하지만, 자연 과학은 다른 자연 조건이 모두 통제된 상황이라면 금속 막대를 측정하는 것과 마찬가지로 결과값이 갑자기 변할 리가 없기 때문에 "예측이 가능할" 것으로 유추 가능하다. 따라서 답은 ①이다.

---

24 윗글의 분위기는 어떻게 묘사가 가능한가?

① 비판적인   ② 객관적인
③ 앙심을 품은   ④ 냉소적인
⑤ 애증이 엇갈리는

| 정답 | ②

| 해설 | 본문은 저자의 어떤 감정이나 의견이 들어가지 않고 객관적으로 사실만을 기술한 글이다. 따라서 답은 ②이다.

25 윗글에서 유추하게 될 가능성이 가장 높은 것은 무엇인가?

① 인간의 편견은 사회 과학자들이 주로 연구하는 연구 대상이다.

② 인간의 행동을 둘러싼 환경은 정확한 통제가 가능하다.

③ 사회 과학은 연구 대상이 다루기 힘들기 때문에 까다로운 것으로 불릴 수 있다.

④ 다니엘 수츠는 자연 과학이 편견에 좌우된다는 주장을 뒷받침하기 위해 인용된다.

⑤ 금속 막대는 자연 환경에 따라서는 길이가 변할 수 있다.

| 정답 | ⑤

| 해설 | "물리학자는 자연 환경이 동일하게 유지되는 한 길이가 늘어나거나 줄어들 일은 없을 것으로 확신한다(he can be quite sure that it will not stretch or shrink in length as long as natural conditions are the same)." 이는 역으로 보면, 자연 환경에 차이가 발생할 경우 길이가 늘어나거나 줄어들 수도 있다는 의미이다. 따라서 답은 ⑤이다.

| 어휘 |

be subject to ~에 좌우되다, ~에 영향을 받다

in contrast to ~와 대조가 된다

assume ⓥ 추정하다, 가정하다

measure ⓥ 측정하다, 재다

shrink ⓥ 줄어들다

predictable ⓐ 예측 가능한

susceptible ⓐ ~에 민감한, ~에 영향 받기 쉬운

immune ⓐ ~의 영향을 받지 않는

formidable ⓐ 가공할, 어마어마한

objective ⓐ 객관적인

cynical ⓐ 냉소적인

stubborn ⓐ 완고한, 다루기 힘든

subject matter 주제, 소재

hydrogen ⓝ 수소

physicist ⓝ 물리학자

stretch ⓥ 늘어나다

quote ⓥ 인용하다

reliable ⓐ 믿을 수 있는

apathetic ⓐ 무관심한

versatile ⓐ 다재다능한

whimsical ⓐ 엉뚱한, 기발한

vindictive ⓐ 앙심을 품은

ambivalent ⓐ 애증이 엇갈리는

PART 02

세부적 이해

CHAPTER 01 내용 일치

CHAPTER 02 특정 정보

CHAPTER 03 문법성 판단

CHAPTER 04 의미 파악

CHAPTER 05 재진술

CHAPTER 06 지시어구

CHAPTER 07 단어와 숙어

연습 문제   01 ②   02 ③   03 ④

01 윗글의 내용과 가장 부합하지 <u>않는</u> 것은? 광운대 2015

성형외과들이 거리를 따라 늘어서 있는 강남은 하루 종일 밤에도 불이 꺼지지 않는다. 중국어로 된 간판은 방문객들을 대상으로 손짓하며 들어오라고 신호를 보내고 있다. 일단 성형외과 안에 들어가 보면 통역사들이 대기하고 있다. 중국의 신흥 부자들이 전 세계를 무대로 꾸준하게 그리고 어디에나 밀려들어 오고 있는 현 상황을 이용할 기회를 잡기 위해, 한국 정부는 쇼핑하고, 먹고, 머무를 수 있는 그리고 어쩌면 성형 수술도 받아볼 수 있는 그런 곳으로 한국을 홍보하고 있다. 그리고 중국인들은, 주로 여성들이 쌍꺼풀 수술 같은 사소한 수술에서부터 안면을 완전히 뜯어고치는 고난이도의 수술에 이르기까지 자신의 신체를 바꾸기 위해 떼를 지어 방문하고 있다. 성형 수술은 중국에서도 널리 이루어지고 있지만, 한국의 성형외과는 비록 더 비싸긴 해도 더 안전하고 위생적인 곳으로 여겨진다.

① 쌍꺼풀 수술은 성형 수술 가운데 좀 사소한 것으로 취급된다.
② 성형 수술은 중국과 비교하면 한국에서는 비싼 수술이 아니다.
③ 중국 여성뿐만 아니라 중국 남성도 성형 수술을 받기 위해 한국에 방문한다.
④ 일부 중국 방문객들은 심지어 얼굴을 완전히 뜯어고치는 수술을 원한다.
⑤ 중국 방문객들은 중국의 병원보다 한국의 병원이 더 깨끗하다고 여긴다.

| 정답 | ②

| 해설 | "Korean hospitals are perceived to be safer and more hygienic, albeit pricier(한국의 성형외과는 비록 더 비싸긴 해도 더 안전하고 위생적인 곳으로 여겨진다)." 여기서 더 비싸다는 말은 말 그대로 '비싸다'는 의미이며, 따라서 성형 수술은 중국에서와 마찬가지로 한국에서도 비싼 수술이다. 때문에 ②가 본문과 거리가 있는 내용이다.

| 어휘 | **plastic surgery** 성형 수술
beckon ⓥ 손짓하다, 부르다, 유인하다
tap ⓥ 이용하다
promote ⓥ 홍보하다
in droves 떼 지어
restructure ⓥ 재구성하다, 개편하다
hygienic ⓐ 위생적인

line ⓥ ~을 따라 늘어서다[줄을 세우다]
seize ⓥ 사로잡다, 장악하다
ubiquitous ⓐ 어디에나 있는, 아주 흔한
nip and tuck 피부 성형 수술(특히 얼굴의)
doble eyelid surgery 쌍꺼풀 수술
perceive ⓥ 인지하다, 여기다
albeit ⓟⓡⓔⓟ 비록 ~일지라도

02 다음 글의 내용과 일치하는 것은?

황금빛 모래사장과 매혹적인 문화, 그리고 친절한 사람들이 모잠비크(Mozambique)에 오는 여행객들을 환영한다. 모잠비크는 아프리카의 동남쪽 해안에 위치해 있다. 수도인 Maputo에는 생기 찬 시장과 노천카페, 나무가 늘어선 널따란 길들을 볼 수 있다. 이 나라의 야생 동물 공원에는 코끼리와 원숭이 및 다른 동물들을 볼 수 있다. 이곳 사람들은 가난한 국가를 재건하기 위해 애쓰고 있다. 약 500년 동안 포르투갈에 식민 지배를 받은 바 있으며, 1975년에 독립을 이루었다. 이후 약 15년 동안 내전으로 모잠비크는 상처로 얼룩졌다. 지금도 많은 사람들이 아프지만 약이나 의사의 치료를 받을 형편이 되지 못한다.

① 모잠비크는 섬나라로 아름다운 해변으로 둘러싸여 있다.
② 수도인 Maputo의 거리에는 다양한 야생 동물들을 볼 수 있다.
③ 모잠비크는 독립 전에 포르투갈의 식민지였다.
④ 모잠비크는 역사적으로 평화로운 국가로 남아 있다.

| 정답 | ③

| 해설 | ①의 경우 아프리카 남동쪽 해안에 위치해 있다고 했으므로, 섬이 아닌 내륙 국가임을 짐작할 수 있으며, ②의 경우 야생 동물은 수도가 아닌 야생 공원에 있다고 언급하고 있다. ③의 경우 본문의 "The country was ruled by Portugal for almost 500 years"라는 구절을 통해 정답임을 알 수 있다. ④의 경우 내전(civil war)으로 인해 나라가 갈기갈기 찢겼다고 했기 때문에 평화로웠다고 할 수 없다.

| 어휘 | **A is home to B** A에는 B가 모여 산다   **wildlife** ⓐ 야생의
independence ⓝ 독립   **tear sth apart** ~을 갈가리 찢어 버리다
can't afford ~을 할 형편이 되지 못하다

03 다음 중 본문에 따르면 맞는 것은 무엇인가?

미국인이 표면상으로 격식 없이 행동하는 것은 종종 외국인을 혼란스럽게 하는데, 왜냐면 그 외국인은 미국인들의 표면상의 격식 없음을 격식이 전혀 없는 것으로 해석하기 때문이다. 외국인은 격식 없음이 어느 지점에서 끝나는지를 이해하지 못한다. 교사는 수업 중에는 친근하고, 즐겁고, 허물이 없더라도, 학생이 공부를 열심히 할 것으로 기대하며 학생 각각에게 비판적이면서 세심하게 점수를 매긴다. 또한 교사는 자신이 존경심을 갖고 대우받을 것으로 기대한다. 비록 학생들은 교사가 한 언급에 관해 자유롭게 질문을 할 수는 있지만, 학생들은 교사에게 반박할 것으로는 기대되지 않는다.

① 미국 학생들은 교사들에게 반박하는 것이 자유롭다.
② 미국 교사들은 자신들의 학생들에게 점수를 후하게 준다.
③ 미국 교사들은 너무 엄격해서 학생들은 종종 교사들을 거역한다.
④ 미국인들은 비록 겉보기에는 격의 없어 보이지만 격식 없는 행위에 제한이 있음을 알고 있다.

| 정답 | ④

| 해설 | 미국인들은 "surface informality(표면상으로 격식 없이 행동)"하지만 외국인들은 이것을 "no formality at all(격식이 전혀 없음)"으로 받아들여서는 안 된다는 것이 본문의 핵심이다. 그리고 외국인들과는 반대로 미국인들이 "understand the point at which informality stops(격식 없음이 어느 지점에서 끝나는지를 이해한다)"는 것의 의미는, 미국인들은 격식 없이 행동하더라도 절대 어떤 선을 넘지는 않는다는 의미이다. 따라서 보기 중에서 답으로 적합한 것은 ④가 된다.

실전 문제

01	①	02	③	03	①	04	③	05	④	06	④	07	③	08	④	09	②	10	④
11	②	12	④	13	③	14	①	15	④	16	②	17	①	18	④	19	①	20	②
21	③	22	④	23	③	24	④	25	③	26	③	27	②	28	④	29	③	30	③
31	⑤	32	④	33	①	34	②	35	②	36	①	37	①	38	①	39	④	40	③
41	④	42	③	43	②	44	①	45	④										

[01~02]

해석

1805년 영국의 외과 의사이자 발명가인 피터 마크 로제(P. M. Roget)는 독특한 취미를 시작했다. 그것은 개념(생각)에 따라 단어들을 분류하는 것이었다. 그의 의도는 그런 단어들을 일종의 어휘 카탈로그 방식으로 제시해 작가들과 언어학자들이 올바른 표현 방식을 찾도록 도와주려는 것이었다. 그는 작업을 하면서 아마도 명실상부한 세계 최초의 주제별 단어집인 고대 산스크리트어 아마라코샤(Amamkosha)나 번역 없이 보편적으로 이해될 수 있도록 단어 배열을 시도한 1797년 출판된 프랑스어 파지그라피(Pasigraphie)를 염두에 두었을 것이다. 로제는 자신의 작품을 '시소러스(thesaurus)'라고 불렀는데, 이 단어는 라틴어로 '보물' 또는 '지식의 보고'라는 뜻을 지닌다.

로제의 취미는 평생의 열정이 되었고, 1852년 73세의 나이로 「Thesaurus of English Words and Phrases, Classified and Arranged so as to Facilitate the Expressions of Ideas and Assist in Literary Composition(생각의 표현을 용이하게 하고 문학작품의 저술을 돕기 위해 분류되고 정리된 영어 단어와 구절의 보고)」을 출판했다. 이 새로운 참고 도서는 엄청난 인기를 끌었고, 초판이 출판된 지 일 년 만에 2차 개정판이 나왔다. 1869년 로제가 사망할 당시, 25개 이상의 개정판과 인쇄본이 출간되었다. 오늘날, 그의 이름은 그의 유의어 사전과 같은 의미를 지닌다.

01 다음 중 글의 요지에 해당하는 것은?

① 영어 유의어 사전의 기원
② 세계 최초의 유의어 사전
③ 로제가 저술한 유의어 사전의 인기
④ 취미와 직업의 관계

| 정답 | ①

| 해설 | 본문은 로제가 저술한 최초의 영어 유의어 사전이 어떻게 태어나게 되었는지에 대해 말하고 있으므로, 정답은 ①이 된다.

| 02 | 다음 중 본문의 내용과 일치하지 <u>않는</u> 것은?

① 오늘날 로제라는 이름은 영어 유의어 사전과 밀접하게 연관되어 있다.

② 로제가 저술한 유의어 사전의 초판은 1년 만에 공급이 부족했다.

③ 최초의 동의어 사전은 외과의사 출신의 언어학자인 로제에 의해 편찬됐다.

④ 로제가 저술한 유의어 사전의 인기는 그가 사망할 때까지 식지 않았던 것으로 보인다.

| 정답 | ③

| 해설 | 첫 번째 문단에서 세계 최초의 주제별 단어집은 고대 산스크리트어로 저술된 아마라코샤(Amamkosha)일 것으로 추정하고 있으므로, 로제가 저술한 동의어 사전이 최초라고 할 수 없고, 'surgeon-turned-linguist'에서와 같이 원래 외과 의사이던 사람이 이후 언어학자가 된 것이 아니라 평생의 취미로 작업을 했으므로 이 부분 또한 적합하지 않다. 따라서 정답은 ③이 된다.

| 어휘 | **surgeon** ⓝ 외과의사

peculiar ⓐ 독특한, 기묘한, 이상한

verbal ⓐ 말의, 구두의

arguably 졷 아마 틀림없이

treasury ⓝ 보고, 금고

pastime ⓝ 취미

facilitate ⓥ 용이하게 하다, 손쉽게 하다

composition ⓝ 작문, 작품

synonymous ⓐ 동의어의, 같은 뜻의

take up (취미나 일 등을) 시작하다

classification ⓝ 분류, 등급 매기기

linguist ⓝ 언어학자

thesaurus ⓝ 유의어 사전

storehouse ⓝ 창고

phrase ⓝ 관용구, 구절

literary ⓐ 문학의

enormously 졷 엄청나게

compile ⓥ 편집하다, 편찬하다

[03~04] 광운대 2015

해석

IQ란 명칭으로도 불리는 지능 지수(intelligence quotient)는 인간의 지능을 평가하기 위해 고안된 여러 가지 표준화된 검사 중 하나에서 유래된 점수를 가리킨다. "IQ"라는 약어는 심리학자 윌리엄 스턴(William Stern)이 독일어 Intelligenz-Quotient로부터 따와서 만든 것으로, 그가 1912년 쓴 자신의 책을 통해 주창한 지능 검사를 위한 점수 산정 방식을 일컫는 용어이다. 현재의 IQ 검사가 개발되었을 당시 규준 표본의 중간값 원점수는 IQ 100으로 정의되었고, 각 상하 표준 편차 점수는 ±15로 정의되었다. 이러한 정의에 따라 총 인구 가운데 대략 3분의 2의 IQ 점수는 85에서 115 사이이며, 약 5퍼센트는 IQ 점수가 125가 넘는다. IQ 점수는 교육적 성취, 특수 요구, 업무 능력 등에 대한 예측 변수로써 활용된다. IQ 점수는 또한 인구 집단 내에서의 IQ 점수 분포를 연구하는 데 사용되며 IQ와 다른 변수 간의 상관관계를 연구하는 데 사용된다. 여러 인구 집단을 대상으로 한 IQ 검사의 원점수는 20세기 초부터 10년 간격으로 평균 3점씩 증가해 왔는데, 이 현상은 플린 효과(Flynn Effect)로 불린다.

| 03 | 윗글의 내용과 가장 부합하지 <u>않는</u> 것은?

① IQ 검사는 심리학자 윌리엄 스턴이 자신의 책에서 고안했다.

② 총 인구의 다수는 IQ 점수가 상하 표준 편차 이내에 들어간다.

③ 총 인구의 대략 5퍼센트는 IQ 점수가 125점이 넘는다.

④ IQ 점수는 한 사람의 학습 능력 및 업무 능력을 예측하는 데 쓰인다.

⑤ 인구 집단은 IQ 점수에 따라 분포가 이루어진다.

| 정답 | ①

| 해설 | 본문을 보면 IQ란 약어가 윌리엄 스턴의 책에서 처음 제시되었다는 내용은 나와 있지만, 본문 어디에도 그가 IQ 검사 자체를 고안했다는 내용은 등장하지 않는다. 따라서 답은 ①이다.

---

04 윗글에서 밑줄 친 the Flynn Effect에 대해 가장 옳게 나타낸 것은?

① 인구 집단 사이에서 IQ 점수가 어떻게 분포되어 있는지를 설명한다.
② 왜 IQ 검사에서 원점수가 중요한 의미를 지니는지 보여 준다.
③ 시간에 따른 IQ 점수의 점진적인 성장을 나타낸다.
④ 왜 IQ로 많은 사회적 현상을 예측할 수 있는지 설명한다.
⑤ 표준 편차가 IQ 점수 규모에 나타내는 영향을 가리킨다.

| 정답 | ③

| 해설 | "여러 인구 집단을 대상으로 한 IQ 검사의 원점수는 20세기 초부터 10년 간격으로 평균 3점씩 증가해 왔다(Raw scores on IQ tests for many populations have been rising at an average rate that scales to three IQ points per decade since the early 20th century)." 여기서 플린 효과는 보기 ③의 "시간에 따른 IQ 점수의 점진적인 성장"을 나타냄을 알 수 있다. 따라서 답은 ③이다.

| 어휘 |
intelligence quotient 지능 지수(IQ)
derive from ~에서 유래하다[파생하다]
assess ⓥ 평가하다, 가늠하다
coin ⓥ (새로운 낱말·어구를) 만들다
median ⓐ 중간값의, 중앙치의
norming sample 규준 표본, 규준 샘플
approximately ⓐⓓ 거의, 대략
educational achievement 교육적 성취
special needs (장애인들을 대상으로 한) 특수 요구[특별한 도움]
job performance 업무 능력
correlation ⓝ 연관성, 상관관계
scale ⓥ 점점 높아지다, (수량 등이) 비례하다 ⓝ 규모, 범위

score ⓝ 점수
standardized ⓐ 표준화된
abbreviation ⓝ 약어
advocate ⓥ 주창하다, 지지하다
raw score 통계 처리하기 전의 숫자, 원점수
standard deviation 표준 편차
predictor ⓝ 예측 변수

distribution ⓝ 분포
variable ⓝ 변수

[05~06]

해석

서구 사회의 기술 과학이 이룬 성취가 눈부시기는 하지만, 그 대가로 자연의 풍요로움을 고갈시키고 파괴해 온 것도 부인할 수 없는 사실이다. 발전, 생산성, 부의 축적을 위해서, 우리는 인간의 친구인 자연과 환경을 수세기 동안 착취해 왔다. 그리고 착취당한 자연이 우리가 예상치 못한 방식으로 보복을 할 수도 있다는 사실을 이제야 깨닫고 있다. 우리는 항상 "같은 것을 더 많이"라는 방식으로 사고하기 때문에, 이 보복에 대한 대응은 오히려 문제를 악화시키는 경향이 있다. 즉, 기술의 폐해에 대한 우리의 대응은 더 많고 더 향상된 기술을 사용하는 것이다. 하천이 오염되고 있다면, 현재 우리가 고안해 내는 해결책이란 더 강력하고 더 비싼 오염 방지제의 개발이다.

05 (A), (B), (C)에 들어갈 말을 순서대로 바르게 짝지은 것은?

① 예상되는 - 약화시키다 - 무해한

② 예상되는 - 개선하다 - 더 생태적인

③ 의외의 - 해결하다 - 더 해로운

④ 의외의 - 약화시키다 - 더 강력한

| 정답 | ④

| 해설 | 문장 간의 논리 관계를 이해하는 것이 출제 의도이다. 자연 착취의 결과는 예상치 못한 부작용일 것이다. 따라서 ①은 "unexpected"가 적절하다. 이 부작용에 대한 인간의 대응이 문제를 오히려 악화시키는 예시가 마지막 문장에 상술되고 있으므로 ②에는 문제를 악화시킨다는 의미를 완성하기 위해 "escalate"가 필요하다. 문제를 악화시키는 이유는 인간이 "같은 것을 더 많이(more of the same)" 사용해서 문제에 대응하려는 사고방식 때문이다. 화학 물질에 의한 하천 오염이라는 문제를 더 강력한 화학 물질인 오염 방지제로 대응한다는 예시가 이어지는 것이 논리적이다.

06 윗글의 내용과 일치하지 <u>않는</u> 것은?

① 서구 사회의 과학 기술은 인류의 삶에 긍정적인 영향과 동시에 부정적인 영향도 미쳤다.

② 우리 인간은 지금 자연을 착취한 것에 대한 대가를 치르고 있다.

③ 서구 사회의 과학 기술이 초래한 문제 중 하나는 환경 착취이다.

④ 오염 방지제 덕분에, 오염되었던 하천은 다시 원래 상태로 복원될 수 있다.

| 정답 | ④

| 해설 | 하천의 오염을 해결하기 위한 오염 방지제의 사용은 과학 기술의 폐해(자연의 보복)를 악화시키는 예이다. 따라서 오염 방지제로 오염된 하천을 회복시켰다는 보기 ④는 지문의 내용과 일치하지 않는다.

| 어휘 | **impressive** ⓐ 인상적인, 대단한

there is no denying that ~라는 사실은 부정할 수 없다

strain ⓝ 긴장, 부담, 압박

in the interest of ~을 위해서, ~의 편에서

productivity ⓝ 생산성

exploit ⓥ 착취하다, 이용하다

kick back 보복하다, 반동하다

kick-back ⓝ 반작용, 역작용

evil ⓝ 악, 폐해

solution ⓝ 해결책

anti-pollutant ⓝ 오염 방지제

achievement ⓝ 성취, 업적

nervous ⓐ 불안한, 예민한

natural riches 천연자원

progress ⓝ 진보, 발전

accumulation ⓝ 축적

wake up to ~을 깨닫게 되다

reaction ⓝ 반응, 대응

in terms of ~의 관점에서

pollute ⓥ 오염시키다

reason ⓥ 추론하다, 생각하다

해석

"구운 흙(baked earth)"이란 의미의 테라코타(terra-cotta)는 본래 로마 제국 전성기에 건축 용도로 사용되었다. 하지만 르네상스 시대에 테라코타는 예술가의 표현 수단으로 훨씬 더 많이 쓰이게 되었다. 예를 들어, 수많은 조각가들은 종종 테라코타로 조각의 "대략적인 초안(rought draft)"을 의미하는 '보제티(bozzetti)'를 만들었는데, 이것은 나중에 돌로 조각되거나 청동으로 주조되었다. 아주 묘하게도, '보제티'는 완성된 작품보다 더 흥미로운 것으로 간주된 경우가 종종 있었는데, 이는 예술 애호가들이 집이나 갤러리에서 전시할 목적으로 테라코타 모델을 수집하기 시작했기 때문이다. 수집가들은 테라코타 모델이 예술가의 재능을 훨씬 더 정확히 나타낸다고 생각했다. 그 결과, 이런 "대략적인 초안" 중 다수가, 이를 기반으로 만든 돌 조각이나 청동 조각보다 종종 더 높은 가격으로 팔리곤 한다.

---

07 본문에 따르면 사실인 것은 무엇인가?

① 조각가들이 '보제티'를 입수하는 것은 쉬운 일이었다.
② 테라코타는 돌이나 청동만큼 견고했다.
③ '보제티'가 수집가들에게는 더 매력적이었다.
④ 르네상스 시대에 테라코타는 그 이전 시대에 비해 건축 용도로 더 많이 사용되었다.

| 정답 | ③

| 해설 | 본문의 "아주 묘하게도(Oddly enough)" 다음 내용은, 왜 수집가들이 보제티에 매력을 느꼈고 심지어 보제티를 기반으로 제작한 조각품보다 원본격인 보제티가 더 많이 팔리는지 설명하고 있다. 이는 ③의 근거가 되며, 따라서 답은 ③이다.
①과 관련된 내용은 본문에 언급된 바 없다. 테라코타는 흙으로 만든 것이고 초안을 잡는 데 쓰이기 때문에 돌이나 청동 조각만큼 단단하다 할 수 없다. 따라서 ②는 답이 될 수 없다. 르네상스 이전 시대에 테라코타는 건축용으로 사용되었고, 르네상스 시대에는 작품 용도로 쓰였다. 따라서 ④는 답이 될 수 없다.

---

08 빈칸 (A)와 (B)에 가장 알맞은 것은 무엇인가?

① 그럼에도 불구하고 – 하지만
② 하지만 – 따라서
③ 따라서 – 게다가
④ 예를 들어 – 그 결과

| 정답 | ④

| 해설 | (A): 빈칸 앞 문장에서는 테라코타가 예술 목적으로 사용되었음이 언급되고, 빈칸이 들어간 문장에서는 "그 예로" 테라코타로 보제티를 만들었음이 언급된다. 따라서 빈칸에 적합한 것은 for example이다.
(B): 빈칸 앞에서는 수집가들이 완성품보다 보제티를 통해 작가의 재능을 더 잘 살필 수 있다고 생각했음이 언급되고, 빈칸이 들어간 문장에서는 "그 결과" 수집가들 사이에서 보제티가 조각품보다 더 비싸게 팔리곤 한다는 점이 언급된다. 따라서 빈칸에 적합한 것은 As a result이다.
이러한 점들을 감안했을 때, 답으로 가장 적합한 것은 ④이다.

| 어휘 | **baked** ⓐ 구운, 햇볕에 탄   **earth** ⓝ 흙
height ⓝ 전성기, 최고조   **medium** ⓝ (화가 · 작가 · 음악가의) 표현 수단
rough ⓐ 거친, 대략적인   **draft** ⓝ 초안
cast ⓥ 주조하다   **oddly enough** 아주 묘한 이야기이지만, 아주 묘하게도

enthusiast ⓝ 애호가, 열광적인 팬
command ⓥ (값에) 팔리다

represent ⓥ 표현하다, 나타내다
sturdy ⓐ 튼튼한, 견고한

[09~10] 서강대 2010

해석

우리는 우정이 전부이면서 동시에 아무것도 아닌 시대에 살고 있다. 이미 현대 특유의 관계가 된 우정은, 최근 수십 년 동안 보편적인 관계로 자리매김했다. 우정은 사람과 사람 사이를 연결 짓는 형식이 되었으며, 이런 우정을 통해 다른 모든 것들이 이해되며, 우정을 척도로 다른 모든 것들의 가치가 부여되며, 우정으로 다른 모든 것들이 해체되어 모이게 된 것이다. 서로 사귀는 이들이 서로를 남자 친구(boyfriend)와 여자 친구(girlfriend)라고 호칭하며, 배우자들은 그들이 서로의 가장 좋은 친구라고 자랑스럽게 말한다. 부모들은 자신들을 친구로 생각해 달라고 어린 자녀들에게는 설득하고, 10대 자녀들에게는 사정한다. 성인이 된 형제자매들은 부모의 재산을 두고 경쟁하던 이전의 관계에서 벗어났다. 과거에는 부모의 재산으로 인해 그들이 결코 친구가 될 수 없었다. [성경에 등장하는 야곱(Jacob)과 에서(Esau)를 생각해 보라.] 하지만 지금은 '친구'라는 용어 등을 그대로 사용해 서로를 대한다. 교사와 성직자 그리고 직장 상사까지도 그들의 권위를 완화시키고 정당화시키기 위해 자신들이 감독하는 이들에게 자신들을 친구로 생각해 달라고 요청한다. 우리는 서로의 이름을 부르며 지내는 절친한 사이가 되었다. 대통령 선거를 할 때도 우리는 스스로에게 후보 중 누구와 함께 맥주를 마시고 싶은지를 묻는다. 인류학자인 Robert Brain이 말한 것처럼, <u>우리는 지금 모두와 친구가 된 것이다.</u>

---

09 본문에 따르면 다음 내용 중 올바른 것은?

① 대통령 선거는 우정에 밀려나는 경향이 있다.
② 우정은 현대 관계를 특징짓는다.
③ 동성애를 우정과 혼동한다.
④ 현대 사회에서는 형제자매들이 우정을 두고 서로 경쟁한다.

| 정답 | ②

| 해설 | 현대 사회에서는 모든 이들의 관계가 우정(friendship)을 기반으로 형성되고 있다고 필자는 주장하고 있다. 따라서 정답은 ②가 된다. ①과 ③에 대한 내용은 본문에 등장하지 않으며, ④의 경우 형제자매들이 서로를 친구라고 생각한다고 본문에서 말한 것을 우정을 두고 여전히 경쟁 관계라고 말했으므로 정답이 될 수 없다.

---

10 다음 내용 중 빈칸에 가장 알맞은 것은?

① 우리는 선출된 정부 관리들에 대해 지나치게 관심을 갖는다
② 우리는 자유만큼이나 우정에 열중한다
③ 우리는 우정을 위해 해외로 나갈 준비가 되어 있다
④ 우리는 지금 모든 사람들과 친구이다

| 정답 | ④

| 해설 | 본문을 보면, 우리는 애인 사이에도 서로 친구이며, 배우자끼리도 서로에게 좋은 친구라고 말한다. 부모와 자식 간의 관계도 친구로 규정하며, 형제자매끼리도 친구가 되었다. 그리고 심지어 교사나 상사, 성직자와도 서로 친구 관계가 되었다고 말하고 있다. 따라서 마지막에 올 말은 우리는 모든 이들과 친구가 되었다는 내용의 ④가 정답이 된다.

characteristically ⓐ 특질상, 특징으로서, 개성적으로

both all and nothing at all 전부이면서 동시에 아무것도 아닌 **cf. all or nothing** 양단간의, 이것 아니면 저것인

in terms of ~ 면에서, ~에 관하여　　　　　　　　　**refer to A as B** A를 B라고 언급하다[호칭하다, 부르다]

spouse ⓝ 배우자　　　　　　　　　　　　　　　**boast** ⓥ 자랑하다

urge ⓥ ~하도록 충고하다, 권고하다　　　　　　　**beg** ⓥ 부탁하다, 간청하다

think of A as B A를 B라고 생각하다[여기다]　　　　**sibling** ⓝ 형제자매

anything but ~이 결코 아닌　　　　　　　　　　　**clergymen** ⓝ 남자 성직자

mitigate ⓥ 완화하다　　　　　　　　　　　　　**legitimate** ⓥ 합법화하다, 정당화하다

authority ⓝ 권위　　　　　　　　　　　　　　　**regard A as B** A를 B라고 생각하다[여기다]

on a first-name basis with (서로 이름을 부르는) 절친한 사이인

vote for ~에게 투표하다　　　　　　　　　　　　**anthropologist** ⓝ 인류학자

push sth aside (싫은 것을) 옆으로 밀치다, (불쾌한 생각을) 피하다, 떨쳐 버리다

characterize ⓥ 특징짓다　　　　　　　　　　　　**be/get mixed up with** 혼동하다, 어울리다

be keen on ~에 매우 열중하여, ~을 아주 좋아하는

[11~12]

해석

인터넷이 조성하거나 강화시킨 더 중요한 것들 중 하나는 언론의 자유와 표현의 자유이다. 인터넷은 전 세계 사람들이 공유하는 매우 거대한 공공 영역이다. 인터넷 이용자의 다양성 덕분에 인터넷상의 언론을 통제할 수 있도록 적용 가능한 단 하나의 표준은 존재하지 않는다. 게다가 인터넷 기술 자체가 정보의 접근을 완전히 차단하는 일을 막는다. 하지만 1990년대 말에 많은 국가들은 인터넷상에서 접근이 가능해진 언론의 자유에 놀라서 이를 제한하려 했다. 싱가포르는 정치적 사이트나 종교적 사이트는 정부에 우선 등록하도록 명령했다. 중국은 모든 인터넷 이용자들에게 경찰에 등록할 것을 명령했다. 그리고 사우디아라비아는 대학과 병원에서만 인터넷 이용을 제한했다. 하지만 인터넷의 속성 덕분에 상기 어떤 노력도 지속적인 효과를 크게 거두지 못했다.

11　밑줄 친 (A), (B)에 들어가기에 가장 적합한 것을 고르시오.

　　① 게다가 – 덧붙여서　　　　　　② 게다가 – 하지만

　　③ 하지만 – 게다가　　　　　　　④ 하지만 – 그럼에도 불구하고

| 정답 | ②

| 해설 | 빈칸 (A)의 앞과 뒤는 서로 모순되거나 반대되는 내용이 아니라 둘 다 인터넷 통제가 어렵다는 점을 증명하고 있다. 따라서 (A)의 답으로 가장 적절한 것은 ①의 in addition이나 ②의 furthermore이다. 빈칸 (B) 앞은 인터넷의 완전한 차단은 어렵다는 내용을 담고 있으나 뒤는 몇몇 국가에서 차단 시도를 감행했다는 내용을 담고 있다. 즉 서로 상반된 내용이다. 따라서 (B)의 답으로 가장 적절한 것은 ②의 however나 ④의 nevertheless이다. 이러한 사항을 모두 종합해 보면 답은 ②이다.

12 다음 중 윗글의 내용과 가장 일치하는 것을 고르시오.

① 인터넷을 통한 정보 접근은 완전히 막을 수 있다.

② 중국에서 인터넷 이용은 대학과 병원에서만 허용된다.

③ 많은 나라에서는 인터넷 이용을 제한하려 했고 이는 성과가 좋았다.

④ 인터넷상에서 언론을 통제할 수 있는 표준을 만들기는 매우 어렵다.

| 정답 | ④

| 해설 | 본문의 "인터넷상의 언론을 통제할 수 있도록 적용 가능한 단 하나의 표준은 존재하지 않는다(no one standard can be applied to govern speech on the Internet)"는 보기 ④의 내용과 일치하며 따라서 답은 ④이다. 보기 ①은 "인터넷 기술 자체가 정보의 접근을 완전히 차단하는 일을 막는다(the Internet's technology itself prevents complete blocking of access to information)"와 상반된 내용이며, ②는 중국이 아니라 사우디아라비아에 관한 내용이므로 답이 될 수 없고, ③은 "상기 어떤 노력도 지속적인 효과를 크게 거두지 못했다(none of these efforts has had much lasting effects)"를 통해 답이 아님을 알 수 있다.

| 어휘 | **foster** ⓥ 조성하다, 발전시키다

alarmed ⓐ 불안해하는, 두려워하는

mandate ⓥ 명령하다, 지시하다

criteria ⓝ criterion의 복수; 표준, 기준

diversity ⓝ 다양성

accessible ⓐ 접근 가능한, 이용 가능한

lasting ⓐ 지속적인, 영속적인

[13~15] 숭실대 2017

해석

혹시 직장 상사에게 인상적인 모습을 보여 주기 위해 휴가를 반납해 본 적이 있는가? 만약 그렇다면 정말 잘못 생각하고 있는 것이다. 최근 연구원들은 더 많은 휴가를 즐기는 것이 실제로는 전반적으로 긍정적인 직장 생활에 해당한다고 밝히고 있다.

조사에 따르면 설문에 참여한 미국 직장인 중 절반 이상이 의도적으로 휴가를 사용하지 않고 남겨 둔 것으로 나타났다. 연구의 저자는 직장인들이 게을러 보이거나 일이 뒤처질 것을 우려한 것으로 의심하며, 휴가를 사용하지 않고 남겨 두어 직장 상사에게 인상적인 모습을 보이려는 의도라고 생각한다.

하지만 사실은 휴가를 내는 것이 노예처럼 일하면서 뇌에 과부하가 걸리게 하는 것보다 생산성 향상에 훨씬 좋다는 것이다. 장기간의 휴가를 보내는 것이 동기 부여를 높여 줄 수 있지만 (그것이 안 된다면) 수시로 하루를 쉬는 것도 집중력 향상에 도움이 된다. "휴가가 정신 건강에 주는 영향은 엄청나다"고 임상 심리학자인 프래신 레더러(Francine Lederer)는 말한다. "대부분의 사람은 설사 24시간의 휴가라고 해도 휴가를 보낸 후 더 나은 인생관을 갖게 되고 목표 달성에 대한 더 많은 동기 부여를 갖게 된다"고 덧붙인다.

심지어 휴가를 포기하는 것이 당신이 승진하지 못한 이유일 수 있다. 〈프로젝트 타임아웃(the Project : Time Out)〉에서 발견한 한 가지 흥미로운 사실은 10일 이하로 휴가를 쓴 사람들이 11일 이상 휴가를 간 사람들보다 최근 3년간 급여 인상이나 보너스를 받을 가능성이 더 낮았다. 이것은 아마도 휴가를 적게 사용해 직장에서의 생산성이 큰 타격을 받은 것일 가능성이 크며, 극도로 피로한 모습이 두드러져 보였을 가능성이 크다. 휴가를 건너뛰지 말고 현명한 전략들을 활용해 상사와의 신뢰 관계를 구축하는 것이 좋다.

여기서 우리가 얻을 수 있는 교훈은 휴가가 개인의 건강과 안녕에 좋을 뿐만 아니라 좋은 직장인이 되는 데 중요한 역할을 수행한다는 것이다. 그리고 더 좋은 소식은 일주일을 휴가 내서 뒤처질 걱정을 할 필요가 없다는 것이다. 대신 연중으로 하루짜리 휴가를 여러 번 내서 아이들의 발표회에 가거나, 집에서 휴식을 취하거나, 공원에서 하루를 보내는 등의 방식으로 사용한다면, 조만간 휴식을 취하는 것이 엄청난 변화를 일으킨다는 사실을 발견하게 될 것이다.

13 직장인들이 휴가를 사용하지 <u>않는</u> 주된 이유에 해당하는 것은?

① 더 많은 돈을 벌기 위해
② 상사의 비위를 맞추기 위해
③ 더 많은 제품을 만들기 위해
④ 일을 즐기기 위해

| 정답 | ②

| 해설 | 직장인들이 휴가를 잘 가지 못하는 이유로 "to impress your boss"나 "they'll look lazy or fall behind on the job, or they think that by leaving the days unused they'll impress the boss" 등의 이유를 들고 있으므로, 이는 ②의 내용에 해당한다.

14 다음 중 본문의 내용과 일치하는 것은?

① 휴가는 생산성과 밀접한 관련이 있다.
② 휴가를 덜 가는 것이 승진을 위해 더 좋다.
③ 휴가는 동기 부여를 높여 주지 않는다.
④ 정신 건강에 휴가는 중요한 부분이 아니다.

| 정답 | ①

| 해설 | 본문의 "taking time off is far better for productivity than slaving away and putting your brain into overdrive"을 통해 휴가가 생산성과 밀접한 관계가 있다는 ①이 정답이 된다. ② 휴가를 많이 가는 것이 승진에 좋다고 했고, ③ "are more motivated to achieve their goals after a vacation" 부분을 통해 휴가는 동기 부여 향상에 더 도움이 된다고 설명하고 있다. ④ 휴가는 건강에 중요하다고 밝히고 있으며, 정신적 건강에 중요한 부분이 아니라는 내용은 본문에 등장하지 않는다.

15 다음 중 본문의 내용과 일치하지 <u>않는</u> 것은?

① 짧은 휴가도 가치 있다.
② 휴가는 모두에게 필요하다.
③ 휴가의 길이는 중요하지 않다.
④ 긴 휴가는 업무 수행을 방해한다.

| 정답 | ④

| 해설 | 본문의 "A day off here and a day off there from the office can improve your concentration" 부분과 "take single days off throughout the year" 부분을 통해 ①과 ③의 내용을 확인할 수 있다. 세 번째 문단의 "… while long breaks boost your motivation"을 통해 긴 휴가가 동기 부여를 더 높여 준다고 했으므로, 업무 수행을 방해한다고 말한 ④가 본문과 다른 내용에 해당한다.

| 어휘 | **turn down** 거절하다

get it wrong 잘못 생각하다, 계산에 틀리다

survey ⓝ 설문 조사 ⓥ 설문 조사 하다

fall behind (~에) 뒤지다[뒤떨어지다]

productivity ⓝ 생산성

overdrive ⓝ 혹사, 과부하; (차량의) 증속 구동

in an effort to ~하기 위해서, ~하려는 노력의 일환으로

positive ⓐ 긍정적인, 확신하는, 확신한

intentionally ⓐⓓ 의도적으로, 고의로

take time off 휴가를 내다

slave away 노예처럼 일하다

boost ⓥ 강화하다, 북돋다

motivation ⓝ 동기

perspective ⓝ 관점

burn out 에너지를 소진하다[소진하게 만들다]

strategy ⓝ 전략, 방법

play a role in -ing ~하는 데 역할을 수행하다

get behind 뒤지다, 밀리다

make all the difference (~에) 중요한 영향을 미치다; 기분이 훨씬 좋아지게 하다

supervisor ⓝ 감독관, 관리자

clinical psychologist 임상 심리학자

promote ⓥ 향상시키다, 승진시키다, 홍보하다

skip out on ~를 저버리다

takeaway ⓝ 교훈; (학습, 회의 등의) 비결; 테이크아웃 음식

book ⓥ 예약(하다)

recital ⓝ 발표회, 연주회

[16~17] 명지대 2010

해석

카프카(Kafka)가 살았던 시대에는 프라하는 오스트리아-헝가리 제국에 속해 있었다. 그 지역 사람들은 주로 체코어를 사용했지만, 상류층이나 사업하는 이들은 독일어를 사용했다. 1910년에 프라하의 인구는 23만이었고, 오스트리아-헝가리 제국 내에서 세 번째로 큰 도시였다. 교외 지역을 포함해서 인구는 60만 정도였다. 인구의 90.7퍼센트가 체코어를 사용하고 나머지가 독일어를 사용했다. 사업하는 엘리트층은 주로 독일어를 사용했다. 독일어를 할 줄 아는 프롤레타리아는 없었다. 그 당시 독일의 여행 안내서에 따르면 "고급 술집이나 식당, 그리고 대형 매장에서는 독일어가 통한다. 마부, 서비스업 종사자, 철도역의 짐꾼들은 그들이 외국인을 대해야 하는 정도의 독일어를 말할 수 있다."고 적고 있다.

오늘날 프라하에서는 체코어가 공식적인 언어이긴 하지만, 프라하에서 국제 상거래의 언어로 영어가 독일어를 대체했다. 프라하의 현재 인구는 대략 130만 명이다. 소수 민족인 독일인들은 거의 사라졌다. 독일어를 사용하는 수많은 사람들이 제2차 세계 대전 이후 강제로 체코를 떠났고, 나머지 대부분의 사람들은 동화되었다.

---

16 빈칸 ㉮에 들어가기에 가장 적절한 것은?

① 카프카는 체코어로 글 쓰는 것을 거부했다.

② 상류층이나 사업하는 이들은 독일어를 사용했다.

③ 체코의 대중문화는 헝가리 전통에 의해 지배되었다.

④ 20세기 초에 체코어는 여행 책자에서 공무상 사용되기 시작했다.

| 정답 | ②

| 해설 | 빈칸의 문장은 although라는 접속사를 사용하여 양보 구조를 나타내고 있다. 양보 문장의 특성은 일부의 사실을 인정하면서 새로운 사실을 제시하는 것이므로, "그 지역 사람들은 주로 체코어를 사용했지만"이라고 한다면, 그와 반대 방향의 진행으로 체코어를 사용한 것과는 다른 이야기가 나와야 한다. 또 하단의 문장에 보면 "인구의 90.7퍼센트가 체코어를 사용하고 나머지가 독일어를 사용했다"는 진술로 미루어 볼 때, 체코에서 주로 체코어를 사용했지만 일부는 독일어를 사용했다는 진술을 끌어낼 수 있다. 그러므로 정답은 "상류층이나 사업하는 이들은 독일어를 사용했다"는 ②가 답이 된다.

17 윗글의 내용과 일치하는 것은?

① 독일 주민들은 점점 줄어들어서 요즈음 프라하에서 독일인들은 거의 없다.

② 1910년에 독일의 여행자들은 체코 국경 내로의 입국이 허용되지 않았다.

③ 1910년 당시 프라하의 독일 소수 민족은 사회적, 경제적 힘이 거의 없었다.

④ 제2차 세계 대전 이후 프라하에서는 영어는 독일어와 더불어 국제적인 언어로 사용되었다.

| 정답 | ①

| 해설 | ②처럼 독일인들의 체코 입국을 불허한다는 것은 본문에 근거가 전혀 없고, ③은 1910년 당시 체코의 상류층이나 사업계에서 독일어를 사용했다는 것은 사회적으로나 경제적으로나 약자는 아니었다는 의미로 받아들일 수 있다. 또한 ④의 경우 영어가 국제어로서 사용되는 것은 맞지만 독일어의 경우는 아니다. 국제 상거래의 언어로 영어가 독일어를 대체했다고 본문에 나와 있다. 이에 반해 독일어를 사용하는 수많은 사람들이 제2차 세계 대전 이후 강제로 체코를 떠났고, 나머지 대부분의 사람들은 동화되었다고 하였으므로, ①처럼 독일 주민들은 점점 줄어들어서 요즈음 프라하에서 독일인들은 거의 없다는 표현은 타당하다.

| 어휘 | **the upper class** 상류층 　　　　　　　　　　　**suburbs** ⓝ 교외(지역)

entrepreneur ⓝ 사업가 　　　　　　　　　**proletariat** ⓝ 프롤레타리아, 무산자(층)

pub ⓝ 술집(bar) 　　　　　　　　　　　　　**coachman** ⓝ 마부(과거 마차를 몰던 사람)

virtually @ 사실상 　　　　　　　　　　　　**assimilate** ⓥ 동화시키다, 동화되다

dominate ⓥ 지배하다, 좌우하다 　　　　　**shrink** ⓥ 줄다

border ⓝ 국경

[18~20]

해석

일상생활에서 우리는 개인 공간이라는 보이지 않는 "막"으로 우리를 둘러싸고 있다. 이 공간은 우리가 자신과 잘 아는 사람들, 친한 친구들을 위해 마련한 공간이다. 이런 개인 공간은 문화권마다 다르며, 각 문화권 안에서도 서로 만나는 사람들의 나이, 인종, 성별, 사회 계층 등의 범주에 따라 달라진다. 예를 들어 중동 사람들은 일반적 만남에서 훨씬 더 가까운 거리를 요구하며, 처음 소개받을 때에도 보통 남자들끼리 포옹을 하거나 볼에 입맞춤을 한다. 하지만 이런 관행은 미국 남성들에게는 매우 어색한 일이 아닐 수 없다. 일본은 인구 밀도가 높은 나라에 살고 있음<u>에도 불구하고</u>, 일본인들은 낯선 사람과 만날 때 더 커다란 사회적 공간을 유지하는 경향이 있다. 일본 남자들끼리 서로 소개받을 때, 서로에게 허리를 숙여 인사를 한다. 이때 서로 머리가 부딪치는 것을 피하기 위해 약 180센티미터 떨어진 거리를 유지한다. 미국에서는 일반적으로 여성들이 남성들보다 훨씬 더 편하게 접촉하고, 포옹하며, 입맞춤을 한다. 그리고 여성들은 친밀한 거리 내에 다른 여성들이 들어오는 것을 보통 허용한다. 하지만 남성들끼리는 혈연관계라 하더라도 다른 남성에게 그런 친밀한 거리를 허용하지 않는다.

18 빈칸 ⓐ에 들어갈 적당한 것은?

① 왜냐하면 　　　　② ~에도 불구하고 　　　　③ ~ 때문에, ~한 이후로 　　　④ 그러나

| 정답 | ②

| 해설 | 일본인들은 인구 밀도가 높은(densely-populated) 곳에서 산다고, 즉 비좁은 공간에서 많은 사람들이 산다고 언급하고 있다. 그리고 뒤에는 일본인들이 유지하는 개인 공간은 다른 나라의 사람들보다 더 크다고 언급하고 있다. 두 내용이 서로 모순을 일

으키고 있기 때문에 ②와 같은 양보의 의미를 지닌 접속사가 사용되어야 한다.

---

19 다음 중 본문과 일치하는 것은?

① 미국 남성들은 동성을 자신의 "막" 안에 들이는 것을 매우 불편해한다고 볼 수 있다.

② 이라크에 사는 남성에게 처음 소개를 받은 자리에서 볼에 입맞춤을 하는 것은 상대방이 불쾌하게 생각할 수 있는 일이다.

③ 일본 문화권에서는 미국에 비해 일반적 만남에서 훨씬 더 가까운 거리를 요구한다.

④ 동일한 문화권에 속한 사람들은 상대방을 대할 때 동일한 크기의 개인 공간을 갖는 경향이 있다.

| 정답 | ①

| 해설 | ①의 경우 본문의 마지막 문장인 "something a man rarely allows from another man, even if they are blood related" 부분을 통해 유추할 수 있으므로 ①이 정답이 된다. ②의 경우 중동 남성들은 훨씬 더 가까운 거리를 유지한다고 했으므로 상대 방이 이를 무례하다고 생각할 리 없다. ③의 경우 일본은 인구 밀도가 높지만 개인 공간이 더 크다고 했으므로 본문과 다르며, ④의 경우 본문 중반에 나온 "These personal spaces vary …… within cultures when people of different age, race, sex, and social class categories interact" 부분을 통해 사실이 아님을 알 수 있다.

---

20 밑줄 친 ⓑ far를 대체할 수 없는 것은?

① 훨씬, 아주 멀리   ② 결석한, 떨어져 있는

③ 너무, 많이   ④ 많이, 상당히

| 정답 | ②

| 해설 | ⓑ의 far는 비교급을 강조해 주는 even, still, much, a lot 등에 해당하는 부사이다. ①의 way는 구어체에 많이 쓰이며, ④의 considerably도 '상당히'라는 의미이므로 가능하다. 따라서 정답은 ②가 된다.

| 어휘 | **invisible** ⓐ 눈에 보이지 않는   **constitute** ⓥ 구성하다

reserve ⓥ (자리 등을) 따로 잡아 남겨 두다; 예약하다   **intimate** ⓐ 친밀한

acquaintance ⓝ 아는 사람   **casual** ⓐ 평상시의, 격식을 차리지 않는

embrace ⓥ 껴안다, 포옹하다   **densely-populated** ⓐ 인구가 밀집된

stranger ⓝ 낯선 사람   **bow** ⓥ (허리를 굽혀) 인사하다

bump ⓥ 부딪히다   **rarely** ⓐ 좀처럼 ～하지 않는

blood related 혈연관계의

해석

당신은 행복의 추구에 대해 어떻게 파악하는가? 많은 이들에게 있어 행복의 추구는 끈질기게 진행되어야 할 여정이고, 더 많이 투입할수록 더 많은 것을 얻어 낼 수 있다. 많은 이들을 감화한 엘리자베스 길버트(Elizabeth Gilbert)의 베스트셀러 회고록인 "먹고 기도하고 사랑하라(Eat, Pray, Love)"에 수록된 다음 에피소드를 생각해 보라. 이 에피소드에서 작가는 자신의 구루가 한 조언에 대해 이야기했다. 작가는 다음과 같이 썼다. "행복은 개인적으로 애쓴 끝에 얻은 결과입니다. 당신은 행복을 얻기 위해 투쟁했고, 행복을 추구했고, 행복을 고집했고, 때로는 행복을 찾아 전 세계를 돌아다녔습니다. 당신은 자신이 받은 축복을 밖으로 드러내는 행위에 집요하리만치 참여해야 합니다. 그리고 당신이 일단 행복한 상태가 되고 나면, 그러한 행복 속에 영원히 잠길 수 있도록 그리고 행복 위에 계속 머무를 수 있도록 열심히 노력해야 합니다. 그렇지 않을 경우 당신 내면의 만족감은 밖으로 새어 나갈 것입니다." 이러한 유형의 태도는 몇몇 사람들에게는 효과가 있을 수 있겠지만, 최근의 과학적 연구에 따르면 <u>그것은</u> 많은 사람들에게 심각한 역효과를 낳을 수도 있는데, 예를 들면 스트레스, 외로움, 개인적인 실패감 등으로 이어질 수 있다. 이러한 견해에 따르면 행복은 겁 많은 새와 같은 존재로 여기는 편이 가장 낫다. 잡으려 노력할수록 더 멀리 날아가는 존재 말이다.

21 밑줄 친 it이 가리키는 것은 무엇인가?

① 행복
② 겁 많은 새
③ 행복해지기 위해 열심히 노력함
④ 최근의 과학적 연구

| 정답 | ③

| 해설 | 문맥상 it은 앞의 this kind of attitude이고, 이 this kind of attitude는 그 앞에 설명된 '개인적으로 행복을 얻기 위해 애쓰고, 투쟁하고, 추구하고, 고집하는 태도이자 행복을 찾아 전 세계를 돌아다닐 수 있는 태도'이다. 이는 ③의 내용과 일치한다.

22 본문에 따르면 다음 중 사실인 것은 무엇인가?

① 저자는 행복을 겁 많은 새와 같다고 여긴다.
② 저자는 행복을 얻기 위해 노력할 것을 권장한다.
③ 저자는 행복은 추구의 대상이 아니라고 주장한다.
④ 저자는 사람들은 행복에 대해 서로 다른 태도를 보인다고 생각한다.

| 정답 | ④

| 해설 | 엘리자베스 길버트 같은 사람들에게 있어 "행복의 추구는 끈질기게 진행되어야 할 여정이고, 더 많이 투입할수록 더 많은 것을 얻어 낼 수 있다." 그런데 "이러한 유형의 태도는 몇몇 사람들에게는 효과가 있을 수 있겠지만, 최근의 과학적 연구에 따르면 많은 사람들에게 심각한 역효과를 낳을 수도 있다." 이를 보면 행복에 대한 태도는 사람들마다 다를 수 있음을 알 수 있다. 따라서 답은 ④이다.

| 어휘 | envisage ⓥ 마음속에 그려보다, 파악하다   pursuit ⓝ 추구, 추적

relentless ⓐ 끈질긴, 가차 없는   inspirational ⓐ 영감[감화/자극]을 주는

memoir ⓝ 회고록   recount ⓥ 이야기하다, 말하다

consequence ⓝ 결과   strive for ~을 얻으려고 노력하다

insist on ~을 고집하다	**relentlessly** ⓐⓓ 가차없이, 집요하게
manifestation ⓝ 드러냄, 징후	**blessing** ⓝ 은혜, 축복
swim ⓥ 가득히 차다, 잠기다	**innate** ⓐ 타고난, 선천적인
contentment ⓝ 만족[자족](감)	**backfire** ⓥ 역효과를 낳다
timid ⓐ 겁 많은, 소심한	

[23~24] 한국외대 2018

해석

비타민 D는 '햇빛 비타민'으로도 알려져 있으며, 그 이유는 우리의 몸이 햇빛에 노출되었을 때 비타민 D가 생성되기 때문이다. 건강을 위해서는 충분한 양의 비타민 D를 섭취하는 것이 필수적이다. 비타민 D는 뼈와 치아의 건강을 유지하는 데 도움을 주고, 면역 체제와 뇌 및 신경계를 뒷받침해 준다. 또한 비타민 D는 암과 당뇨병 및 경화증 등 다양한 질병으로부터 우리를 보호한다. 비타민 D라는 이름에 속을 수도 있지만, 비타민 D는 <u>실제로는 비타민이 아니라 프로호르몬의 일종</u>이다. 비타민은 우리의 몸에서 생성되지 못하며 대신 반드시 식사를 통해 섭취되어야 하는 영양소로 정의된다. 하지만 우리의 몸은 일주일에 2~3번 직사광선에 5~10분 정도 노출되면 '비타민' D를 생성할 수 있다. 전문가들은 노출되는 햇빛의 양이 대체로 줄어드는 겨울에는 비타민 D가 매우 빨리 분해된다고 경고한다. 전문가들은 저장된 비타민 D가 고갈되지 않으려면 식사나 영양 보충제를 통해 비타민 D의 섭취량을 늘려야 한다고 권고한다.

---

23 본문에 따르면 다음 중 비타민 D에 대해 사실이 <u>아닌</u> 것은 무엇인가?

① 충분한 양의 비타민 D는 뼈 구조를 건강하게 하기 위해 필수적이다.
② 비타민 D는 프로호르몬의 일종으로 우리의 몸에서 생성할 수 있다.
③ 충분한 양의 비타민 D를 생성하려면 매일 햇빛에 노출될 필요가 있다.
④ 비타민 D가 들어간 영양 보충제는 겨울에 섭취가 권장된다.

| 정답 | ③

| 해설 | ③에서 말하는 것과 달리 "우리의 몸은 일주일에 2~3번 직사광선에 5~10분 정도 노출되면 '비타민' D를 생성할 수 있다(our bodies are capable of creating 'Vitamin' D if exposed to direct sunlight for five to ten minutes, two or three times a week)." 따라서 답은 ③이다.
"비타민 D는 뼈와 치아의 건강을 유지하는 데 도움을 주고(Vitamin D helps us maintain healthy bones and teeth)"는 ①의 근거가 되며, 위에 인용된 문장은 ②의 근거가 되고, "전문가들은 노출되는 햇빛의 양이 대체로 줄어드는 겨울에는 비타민 D가 매우 빨리 분해된다고 경고한다. 전문가들은 저장된 비타민 D가 고갈되지 않으려면 식사나 영양 보충제를 통해 비타민 D의 섭취량을 늘려야 한다고 권고한다(Experts warn that in the winter, when we are generally exposed to less sunlight, Vitamin D can break down very quickly. They recommend that in order to prevent stores from running low, we should increase our intake of Vitamin D through food or nutritional supplements)"는 ④의 근거가 된다.

24 (A)에 가장 알맞은 것은 무엇인가?

① 비타민일 뿐만 아니라

② 드문 종류의 비타민이다

③ 여러 가지 다양한 형태를 지닌다

④ 실제로는 비타민이 아니다

| 정답 | ④

| 해설 | 비타민은 우리 몸에서 생성되지 못하고 대신 반드시 식사를 통해 섭취되어야 하는 물질인데, 비타민 D는 우리 몸에서 생성된다. 그래서 본문에서는 비타민을 프로호르몬이라고 칭하고 있는 것이다. not A but B 구문을 염두에 두고 생각해 보면, 보기 중에서 ④를 답으로 볼 수 있다.

| 어휘 | **immune system** 면역 체제　　　　　　　**nervous system** 신경계

a wide range of 광범위한, 다양한　　　　　**sclerosis** ⓝ 경화증

pro-hormone ⓝ 프로호르몬　　　　　　　**nutrient** ⓝ 영양소

break down 분해하다　　　　　　　　　　**run low** 고갈되다, 모자라게 되다

intake ⓝ 섭취량　　　　　　　　　　　　**supplement** ⓝ 보충제

skeletal ⓐ 뼈대[골격]의

[25~26] 단국대 2017

해석

어른이 된 이후의 모든 삶은 두 가지의 커다란 사랑 이야기로 규정된다고 말할 수 있다. 성적인 사랑을 찾아가 는 첫 번째 이야기는 잘 알려져 있고, 지도도 잘 그려져 있고, 사회적으로 수용되며, 거기서 나오는 기발한 행동은 음악과 문학에서 기념된다. 세상이 주 는 사랑을 찾아가는 이야기인 두 번째 이야기는 첫 번째보다 더 은밀하고 부끄러운 이야기이다. 입에 올린다 해도 비난하거나 조롱 할 때만 그러는 경우가 많다. 그런 사랑은 질투심이 많거나 결함이 있는 사람들의 관심사로 여긴다. 아니면 높은 지위의 추구는 경 제적 의미로만 해석해야 한다고 생각하는 것 같기도 하다. 하지만 이 두 번째 사랑 이야기는 첫 번째 이야기만큼이나 강렬하며, 또 첫 번째 이야기만큼이나 복잡하고, 중요하고, 보편적이다. 그리고 이 사랑을 이루지 못할 때도 첫 번째 사랑을 이루지 못할 때만큼 이나 고통스럽다. 여기에도 가슴 아픈 상처가 있다.

25 다음 중 본문의 내용과 일치하지 않는 것은?

① 세상이 주는 사랑은 모든 성인들의 삶에서 추구되는 두 가지 중요한 사랑 중 하나이다.

② 세상이 주는 사랑에 대한 욕구는 조롱받는 경향이 있으며 질투심이 많은 사람들의 관심사로 여겨진다.

③ 세상이 주는 사랑을 추구하는 것은 성적인 사랑의 추구보다 덜 고통스럽다.

④ 성적인 사랑에 대한 추구는 훨씬 더 공개적으로 논의되고 기념된다.

| 정답 | ③

| 해설 | 본문에서는 성인들이 추구하는 사랑을 두 가지로 분류한다. 첫 번째는 연인과의 로맨틱한 사랑이고, 두 번째는 세상으로부터 받는 사랑이라고 말한다. 그런데 후반부에 세상으로부터 받는 사랑도 첫 번째의 사랑만큼 강렬하고, 복잡하고, 중요하고, 보편 적이며, 고통스럽다(no less painful)고 했으므로, '덜 고통스럽다'고 말한 ③이 본문과 일치하지 않는 내용이 된다.

26 다음 중 빈칸에 올 수 있는 가장 적합한 것은?

① 그런 이유로   ② 하지만

③ 필연적으로   ④ 여담이지만

| 정답 | ②

| 해설 | 빈칸 앞부분에서는 세상으로부터 받는 사랑을 추구하면 사람들에게 '비난받거나 비웃음'을 받으며, '돈'과 관련한 관점에서 해석되는 등 부정적으로 여겨진다고 말한다. 하지만 빈칸 뒷부분에서는 두 번째 종류의 사랑도 첫 번째 종류의 사랑만큼 '강렬하고, 복잡하고, 중요하고, 보편적이며, 고통스럽다'고 말하면서, 본질적으로 유사함을 말한다. 즉 앞서의 비난이나 비웃음을 받을 만한 이유가 없다는 내용이므로, 앞의 내용과 대조의 관계를 보이는 ②가 정답이 된다.

| 어휘 |
define ⓥ 정의하다   **quest** ⓝ 추구

vagary ⓝ (날씨) 예측 불허의 변화[변동]; 엉뚱한 짓; 변덕   **shameful** ⓐ 수치스러운, 창피한

caustic ⓐ 신랄한, 비꼬는; 가성의, 부식성의   **mocking** ⓐ 비웃는[조롱/조소하는]

envious ⓐ 부러워하는, 선망하는   **deficient** ⓐ 부족한

drive ⓝ 투지, 추진력; 충동, 욕구   **status** ⓝ 지위, 신분

interpret ⓥ (의미를) 설명[해석]하다   **complicated** ⓐ 복잡한, 정교한

universal ⓐ 보편적인   **setback** ⓝ (일시적) 후퇴, 차질, 방해, 좌절

A is no less ~ than B A는 B보다 ~에 있어 결코 덜하지 않다

[27~28] 한양대 2012

해석

청소년 폭력을 줄이기 위해서는 모든 아이들에게 갈등 해결 기술을 가르쳐야 한다. 총을 쉽게 구할 수 있는 위험한 사회에서 많은 젊은이들은 모욕이나 논쟁에 폭력으로 대응하는 수밖에 없다고 생각한다. 전국에 있는 수많은 프로그램과 강좌에서 10세에서 19세까지 아이들에게 폭력 없이 의견 충돌을 해결하는 방법을 가르쳐 주고 있다. 비록 갈등 해결은 모든 연령대에서 유용하지만, 전문가들은 호르몬과 중학교라는 갑작스런 이중의 충격을 당하기 전에 학생들이 갈등 해결 기술에 우선 접할 수 있도록 해야 한다는 점에 동의한다.

비록 반대론자들은 이런 갈등 해결 기술은 10대 폭력의 근본 원인인 (몇 가지 예를 들면) 가난·문제 많은 가정·마약 등을 해결하지 못하는 미봉책에 불과하다고 주장하지만, 실제로 이제는 갈등 해결 훈련은 생명을 구한다. 물론 더 큰 사회적 문제도 해결되어야 하겠지만 이런 문제는 해결하는 데 오랜 시간이 걸린다. 반면에 학생들에게 새로운 태도와 "사람 다루는 기술"을 가르쳐 주면 학생들에게 즉각적으로 힘이 되고 평생 동안 유용하게 쓰일 수 있다. 젊은이들을 폭력으로부터 보호할 수 있도록 도와주는 입증된 하나의 방법은 바로 초기에 시작되는 갈등 해결 훈련이다.

---

27 밑줄 친 "a Band-Aid solution"이 의미하는 것을 고르시오.

① 대역   ② 미봉책   ③ 대체물   ④ 수정

| 정답 | ②

| 해설 | 본래 'Band-Aid'는 일회용 반창고를 의미하며, 문맥상으로는 "10대 폭력의 근본 원인을 해결하지 못하는(does not address the root causes of teen violence)" 방법, 즉 미봉책을 의미한다. 따라서 답은 ②이다.

28 윗글의 내용과 일치하는 것을 고르시오.

① 가난과 마약 사용은 젊은이의 폭력과 관계가 거의 없다.
② 총기 통제는 갈등 해결을 위한 더욱 근본적인 예방책이다.
③ 갈등 해결 기술은 일단 아이가 성년이 되면 유용하지 않다.
④ 학생이 어렸을 때부터 갈등 해결 훈련을 받을수록 갈등 해결 훈련이 더욱 실질적으로 학생들에게 도움이 된다.

| 정답 | ④

| 해설 | 갈등 해결 능력은 "즉각적으로 힘이 되고 평생 동안 유용하게 쓰일 수 있는(empower them immediately and serve them for a lifetime)" 방책이고, "젊은이들을 폭력으로부터 보호할 수 있도록 도와주는 입증된 하나의 방법은 바로 초기에 시작되는 갈등 해결 훈련이다(One proven way to help youngsters protect themselves from violence is conflict resolution training that begins early)." 만약 아이들이 갈등 해결 능력을 일찍 배웠다면 바로 써먹을 수 있기 때문에 더 큰 도움이 될 것이다. 따라서 답은 ④이다.

| 어휘 |

resolution ⓝ 해결
teen ⓝ 10대(13~19세 사이의 아이들)
jolt ⓝ 정신적 충격, (갑작스럽고 예기치 않은) 좌절
to name a few 몇 가지 예를 들면
people skill 대인 관계 기술, 사람 다루는 기술
makeshift ⓝ 임시변통, 미봉책
amendment ⓝ 수정, 개정

readily ⓐ 손쉽게
preteen ⓝ 10~13세 사이의 아이들
Band-Aid ⓝ 임시 처방, 미봉책
troubled ⓐ 문제 많은
stand-in ⓝ 대리인, 대역
substitute ⓝ 대신하는 사람, 대체물
preventive ⓐ 예방을 위한

[29~30] 이화여대 2014

> **해석**
>
> 에드거 앨런 포와 아서 코난 도일 경이 작성한 최초의 탐정 소설은 19세기 중반에 처음 등장했으며 그 당시는 과학 발전에 대한 대중의 관심이 엄청났다. 당시 신문은 계속해서 가장 최근에 이루어진 과학적 발전을 알려 줬고 과학자들은 당대의 영웅으로 칭송받았다. 포와 코난 도일은 과학자들이 실험 과정에서 활용한 단계적이고 논리적인 접근법에 매료되었고, 과학적 추론을 통한 뛰어난 능력을 자신들이 쓴 탐정 소설의 주인공들에게 서서히 주입시켰다.
> 예를 들어 셜록 홈즈라는 등장인물은 과학적 사고에 대한 코난 도일의 동경을 담고 있다. 셜록 홈즈는 수사하는 각각의 사건마다 상대방을 추적하기 위해 가장 실체 없는 증거를 활용한다. 홈즈는 끊임없이 움직이는 눈과 기발한 추리력을 활용하여 <u>손 편지에 사용된 잉크의 종류</u> 같이 특별할 것 없는 세부적인 정보를 가지고 범인의 신원을 종합한다. 사실 홈즈가 세부적인 정보에 공들여 집중하는 모습은 독자들에게 작품보다 대략 20년 전에 발표된 찰스 다윈의 "종의 기원"을 종종 연상시킨다.

29 다음 중 윗글에 관해 사실인 것은 무엇인가?

① 홈즈의 적은 범죄 현장에 아무 흔적도 남기지 않았다.
② 홈즈라는 등장인물은 찰스 다윈에 기반을 두고 있다.
③ 탐정 소설의 등장은 사람들이 과학에 매혹된 것과 관련이 있다.
④ 실제 탐정들은 아무도 홈즈의 사건을 풀 수 있는 능력이 없다.
⑤ 도일과 동시대 사람들은 모두 다윈의 작품에 친숙하다.

| 정답 | ③

| 해설 | 탐정 소설이 본격적으로 등장한 시기는 19세기 중반의 과학 발전에 대한 대중의 관심이 높은 시기였다. 에드거 앨런 포와 아서 코난 도일은 탐정 소설에 과학 실험에서 도입된 논리적이고 단계적인 접근법을 활용하였고, 소설 속 주인공들이 과학적 추론을 활용할 수 있도록 하였다. 따라서 답은 ③이 된다.

---

30 [A]에 가장 알맞은 것은 무엇인가?

① 용의자의 알리바이　　　　　　② 희생자의 혈액형

③ 문고리에 찍힌 지문　　　　　　④ 손 편지에 사용된 잉크의 종류

⑤ 목격자의 증언

| 정답 | ④

| 해설 | [A]는 "특별할 것 없는 세부적인 정보(unremarkable details)"의 사례이며, 보기 중에서 이런 별 것 아닌 정보에 해당되는 것은 ④이다.

| 어휘 | **enormous** ⓐ 거대한, 막대한

fascination ⓝ 매력, 매료

insubstantial ⓐ 대단찮은, 실체 없는

ingenious ⓐ 기발한

painstaking ⓐ 공들인, 힘들여

acclaim ⓥ 칭송하다

instill ⓥ 서서히 주입시키다, 스며들게 하다

restless ⓐ 가만히 못 있는, 끊임없이 움직이는

unremarkable ⓐ 특별할 것 없는, 평범한

[31~32] 인하대 2016

해석

후추는 3,000년이 넘도록 지금까지도 전 세계에서 가장 폭넓게 거래되는 향신료이다. 후추 거래는 전 세계 향신료 거래의 25퍼센트 이상에 해당되지만, 그럼에도 불구하고 적도 기준 15도 이내에 위치한 소수의 국가들만이 생산한다. 인도의 경우 말라바르 해안(Malabar Coast)에서 세계 최대 규모로 후추를 생산하며 그 외에도 스리랑카 · 베트남 · 말레이시아 · 인도네시아 또한 주요 생산국이다. 후추는 또한 남북아메리카 대륙(신세계)에서도 재배되며 브라질이 주요 수출국이다.

후추는 고대 이집트 및 로마 시대에 사용되었다. 이들에게 후추를 공급한 사람들은 아랍의 해양 무역상들이었고, 무역상들은 후추의 원산지를 비밀로 했다. 이후 후추는 실크로드를 따라 육로를 통해 공급되었다. 어느 시점에서 그리스인들이 그리고 그 후에는 로마인들이 이 귀중한 향신료의 원산지를 알게 되었고, 경쟁이 시작되었다. 이 귀중한 향신료를 얻기 위한 경쟁은 2천 년이 넘도록 격렬하게 진행되었고 크리스토퍼 콜럼버스(Christopher Columbus)에 의한 신대륙 탐험 및 발견의 원동력이 되었다. 무역이 처음에는 포르투갈들에게 의해 이후엔 네덜란드인들에 의해 독점되었던 중세 시대에, 후추는 너무나 귀중한 품목이었기 때문에 무게로 따졌을 때 금보다 더 가치가 높았고 알후추 낱알이 법정 통화로 널리 채택되었다. 후추를 취급하던 노동자들에게는 도난 방지를 위해 주머니나 소맷동이 달리지 않은 옷이 지급되었다.

31 다음 중 상자 안의 문장이 들어갈 만한 곳은 어디인가?

> 후추를 취급하던 노동자들에게는 도난 방지를 위해 주머니나 소맷동이 달리지 않은 옷이 지급되었다.

① [A] ② [B] ③ [C]
④ [D] ⑤ [E]

| 정답 | ⑤

| 해설 | 상자 안의 문장은 후추 노동자들이 작업 중간에 후추를 빼돌리지 못하도록 조치가 취해졌다는 내용이며, 이는 후추가 그만큼 귀중했음을 의미한다. "후추는 너무나 귀중한 품목이었기 때문에 무게로 따졌을 때 금보다 더 가치가 높았고 알후추 낱알이 법정 통화로 널리 채택되었다(pepper was so valuable that it was worth more than gold by weight, and individual peppercorns were widely accepted as legal currency)"를 보면, 후추가 돈으로 쓰일 만큼 귀중했음을 알 수 있다. 때문에 노동자들이 그만큼 귀중한 후추를 빼돌리지 못하도록 조치가 취해졌다는 내용의 상자 안의 문장이 위의 문장 다음에 와야 할 것이다. 따라서 답은 ⑤이다.

32 본문에 따르면 다음 중 사실이 <u>아닌</u> 것은 무엇인가?

① 옛날에는 후추의 원산지가 무역상들에 의해 비밀로 유지되었다.
② 후추는 전 세계의 향신료 무역 시장의 25퍼센트 이상을 차지한다.
③ 아랍 무역상들은 고대에 이집트와 로마에 후추를 공급했다.
④ 후추는 2000년 전에 포르투갈 무역상들 사이에서 법정 통화 역할을 했다.
⑤ 남북아메리카 대륙의 발견은 후추를 손에 넣기 위한 경쟁의 결과였다.

| 정답 | ④

| 해설 | 법정 통화 역할을 한 시기는 중세 시대이지 2000년 전이 아니다. 따라서 답은 ④이다.
"후추는 고대 이집트 및 로마 시대에 사용되었다. 이들에게 후추를 공급한 사람들은 아랍의 해양 무역상들이었고, 무역상들은 후추의 원산지를 비밀로 했다(Pepper was used in ancient Egypt and in Roman times, supplied by Arab sea traders who kept the source secret)"는 ①과 ③의 근거가 된다. "후추 거래는 전 세계 향신료 거래의 25퍼센트 이상에 해당된다(It represents more than 25퍼센트 of the world trade in spices)"는 ②의 근거가 된다. "이 귀중한 향신료를 얻기 위한 경쟁은 2천 년이 넘도록 격렬하게 진행되었고 크리스토퍼 콜럼버스 (Christopher Columbus)에 의한 신대륙 탐험 및 발견의 원동력이 되었다(The competition for this valuable spice has been fierce for over 2,000 years and spurred exploration and discovery of the New World by Christopher Columbus)"는 ⑤의 근거이다.

| 어휘 | **represent** ⓥ (~에) 해당[상당]하다
cultivate ⓥ 재배하다, 경작하다
overland ⓐ 육로[육상]의
spur ⓥ 원동력[자극제]이 되다
peppercorn ⓝ 말린 후추 열매, 알후추
cuff ⓝ 소맷동

and yet 그럼에도 불구하고
New World 신세계, 남북아메리카
fierce ⓐ 격렬한, 맹렬한
monopolize ⓥ 독점하다
currency ⓝ 통화

해석

NASA의 연구에 따르면, 무중력 상태의 우주에서 우주 비행사들이 12주 동안 지내면서 이들의 키가 평균 2인 치가 자랐다고 밝혔다. 무중력 상태에서 왜 이 같은 급격한 성장이 일어날까? 이에 대한 답변으로, 중력이 척추에 미치는 영향을 관찰해 보는 것이 한 방법일 수 있다. 아침과 저녁 사이에, 중력에 의해 가능한 앉기나 서기, 걷기 등의 모든 체중 지지 운동은 척추에 압축이 일어나게 한다. 이 같은 압축으로 인해 척추 디스크에서 수액이 근처의 연조직으로 빠져나간다. 하루가 끝날 때쯤이면 디스크에서 빠져나간 수액으로 인해 사람의 키가 1/2~3/4인치 가량 줄어들게 된다. 자신의 체중을 지탱할 필요가 없는 수면의 상태에서 수액이 다시 디스크로 빨려 들어오면서 사람의 키가 그전의 상태로 돌아가게 된다.

우주에서도 지구에서 그러하듯 혈류로부터 수액이 척추 디스크에 모인다. 하지만 우주에서는 중력이 없기 때문에 압축이 발생하지 않는다. 디스크에서 수액이 빠져나가지 않는 것이다. 수액이 디스크에 머무르면서 디스크는 퉁퉁한 상태를 유지하며 결과적으로 사람의 키가 더 크도록 해 준다. 대부분의 사람들은 아마 키가 1~2인치 더 커져서 높은 선반의 물체를 쉽게 잡을 수도 있는 것에 별로 신경을 쓰지 않을 것이다. 하지만 무중력 상태에서 발생하는 신장의 증가와 척추의 당김 현상은 종종 허리 통증이나 신경 염증이라는 부작용을 동시에 수반한다. 뿐만 아니라 사람의 뼈대와 근육 조직은, 중력이 당기는 힘과 반대되는 방향으로 신체를 수직으로 유지해야 하기 때문에 강한 상태를 유지해야 한다. 하지만 무중력 상태에서는 근육과 뼈가 사용되지 않아서 약해지게 된다. 우주에 있을 경우에 우주 비행사는 주기적으로 운동을 엄격하게 실시해 이에 대처한다.

33 빈칸에 들어가기에 가장 적합한 것을 고르시오.
   ① 중력이 척추에 미치는 영향
   ② 일상 활동과 체중과의 관계
   ③ 근육 조직이 중력의 당김에 대항하기 위해 작동하는 방식
   ④ 척추 디스크를 둘러싼 연조직이 체중을 지탱하기 위해 발달하는 방식

| 정답 | ①

| 해설 | 무중력 상태에서 키가 더 커지는 현상을 이해하려면 어떤 것을 관찰해 보면 될 것인가를 묻고 있다. 본문에서 빈칸 뒤의 내용을 보면 중력이 척추에 미치는 영향으로 척추 디스크의 수액이 빠져나가 키가 작아졌다가 수면 중에 수액이 다시 돌아와 키가 이전 상태로 돌아간다고 나온다. 우주에서는 이런 중력의 당김이 척추에 작용하지 않기 때문에 키가 커진다고 나온다. 따라서 척추와 중력과의 관계에 대한 내용인 ①이 정답이 된다.

34 윗글의 내용과 일치하지 않는 것으로 가장 적합한 것을 고르시오.
   ① 지구에서 사람은 저녁보다는 아침에 키가 더 크다.
   ② 우주에서 우주 비행사는 수면 후 키가 이전 상태로 되돌아온다.
   ③ 우주 비행사는 우주에서 키가 더 자라는데, 이는 척추 디스크에서 수액을 함유하고 있기 때문이다.
   ④ 무중력 상태는 종종 신체에 부정적인 영향을 유발한다.

| 정답 | ②

| 해설 | ①의 경우 중력의 당김이 덜한 아침에 키가 크다가, 서서 활동하는 동안 중력으로 인해 척추 디스크에서 수액이 빠져나가 키가 작아지게 되므로 옳은 설명이다. ②의 경우는 수면과 무관하게 중력이 작용하지 않기 때문에 키가 이전 상태로 돌아오지 않는다. 따라서 정답은 ②가 된다. ③은 우주 비행사가 우주에서는 키가 더 자란다고 했기 때문에 올바른 설명이며, ④의 경우도 본문에 등장한다. 본문에서는 허리 통증이나 신경 염증 등의 부작용을 일으킨다고 설명하고 있다.

gravity-free ⓐ 무중력의(= weightless)

compression ⓝ 압축

squeeze ⓥ 쥐어짜다

soak ⓥ 담그다, 흠뻑 적시다

plump ⓐ 통통한, 포동포동한

concurrent ⓐ 동시에 발생하는

musculature ⓝ 근육 조직

weight-bearing ⓐ 체중을 지지하는

spine ⓝ 척추

spinal disc 척추 디스크

lengthen ⓥ 길어지다, 늘어나다, 늘이다

accompany ⓥ 동반하다

nerve irritation 신경 염증

rigorous ⓐ 철저한, 엄격한

[35~37]

해석

1970년대 후반과 1980년대 및 1990년대 초반에 건설된 스포츠 시설은 일상적으로 시설 내 경험을 강화하는 방향으로 설계되었지만, 주변의 부동산에서 벌어질 수 있는 관련된 경제적 활동을 활용할 수 있는 잠재력은 일상적으로 무시했다. 이 당시 건립된 시설은 상당한 규모의 공공 투자를 통해 건설되었다. 부동산 가치를 높이고 장소 내에서 벌어지는 경제적 활동을 활용하지 못한 결과 새로운 장소를 확보하려는 스포츠팀의 노력을 지지한다는 결정을 두고 상당히 높은 불만이 생겨났다. 그 결과 장소 건립으로 인한 모든 혜택이 팀 소유주 및 스포츠 업계와 연계된 이들에게 축적되었다. 공공부문의 파트너들에게는 금전적 이득이 설사 있다 하더라도 거의 돌아가지 않았다. 이러한 상황은 팀 소유주에게 새로 건립된 최신 시설을 통해 창출된 수익원을, 전부는 아니더라도 대부분 유지하도록 허용함으로써 더욱 악화되었다.

35 다음 중 밑줄 친 부분이 적절하지 않은 것은 무엇인가?

① (A)

② (B)

③ (C)

④ (D)

| 정답 | ②

| 해설 | 스포츠 시설 내에서 벌어지는 경제적 활동을 활용(capitalize on)하는 것과 부동산 가치를 "낮추는" 것 간의 관계는 모순적이다. 부동산 가치를 "높이고" 시설의 경제적 활동을 활용함으로써 스포츠 시설의 가치를 높여야 새로운 시설을 건립하는 것이 지지를 받을 것이나, 활용 및 가치 상승이 제대로 이루어지지 않는 바람에 시설 건립에 대해 불만이 생겨난다는 것이 본문의 내용이다. 따라서 (B)diminish는 elevate나 같은 의미의 다른 동사로 바꿔야 한다.

36 빈칸에 가장 알맞은 것은 무엇인가?

① 그 결과

② 그럼에도 불구하고

③ 그렇지 않으면

④ 대조적으로

| 정답 | ①

| 해설 | 빈칸 뒤를 보면 시설 건립의 혜택이 공공부문이 아닌 스포츠팀 소유주 및 스포츠 업계 관계자들에게 갔음을 알 수 있다. 그 원인은 앞 문장에서 나와 있듯이, 팀 차원에서는 경기장을 지으려 노력하는 데 반해 아직 시설을 통해 경제적 활동으로 이득을 보거나 부동산 가치가 상승하는 등의 혜택을 보기 힘든 관계로, 시설을 건립하는 스포츠팀에 대한 지지가 약하고, 때문에 스포츠팀 소유주 및 관계자들이 건립에 대한 책임을 맡는 대신 혜택 또한 가져가는 식이 되었음을 유추할 수 있다. 즉 빈칸 앞의 상황으로 인한 "결과"가 빈칸 뒤의 내용으로 이어지는 것이다. 따라서 답은 ①이다.

37 본문에 따르면 사실인 것은 무엇인가?

① 새로운 스포츠 시설의 건립을 통한 혜택은 공정하게 분배되지 않았다.

② 스포츠팀이 새로운 시설을 찾기엔 어려움이 따른다.

③ 현대의 스포츠 업계에 있어 가장 중요한 것은 재무 관리이다.

④ 팀 소유주는 공공부문의 투자를 받은 스포츠 업계의 발전에 기여했다.

| 정답 | ①

| 해설 | "그 결과 장소 건립으로 인한 모든 혜택이 팀 소유주 및 스포츠 업계와 연계된 이들에게 축적되었다. 공공부문의 파트너들에게는 금전적 이득이 설사 있다 하더라도 거의 돌아가지 않았다." 여기서 건립을 통한 혜택이 불균등하게 돌아갔음을 알 수 있으며, 이는 ①의 내용과 일치한다. 따라서 답은 ①이다.

"새로운 장소를 확보하려는 스포츠팀의 노력을 지지한다는 결정"에 대해 불만이 생겨났다는 내용은 있지만 시설을 찾는 데 어려움이 있는지 여부는 본문에 언급되지 않으며, 따라서 ②는 답이 될 수 없다. 본문 어디에도 ③과 관련된 사항이 등장하지 않는다. 마지막으로 스포츠 시설 건립에 있어 공공부문의 투자를 받았음은 본문에 나와 있지만, 팀 소유주가 업계의 발전에 기여했다는 ④와 관련된 사항은 본문에 언급된 바 없다.

| 어휘 |

routinely ⓐ 일상적으로

adjacent ⓐ 인접한, 주변의

elevate ⓥ 증가시키다, 들어올리다

venue ⓝ 장소

accrue ⓥ 누적되다, 축적되다

nevertheless ⓐ 그럼에도 불구하고

harness ⓥ 이용하다, 활용하다

substantial ⓐ 상당한

capitalize (on) ⓥ ~을 활용하다[기회로 삼다]

discontent ⓝ 불만

revenue stream 수익원

contribute (to) ⓥ ~에 기여하다

[38~39] 에리카 2014

해석

범죄가 일어났다. 경찰은 자신들이 진범을 구금하고 있다고 확신한다. 어쨌든 경찰은 목격자를 확보하였다. 하지만 이렇게 확신해도 괜찮은 것일까? "그렇지 않다"고 목격자 증언에 관해 연구하는 심리학자들은 주장한다. 서섹스대학 심리학자인 다니엘 라이트는 목격자들이 사건 이후 사실을 호도하는 정보를 제공받았을 경우, 일부 목격자는 새로운 정보를 수용하기 위해 자신의 기억을 조정한다는 사실을 발견했다. 한 실험에서, 두 명의 남성이 당구장에서 만났고 나중에 한 명의 여성이 한 남성의 지갑을 훔친 것을 보여 주는 그림책을 40명의 학생들에게 보여 줬다. 학생 각자가 혼자서 그림책을 살펴봤다. 실험 참여 집단 가운데 반쪽은 다른 반쪽과 비교해 약간 다른 정보를 제공받았는데, 이를 실험 지원자 중에서는 아무도 알지 못했다. 20명의 학생들은 여성이 범죄를 저지르기 이전에 혼자 당구장 밖을 배회하는 모습을 보여 주는 그림책을 봤다. 다른 나머지 20명의 학생들은 여성이 공범과 함께 배회하는 그림을 봤다. 나중에 여성에게 공범이 있었는지를 각각 물어봤을 때 40명 학생 가운데 39명은 올바로 대답했다.

이후 학생들을 한쌍씩 짝을 지었는데, 각 쌍은 한 사람은 공범이 등장하는 그림을 본 사람으로 다른 한 사람은 공범이 등장하지 않는 그림책을 본 사람으로 구성되었다. 각 쌍은 무엇을 봤는지 서로 상의하고 다음의 질문에 같이 대답해 달라는 요청을 받았다. "여성에게 공범이 있었는가?" 각 쌍의 두 명의 구성원이 서로 다른 시나리오를 접했기 때문에 합의를 이룬 사람은 아무도 없었어야 했다. 실제로는 15쌍이 타협안을 도출했다. 다른 말로 하자면 15명의 목격자는 동반자의 말에 좌우된 것이다.

38 윗글의 빈칸에 들어갈 가장 알맞은 것을 고르시오.

    ① 좌우된   ② 무시된

    ③ 패배된   ④ 사로잡힌

| 정답 | ①

| 해설 | 한쌍으로 짝지어진 두 사람 중에 한 명은 공범이 없는 그림을 봤고 다른 한 명은 공범이 있는 그림을 봤다. 서로 공범 여부에 관해 알고 있는 내용이 다르므로 원칙적으로 결코 의견이 일치할 수 없다. 그런데 20쌍 가운데 15쌍이나 합의에 도출했다는 것은, 결국 15명이 상대방의 의견에 휩쓸렸다는 것이다. 따라서 답은 ①이다.

39 윗글의 내용과 맞지 않는 것을 고르시오.

    ① 심리학자들은 목격자 증언에 관해 연구하고 있다.

    ② 목격자는 때로는 사실을 호도하는 정보를 받을 경우 이야기를 바꾸기도 한다.

    ③ 최초 실험에서 질문을 받은 학생 40명 가운데 오직 한 명만이 틀렸다.

    ④ 두 번째 실험에서 거의 모든 쌍의 학생들이 즉시 합의에 도달했다.

| 정답 | ④

| 해설 | 20쌍 가운데 15쌍이 합의를 도출했음을 "거의 모든 쌍(virtually every pair)"으로 표현할 수는 없으며, 또한 서로 이견이 있었을 것이므로 "즉시(instantly)" 합의에 도달했다고 할 수는 없다. 따라서 답은 ④이다.

| 어휘 | **in custody** 구금하다, 감금하다   **misleading** ⓐ 사실을 호도하는, 오해의 소지가 있는

       adapt ⓥ 조정하다, 맞추다   **accommodate** ⓥ 수용하다, 부응하다

       pool hall 당구장   **loitering** ⓥ 어슬렁거리다, 배회하다

       accomplice ⓝ 공범   **pair off** 짝을 짓다

       compromise ⓝ 절충, 타협

       sway ⓥ (마음, 의견 따위를) 동요시키다; (남의 의견·결심 등을) 좌우하다

       virtually ⓓ 사실상, 거의   **instantly** ⓓ 즉시

[40~42] 한국외대 2017

해석

'거북목(text neck)'은 목과 어깨의 통증을 유발하는 과도한 휴대기기 사용 증후군을 지칭한다. 간단히 말해, 거북목은 휴대폰을 너무 많이 내려다보면서 사용해 발생하는 고통과 부상을 의미한다. 이런 행동은 모든 연령대의 사람들에게 영향을 미칠 수 있지만, 특히 어린이와 청소년에게 위험하다. 이는 젊은 사람들이 휴대기기를 오랫동안 사용하는 경향이 있을 뿐만 아니라 성장 중인 목과 등뼈가 비정상적인 힘에 더 취약하기 때문이다. 거북목을 피하는 확실한 방법은 휴대폰을 내려놓는 것이다. 그러나 문자 메시지를 기꺼이 중지하려는 사람은 거의 없기 때문에 이보다 더 현실적인 방법은 휴대폰을 잡는 방식을 변경하는 것이다. 목을 직립 자세로 유지할수록 거북목이 덜 발생할 수 있다. 이상적으로는, 어깨선과 나란히 머리와 귀의 위치를 유지하고, 휴대폰을 눈높이까지 드는 것이다. 목이 구부러질수록 목에 걸리는 힘이 커진다. 거북목이라고 하면 일시적 유형처럼 들릴지 모르지만, 확실히 거북목은 진짜 문제이다. 거북목의 자세는 디스크 균열, 디스크 협착증, 신경의 눌림 등과 같은 증상을 유발할 수 있다. 평균적인 머리는 중립 자세에서 약 10~12파운드의 무게가 나갈 수 있으며, 15도 아래로 내려다보면 목에 미치는 영향이 27파운드나 증가할 수 있다.

40 다음 중 빈칸 (A)와 (B)에 들어갈 단어의 쌍으로 가장 적합한 것은?

① 개조한 – 중립의
② 해로운 – 수직의
③ 취약한 – 직립의
④ 취약한 – 옆으로

| 정답 | ③

| 해설 | (A)의 경우, 청소년기와 같은 신체가 성장하고 있는 경우 목과 등뼈가 비정상적 힘에 취약(susceptible, vulnerable)하다는 내용이 와야 한다. (B)의 경우 바로 뒤의 내용인 "you would hold your head with your ears in line with your shoulders, holding your device at eye level."을 통해 유추가 가능하다. 즉 목을 최대한 세우고 휴대기기를 드는 방식을 의미하므로 허리를 곧게 세우는(upright, vertical) 것을 의미한다. 이를 종합하면 정답은 ③이 된다.

41 다음 중 본문의 내용과 일치하는 것은?

① 거북목은 최근 유행하는 일시적 문제이다.
② 거북목으로 인한 의학적 증상은 치료가 불가능하다.
③ 휴대기기는 그 가치보다 훨씬 더 고통스럽다.
④ 자세의 변화가 거북목을 완화시킨다.

| 정답 | ④

| 해설 | 거북목은 일시적 문제가 아닌 현실의 실제 문제라고 했으며, 휴대폰의 기기를 잡는 방식을 변경해서 문제를 줄일 수 있다고 했으므로 정답은 ④가 된다.

42 다음 중 본문의 내용과 일치하는 것은?

① 어른들은 십 대보다 더 오래 스마트폰을 사용한다.
② 목이 구부러지면 목에 영향이 덜 미친다.
③ 거북목은 협착과 신경 눌림의 결과를 가져올 수 있다.
④ 곧은 목은 목에 힘을 증가시킨다.

| 정답 | ③

| 해설 | 본문의 "Posture issues from text neck can lead to conditions such as cracks in the discs, stenosis, pinched nerves, and more." 부분을 통해 거북목이 협착과 신경 눌림을 유발할 수 있다는 것을 알 수 있으므로 정답은 ③이 된다.

| 어휘 |

turtle neck 거북목
simply put 간단히 말하면
trendy ⓐ 최신 유행의
crack ⓝ (무엇이 갈라져 생긴) 금
pinched ⓐ 꽉 죄어진; (허기 따위로) 초췌한, 야윈
detrimental ⓐ 해로운
vulnerable ⓐ (~에) 취약한, 연약한
alleviate ⓥ 완화하다

trigger ⓥ 일으키다, 유발하다
spine ⓝ 등뼈, 척추
posture ⓝ (사람이 앉거나 서 있는) 자세
stenosis ⓝ 협착(증)
neutral ⓐ 중립의, 중간의
susceptible ⓐ 영향을 받기 쉬운, 민감한, 예민한
incurable ⓐ 불치의

해석

공리주의자들은 결정을 내려야 할 일에 직면할 경우 장단점의 목록을 작성하는 것을 선호한다. 주요한 윤리 이론 중의 하나인 공리주의는 어떤 행동을 도덕적으로 옳거나 그르게 만드는 관건은 그 행위의 결과라고 가정한다.

우리의 의도가 좋거나 나쁜 것은 무관한 것이다. 중요한 것은 우리 행위의 결과가 좋은가 나쁜가에 달려 있다. 행복이란 인간의 궁극적 목표이며, 가장 도덕적인 수준의 선이다. 따라서, 만약 어떤 행위로 인해 커다란 불행이 발생한다면, 그 행위는 도덕적으로 나쁜 것이라고 말할 수 있다. 공리주의자들은 우리가 어떤 행동을 취하기에 앞서 행동의 잠재적 결과를 신중하게 따져 보아야 한다고 믿는다.

공리주의의 또 다른 문제가 있는 측면은, 목적을 위해서 다른 사람을 수단으로 사용하는 것과 다수의 행복을 위해서 하나 혹은 소수의 행복을 희생하는 것이 모두 받아들여질 수 있다고 간주한다는 점이다.

43 다음 중 빈칸 (A)에 올 수 있는 가장 적합한 것을 고르시오.

① 부인하다
② 가정하다, 단정하다
③ 의문을 제기하다
④ 신임을 떨어뜨리다, 신빙성을 없애다

| 정답 | ②

| 해설 | 어떤 행동을 도덕적으로 옳거나 그르게 만드는 것은 의도가 아닌 행위의 결과라고 주장하는 사람들이 공리주의자들이다. 따라서 빈칸에는 주장하다에 해당하는 단어가 와야하므로, '가정하다, 단정하다'에 해당하는 ② posits가 정답이 된다.

44 다음 중 본문의 내용과 일치하는 것은?

① 도덕적 결정을 내리기 위해 공리주의를 사용하는 것은 항상 쉬운 일은 아니다.
② 공리주의자들은 결과는 무의미하다고 믿는다.
③ 공리주의자들에게 장단점 목록은 올바른 결정을 내릴 수 있게 만들어 주는 유일한 방법이다.
④ 공리주의자들은 인생에서 희생이 반드시 필요한 것은 아니라고 믿는다.

| 정답 | ①

| 해설 | 공리주의자들에게는 행위의 의도보다는 행위의 결과가 중요하다. 또한 다수의 행복을 위해 소수의 행복을 희생할 수 있다고 생각한다. 마지막 문단에서 "목적을 위해서 다른 사람을 수단으로 사용하는 것과 다수의 행복을 위해서 하나 혹은 소수의 행복을 희생하는 것이 모두 받아들여질 수 있다고 간주한다"라고 했으므로, 도덕적 결정을 내리기 위해 공리주의를 사용하는 것은 쉬운 일이 아니라는 것을 알 수 있다. ③의 경우, 첫 번째 문장인 "When faced with a decision to make, utilitarians prefer to create a list of pros and cons."을 통해 장단점 목록은 공리주의자들이 특정 결정을 내리는 데 선호하는 것이라고 했지만, '유일한' 방법인지의 여부는 알 수 없다.

45 다음 중 본문의 내용과 일치하지 <u>않는</u> 것은?

① 공리주의자들은 목적에 대한 수단으로 사람을 사용할 수 있다.

② 공리주의자들은 많은 불행을 만드는 행위는 도덕적으로 올바르지 못한 것이라고 생각한다.

③ 공리주의자들은 좋거나 나쁜 의도를 가지고 있는 것은 중요하지 않다고 주장한다.

④ 공리주의자들은 잠재적 결과는 행위를 취한 후에 따져 보아야 한다고 생각한다.

| 정답 | ④

| 해설 | 본문의 "Utilitarians believe that people should carefully weigh the potential consequences of an action before they take it."을 통해 공리주의자들은 잠재적 결과는 행위를 취한 후가 아닌 취하기 전에 따져 보아야 한다고 생각하므로, 정답은 ④가 된다.

| 어휘 |

be faced with ～에 직면하다

pros and cons 찬반 양론, 장단점

theory ⓝ 이론

morally ⓐⓓ 도덕[도의]적으로

intention ⓝ 의도

matter ⓥ 중요하다

human being ⓝ 인간

problematic ⓐ 문제가 있는

deem ⓥ ～로 여기다, 생각하다

means ⓝ 수단

sacrifice ⓥ 희생하다

question ⓥ 의문을 제기하다; 심문하다

discredit ⓥ 존경심[신임]을 떨어뜨리다, 신빙성을 없애다 ⓝ 불신, 불명예

utilitarian ⓝ 공리주의자 ⓐ 공리주의의, 실용의, 실익의

ethical ⓐ 윤리적인, 도덕적인

utilitarianism ⓝ 공리주의

consequence ⓝ 결과, 중대성

irrelevant ⓐ 무관한, 상관없는

ultimate ⓐ 궁극적인, 최종적인, 근본적인

weigh ⓥ 따져 보다, 저울질하다

aspect ⓝ 양상, 국면, 측면

acceptable ⓐ (사회적으로) 용인되는[받아들여지는]

end ⓝ 목적

posit ⓥ 가정하다, 단정하다

| 연습 문제 | 01 ③ 02 ③ 03 ④ |

01 번호 자물쇠의 번호는 몇 번인가?

다른 한 남자와 난 직장에서 로커를 공유한다. 로커에 새 번호 자물쇠가 필요하다는 것을 인지한 서른 살의 내 동료는 다음 날 출근하는 길에 하나 가져오겠다고 말했다. 나중에 내가 아침에 그를 보지 못할 수도 있음이 머릿속에 떠올랐다. 나는 어떻게 해야 번호를 알 수 있을까? 난 걱정할 필요가 없었다. 출근하니 그가 나보다 먼저 로커를 사용한 다음에 메모를 남겨 놓은 것을 발견했다. 그 메모에는 "첫 번째 자리 숫자는 내 나이에서 21을 뺄 것. 두 번째 자리 숫자는 첫 번째 자리 숫자보다 6이 적은 수임. 세 번째 자리 숫자는 두 번째 자리 숫자에서 2를 뺄 것."

① 860   ② 862
③ 931   ④ 942

| 정답 | ③

| 해설 | 첫 자리 번호는 "subtract 21 from my age(내 나이에서 21을 뺀 것)"이므로 30−21에서 9가 된다. 두 번째 자리 번호는 "6 less than that(첫 번째 자리 숫자보다 6이 적은 수)"이므로 9−6에서 3이 된다. 세 번째 자리 숫자는 "subtract 2 from the second(두 번째 자리 숫자에서 2를 뺀 것)"이므로 3−2에서 1이 된다. 따라서 암호는 931이고 답은 ③이다.

| 어휘 | **combination lock** 번호 자물쇠   **occur to** ~에게 떠오르다
subtract ⓥ 빼다

02 다음 중 왜 우리 사회에서 패션이 급속히 변화하는지 그 이유가 될 수 <u>없는</u> 것은 무엇인가?

패션이 금방 유행이 다하는 한 가지 이유는 우리 사회가 새로움에 가치를 두기 때문이다. 새로운 것들은 기존 전통의 위협으로 간주되기보다 바람직한 것으로 간주된다. 또 다른 이유로는 인기 있는 새 스타일을 만들어 이득을 취하는 디자이너나 의류업체가 변화를 조장하기 때문이다. 마지막으로, 새로운 패션은 매력적으로 보이고자 하는 수단일 뿐 아니라 사회적 지위를 나타내는 수단이기도 하다. 최신 스타일은 그 스타일을 감당할 재력이 있는 부유층에 의해 처음으로 채택된다. 나중에는 수입이 낮은 사람들이 구매할 수 있도록 비싸지 않은 복제품이 제조된다. 그러나 때로는 정반대의 과정도 벌어진다. 청바지는 오랜 기간 동안 노동자 계급의 전통 복장이었다. 오늘날 청바지는 중산층 및 상류층 사이에서도 매우 인기 있다.

① 새로운 것이 가치 있게 여겨진다.
② 새로운 패션의 착용이 사회적 지위를 보여 준다.
③ 상류층은 다른 계급 사람들보다 자신의 옷에 더욱 쉽게 싫증낸다.
④ 의류 디자이너들과 제조 업체는 돈을 더 벌고자 스타일을 바꾼다.

| 정답 | ③

| 해설 | 본문에 따르면 패션이 급속히 변하는 이유로는 세 가지를 들고 있다. 첫째 "우리 사회가 새로움에 가치를 두기 때문

(our society values novelty)"은 보기 ①의 내용이기도 하다. 둘째 "인기 있는 새 스타일을 만들어 이득을 취하는 디자이너나 의류업체가 변화를 조장하기 때문이다(designers and apparel makers, who profit by producing popular new styles, encourage change)"는 보기 ④의 내용이기도 하다. 셋째 "새로운 패션은 매력적으로 보이고자 하는 수단일 뿐 아니라 사회적 지위를 나타내는 수단이기도 하다(new fashions are a means of showing social status, as well as appearing attractive)"는 보기 ②의 내용이기도 하다. 따라서 유일하게 언급되지 않은 것은 보기 ③이다.

| 어휘 | **out-of-date** ⓐ 유행이 지난, 유행이 다한   **value** ⓥ ~를 가치 있다 여기다
novelty ⓝ 새로움, 참신함   **desirable** ⓐ 바람직한
established ⓐ 자리를 잡은, 기존의   **apparel** ⓝ 의류
means ⓝ 수단; 재력, 수입   **reverse** ⓐ 정반대의

03 다음 중 식초에 관해 언급되지 <u>않은</u> 것은 무엇인가? 명지대 2014

식초는 과일, 산딸기류 열매, 감자, 근대, 맥아, 곡물 여기에 심지어 코코넛 등의 다양한 산물을 통해 만들 수 있다. 이들 산물에 함유된 천연 당분이 발효하면서 알코올을 생성하고 이를 통해 2차 발효가 계속되어 알코올이 산으로 바뀌게 되면서 식초가 만들어진다. 식초가 우리 주변에 등장한 지는 만 년이 넘었다. 원래는 통 안에 담긴 포도주가 가장 맛좋을 시기를 지나 (프랑스어로 '신맛이 나는 포도주'란 의미의) vin aigre로 변했을 때 식초를 발견하게 되었다. 발사믹 식초는 요리법에 풍미를 주기 위한 좋은 선택이다. 발사믹 식초는 비록 산도는 높아도 요리에 그윽한 풍미를 부여하며 왜냐하면 식초의 달콤한 맛이 시큼한 맛과 조화를 이루기 때문이다. 발사믹 식초는 딸기나 망고에 곁들이는 편이 가장 좋다. 시나몬, 정향, 육두구 같이 새로운 향신료가 첨가된 식초도 요리에 흥미로운 풍미를 부여한다.

① 식초가 만들어지는 방법   ② 식초는 처음 어떻게 만들어졌는가
③ 식초라는 단어는 프랑스어로 어떤 의미를 갖는가   ④ 식초를 가장 잘 보존하는 방법

| 정답 | ④

| 해설 | 첫 문장과 두 번째 문장은 식초가 만들어지는 방법에 관해 말하고 있고(①), 네 번째 문장에서는 식초는 처음 어떻게 만들어졌는지를 말하고 있으며(②) 이와 함께 식초의 프랑스어 어원에 관해 말하고 있다(③). 하지만 본문 어디에도 식초의 보관법에 관해서는 나와 있지 않다. 따라서 답은 ④이다.

| 어휘 | **vinegar** ⓝ 식초   **a range of** 다양한
berry ⓝ 산딸기류 열매   **beet** ⓝ 근대, 사탕무우
malt ⓝ 맥아   **ferment** ⓥ 발효하다
secondary ⓐ 2차적인, 부수적인   **fermentation** ⓝ 발효
cask ⓝ (특히 술을 담아 두는 나무로 된) 통   **prime** ⓝ 전성기, 한창때
impart ⓥ (특정한 특성을) 주다   **flavor** ⓝ 풍미
recipe ⓝ 조리법, 요리법   **lend** ⓥ (어떤 특질을) 주다[부여하다]
mellow ⓐ 달콤한, 그윽한   **tartness** ⓝ 산미, 시큼함
infuse ⓥ 불어넣다, 스미게 하다   **clove** ⓝ 정향(유)
nutmeg ⓝ 육두구   **preserve** ⓥ 보존하다, 관리하다

01	①	02	④	03	③	04	③	05	④	06	①	07	②	08	③	09	②	10	②
11	④	12	①	13	④	14	①	15	③	16	③	17	⑤	18	④	19	③	20	①
21	③	22	②	23	①	24	⑤	25	③	26	③	27	②	28	③	29	④	30	①
31	①	32	②	33	②	34	①	35	③	36	④	37	①	38	②	39	④	40	①
41	②	42	③	43	②	44	②	45	③												

[01~02]

해석

슈퍼컴퓨터의 예측에 따르면 기온은 매년 0.2℃ 상승할 것이다. 이 추세는 10,000년 전 마지막 빙하기가 끝난 이래로 가장 빠른 온도 상승이다. 독일의 또 다른 슈퍼컴퓨터도 같은 예측을 내놓았다. 기온은 훨씬 더 중요한 강우량과 더불어 빠르게 변화해서 농경, 삼림, 자연 생태계를 파괴할 것이다. 슈퍼컴퓨터는 공해로 인해 지구가 어떻게 온난화는 물론이고 한랭화되는지 보여 줌으로써 기온 변화를 예측한다. 기온 상승의 원인은 열을 가두는 온실가스의 증가이다. 이 온실가스는 화석 연료와 숲을 태울 때 발생한다. 그러나 산성비의 원인 등 다른 유형의 공해들은 태양빛이 지구를 온난화하기 전에 빛을 반사시켜서 지구를 한랭하게 한다. 전 기상청장 John Houghton 경은 "온실가스 배출을 제한하기 위해서는, 쉽게 취할 수 있는 조치부터 당장 시행해야 한다."고 말했다.

01 새로운 슈퍼컴퓨터의 예측에 따르면 _____.

① 지구는 온난화될 것이다.　　　　② 지구에는 기후가 있다.
③ 기상이 악화되었다.　　　　④ 온도가 0.5도 상승할 것이다.

| 정답 | ①

| 해설 | 첫 문장에 착안한 문제이다. 슈퍼컴퓨터는 매년 0.2도씩 기온이 상승할 것을 예측하고 있으므로 ①이 적절하다. 지구 온난화에 비해 기상 악화는 지엽적인 기상 현상이므로 ③을 선택하지 않도록 주의한다.

02 기온 상승은 _____.

① 새로운 슈퍼컴퓨터가 10년 전에 예측했다.
② 산성비가 원인일 수도 있다.
③ 주로 태양빛의 반사가 원인이다.
④ 온실가스 배출 제한을 통해 막을 수 있다.

| 정답 | ④

| 해설 | 지구 온난화의 심각성과 온실가스 감축 필요성을 강조하는 글이다. 기온 상승에 대한 대비책으로서 온실가스 감축을 주장하는 마지막 문장을 참조한다. 공해로 인한 태양빛 반사는 기온 상승(온난화)이 아니라 한랭화의 원인이므로 ③을 선택하지 않도록 주의한다.

| 어휘 | **predict** ⓥ 예상(예측)하다　　　　**temperature** ⓝ 온도, 기온　　　　**decade** ⓝ 10년

ice age 빙하기	**combined with** ~와 결합되어	**rainfall** ⓝ 강우
rapid ⓐ 빠른	**agriculture** ⓝ 농업	**buildup** ⓝ 증강, 축적, 강화
heat-trapping ⓐ 열을 가두는	**fossil fuel** 화석 연료	**pollution** ⓝ 공해, 오염
acid rain 산성비	**reflect** ⓥ 반사하다, 숙고하다	**warm** ⓥ 데우다
former ⓐ 전직의, 이전의	**Meteorological Office** (영) 기상청	**chief executive** 최고 책임자
take action 조치를 취하다	**emission** ⓝ (빛, 열, 가스 등의) 배출, 배기가스	

[03~04]

초기 빅토리아 시대의 의상은 여성을 약하고 무력한 존재로 보이도록 만들 뿐 아니라 실제로도 약하고 무력하게 만들었다. 이러한 신체적 쇠약함의 주범은 코르셋이었고, 당시 코르셋은 단순한 패션 아이템으로 여겨진 게 아니라 의학적 필수품으로 여겨졌다. 당시에는 여성의 "뼈대"는 극도로 연약하다고 여겨졌으며, 여성의 근육은 보조 없이 신체를 지탱할 수 없다고 생각되었다. 가정 교육을 잘 받은 소녀들은 빠르게는 3~4살 때부터 아이들용 코르셋으로 허리가 죄어진다. 점차 코르셋은 길어지고, 뻣뻣해지고, 더 세게 죄어진다. 소녀가 사춘기 말에 다다르면 무거운 캔버스 천에 강철로 보강된 우리 같은 코르셋을 입으며, 착용자의 등 근육은 코르셋의 지탱 없이 오랫동안 앉거나 서 있을 수 없을 정도로 위축된다. 코르셋은 또한 내장의 형태를 변형시키고 숨을 깊게 들이쉬지 못하게 만든다. 결과적으로 세련되게 차려입은 숙녀들은 쉽게 기절하고, 소화기 질환으로 고통받고, 격심한 활동을 하면 힘이 없고 진이 다 빠진 기분이 든다.

03 본문에 따르면 왜 사람들은 여성에겐 코르셋이 필요하다고 생각했는가?

① 여성들은 아름답게 보여야만 하기 때문에
② 여성들은 약하고 무력해 보이길 원했기 때문에
③ 여성들은 연약한 신체를 지탱해야 했기 때문에
④ 여성들은 코르셋을 입도록 강요받았기 때문에
⑤ 여성들은 등이 뻣뻣했기 때문에

| 정답 | ③

| 해설 | 문제 해결을 위한 핵심 문장은 "당시에는 여성의 '뼈대'는 극도로 연약하다고 여겨졌으며, 여성의 근육은 보조 없이 신체를 지탱할 수 없다고 생각되었다(Ladies' "frames," it was believed, were extremely delicate; their muscles could not hold them up without assistance)."이다. 즉 여성은 코르셋이 없으면 자신의 신체를 지탱할 수 없을 정도로 약한 존재로 여겨졌다는 의미이다. 따라서 답은 ③이다.

04 다음 중 코르셋을 입어 생긴 영향으로 언급되지 <u>않은</u> 것은?

① 피로 　　　　　　　　　　② 소화 불량
③ 식욕 부진 　　　　　　　　④ 빈번한 기절
⑤ 연약한 등 근육

| 정답 | ③

| 해설 | 본문에 따르면 여성은 코르셋을 입어서 "힘이 없고 진이 다 빠진 기분(felt weak and exhausted)"이 들고, "소화기 질환으로 고통받고(suffered from digestive complaints)", "쉽게 기절하고(fainted easily)", "등 근육이 위축된다(their back muscles had often atrophied)." 이는 각각 ①, ②, ④, ⑤에 대응한다. 그러나 본문에는 식욕이 떨어지는 부작용은 언급된 바 없다. 따라서 답은 ③이다.

| 어휘 |
agent ⓝ 요인, 동인
necessity ⓝ 필수품
delicate ⓐ 연약한
well-brought-up ⓐ 가정 교육을 잘 받은
juvenile ⓐ 청소년의, 아이의
stiffen ⓥ 뻣뻣하게 만들다
cage ⓝ 우리
atrophy ⓥ 위축되다
internal organ 내장
complaint ⓝ 불편, 질환
exertion ⓝ 힘든 일, 격심한 활동

debility ⓝ 쇠약함
frame ⓝ 뼈대
hold up 지지하다, 떠받치다
lace ⓥ (코르셋의 끈으로) ~의 허리를 졸라매다
stay ⓝ (코르셋·칼라 등의 보강에 사용되는) 망; 코르셋
adolescence ⓝ 사춘기, 청소년기
canvas ⓝ 캔버스 천
deform ⓥ 형태를 변형시키다
digestive ⓐ 소화기의
strenuous ⓐ 힘이 많이 드는, 격렬한
weariness ⓝ 피로

[05~07]

해석

기억 상실증의 주 원인은 신체적이거나 정신적이다. 전향적(antegrade) 기억 상실증에 걸린 환자는 쇼크나 뇌 손상 이후에 발생하는 일을 기억하지 못한다. 반면, 과거의 기억은 사라지지 않는다. 역행성(retrograde) 기억 상실증에 걸린 환자는 트라우마 이후에 발생하는 일들은 기억할 수 있다. 그러나 흥미롭게도 쇼크 이전에 저장된 기억은 사라지고 결코 회복되지 않는다. 유사 기억 상실증에 걸리면 저장된 기억이 왜곡된다. 심인성 둔주 (psychogenic fugue: 건망증이 전반적일 뿐 아니라 가정 및 직장을 떠나서 새로운 사람으로 행동하는 장애)를 겪고 있는 환자는 두려운 기억을 억누르기 위해 자신의 생활을 바꾸려 한다. 심인성 둔주를 겪는 동안에 발생한 일들에 대한 기억은 되살릴 수 없다. 그러나 발병 이전의 기억은 되살릴 수 있다. 심인성 기억 상실증을 치료하는 가장 일반적인 치료법은 심리 치료와, 약물 처방, 최면이다.

05 다음 글의 주제는 무엇인가?
① 기억 상실증의 주원인들
② 기억 상실증의 일반적 치료법
③ 기억 상실증으로 인한 기억 장애
④ 기억 상실증의 종류

| 정답 | ④

| 해설 | 기억 상실을 전향적 기억 상실, 역행성 기억 상실, 유사 기억 상실, 심인성 기억 상실로 분류해서 설명하는 글이므로 ④가 적절한 주제이다.

06 밑줄 친 단어 trepidation을 가장 잘 대체할 수 있는 것은 _____이다.
① 불안
② 자제
③ 위협
④ 자기 부정

| 정답 | ①

| 해설 | trepidation (앞으로 일어날 일에 대한) 공포, 두려움, 불안 ① anxiety 불안 ② restraint 자제, 통제 ③ intimidation 위협 ④ selfdenial 자기 부정

---

07 심인성 둔주를 겪고 있는 환자의 기억은 _____.

① 왜곡되고 불분명하다   ② 사라진다

③ 일시적으로 불분명하다   ④ 곧 회복될 수 있다

| 정답 | ②

| 해설 | "심인성 둔주를 겪고 있는 동안의 일은 기억을 되찾을 수 없다.(The events happening during psychogenic fugue are non-retrievable.)"는 언급이 있으므로 "(기억이 완전히) 사라진다"는 ②가 적절하다.

| 어휘 |

leading ⓐ 주요한, 주도적인   **amnesia** ⓝ 기억 상실증   **physical** ⓐ 신체적인, 물리적인

psychological ⓐ 심리적인   **antegrade** ⓐ 전향적인   **subject** ⓝ 환자, 피실험자

lost ⓐ 사라진   **retrograde** ⓐ 역행성의   **recall** ⓥ 기억하다

store ⓥ 저장하다   **retrieve** ⓥ 되찾아오다, 복구하다   **para-** 유사의, 비슷한

established ⓐ 확실히 자리 잡은, 인정받는

contort ⓥ 뒤틀다, 일그러뜨리다   **psychogenic** ⓐ 심인성의(심리적 원인이 있는)

psychogenic fugue 심인성 둔주(건망증이 전반적일 뿐 아니라 가정 및 직장을 떠나서 새로운 사람으로 행동하는 장애)

venture into ~ 대담하게 ~하다   **repress** ⓥ 억누르다, 탄압하다   **trepidation** ⓝ 공포, 두려움, 불안

non-retrievable ⓐ 되찾을 수 없는, 복구할 수 없는

onset ⓝ 발병, 시작   **recover** ⓥ 회복하다, 복구하다   **popular** ⓐ 일반적인, 대중적인

related ⓐ 관련 있는   **psychotherapy** ⓝ 심리 치료   **hypnosis** ⓝ 최면

[08~09] 성균관대 2017

해석

1차 세계 대전 도중 개발된 대부분의 의학적 혁신은 동일하게 발달된 군사적 혁신에 대한 대응으로 나타난 것이었다. 이러한 혁신적 무기 중 하나는 독가스로, 1915년 독일군의 대규모 공격에서 처음 사용되었다. 독극물과 독극물을 사용한 무기는 이미 전쟁 범죄로 간주하였지만 — 이 무기들은 1899년의 헤이그 선언과 1907년의 헤이그 협약을 통해 이미 금지 결정이 내려진 바 있었다 — 어떤 면에서 독가스의 사용은, 참호로 구축된 최전선 너머로 어떻게 공격을 가할 것인지를 놓고 지휘관들을 혼란에 빠트린 참호전과 같은 전쟁 유형에서는, 충분히 예측 가능한 결과였다.

하지만 1915년 봄 독일군이 연합군을 상대로 염소(chlorine) 가스를 처음 사용했을 때, 영국의 의료진들은 불과 몇 시간 만에 희생자들의 폐와 호흡기를 망가뜨리는 새로운 무기에 대응할 준비가 되어 있지 않았다. 첫 공격이 있고 얼마 지나지 않아, 과학자인 존 스콧 홀데인(John Scott Haldane)은 그 가스가 무엇인지 그리고 최악의 상황을 막을 방법은 무엇인지 알아내기 위해 전선으로 향했다. 그가 발명한 것 중 하나는 산소 기구였다. 이 기구는 혈액의 산소 농도를 증가시키는 것이 폐를 손상시키는 치명적인 독가스에 대응할 수 있는 가장 좋은 방법 중 하나라는 연구 결과에 근거한 것이었다. 이 산소 기구는 동시에 네 명을 치료할 수 있었다. 이 기구는 최전선 인근에 곧 배치되었던 독가스 치료 장치의 핵심적인 혁신이 되었다.

08 다음 중 빈칸 Ⓐ와 Ⓑ에 올 수 있는 가장 적합한 것을 고르시오.

① 국내의 – 해외의   ② 화학의 – 공업의

③ 의학적인 – 군사적인   ④ 무장한 – 군사적인

⑤ 민간인의 – 전쟁의

| 정답 | ③

| 해설 | 빈칸의 문장이 본문의 주제문으로, 이후 이어지는 전체 내용을 요약하고 있다. 이어지는 내용을 통해, 군사적 혁신(독가스 공격)의 증가에 대응해 의학적 혁신(산소 기구)의 증가가 나타났다는 것을 알 수 있으므로, 정답은 ③이 된다.

09 다음 중 독가스에 중독된 군인을 치료할 수 있는 가장 좋은 방법은 무엇인가?

① 출혈을 멈추고 수혈을 실시하는 것

② 군인의 혈액 속 산소의 농축 비율을 높이는 것

③ 군인의 호흡기를 최대한 빨리 열어 놓는 것

④ 군인을 최대한 빨리 가장 가까운 병원으로 이송하는 것

⑤ 산소와 에테르 혼합 물질을 지속적으로, 그리고 정밀하게 계속해서 주입하는 것

| 정답 | ②

| 해설 | 마지막 문단의 "increasing the blood's concentration of oxygen was one of the best ways to work against the deadly gases"를 통해 독가스에 중독된 군인을 치료할 수 있는 가장 좋은 방법은 '혈액의 산소 농도를 증가시키는 것'이라는 사실을 알 수 있다. 따라서 정답은 ②가 된다.

| 어휘 |

innovation ⑪ 혁신, 쇄신

equally ⒜ 똑같이, 동일[동등]하게

war crime 전쟁 범죄, 전범

the Hague Declaration 헤이그 선언

warfare ⑪ 전쟁

entrenched ⒜ 깊게 뿌리 박힌

chlorine ⑪ 염소

respiratory ⒜ 호흡기의, 호흡기와 관련된

apparatus ⑪ 기구, 장치

simultaneously ⒜ 동시에

station ⓥ (특히 군인을) 배치하다[주둔시키다] ⑪ 계급, 신분, 지위

domestic ⒜ 가정의; 국내의; 길들여진, 애완용의

civilian ⒜ 민간인의 ⑪ 민간인

transfusion ⑪ 수혈

in response to ~에 대한 반응으로, ~에 대항해서

assault ⑪ 공격 ⓥ 공격하다

forbid ⓥ 금지하다

the Hague Convention 헤이그 협약

confound ⓥ 혼동하다, 당황시키다

front line 최전선, 최전방

personnel ⑪ (집합적) 직원, 인원, 인사부

oxygen ⑪ 산소

deadly ⒜ 치명적인

crucial ⒜ 중대한, 결정적인

armed ⒜ 무장한

martial ⒜ 전쟁의, 호전적인

해석

왜 그런지 이유를 댈 수는 없지만, 스타트업 기업들은 매우 반직관적이다. 이는 어쩌면 단지 스타트업에 대한 지식이 아직 우리의 문화에 완전히 스며들지 못 했기 때문일 수도 있다. 하지만 이유를 불문하고 스타트업을 시작하는 일은 직감을 항상 믿어서는 안 되는 일이다. 스타트업을 시작하는 것은 스키를 타는 것과 비슷하다. 우리는 처음 스키를 타기 시작하고 속도를 늦추려 할 때 본능적으로 상체를 뒤로 젖히게 된다. 하지만 스키를 탄 채로 상체를 뒤로 젖히게 되면 언덕에서 통제 불능 상태로 아래로 떨어지고 만다. 따라서 스키를 배우는 것은 일부는 상체를 뒤로 젖히고 싶다는 충동을 억제하는 법을 배우는 것이다. 결국에는 새로운 습관을 배우게 되지만, 처음에는 의식적으로 노력을 기울여야 한다. 처음 시작할 때는 마치 언덕을 내려가기 시작할 때와 같이 기억해야 할 몇 가지 것들이 담긴 목록이 존재한다. 스타트업은 스키를 타는 것과 마찬가지로 자연스러운 것이 아니다. 따라서 스타트업이 기억해야 할 몇 가지 것들이 담긴 목록이 존재한다. 스타트업은 너무나 기이한 존재이기 때문에 직감을 신뢰하다가는 수많은 실수를 범하게 된다. 나는 종종 내 역할은 스타트업의 창업주들이 무시하고 말 것들을 창업주들에게 말하는 것이라고 농담 삼아 말하곤 한다. 근데 사실이 그렇다. 스타트업 창업주들은 왜 조언자의 말을 진지하게 고려하지 않을까? 어쩌면 반직관적 생각이란 바로 이런 것일 것이다. 반직관적인 생각은 당신의 직감과는 반대되는 것이다. 당신에게 필요한 사람은 오로지 당신을 놀라게 하는 조언을 하는 사람뿐이다. 바로 이 때문에 스키 강사는 많아도 달리기 강사는 많지 않은 것이다.

---

10 스타트업은 스키를 타는 것에 비유되었고, 그 이유는 둘 다 _____ 때문이다.

① 제어하기 쉽기
② 우리의 직관과 모순을 일으키기
③ 집중적이고 광범위한 훈련을 필요로 하기
④ 효과적인 달리기와 같은 전략을 필요로 하기

| 정답 | ②

| 해설 | 스키를 배울 때 우리는 상체를 뒤로 젖히고 싶다는 충동을 억제하는 법을 배우게 된다. 자연스러운 일은 아니기 때문에 의식적으로 노력을 기울여야만 하는 일이다. 직감을 신뢰했다가는 오히려 실수를 범하고 만다. 그리고 스타트업은 스키를 타는 것과 마찬가지로 자연스러운 일이 아니다. 즉 스키와 스타트업 모두 "우리의 직관과 모순을 일으키는 일"이다. 따라서 답은 ②이다.

---

11 (A)에 가장 알맞은 것은 무엇인가?

① 새로운 습관을 얻다
② 경험에 의존하다
③ 전문 지식을 활용하다
④ 직감을 믿다

| 정답 | ④

| 해설 | 앞서 문제를 설명하는 과정에서 알 수 있듯이, 스타트업은 스키와 마찬가지로 우리의 직관과 모순을 일으킨다. 즉 "직감을 항상 믿어서는 안 되는" 일이다. (A) 앞의 not always를 감안하고 보기의 구문을 빈칸에 대입해 보면 답으로 가장 적절한 것은 ④이다.

12 다음 중 저자가 스타트업의 창업주들이 해야 할 일로 제안한 것은 무엇인가?

① 조언자의 말을 듣는다   ② 심화 과정을 수강한다

③ 창조적인 생각의 목록을 만든다   ④ 우선 성공적인 스타트업을 관찰한다

| 정답 | ①

| 해설 | 스타트업이 스키와 마찬가지로 반직관적이라는 말은, 스타트업의 창업주들은 자신의 직감을 믿고 섣부르게 일을 진행하지 말라는 의미이다. 스타트업은 너무나 기이한 존재이기 때문에 직감을 신뢰하다가는 수많은 실수를 범하게 되기 때문이다. 창업주들이 해야 할 일은 따라서 직감을 믿는 것이 아니라 남의 말에 귀를 기울이는 것 즉 "조언자의 말을 진지하게 고려하는(consider the advisor's advice seriously)" 것이다. 때문에 저자는 "당신에게 필요한 사람은 오로지 당신을 놀라게 하는 조언을 하는 사람뿐이다(You only need other people to give you advice that surprises you)"라고 말한 것이다. 따라서 답은 ①이다.

| 어휘 | **counterintuitive** ⓐ. 반(反)직관적인, 직관에 어긋나는

instinct ⓝ 직감, 본능

impulse ⓝ 충동

conscious ⓐ 의식하는, 자각하는

function ⓝ 직무, 역할

liken (to) ⓥ ~에 비유하다

intensive ⓐ 집중적인

expertise ⓝ 전문 지식

permeate ⓥ 스며들다, 퍼지다

suppress ⓥ 억누르다, 억제하다

eventually ⓐⓓ 결국, 종내

weird ⓐ 기이한, 기묘한

opposite (to) ⓐ 반대의

contradict ⓥ 모순되다

extensive ⓐ 광범위한

in-depth ⓐ 심층적인, 심화된

[13~15]

해석

귀소성 비둘기는 신비한 체내 나침반으로 유명하지만 새로운 연구에 따르면 이 새들도 우리 인간과 같은 방식으로 둥지를 찾는다. 그들도 길을 따라가는 것이다. 영국 Oxford University의 Tim Guilford와 Dora Biro는 스위스와 이탈리아 연구자들이 개발한 GPS 추적 장치를 이용해서 3년간 비둘기들을 추적 연구했다. "우리는 새들이 가장 에너지 효율적인 경로를 찾으리라 기대했습니다. 그 과정에서 비둘기들이 이용하는 지형적 특징을 찾고 싶었죠."라고 Guilford는 말했다.

연구 결과는 놀라웠다. 둥지에서 10킬로미터 이내에서는, 비둘기는 태양의 위치나 지구 자기장을 알아내 길을 찾는 놀라운 능력을 덜 사용했다. 대신에 도로, 철로, 울타리 등 지형의 선형적 형태의 특징들을 따라가는 습관적인 경로를 택했고, 심지어는 그 경로가 둥지로 가는 가장 가까운 직선 경로가 아닐 때도 있었다.

13 Oxford University 연구자들이 처음에 관심을 가진 것은 _____이다.

① 비둘기들이 둥지로 돌아가는 효율적인 경로를 찾는지

② 어떻게 비둘기들이 몸에 있는 추적 장치를 인식하는지

③ 어떤 선천적인 능력이 비둘기들을 가장 효율적으로 날게 하는지

④ 어떤 지형적 특징을 비둘기들이 가장 효율적인 경로를 찾기 위해 이용하는지

| 정답 | ④

| 해설 | 첫 단락 마지막 문장에 연구의 목적이 언급되었다. 연구의 목적은 비둘기들이 길 찾기에 이용하는 지형적 특징이다. "And we were interested in finding out what land features they used to do that" 참조.

---

14 비둘기들이 둥지 근처에서 사용하는 방법은 _____이라는 것이 밝혀졌다.

① 습관적

② 가장 효율적

③ 가장 직선적

④ 간접적

| 정답 | ①

| 해설 | 연구 결과를 묻는 문제이다. 두 번째 단락 마지막 문장에서 "비둘기들은 둥지에서 가까운 범위 내에서는 습관적인 경로를 이용한다."는 것을 알 수 있다. 이 경로는 직선 경로(가장 가까운 경로)가 아닐 때도 있으므로 ③을 선택하지 않도록 주의한다. "Instead they opted for a habitual route that followed the linear features in the landscape" 참조.

---

15 귀소성 비둘기들은 _____는 점에서 인간과 비슷하다.

① 집으로 가는 길을 자주 잃는다

② GPS를 이용해 길을 찾는다

③ 가끔은 선형적인 경로를 고집한다

④ 태양의 위치와 자기장을 알아내서 길을 찾는다

| 정답 | ③

| 해설 | 지문의 주제를 다른 말로 표현하는 것이 출제 의도이다. 첫 문장에서 말하는 인간과 비슷한 방식이란 "선형적 지형지물을 따라 가는 습관적 경로"를 택하는 방식이다. 따라서 ③이 적절하다.

| 어휘 |
homing pigeon 귀소성 비둘기
route ⓝ 경로
well-known ⓐ 유명한
magnetic field 자기장
habitual ⓐ 습관적인

uncanny ⓐ 이상한, 묘한
feature ⓝ 특징
decode ⓥ 해독하다(= decipher 해독하다)
navigate ⓥ 길 찾다, 항해하다
linear ⓐ 선형적인, 직선의, 1차적인

tracking device 추적 장치
rely on 의존하다
opt for 선택하다
hedge ⓝ 울타리

[16~19] 숙명여대 2010

해석

기원전 399년 봄, 한 유명한 그리스 철학자가 2개의 죄명으로 재판에 회부되었다. 하나는 국가의 신들에 대한 불경죄였고, 다른 하나는 젊은이들에게도 불경을 가르쳐서 그들을 타락시켰다는 죄명이었다. 이러한 고발에 대해 유죄 판결이 날 경우 사형까지 가능한 중대한 범죄였다. 그 죄수의 이름은 소크라테스였고, 그는 당시 70세였다. 소크라테스를 심판하려는 데에는 다른 이유, 즉 정치적 이유도 있었다. 그는 민주 정권에 의해 전복된 이전 귀족정과 관계가 있었고, 현재의 민주 정권에 대한 비판자라는 의심을 받고 있었다. 다른 모든 비판 중에서도, 심지어 정치가들도 그들이 무엇을 하고 있는지는 알아야 한다는 그의 이상한 교리 때문에 대중들로부터 인기가 없었다. 소크라테스는 그의 시대에 가장 현명한 사람이라고 평판이 나 있었다. 그는 스스로를 무지한 사람으로 여겼으며, 인간의 행복과 인간의 운명이라는 궁극적 질문들에 대한 답을 알지 못한다고 생각했기 때문에, 사람들의 이런 평판에 그는 놀랐다고 주장했다. 그러나 그는 또한 다른 어느 누구도 이런 문제들에 대한 해답을 모를 것이라고 확신했고, 이것은 현인이라는 그의 명성에 대한 설명을 부여해 주는 것이었다. 그는 무지했지만 그 혼자서 자신이 무지하다는 사실을 알았던 반면, 다른 무지한 사람들은 그들이 모든 해답을 알고 있다고 생각하면서 자신들이 무지하다는 사실을 깨닫지 못했다.

16 소크라테스는 국가의 신들에 대한 불경과 _____ 때문에 재판에 회부되었다.

① 무례한 행동
② 민주주의에 반하는 저작
③ 청년들의 타락
④ 절도
⑤ 궁극적 질문들에 대한 무지함

| 정답 | ③

| 해설 | 본문 초반부에 소크라테스의 두 죄명이 등장한다. 하나는 문제에 주어진 것이며, 다른 하나는 "the other was the corruption of youth, by teaching them impiety"이라고 나오므로 정답은 보기 ③의 "corruption of youth(청년들의 타락)"이 된다.

17 정치적으로 소크라테스는 _____.

① 새로운 민주 정권에 우호적이었다
② 혁명론자
③ 공산주의자
④ 군주주의자
⑤ 새로운 정권에 반대하였다

| 정답 | ⑤

| 해설 | 소크라테스가 재판을 받은 이유로는 정치적인 이유도 있었다고 말하면서, 현재의 민주 정권에 의해 전복된 과거 귀족정(aristocratic regime)과 친분이 있었으며, 현재의 민주 정권에 대한 비판자(a critic of the democracy)라는 의심을 받았다고 했으므로, 정답은 지금의 정권(the new regime)에 대해 우호적(for)이 아닌 비판적(against) 입장을 취했을 것으로 유추할 수 있다. 따라서 답은 ⑤가 된다.

18 소크라테스는 스스로를 ＿＿＿＿＿＿＿＿(이)라고 생각했다.

① 당대의 가장 현명한 사람들 중에 한 명
② 당대의 가장 무지한 사람들 중에 한 명
③ 보통의 사상가
④ 그가 특정한 궁극적 질문들에 대한 해답을 내놓을 수 없었기 때문에 무지하다
⑤ 그의 교리가 다른 정치가들에게 반대를 받았기 때문에 인기가 없다

| 정답 | ④

| 해설 | 참고로 문제에서 hold는 '～라고 생각하다'는 뜻의 동사로 사용되었다. 소크라테스를 '당대의 가장 현명한 사람'이라고 생각한 것은 당대의 사람들이지 소크라테스 자신이 아니었다.(Socrates was reputed to be the wisest man of his time.) 사실 소크라테스는 이런 평판에 놀랐다고 나온다.(This reputation surprised him ......) 왜냐하면 그는 스스로를 무지한 사람이라고 생각했으며, 자신뿐만 아니라 다른 이들도 그가 생각한 궁극의 문제에 대한 해답을 제시할 수 없다는 것을 알았기 때문에 무지하다고 생각했다. 그리고 이런 사실이 그를 현자라는 사실을 설명(this furnished him with an explanation of his reputation as a wise man)해 준다는 부분은 소크라테스나 당대의 사람들이 아닌 본문을 기술한 '필자'의 생각이다. 따라서 답은 ④가 된다.

19 ㉮와 ㉯에 들어갈 가장 적절한 단어 쌍은 무엇인가?

① how – As
② that – If
③ what – Though
④ if – Despite
⑤ what – Whether

| 정답 | ③

| 해설 | 먼저 ㉮에 들어갈 단어는, doing의 목적어이면서 동시에 본동사 know의 목적어에 해당하는 명사구를 이끌 수 있는 단어가 들어가야 한다. 따라서 선행사를 포함하는 관계 대명사인 what이 적절하다. 따라서 답은 ③과 ⑤ 중 하나가 된다. ㉯는 접속사가 올 자리로 빈칸이 들어 있는 문장의 내용을 보면, 소크라테스는 무지했고, 자신도 이런 사실을 알았다고 말하면서, 이런 반면(whereas) 다른 이들은 그렇지 않았다고 말하고 있다. 따라서 ⑤의 'Whether(～인지 아닌지)'보다는 'Though(～에도 불구하고)'의 양보의 뜻이 적절하다. 따라서 답은 ③이 된다.

| 어휘 | **commit a crime** 범죄를 저지르다
corruption ⓝ 타락, 부패
charge ⓝ 혐의, 비난
regime ⓝ 정권, 체제
doctrine ⓝ 원칙, 교리
ignorant ⓐ 무지한
furnish A with B A에게 B를 제공하다
theft ⓝ 절도

impiety ⓝ 불경, 불손
conviction ⓝ 유죄 판결, 확신
aristocratic ⓐ 귀족의
overthrow ⓥ 전복하다, 타도하다
be reputed ～라는 평판을 듣다, ～라고 알려지다
supreme ⓐ 궁극의, 최고의
conduct ⓝ 행위, 행동
hold ⓥ (신념·의견 등을) 가지다, ～라고 여기다, 생각하다

해석

거의 100년 전에 시작된 제1차 세계대전은 그 나름의 생체공학 인간을 등장시켰다. 1차 세계대전 이전 전쟁에서는 심각한 부상을 당한 군인은 자주 괴저와 감염으로 인해 죽곤 했다. 하지만 더욱 발달한 외과의술 덕분에 많은 군인들이 살아남았다. 독일측의 경우에만 200만 명의 사상자가 발생했는데, 이 중 64%는 팔이나 다리에 부상을 입었다. 약 67,000명이 팔다리를 절단해야 했다. 전쟁에 참여한 모든 국가에서 소위 "전쟁으로 인해 불구가 된 사람"으로 구성된 세대가 등장하였고, 이들의 존재는 연금제도 및 복지제도에 불길한 기운을 풍기며 떠올랐으며, 많은 정부 관료와 군 지도자 및 민간인들은 이들의 장기적인 운명에 대해 걱정했다. 한 가지 해결책은 불구가 된 군인들을 일터로 복귀시키는 것이었다. 마침내 이를 가능케 하고자 다양한 의지가 고안되었다.

20 빈칸에 가장 알맞은 표현은 '＿＿＿＿＿＿＿＿＿＿'이다.

① 전쟁으로 인해 불구가 된 사람　　　　② 참전용사
③ 장애인　　　　④ 전쟁 신경증 환자
⑤ 정신 이상자

| 정답 | ①

| 해설 | 팔이나 다리에 부상을 입고 팔다리를 절단해야 했던 사람들은 "전쟁으로 인해 불구가 된 사람"이라 한다. 따라서 답은 ①이다.

21 본문에 따르면, 제 1차 세계대전은 의수 및 의족 기술의 발전으로 이어졌다.

① 외과의술의 의학적 발전
② 복지 정책의 주목할 만한 변화
③ 의수 및 의족 기술의 발전
④ 참전용사들의 장기적인 운명
⑤ 기존의 확립된 사회제도에 대한 여성의 반란

| 정답 | ③

| 해설 | "불구가 된 군인들을 일터로 복귀시키는" 방법은 의지의 개발, 구체적으로는 "의수 및 의족 기술의 발전"에 달려있다. 따라서 답은 ③이다.

| 어휘 | **a crop of** (동시에 같은 일을 하는 사람들의) 무리[집단]　　**bionic** ⓐ 생체공학적인
succumb (to) ⓥ (병·부상·노령 따위에) 지다, (~으로) 쓰러지다; 죽다
gangrene ⓝ 괴저　　**surgery** ⓝ 외과의술
casualties ⓝ 사상자　　**limb** ⓝ (하나의) 팔[다리]
amputee ⓝ 팔[다리] 절단 수술을 받은 사람　　**cripple** ⓝ 불구자
loom over (불길하게) 다가오다, 떠오르다　　**ominously** ⓐⓓ 불길하게, 기분 나쁘게
bureaucrat ⓝ (정부) 관료
mutilate ⓥ (인체를 심하게) 훼손하다, (특히 팔·다리를 절단하여) 불구로 만들다
prosthesis ⓝ (의족·의안·의치 같은) 인공 기관[삽입물]; 의지(義肢)
neurotic ⓝ 신경증[노이로제] 환자　　**prosthetic** ⓐ 보철의; 인공 기관의
prosthetic limbs 의수, 의족

해석

커피는 사람들이 야간에 운전하거나 기말시험 전 벼락치기를 할 때 잠들지 않기 위한 강력한 각성제로 잘 알려져 있다. 커피의 카페인은 활력을 증진하고, 주의력을 강화하고 반응 시간을 단축시킨다. 또한 기분 전환제이기도 해서 경미한 우울증에 도움이 된다. 최근 University of Bristol 연구진들은 카페인이 지각과 기분에 미치는 영향에 대한 10년간의 연구를 분석했다. 이 분석에 따르면, 커피 한 잔은 지속적인 집중을 요하는 업무 수행에 효과적일 뿐 아니라, 점심 식사 후나, 밤에, 감기에 걸렸을 때 등 집중력이 저하되는 상황에도 도움이 된다.

커피의 건강상의 이점은 기분 전환이나 활력 증진에 그치지 않는다. 일부 일반 감기약에는 항히스타민 성분의 진정 효과를 억제하기 위한 카페인이 함유되어 있다. 또한 카페인은 기관지를 확장시켜 감기와 독감으로 인한 코 막힘을 완화시킨다. 기관지 확장제 기능을 하는 커피는 천식 발작을 예방하는 데도 효과적이다. 뿐만 아니라, 여러 연구에 따르면, 아스피린만 복용했을 경우와는 달리 아스피린과 카페인을 함께 복용하면 아스피린만 복용했을 때보다 진통 효과가 훨씬 뛰어나다. 마지막으로, 저널 The Physician and Sports Medicine에 실린 기사에 따르면, 커피는 체력도 강화시킨다. 커피의 효과를 원하는 운동선수들은 경기 전 1~2시간 동안 보통 3~4잔의 커피를 마신다.

22 다음 중 빈칸 ⓐ에 가장 적절한 것은?

① 측정하다
② 강화하다
③ 억제하다
④ 증명하다
⑤ 생산하다

| 정답 | ③

| 해설 | 커피는 강력한 각성제(powerful stimulant)이므로, 항히스타민의 진정 효과(sedative effects)를 상쇄하거나 막을 것이다. 각성 효과와 진정 효과가 서로 길항 작용을 하는 상반된 효과라는 점에 착안한 문제이다. "counteract(대항하다, 억제하다)"가 빈칸에 적절하다.

23 다음 중 커피의 효능으로 언급되지 <u>않은</u> 것은?

① 신진대사 촉진
② 반응 시간 단축
③ 주의력 강화
④ 체력 증진
⑤ 기분 전환

| 정답 | ①

| 해설 | 지문에 순서대로 나열되는 카페인의 효과를 범주화하는 것이 출제 의도이다. ②, ③, ⑤는 첫 단락에, ④는 두 번째 단락에 제시된 효과이다. ① speeding up metabolism(신진대사 촉진)은 언급되지 않았다.

24 다음 중 지문에서 언급되지 <u>않은</u> 것은?

① 연구에 따르면, 커피는 스트레스 감소에 도움이 된다.

② 카페인은 감기와 독감으로 인한 코 막힘을 해소하는 데 도움이 된다.

③ 커피는 지속적인 집중이 필요한 업무를 하는 데 도움이 된다.

④ 몇몇 운동선수들은 경기 전에 커피를 마신다.

⑤ 커피는 그 자체만으로도 강력한 진통제이다.

| 정답 | ⑤

| 해설 | 커피만으로는 강력한 진통제가 아니라, 커피와 아스피린을 함께 마실 때만 진통 효과가 뛰어나다. "the combination of aspirin and caffeine relieves pain significantly better than aspirin alone" 부분에 단서가 나와 있다.

| 어휘 |

stimulant ⓝ 자극제, 각성제	**awake** ⓐ 깨어 있는	**cram** ⓥ 벼락치기하다
boost ⓥ 강화하다	**alertness** ⓝ 주의력	**quicken** ⓥ 빠르게 하다, 촉진하다
depression ⓝ 우울증	**cognition** ⓝ 지각	**sustained** ⓐ 지속적인
have a cold 감기에 걸리다	**confine** ⓥ 한정하다	
over-the-counter ⓐ 처방전 없이 살 수 있는, 일반 의약품의		**cold formula** 감기약
sedative ⓐ 진정의 ⓝ 진정제	**antihistamine** ⓝ 항히스타민제(천식, 알레르기 치료제의 일종)	
bronchial tubes 기관지	**congestion** ⓝ 막힘(코 막힘), 충혈, 혼잡	
bronchodilator ⓝ 기관지 확장제	**asthma** ⓝ 천식	**attack** ⓝ 발작
relieve ⓥ 완화하다	**stamina** ⓝ 체력, 지구력	**gauge** ⓥ 측정하다
counteract ⓥ 억제하다, 대응하다	**demonstrate** ⓥ 증명하다, 시위하다	**metabolism** ⓝ 신진대사
boost ⓥ 강화하다		

[25~27]

해석

전통적인 미국의 추수 감사절은 1621년으로 거슬러 올라간다. 그해 Massachusetts의 Plymouth에서는 특별한 축제가 준비되었다. 그 지역 정착민들은 종교적 자유를 거부당했기 때문에 영국을 떠난 사람들이다. Mayflower호를 타고 신대륙을 향하는 항해에서 그들은 많은 어려움을 겪었다. 북대서양은 폭풍우가 심해서 항해하기 어려웠다. 신대륙에 도착한 후에는 토착 인디언들에게 정착하는 법을 배웠다. 청교도로 불리던 정착민들에게는 크게 감사할 일이 있었는데 그들은 더 이상은 정부로부터 종교 활동 때문에 비난을 받지 않았다. 그들의 농경 방식은 새로운 기후와 토양에 맞추어 적용되었다. 그들은 11월 네 번째 목요일을 추수 감사제로 정해서, 이웃과 인디언들을 초대해 함께 식사하고 기도하며 새로운 삶을 도와준 인디언들에게 감사의 뜻을 전했다. 또한 Mayflower호를 타고 영국을 떠났던 102명의 남녀와 어린이들을 떠올리며, Massachusetts 해안에 도착하기 전에 죽은 이들을 추모하고 자신들의 강인함을 시험했던 65일간의 여정을 반추했다.

25 다음 중 빈칸에 적절한 것을 고르시오.

① 희생   ② 의무

③ 자유   ④ 기념

| 정답 | ③

| 해설 | 청교도들이 영국을 떠난 이유를 추론한다. "Their religious practices were no longer a source of criticism by the government.(신대륙에서는 종교 활동이 자유롭다.)"가 힌트이다. 신대륙에서는 종교 활동이 자유로우므로, 영국에서는 종교의 자유가 없었음을 유추할 수 있다.

26 정착민들이 인디언들을 저녁 식사에 초대한 이유는 _____.

① 인디언들에게 영국 요리를 가르치기 위해서이다

② 배고픈 인디언에게 식사를 대접하기 위해서이다

③ 인디언들에게 깊은 감사의 뜻을 전하기 위해서이다

④ 인디언과의 전쟁을 피하기 위해서이다

| 정답 | ③

| 해설 | 정착민들을 정착 생활을 도와준 인디언에게 감사의 뜻을 전하기 위해 식사에 초대했다. 본문의 "they invited their neighbors, the Indians, to join them for dinner and prayer and to express gratitude to the Indians for helping them in their new life"가 근거가 된다.

27 정착민들은 감사의 뜻을 전하며, _____을 추모했다.

① 영국에 남은 사람들

② 항해 도중 사망한 동료들

③ 과거의 종교적 관습

④ 인디언 친구들을 초대할 것을

| 정답 | ②

| 해설 | 추수 감사절의 목적을 묻는 문제이다. 추수 감사절은 이웃과 인디언들에게 감사하고, 항해 중 사망한 사람들을 추모하는 것이다. "They recalled the group of 102 men, women, and children who left England." 참조.

| 어휘 | **Thanksgiving Day** 추수 감사절
colonist ⓝ 식민지인
Puritan ⓝ 청교도
religious practice 종교 활동
source ⓝ 원천, 원인
soil ⓝ 토양
gratitude ⓝ 감사
obligation ⓝ 의무

celebration ⓝ 기념, 축제
settle ⓥ 정착하다, 해결하다
be thankful for ~에 대해 감사하다
no longer ~ 더 이상은 ~하지 않다
adjust ⓥ 적응시키다, 바꾸다
select ⓥ 선택하다
recall ⓥ 기억하다

feast ⓝ 축제
deny ⓥ 거부하다, 주지 않다

climate ⓝ 기후
prayer ⓝ 기도
sacrifice ⓝ 희생

해석

"왜 하품이 나는지 아무도 모릅니다."라고 State University of New York at Albany의 심리학 교수 Andrew Gallup은 말한다. Gallup과 동료 연구진들은 새로운 이론을 제시한다. 하품은 신체가 뇌를 식히는 방법이라는 것이다. 그들이 Evolutionary Psychology 5월호의 논문에서 밝힌 바에 의하면, 피험자들은 뇌가 열을 내기 쉬운 상황에서는 더 자주 하품을 했다. 다른 신체 시스템으로는 뇌 온도를 조절하기 충분치 않을 때 하품이 그 역할을 한다는 이론을 입증하기 위해, 연구진들은 사람들이 주변 사람들이 하품을 하면 따라서 하품을 한다는 잘 알려진 경향을 이용했다. 피험자들은 방에 혼자 들어가서 사람들이 감정을 드러내지 않으며 그저 웃거나 하품하는 비디오를 시청했다. 한쪽 방향에서만 보이는 거울을 통해서 관찰자들은 피험자들의 하품 횟수를 셌다. 일부 관찰자들을 비디오를 시청하는 동안 오직 코로만 숨을 쉬도록 했다. 이후에는 따뜻한 팩이나 차가운 팩을 이마에 대도록 했다. 뇌를 식히는 데 도움이 되는 두 가지 조건(코로 호흡하는 것과 이마를 식히는 것)이 충족되면 하품을 따라하는 현상은 일어나지 않았다. 이 연구는 또한 왜 하품이 전염되는지도 설명해 준다. Gallup은 뇌는 시원할수록 정신이 더 맑다고 한다. 따라서 하품은 더 또렷한 정신을 유지하려는 방법인 듯하다. 그리고 하품이 전염되는 현상이 진화해서 집단이 민첩하게 위험을 경계하는 데 도움이 되었을 것이다.

28 다음 중 윗글에 나타난 Gallup과 그의 동료들의 연구 결과와 가장 일치하는 것을 고르시오.

① 하품은 웃음과 관계있다.   ② 하품은 졸음과 관계있다.
③ 하품은 코로 숨 쉬는 것과 관계있다.   ④ 하품은 혈중 산소 수치와 관계있다.

| 정답 | ③

| 해설 | 실험의 변수는 코로 숨 쉬는 것과 이마에 팩을 대는 것이고 실험의 결과는 하품이 나지 않았다는 것이다. 변수와 결과의 관계를 옳게 표현한 보기는 ③이다. 비디오에 웃거나 하품하는 장면이 있다는 사실을 비약에서 보기 ①을 선택하지 않도록 주의한다.

29 밑줄 친 ⓐ와 ⓑ에 공통적으로 들어가기에 가장 적합한 것을 고르시오.

① 높은 온도   ② 뇌 온도의 상승   ③ 뇌의 주의력   ④ 전염되는 하품

| 정답 | ④

| 해설 | 첫 문장에서 하품을 통해 뇌 온도를 낮춘다는 것을 알 수 있다. 코로 숨을 쉬거나 이마에 팩을 대면 뇌 온도가 낮아지므로 하품을 할 필요가 없을 것이다. 따라서 첫 번째 빈칸은 '하품이 사라졌다.'는 내용을 완성해야 논리적이다. 두 번째 빈칸 역시 그 앞 문장과 부연 관계에 있는 문장을 완성해야 하므로 '하품이 진화해 집단이 위험을 경계'하도록 뇌를 각성시키는 역할을 했다는 결론이 적절하다.

| 어휘 |

yawn ⓥ 하품하다	**psychology** ⓝ 심리학	**fellow** ⓝ 동료
cool ⓥ 식히다	**report** ⓥ 보도하다, 밝히다	**be likely to** ~하기 쉽다
prove ⓥ 입증하다	**regulate** ⓥ 조절하다	**take advantage of** 이용하다
tendency ⓝ 경향	**step into** 들어서다	
neutrally 감정을 드러내지 않고, 중립적으로		
count ⓥ 세다	**breathe** ⓥ 숨 쉬다	**press** ⓥ 바짝 대다, 누르다
forehead ⓝ 이마	**condition** ⓝ 조건, 상황	**promote** ⓥ 향상시키다, 촉진하다
eliminate ⓥ 제거하다	**spread** ⓥ 확산하다	**clear** ⓐ 냉철한, 정신이 또렷한
alert ⓐ 경계하는, 민첩한	**evolve** ⓥ 진화하다, 발달하다	**vigilant** ⓐ 바짝 경계하는

해석

2020년은 떠들썩한 해였고, 2021년을 고대하는 지금 시점에 우리가 현재 처한 'K자형' 경제 회복은 무시할 수 있는 것이 아니다. 이러한 유형의 경제 회복은 그렇게까지 새로운 것은 아니다. 실제로는 2008년에 전 세계가 이러한 형태의 회복을 목격했다. 경제가 불황에서 벗어나 회복되면서 다시 팽창되기 시작할 때, 경제학자들은 언급된 불황과 회복에 관해 설명하기 위해 한 글자의 알파벳을 사용한다. 'K자형' 경제 회복은 경제 회복의 속도에 있어 극명한 분열을 그 특징으로 삼는다. 즉 일부 경제 부문은 다른 나머지에 비해 훨씬 빠른 속도로 앞서나가면서 다시 회복하는 반면, 다른 부문은 계속 하향 궤도를 탄다. 따라서 경제 회복에서 발생한 이러한 분열은 'K'자와 흡사하다. 이는 다음의 질문을 제기한다: 좋은 성과를 내는 산업은 무엇이고 그렇지 않은 산업은 무엇인가? 상승 곡선을 기록하는 산업은 기술 부문의 기업, 대기업, 정부, 공익사업 등이 있다. 이러한 산업은 다른 나머지 산업보다 보다 빨리 회복될 수 있지만, 하강곡선을 타는 산업은 팬데믹으로 인한 타격으로 고통받는 산업으로, 여행, 연예, 식품 서비스업 등이 있다. 하지만 대부분의 부문이, 심지어 하강곡선을 타고 있는 부분이라 할지라도, 번성할 수 있는 방법을 찾아낼 수 있는 수단이 존재한다.

30 본문에 따르면 다음 중 'K'의 상단에 위치한 산업의 경제 활동을 가장 그럴듯하게 나타낸 것은 무엇인가?
① 이들은 빠르게 회복할 가능성이 높다.
② 이들의 회복은 계속 하향성을 띨 것이다.
③ 이들의 경제 활동은 떠들썩한 경제 상황에 영향을 받지 않는다.
④ 정부 개입을 통해 이들의 경제 회복이 보장된다.

| 정답 | ①

| 해설 | K자에서 상단에 위치한 경제 부문은 "다른 나머지에 비해 훨씬 빠른 속도로 앞서나가면서 다시 회복"한다. 따라서 답은 ①이다.

31 본문에 따르면 다음 중 'K'의 하단에 위치한 산업의 미래로 가장 가까운 것은 무엇인가?
① 이들은 'K'의 상단에 위치한 산업의 도움이 있어야만 회복할 수 있다.
② 이들에게도 생존할 방안이 존재하지만, 본문의 저자는 그 방안이 무엇인지 언급하지 않았다.
③ 여행, 연예, 식품 서비스업 같은 산업은 정부의 지원이 있어야만 회복이 가능하다.
④ 'K'의 하단에 위치한 여러 산업은 결코 회복하지 못한다.

| 정답 | ②

| 해설 | "대부분의 부문이, 심지어 하강곡선을 타고 있는 부분이라 할지라도, 번성할 수 있는 방법을 찾아낼 수 있는 수단이 존재한다" 를 보면, 하단에 속한 부문에게도 생존할 수 있는 방안이 존재한다는 것은 알 수 있지만, 저자는 구체적으로 무슨 방법이 존재 하는지에 관해서는 언급하지 않았다. 따라서 답은 ②이다.

| 어휘 | **tumultuous** ⓐ 떠들썩한, 격동의
recession ⓝ 불황, 경기 후퇴
be characterized by ~을 특징으로 한다
split ⓝ 분열, 분할
trajectory ⓝ 궤적, 궤도
public utility 공익사업
pandemic ⓝ 전국[전 세계]적인 유행병, 팬데믹

bounce back 다시 회복되다
said ⓐ 앞서 말한[언급된]
stark ⓐ (차이가) 극명한; 완전한
sector ⓝ (특히 국가 경제 활동) 부문[분야]
beg the question 질문을 하게 만든다
fallout ⓝ 방사능 낙진, 좋지 못한 결과
intervention ⓝ 개입, 참가

해석

1997년 8월의 이른 아침 대한항공 801편은 착륙을 위해 괌 국제공항으로 향하는 중이었다. 악천후가 빈발하던 상태였으나, 기상이 나쁜 것 그 자체가 문제될 것은 없었다. 하지만 공항의 유도 시스템이 먹통이었고, 기장은 (지쳐서) 기진맥진한 상황이었다. 기장은 과거 괌 국제공항에 착륙한 적이 많이 있었지만, 큰 언덕이 활주로로 접어드는 길을 막고 있다는 점을 잊고 있었다. 기장은 비행기를 언덕으로 곧장 유도했고, 228명이 사망했다. 문제를 분석하고자 초빙된 자문 위원은 문제의 놀랄 만한 원인을 발견했다. 상급자에게 과도할 정도로 공손한 태도를 취하는 한국의 문화적 성향이 원인이었던 것이다. 부기장과 기관사는 위험 신호를 감지했지만, 차마 기장을 직접적으로 대면하거나 기장으로부터 항공기의 제어를 이어받을 엄두를 내지 못했다. 이 문제는 자문 위원이 대한항공의 조종석에 있는 모든 사람은 영어로 말할 것을 요구하면서 사라졌다. 한국어에서 사용되는 존댓말 호칭이 사라지면서, 승무원들은 더 단도직입적으로 말을 할 수 있었고, 그 결과 대한항공은 항공사 중에서 최고의 안전 기록을 달성한 곳 중 하나가 되었다.

32 다음 중 대한항공 801편의 사고 원인이 아닌 것은 무엇인가?

① 괌 국제공항의 유도 시스템이 고장났다.

② 기장은 괌 국제공항을 잘 몰랐다.

③ 항공기의 부기장은 기장을 직접적으로 대면하지 않았다.

④ 기상 상태가 좋지 못했다.

| 정답 | ②

| 해설 | "기장은 과거 괌 국제공항에 착륙한 적이 많이 있었지만, 큰 언덕이 활주로로 접어드는 길을 막고 있다는 점을 잊고 있었다 (Even though he'd landed at this airport many times in the past, he forgot that there was a big hill blocking the approach to the runway)"라는 문장에서 주의할 점은 "잊었다(forget)"는 동사이다. 언덕이 있는 것을 '잊었던' 것과 애초에 '잘 몰랐던' 것과는 차이가 있으며, 기장은 과거 괌 국제공항에 착륙했던 경험이 "많이 있던(many times)" 사람이었으므로 괌 국제공항을 기장이 '잘 몰랐다'고 보기엔 무리가 있다. 따라서 답은 ②이다. 사고 당시 "공항의 유도 시스템은 먹통이었고(the airport's guidance system was down)", 부기장이나 기관사는 뭔가 문제가 있음을 눈치챘어도 "차마 기장을 직접적으로 대면할 수 없었고(couldn't bring themselves to confront the pilot directly)", 기상 상태는 "악천후가 빈발하던(a spate of heavy weather)" 상태였다. 따라서 ①, ③, ④ 모두가 사고의 한 원인을 차지했음을 알 수 있다. 여기서 "기상이 나쁜 것 그 자체는 문제될 것은 없었다(which wouldn't have been a problem in itself)"고 명시되어 있기 때문에 ④는 사고의 원인이 아니며 따라서 답이 된다고 생각할 수는 있다. 그런데 바로 뒷부분을 보면 "하지만 공항의 유도 시스템이 먹통이었고, 기장은 (지쳐서) 기진맥진한 상황이었다(But the airport's guidance system was down, and the pilot was dog-tired)"라고 명시되어 있으며, 이는 악천후 그 자체(in itself)가 문제될 것은 아니었지만 유도 시스템 문제나 피로 등 다른 문제랑 결합되면서 악천후 또한 사고에 한몫했음을 의미한다. 따라서 ④ 또한 사고의 원인으로 볼 수 있다.

33 본문에 따르면 무엇을 통해 대한항공의 안전 기록을 바꿨는가?

① 안전 장비에 거액을 투자함

② 조종석 승무원들이 상급자에게 더 단도직입적으로 말하게 함

③ 훈련을 늘려 조종석 승무원들이 있을 수 있는 위험을 더 잘 알아채게 함

④ 직원들이 안전 연수회를 받게 함

| 정답 | ②

| 해설 | 문제의 안전 기록을 바꿨다는 것의 의미는 "최고의 안전 기록을 달성(achieve one of the best safety records)" 했다는 것이다. 이는 자문 위원이 조종석 내에서 "한국어에서 사용되는 존댓말 호칭이 없는(without the deferential forms of address used in Korean)" 영어를 쓰도록 요구한 덕분에 "승무원들은 더 단도직입적으로 말을 할 수 있어서(the crew was able to speak more directly)" 가능했다. 따라서 답은 ②가 된다.

| 어휘 |

spate ⓝ (불쾌한 일의) 빈발

dog-tired ⓐ 기진맥진한, 매우 피곤한

deferential ⓐ 공손한

flight engineer 기관사

address ⓝ 호칭

workshop ⓝ 워크숍, 연수회

heavy weather 악천후

runway ⓝ 활주로

first officer 부기장

bring oneself to + 동사원형 차마 ~을 할 엄두를 내다

go on to (이어서) ~을 하게 되다

[34~36]

해석

비타민(vitamin)이란 명칭은 원래 Funk가 사용한 "vital amine"라는 용어에서 나왔다. 1912년 Funk는 Christian Eijkman의 각기를 예방할 수 있는 정미로부터 추출한 아민(amine)의 발견을 인용했다. 반각기 요소가 생존에 주요하다는 Funk의 인식은 사실 정확한 것이었다. 그 이후 연구가들은 비타민이 인체에서는 합성하지 못하는 주요한 유기 화합물이라는 사실을 발견했다. 각기 다른 두 팀(예일대학의 Osborne과 Mendel 팀과 위스콘신대학의 McCollum과 Davis 팀)이 1913년 비타민 A를 동시에 발견했다.

비타민 A는 시력(특히 암순응), 면역 체계 반응, 뼈 발육, 생식, 안구 외벽의 유지, 상피 세포 성장과 치유, 호흡 · 소변 · 장 기관의 상피 조직의 정상화(epithelial integrity)에 매우 중요한 역할을 담당한다. 또한 비타민 A는 배아의 성장과 성인 유전자의 조절에도 중요하다. 비타민 A의 부족 현상은 미국의 경우 영양실조에 걸리거나, 노인들, 만성 질병에 걸린 이들에게서 나타나지만, 개발 도상국에서 보다 만연해 있는 현상이다. 어둠에서의 비정상적 암순응, 건성 피부, 건성 모발, 손톱의 깨짐, 감염에 대한 낮은 저항 등이 비타민 A 부족(VAD)의 첫 증상의 일부라고 할 수 있다.

34 윗글의 제목으로 가장 적당한 것은?

① 비타민 A와 비타민 A의 부족과 관련된 증상

② 비타민 A 연구의 기원

③ 비타민 A의 종류와 이들의 역할

④ 비타민 A 부족의 결과들

| 정답 | ①

| 해설 | 본문에서는 비타민 A의 명칭과 연구의 기원에 대해 다루고 있으며, 비타민 A가 어디에 중요하게 사용되는지에 대해서도 서술하고 있다. 또한 후반부에는 비타민 A의 부족이 가져올 수 있는 증상에 대해서도 다루고 있다. 따라서 이런 내용을 모두 포괄하는 것이 제목이 되어야 하므로 ①이 정답이 된다. ③은 본문과 무관하며, ②와 ④는 본문의 초반과 후반만을 언급한 내용들이므로 제목이 되기에는 충분하지 않다.

35 문맥상 빈칸 ㉮에 알맞은 것은?

① 제한된   ② 흔하지 않은

③ 만연한   ④ 고립된

| 정답 | ③

| 해설 | VAD 현상이 미국에서는 제한적으로 나타나지만, 개발 도상국에서는 보다 보편적인 사람들에게서 나타나는 증상이란 뜻이 와야 하기 때문에, '만연한'의 의미인 ③ prevalent가 적당하다. 나머지 보기는 모두 이와 반대의 의미를 담고 있다.

36 윗글에서 vitamin A deficiency의 결과로 나타나는 증상으로 언급되지 <u>않은</u> 것은?

① 비정상적인 암순응   ② 면역 반응의 저하

③ 손톱의 부러짐   ④ 상피 세포 증가

| 정답 | ④

| 해설 | 글의 후반에 VAD에 대한 내용이 나열되어 있지만, 상피 세포에 관한 내용은 언급되어 있지 않으므로 정답은 ④가 된다.

| 어휘 | **derive from** ~로부터 유래하다   **term** ⓝ 용어   **refer to** ~을 인용하다, 참고하다

       amine ⓝ [화학] 아민   **extract** ⓥ 추출하다   **rice polishing** ⓝ 정미

       beriberi ⓝ [의학] 각기병   **organic compound** 유기 화합물   **synthesize** ⓥ 합성하다

       dark adaptation [생리] 암순응(암순응은 밝은 곳에서 어두운 곳으로 들어갔을 때, 처음에는 보이지 않던 것이 시간이 지남에 따라 차차 보이기 시작하는 현상을 의미한다.)

       epithelial ⓐ 상피의   **respiratory** ⓐ 호흡기의   **urinary** ⓐ 소변의

       intestinal ⓐ 장의   **embryonic** ⓐ 배아의   **deficeincy** ⓝ 부족

[37~39]

해석

열대 저기압은 1945년부터 공식적으로 명칭이 부여되었으며, 그 이유로는 기상 예보, 경보, 주의보 등이 발령되었을 때 기상 예보 관과 일반 대중 간의 의사소통을 촉진하기 위한 것 등 여러 가지가 존재한다. 한 지역에 동시에 둘 이상의 열대성 저기압이 발생할 수 있으므로, 명칭은 어떤 폭풍을 가리키는지에 대한 혼동을 줄여 준다. 열대 저기압에 명칭을 부여하는 관행은 공식적으로 서태평양 내에서 1945년에 시작되었고, 이는 인도 기상청이 북인도양 내에서 발생하는 저기압성 폭풍에 명칭을 부여하기 시작한 2004년 까지 서서히 확장되어 왔다.

열대 저기압에 명칭을 부여하는 관행이 공식적으로 시작되기 전에는 규모가 큰 열대 저기압의 명칭은 짜증스러운 정치인, 신화 속 창조물, 성자, 장소명 등을 따라서 지어졌다. 사전에 결정된 목록에서 이름을 뽑았고, 발생 지역이 어디냐에 따라, 65km/h (40mph) 을 넘는 속도로 바람이 1분이나 3분 또는 10분 동안 지속되는 열대 저기압에 명칭이 부여되었다. 하지만 수역마다 기준이 다른 관 계로, 서태평양에서는 일부 열대성 저기압에 명칭이 부여되지만 남반구 지역에서는 열대 저기압 중심부 주변에 상당한 규모의 강풍 이 불어야만 따로 명칭이 부여된다.

37 다음 중 본문의 제목으로 가장 좋은 것은 무엇인가?

① 열대 저기압의 명칭 부여

② 열대 저기압 식별의 다양성

③ 서태평양의 열대 저기압 명칭 부여 관행

④ 남반구 열대 저기압의 명칭

| 정답 | ①

| 해설 | 본문은 열대 저기압에 명칭을 붙이는 문제에 관해, 구체적으로는 명칭을 언제 붙이게 되었는지, 기준은 무엇인지, 어떤 명칭을 붙이는지 등에 관해 말하고 있다. 따라서 답은 ①이다.

38 열대 저기압에 명칭을 부여하던 과거의 방식은 _____.

① 번호순에 따라 식별한다

② 정치인, 성자, 장소의 이름을 따서 지었다

③ 지속 시간에 따라 식별한다

④ 발생 지역의 이름을 부여했다

| 정답 | ②

| 해설 | "열대 저기압에 명칭을 부여하는 관행이 공식적으로 시작되기 전에는 규모가 큰 열대 저기압의 명칭은 짜증스러운 정치인, 신화 속 창조물, 성자, 장소명 등을 따라서 지어졌다(Before the official practice of naming of tropical cyclones began, significant tropical cyclones were named after annoying politicians, mythological creatures, saints and place names)." 따라서 답은 ②이다.

39 열대 저기압에 명칭을 부여하는 데 있어 언급되지 <u>않은</u> 속성은 무엇인가?

① 지속 시간　　　　　　　　　　　　② 풍속

③ 강풍 규모　　　　　　　　　　　　④ 수역의 명칭

| 정답 | ④

| 해설 | "시속 65킬로미터(시속 40마일)를 넘는 속도로 바람이 1분이나 3분 또는 10분 동안 지속되는 열대 저기압[tropical cyclones with one-, three-, or ten-minute sustained wind speeds of more than 65 km/h (40 mph)]"은 ①과 ②에 해당되며, "남반구 지역에서는 열대 저기압 중심부 주변에 상당한 규모의 강풍이 불어야만 따로 명칭이 부여된다(within the Southern Hemisphere tropical cyclones have to have a significant amount of gale-force winds occurring around the center before they are named)"는 ③에 해당된다. 따라서 답은 ④이다.

| 어휘 | **tropical cyclone** 열대 저기압

meteorological ⓐ 기상의

predetermined ⓐ 미리[사전에] 결정된

basin ⓝ 분지, 수역

gale-force wind 강풍

numerical order 번호순

forecaster ⓝ 기상 예보관

cyclonic storm 저기압성 폭풍

sustained ⓐ 지속되는

tropical depression 열대성 저기압

diversity ⓝ 다양성

해석

미국 내에서 적어도 인종 및 민족 집단을 기술하는 목적으로 쓰이는 "소수 민족"이라는 용어는 곧 사용을 중지하거나 정의를 다시 생각해야 할 것으로 보인다. 2012년 인구조사국에서 발표한 예상에 따르면 2010년대 말이 되면 18세 미만의 아동 가운데 단일 인종 또는 단일 민족으로 구성된 집단이 과반수를 이루는 경우는 없을 것이다. 그리고 대략 30년이 지나면 미국은 대체로 "소수 민족이 과반수가 되는 인구 구성"을 지니게 될 것이다. 인구 조사국에 따르면 미국은 다양성이 커지면서 "복수 민족으로 구성된 국가"로 변하고 있다. 인구조사국의 직무 대행자에 따르면 "현재 지속되는 이러한 경향에 있어 앞으로 닥칠 50년이 중요한 역할을 할 것입니다. 미국은 복수 민족으로 구성된 국가로서 비히스패닉 백인이 전체 인구 가운데 가장 큰 비중을 차지하지만 그 어떤 집단도 과반수를 차지하지 못하게 될 것입니다." 미국 아이들의 다양성은 과거 예측했던 것보다 더 빠르게 증가하고 있다. 인구조사국의 예측에 따르면 아동 인구에 있어 소수 민족이 과반수가 되는 형태로의 인구학적 변화가 2018년에 닥칠 것이고, 이는 과거 예측했던 것보다 몇 년이 빠른 것이다. 인구조사국은 과거 전망했던 것보다 1년이 늦은 2043년에 전체적으로 미국 내에 과반수를 차지하는 단일 인구 집단은 존재하지 않을 것이며, 그 이유는 비히스패닉 백인의 비율이 50퍼센트 이하로 떨어지기 때문으로 예측하고 있다.

---

40 다음 중 본문의 주제는 무엇인가?

① 인구학적 변화   ② 문화적 다양성
③ 소수 민족 집단   ④ 인구 증가

| 정답 | ①

| 해설 | 본문은 미국이 앞으로 소수 민족이 과반을 넘는 인구학적 변화가 있을 것임을 말하고 있다. 따라서 답은 ①이다.

---

41 다음 중 "소수 민족이 과반수가 되는 인구 구성"을 나타내려면 비율이 어떻게 되어야 하는가?

① 인종 A 23퍼센트 인종 B 55퍼센트 인종 C 14퍼센트 기타 8퍼센트
② 인종 A 35퍼센트 인종 B 40퍼센트 인종 C 18퍼센트 기타 7퍼센트
③ 인종 A 52퍼센트 인종 B 17퍼센트 인종 C 16퍼센트 기타 15퍼센트
④ 인종 A 26퍼센트 인종 B 60퍼센트 인종 C 7퍼센트 기타 7퍼센트

| 정답 | ②

| 해설 | "소수 민족이 과반수가 되는 인구 구성"은 역으로 말하면 그 어떤 민족도 과반을 넘지 못하는 인구 구성을 의미한다. 보기 중에서 어느 쪽도 과반을 넘지 못하는 ②를 답으로 볼 수 있다.

---

42 다음 중 2020년의 미국 인구에 관해 맞는 것은 무엇인가?

① 히스패닉 백인을 포함해 백인 미국인은 더 이상 다수가 되지 못한다.
② 히스패닉 인구가 백인 인구를 넘어설 것으로 예측된다.
③ 18세 미만의 아동 가운데 비히스패닉 백인은 다수가 되지 못한다.
④ 전체 인구 가운데 다수를 차지하는 쪽은 아무도 없을 것이다.

| 정답 | ③

| 해설 | "2012년 인구조사국에서 발표한 예상에 따르면 2010년대 말이 되면 18세 미만의 아동 가운데 단일 인종 또는 단일 민족으로 구성된 집단이 과반수를 이루는 경우는 없을 것이다(By the end of this decade, according to Census Bureau projections released in 2012, no single racial or ethnic group will constitute a majority of children under 18)." 즉 ③과 같이 비히스패닉 백인이든 아니든 어느 쪽도 과반을 넘지는 못한다는 의미이다. 따라서 답은 ③이다.

| 어휘 | **minority** ⓝ 소수 민족

constitute ⓥ ~을 구성하다[이루다]

plurality ⓝ 복수, 다수

mark ⓥ ~일 것임을 보여 주다, (새로운 일이 일어날) 전조이다

demographic ⓐ 인구학의

projection ⓝ 예상

diverse ⓐ 다양한

acting director 국장 대리, 직무 대행자

ethnic minority 소수 민족 집단

[43~45] 경기대 2017

해석

우울증은 단순히 약간 우울하거나 격한 감정에 휩싸이는 기분 그 이상을 말한다. 최악의 경우, 우울증은 사람을 쇠약하게 만드는 질병으로, 우울증을 겪는 사람들은 잠을 자거나 먹을 수 없고, 극도의 슬픔과 죄책감으로 가득 차게 된다. 우울증은 가끔 현대인의 질병으로 여겨지며, 부유한 국가의 사람들이 한가롭게 자신에게 집착해서 생겨난 결과라고 생각하기도 한다. 하지만 그것은 전혀 사실이 아니다. 우울증은 한때 'melancholia'라고 불렸으며, 히포크라테스(Hippocrates)와 같은 철학자들이 기원전 5세기경에 진단한 내용이 기록으로 남아 있다. 아레테우스(Aretaeus)는 현대 임상의에게 너무도 익숙한 다음과 같은 증상들을 기술했다. '환자들이 둔하거나 심각한 상태가 되며, 실의에 빠지거나 지나치게 무감각한 모습을 보인다. 그들은 또한 신경질적이고, 의기소침하며, 수면을 방해받는 상태에서 깨어나기도 한다.' 우울증은 또한 개발 도상국에 사는 사람들에게도 실재한다. 우간다의 에이즈가 닥친 지역들을 조사한 내용을 보면, 주민들의 21퍼센트가 임상적으로 우울증을 앓고 있다는 사실을 보여 주며, 파키스탄의 한 마을에 대한 조사에서는 전체 주민 중 44퍼센트가 우울증과 관련한 질환으로 고통을 겪고 있다는 사실을 알 수 있다.

43 다음 중 빈칸 ⒜에 올 수 있는 가장 적합한 것은?

① 마음 산란한　　　　　　　　　② 더 나아가

③ 숨겨진　　　　　　　　　　　④ 구한

| 정답 | ②

| 해설 | 가정법을 이용한 최상급 표현에 관한 문제로, 'nothing could be further from the truth'는 '그보다 사실과 더 거리가 먼 것은 없다. 즉 그것은 전혀 사실이 아니다'를 의미하는 숙어이다. 따라서 빈칸에는 ② further가 정답으로 적합하다.

44 다음 중 본문에서 우울증의 증상으로 언급된 것이 아닌 것은?

① 실망　　　　　　　　　　　② 자살

③ 무기력　　　　　　　　　　④ 짜증

| 정답 | ②

| 해설 | 본문 중간에 나오는 "환자들이 둔하거나 심각한 상태가 되며, 실의에 빠지거나 지나치게 무감각한 모습을 보인다. 그들은 또한 신경질적이고, 의기소침하며, 수면을 방해받는 상태에서 깨어나기도 한다." 부분을 통해 우울증 환자들의 증상을 확인할 수 있

다. 실의에 빠지는 것(dejected)이 ① disappointment를 의미하고, 둔하거나 무감각한 모습(dull, torpid) 등이 ③ inactivity 를 의미한다. 또한 신경질적(peevish)이라는 부분이 ④ irritation이 된다. 따라서 증상으로 언급된 것이 아닌 것은 ② suicide 가 된다.

---

45 다음 중 본문의 내용과 일치하는 것은?

① 우울증은 인간 역사에서 최근 들어 진단되었다.
② 요즘 사람들은 과거보다 우울증에 더 많이 시달린다.
③ 우울증의 증상은 과거와 현재 모두 비슷해 보인다.
④ 우울증은 부유한 국가보다 개발 도상국에서 더 심각하다.

| 정답 | ③

| 해설 | 본문의 "Aretaeus described symptoms that sound all too familiar to modern clinicians" 부분을 통해 우울증 증상이 과거와 현재 모두 비슷하다는 것을 알 수 있으므로, 정답은 ③이 된다. 참고로 우울증이 선진국에서만 나타나는 증상이 아니라고 설명하면서 본문 후반부에 "Depression is a reality for people in the developing world, too"라고 말하고 있다. 하지만 더 심각하다는 내용은 본문에 등장하지 않는다.

| 어휘 | **depression** ⓝ 우울증; (경제) 침체, 공황

overwhelmed ⓐ (격한 감정에) 압도된

immense ⓐ 광대한, 거대한, 막대한

think of A as B A를 B로 생각하다

leisurely ⓐ 한가한, 여유로운, 느긋한

refer to A as B A를 B로 지칭하다

diagnosis ⓝ 진단

clinician ⓝ 임상의(직접 환자를 상대하는 의사)

dull ⓐ (감각이) 무딘, 둔한, 어리석은, 우둔한 ⓥ 둔해지다, 약해지다

stern ⓐ 엄중한, 근엄한; 심각한

torpid ⓐ 활기 없는, 둔한, 마비된, 무감각한

dispirited ⓐ 의기소침한

survey ⓝ 설문 조사 ⓥ 설문 조사 하다

distract ⓥ 주의를 산만하게 하다, 즐겁게 하다

irritation ⓝ 짜증, 화

down ⓐ 우울한

debilitating ⓐ 쇠약하게 하는

guilt ⓝ 죄책감

affliction ⓝ 고통, 병, 불행, 역경

preoccupation ⓝ 사로잡힘, 집착

melancholia ⓝ (구식) 우울증

symptom ⓝ 징후, 증상

dejected ⓐ 실의에 빠진, 낙담한

peevish ⓐ 짜증[화]을 잘 내는

disturbed sleep 수면 방해

stricken ⓐ (~에) 시달리는, (피해 · 질병 등에) 걸린

inactivity ⓝ 무기력, 활동하지 않음, 나태

연습 문제   01 ③   02 ②   03 ④   04 ④

[01~02]

| 해석 |

개인의 문제이든 학업의 문제이든 하여튼 모든 문제 해결은 의사 결정을 수반한다. 문제를 해결하기 위해서는 결정을 내려야 한다. 그렇지만 어떤 문제들은 당신이 내린 결정으로 인하여 발생할 수도 있다. 학교 생활에서 당신은 아마도 수학과 과학을 너무 어렵다는 이유로 공부하지 않기로 결정을 내릴 수도 있다. 이러한 결정 때문에 당신은 장래 어떤 일들은 못할 수도 있다. 당신은 당신 인생에서 많은 사건들이 그저 단순히 발생하는 것은 아니라는 것을 볼 수 있는데, 이는 당신의 선택과 결정의 결과이다. 비판적인 사고와 창의력은 당신이 개인의 문제와 학업의 문제를 해결하는 데 도움을 줄 수 있다.

01 빈칸 ⓐ에 문맥상 가장 적합한 단어를 고르시오.

① 할 것이다   ② 할 것이다
③ 할 수도 있다   ④ 해야 한다

| 정답 | ③

| 해설 | 학교 생활에서 발생할 수 있는 가능성에 대하여, 예를 들어 설명한다. 그 다음에 구체적인 사례로 나오는 것이므로 확실성이 아닌 가능성에 해당하는 may가 적당하다.

02 빈칸 ⓑ에 문맥상 가장 적합한 단어를 고르시오.

① to be solved   ② solve
③ solving   ④ solved

| 정답 | ②

| 해설 | help가 5형식으로 목적격 보어를 동사원형이나 to를 동반한 동사원형으로 받는다. 목적어와 목적보어와의 관계를 고려하면 능동 구조가 와야 하고, 그러므로 정답은 ②이다.

| 어휘 | **critical** ⓐ 비판적인, 평론의   **creativity** ⓝ 창의성, 창조력

03 밑줄 친 표현 중 문법적으로 <u>틀린</u> 것을 고르시오.

당신이 차를 수리하거나 방에 도색을 할 때 입는 옷은 구직 면접 자리에는 적절하지 않다. 당신이 친구들 과 있을 때 사용하는 표현들 역시 당신이 경찰관을 감동시켜야 하는 상황에서 사용하기에는 적절하지 않다. 따라서 좋은 작가가 되기 위해서는, 영어의 표준 문어체 원칙들을 따라야 한다. 다시 말해 이는 작업에 맞는 언어를 사용하는 것을 의미한다. 만약 당신의 글이 이 원칙을 따르지 않는다면, 예를 들어 문법이나 철자, 구두점에 오류가 있다면, 이는 독자를 혼란스럽게 하고 오도할 수 있다. 심지어는 당신과 당신의 생각들을 진지하게 받아들일 필요가 없다는 확신을 그들에게 줄 수도 있다.

① working on   ② speak to
③ whom   ④ not
⑤ him or her

| 정답 | ④

| 해설 | ①의 'work on a car'라고 하면 '차를 손보고 있다'는 뜻이 되어 수리한다는 의미가 된다. ②의 경우 speak 뒤에 사람이 오는 경우 to와 with를 모두 사용할 수 있는데, 'speak to'의 경우는 '잘못을 바로잡기 위해 ~와 이야기하다'는 뜻이 있고, 'speak with'는 '상대방과 대화나 논의하다'의 의미를 지닌다. ③의 whom은 목적격 관계대명사로 바로 앞의 officer를 선행사로 받는다. 정답은 ④가 되는데, dash를 사용해 앞의 내용을 부연 설명하고 있는 문장이므로 문맥상 not이 없어야 한다. ⑤는 독자(reader)를 지칭하고 있으며, 남자 독자 혹은 여자 독자를 지칭하기 위해 사용했다.

| 어휘 | **appropriate** ⓐ 적절한
speak to somebody (about something) (잘못을 바로잡거나 무엇을 못 하게 하기 위해) ~와 (~에 대해) 이야기를 하다
punctuation ⓝ 구두점   **mislead** ⓥ 오해시키다, 잘못 인도하다
convince ⓥ 확신시키다
take sth seriously ~을 진지하게 생각하다, ~을 진지하게 받아들이다

04 밑줄 친 ⓐ, ⓑ, ⓒ를 내용과 문법에 맞게 가장 정확히 배열한 것은?

쉬운 영어로 글을 쓴다는 것은 어려운 일이다. 어느 누구도 지금껏 교과서에서 문학을 배우지 못했다. 나는 글쓰기 수업을 들은 적이 없다. 나는 자연스럽게 스스로 글 쓰는 법을 배웠다. 나는 우연히 성공한 것은 아니다. 나는 인내를 가지고 어려운 일을 통해서 성공했다. 말솜씨가 좋은 책을 만드는 것이 아니다. 지나치게 많은 작가가 자신이 쓰고 있는 등장인물보다 자신의 글의 스타일에 관심을 둔다. 종종 장황한 말과 젠체하는 것으로 인해 자신의 스타일이 훼손된 작가가 너무 많다. 위대한 작가의 대부분은 훌륭한 언어 구사력이 없다. 훌륭한 작가에게서 뺄 수 없는 특징은 명료함을 특징으로 하는 스타일이다. 훌륭한 작가는 자신이 선택하는 주제에 대해 현명하고, 재료를 모으는 데 철저하다. 훌륭한 작가는 자기 자신과 의견에 솟구치는 자신감을 가지고 있어야 한다. 훌륭한 작가는 정보의 홍수에서 중요한 사실을 발굴할 수 있는 능력을 안다. 작가에게 있어 가장 어려운 것은 지칠 줄 모르는 독창적인 상상력을 유지하는 것이다. 대부분의 작가는 단순히 천재 작가에게서 빼놓을 수 없는 특징이 없기에 실패한다. 이들은 심할 정도로 선입견을 지닌다. 자신의 교육에도 불구하고, 이들의 시야는 아주 좁다.

	ⓐ	ⓑ	ⓒ
①	are writing	– to mark	– maintaining
②	wrote	– marked	– to maintain
③	wrote	– to mark	– maintaining
④	are writing	– marked	– to maintain

| 정답 | ④

| 해설 | ⓐ의 경우 작가가 '다루고 있는'의 의미이므로 'are writing'의 진행의 형태를 취하고, ⓑ의 경우 'by'와 함께 수동태를 취하는데, 관계대명사+be동사가 생략된 과거 분사의 형태이다. ⓒ의 'maintain'은 'the toughest thing for a writer is 다음의 보어에 해당하는 to maintain이 되어야 한다.

| 어휘 | **plain** ⓐ 평평한, 명백한, 쉬운

verbal ⓐ 말의

mar ⓥ 손상시키다, 훼손하다

have a command of ~을 자유자재로 구사하다

lucidity ⓝ 명료함

accumulation ⓝ 축척

irrepressible ⓐ 억누를 수 없는

excavate ⓥ ~에 구멍을 파다, 발굴하다

maintain ⓥ 주장하다, 유지하다

fertility ⓝ 기름짐, 비옥, 다산

indispensable ⓐ 불가결의, 없어서는 안 될

prejudiced ⓐ 편견을 가진, 편파적인

narrow ⓥ 좁게 하다, 좁히다, 제한하다

by accident 우연히

dexterity ⓝ 솜씨 좋음, 기민한, 빈틈없는

verbosity ⓝ 말이 많은, 다변의, 장황한

indispensable ⓐ 불가분의

exhaustive ⓐ 전부를 다 하는, 남김없이, 소모적인

material ⓝ 재료, 내용

confidence ⓝ 자신감

masses of information 엄청난 양의 정보

vigor ⓝ 활기, 정력, 힘, 생기

imagination ⓝ 상상력

genuine ⓐ 진짜의, 성실한, 진심에서 우러난

horizon ⓝ 수평선, 시야, 범위

01	①	02	⑤	03	①	04	③	05	④	06	③	07	②	08	③	09	④	10	③
11	③	12	①	13	④	14	③	15	③	16	④	17	④	18	④	19	①	20	①

[01~02]

해석

새로운 기술을 통해 의사의 처방을 감시할 수 있게 되면서, 긍정적 결과와 부정적 결과가 함께 나타났다. 일부 감독 기관들은 이것을 이용해서, 의사가 환자의 병을 가장 잘 치료할 수 있는 약을 선택하도록 한다. 그러나 또 다른 일부 감독 기관들은 이것을 이용해서 의사에게 압력을 가해 가장 효과적인 약이 아니라 가장 저렴한 약을 처방하게 만든다. 이와 마찬가지로, 환자의 병력을 알려주는 디지털 의료 기록은 치료법을 향상시키고 전염병 연구를 촉진할 수 있다. 반면에 환자의 프라이버시를 침해할 수도 있다. 컴퓨터는 교실에 새로운 지식의 영역을 들여왔지만, 더 필요한 교구들을 구입하는 데 쓰일 소중한 자원을 다른 곳에 투입함으로써 부유한 학교와 빈곤한 학교의 격차를 심화시킬 수도 있다. 컴퓨터 기술이 동시에 갖고 있는 장점과 단점의 예는 계속된다.

01 다음 중 제목으로 가장 적절한 것은?

① 정보화 시대의 딜레마
② 현대적 교육을 위한 컴퓨터의 효과적 이용
③ 좋은 점과 나쁜 점을 구별하는 방법
④ 공공 정책이 개인의 프라이버시에 미치는 영향
⑤ 어떻게 현대 기술이 인권을 신장시켰는가

| 정답 | ①

| 해설 | 컴퓨터 기술(정보화 기술)의 장단점이 디지털 의료 정보 시스템의 장단점, 교육용 컴퓨터 도입의 장단점으로 예시되고 있으므로 ①이 적절하다.

02 빈칸에 들어갈 알맞은 전치사는?

① by　　　　② without　　　　③ with　　　　④ at　　　　⑤ from

| 정답 | ⑤

| 해설 | 문맥상 컴퓨터 기술(정보화 기술)이 교육에 미치는 부정적 영향이 언급되어야 하므로 소중한 재원이 정작 더 중요한 교구 구입에 쓰이지 못하고 다른 곳에 사용된다는 내용이 이어져야 자연스럽다. "divert A from B[A를 B로부터 다른 곳으로 돌리다, (돈 등을) 다른 곳으로 유용하다]"를 사용해 문장을 완성한다.

| 어휘 | **monitor** ⓥ 감시하다
consequence ⓝ 결과
make sure that 반드시 ~하게 하다
pressure ⓥ 압력을 가하다
track ⓥ 추적하다
enhance ⓥ 강화하다, 개선하다
promote ⓥ 촉진하다

prescription ⓝ 처방(전) → **prescribe** ⓥ 처방하다
oversee ⓥ 감시하다
ailment ⓝ 병
effective ⓐ 효과적인
medical history 병력
treatment ⓝ 치료(법)
epidemiological ⓐ 전염병학의

lead to 초래하다

realm ⓝ 영역

educational tool 교구

divide ⓝ 격차

good news-bad news 사물(현상)의 좋은 면과 나쁜 면, 장단점

invasion of privacy 사생활 침해

divert A from B B로부터 A를 다른 곳으로 돌리다

deepen ⓥ 심화하다

go on and on 계속되다

[03~04] 국민대 2016

해석

중국의 난징대학교 의과대학(Nanjing University of Medicine)에서 실시한 설문 조사에 따르면, 단백질을 더 많이 섭취하는 사람들, 특히 해산물을 통해 단백질을 더 많이 섭취하는 사람들은 뇌졸중을 일으킬 가능성이 적다. 미국 신경과학회(the American Academy of Neurology)의 의학 저널인 신경학(Neurology) 학회지에 게재된 이번 연구는 254,489명의 사람들을 대상으로 한 7건의 개별 연구를 포함하고 있으며, 매일 20그램의 단백질을 섭취하면 뇌졸중의 위험이 26퍼센트 낮아지는 것으로 나타났다. 전반적으로 단백질 섭취량이 가장 많은 참가자는 식단에 가장 적은 양의 단백질을 섭취 한 참가자보다 뇌졸중 발생 가능성이 20퍼센트 낮게 나타났다. 곡물이나 붉은 고기보다는 해산물에서 단백질을 얻는 사람들에게 이런 관련성이 가장 높게 나타났다. 생선의 단백질과 지방산은 혈압을 낮추어 뇌졸중을 예방하는 데 도움을 준다.

03 다음 중 문법적으로 올바르지 <u>못한</u> 부분은?

① Ⓐ   ② Ⓑ   ③ Ⓒ   ④ Ⓓ

| 정답 | ①

| 해설 | Ⓐ 앞의 the study가 주어가 되고 involved가 동사이므로, Ⓐ는 앞의 주어를 시식하는 분사가 되어야 한다. 하지만 의미상 '학회지에 출간된'이라는 뜻의 수동태가 와야 하므로 현재분사가 아닌 과거분사 published로 수정되어야 한다.

04 다음 중 본문의 제목으로 가장 적합한 것은?

① 생선 섭취를 증가시키는 방법

② 붉은 고기와 곡물을 피하는 방법

③ 뇌졸중의 위험을 줄일 수 있는 방법

④ 혈압을 정기적으로 확인하라

| 정답 | ③

| 해설 | 본문 서두의 "People who eat more protein … may be less likely to have a stroke" 부분을 통해 단백질 섭취가 뇌졸중 방지와 관련이 있다는 내용이 주제문으로 와야 한다. 따라서 이와 가장 유사한 ③이 제목으로 적합하다.

| 어휘 | **protein** ⓝ 단백질

neurology ⓝ 신경학

grain ⓝ 곡물

stroke ⓝ 뇌졸중

lower ⓥ 낮추다

fatty acid 지방산

publish ⓥ 출판하다, 출간하다

intake ⓝ 섭취

해석

Rodrigo Bonilla는 보트의 모터를 끈다. 우리는 보트에서 내려 길을 따라 열대 우림 속으로 그를 따라간다. 우리 위로는 새끼와 함께 있는 원숭이가 나무에 매달려 있다. 이렇게 더운 1월의 어느 날, Rodrigo는 야생 동물을 찾고 있는 것이 아니라 약초, 즉 질병을 고쳐 주고 치료해 줄 수 있는 식물을 찾고 있다. Rodrigo는 코스타리카 사람이다. 그는 그의 할머니로부터 정글의 약에 대해 배웠다. 그는 우리에게 로뎀나무와 같은 많은 다른 식물을 보여 준다. 그는 우리에게 로뎀나무의 일부가 지혈에 도움이 될 수 있다는 사실을 알려 준다. 사람들은 항상 천연 산물들을 약으로 이용해 왔다. 사실 아스피린과 같은 서양 의약품의 약 50퍼센트는 천연자원으로부터 나온다. 그리고 몇몇 동물들은 그들이 아플 때 특정 종류의 식물을 먹는다. 이것이 의학 연구자들이 약초에 그렇게 관심이 많은 이유이다. 많은 기업들이 현재 지방 정부와 협력하여 열대 우림에서 약초를 찾고 있다. 지금까지 찾아본 결과 새로운 약초는 발견하지 못했다. 하지만 계속 찾아보는 것은 좋은 생각이다. 그것이 우리가 현재 코스타리카 열대 우림에 있는 이유이다.

05 빈칸에 들어갈 가장 알맞은 것을 고르시오.

① help stop bleed
③ help stop to bleeding
② help to stop bleed
④ help stop bleeding

| 정답 | ④

| 해설 | 'help'는 준사역동사로 뒤에 동사원형이나 to부정사가 올 수 있다. 'stop' 뒤에 '~을 중단하다'의 의미로 사용할 경우 동명사만 와야 한다. 따라서 'help (to) stop -ing'의 구조이어야 하므로 정답은 ④가 된다.

06 윗글의 내용과 맞지 <u>않는</u> 것을 고르시오.

① 새로운 약초를 발견하는 것은 쉬운 일이 아니다.
② Rodrigo는 약초를 찾기 위해 원정을 이끌고 있다.
③ 약들은 전부 천연 공급원으로부터 만들어진다.
④ 몇몇 동물은 치료를 위해 약초를 사용한다.

| 정답 | ③

| 해설 | 본문 중반에서 "서양 의약품의 약 50퍼센트가 천연자원으로부터 나온다"고 했으므로 전부(entirely) 천연 공급원에서 나온다는 ③이 본문과 일치하지 않는다.

| 어휘 | **medicinal** ⓐ 약효[치유력]가 있는   **cure** ⓥ 치료하다   **broom tree** 로뎀나무
bleed ⓥ 피를 흘리다, 출혈하다   **expedition** ⓝ 탐험, 원정; 신속함   **entirely** ⓐⓓ 전적으로, 완전히, 전부

해석

폭풍에 대한 새로운 공식이 낙뢰에 대해 새로운 정보를 제공해 주고 있다. 데이비드 롬프스(David Romps)와 그의 동료들은 낙뢰를 예측하는 데 있어 지금까지 가장 정확하다고 주장하는 모델을 고안해 냈다. 그런 다음 그들은 그 모델을 사용하여 지구 온난화가 계속될 경우, 어떻게 낙뢰가 증가할 것인지, 그리고 이것이 어떻게 더 많은 산불로 이어질 수 있는지를 예측했다. 폭풍이 번개로 알려진 갑작스러운 전기 방전을 일으키기 위해서는 액체 상태의 물과 얼음, 그리고 이 둘을 모두 공중에 떠 있게 유지할 수 있을 만큼의 빠른 상승 기류가 존재해야 한다. 롬프스는 이러한 요인들을 방정식에 대입해, 낙뢰가 얼마나 자주 발생하는지를 계산할 수 있다고 이론화했다. 그는 측정된 강수량을 대류 가능한 위치 에너지(폭풍우 구름이 얼마나 빨리 상승할 수 있는지)에 곱했다. 2011년 데이터를 사용한 그의 계산은 기록된 낙뢰 현상과 77퍼센트 일치했다. 기존의 모델은 39퍼센트의 정확도만을 보였다. 공기가 더 따뜻할수록 폭풍을 유발하는 더 많은 수증기를 함유한다. 지구 온난화로 지구가 섭씨 1도가 상승할 경우, 미국에서 낙뢰는 약 12퍼센트 증가할 것이라고 롬프스는 주장한다. 이산화탄소 배출량이 현재의 비율로 계속된다면 2100년까지 낙뢰가 50퍼센트 이상 발생할 수 있다.

07 다음 중 주어진 문장이 들어가기에 가장 적합한 곳은?

롬프스는 이러한 요인들을 방정식에 대입해, 낙뢰가 얼마나 자주 발생하는지를 계산할 수 있다고 이론화했다.

① Ⓐ ② Ⓑ ③ Ⓒ ④ Ⓓ

| 정답 | ②

| 해설 | 제시된 문장에서 'those factors'가 앞의 내용을 지칭하고 있으므로 제시문 앞에는 이런 요인들이 나열되어 있어야 한다. Ⓑ 앞에 나오는 'liquid water', 'ice', 'updrafts' 등이 이러한 요인들에 해당하므로 정답은 Ⓑ가 된다.

08 다음 중 문법적으로 올바르지 않은 것은?

① ⓐ ② ⓑ ③ ⓒ ④ ⓓ

| 정답 | ③

| 해설 | ⓒ는 간접의문문에 해당하므로 밑줄 친 부분이 'how fast a storm cloud can'으로 수정되어야 한다.

09 다음 중 빈칸 ㉠에 들어갈 단어로 가장 적합한 것은?

① 다다르다 ② 차지하다
③ 급락하다 ④ 증가하다

| 정답 | ④

| 해설 | 빈칸 바로 앞 문장에서 "The warmer the air is, the more storm-fueling water vapor it can hold."라고 설명하고 있다. 공기가 더 따뜻할수록 폭풍을 유발하는 더 많은 수증기를 함유한다는 것이다. 따라서 지구의 온도가 1도 상승할 경우 '폭풍을 유발하는 수증기'가 늘어날 것이고, 이는 더 많은 낙뢰로 이어질 수 있으므로 정답은 '증가한다'는 ④가 된다.

| 어휘 | **novel** ⓐ 새로운   **shed new light on** ~에 새로운 해결의 빛을 던지다; 새로운 정보를 주다

lightning ⓝ 번개
multiply ⓥ 늘어나다, 곱하다
precipitation ⓝ 강수량
vapor ⓝ 증기

devise ⓥ 고안하다
electric discharge 방전
convective ⓐ 대류성의
carbon dioxide emissions 이산화탄소 방출

project ⓥ 예상[추정]하다
updraft ⓝ 상승 기류
conventional ⓐ 기존의, 전통적인

[10~11] 단국대 2011

해석

몇몇 박물관들이 출처에 의문이 드는 유물들의 수락을 거절하는 이유는, 그것이 유물 발굴 현장이나 다른 박물관에서 도난당했을 가능성이 있기 때문이다. 최근 아프가니스탄이나 이라크 전쟁에서 볼 수 있듯이, 전쟁 중이나 정치적 격동기에 유물들이 도난을 당하거나 최고 가격을 부른 입찰인에게 판매가 되는 경우가 흔히 발생한다. 그러나 몇몇 박물관장들은 출처를 알 수 없는 유물을 받아들이는 것도 좋은 근거들이 있다고 주장한다. 예를 들어 큐레이터들은 몇 세대에 걸쳐 개인 소장품으로 간직된 유물들을 받아들이지 않고 거부하는 것을 꺼린다. 여러 세대에 걸쳐 관련 서류를 계속 보유한다는 것이 어렵기 때문에, 서류가 미비한 것이 꼭 유물을 기증한 이들이 불법적인 방법으로 유물을 소유한 것을 의미하는 것은 아니라고 이들은 주장한다. 출처가 불분명한 유물을 적극적으로 전시하려고 하는 큐레이터들은 만약 자신들이 그런 유물들을 전시하지 않는다면, 그것은 대중에게 고대 문화에 대한 역사적인 정보를 제공해야 하는 그들의 의무를 다하지 못하는 것이라고 주장한다. 예를 들어 메트로폴리탄 미술관(The Metropolitan Museum of Art)은 지금의 아프가니스탄 지역에 위치했던 고대 도시인 Bactria의 유물 전시회 때 출처가 불분명한 유물을 전시했었다.

10 본문의 제목으로 가장 적절한 것은?

① 큐레이터의 역할　　　② 출처 미상　　　③ 박물관의 딜레마　　　④ 유물의 전시

| 정답 |　③

| 해설 |　본문은 단순히 유물을 전시하는 것에 초점을 맞추고 있는 글이 아니다. 유물은 유물이되 출처가 불분명한 유물을 박물관에서 어떻게 보는지에 대해 다루고 있다. 몇몇 박물관은 출처 미상의 유물을 받지 않지만, 이런 유물을 적극적으로 받는 박물관도 있다고 소개하고 있다. ①의 경우 큐레이터가 박물관에서 어떤 일을 하는지 소개하는 글이 아니므로 정답이 될 수 없고, ②의 경우 출처 미상만으로는 글의 의도를 파악하기 어렵다. ③의 경우 박물관에서 출처 미상의 유물을 두고 앞서 말한 어려움이 있다는 것을 담고 있으므로 정답에 가깝다. ④의 경우 단순한 유물 전시는 너무 포괄적인 말이기 때문에 제목이 될 수 없다.

11 다음 중 빈칸에 가장 적합한 것은 무엇인가?

① 비록 이들이 그렇게 하지 않았다 하더라도
② 이들이 그렇게 하지 않았을 때
③ 만약 이들이 그렇게 하지 않았다면
④ 그들이 그렇게 하지 않았기 때문에

| 정답 |　③

| 해설 |　밑줄 뒤에 나온 문장을 보면 "wouldn't be fulfilling ..."이라는 부분을 통해 가정법 과거임을 알 수 있으며, 문맥을 통해서도 짐작할 수 있다. 따라서 가정법 과거에 적합한 ③이 정답이 되며, 가정법 과거이기 때문에 현재 사실에 대한 가정을 하고 있는 것도 확인할 수 있다.

| 어휘 | provenance ⓝ 출처, 기원, 유래   archaeological ⓐ 고고학의   loot ⓥ 훔치다, 약탈하다

times of war 전시   upheaval ⓝ 격변, 대변동

political upheaval ⓝ 정변, 쿠데타, 혁명

highest bidder ⓝ 최고 입찰인   insist ⓥ 주장하다   reluctant ⓐ 꺼리는, 마지못한

turn down ~을 거부하다   fulfill ⓥ 다하다, 이행하다

[12~14]

해석

초기에는, 지구 온난화가 실제로 일어나고 있는 현상인지 아닌지에 관한 논쟁이 있었지만 이제 우리는 지구 온난화가 실제로 일어나고 있음을 알고 있다. 오늘날의 논쟁은 지구 온난화의 원인이 인간인지 아닌지에 관한 것이다. 일반적으로, 사람들이 자신은 지구 온난화를 믿지 않는다고 말하는 것은 자동차 운전, 숲의 개간, 늪지의 간척은 지구 온난화의 원인이 아니라고 말하는 것과 같다. 또는 설사 그렇다 할지라도 일부 사람들이 생각하는 만큼 심각한 위협은 아니라고 말하는 것과 같다. 안타깝게도 그들은 부정하고 있다. 그들은 그저 말하고 싶을 뿐이다 <u>"우리는 책임이 없다."</u>고.

오늘날에는 지구 온난화를 전혀 믿지 않는다는 말은 그야말로 타당하지 않다. 물론 그렇게 말할 수는 있다. 그러나 지구가 우주의 중심이라는 말처럼, 우리가 알고 있는 모든 것과 모순되는 말이다. 인간이 지구 온난화의 최대 원인임을 믿지 않은 사람들도 마찬가지이다. 물론 자연은 강인하기 때문에 엄청난 변화에도 적응할 수 있고, 지구 온난화 때문에 세계가 무너지지는 않을 것이다. 하지만 인간처럼 강력한 새로운 요소가 생태계에 들어온 적은 없었다. 우리는 이제 지질학적 행위자로서 기후 형성 과정에 영향을 미치고 있다. 지구상에 인간이 얼마나 많은지 생각해 본다면 놀라운 일도 아니다.

---

12 빈칸 (A)에 가장 알맞은 것은?

① 우리는 책임이 없다

③ 너무 점잖은 척하지 마라

② 모든 책임은 내가 진다

④ 낭비하지 않으면 부족함도 없다.

| 정답 | ①

| 해설 | 지구 온난화의 원인이 인간이 아니라는 주장은 곧 인간은 지구 온난화에 책임이 없다는 것이다. '우리는 책임이 없다'는 의미로는 ①이 적절하다. "be to blame for ~"은 "~에 책임이 있다"는 표현이다.

---

13 밑줄 친 부분 (가)~(라) 중 문법적으로 틀린 것은?

① (가)

② (나)

③ (다)

④ (라)

| 정답 | ④

| 해설 | 출제 의도는 ④의 "such+a+형용사+명사" 용법을 확인하는 것이다. "such huge a new factor"를 "such a huge new factor"로 바꾸어야 옳은 표현이다.

---

14 윗글의 제목으로 가장 알맞은 것은?

    ① 부인: 위험한 정신 상태

    ② 지구 온난화: 사실인가 허구인가?

    ③ 인간이 지구 온난화에 미치는 영향

    ④ 인구 폭발: 전 지구적 재난

| 정답 | ③

| 해설 | 지문의 주제는 "지구 온난화의 원인은 인간"이라는 것이다. 주제를 강조하기 위해, 지구 온난화에 대한 인간의 책임을 부정하는 관점을 비판하고 있다. 주제를 가장 포괄적으로 전달하는 보기는 ③이다. 지구 온난화가 사실인지 아닌지에 대한 논쟁은 과거에 이미 끝났으므로 보기 ②를 선택하지 않도록 주의한다.

| 어휘 |

debate ⑪ 논쟁, 논한	**global warming** 지구 온난화	**believe in** (사실, 존재를) 믿다
clear ⓥ 개간하다, 없애다	**drain** ⓥ 배수하다	**marsh** ⑪ 늪지
be responsible for ~에 책임이 있는, ~의 원인이 되는		**make out** 이해하다
in denial 부정하는	**be blame to** ~에 책임이 있는	**state** ⓥ 언급하다, 말하다
resonable ⓐ 합리적인, 타당한	**go against** ~와 모순되다, ~에 불리하다	
prime ⓐ 주요한, 최고의	**factor** ⑪ 요소, 요인	**hardy** ⓐ 강한, 강인한
adapt to ~에 적응하다	**crumble** ⓥ 무너지다, 가루가 되다	**geological agent** 지질학적 주체
affect ⓥ 영향을 미치다	**determine** ⓥ 결정하다	**hardly** ⓐⓓ 거의 ~하지 않다

[15~17]

해석

> 1990년대 초반까지만 해도 휴대폰은 귀한 사치품이었다. 그러나 1990년대 후반부터 휴대폰은 업무용으로, 가정용으로, 심지어 패션 액세서리로서 다른 모든 전자 제품보다 더 많이 팔렸다. 더 작은 크기에 더 많은 전력을 더 오래 저장할 수 있도록 기능이 향상된 충전 배터리와, 전력을 덜 소모하는 더 효율적인 전자 장치 덕분에 휴대폰의 크기도 작아졌다. 휴대폰은 기본적으로 저출력 라디오 송수신기에, 음성을 전기 신호로 변환하는 소형 마이크와 그 반대 기능을 하는 소형 스피커가 장착된 것이다. 액정 디스플레이(LCD)는 숫자, 문자, 부호를 보여 준다. 최신 모델의 휴대폰은 더 큰 화면에 더 화려한 영상 이미지를 구현한다. 인터넷, 라디오, 오디오 플레이어 기능이 추가된 모델도 있다. 휴대폰이 작동할 때는 무선 전파를 송출하고 전파를 수신한 주변의 기지국 안테나 송수신기는 응답 신호를 보낸다. 휴대폰은 가장 뚜렷한 신호를 추적해서 통화 영역권[각 송신기의 통화 영역권을 셀(cell) 이라고 한다.] 안에서 사용한다. 휴대폰은 신호 강도를 계속 모니터하다가 필요한 경우 대체 가능한 송신기로 전환한다.

---

15 밑줄 친 ⓐ~ⓓ 중 어법상 잘못된 것은?

    ① ⓐ   ② ⓑ   ③ ⓒ   ④ ⓓ

| 정답 | ③

| 해설 | ⓒ의 대명사 some은 some models를 대신하는 대명사로, 복수이므로 incorporates과는 수가 일치하지 않는다. 따라서 incorporate로 바꾸어야 한다.

16 빈칸 ⓔ에 가장 알맞은 것은?

① 부적절한 　　　　　　　　　② 애매한

③ 양면적인 　　　　　　　　　④ 대체의

| 정답 | ④

| 해설 | 휴대폰은 통화 영역권 내에서 기지국 송신기의 신호를 사용한다. 따라서 신호 강도가 약해지면 다른(alternative) 송신기로 바꿀 것을 유추할 수 있다. 나머지 보기는 휴대폰 통화 원리와 무관한 형용사이므로 선택하지 않도록 주의한다.

17 윗글의 내용과 가장 일치하지 않는 것은?

① 휴대폰은 항상 가장 뚜렷하고 강한 신호를 찾으려 한다.

② 1990년대 휴대폰은 거의 모든 다른 전자 제품보다 많이 판매되었다.

③ 휴대폰의 크기는 충전 배터리의 용량이 늘어나면서 점차 작아졌다.

④ 최신 모델의 휴대폰은 인터넷, 오디오 플레이어, 카메라 등의 많은 추가적인 기능을 갖추고 있다.

| 정답 | ④

| 해설 | 일부 최신 휴대폰에는 인터넷, 라디오, 오디오 플레이어 기능이 추가되어 있지만 카메라 기능은 포함되지 않았으므로 ④는 내용과 일치하지 않는다. "some incorporate other functions such as internet access, radio, and an audio player." 부분을 참조한다.

| 어휘 | **rare** ⓐ 드문, 귀한

gadget ⓝ 장치, 도구

typical ⓐ 전형적인, 일반적인

rechargeable ⓐ 재충전할 수 있는

electronics ⓝ 전자 장치, 전자 공학, 전자 제품

radio ⓝ 전파

convert ⓥ 변환하다, 개종하다

complex ⓐ 복잡한, 정교한

radio pulse 라디오 펄스(전파 파동)

range ⓝ 범위, 영역

alternative ⓐ 대체 가능한, 대안

luxury ⓝ 사치품

domestic ⓐ 가정의, 국내의

shrink ⓥ 줄어들다

store ⓥ 저장하다

receiver ⓝ 수신기

reverse ⓝ 반대, 역

incorporate ⓥ 통합하다

mast ⓝ (안테나용) 철탑, 기둥

monitor ⓥ 감시하다

outsell ⓥ 더 많이 팔리다

convenience ⓝ 편리, 편익

due to ~ 때문에

electricity ⓝ 전기

low-power ⓐ 저출력의

transmitter ⓝ 송신기

symbol ⓝ 부호

activate ⓥ 활성화하다

lock onto 추적하다, 따라가다

switch to ~로 바꾸다

해석

미국 독립 혁명(American Revolution)은 시민의 권리와 국가의 권리 사이의 관계를 상징했다. 자유 시민은 스스로를 통치할 권리가 있었고, 따라서 자유 시민으로 이루어진 공동체 전체는 스스로를 통치할 권리가 있었다. 이는 아직은 현대의 국가주의는 아니었다. 미국인들은 스스로를 하나의 국가를 이룬 집단이 아니라 어느 한 명제에 헌신한 자유인들로 이루어진 하나의 공동체로 봤다. 하지만 20년 만에 스스로가 어떤 존재인지를 인지하게 되었다.

인간의 권리(Rights of Man)를 선포한 프랑스 혁명(French Revolution)이 새로운 방식의 국가를 형성했다. 유럽의 낡은 왕국군을 격파한 국민개병(levée-en-masse)은 주권국가의 기초로서 완전한 국가 통합이 최초로 표현된 사례이다. 인간과 국가가 동등한 자결권을 갖춘 것이다. 인간은 자신이 속한 국가 공동체가 자유롭지 않다면 그 또한 자유로울 수 없는 것이다.

동일한 혁명을 통해 반대의 경우는 사실이 아닐 수 있음이 빠르게 증명되었다. 국가는 자국민을 노예화하면서 다른 국가와의 거래에 있어 제약을 전혀 받지 않을 수 있다. 사실 국가를 과도하게 예찬할 경우 개인의 권리를 불가피하게 소멸시킬 수 있다. 시민은 국가가 의지를 표현하는 도구가 될 수 있다. 하지만 혁명의 열정이 최초로 폭발했을 때, 인간의 권리와 국가의 권리(Rights of the Nation)에 대한 생각은 서로 어우러졌다. 그리고 이 두 권리는 공식적으로는 현재에도 그러한 위치에 있다.

---

18 다음 중 괄호 (A) 안에 가장 알맞은 것은 무엇인가?

① 둘 다 상호 보완적일 수 있다
② 반대의 경우는 사실일 수도 있다
③ 둘 다 완전히 모순될 수 있다
④ 반대의 경우는 사실이 아닐 수 있다

| 정답 | ④

| 해설 | 우선 빈칸이 들어간 문장에서 the same revolution은 "프랑스 혁명"을 의미한다. 프랑스 혁명이 무엇을 증명했는지가 빈칸에 들어갈 답이다. 빈칸 앞 문장을 보면, 프랑스 혁명의 결과 "인간은 자신이 속한 국가 공동체가 자유롭지 않다면 그 또한 자유로울 수 없음"을 알게 되었다. 즉 국가 공동체의 자유가 개인의 자유로 이어진 것이다. 그런데 빈칸 뒤를 보면 국가가 개인을 억압하고 있음을 알 수 있다. 즉 프랑스 혁명을 통해 국가는 자유를 얻었지만, 개인은 자유를 얻기보다 오히려 억압을 당하게 되었던 것이다. 여기서 ④의 "반대의 경우" '개인이 자유롭지 않다면 국가 또한 자유로울 수 없다'는 사실이 아닐 수 있음을 말하는 것임을 알 수 있다. 따라서 답은 ④이다.

---

19 다음 중 본문의 핵심어는 무엇인가?

① 개인주의와 국가주의
② 개인의 권리와 국가의 번영
③ 혁명과 자유 시민
④ 주권국가와 국가주의

| 정답 | ①

| 해설 | 첫 번째 단락의 미국 독립 혁명은 스스로를 통치할 권리를 가진 개인의 등장을 상징하며 이는 개인주의와 관련이 있다. 두 번째 단락의 프랑스 혁명은 주권국가의 기초로서의 완전한 국가 통합 즉 국가주의의 등장과 관련이 있다. 그리고 마지막 단락은 국가의 권리와 개인의 권리가 서로 공존하고 있음을 말하고 있다. 즉 본문은 개인주의와 국가주의의 등장 및 그 공존에 관해 말하고 있다. 따라서 답은 ①이다.

20 다음 중 괄호 (B) 안에 가장 알맞은 것은 무엇인가?

① where

② what

③ which

④ that

| 정답 | ①

| 해설 | 우선 빈칸 뒤를 보면 동사가 자동사인 remain이므로 빈칸 뒤 생략된 부분은 없음을 알 수 있다. 따라서 빈칸에는 관계부사가 와야 한다. they는 빈칸 앞 문장의 인간의 권리(Rights of Man)와 국가의 권리(Rights of the Nation)를 가리키고, 이 둘이 과거에 서로 어우러졌고(went together), 지금도 계속 그러한 위치에 있음(remain)을 알 수 있다. 여기서 그런 위치에 계속 있다는 의미에서 장소를 의미하는 관계부사 where가 와야 문맥상 무리가 없다. 따라서 답은 ①이다.

| 어휘 | **symbolize** ⓥ 상징하다

nationalism ⓝ 국민주의, 국가주의

proposition ⓝ 명제; (처리해야 할) 문제[과제]

proclaim ⓥ 선언하다, 선포하다

sovereign state 주권국가

unfettered ⓐ 제한받지 않는, 제약 없는

enslave ⓥ 노예화하다, 노예로 만들다

inevitably ⓐ 불가피하게, 필연적으로

ardour ⓝ 열정

contradictory ⓐ 모순되는

govern ⓥ 지배하다, 통치하다

dedicated to ~에 헌신하는

identification ⓝ (존재·중요성 등의) 인지[발견]

dynastic ⓐ 왕조의, 왕가의

self-determination ⓝ 자결권, 자결 능력

dealing ⓝ 거래

glorification ⓝ 예찬, 찬송

extinction ⓝ 소멸

complementary ⓐ 보완적인

prosperity ⓝ 번영, 번창

연습 문제	**01** ① **02** ① **03** ④

01 밑줄 친 부분의 의미는 무엇인가?

나이 든 두 부부가 친근한 대화를 즐기던 와중에 남편 중 한쪽이 다른 남편에게 물었다. "Fred, 지난달 자네가 다녀온 기억 장애 치료소는 어땠나?" Fred는 "끝내줬지"라고 답했다. "그들은 내게 구상화, 연상 등과 같은 모든 심리학적 테크닉을 알려 줬네. 그건 내게 큰 변화를 가져다줬지." "그거 대단하군! 그 치료소의 이름이 뭐지?" Fred는 멍해져서 아무것도 기억하지 못했다. 그는 생각하고 또 생각했지만 이름을 떠올릴 수 없었다. 그러다가 얼굴에 미소를 머금으면서 "긴 줄기에 가시가 달린 꽃을 뭐라 부르지?"라고 물었다. "장미(rose)를 말하는 건가?" "그래 바로 그거야!" 그러고 나서 Fred는 부인을 돌아보면서 "Rose, 그 치료소 이름이 뭐였지?"라고 물었다.

① 그는 그 치료소의 이름을 부인에게 물을 예정이었다.
② 그는 그 치료소의 이름이 꽃과 연상됨을 깨달았다.
③ 그는 기억 장애 치료소에게 도움을 요청할 예정이었다.
④ 그는 Rose가 그 치료소의 이름임을 깨달았다.

| 정답 | ①

| 해설 | Fred는 방법이 생각난 듯 미소를 지은 후에, 장미(Rose)가 어떻게 생긴 꽃인지 친구에게 물었다. 친구는 Rose가 치료소의 이름인가 생각했지만, 사실 Fred는 부인인 Rose의 이름이 기억이 나지 않아서 친구에게 물은 것이었다. Rose란 이름을 듣고 나서 부인에게 치료소의 이름을 물은 것으로 봐서 Fred는 치료소의 이름을 부인에게 물어야겠다는 생각이 나서 미소를 지은 것임을 유추할 수 있다. 따라서 답은 ①이다.

| 어휘 | **memory clinic** 기억 장애 치료소　　　　　**visualization** ⓝ 구상화, 시각화
association ⓝ 연상　　　　　　　　　　　**go blank** 멍해지다, 아무 기억이 안 나다

02 본문의 "what was underneath"에 해당하는 것은 무엇인가? 인하대 2016

미사여구는 말의 설득력을 높여 준다. 미사여구는 당신이 무슨 말을 하든 다른 이들의 동의와 감탄을 이끌어내는 갖가지 수단으로서 이용된다. 당신은 말을 통해 힘을 얻을 수 있다. 미사여구는 음식 위에 소스와 향신료를 수북이 담아 그 아래에 있는 것을 감추는 옛날 방식의 요리 같은 식사가 되었다. 사람들이 미사여구를 즐기는 이유는 매료당하는 것을 즐기기 때문이며 이들은 자신들이 아름다움이라 생각한 것의 노예가 되었다. 논쟁에 승리하는 것은 진실을 발견하는 것을 대신하게 되었다. 다른 이들에게 동의하도록 강요하는 것이 자부심의 근원이 되었다. 미사여구는 수많은 사람들을 예속시키는 전쟁 무기가 되었다.

① 진실　　　　　② 말　　　　　③ 아름다움　　　　　④ 미사여구　　　　　⑤ 갖가지 수단

| 정답 | ①

| 해설 | 우선 미사여구는 "당신이 무슨 말을 하든 다른 이들의 동의와 감탄을 이끌어 내는 갖가지 수단(a bag of tricks which got others to agree and to admire, whatever you said)"인데, 이 "당신이 무슨 말을 하든"에서 미사여

구는 당신의 '실제 의도'를 감추고 더 좋게 보이게 하기 위해 포장하는 수단임을 알 수 있다. 이를 요리에 비유하면 "소스와 향신료(sauce and spice)"라 할 수 있다. 소스와 향신료는 부정적 관점에서 보면 '요리의 본래 맛'을 가려 버려서 먹는 사람이 실제 맛을 느끼지 못하게 만든다. 여기서 미사여구는 '실제 의도'를 감추고 '본래 맛'을 가리는 것, 즉 사람들이 "진실"을 인식하지 못하게 막는 것임을 알 수 있다. 그리고 소스와 향신료에 가려진 "그 아래에 있는 것(what was underneath)" 또한 "진실"에 해당되는 것임을 유추할 수 있다. 따라서 답은 ①이다.

| 어휘 |　**correspond to** ~에 해당하다, ~에 일치하다　　　　**rhetoric** ⓝ 미사여구, 수사법[학]

　　　　persuasive ⓐ 설득력 있는　　　　　　　　　　**bag of tricks** 갖가지 수단[방법], 모두

　　　　diet ⓝ 식사, 음식　　　　　　　　　　　　　　**heap** ⓥ 쌓아 올리다[수북이 담다]

　　　　conceal ⓥ 감추다, 숨기다　　　　　　　　　　**charm** ⓥ 매혹[매료]하다

　　　　substitute ⓝ 대용물[품], 대체물　　　　　　　**self-esteem** ⓝ 자부심

　　　　subjugate ⓥ 예속시키다, 지배하에 두다

03　**다음 글에서 밑줄 친 문장이 뜻하는 것을 고르시오.**

> 세계 인구가 급격히 늘어나고 있지만, 모든 지역에서 같은 비율로 늘어나고 있는 것은 아니다. 상대적으로 더 부유하고, 보다 선진화된 국가들은 감소 추세의 출산율을 보이는 경향이 있는 반면, 개발 도상국들은 여전히 기하급수적으로 출산율이 증가하고 있는 경향을 보이고 있다. 이 같은 차이가 나는 이유는 선진국의 교육 수준이 높은 여성들이 더 이상 이전과 같이 많은 아이를 갖기 원하지 않기 때문이다. 이들은 또한 가정에서 아이들을 양육하는 대신 일하기를 희망한다. 개발 도상국에서는, 부족한 교육과 산아 제한의 지식 부족으로 아직도 많은 아이들을 출산하고 있다. 결과적으로 이에 따른 문제는 보다 많은 이들이 보다 적은 자원을 두고 경쟁하고 있다는 사실이다. 선진국의 경우 또한 감소 추세의 출산율이 문제가 되고 있다. 노령 인구가 늘어나고 노동력이 줄어드는 가운데, 경제학자들은 종국에 가서는 노인들을 돌볼 젊은 노동자들이 충분하지 않게 될 것이라고 예측한다. <u>이와 같은 경향에 미국이 유일한 예외이다.</u>

① 미국의 인구는 급격하게 늘고 있지 않지만, 개발 도상국들과 같은 비율로 증가하고 있다.
② 미국의 인구는 다른 선진국들과는 달리 출산율이 감소하는 경향이 있다.
③ 미국의 교육 수준이 높은 여성들은 계속 일하면서 많은 아이들을 키우기 원한다.
④ 미국은 노인들을 부양할 많은 수의 젊은 노동자들이 있을 것이다.
⑤ 미국은 다른 선진국과 개발 도상국 국가들과 보다 적은 자원을 두고 경쟁하지 않을 것이다.

| 정답 |　④

| 해설 |　바로 앞의 내용에 대해 미국은 예외라는 내용이므로 앞의 내용을 주목해야 한다. 개발 도상국이 아닌 선진국의 인구 감소에 따른 미래의 문제에 대해 말하고 있으며, 노인들을 부양할 젊은이들의 수가 부족하다는 내용이므로 정답은 ④가 된다.

| 어휘 |　**at the same rate** 같은 비율로　　　　　　　　**developed countries** 선진국

　　　　developing countries 개발 도상국　　　　　　**declining** ⓐ 줄어드는, 감소 추세의

　　　　exponentially ⓐⓓ 기하급수적으로, 급격히　　　**no longer** 더 이상 ~하지 않다

　　　　inadequate ⓐ 충분하지 않은　　　　　　　　**birth control** 산아 제한, 피임

　　　　exception ⓝ 예외

01	①	02	③	03	①	04	③	05	④	06	③	07	④	08	①	09	①	10	①
11	④	12	④	13	③	14	④	15	②	16	①	17	④	18	④	19	③	20	③

[01~03]

해석

프랑스의 유명 철학자인 드니 디드로(Denis Diderot)는 거의 평생을 가난 속에 살았지만 1765년에 이 모든 상황이 바뀌게 되었다. 당시 디드로는 52세였고 딸이 결혼을 앞두고 있었지만, 디드로에게는 지참금을 마련할 금전적 형편이 안 됐다. 러시아의 여제 예카테리나 2세(Catherine the Great)는 디드로가 재정적 어려움을 겪고 있다는 소식을 듣자 큰돈을 주고 디드로에게서 그의 장서를 사 들이겠다고 제안했다. 디드로에게는 갑작스럽게 여윳돈이 생겼다. 이렇게 운 좋게 장서를 판매한 지 얼마 지나지 않아, 디드로는 진홍색 가운을 새로 구했다. 그 진홍색 가운이 너무나 아름다웠던 나머지 디드로는 그 진홍색 가운이 자신의 평범한 나머지 소지품에 둘러싸인 생태에서 보면 너무나 어울리지 않는다는 사실을 곧바로 깨닫게 되었다. 디드로는 곧바로 가운의 아름다움에 걸맞은 새로운 물건을 구매해야겠다는 충동이 들었다. 디드로는 오래된 융단을 다마스쿠스에서 수입된 새 융단으로 교체했다. 디드로는 집을 아름다운 조각품과 더 좋은 식탁으로 꾸몄다. 이처럼 반응에 따른 구매 행위는 디드로 효과(Diderot Effect)로 알려지게 되었다. 디드로 효과는 새로운 소지품의 구입이 새로운 것을 더 많이 구매하게 되는 소비의 악순환을 낳는 일이 종종 있음을 말한다. 그 결과 우리는 과거의 우리가 행복함이나 충족감을 느끼기 위해, 필요하지 않았던 것들을 결국 구매하고 마는 것이다.

---

01 다음 중 본문의 제목으로 가장 알맞은 것은 무엇인가?

① 디드로 효과 : 우리는 왜 필요 없는 것을 사는가
② 디드로의 기발한 재주: 우리는 가난을 어떻게 극복하는가
③ 디드로의 프라이버시 : 알려지지 않은 사실
④ 디드로의 이중생활 : 가난하면서도 사치스러운 인간

| 정답 | ①

| 해설 | 본문은 물건의 구입이 별 쓸모없는 다른 물건의 연속적인 구입으로 이어지는 "디드로 효과"에 관해 말하고 있다. 따라서 답은 ①이다.

---

02 다음 중 빈칸 ⑧ 에 가장 알맞은 것은 무엇인가?

① 초점이 벗어난   ② 비수기의
③ 어울리지 않은   ④ 불가능한

| 정답 | ③

| 해설 | 빈칸 앞을 보면 새로 구입한 진홍색 가운은 매우 아름답고, 빈칸 뒤를 보면 집의 나머지 물건은 평범함을 알 수 있다. 집 안에 진홍색 가운을 둘 경우, 나머지 물건과 비교해 진홍색 가운은 "어울리지 않을" 것이다. 따라서 답은 ③이다.

03 다음 중 ⑧와 의미상 가장 가까운 것은 무엇인가?

① 결국 물건을 사게 되었다
② 단호히 물건 구매를 중지하다
③ 무심결에 물건 구매를 연기하다
④ 물건 구매를 항상 주저하다

| 정답 | ①

| 해설 | ⑧는 해석하면 "결국 구매하고 만다"란 의미를 갖는다. 이는 보기 ①의 의미와 일치한다.

| 어휘 | **dowry** ⓝ 지참금 **money to spare** 여윳돈
scarlet ⓝ 진홍색 **out of place** 어울리지 않는, 부적절한
possession ⓝ 소지품 **reactive** ⓐ 반응[반작용]을 보이는
spiral ⓝ 연쇄적 변동, 악순환 **end up** 결국 ～하게 되다
ingenuity ⓝ 기발한 재주, 재간 **out of the question** 불가능한
decisively ⓐⓓ 단호히, 결정적으로 **unconsciously** ⓐⓓ 무의식적으로; 무심결에
suspend ⓥ 연기하다, 유예하다 **hesitate** ⓥ 주저하다, 망설이다

[04~05] 성균관대 2017

해석

고양이들이 하는 모든 행동은 조금은 이기적이고, 약간은 자기중심적이라는 인식이 보편적으로 자리 잡고 있다. 하지만 근거 없는 고정관념에 만족할 수 없는 우리는 독자 포럼에 "고양이들은 이기적인가?"라는 짧은 질문을 올렸다.

몇몇 사람들은 이런 질문 자체를 좋아하지 않았다. "이기심은 인간의 특성이다"고 Ann Halim은 주장했다. "'이기적'이라는 단어는 인간을 제외한 다른 동물들에게는 적용하기 어렵다"고 Kevin Bonin은 동의했다. 확실히 어려운 질문이긴 하지만, 그래도 우리는 질문을 포기하지 않았다. 찰스 다윈은 1871년 자신의 저서인 인간의 유래(The Descent of Man)에서 동물의 마음이 여러 면에서 우리의 마음과 유사하다고 주장했다. "인간과 고등 동물 간 마음의 차이는 분명 정도의 차이이지 종류의 차이는 아니다."라고 서술한 바 있다. 만약 그것이 사실이라면, 당연히 고양이 또는 다른 고등 동물도 이기적이라는 정의를 충족할 수 있을 것이다.

많은 이들이 고양이들은 자신만 생각한다는 견해에 공감을 표했다. "고양이는 이기적인가? 그것은 마치 교황은 발코니를 가지고 있는가라고 질문하는 것과 같다."라고 Jane Ramsden은 말한다. "고양이라는 단어 안에는 당연히 I가 들어 있다."라고 Dan Oken은 말한다.

04 다음 중 빈칸에 올 수 있는 가장 적합한 것은?

① 자신의 기질을 더 나은 상태로 진화시키다
② 고정관념에 대한 일반적인 생각을 부인하다
③ 이기적이라는 정의를 충족하다
④ 인간 특성의 범주로 확인되지 않는다
⑤ 다른 이들에게 이타적인 행동을 한다

| 정답 | ③

| 해설 | 앞서 다윈은 '동물의 마음과 인간의 마음은 비슷하다'고 말했으므로, 다윈의 견해에 따라 고양이라는 동물도 인간의 이기적인 마음과 비슷한 것을 소유하고 있을 것으로 추정할 수 있다. 따라서 고양이도 이기적이라는 내용이 와야 하므로, '이기적이라는 정의를 충족'한다는 ③이 정답이 된다.

---

05 다음 중 밑줄 친 "그것은 마치 교황은 발코니를 가지고 있는가라고 질문하는 것과 같다."가 의미하는 것은?

① 그것은 정말 터무니없는 말이다!
② 그것은 내가 상관할 일이 아니다!
③ 누가 알겠는가?(아무도 모른다)
④ 분명히 그럴 것이다!
⑤ 누가 그랬지?

| 정답 | ④

| 해설 | 마지막 문단의 첫 문장인 "Many of you identified with the idea that cats are out for themselves."를 통해 '고양이가 이기적이라고 많은 사람들이 생각한다'는 내용의 예시로 두 명이 말하는 내용 중 하나에 해당한다. 따라서 '교황이 사는 곳에도 발코니가 있을까'라는 질문은 너무도 당연한 질문이 되므로, "분명히 그럴 것이다!"라는 ④가 정답이 된다.

| 어휘 |

perception ⑪ 인지, 지각, 이해	self-serving ⓐ 자기 잇속만 차리는, 이기적인
a touch 약간, 조금	self-centered ⓐ 자기중심적인, 이기적인
be content with ~에 만족하다	idle ⓐ 무의미한, 무가치한; 이유[근거]가 없는
stereotype ⑪ 고정관념, 정형화된 생각, 틀에 박힌 문구	selfish ⓐ 이기적인
trait ⑪ 특징, 특성	descent ⑪ 가계, 혈통; 하강
identify with ~와 동일시하다, 동질감을 갖다	be out for oneself 자기 일만 생각하고 있다
temperament ⑪ 기질, 성질, 성미	confirm ⓥ 확인하다, 확증하다
altruistic ⓐ 이타주의의	none of my business 내가 상관할 일이 아니다

[06~08] 한국외대 2011

해석

Denver의 Stapleton 공항이 폐쇄되기 직전 며칠 사이에, 승객으로 가득 찬 United 항공사 한 편이 결항된 적이 있었다. 공항 직원 한 사람만이 한 줄로 길게 늘어서서 불편함을 겪던 여행객들의 항공권을 재예약해 주던 중이었다. 갑자기 분노한 승객 한 사람이 데스크로 사람들을 밀치며 와서는 항공권을 카운터에 내던지고 나서 "난 무조건 이 비행기 탈 거니까 그렇게 알고 무조건 1등석으로 내놔"라고 말했다. 직원은 "죄송합니다 고객님. 정말 도와드리고 싶지만 여기 먼저 계신 분들을 우선 도와드려야 합니다. 그리고 나서 고객님의 문제를 해결해 드리겠습니다"라고 답했다. 그 승객은 그러한 답변에 화가 났다. 그는 <u>"내가 누군지는 알고 하는 소리야?"</u>라고 뒤에 있는 승객들이 들을 수 있을 정도로 큰 소리를 지르며 물었다. 주저하는 기색 없이 게이트 직원은 미소 지으면서 공항 안내 방송용 마이크를 집어 들었다. 그녀는 "승객 여러분 잠시만 주목해 주시기 바랍니다"라면서 방송을 시작했고, 그녀의 목소리가 터미널 전체에 울려 퍼졌다. <u>"여기 게이트에 자신이 누군지 모르시는 승객분께서 와 계십니다. 혹시 이 승객분이 자신의 신원을 파악하는 데 도움을 주실 수 있는 분이 계시다면 게이트로 와 주시기 바랍니다."</u> 그 화난 승객 뒤에 줄 서 있던 사람들은 모두 미친 듯이 웃었다.

06 화난 승객이 ㉮라고 말한 가장 그럴 듯한 이유는 무엇인가?

① 그가 자신의 신원을 알고 싶었기 때문이다.
② 그가 자기 뒤의 승객들을 즐겁게 해 주고 싶었기 때문이다.
③ 그가 게이트 직원을 위협하고 싶었기 때문이다.
④ 그가 자기 뒤의 승객들을 화나게 하고 싶었기 때문이다.

| 정답 | ③

| 해설 | ㉮를 직역하면 '너는 내가 누군지 전혀 모르는가?'인데, 그 승객은 자신이 누군지 몰라서 직원에게 ㉮처럼 물은 것이 아니다. 실제로는 '너 내가 누군지나 알고 이런 식으로 날 대하는 거냐?'라고 직원을 겁주기 위해 한 말이다. 따라서 답은 ③이다.

07 게이트 직원이 ㉯라고 말한 가장 그럴듯한 이유는 무엇인가?

① 그녀는 그 화난 승객을 웃기고 싶었기 때문이다.
② 그녀는 그 화난 승객의 이름을 알고 싶었기 때문이다.
③ 그녀는 그 화난 승객이 자신의 신원을 알도록 돕고 싶었기 때문이다.
④ 그녀는 그 화난 승객을 놀리고 싶었기 때문이다.

| 정답 | ④

| 해설 | 화난 승객은 '너 내가 누군지나 알고 이런 식으로 날 대하는 거냐?'라는 의미로 직원에게 말을 내뱉었는데, 직원은 능청스럽게 승객이 '나는 나 자신이 누군지 모르겠다. 너는 내가 누군지 전혀 모르는가?'라고 자신에게 물은 것처럼 '여러분 여기 자기가 누군지 모르는 분이 오셨습니다'라고 전체 방송을 해 진상 승객의 무리한 요구에 대응했다. 그리고 이런 직원의 행동에 다른 승객들은 웃음으로 화답했다. 따라서 직원의 의도는 화난 승객을 놀리기 위한 것이었음을 알 수 있으며 ④가 답이 된다.

08 다음 중 본문의 특징을 가장 잘 나타낸 것은 무엇인가?

① 재미있는 ② 슬픈 ③ 유익한 ④ 단조로운

| 정답 | ①

| 해설 | 본문 마지막의 사람들의 반응을 봐도 그렇고, 본문이 말의 미묘한 뉘앙스를 소재로 웃음을 주는 글이기 때문에 답은 ①임을 알 수 있다.

| 어휘 | **rebook** ⓥ 재예약하다
work out (문제를) 해결하다
public address 장내 방송
identity ⓝ 신원, 정체
intimidate ⓥ 겁을 주다, 위협하다

slap ⓥ (화가 나서) 툭 내던지다
unimpressed ⓐ ~에 감명받지 않는, ~에 화난
bellow ⓥ 큰 소리를 내다, 크게 울리다
utter ⓥ 말을 하다

해석

자동화는 점차적으로 유능해지고 있다. 자동화 시스템은 적절한 기온을 유지하거나, 앞 차와 올바른 거리를 유지하면서 할당된 차선을 벗어나지 않고 자동적으로 차량을 운전하거나, 항공기가 이륙에서 착륙까지 저절로 비행할 수 있도록 하거나, 선박이 저절로 항해할 수 있도록 하는 등 과거 인간들이 행한 업무를 대체하고 있다. 자동화가 이루어지는 중에는 사람들이 할 때만큼의 성과가 나오거나 사람들이 할 때보다 더 좋은 성과가 나온다. 게다가 자동화는 사람들이 지루하고 따분한 판에 박힌 일들을 하지 않아도 되게 해 주며 이를 통해 시간을 좀 더 유용하게 생산적으로 활용할 수 있게 해 주고 피로와 실수를 줄여 준다. 하지만 업무가 너무 복잡해질 경우 자동화가 제대로 되지 않는 경향이 있다. 여기서 자동화는 지루하고 따분한 업무를 대체할 수는 있어도 복잡한 업무를 대체할 수는 없다는 모순이 생겨난다. 자동화가 실패할 경우, 종종 사전 경고 없이 그런 현상이 발생할 때도 있다. 자동화의 실패가 벌어질 당시 "인간은 자동화로 인해 전체적인 상황으로부터 벗어나 제대로 된 상황 파악을 못하는 상황이다." 이는 즉 인간이 업무 진행 상황에 제대로 관심을 기울이지 않고 있다 보니 실패했음을 알아채고 평가하는 데 시간이 걸리고 따라서 대응 방법을 결정하는 데에도 시간이 걸리게 된다는 의미이다.

09 윗글의 제목으로 가장 알맞은 것은 무엇인가?

① 자동화의 모순 ② 자동화의 효율성 향상

③ 자동화의 순서 ④ 자동화의 실패에 대처하는 방법

| 정답 | ①

| 해설 | 본문은 자동화의 장점에 관해 언급한 후, 자동화가 지루한 일은 할 수 있을지 모르나 인간이 기계를 통해 맡겨 버리고 싶어 하는 복잡한 일은 오히려 하지 못하고 오류에 직면할 수도 있음을 말하고 있다. 즉 자동화의 모순된 점을 말하고 있는 것이다. 따라서 답은 ①이다.

10 자동화의 실패에 있어 "the human is out of the loop"라는 문구는 다음의 의미를 지닌다.

① 매우 숙련된 운전자도 사고를 피하려면 몇 분의 일 초밖에 시간이 없을 것이다.

② 잘 훈련된 조종사는 자동화 실패를 즉각 알아채고 상황에 대처할 수 있다.

③ 범지구위치결정시스템(GPS)의 도움 없이도, 유람선에서는 수동으로 위치 파악을 할 수 있다.

④ 우리는 속도와 이동 방향을 근거로 배의 위치를 파악할 수 있다. 비록 항해의 경우 해당 측정값이 정확하지는 않더라도 말이다.

| 정답 | ①

| 해설 | out of the loop는 "잘 모르는, 배제된, 소외된" 등의 의미를 가지며, 문맥상 자동화가 진행된 상태에서 오류가 발생하면 인간은 기계에 모든 것을 맡겨 놓은 상태에서 상황을 제대로 파악 못하고, 배제되고, 소외된 처지에 놓여 있게 됨을 의미한다. 그리고 이 문구 뒤를 보면 "이는 즉 인간이 업무 진행 상황에 제대로 관심을 기울이지 않고 있다 보니 실패했음을 알아채고 평가하는 데 시간이 걸리고 따라서 대응 방법을 결정하는 데에도 시간이 걸리게 된다는 의미이다(This means that the person has not been paying much attention to the operation, and it takes time for the failure to be noticed and evaluated, and then to decide how to respond)"라고 해설이 되어 있고, 여기는 '제대로 상황 파악을 못하고 있다가 대응에 시간이 걸린다'는 점이 강조된다. 보기 중에서 문제에 제대로 대응할 시간이 없다는 취지로 작성된 것은 ①이며, 따라서 답은 ①이다.

11 윗글에서 유추할 수 있는 것은 무엇인가?

① 엄청나게 복잡한 문제를 상당히 많이 안고 있을 경우, 자동화된 기계를 갖추고 있으며 점차적으로 네트워크화가 이루어 지는 발전 시스템의 필요성을 깨닫게 될 것이다.

② 소규모 점검 및 모의 실험은 실제 시스템 장애의 특징이라 할 수 있는 복잡성과 예측할 수 없는 사건 발생을 감소시킬 수 있다.

③ 주요 자동차 공급업체들은 운전자가 얼마나 잘 대응할 수 있을지를 시험하기 위해 최종 생산물에다 의도적으로 오류를 발생시킬 필요가 있다.

④ 공장 및 항공 분야의 자동화는 업무가 단순할 경우 효율성을 높이면서 실수를 범할 비율을 낮춰 준다.

| 정답 | ④

| 해설 | "자동화가 이루어지는 중에는 사람들이 할 때만큼의 성과가 나오거나 사람들이 할 때보다 더 좋은 성과가 나온다. 게다가 자동화는 사람들이 지루하고 따분한 판에 박힌 일들을 하지 않아도 되게 해 주며 이를 통해 시간을 좀 더 유용하게 생산적으로 활용할 수 있게 해 주고 피로와 실수를 줄여 준다(When the automation works, the tasks are usually done as well as or better than by people. Moreover, it saves people from the dull, dreary routine tasks, allowing more useful, productive use of time, reducing fatigue and error)." 여기서 자동화를 통해 효율을 높이고 오류를 줄일 수 있음을 알 수 있다. 보기 중에서 이러한 내용과 뜻이 통하는 것은 ④이다.

| 어휘 | **take over** 인계받다, 대체하다

lane ⓝ 차선

landing ⓝ 착륙

save ⓥ 피하게[~하지 않아도 되게] 하다

routine ⓐ 판에 박힌, 지루한

sequence ⓝ 순서, 차례

fraction ⓝ 일부, 분수

manual ⓐ 수동의

substantial ⓐ 상당한

characterize ⓥ 특징이 되다, 특징짓다

aviation ⓝ 항공(술)

assign ⓥ 할당하다

takeoff ⓝ 이륙

navigate ⓥ 항해하다

dreary ⓐ 음울한, 따분한

out of the loop 잘 모르는, 배제된, 소외된

expert ⓐ 전문적인, 숙련된

global positioning system 범지구위치결정시스템(GPS)

cruise ship 유람선

necessity ⓝ 필요(성)

intentional ⓐ 의도적인, 고의로

해석

위기로 몸살을 앓고 있는 미 항공 산업에 대한 얼마 되지 않는 좋은 소식 중에 하나는 미 정부가 상업용 비행기 조종사의 의무 은퇴 연령을 마침내 60세에서 65세로 올렸다는 것이다. 사실상 거의 대부분의 국가들이 이 문제에 대해 우리보다 선수를 쳤다. 지난달 대통령이 서명한 특별 법안을 의회가 제정하지 않았었다면, 이들의 은퇴 연령은 한동안 60세에 머물러 있게 됐을 것이다.

이는 도의적 측면에서나 실용적 측면에서 올바른 조처라고 할 수 있다. 항공기 조종사들이 부족한 상황에서, 이들처럼 숙련된 인력을 은퇴하도록 강요하는 상황이 계속되는 것은 위험하기 짝이 없는 변덕스런 조치이다. 해마다 60세에 이르는 비행사는 대략 3,000명으로, 이제 그중 절반 이상이 빈번한 신체검사와 정기 비행 시험을 통과하는 한 계속 남아 있을 것으로 예상된다. 하지만 이 부분에 대해 의회가 할 일이 한 가지 더 있다. 그것은 바로 이 법안이 제정되기 전에 60세가 됐지만 아직 65세는 넘지 않은 조종사들을 위한 대안을 도출하는 것이다. 현재로서는 이들이 복직을 원할 경우, 이들의 하던 일이나 근속 연수를 다시 찾을 수 없다. 현 규정대로라면 이들은 노련한 베테랑 조종사가 아니라 갓 들어온 신참으로 취급받게 된다. 그들 중 다수가 국내 항공사 대신 외국 항공사와 계약을 하고 있는 점은 놀라운 일이 아니다. 이들이 주요 시험들을 통과할 수 있다면, 근속 연수를 유지하면서 이들이 우리 항공업계를 위해 일하게 하는 것이 맞지 않을까?

---

12 빈칸 ⓐ에 가장 알맞은 것은?

① remained
② have remained
③ will remain
④ would have remained

| 정답 | ④

| 해설 | if절이 "if Congress hadn't enacted special legislation"와 같이 'had+p.p.'로 가정법 과거 시제로 사용되었으므로 주절의 시제도 'would/could/might have+p.p.'가 되어야 하므로 정답은 ④가 된다.

---

13 밑줄 친 ⓑ these individuals가 가리키는 것은?

① 60세에 퇴직한 조종사들로, 현재 새로 들어온 조종사들을 훈련하고 있는 이들
② 신체검사와 비행 시험을 통과했으며 현재 65세 이상인 조종사들
③ 법안이 제정되기 전에 60세가 지났지만 아직 65세가 되지 않은 조종사들
④ 60세가 되었지만 퇴직 규정에 동의한다는 서명하길 원하지 않은 조종사들

| 정답 | ③

| 해설 | 앞 문장에서 "those pilots who turned 60 before this legislation was enacted and are not yet 65"라고 한 이들을 지칭한다. 새로 생긴 법안의 혜택을 받을 수 없는 사람들로, 이미 퇴직을 해 버렸기 때문에 조종사가 되려면 새로 들어와야 해서 지금까지의 근속 연수를 우대받을 수 없는 조종사들을 말한다.

14 빈칸 ⓒ와 ⓓ에 가장 알맞은 것은?

	ⓒ	ⓓ
①	지방 정부의	– 연방 정부의
②	시골의	– 도시의
③	새로 태어난	– 경험 많은
④	외국의	– 국내의

| 정답 | ④

| 해설 | 바로 앞 문장이 힌트가 되는데 "Under current rules, these individuals would be treated as spanking-new hires instead of the seasoned veterans they are."를 보면 현재 미국의 규정으로는 이미 퇴직한 조종사들의 경우 혜택을 받을 수 없다고 하면서, 빈칸이 들어간 문장과 같이 조종사들이 계약하고 있는 현실이 놀라울 것이 없다고 말하고 있다. 따라서 빈칸에는 지방 정부/연방 정부, 시골/도시 등으로 대조가 적합하지 않다. 모두 미국 내에 포함되기 때문이다. ③은 항공사를 수식하는 형용사로 적합하지 않고 의미상으로도 부적절하다. 따라서 정답은 ④가 되며, 상황이 이렇기에 아까운 인재들이 외국으로 유출되고 있기 때문에 필자는 규정을 바꿔서라도 자국의 항공사에 복무하게 하는 것을 원하고 있다.

15 윗글의 내용과 일치하는 것은?

① 미국을 제외한 세계 모든 나라에서 조종사는 60세에 정년 퇴임한다.
② 60세 이상인 조종사들이 정기 비행 시험을 통과하지 못하는 경우 퇴직해야 한다.
③ 의무 퇴직 연령에 관한 특별법이 아직 논의 중이다.
④ 매년 대략 3,000명에 달하는 노년 조종사들이 신입으로 다시 복귀할 것으로 예상된다.

| 정답 | ②

| 해설 | ①의 경우를 보면, 미국은 항공사 정년이 60세이지만 다른 나라의 경우 "Virtually every other nation in the world beat us to the punch on this"라고 하면서, 이 문제에 대해 다른 나라의 사정이 더 낫다고 표현하고 있으므로 ①은 다른 나라들과 미국 모두 맞지 않는 말이 된다. ③의 경우 특별법이 통과됐다고 나오므로 논의 중이라는 말은 사실과 다르며, ④의 경우 3,000명이라는 숫자는 매년 신참 사원으로 복직할 조종사의 수가 아니라 매년 60세에 이르는 조종사의 수이므로 사실이 아니다. 정답은 ②로 "as long as they continue to pass their frequent physicals and regular piloting exams"를 통해 알 수 있다.

| 어휘 | **crisis-plagued** ⓐ 위기로 몸살을 앓고 있는   **airline industry** 항공 산업

mandatory ⓐ 의무의, 강제적인   **commercial pilot** 상업용 항공기 조종사

virtually ⓐⓓ 사실상

beat somebody to the punch ~보다 먼저 선수를 치다, 먼저 펀치를 먹이다

enact ⓥ (법을) 제정하다   **legislation** ⓝ (의회에서 통과되는) 제정법

for the foreseeable future 예측 가능한 미래에; 가까운 장래에

morally ⓐⓓ 도의적으로, 도덕적으로   **practically** ⓐⓓ 실용적으로

an experienced hand 경험자, 숙련된 사람   **capricious** ⓐ 변덕스러운, 잘 변하는

physical ⓝ 신체검사, 건강 진단   **as things stand** 현 상태로(는), 그대로(는)

reclaim ⓥ 되찾다   **seniority** ⓝ (근무 햇수에 따른) 연공서열

(brand) spanking-new ⓐ 매우 새로운, 구입한 후 아직 한 번도 사용하지 않은

seasoned ⓐ 경험 많은, 노련한   **carrier** ⓝ 항공사

intact ⓐ (하나도 손상되지 않고) 온전한, 전혀 다치지 않은

해석

틸버그대학교의 파올라 아세베도(Paota Acevedo) 교수와 취리히대학교의 스티븐 온게나(Steven Ongena) 교수가 발표한 새로운 논문에 따르면, 정신적 외상을 입은 은행원들의 경우 그들이 이후 업무를 처리하는 방식에 영향을 준다고 말한다. 논문의 두 저자들은 2003년에서 2011년 사이 835건의 은행 강도 사건이 발생한 콜롬비아에서, 강도 사건이 발생한 후 은행 대출이 어떻게 달라졌는지 면밀히 관찰했다. 그들은 대출 담당자들이 무장 강도를 당한 후에 대출을 받고자 하는 사람들을 다르게 대우한다는 것을 확인했다. 대출 규모가 달라지지는 않았지만, 권총 강도 후 첫 90일 동안 승인된 대출의 경우 대출 기간이 70퍼센트 더 늘어났다. 콜롬비아의 평균 대출은 5.4개월 후에 만기가 도래하지만, 이제 갓 금고를 털린 은행의 경우 일반적으로 대출 기간이 8.7개월에 달했다. 이 외에도 정신적 외상을 입은 대출 담당자들은 대부분 더 많은 담보를 요구했지만, 평소보다 약간 낮은 금리를 제공했다. 이런 변화 모두 새로운 고객을 직접 상대해야 할 필요성을 줄여 준다. 대출 기간을 늘려 주는 것은 대출 상환을 위해 만나는 일을 더 먼 미래로 늦춰 준다. 더 많은 담보를 잡는 것은 고객을 철저하게 심사해야 할 필요성을 줄여 준다. 그리고 금리가 낮다는 것은 대출 담당자들이 이율 문제로 서로 실랑이를 벌이는 데 드는 시간을 줄여 준다는 것을 의미한다. 이런 행동이 외상 후 스트레스 장애의 전형적인 증상이다.

16 무장 강도를 당한 후 은행원들은 _____.

① 더 좋은 조건으로 대출을 해 주었다
② 대출 기간을 줄여 주는 경향이 있었다
③ 새로운 고객들에게 대출을 해 주지 않으려고 했다
④ 그 어떤 담보도 요구하지 않았다
⑤ 고객에게 매우 높은 이율을 청구했다

| 정답 | ①

| 해설 | 무장 강도를 당한 후 대출 담당자들은 고객들에게 대출 기간을 늘리고, 더 많은 담보를 요구했으며, 낮은 금리를 적용해 고객과 실랑이를 벌일 가능성을 낮추었다. 따라서 정답은 ①이 되며, 여기서 더 좋은 조건이란 금리를 낮춰 준 것을 의미한다.

17 밑줄 친 표현, 'This behaviour'가 의미하는 것은?

① 고객들에 대한 공격적인 태도
② 고객들에 대한 애매모호한 태도
③ 고객들을 즐겁게 해 주려는 경향
④ 고객들을 피하려고 하는 경향
⑤ 고객들을 불신하는 경향

| 정답 | ④

| 해설 | 밑줄 친 부분은 바로 앞 문장의 낮은 금리 적용으로 "loan officers spend less time haggling"하려고 하는 경향을 말하며, 이는 고객들과의 직접적인 대면을 회피하는 행동이므로 정답은 ④가 된다.

| 어휘 | **trauma** ⓝ 정신적 외상   **heist** ⓝ 강도, 노상강도   **loan officer** 대출 담당 직원
     would-be ⓐ ~할 작정인   **in the aftermath of** ~의 여파로, ~의 결과로
     armed robbery 무장 강도   **stickup** ⓝ 권총 강도   **mature** ⓥ (어음 등이) 만기가 되다

burgle ⓥ 은행이 털리다   collateral ⓝ 담보   in person 직접 일대일로

vet ⓥ 조사[심사]하다, 점검하다   haggle ⓥ (특히 물건값을 두고) 실랑이를 벌이다, 흥정을 하다

[18~20] 광운대 2018

해석

이메일은 비즈니스 업계에서 문서로 주고받는 가장 일반적인 형식의 의사소통이다. 이메일이 비록 업무상 서신 보다 덜 격식을 갖춘 것으로 생각되지만, 그래도 이메일은 어조와 구성 면에서 전문적이어야 하고, 친구나 가족에게 보내는 일상적 메시지와는 상당한 차이가 있다. 하지만 업무상 이메일은 컴퓨터를 이용해 보낸 편지만은 아니다. 이메일만의 형식이 있으며 이것을 이해하는 것은 중요하다. 비즈니스 파트너에게 이메일을 보낼 때 기억해야 할 가장 중요한 사항 중 하나는 간결해야 한다는 것이다. 많은 전문직 종사자들은 온종일 수많은 이메일을 받기 때문에 모든 서신을 꼼꼼히 읽어 볼 시간이 없다. 수신자마다 전송된 이메일 중 어떤 것이 가장 우선순위가 높은지 검토할 수 있기 때문에, 이메일의 제목을 신중하게 선택해야 하고 이를 이용해 이메일을 보낸 목적을 분명히 밝힐 수 있어야 한다. 회사 외부로 전송되는 이메일의 경우, 발신자의 전체 이름과 회사 소속을 포함한 마감 서명이 끝에 위치해야 한다. 대부분의 이메일 프로그램에는 마감 서명을 새로 작성할 것인지 아니면 외부로 전송되는 모든 이메일에 대해 자동으로 마감 서명을 첨부하도록 할 것인지 선택하는 옵션이 제공된다. 또한 '새 메일쓰기' 페이지를 여는 것보다 기존 이메일에 '답장하기' 옵션을 사용하는 것이 바람직한 업무 방식이다. '답장하기'는 수신자에게 흔히 스레드(thread)라고 하는 기존 이메일에 대한 링크와 한 메시지에 대한 답장이 여러 개 쌓이게 될 경우 이를 추적할 수 있는 경로를 제공해 준다. 아니면 전송된 메시지가 길고 특정 항목만 답장을 보낼 필요가 있다면, 수신자는 메시지에서 관련된 부분만 '새 메일 쓰기'에 복사한 후 적절한 답변을 입력하는 것이 좋다.

---

18 글의 내용에 의하면, 업무상 이메일이 간결해야 하는 이유는?

① 이메일이 비즈니스 업계에서 가장 보편적인 문자 커뮤니케이션의 형태이기 때문이다.
② 이메일이 비즈니스 업계에서 여전히 전문적인 의사소통의 수단으로 간주되기 때문이다.
③ 이메일이 특정 방식을 따를 때 컴퓨터가 더 효율적으로 처리할 수 있기 때문이다.
④ 많은 전문직 종사자들이 바쁜 나머지 매일 받는 이메일을 일일이 모두 읽을 수 없기 때문이다.
⑤ 비즈니스 파트너에게 긴 이메일을 작성하는 것이 예의에 맞지 않고 효과적이지도 않기 때문이다.

| 정답 | ④

| 해설 | 이메일이 간결해야 하는 이유 뒤에 오는 "Many professionals receive a multitude of emails throughout the day and often don't have the time to read thoroughly each piece of correspondence." 부분을 통해, ④가 정답임을 알 수 있다.

---

19 밑줄 친 the 'reply' option과 가장 잘 부합하는 것은?

① 기존의 메시지 대신 새로운 메시지에 답변을 보내는 것이 더 좋다.
② 원본 메시지에 대한 링크나 스레드가 보이는 모든 메시지에 답장을 보내는 것이 더 좋다.
③ 답장에 기존 메시지를 포함시키고, 이전 메시지들로 안내해 주는 경로를 포함시키는 것이 좋다.
④ 여러 메시지를 보냈다고 하더라도 수신자에게 하나의 답변만 보내는 것이 더 좋다.
⑤ 원본 메시지가 긴 경우에도 적절한 답변과 함께 모든 원본 메시지를 포함시켜 답변하는 것이 더 좋다.

| 해설 | 밑줄 친 부분 다음 문장인 "The 'reply' gives the recipient a link, commonly called a thread, to the original message, and a path to follow if several replies to one message pile up." 부분을 통해 답장하기 옵션과 스레드를 알 수 있다. 업무상 이메일을 주고받는 경우 매번 새롭게 이메일을 작성하는 것보다 기존 이메일에 답장하기 형식으로 보낼 경우 이전에 주고받은 내용들이 스레드라는 하나의 틀로 묶이기 때문에 업무에 유용하다고 말한다. 따라서 '답장에 기존의 메일과 이전 메일들의 경로가 모두 포함된 것'이라는 ③이 정답이 된다.

---

20 윗글의 내용과 부합하지 <u>않는</u> 것은?

① 업무상 이메일은 친구나 가족에게 보내는 일상적인 이메일에 비해 전문적으로 작성해야 한다.
② 많은 전문가 사이에서 간략한 업무용 이메일이 긴 이메일보다 선호된다.
③ 이메일의 제목이 들어가는 부분에 내용의 우선순위 정도를 표시해야 한다.
④ 마감 서명을 동봉할 때에는 발신자의 이름과 회사명이 명시되어야 한다.
⑤ 수신되는 이메일이 긴 경우 내용 중 관련된 부분만 새 페이지로 회신할 수 있다.

| 정답 | ③

| 해설 | 본문의 "Because the recipient may have to evaluate which incoming messages have the greatest priority, choose the contents of the subject line carefully and use it to give a clear summary of the email's purpose." 에서 이메일 제목을 세심하게 선정해서 이메일을 보낸 목적의 개요가 잘 드러나야 한다고 설명한다. 하지만 ③과는 달리 이메일의 우선순위는 수신인이 판단해야 하는 문제라고 했고, 발신인이 이메일의 우선순위를 지정해서 보내야 한다고 말하지 않았다.

| 어휘 |

formal ⓐ 공식의, 형식적인
tone ⓝ 어조, 말투
casual ⓐ 평상시의; (관계가) 가벼운, 우연한
colleague ⓝ 동료
multitude ⓝ 다수
correspondence ⓝ (남과 주고받는) 서신, 편지
evaluate ⓥ 평가하다
summary ⓝ 요약
affiliation ⓝ 소속
append ⓥ 첨부하다, 첨가하다
email thread 이메일 스레드(하나의 주제에 관해 서로 대화를 나눈 이메일 대화 목록)
pile up 많아지다, 쌓이다
key in (데이터를) 입력하다

business letter 업무용 서신
structure ⓝ 구조, 구성
via ⓟⓡⓔⓟ (어떤 장소를) 경유하여[거쳐]
concise ⓐ 간결한, 간명한
thoroughly ⓐⓓ 철저히
recipient ⓝ 수신자, 수상자, 수용 기관
priority ⓝ 우선순위, 우선권
signature ⓝ 서명; 자신만의 독특한 것, 특징
whereby ⓐⓓ (그것에 의하여) ~하는
practice ⓝ 관행, 관습 ⓥ 시행하다
relevant ⓐ 관련 있는, 적절한; 의의가 있는, 유의미한
appropriate ⓐ 적합한, 적절한

| 연습 문제 | 01 ⑤ 02 ③ 03 ① 04 ② |

01 밑줄 친 표현은 <u>사소한 것들이 끔찍한 말다툼으로 발전할 수 있음</u>을 나타낸다.

> 내가 지금까지 가졌던 최고의 이웃은 이탈리아 음식점이었다. 밤이든 낮이든 즉석에서 라자냐를 먹을 수 있었고, 일요일마다 코인 빨래방에 필요한 잔돈도 구할 수 있었고, 불청객들이나 주차 위반 티켓을 쥔 경찰관들로부터 막아 줄 상주 경비원도 있었다. 비록 음식점에서 에스프레소 기계에 물을 채울 때마다 4층 욕실의 목욕물이 안 나오곤 했지만, 아직도 난 그때 그런 것들이 그립다. 나쁜 이웃은 썩어 가루가 된 목재보다 더 집을 망치지만, 그런 이웃에 대비한 보호 수단은 존재하지 않고, 적절히 조심하며 너무하다 싶을 정도로 기상에만 국한해 대화를 나누는 경우를 제외하면 강제적으로 (나쁜 이웃과) 인접한 상황에서 효과적인 방어벽은 존재하지 않는다. 그리고 진부한 이야기로 에워싼 벽에 자그마한 틈이 생기면 괴롭힘과 격노로 가득한 끔찍한 드라마가 펼쳐진다.

① 아무 반응을 보이지 않으면 이웃을 행복하게 한다.
② 폭력적으로 변하는 것은 적대적 관계를 개선하는 데 도움이 되지 않는다.
③ 같이 영화를 보는 것이 문제를 해결하는 좋은 방법이 될 수 있다.
④ 극단적인 행동을 취하는 사람이 성공한다.
⑤ 사소한 것들이 끔찍한 말다툼으로 악화될 수 있다.

| 정답 | ⑤

| 해설 | 밑줄 친 문장에서 'take ~ to …' 구문은 '…하기 위해서 ~이 필요하다'는 의미이다. 그리고 "진부한 이야기로 에워싼 벽(the wall of platitudes)"이 가리키는 것은 "기상에만 국한된 대화(conversation restricted to matters of meteorology)"임을 유추할 수 있다. 또한 "괴롭힘과 격노로 가득한 끔찍한 드라마(appalling dramas of persecution and passion)"가 펼쳐지기 위해 "자그마한 틈(a tiny bleach)"이 필요하다는 것은, 나쁜 이웃과 날씨 얘기만 하면서 진부한 대화만 하다가 어쩌다 날씨 이외의 별일 아닌 "사소한 것(trivial things)"에 관해 대화를 나눴다가는 말이 씨가 되어 서로 싸우고 나쁜 이웃으로부터 괴롭힘을 받거나 고통을 받을 수 있음을 의미한다. 따라서 답은 ⑤가 된다.

| 어휘 |

change ⓝ 잔돈	**launderette** ⓝ 코인 빨래방	**door-keeper** ⓝ 경비원
gatecrasher ⓝ 불청객	**blight** ⓥ 망치다, 엉망으로 만들다	**dry rot** 썩어 가루가 된 목재
barricade ⓝ 방어벽	**compulsory** ⓐ 강제적인	**intimacy** ⓝ 친밀함, 가까이 지냄
ruthlessly ⓐⓓ 무자비하게	**restricted to** ~로 국한된	**meteorology** ⓝ 기상(학)
breach ⓝ 틈, 구멍	**platitude** ⓝ 진부한 이야기	**unleash** ⓥ 촉발시키다, 불러일으키다
appalling ⓐ 간담을 서늘케 하는, 끔찍한		
persecution ⓝ 박해, 학대, 괴롭힘	**passion** ⓝ 격정, 격노	**sort out** 문제를 해결하다
escalate ⓥ 악화되다, 악화시키다	**prefer A to B** B보다 A를 더 선호한다	
confrontation ⓝ 대립, 대치	**compensation** ⓝ 보상, 보답	**irritating** ⓐ 짜증 나는

02 밑줄 친 "지역 신문에 몇 줄 보도되지도 못했다"가 의미하는 것은?

> 작년 여름 Martin Torres는 텍사스주 오스틴에서 요리사로 일하고 있었다. 8월 23일 오전 그는 친척으로부터 전화 한 통을 받았다. 그의 17살 조카인 Emilio가 살해됐다는 것이었다. 경찰에 따르면 Emilio는 시카고의 South Side의 거리를 걷고 있었는데 누군가 가슴을 쐈고, 아마도 지속되던 분쟁 끝에 나타난 결과일 것이었다. 많은 살해 사건과 마찬가지로 Emilio의 사건은 지역 신문에 몇 줄 보도되지도 못했다. 조카인 Emilio와 무척 가까웠던 Torres는 시카고로 가는 Greyhound 고속버스 첫차를 탔다. 그는 슬퍼하면서 보복을 계획했다. 최근 그는 내게 "기자 선생, 난 내 할 일을 할 거요. 이게 내가 사는 방식이지. 난 사냥을 나섰소. 내 조카는 내 피와 같은 존재라오."

① 짧은 편지를 받았다.　　　　　　　　　② 위로의 말을 조금 들었다.
③ 거의 주목받지 못했다.　　　　　　　　④ 며칠간 수감되었다.
⑤ 편지를 몇 장 써 달라는 부탁을 받았다.

| 정답 | ③

| 해설 | 조카인 'Emilio'의 죽음이 "received just a few sentences(몇 문장밖에 받지 못했다)"는 것은 신문 지상에서 '몇 줄 실리지 못했다'는 의미이고, 이는 '몇 줄 보도되지도 못했다'는 의미가 된다. 결국 신문에서 몇 줄 정도의 단신으로 처리될 만큼 거의 주목받지 못했다는 것이며, 따라서 답은 ③이다.

| 어휘 | **relative** ⓝ 친척　　　　　　　　　　**culmination** ⓝ 어떤 일의 정점 또는 결과
　　　 ongoing ⓐ 지속되는　　　　　　　　**grieve** ⓥ 슬퍼하다
　　　 consolation ⓝ 위안, 위로　　　　　　**be sentenced to** ~의 형을 선고받다
　　　 conspiracy ⓝ 음모　　　　　　　　　**retribution** ⓝ 보복

[03~04]

원래 문장으로부터 재진술하거나 추론할 수 있는 문장들로 구성된 보기를 선택하시오.

03 인간의 유아는 다른 하등 동물과 비교해 태어난 첫 몇 년 동안 독립적 생존에 적합한 능력을 갖추고 있지 않지만, 자라면서 놀라운 기억력을 지닌 뇌 덕분에 다른 동물에 비해 생존에 훨씬 더 능숙한 모습을 보이게 된다.

> Ⓐ 인간의 유아는 처음 태어났을 때 대체로 무기력하다.
> Ⓑ 하등 동물은 생존에 필요한 능력을 갖추어 태어난다.
> Ⓒ 인간은 더 나은 진화 과정의 산물이다.
> Ⓓ 인간의 유아는 최소한의 학습만으로도 삶에 참여할 수 있도록 잘 준비되어 있다.

① Ⓐ & Ⓑ　　　　　　　　② Ⓐ & Ⓓ　　　　　　　　③ Ⓑ & Ⓒ
④ Ⓑ & Ⓓ　　　　　　　　⑤ Ⓐ, Ⓑ & Ⓒ

| 정답 | ①

| 해설 | 다른 동물과 비교해 인간의 유아는 혼자서 생존할 수 없는 '무기력한' 상태로 태어나지만, 자라면서 독자적 생존 능력이 다른 동물에 비해 급격하게 높아 간다는 내용이다. 따라서 Ⓐ는 반드시 포함되어야 하고, Ⓓ는 인간의 유아가 아닌 하등 동물의 새끼에 더 적합한 내용이므로 정답에 포함되어서는 안 된다. 따라서 ①과 ⑤가 남게 되며, Ⓐ와 Ⓑ가 동일

하게 포함되므로, ⓒ를 통해 정답을 도출한다. ⓒ에서 말한 '더 나은 진화 과정의 산물'은 태어나자마자 생존에 적합하게 태어난 하등 동물에 해당하는 내용이므로 정답에서 제외된다. 따라서 정답은 ①이 된다.

| 어휘 | infant ⓝ 유아

compared to ~와 비교하여

thanks to ~ 덕분에[때문에]

helpless ⓐ 무기력한

evolutionary ⓐ 진화의

ill-equipped ⓐ 장비[기술]를 제대로 갖추지 않은

adept ⓐ 숙련된, 정통한 ⓝ 숙련자, 명인

capacity ⓝ 능력, 재능; 수용 능력

ready-made ⓐ 이미 만들어져 나오는, 기성품의

minimum ⓐ 최소의 ⓝ 최소

04 연구에 따르면 공격적 행동은 공격적 행동에 대한 모방과 긍정적 강화의 조합을 통해 획득될 수 있다. 아이들은 실제 혹은 가상의 역할 모델의 공격적 행동을 목격한 이후 공격적 행동에 대한 긍정적 강화를 목격하거나 혹은 공격적 행동에 대한 부정적 강화의 결여에 영향을 받는다.

> Ⓐ 공격성은 학습된 행동으로 볼 수 있다.
> Ⓑ 아이들은 공격성이 부정적으로 강화되는 경우에도 공격성을 배운다.
> ⓒ 가상의 역할 모델의 공격성이 실제의 역할 모델의 공격성보다 더 큰 영향을 미칠 수 있다.
> Ⓓ 아이들은 공격적 행동이 보상을 받거나 처벌받지 않는 것을 보면서 공격적 행동을 배울 수 있다.

① Ⓐ & Ⓑ

② Ⓐ & Ⓓ

③ Ⓑ & ⓒ

④ Ⓑ & Ⓓ

⑤ Ⓐ, ⓒ & Ⓓ

| 정답 | ②

| 해설 | 공격적 행동은 공격적 행동에 대한 모방과 긍정적 강화의 조합을 통해 획득되는(acquired) 것이므로, Ⓐ와 같이 선천적 행위가 아닌 후천적 학습에 의한(learned) 행동이라는 것을 알 수 있다. 또한 아이들은 공격적 행동을 목격한 이후 그 행동이 긍정적 강화를 받거나 혹은 부정적 강화를 별로 받지 않는 것을 보면서 공격적 행동을 배운다고 했으므로, 이 부분은 Ⓓ의 내용에 해당한다. 따라서 Ⓐ와 Ⓓ가 동시에 들어간 ② 혹은 ⑤로 정답을 좁힐 수 있다.

ⓒ의 경우 주어진 지문에는 "실제 혹은 가상의 역할 모델의 공격적 행동"이라고 서술하고 있으므로, 어느 한쪽이 더 큰 영향을 미치는지에 대해서는 알 수 없으므로 ⓒ는 정답에서 제외되어야 한다. 따라서 정답은 ②가 된다.

| 어휘 | aggressive ⓐ 공격적인, 적극적인

positive reinforcement 긍정적 강화

role model 역할 모델, (존경하며 본받고 싶도록) 모범이 되는 사람

aggression ⓝ 공격성

combination ⓝ 조합

fictional ⓐ 허구적인

learned ⓐ 학습된, 후천적인

01	④	02	⑤	03	③	04	①	05	②	06	④	07	③	08	②	09	①	10	④
11	④	12	①	13	②	14	①	15	③	16	④	17	③	18	③	19	④	20	③
21	①	22	④	23	④	24	②	25	①	26	①	27	①	28	②	29	④	30	②

[01~03] 아주대 2016

다음 중 원래 주어진 문장에 대해 재진술되어 있거나 추론 가능한 문장에 해당하는 것을 모두 선택하시오.

01 조증, 정신분열증 및 심한 우울증과 같은 심각한 정신 질환은 일반 인구의 남성보다 감옥에 수감되어 있는 남성에게서 2~3배 더 흔하게 발견된다.

Ⓐ 감옥에 있는 남성 대부분은 심각한 정신 질환에 취약하다.
Ⓑ 심각한 정신 질환을 가진 사람들은 일반인보다 감옥에 더 자주 수감된다.
Ⓒ 특정 정신 질환을 앓고 있는 일반인보다 그런 정신 질환을 앓고 있는 수감자가 더 많다.
Ⓓ 개인의 정신 질환과 수감의 원인이 되는 반사회적 행동 사이에는 직접적인 연관성이 있다.

① Ⓐ & Ⓑ 　　　　　　　　　　② Ⓐ & Ⓒ
③ Ⓑ & Ⓒ 　　　　　　　　　　④ Ⓑ & Ⓓ
⑤ Ⓑ, Ⓒ & Ⓓ

| 정답 | ④

| 해설 | 주어진 문장을 보면 '일반 남성들'보다 '남성 수감자들'이 정신 질환을 가지고 있는 비율이 더 높다는 내용이다. 예를 들어 정신 질환을 가지고 있는 일반 남성의 비율이 10~20퍼센트라고 하면, 남성 수감자의 경우는 30~40퍼센트에 이른다는 말이 된다. Ⓐ의 경우 수감자 대부분이 정신 질환에 취약하다고 서술해서, 일반인과 수감자의 비율에 대한 원문의 내용을 반영하지 못하고 있다. Ⓒ의 경우 얼핏 보면 재진술로 보이지만, Ⓒ에서는 비율(ratio)이 아닌 숫자(number)를 의미하고 있으므로 재진술이나 추론에 해당되지 않게 된다. 정답은 Ⓑ와 Ⓓ로, Ⓑ에서는 정신 질환을 앓고 있는 경우 일반인보다 수감될 확률이 더 높다고 설명하고 있으며, Ⓓ에서는 정신 질환과 수감의 원인(반사회적인 범죄 행위) 사이에 직접적인 연관성이 있다고 설명하고 있으므로, 추론 가능한 내용이 된다.

| 어휘 | **mental disorder** 정신병
schizophrenia ⓝ 정신분열증
the general population 일반 대중
anti-social behavior 반사회적 행위

mania ⓝ 열광, 열중, 조병, 조증
depression ⓝ 우울증, 불경기
be vulnerable to ~에 취약한, 비난받기 쉬운
imprisonment ⓝ 투옥, 감금

02 밤새 시험공부를 하느라 잠을 자지 못한 최악의 경우를 떠올려 보자. 그런 후 최악의 독감에 걸렸던 경우를 떠올려 보라. 이 두 경우가 합쳐지고, 여기에 이런저런 것들이 합쳐진 것이 바로 만성피로증후군 (CFS)이 평소에 어떤 느낌인지를 보여 주는 것이 된다.

Ⓐ 만성피로증후군을 가진 환자들은 수면 부족에 시달린다.
Ⓑ 만성피로증후군을 겪는 것은 독감에 걸리는 것보다 훨씬 더 나쁘다.
Ⓒ 만성피로증후군은 일반적으로 독감의 특징적인 증상을 수반한다.
Ⓓ 당신이 심한 독감 증상을 가지고 있다면, 만성피로증후군에 걸릴 위험이 더 크다.

① Ⓐ & Ⓒ
② Ⓐ & Ⓓ
③ Ⓑ & Ⓒ
④ Ⓑ & Ⓓ
⑤ Ⓐ, Ⓑ & Ⓒ

| 정답 | ⑤

| 해설 | 주어진 문장은 만성피로증후군의 일반적 느낌을 서술한 것으로, 이는 최악의 수면 부족의 느낌과 최악의 독감의 느낌을 합한 것 그 이상이 된다는 내용으로, 여기서 느낌은 그런 증상(symptom)을 보인다는 것을 의미한다. 다시 말하면 만성피로증후군의 증상은 수면 부족의 증상과 독감의 증상을 합친 것 이상이라는 설명이다. Ⓐ에서는 수면 부족의 증상을 보인다는 내용이고, Ⓒ에서는 독감의 증상을 보인다는 설명이므로 추론 가능하다. Ⓑ는 만성피로증후군의 증상이 독감의 증상보다 더 심하다는 내용이므로 이 또한 추론 가능하다. Ⓓ의 경우 독감 증상이 있는 경우 만성피로증후군에 걸릴 위험이 더 크다는 내용으로 인과 관계를 설명하고 있는데, 이는 제시된 문장으로 추론할 수 있는 내용이 아니므로 정답에서 제외되어야 한다.

| 어휘 | **stay up all night** 밤을 새다
and then some ~보다 훨씬 더 많은 것, 그 외에도 더 많은 것들
chronic ⓐ 만성적인
chronic fatigue syndrome 만성피로증후군(CFS)
symptom ⓝ 증상, 징후, 조짐
combination ⓝ 조합
fatigue ⓝ 피로
characteristic ⓐ 특유의

[03~04] 국민대 2016

해석

전 세계 대학의 수학과에서는 유명한 문제를 풀었다고 주장하는 아마추어 수학자들의 편지를 정기적으로 전해 받는다. 그들이 보낸 '해법들'은 사실상 예외 없이 단순히 잘못된 정도가 아니라 우스꽝스러울 정도로 잘못된 것들 이다. 어떤 해법들은 완벽히 잘못된 것이라고 말할 수는 없지만 실제 올바른 해법과는 너무도 달라서 실제로 전혀 시도되지 않는 해법들이다. 수학 발표의 통상적인 관례들을 일부라도 따르는 해법들은 매우 초보적인 논증을 사용하고 있어서, 설사 올바른 해법이라면 수백 년 전에 발견되었을 법한 내용들이다. 이런 편지를 쓰는 사람들은 수학 연구가 얼마나 어려운지 모르며, 중요한 독창적 연구를 수행하기 위해서 충분한 전문 지식을 개발하는 데 필요한 수년간의 노력에 대해서도 알지 못하며, 어느 정도까지 수학이 집단적인 활동인지에 대한 개념도 없는 사람들이다.

03 다음 중 밑줄 친 Ⓐ mathematics is a collective activity에 대한 재진술로 적합하지 않은 것은?

① 수학자들의 공동의 노력은 대개 수학 발전을 이끌어 낸다.

② 많은 수학자들이 수학 문제 해결에 동시에 참여하고 있다.

③ 특히 어려운 수학 문제를 풀기 위해서는 수학 분야의 천재가 필요하다.

④ 많은 수학자들이 장기간에 걸쳐 수학 발전에 기여했다.

| 정답 | ③

| 해설 | Ⓐ는 수학이 집단적인(collective) 행위라고 서술하고 있다. 하지만 ③의 경우 집단이 아닌 천재적인 수준의 개인이 필요하다고 했으므로 재진술로 적합하지 않은 내용이 된다.

04 다음 중 본문의 내용과 일치하는 것은?

① 아마추어가 유명한 수학 문제를 해결하는 것은 사실상 불가능하다.

② 수학적 연구에서 독창성은 지속적 노력만큼 중요하게 생각되지 않는다.

③ 아마추어도 종종 독창적인 연구를 수행하기에 충분한 전문 지식을 갖추고 있다.

④ 아마추어도 종종 어려운 수학 문제를 푸는 데 중요한 돌파구를 마련한다.

| 정답 | ①

| 해설 | 아마추어 수학자들이 보내온 해법들은 예외 없이 실제 수학의 해법과는 거리가 먼 것들이라고 했으므로 ①의 내용과 일치한다.

| 어휘 | **virtually** ⓐⓓ 사실상
solution ⓝ 해법, 풀이
expertise ⓝ 전문 지식
simultaneously ⓐⓓ 동시에
tackle ⓥ (힘든 문제 또는 그런 상황과) 씨름하다
be equipped with 장비를 갖추다

without exception 예외 없이
convention ⓝ 관습, 관례, 전통[관습](적인 방식)
collective ⓐ 집단적인
be engaged in ~에 관여하다, 참여하다
contribute to 기여하다, 공헌하다
breakthrough ⓝ 돌파구, 비약적인 전진

[05~06] 단국대 2017

해석

자연에서 동물들은 자신의 생존과 종의 생존을 보장하기 위해 여러 종류의 기법을 사용한다. 가장 일반적인 생존 적응 중 하나는 천적으로부터 숨기 위해 많은 동물이 사용하는 자연 위장이다. 위장은 동물의 환경, 생리, 행동에 따라 다르게 전개된다. 가장 간단한 위장 기법은 동물이 주변 환경과 섞이는 것이다. 그러한 경우, 동물의 자연 서식지의 요소들이 위장의 모델이 된다. 예를 들어, 개구리의 피부는 주변에 있는 나뭇잎과 비슷한 색과 질감을 갖는다. 생리 및 행동 측면에서 보면, 동물의 생활 방식이나 신체적 특징에 따라 위장의 유형이 결정된다. 털이 난 동물은 비늘이 있는 동물과는 다른 종류의 위장을 만들 것이다. 어떤 동물들은 털갈이를 하면서 계절별로 털의 색상을 바꾼다.

05 다음 중 밑줄 친 부분과 가장 가까운 의미를 가지는 것은?

① 동물들은 천적으로부터 모습을 감추기 위해 주변 환경을 바꾼다.

② 동물들의 생김새는 주변 환경을 모방하거나 혹은 주변에서 흔히 발견할 수 있는 대상을 모방한다.

③ 동물들이 주변 환경의 다른 동물들과 비슷하게 행동한다.

④ 동물들이 주변 환경의 물체를 가지고 자신을 가려서 주변의 나무와 조화를 이룬다.

| 정답 | ②

| 해설 | 바로 앞 내용이 '주변 환경과 조화를 이루며 섞여 들어가다'는 뜻으로 "blend in with its environments"라고 설명하며, 그런 경우 서식처의 요소들을 모델로 삼아 모방한다는 뜻이므로, 정답은 ②가 된다. 주변을 바꾸는 것이 아니라 자신을 주변에 맞추는 것이므로 ①은 정답이 될 수 없다. ③의 경우는 행동에 관한 내용이므로 혹시라도 나온다면 다음 내용에서 등장해야 한다.

06 다음 중 빈칸에 올 수 있는 가장 적합한 것은?

① 결과적으로   ② 그렇지 않다면   ③ 그럼에도 불구하고   ④ 예를 들어서

| 정답 | ④

| 해설 | 주변의 대상을 모방해 몸을 감추는 자연 위장에 대한 예로, 개구리의 피부를 들고 있으므로 예시에 해당하는 ④가 정답이 된다.

| 어휘 | **ensure** ⓥ ~을 보장하다, 확실하게 하다   **adaptation** ⓝ 적응

camouflage ⓥ 위장하다, 속이다 ⓝ 위장   **predator** ⓝ 포식 동물, 포식자

physiology ⓝ 생리학   **blend in with** 조화를 이루다; (주위 환경에) 섞여 들다

natural habitat 자연 서식지   **texture** ⓝ 질감

fur ⓝ 털

scale ⓝ 저울, 규모, 비늘, 치석 ⓥ 비늘을 벗기다, 치석을 제거하다, 올라가다

molting ⓝ 털갈이   **vegetation** ⓝ 초목, 식물

[07~10]

해석

여름이 한창인 몽고에서는 소위 남자다운 세 가지 스포츠인 씨름, 경마, 활쏘기가 가장 각광받는 올림픽 비슷한 축제인 에린 구르반 나담 축제가 지금 개최될 예정이다. 나담 축제는 매년 7월 11일부터 13일까지 열린다. 이 시기는 경쟁 관계인 중국과 러시아 세력으로부터 몽고가 독립을 쟁취했던 1921년 몽고 혁명 기념일과 일치한다. 이 축제의 기원은 칭기즈 칸이 이끄는 몽고군이 전성기엔 강역이 유라시아 전역에 펼쳐졌던 제국을 설립했던 시기인 12세기로 거슬러 올라간다. 전장에서 성공하려면 씨름, 경마, 활쏘기는 꼭 필요한 기술이었다. 이들 기술을 스포츠의 영역으로 편입시킴으로써 전사들을 더 훌륭한 전사로 훈련시킬 수 있었다. 나담 축제는 전통적으로는 한 해 동안 훈련했던 남자들이 이들 기술들을 숙달하고 있음을 과시하는 시기였다. "남자다운 스포츠"라고 종종 기술되곤 하던 이 나담 축제의 행사는 원래는 남자에게만 국한된 것이었다. 오늘날에는 여성들도 승마와 활쏘기 경기에 참가할 수 있고, 특히 소년 소녀는 경마에 참여한다. 몽고의 이 국가적 축제는 뿔뿔이 흩어진 유목민들을 한데 모이도록 끌어들이고, 이들은 축제에서 다 함께 우호를 다지는 경기에 참여하고, 발효 말젖을 마시고, 다양한 유제품을 마음껏 먹는다. 오늘날 이들 기술은 대체로 운동 경기 및 동지애를 다지기 위한 용도로 남아 있다. 하지만 나담 축제를 둘러싼 명성 및 민족주의적 자부심은 여전히 밝게 빛나고 있다.

07 에린 구르반 나담 축제에 대한 내용이 담긴 본문에서 유추할 수 있는 것은 무엇인가?

① 칭기즈 칸 시대부터 매년 열린다.
② 원래 목적은 유라시아 전역에 흩어진 몽고인들을 모으는 것이다.
③ 여성과 아이들은 현재 일부 경기에 참여할 수 있다.
④ 과거에는 전문 운동선수들이 훈련받던 군대 기지에서 열렸다.

| 정답 | ③

| 해설 | 과거에 이 축제는 남성만의 전유물이었지만 "오늘날에는 여성들도 승마와 활쏘기 경기에 참가할 수 있고, 특히 소년 소녀는 경마에 참여한다(Today women participate in both the horse racing and archery competitions, and young boys and girls in particular take to the horse racing)." 따라서 답은 ③이다. 축제의 기원이 칭기즈 칸 시대라는 말은 있으나 그때부터 계속 개최되었다는 언급은 없기 때문에 ①은 답으로 볼 수 없다. 원래 축제의 목적은 몽고인들을 한데 모으는 것이 아니라 전사들을 훈련시키는 것이기 때문에 ②도 답으로 볼 수 없다. ④에 관해서는 본문에 언급된 사항이 없기 때문에 답으로 볼 수 없다.

08 다음 중 빈칸 ⓒ에 가장 알맞은 것은 무엇인가?

① 기억하다　　　② 과시하다　　　③ 계속 고수하다　　　④ 가정하다

| 정답 | ②

| 해설 | 문맥상 남성들은 자신들이 "이들 기술들을 숙달하고 있음(they have mastered these skills)"을 보여 주기 위해 축제에 참가했을 것이다. 따라서 답은 ②이다.

09 밑줄 친 구문 ⓐ는 나담 축제를 _____과 연계한다.

① 민족주의적 자존심　　　　　② 유목민의 문화 전통
③ "남자다운 스포츠"의 전통　　④ 운동 경기 및 동지애

| 정답 | ①

| 해설 | 나담 축제의 개최 시기는 ⓐ에 따르면 "경쟁 관계인 중국과 러시아 세력으로부터 몽고가 독립을 쟁취(gained independence from competing Chinese and Russian forces)"한 "1921년 몽고 혁명 기념일(the anniversary of the 1921 Mongolian Revolution)"과 일치한다. 독립은 '민족주의적 자존심'과 연계되는 개념이며, 이 시기에 열리는 나담 축제에 민족주의적 색채가 강할 것임은 유추 가능하다. 따라서 답은 ①이다.

10 밑줄 쳐진 문장 ⓑ는 _____는 의미이다.

① 전사들은 운동선수로 변했다.
② 군대는 관중이 많은 스포츠를 즐겼다.
③ 고대 몽고인들은 스포츠와 오락을 좋아했다.
④ 스포츠는 군사 훈련의 과정으로 사용되었다.

| 정답 | ④

ⓑ의 의미는 '이들 기술을 스포츠의 영역으로 편입시킴으로써 전사들을 더 훌륭한 전사로 훈련시킬 수 있었다'이다. 즉 축제를 통해 스포츠화한 씨름, 경마, 활쏘기는 남자들을 단련시키고 더 훌륭한 전사로 육성하는 데 도움이 되었다는 의미이다. 따라서 답은 ④이다.

| 어휘 |

take center stage 주목받다, 각광받다	be set to ～하도록 예정되어 있다
coincide ⓥ 동시에 일어나다, 일치하다	trace ⓥ (유래를) 더듬다, 거슬러 올라가다
stretch ⓥ 펼쳐지다	master ⓥ 숙달하다, 통달하다
take to ～에 전력하다, ～하기 시작하다; ～를 좋아하게 되다	
scattered ⓐ 뿔뿔이 흩어진	nomadic ⓐ 유목의, 방랑의
herder ⓝ 목동	fermented ⓐ 발효된
feast on 마음껏 먹다	camaraderie ⓝ 동지애
luster ⓝ 명성	nationalistic ⓐ 민족주의적인
show off 과시하다	hold fast 굳게 유지되다, ～을 계속 고수하다
shape into ～을 만들다, 다른 형상으로 변하다	
spectator sport 관중 동원력이 큰 스포츠, 많은 관중이 보는 스포츠	

[11~13] 단국대 2018

해석

연구자들에 따르면, 가십(gossip)은 일부 이점을 가진다고 한다. 정보를 주고받는 것이 건강한 관계를 형성할 수 있다. 또한, 용인되는 행위와 용인되지 않는 행위에 대해 기준을 세울 수 있다. 사회를 발전시킬 수도 있다. 마찬가지로, 가십은 비즈니스 업계에서도 유용하다. 가십 연구자인 Frank McAndrew 교수는 "다른 사람들이 행한 좋은 일들을 사람들이 이야기하면 우리는 그런 좋은 행동을 모방하고 싶어 한다. 그것은 사람들을 사회적으로 통제하는 좋은 방법에 속한다."라고 말한다. 회사가 어려운 시기에 직면했을 때, 직원들의 미래에 대한 가십은 두려움과 불확실성을 감소시킬 수 있다. 그것은 또한 유대감도 생성해 줄 수 있다.

하지만 다른 사람들의 사생활에 관한 부정적인 말인 나쁜 가십은 파괴적일 수 있다. 매우 안타깝게도, 연구자들은 악의의 이런 행태를 연구하는 데 시간을 투자하지 않는다. 사람들은 몇 가지 이유에서 나쁜 가십에 동참한다. 나쁜 가십을 나누면서 서로 간에 유대관계를 쌓을 수도 있다. 또는 시간을 보내기 위해서거나 문제를 부정하기 위해서일 수도 있다. 남들과의 비교를 통해 자신을 포장하기 위해 가십에 참여할 수도 있고, 다른 사람을 상처를 주기 위한 것일 수도 있다.

11 다음 중 빈칸 (A)와 (B)에 들어갈 것으로 가장 적합한 것은?

① 그럼에도 불구하고 – 하지만
② 하지만 – 이와 유사하게
③ 하지만 – 그럼에도 불구하고
④ 마찬가지로 – 하지만

| 정답 | ④

| 해설 | (A) 앞에서는 가십의 긍정적인 면을 언급하고 있다. 남들과 건강한 관계를 맺게 하거나 용인되는 행위에 대한 기준을 형성하고 사회를 향상시키는 것에 대해 언급하고 있다. (A) 뒤의 내용도 useful이라는 단어를 통해 기업에서도 유용하게 사용될 수 있음을 언급하고 있으므로, 역접의 연결사는 부적합하므로 Similarly만이 가능하다. (B)의 경우, 첫 번째 문단의 좋은 가십과 두 번째 문단의 나쁜 가십이 나누어지는 부분이므로, 역접의 연결사인 However가 와야 한다. 따라서 정답은 ④가 된다.

12 다음 중 본문의 밑줄 친 부분이 의미하는 것은?

① 좋은 행동을 모방하기 위해서
② 좋은 행동을 비난하기 위해서
③ 좋은 행동을 개화하기 위해서
④ 좋은 행동을 주목하기 위해서

| 정답 | ①

| 해설 | 밑줄 친 부분에서 emulate가 누군가를 모방한다는 뜻이므로, 이와 유사한 imitate가 들어간 ①이 정답이 된다.

13 다음 중 본문의 요지로 적합한 것은?

① 사람들은 가십이 얼마나 파괴적일 수 있는지에 대해 깨닫지 못한다.
② 가십은 사회와 사람들의 삶에 유익할 수도 부정적일 수도 있다.
③ 직원들이 가십을 통해 유대감을 형성할 수 있기 때문에 가십은 필요하다.
④ 사람들은 다양한 이유로 나쁜 가십에 참여할 수 있다.

| 정답 | ②

| 해설 | 첫 번째 문단에서는 가십의 긍정적인 면에 대해 말하고 있고, 두 번째 문단에서는 나쁜 가십에 대해 말하면서 가십의 파괴적인 측면을 말하고 있으므로, 이 둘을 모두 언급한 ②가 요지로 적합하다.

| 어휘 | **gossip** ⓝ (남의 사생활에 대한 좋지 않은) 소문, 험담
improve ⓥ 향상시키다
destructive ⓐ 파괴적인
engage in 참여하다; 참여하게 만들다
pass the time 빈 시간을 아무 생각 없이 보내다
comparison ⓝ 비교, 비유
civilize ⓥ 개화[교화]하다; (태도를) 세련되게 하다

acceptable ⓐ (사회적으로) 용인되는[받아들여지는]
emulate ⓥ (흠모하는 대상을) 모방하다
malice ⓝ 악의, 적의
bond with 유대관계를 맺다
build up ～을 과대 포장[광고]하다
imitate ⓥ 모방하다, 모조하다
beneficial ⓐ 유익한, 이익을 가져오는

[14~15]

> 해석

컴퓨터 바이러스 및 보안 기술 전문가인 Sarah Gordon은 1992년부터 바이러스 개발자들의 심리에 대해 연구했다. "바이러스 개발 자나 해커는 그저 평범한 우리 이웃들과 같다"고 그녀는 말한다. "혹은 계산대에서 장바구니에 물건을 담아 주는 아이와 같다. 일반 해커들은 결코 온통 검은 옷을 입고, 코에 피어싱을 한 고스(goth) 타입의 사람들이 아니다"고 그녀는 덧붙였다. Gordon이 알게 된 바이러스 개발자들은 다양한 배경을 가지고 있었다. 그들은 체격이 좋은 운동선수 스타일도 있으며, 지극히 학구적인 이들도 있다. 그들 대부분이 부모님이나 가족들과 좋은 관계를 유지하며, 친구들에게도 인기가 많다. 그들이 대부분의 시간을 지하실에서 보내는 것도 아니다. 한 바이러스 개발자는 그 지역의 도서관에서 자원봉사를 하며 노인들과 함께 일을 한다. 그들 중에는 시인이나 음악가 도 있으며, 전기 기술자도 있다. 이들이 일렬로 쭉 서 있다면 우리들은 이들 사이에서 범인으로 그들을 골라 낼 수 없을 것이다.

14 밑줄 친 ㉮를 가장 잘 설명한 것은?

① 일반적으로 해커나 바이러스 개발자들은 평범해 보여서, 이들을 외모로 가려내기는 어렵다.

② 해커나 바이러스 개발자들은 좋은 이미지 안에 자신을 숨기기 때문에 우리는 이들에게 쉽게 속을 수 있다.

③ 대부분의 해커나 바이러스 개발자들은 굉장히 똑똑하고 지적이나, 종종 좌절감을 겪기도 한다.

④ 대부분의 해커나 바이러스 개발자들은 비슷한 직업을 갖고 있기 때문에, 이들의 일반적인 직업적 성격을 규정하기 쉽다.

| 정답 | ①

| 해설 | 라인업(lineup)이란 수사 기관이 범인을 수사하는 경우 용의자(suspect)들을 일렬로 세워 놓고 목격자가 이들 중에서 진짜 범인을 지명하도록 한다. 이때 비슷하게 생긴 이들(filler)을 섞어 놓아 목격자의 기억이 정확한지를 확인한다. 밑줄 친 부분은 이를 비유한 것이다. 흔히들 해커라고 하면 떠오르는 이미지가 있어서 여러 사람 중에 쉽게 골라낼 수 있을 것 같지만 사실은 그렇지 않다는 내용이다. 따라서 해커들은 평범하게 생겨서 외모로만 식별하기는 어렵다는 내용의 ①이 정답이 된다.

15 윗글에서 다른 의미로 쓰인 구절은?

① 계산대에서 장바구니를 담아 주는 아이

② 당신의 이웃

③ 검은 옷을 입은 고스 스타일의 사람

④ 시인과 음악가

| 정답 | ③

| 해설 | ③은 보통 사람들이 생각하는 해커의 이미지이고, 나머지 보기는 모두 주변의 보통 사람들을 지칭하는 구절이므로 정답은 ③이 된다.

| 어휘 | **expert** ⓝ 전문가

psychology ⓝ 심리학, 심리

goth ⓝ 고스(1980년대에 유행한 록 음악의 한 형태. 가사가 주로 세상의 종말, 죽음, 악에 대한 내용을 담음), 고스 음악 애호가(검은 옷을 입고, 흰색과 검은색으로 화장을 함)

peer ⓝ 동료, 또래

perpetrator ⓝ 범인

deceive ⓥ 속이다, 기만하다

define ⓥ 규정하다, 분명히 밝히다

security technology ⓝ 보안 기술

bag ⓥ 봉지에 넣다

electrical engineer ⓝ 전기 기술자

render ⓥ (어떤 상태가 되게) 만들다

frustration ⓝ 불만, 좌절감

해석

Eisenhower는 모든 사항을 책임졌다. Eisenhower가 시행한 권한 위임은 유사 위임이었다. 따라서 대부분의 사람들은 Eisenhower가 국내 문제를 주로 비서실장이자 전직 뉴햄프셔주 주지사인 Sherman Adams에게 맡겼다고 생각했다. Adams 자신도 그런 착각을 다른 이들과 공유했던 것으로 보인다. Adams는 Eisenhower가 주요 인물 중에서는 전화를 사용하기를 적극 싫어하고 피했던 마지막 인물이라고 말했다. 하지만 통화 기록을 보면 Eisenhower는 Admas가 모르는 일에 대해 전화를 아주 많이 걸었음이 나타난다. 외교 문제의 경우 Eisenhower가 활용한 조언과 정보의 출처는 마찬가지로 Dulles가 모르던 출처였다. Eisenhower는 근면한 Dulles를 우수한 하인으로 활용했고, Dulles는 백악관에서 Eisenhower 대통령이랑 자주 밤늦게까지 일했는데도 '한 번도 가족 식사에 초대된 적이 없었다'고 불평을 표했다. Adams와 Dulles가 Eisenhower 행정부의 주역이라는 생각은 의도적으로 Eisenhower에 의해 홍보된 것이며, 그 이유는 실수가 밝혀지면 이 두 사람이 비난을 받고, 따라서 대통령실은 보호받기 때문이다.

---

16 다음 중 본문의 주제로서 빈칸 ㉮에 가장 알맞은 것은 무엇인가?

① Eisenhower의 대리인들은 과도한 권력을 지녔다.
② Eisenhower는 매우 인도적인 정치가였다.
③ Eisenhower는 모든 일을 참모들에게 맡겼다.
④ Eisenhower는 모든 사항을 책임졌다.

| 정답 | ④

| 해설 | 이 글은 Paul Johnson이 저술한 Modern Times에 나오는 글로 Eisenhower의 정치적인 특성에 대한 언급이다. 실제로는 자신이 모든 사항을 책임지면서도, 모든 권한을 부하들에게 위임한 듯 외관을 보여 문제점이 생기면 자신은 빠져나갈 수 있는 장치를 만들었다는 내용이다. 그러므로 글의 앞부분에 도입이 되는 이야기는 실상은 Eisenhower 자신이 모든 사항을 책임졌다는 것이 올바른 내용이 된다.

---

17 밑줄 친 ㉯는 무엇을 언급한 것인가?

① Eisenhower가 유사 권한 위임을 시행한 것
② 대부분의 사람들이 정치에 관심을 보였던 것
③ Adams가 국내 문제를 책임졌다는 것
④ Adams가 뉴햄프셔주의 전직 주지사였다는 것

| 정답 | ③

| 해설 | "대부분의 사람들은 Eisenhower가 국내 문제를 주로 비서실장이자 전직 뉴햄프셔 주 주지사인 Sherman Adams에게 맡겼다고 생각했다(most people thought he left domestic matters largely to his chief of staff, the former governor of New Hampshire)." Adams 자신도 그렇게 생각했기 때문에 "Eisenhower를 주요 인물 중에 서는 전화를 사용하기를 적극 싫어하고 피했던 마지막 인물(Eisenhower was the last major figure who actively disliked and avoided using the phone)", 즉 자신에게 권한을 넘겨주고 전화하지 않는 인물로 봤을 것이다. 그런데 ㉯의 illusion은 '착각'을 의미한다. 실제로 Eisenhower 대통령은 통화 기록에 따르면 "Adams가 모르는 일에 대해 전화를 아주 많이 거는(made multitudes of calls about which Adams knew nothing)" 대통령이었다. Adams 자신은 권한을 위임받고 국내 문제를 전담했다고 '착각'했으나, 실제로는 대통령은 모든 일을 맡기고 한발 물러나긴커녕 적극적으로 전화하고 알아보던 사람이었던 것이다. 이러한 점을 고려해 보면 정답은 ③이다.

18 밑줄 친 ⓓ가 의미하는 것은 무엇인가?

① Adams와 Dulles는 오페라를 매우 좋아했다.

② Adams와 Dulles는 하인 취급을 받았다.

③ Adams와 Dulles는 주요 역할을 맡았다.

④ Adams와 Dulles는 많은 실수를 저질렀다.

| 정답 | ③

| 해설 | 프리마 돈나는 오페라의 주역을 의미한다. Adams와 Dulles가 프리마 돈나, 즉 행정부의 주역이라는 의미는 Eisenhower 대통령이 (비록 착각이지만) Adams에게는 국내 문제를 전담시키고, Dulles에게는 국외 문제를 전담시켰음을 의미한다. 따라서 답은 ③이다.

19 다음 중 빈칸 ⓔ에 가장 적절한 것은 무엇인가?

① Eisenhower의 명예에 크나큰 손상을 초래할 뿐이었다.

② 하지만 Eisenhower는 Adams와 Dulles의 정치 경력을 유지하도록 도왔다.

③ Eisenhower가 의도한 것과는 정반대로

④ 따라서 대통령직은 보호받는다.

| 정답 | ④

| 해설 | Adams와 Dulles에 권한을 넘겨줬다는 '착각'은 "의도적으로 Eisenhower에 의해 홍보된 것(was deliberately promoted by Eisenhower)"이다. "실수가 밝혀지면 이 두 사람이 비난을 받는다(they could be blamed when mistakes were uncovered)"는 문장의 의미는, 설사 행정 집행 과정에서 실수가 발생하면 권한이 두 사람에게 있었으니 실제 책임질 사람도 대통령이 아니라 이 두 사람이라는 의미이다. 그렇게 되면 당연히 책임은 두 사람에게 가지만 대통령에게 책임이 가지는 않을 것이다. 따라서 답은 ④가 된다.

| 어휘 | **pesudo-** ⓐ 가상의, 유사의

chief of staff 수석 보좌관, 비서실장

major figure 주요 인물

multitudes of 다수의

prima donna 주역, 프리마 돈나

delegate ⓝ 대표, 사절, 대리인

incur ⓥ 초래하다

contemptuous ⓐ 경멸하는

delegation ⓝ (권한 등의) 위임; 대표단

illusion ⓝ 환상, 착각

log ⓝ 기록, 일지

industrious ⓐ 근면한

deliberately ⓐⓓ 의도적으로, 고의로

humane ⓐ 인도적인

contrary to ~와는 반대로

해석

영국의 한 연구는 크리스마스와 새해 연휴에 남성들의 심장 마비사가 크게 증가하고 있다는 것을 보여 준다. 이것은 사람들이 휴일에 병원을 찾는 번거로움 때문에 증세를 무시하고 병원에 가는 것을 미루기 때문이다. 또는 여행 중인 사람들은 적절한 의료 서비스를 찾는 데 더 오래 걸릴 수도 있다. British Heart Foundation의 간호사 Ellen Mason은 "잘 알다시피, 추운 날씨에는 피의 농도가 더 진해져서 심장 마비 위험이 커지죠. 하지만 연휴에 의료적 도움을 받는 것을 미루기 때문에 사망자가 더 증가하는 것 같아요."라고 말한다. 남성 건강 전문가 Dr. Mike Ingram은 크리스마스 시즌이 특히 남성들의 심장 마비 위험을 크게 증가시키기 때문에 위험하다고 경고한다. 크리스마스 시즌이 호흡 곤란을 일으키는 계절성 감기와 독감의 증가, 무리한 신체 활동, 과식, 추위, 수면 부족, 정서적 스트레스, 염분 과다 섭취와 과음의 원인이라는 것이다. Dr. Ingram은 "남성이 사망하는 가장 큰 원인은 심장 질환입니다. 너무나 많은 남성들이 위험에 제대로 대처하지 못한 채 심장 질환으로 사망하고 있습니다."라고 말했다. 그는 남성들의 가장 위협적인 적은 바로 남성 자신이라고 말하며 덧붙였다. "장수하는 건강한 삶을 누리고 싶은 남성이라면, 심장 마비 위험 요소를 줄이는 데 더 신경을 써야 합니다. 담배는 끊고, 술은 적당히 마시고, 고지방 음식은 줄이고, 규칙적으로 운동하고, 혈압에 주의해야 합니다. 이런 것들이 너무 어려운가요? 그렇다면 염분을 줄이는 것부터 시작하세요."

20 지문에서 분명하게 언급된 것은 _____.

① 여성보다 훨씬 많은 남성들이 겨울철에 사망한다
② 염분은 특히 건강에 해롭다
③ 겨울철 남성 사망률 증가에는 다양한 요인들이 있다
④ 추운 날씨에 발생하는 심장 마비는 거의 항상 치명적이다

| 정답 | ③

| 해설 | 겨울에 남성 심장 마비가 크게 증가하는 복합적 원인들을 밝히는 글이므로 ③이 적절하다. ①, ②는 비약이므로 선택하지 않도록 주의한다.

21 지문에서 분명하게 언급된 것은 _____.

① 심장 마비는 발생 즉시 치료를 받아야 한다
② 영국의 병원들은 크리스마스에는 보통 문을 닫는다
③ 심장 마비 증상이 있는데도 여행을 하는 것은 현명치 못하다
④ 어떤 사람들은 겨울에는 병원에 가는 것을 꺼린다

| 정답 | ①

| 해설 | 지문의 전반부에 연휴 기간 동안 심장 마비사가 크게 증가하는 1차적 원인인 "연휴 기간 동안 증상을 무시하고 병원을 찾지 않는 것"의 위험성이 상술되어 있으므로 ①이 적절하다. "but it is likely that the delay in seeking medical assistance over the holidays may lead to more deaths" 참조. 심장 마비 치료가 지연되는 것은 병원이 문을 닫아서가 아니라 환자가 병원을 찾지 않기 때문이므로 ②를 선택하지 않도록 주의한다. 휴일에 병원에 가는 것을 꺼리는 사람들은 있지만, 겨울에 병원에 가는 것을 꺼리는 사람들이 있다는 것은 비약이므로 ④도 선택하지 않도록 주의한다.

22 밑줄 친 "men could be their own worst enemies"가 의미하는 것은 _____.

① 남성들은 자신에게 일어난 일들에 대해 서로를 심하게 탓한다

② 자신의 건강 관리는 스스로 해야 한다

③ 남을 싫어하는 것은 당신의 건강에 해롭다

④ 남성이 해로운 생활 방식을 고집한다면, 그 결과에 대한 책임은 그 자신에게 있다

| 정답 | ④

| 해설 | 문맥상 심장 질환은 남성들의 무절제한 생활 방식이 원인이므로 ④가 문맥에 맞는다. 나머지 보기는 주체가 남성들이 아니거나, 건강과 무관한 내용이므로 선택하지 않도록 주의한다.

23 지문에서 알 수 있거나 유추할 수 없는 것은 _____.

① 남성 사망의 가장 큰 원인은 심장 질환이다

② 호흡 곤란은 심장 질환을 야기할 수 있다

③ 사람들은 크리스마스 시즌에 자주 과음한다

④ 노인 남성이 심장 마비를 피하는 것은 불가능하다

| 정답 | ④

| 해설 | ④는 "겨울철 남성 심장 마비 증가의 원인과 예방"이라는 지문의 주제와 무관한 내용이므로, 지문에서 알 수 있거나 유추할 수 없다.

24 마지막 문장은 염분 섭취를 줄이는 것으로 시작할 권을 권하고 있다. 왜냐하면 _____.

① 염분은 특히 위험하기 때문이다

② 그것이 쉬운 첫 단계이기 때문이다

③ 그것이 특히 하기 어려운 일이기 때문이다

④ 염분 없는 음식이 더 맛있기 때문이다

| 정답 | ②

| 해설 | "Too challenging?"에 주의한다. 앞에서 언급한 예방책들이 너무 어렵다면 쉬운 첫 단계로 염분을 줄이라는 권고이다. 염분을 줄이는 것부터 시작하는 것은 쉽기 때문이지 염분이 특히 위험하기 때문이 아니므로 ①을 선택하지 않도록 주의한다.

| 어휘 | significant ⓐ 상당한

be attributed to ~ 때문이다

inconvenience ⓝ 불편

lead to 초래하다

blame A on B B에 대해서 A를 비난하다

cold ⓝ 감기

physical exertion 무리한 활동, 격렬한 운동

excess ⓐ 과도한

tackle ⓥ 대처하다, 처리하다

hear attack 심장 마비

symptom ⓝ 증세, 증상

thick ⓐ 농도가 짙은, 진한

festive period 크리스마스 시즌

seasonal ⓐ 계절성의

flu ⓝ 독감

overeating ⓝ 과식

condition ⓝ 병, 병세

focus on 초점을 맞추다, 역점을 두다

factor ⓝ 요인, 요소

in moderation 적당히

cut out 줄이다

blood pressure 혈압

[25~27]

해석

일부 사실은 특정한 유전적 특성을 발현시키는 분자 과정을 지배하는 것은 오직 DNA 유전자뿐이라는 센트럴 도그마의 가장 중요한 격언과 모순을 일으킨다. 대부분의 분자생물학자들은 구식 이론에 몰두하는 관계로, 이들은 DNA가 생명의 비밀이라는 가정하에서 행동하지만, 반면에 생명 과정의 체계를 면밀하게 관찰해 보면 사실은 그 반대라는 점이 강력하게 시사된다. 그렇다면 센트럴 도그마가 여전히 유효한 이유는 무엇인가? 어느 정도는 이 이론은, 반대 또는 단순히 기존의 것과 조화되지 않는 사실의 발견은 처벌이 가능한 위반 사항이며 전문가들로부터 배척받기 쉬운 이설에 불과하다고 보는, 과학보다는 종교와 더 공통점이 많은 시각을 통해 비판으로부터 보호받아 왔기 때문이다. 이러한 편견 가운데 상당 부분은 제도적인 타성, 즉 엄격한 규칙 적용에 실패한 탓에 기인한다고 볼 수 있지만, 분자 유전학자들이 왜 현 상황에 만족하는지에 관해 그 외 다른 은밀한 이유도 존재한다. 그것은 센트럴 도그마가 학자들에게 유전에 대해, 만족스러우면서 마음을 사로잡는, 매우 단순화된 설명을 제공하기 때문이다.

25 윗글의 내용과 일치하지 않는 것은?

① 분자 과정을 지배하는 DNA 이론은 유효한 것으로 입증되었다.
② 유전 공학은 거짓된 근거를 바탕으로 두고 있다.
③ 종교와 마찬가지로 과학에서도 배타적인 주의가 단단히 자리 잡혀 있다.
④ 환원주의는 DNA를 둘러싼 도그마에 대한 근거 없는 믿음의 중심에 있다.

| 정답 | ①

| 해설 | "일부 사실은 특정한 유전적 특성을 발현시키는 분자 과정을 지배하는 것은 오직 DNA 유전자뿐이라는 센트럴 도그마의 가장 중요한 격언과 모순을 일으킨다(Some facts contradict the central dogma's cardinal maxim : that a DNA gene exclusively governs the molecular processes that give rise to a particular inherited trait)." 이는 즉 분자 과정을 지배하는 DNA 이론이 흔히 통용되는 것과는 달리 유효하지 않다는 의미이다. 따라서 답은 ①이다.

26 윗글의 문맥상 빈칸 ⓐ에 가장 알맞은 단어는?

① 조화되지 않는   ② 공정한   ③ 반박 가능한   ④ 짜증 나는

| 정답 | ①

| 해설 | "반대(dissent)"되는 내용을 주장하는 것을 처벌 가능한 위반 사항이자 이설로 취급하는 것이 문제라는 주장을 본문에서 하고 있는데, 문맥상 "반대"와 "단순히 ⓐ _____인 사실의 발견(merely the discovery of a ⓐ _____ fact)"은 or로 연결되어 서로 유사한 의미를 지닌 것으로 볼 수 있다. 즉 "조화되지 않는(discordant)" 또는 기존의 의견과 맞지 않는 것을 주장하는 것을 금기시하는 것이 문제가 된다는 것이다. 따라서 답은 ①이다.

27 다음 중 밑줄 친 ⓑ가 의미하지 <u>않는</u> 것은?

① 의미를 다시 규정하여 새로운 사실을 주류 이론에 포함시킴
② 보다 최근에 관찰된 사항이 편의에 따라 빠져 있음
③ 명망 있는 전통적인 과학적 질서
④ 주류 이론과 다른 사실에 영향을 받지 않는

| 정답 | ①

| 해설 | 밑줄 친 부분은 '현 상황'을 의미하며, 문맥상 '주류 의견에 반대하는 것을 받아들이지 않는 경향'을 의미한다. 그러나 ①은 기존과 다른 새로운 사실을 받아들이는 것을 의미하며, 따라서 나머지 보기와도 다른 내용을 담고 있다. 따라서 답은 ①이다.

| 어휘 | **central dogma** 센트럴 도그마; 유전 정보의 흐름을 나타내는 분자 생물학의 기본 원리

dogma ⓝ 신조, 도그마

maxim ⓝ 격언, 금언

give rise to ~이 생기게 하다

obsolete ⓐ 구식의, 한물간

the other way around 반대로, 거꾸로

dissent ⓝ 반대

heresy ⓝ 이단, 이설

be attributed to ~에 기인하다

rigor ⓝ (법·규칙 등의) 엄격한 적용, 엄격함

the status quo 현재의 상태[상황]

heredity ⓝ 유전

valid ⓐ 유효한, 타당한

tenet ⓝ 주의, 교리

reductionism ⓝ 환원주의; 복잡한 사물은 자신을 구성하고 있는 가장 단순한 것으로부터 이해될 수 있다는 주장

impartial ⓐ 공정한

conveniently ⓐⓓ 편의대로, 간편하게

economy ⓝ (조직·구조의) 유기적 통일[조직]; (자연계의) 질서

prestige ⓝ 위신, 명망

divergent ⓐ 갈라지는, 다른

cardinal ⓐ 가장 중요한, 기본적인

exclusively ⓐⓓ 오직, 독점적으로

inherited ⓐ 유전의

hierarchy ⓝ 계층, 체계

stand ⓥ 아직도 유효하다[변함없다]

discordant ⓐ 조화를 이루지 못하는, 불협화음의

ostracism ⓝ 외면, 배척

inertia ⓝ 타성, 관성

insidious ⓐ 은밀한, 서서히 퍼지는

seductively 매혹적으로, 마음을 끄는

simplistic ⓐ 지나치게 단순화한

spurious ⓐ 거짓된, 겉으로만 그럴싸한

entrenched ⓐ 단단히 자리 잡은

refutable ⓐ 반박 가능한

devoid of ~이 없는

immune to ~에 영향을 받지 않는

해석

인간이 자연을 대하는 방식이 근본적으로 변하지 않을 경우, 미래에 팬데믹이 보다 자주 발생하고, 팬데믹으로 인해 더 많은 사람이 사망하고, 세계 경제에 코로나19보다 더 큰 피해를 입힐 것이다. 신종 코로나바이러스처럼 동물에 존재하는 바이러스가 최대 850,000종에 달하고 이런 바이러스가 사람을 감염시킬 수 있다고 경고한, IPBES라는 명칭의 전문가 패널에서는 팬데믹이 인류에게 있어 실존적인 위협을 나타낸다고 말한다.

'생물다양성과 팬데믹에 관한 특별보고서'의 저자들은 서식지의 파괴와 만족할 줄 모르는 소비로 인해 동물 매개 질환이 미래에는 사람들에게 옮겨갈 가능성이 훨씬 커졌다고 말한다. 코로나19 팬데믹의 원인에 관해서는 그다지 수수께끼가 될 만한 것이 없다. 기후변화와 생물다양성의 상실을 촉발시킨 것과 동일한 인간의 활동이 우리의 농업에 미치는 영향을 통해 팬데믹의 위험을 촉발시키고 있다.

코로나19는 1918년의 인플루엔자 발발 이후 여섯 번째의 팬데믹이다. 이러한 팬데믹은 전적으로 인간의 활동을 통해 촉발되었다. 이러한 인간의 활동에는 삼림 벌채, 농업 확대, 야생동물의 거래, 소비 등을 통한 환경의 지속 불가능한 착취가 포함된다. 이 모든 착취로 인해 인간은 야생동물 및 사육동물 그리고 이들이 품고 있는 질병과 점차적으로 가까이 접촉하게 되었다.

에볼라, 지카, HIV/AIDS같은 최근 생겨난 질병의 70%는 인수공통 질병으로, 이는 즉 질병이 인간에게 옮겨지기 전에 동물들 사이에서 돌았음을 의미한다. 매년 약 5개의 새로운 질병이 인간들 사이에서 발생하며, 이러한 질병이 팬데믹이 될 가능성은 모두에게 존재한다.

---

28 본문 두 번째 문장의 "an existential threat to humanity"를 가장 잘 패러프레이즈한 것은?

① 인간에 대한 가상의 위험

② 인간 생존에 있어 실질적인 위험

③ 생물체에는 임박한 위험이지만 인간에게는 아닐 수 있음

④ 인간에 대한 이전에도 존재했던 위험

| 정답 | ②

| 해설 | 밑줄 친 부분은 해석하면 "인류에게 있어 실존적인 위협"이며, 문맥상 이 위협은 많은 사람들을 감염시키고 사망시킬 수 있으므로 "인간 생존에 있어 실질적인 위험"이 될 수 있다. 따라서 답은 ②이다.

---

29 본문에 따르면 다음 중 코로나19 팬데믹에 관해 사실인 것은 무엇인가?

① 그 원인과 유래가 에볼라, 지카, HIV/AIDS 등의 다른 질병과 달리 인수공통이 아니다.

② 코로나19는 다소 독특한 질병이기 때문에 미래에 코로나19와 유사한 팬데믹이 발생할 가능성은 낮다.

③ 코로나19의 원인은 여전히 과학자들에게 알려진 바 없다.

④ 코로나19의 근본 원인은 서식지 파괴와 만족할 줄 모르는 소비이다.

| 정답 | ④

| 해설 | 본문 세 번째 단락, 구체적으로는 "이러한 팬데믹은 전적으로 인간의 활동을 통해 촉발되었다. 이러한 인간의 활동에는 삼림 벌채, 농업 확대, 야생동물의 거래, 소비 등을 통한 환경의 지속 불가능한 착취가 포함된다"는 코로나19 팬데믹에 관해 보기 ④의 내용과 일치한다. 따라서 답은 ④이다.

본문에서 코로나19가 인수공통인지 여부가 언급되지는 않지만 네 번째 단락을 보면 코로나19 팬데믹은 인간의 활동을 통해

촉발되었다는 것을 알 수 있고, 여기서 ①의 내용은 답으로 보기 힘들다는 점을 알 수 있다. "인간이 자연을 대하는 방식이 근본적으로 변하지 않을 경우, 미래에 팬데믹이 보다 자주 발생하고, 팬데믹으로 인해 더 많은 사람이 사망하고, 세계 경제에 코로나19보다 더 큰 피해를 입힐 것이다"는 보기 ②가 답이 아닌 이유를 설명한다. "코로나19 팬데믹의 원인에 관해서는 그다지 수수께끼가 될 만한 것이 없다"는 ③이 답이 될 수 없는 이유가 된다.

---

30 본문에 따르면, 기후변화와 생물다양성의 상실 및 팬데믹 모두의 공통점은 무엇인가?

① 현재로는 과학자들에게 있어 원인이 크나큰 수수께끼이다.

② 모두 인간의 활동으로 인해 야기되었다.

③ 이들의 위험은 최근이 되어서야 알게 되었다.

④ 저자는 이러한 현상의 공통점에 관해 언급하지 않았다.

| 정답 | ②

| 해설 | "기후변화와 생물다양성의 상실을 촉발시킨 것과 동일한 인간의 활동이 우리의 농업에 미치는 영향을 통해 팬데믹의 위험을 촉발시키고 있다"를 보면, 기후변화와 생물다양성의 상실 및 팬데믹 모두 인간의 활동으로 인해 야기되었음을 유추할 수 있다. 따라서 답은 ②이다.

| 어휘 | **pandemic** ⓝ 전국[전 세계]적인 유행병, 팬데믹

novel ⓐ 새로운, 신종의

existential ⓐ (인간의) 존재에 관한, 실존주의적인

habitat ⓝ 서식지

animal-borne ⓐ 동물 매개의, 동물이 원인이 되는

outbreak ⓝ 발생, 발발

exploitation ⓝ 착취, 개발

farm ⓥ (동물을) 기르다[사육하다]

emerging ⓐ 최근 발생한[생겨난]

potential ⓝ 가능성

imminent ⓐ 임박한, 목전의

commonality ⓝ 공통성, 평범

wreak ⓥ (큰 피해 등을) 입히다[가하다]

represent ⓥ 나타내다, 대변하다

biodiversity ⓝ 생물다양성

insatiable ⓐ 채울[만족시킬] 수 없는, 만족할 줄 모르는

drive ⓥ 촉발시키다, (어떤 결과를 낳도록) 몰아가다

entirely ⓐⓓ 전적으로, 전부

deforestation ⓝ 삼림 벌채[파괴]

harbor ⓥ 품다

zoonotic ⓐ 동물원성의, (감염병이) 인수공통의

hypothetical ⓐ 가상의, 가설의

underlying ⓐ 근본적인, 근원적인

연습 문제   01 ②   02 ④   03 ②

---

01 밑줄 친 Three가 언급하는 것은 무엇인가?

> 학교의 축구 감독으로서 나는 운동하는 학생들이 스포츠에만 집중하는 성향이 있음을 알고 있다. 동료 감독인 Bob은 그런 선수 한 명에 관해 말하고 있었다. 그 학생은 Bob의 집에 밤에 전화를 했는데, Bob의 아내가 Bob은 집에 없다고 하자 그 학생은 극도로 흥분하더니 당장 감독님과 통화를 해야 한다고 말했다. 감독의 부인은 그 학생에게 "진정하렴. 남편이 집에 오면 바로 네게 전화하도록 할게"라고 말했다. "번호가 어떻게 되니?" 허둥거리는 그 학생은 "3번이요."라고 답했다.

① 학생의 전화번호   ② 학생의 등 번호
③ 학생의 방 번호   ④ 동료 팀원의 수

| 정답 | ②

| 해설 | 우선 운동하는 학생들이 "end to focus too much on sports(스포츠에만 집중하는 성향이 있음)"를 먼저 제시한 후, 그 예로 "What's your number?(번호가 무엇이니?)"라고 물으니까 "3번이요."라고 답한 학생을 들고 있다. 감독의 부인이 말하는 'number'는 남편이 들어오면 학생에게 전화하기 위해 필요한 '전화번호'이지만, 운동에 너무 집중하는 학생이라면 'number'라는 말을 들었을 때 전화번호가 아니라 자신의 등 번호를 말하는 것으로 착각했을 것이고 그래서 자신의 등 번호인 "3번"을 말했으리라 유추할 수 있다. 따라서 답은 ②가 된다.

| 어휘 | **frantic** ⓐ 제정신이 아닌, 극도로 흥분한   **flustered** ⓐ 허둥거리는

---

02 다음 중 밑줄 친 Ⓐ silent heroes가 가리키는 것은? 가천대 2019

> 자동차가 출현한 이래 자동차로 인한 기록상의 사망자 수는 2천만 명이 넘는다. 1950년대까지만 해도, 자동차 제조업체는 충돌로 인한 물리적 힘은 극복하기엔 너무나 크기 때문에 차량을 그 당시보다 더 안전하게 만드는 것은 불가능하다는 주장을 고수했다. 동시에 사체를 가지고 실험을 한 후, 최초의 충돌시험 더미가 공개되었다. 충돌시험 더미는 실물 크기의 인간형 시험장치(ATD)로 체중과 신체 비율 및 움직임 차원에서 인체와 유사하다. 오늘날 더미는 핵심적인 충돌 데이터를 제공하는 고감도의 첨단 센서를 장착하고 있다. 이러한 말 없는 영웅들 덕에 인류는 과거 어느 때보다도 치명적인 사고에서 생존할 기회가 더 높다.

① 사망자 수   ② 제조업체
③ 사체   ④ 더미

| 정답 | ④

| 해설 | Ⓐ 다음을 보면, Ⓐ 덕분에 치명적인 사고에서 생존할 기회가 높아졌다는 것을 알 수 있고, 여기서 Ⓐ는 충돌시험의 대상이 되어 차량의 안전을 높이는 데 기여한 "충돌시험 더미"를 가리키는 것으로 볼 수 있다. 따라서 답은 ④이다.

| 어휘 | **advent** ⓝ 등장, 출현   **fatalities** ⓝ 사망자 수

03 밑줄 친 ⓐ~ⓓ 중 가리키는 대상이 나머지 셋과 <u>다른</u> 것은?

심지어 오늘날 가장 구제할 수 없을 정도로 심한 정크 푸드 중독자들도 어떤 형태의 지방이건 건강과 허리둘레에 나쁘다는 것을 알고 있지만, 트랜스 지방은 두 배는 더 나쁘다. 액상 기름에 수소가 첨가되어 고체화될 때 생기는 트랜스 지방은 나쁜 콜레스테롤의 수치를 증진시키고 좋은 콜레스테롤의 수치를 억누른다. 최근의 연구에 따르면 가공 식품과 가공유가 미국의 트랜스 지방 섭취의 80퍼센트를 차지한다고 한다. 학자들은 사람들이 가능한 한 트랜스 지방 섭취를 줄일 것을 권하고 있다. 이와 별도로 행한 연구에 따르면 경화유를 제거하는 것은 조기 관상 동맥 사망자 수를 10만 명이나 줄여 놓을 것이라고 결론 지었다.

① ⓐ   ② ⓑ   ③ ⓒ   ④ ⓓ

| 정답 | ②

| 해설 | 나머지는 트랜스 지방을 가리키는데, ② liquid oils는 수소 첨가 이전의 상태를 뜻한다.

| 어휘 | **trans fat** 트랜스 지방   **liquid oil** 액상 기름
     coronary ⓐ 관상 동맥의

실전 문제

01	③	02	④	03	③	04	①	05	③	06	⑤	07	①	08	②	09	⑤	10	④
11	②	12	③	13	②	14	③	15	④	16	②	17	②	18	④	19	③	20	①
21	③	22	④	23	②	24	④	25	④	26	④	27	③	28	④	29	③	30	①

[01~02]

해석

마태복음은 세 명의 현자(동방 박사)에 대해 조금이라도 언급한 유일한 복음서이며, 다른 복음서에서는 아기 예수에게 선물을 가져다준 동방 박사가 몇 명이었는지에 대해서 언급이 없다. 마태복음은 단지 "동양에서 예루살렘으로 현자들이 왔다"고만 기록되어 있다. 현자(동방 박사)는 오직 세 명뿐이라고 여긴 것은 선물이 황금과 유향과 몰약 등 세 종류였기 때문이다. 성경의 이야기를 교회의 석벽에 성화로 그려 넣을 때, 하나의 선물을 한 명의 동방 박사가 가져오는 게 자연스러웠을 것이다. 그렇지만 아마도 더 많은 사람들과 더 많은 선물이 있었을 수 있다.

윗글의 내용과 일치하지 않는 것은?

① 동방 박사들은 예루살렘이 고향이 아니다.

② 동방 박사들은 각각 다른 선물을 가져왔다고 추정된다.

③ 성경의 많은 복음서들은 오직 세 명의 동방 박사라고 적고 있다.

④ 동방 박사가 세 명 이상일 가능성이 있다.

| 정답 | ③

| 해설 | 마태복음만이 세 명의 동방 박사에 대해 조금이라도 언급한 유일한 복음서이며, 다른 복음서에서는 아기 예수에게 선물을 가져다준 동방 박사가 몇 명이었는지에 대해서 언급이 없다.

02 **밑줄 친 ㉮가 지칭하는 것은?**

① 동방 박사의 여정   ② 예수님의 삶

③ 교회   ④ 마태복음

| 정답 | ④

| 해설 | 앞에 언급된 단수 형태를 찾는 것이므로 마태복음을 지칭한 것이다.

| 어휘 | **creep** ⓥ 기다, (생각이) 들다   **frankincense** ⓝ 유향   **myrrh** ⓝ 몰약

[03~05]

해석

한 세기 전에는 인간이 어떻게 사고하는지를 설명할 방법은 사실상 없었다. 그 후 Sigmund Freud와 Jean Piaget 같은 심리학자들이 아동 발달 이론들을 내놓았다. 이어서 기계적 측면에서는 Kurt Godel과 Alan Turing 같은 수학자들은 당시까지는 알려지지 않았던, 기계가 할 수 있는 일의 영역을 밝혀냈다. Warren McCulloch와 Walter Pitts가 어떻게 기계를 보고, 생각하고, 기억하게 만들 수 있는지를 보여 준 19040년대가 되어서야 이 두 사상의 조류는 결합되기 시작했다. 현대 인공 지능 과학 연구는 현대식 컴퓨터의 발명에 힘입어 1950년대에야 등장했다. 이 연구의 영향을 받아, 기계가 어떻게 예전에는 오직 정신만이 했던 일을 할 수 있는지에 관한 새로운 아이디어들이 쏟아지기 시작했다.

03 **빈칸 ⓐ에 문맥상 가장 적합한 단어를 고르시오.**

① 컴퓨터   ② 정신

③ 기계   ④ 인공 지능

| 정답 | ③

| 해설 | 글은 한 세기 전 등장한 사고에 대한 새로운 심리학적, 기계적 통찰이 상호 결합하면서 생각하는 기계가 탄생하는 과정을 설명하고 있다. 문맥상 빈칸 ⓐ는 지문의 소재인 기계(machine)이다. 1940년대는 기계와 사고 능력이 결합하기 시작하는 초기이므로 일반적인 의미의 computer는 문맥에 맞지 않는다.

04 밑줄 친 ⓑ가 지시하는 핵심 단어를 고르시오.

① 연구
② 컴퓨터
③ 발명
④ 해당 없음

| 정답 | ①

| 해설 | 밑줄이 지시하는 것은 문맥상 앞 문장의 인공 지능 연구이므로 ①이 가장 적절하다. 인공 지능 연구가 시작되면서 그 결과, 과거에는 인간의 정신만이 할 수 있던 일을 이제는 기계가 어떻게 할 수 있는지에 대한 새로운 아이디어가 쏟아졌다. "Research in the modern science of Artificial Intelligence started only in the 1950s, stimulated by the invention of modern computers." 참조.

05 빈칸 ⓒ에 문맥상 가장 적합한 단어를 고르시오.

① 겉으로는
② 지나치게
③ 예전에는
④ 급속하게

| 정답 | ③

| 해설 | 생각하는 기계는 최근에 등장했다. 따라서 인간의 정신만이 할 수 있는 일, 즉 사고(thinking)가 인간만의 영역이었던 때는 과거임을 유추할 수 있다. 과거 인간만이 할 수 있었던 사고를 이제는 기계도 할 수 있게 되었다는 것이 이 문장의 함의이므로, 과거와 현재의 대조가 중요하므로 ③이 적절하다. ①은 이 문장의 함의와도 전체 주제와도 무관한 키워드이므로 선택하지 않도록 주의한다.

| 어휘 | **work** ⓥ 작동하다, 효과를 발휘하다
child development 아동 발달
reveal ⓥ 드러내다, 밝히다
range ⓝ 범위, 영역
reason ⓥ 추론하다, 생각하다
stimulate ⓥ 자극하다, 격려하다
a flood of 쇄도하는, 다량의

psychologist ⓝ 심리학자
somewhat 뒈 약간, 다소, 어느 정도
hitherto 뒈 지금까지는
merge ⓥ 합쳐지다, 통합하다
Artificial Intelligence 인공 지능
inspire ⓥ 영감을 주다, 격려하다

[06~08] 성균관대 2016

해석

종교 권장을 위해 종종 사용되는 주장 중 하나는, 예수의 말씀을 담고 있는 마태복음의 내용을 쉽게 풀어서 설명하자면, 종교를 통해 사람들이 이웃을 자신의 몸과 같이 사랑하도록 이끌어 낼 수 있다는 것이다. 만일 이것이 사실이라면, 이것은 강력한 주장이 될 것이다. 그러나 이것이 정말 사실일까? 이와 같은 물음은 시카고 대학의 발달신경과학자인 장 데서티(Jean Decety) 교수가 Current Biology 지에 발표한 한 연구 논문을 통해 던진 질문이다.

종교와 이타주의 간의 관계에 대해 과학적 접근 방식으로 의문을 제기한 인물이 데서티 교수가 처음은 아니다. 하지만 심리학자들이 선호하는 일반적이지만 특별한 실험용 동물인 학부생들에게 의존하지 않고 실험을 수행한 것은 데서티 교수가 최초이다. 그는 학부생들 대신 5~12세 사이의 아이들과 이들 가족들을 조사하기 위해서, 미국의 동료뿐만 아니라 캐나다, 중국, 요르단, 남아프리카 공화국, 터키 등의 연구원들과도 공동으로 이 연구를 수행했다.

06 다음 중 밑줄 친 'it'이 의미하는 것은?

① 대부분의 사람들은 종교적이다.

② 신앙의 대상은 중요한 것이 아니다.

③ 예수는 사람들의 사랑을 강조했다.

④ 과학과 종교는 다르지 않다.

⑤ 종교는 사람들이 다른 이들을 돕도록 만든다.

| 정답 | ⑤

| 해설 | it는 바로 앞 문장의 "it leads people to love their neighbors as themselves"을 의미한다. 내 이웃을 내 몸과 같이 사랑하라는 예수의 말씀처럼 종교가 이런 이타심을 이끈다는 것이다. 이와 가장 유사한 것으로 ③과 ⑤의 보기를 고려할 수 있다. ③도 의미는 유사하지만 정답으로 되기에 문장의 내용이 모호하다. 사물이 아닌 사람의 사랑을 강조한 것인지, 사랑을 한다면 어느 정도로 사랑을 하라는 말인지가 담겨 있지 않다. 그런 이유로 이 문제의 정답은 ⑤가 된다.

07 다음 중 빈칸에 들어갈 가장 적절한 것은?

① 이타주의　　　　　　　　　② 개인주의

③ 이기주의　　　　　　　　　④ 자본주의

⑤ 자아도취

| 정답 | ①

| 해설 | 주어진 지문의 주제에 해당하기 때문이다. 내 이웃을 내 몸과 같이 사랑한다는 말은 이기심을 버리고 이타심을 발휘하라는 내용이므로 정답은 ①이 된다.

08 본문에 의하면, 심리학자들이 가장 선호하는 실험 대상은 무엇인가?

① 아이들　　　　　　　　　　② 대학생

③ 미국인　　　　　　　　　　④ 동물

⑤ 연구원

| 정답 | ②

| 해설 | 본문 후반의 "that standard but peculiar laboratory animal beloved by psychologists, the undergraduate student"를 통해 심리학자들의 사랑을 받는 일반적이지만 다소 이상한 연구소 동물은 바로 학부생이라고 했으므로, 심리학자들은 대학생을 실험 대상으로 즐겨 사용한다는 것을 알 수 있다.

| 어휘 | **encouragement** ⓝ 격려[고무]　　　　　　**neuroscientist** ⓝ 신경 과학자

without recourse ~에 의지하지 않고　　　**undergraduate student** 학부생

altruism ⓝ 이타주의　　　　　　　　　　**individualism** ⓝ 자본주의

egoism ⓝ 이기주의　　　　　　　　　　　**capitalism** ⓝ 자본주의

narcissism ⓝ 자아도취

[09~10]

프라하 성(Prague Castle)은 역사적 유적의 아름다운 복합체일 뿐만 아니라 우리나라의 정치적, 법적 발전과 밀접한 관계가 있는 곳이다. 이 벽 안에는 위대하고 비극적인 사건들이 모두 반영되어 있다. 이 성은 건축된 이후 수많은 기능을 수행했다. 이곳은 군주의 거주지, 군사 요새, 부족의 성역, 기독교의 중심지, 지방의회의 소재지, 법원 및 행정 사무소들이 모여 있는 중심지였다. 특히 이곳은 체코 왕실의 무덤과 체코 왕관 보석의 보관소 기능을 담당하고 있는데, 이는 여전히 체코의 국가 상징이다. 1918년 이후로 이곳은 공화국 대통령의 거처이자 집무실이며, 1000년 이상 지속되며 국가 원수의 거처로써의 프라하 성의 전통을 이어 가고 있다. 대통령 거처의 상징은 프라하 성 위에서 펄럭이는 공화국 대통령의 국기이며, 이는 체코의 국가 상징물 중 하나로, 이것의 중앙에는 거대한 국가 문장이 있으며, "진실은 승리한다"라는 뜻을 가진 문구인 'Pravda vitezi'가 쓰여 있다.

09 밑줄 친 (A)~(E) 가운데 가리키는 것이 다른 하나는?

① (A)　　　　② (B)　　　　③ (C)　　　　④ (D)　　　　⑤ (E)

| 정답 | ⑤

| 해설 | ①~④는 모두 프라하 성을 지칭하고 있지만, ⑤는 프라하 성 위의 국기를 지칭하고 있다.

10 밑줄 친 a number of functions의 예로 언급되지 않은 것은?

① 최고 통치자의 거소(居所)　　　　② 국가적 상징물의 보관소
③ 왕실의 무덤　　　　④ 문화예술 공연장
⑤ 군사 요새

| 정답 | ④

| 해설 | 프라하 성이 기능이 뒤에 나열되어 있는데, '군주의 거주지, 군사 요새, 부족의 성역, 기독교의 중심지, 지방의회의 소재지, 법원 및 행정 사무소들이 모여 있는 중심지' 역할을 담당했다. 그리고 뒤이어 '국가 원수의 거처'였다는 내용이 이어진다. 또한 왕실의 무덤이자 왕관 보석의 보관소로 국가적 상징물을 보관하는 곳이기도 하다. 정답은 ④로, '문화예술 공연장'의 기능은 언급되어 있지 않다.

| 어휘 | **be connected with** ~와 관계가 있다
legal ⓐ 합법의, 법률의
tragic ⓐ 비극적인
a number of 다수의
residence ⓝ 주택, 거주지
tribal ⓐ 부족의, 종족의
christianity ⓝ 기독교
provincial ⓐ 지방의
court ⓝ 궁궐, 법정
not least 특히
repository ⓝ 저장소, 창고
coat of arms 문장

political ⓐ 정치적인
reflect ⓥ 반영하다, 나타내다
fulfill ⓥ 성취하다, 이행하다, 실행하다
monarch ⓝ 군주
fortification ⓝ 성채, 요새
sanctuary ⓝ 성소, 은신처
seat ⓝ 중심지, 소재지
council ⓝ (지방 자치 단체의) 의회, 회의, 협의회
administrative ⓐ 관리상의, 행정상의
burial ⓝ 매장
statehood ⓝ 국가의 지위, 주의 지위
prevail ⓥ 우세하다, 이기다

해석

TV는 역사상 가장 효과적인 마케팅 수단이다. 많은 광고들이 우리의 불안과 욕망에 호소하면서 인간의 기본적인 심리를 이용한다. 광고는 예전엔 사치품이라고 생각했던 것들을 이제는 필수품으로 여기게 한다. TV는 광고뿐 아니라 프로그램에서도 풍요로운 이미지를 만들어 내는 데 탁월하다. 세밀한 시장 조사를 통해, 프로그램 제작자와 광고주들은 물질적 부를 추구하는 삶의 모습을 그려 낸다. 이런 삶은 화려하고 바람직해 보일 수도 있지만, 그것은 전적으로 인간관계의 희생을 대가로 한 것이다.

알다시피, 나는 이 매체를 비판하는 사람들에 동의한다. 광고는 거짓된 욕구를 만들어 내며, 우리에게 정말 필요한 물건들은 광고할 필요가 없다. TV는 소비주의를 조장한다. TV는 우리에게 끝없이 많은 상품들을 보여 주며 탐욕과 부러움을 부추긴다. TV는 물건이 낡기도 전에 버려지는 낭비 사회를 만드는 데 일조한다.

11 밑줄 친 ⓐ, ⓑ, ⓒ, ⓓ 중에서 가리키는 바가 **다른** 것은?

① ⓐ   ② ⓑ   ③ ⓒ   ④ ⓓ

| 정답 | ②

| 해설 | 문맥상 ⓑ it은 앞 문장의 "This kind of life"를 지칭하고, 나머지 보기는 모두 TV를 지칭한다.

12 빈칸 (가)에 들어갈 가장 적절한 것은?

① 광고는 우리의 불안에 무관심하다.
② 광고는 우리 내면의 욕망을 은폐한다.
③ 광고는 거짓된 욕구를 만들어 낸다.
④ 광고는 인간관계를 드러낸다.

| 정답 | ③

| 해설 | 빈칸 다음의 절이 연결어 없이 이어지므로, 다음 절은 빈칸에 대한 부연이다. 빈칸은 "products we really need don't require advertising"과 같은 내용이 되도록 완성한다. '광고는 거짓된 욕구를 만들어 낸다. = 우리에게 정말 필요한 물건은 광고할 필요가 없다.'

13 빈칸 (나)에 들어가기에 적절하지 **않은** 것은?

① 사치스러운   ② 검소한
③ 비경제적인   ④ 낭비하는

| 정답 | ②

| 해설 | where 이하의 내용이 빈칸에 대한 부연 설명이다. "낡기도 전에 물건을 버리는 사회(where things are thrown out long before they are worn out)"는 '낭비하는' 사회이므로 빈칸에 적절치 않은 것은 "frugal(검소한)"이다.

14 윗글의 내용과 일치하지 <u>않는</u> 것은?

① TV는 건전한 소비 풍토에 방해물일 수 있다.

② TV는 소비주의 문화를 조장한다.

③ TV는 광고 산업에 부정적인 영향을 미친다.

④ TV는 풍요로운 사회의 이미지를 보여 준다.

| 정답 | ③

| 해설 | 'TV가 소비 풍토에 부정적인 영향을 미친다.'는 주제와 무관한 내용은 보기 ③이다. TV가 광고 산업에 영향을 미치는 것이 아니라, TV가 광고와 프로그램을 통해 소비 풍토에 영향을 미친다는 것에 주의한다.

| 어휘 |

sort of 일종의

insecurity ⓝ 불안

luxury ⓝ 사치품, 사치

be skilled at ~에 능하다

as well 또한

be centered on ~을 중심으로 하다

glamorous ⓐ 화려한

agree with ~에 동의하다

consumerism ⓝ 소비주의

greed ⓝ 탐욕

throw out 버리다

extravagant ⓐ 사치스러운

uneconomical ⓐ 사치스러운, 비경제적인

appeal to ~에 호소하다

convince ⓥ 설득하다, 확신시키다

necessity ⓝ 필수품, 필요

affluence ⓝ 풍요

sophisticated ⓐ 정교한, 세밀한, 세련된

material possession 물질적 소유(부)

at the expense of ~을 대가로

promote ⓥ 조장하다, 촉진하다

encourage ⓥ 조장하다, 권유하다

envy ⓝ 부러움, 시기

wear out 낡다

frugal ⓐ 절약하는

[15~16]

해석

이 약물이 과학계에서 항상 그렇게 논란이 많았던 것은 아니다. 1820년에 편찬되기 시작한 의사들의 약재 목록인 미국 약전(U.S. Pharmacopeia)에는 1870년 최초로 카나비스(마리화나, 대마초)가 약재 목록에 포함되었다. 1937년 카나비스가 금지된 이후 처음으로 출간된 1942년 판은 카나비스를 목록에서 제외했다. 결국엔 대부분의 의사들이 이 약물을 조잡한 흥분제에 불과하다고 생각하기 시작했다. 그들은 제약 회사에서 순수한 화학 성분으로 정제한 신약들을 더 선호했다. 반면 천연 마리화나에는 400여 가지 복합 성분이 있다. 70년대에 이르러서야, 카나비스의 의학적 효능이 현대적 방식을 통해 테스트되었다. Earleywine에 따르면, 대마초가 동공을 확장시킨다는 경찰 보고서를 검증하기 위한 UCLA 연구는 오히려 대마초가 동공을 미세하게 축소시킨다는 것을 발견했다. 이를 통해, 의사들은 대마초가 안압을 낮춤으로써 녹내장 환자들에게 도움을 줄 수도 있다는 것을 알게 되었다.

15 밑줄 친 ⓐ The drug이 가리키지 <u>않는</u> 것은?

① 마리화나

② 카나비스(마리화나)

③ 마리화나

④ 흥분제

| 해설 | 지문의 ①, ②, ③ 모두 지문의 소재인 마리화나를 뜻한다. ④ intoxicant(흥분제)는 다른 약물까지 포함하는 더 포괄적인 단어이므로 마리화나를 지칭하지 않는다.

---

16 윗글의 내용에서 추론할 수 없는 것은?

① 예전에는 마리화나의 사용이 불법은 아니었다.

② 마리화나는 동공을 확장시킨다.

③ 녹내장 환자들은 안압이 더 높다.

④ 마리화나는 녹내장 환자들에게 도움이 된다.

| 정답 | ②

| 해설 | UCLA 연구는 마리화나가 동공을 미세하게 축소시킨다는 것을 발견했으므로 ②는 사실과 일치하지 않는다. 마리화나가 동공을 확장시킨다는 경찰 보고는 이 연구에 의해 반박되었음을 유추할 수 있다. "a UCLA study designed to confirm police reports that pot dilates pupils found instead a slight constriction." 참조.

| 어휘 |
controversial ⓐ 논쟁적인

pharmacopeia ⓝ 약전

cannabis ⓝ 카나비스, 대마초

outlaw ⓥ 금지하다

view A as B A를 B라고 간주하다

intoxicant ⓝ (술, 마약 등) 취하게 하는 것

new-fashioned ⓐ 새로운

chemical ⓝ 화학 물질

compound ⓝ 화합물

recount ⓥ 자세히 설명하다

pot ⓝ 마리화나

pupil ⓝ 동공, 학생

glaucoma ⓝ 녹내장

scientific establishment 과학계

remedy ⓝ 치료제

drop ⓥ 제외하다

physician ⓝ 의사

crude ⓐ 조잡한, 조악한

favor ⓥ 선호하다

refine ⓥ 정제하다, 다듬다

marijuana ⓝ 마리화나, 대마초

apply ⓥ 적용하다, 응용하다

confirm ⓥ 확인하다, 공식화하다

dilate ⓥ 확대(확장)하다

constriction ⓝ 축소

intraocular pressure 안압

해석

웨스트베리(Westbury) 교수는 언어 장애와 뇌 기능의 연관성을 탐구하면서 중요한 연구를 수행해 오고 있다. 연구 조사의 일환으로 웨스트베리 교수는 실어증 환자들(단어와 말에 대한 이해력이 떨어지는 환자들)에게 일련의 글자들을 나열해 제시하면서 이 글자들이 실제 영어 단어인지를 물어보는 실험을 실시했다. 하루는 한 대학원생이 흥미로운 부분을 지적했다. 말도 안 되는 특정 단어들이 일관되게 환자들을 미소 짓게 만들거나 심지어 박장대소하게 만들었던 것이다. 특히 웨스트베리는 "snunkoople"이라는 단어가 그랬다고 말한다. 그는 친구들과 동료들도 이 단어에 같은 반응을 보이는지 확인하기 시작했고, 그 반응은 모두 같은 것으로 나타났다. snunkoople 이란 단어는 우스웠다. 하지만 왜 그런 것일까? 웨스트베리는 자신이 정답으로 생각하는 것을 내놓는다. 그것은 바로 단어 혹은 적어도 문맥이 없는 비단어가 갖는 고유한 우스꽝스러움이 정량화될 수 있으며, 터무니없는 단어라도 모두 동일하게 만들어지지 않았다는 사실이다. 웨스트베리에 따르면 통계적으로 볼 때 특정 글자 모음이 영어로 실제 단어를 형성할 확률이 낮을수록 더 우스꽝스럽게 들린다. 극작가 닐 사이먼(Neil Simon)은 1972년 작품 '선샤인 보이즈(Sunshine Boys)'에서 암묵적으로 이것을 파악한 것으로 보인다. 나이 든 한 등장인물이 자신의 조카에게 "단어 안에 'k'가 없다면 우습게 들리지 않아. 'k'는 알파벳 중 매우 흔하게 사용되는 문자가 아니기 때문에 그렇지."라고 말하는 대목이 나온다.

17 윗글의 제목으로 가장 적절한 것은?

① 실어증: 우리가 웃는 방식
② 왜 어떤 단어는 우스운 것일까?
③ 애매하게 말하는 기술로서의 유머
④ 특이한 문자 조합인 'snunkoople'

| 정답 | ②

| 해설 | 본문에서 snunkoople은 주제의 한 예로 사용된 것으로, 이 단어가 웃기게 들리는 이유에 대한 분석인 ②가 주제로 적합하다.

18 밑줄 친 "this"가 의미하는 것으로 적절하지 않은 것은?

① 웃음은 일종의 부조화의 부산물이다.
② 단어가 그럴듯하게 들리지 않으면 않을수록 우리는 그 단어를 더 우스꽝스럽게 여긴다.
③ 웃음은 기대가 갑자기 어긋날 때 발생한다.
④ 웃음은 단어가 직관적으로 우리의 기대와 일치할 때 제대로 작용한다.

| 정답 | ④

| 해설 | 특정 단어가 우습게 들린다는 것은 그 단어를 구성하는 문자의 조합이 가장 그럴듯하지 않을 때 발생한다고 말하고 있다. 이것이 바로 부조화(incongruity)를 의미하며, 우리의 기대와 어긋나는 것을 말한다. 정답은 ④로 단어가 우리의 직관과 일치할 경우 웃음이 나지 않아야 하므로 반대로 서술한 문장이 된다.

| 어휘 | **inquiry** ⑪ 연구, 탐구, 조사 **aphasia** ⑪ 실어증 **impaired** ⓐ 손상된
unanimous ⓐ 만장일치의 **inherent** ⓐ 내재하는, 고유한 **quantified** ⓐ 정량화된
grasp ⓥ 이해하다 **implicitly** ⓓ 암암리에, 함축적으로 **equivocation** ⑪ 얼버무리기
cluster ⑪ 무리, 다발, 송이 **by-product** ⑪ 부산물 **incongruity** ⑪ 부조화, 모순
plausible ⓐ 타당한 것 같은, 이치에 맞는, 그럴듯한 **deem** ⓥ ~라고 여기다
square with ~와 아귀가 맞다, 일치하다

해석

일반적인 통념과는 반대로, 1991년 Sports Medicine이라는 잡지에서 발표된 연구에 따르면 운동과 추위에서의 노출이 결합되어도 지방의 신진대사를 촉진하도록 시너지 효과를 일으키지는 않는다. Maryland주 Bethesda에 위치한 Naval Medical Research Institute의 Hyperbaric Environmental Adaptation Program에서 시행된 이 연구는 비교적 추운 날씨가 인간의 조직에 미치는 영향으로 인해 지방의 신진대사와 연관되는 신체 과정 중 일부가 둔화된다는 점을 발견했다. 연구자들은 추위 속에서 운동을 할 때 말단부의 지방 조직의 혈관이 수축되는 것과 신진대사 과정의 둔화가 연관되어 있을 수 있음을 시사했다. 이 연구는 1분간 들이쉬고 내쉬는 공기의 양이 처음 추위에 노출되었을 때엔 증가하지만 오랫동안 격심한 운동을 하면 따뜻한 공기에서 운동할 때의 비율과 비슷한 비율로 돌아갈 수 있다는 점도 발견했다. 이 연구는 심장 박동 수는 항상 그런 것은 아니지만 추운 날씨에서 운동할 때는 낮아지며 반면 산소 흡수율은 늘어나는 것 같음을 발견했고, 연구진들은 이것이 어느 정도는 최소한 몸을 부르르 떠는 결과로 인한 것일 수 있음을 시사했다.

---

19 본문의 연구를 통해 알 수 있는 것은 무엇인가?

① 사람들은 더운 날씨보다 추운 날씨에서 운동할 때 지방을 더 많이 연소한다.
② 따뜻한 날씨에서 운동하는 것은 들이마시는 공기의 양을 늘린다.
③ 추운 날씨는 일부 신진대사 과정의 둔화를 야기한다.
④ 몸을 떨어서 산소의 흡수율이 늘어나면 심장 박동 수가 높아진다.

| 정답 | ③

| 해설 | 본문에 "비교적 추운 날씨가 인간의 조직에 미치는 영향으로 인해 지방의 신진대사와 연관되는 신체 과정 중 일부가 둔화된다(some of the bodily processes involved in fat metabolism were actually slowed down by the effects of relatively cold temperatures on human tissue)"라고 명시되어 있으며 이는 ③의 내용과 일맥상통한다.

①의 경우는, "운동과 추위에의 노출이 결합되어도 지방의 신진대사를 촉진하도록 시너지 효과를 일으키지는 않는다(the combination of exercise and cold exposure does not act synergistically to enhance metabolism of fats)"는 점에서 사실이 아님을 알 수 있다. ②의 경우는, "1분간 들이쉬고 내쉬는 공기의 양이 처음 추위에 노출되었을 때엔 증가(the volume of air inhaled and exhaled in one minute increases upon initial exposure to the cold)"한다는 언급은 본문에 있으나 더위에 노출되었을 때 들이마시는 공기의 양이 늘어난다는 언급은 없었으므로 답이 될 수 없다. ④의 경우는, "추운 날씨에 운동하면 산소 흡수율은 늘어나지만 심장 박동 수는 항상 그런 건 아니긴 해도 줄어든다(the heart rate is often, but not always, lower during cold-weather exercise ... while oxygen uptake may increase)"라고 언급되어 있으므로 ④ 또한 답이 될 수 없다.

---

20 밑줄 친 'those'가 나타내는 것은 무엇인가?

① 비율   ② 신진대사 과정
③ 증가   ④ 지방 조직

| 정답 | ①

| 해설 | those가 복수이므로 문장 내에서 복수형인 것을 찾아야 하며 동시에 보기에 제시된 것 중에서 대입했을 때 문맥상 가장 적합한 것을 골라야 한다. 또한 A is comparable to B에서 A와 B를 비교하고 있으므로, A와 B는 동등한 자격의 것이 와야 한다.

A가 '비율(rates)'이라면 B에 들어올 것 역시 '비율'이어야 한다. 이러한 조건에 부합되는 것은 ①뿐이다.

| 어휘 | conventional wisdom 일반적인 통념

metabolism ⓝ 신진대사

adaptation ⓝ 적응

constriction ⓝ 수축

inhale ⓥ 숨을 들이마시다

comparable to ～와 비슷한

exertion ⓝ 격심한 운동

shiver ⓥ (추위로 몸을) 떨다

synergistically ⓐⓓ 시너지 효과를 일으키는

hyperbaric ⓐ 고압성의

tissue ⓝ 조직

peripheral ⓐ 말단부의

exhale ⓥ 숨을 내쉬다

prolonged ⓐ 오래 지속되는

uptake ⓝ 흡수율

bring about ～을 야기하다, 초래하다

[21~24] 한성대 2010

해석

소음은 오늘날 가장 만연한 오염원이지만 동시에 일시적인 오염원이기도 하다. 소음 공해를 대략적으로 정의하자면, 우리 일상 생활에 지나칠 정도로 침범해 들어오는 달갑지 않거나 짜증을 유발하는 소리라고 할 수 있다. 우리는 소음을 여러 방식으로 경험한다. 어떤 경우에는 우리는 소음의 가해자이면서 동시에 소음의 피해자가 될 수도 있다. 예를 들어 소음을 유발하는 가전제품이나 장비를 직접 작동시키는 경우를 생각해 보면 된다. 또한 사람들이 간접흡연을 경험하는 것처럼 타인에 의해 발생한 소음을 간접적으로 경험하는 경우도 있다. 두 경우 모두 소음은 신체에 동일하게 손상을 준다. 하지만 간접 소음이 일반적으로 더 큰 문제가 되는데, 그 이유는 소음이 우리 동의 없이 타인에 의해 환경에 더해지기 때문이다.

간접 소음이 방출되거나 그것이 이동하는 데 필요한 대기는 "공유재(commons)"에 해당한다. 대기는 특정 개인이나 집단에 속한 것이 아니라 우리 모두의 것이다. 그러므로 사람들과 기업들, 기관들은 자신들이 원하는 대로 간접 소음을 무제한적으로 내보낼 수 있는 특권을 갖고 있는 것이 아니다. 이와는 반대로 그들에게는 공유재를 타인의 사용과 양립해서 이용할 의무가 있다. 소음 공해를 유발하면서 타인의 공유재 사용을 "방해하지 않을" 의무를 저버리는 이들은 마치 학교 교정에서 약자를 괴롭히는 불량배와 같이 행동하고 있는 것이다. 비록 자신도 모르는 사이에 이런 행동을 한다 할지라도, 그들은 타인의 권리를 무시하고 있는 것이며 자신들의 소유가 아닌 권리를 자신들을 위해 요구하고 있는 것이다.

---

21 밑줄 친 ⒜ transient와 의미가 가장 비슷한 것은?

① 투명한　　　　② 이동 가능한　　　　③ 일시적인　　　　④ 초월적인

| 정답 | ③

| 해설 | 'transient'는 '일시적인'이란 의미를 지니므로, 정답은 ③의 transitory가 된다.

---

22 밑줄 친 ⒝와 ⒞의 it이 각각 지칭하는 것은?

① 대기, 간접 소음　　　　　　　② 대기, 대기

③ 간접 소음, 대기　　　　　　　④ 간접 소음, 간접 소음

| 정답 | ③

| 해설 | 우선 ⒝의 it은 바로 앞의 "the air" 또는 "secondhand noise" 중에서 하나를 받을 것으로 추측할 수 있다. 그리고 "into

which secondhand noise is emitted"와 "on which it travels" 부분이 병렬 구조를 이루면서 앞의 "the air"라는 선행사를 꾸미고 있다는 것을 알 수 있다. 따라서 앞쪽의 내용은 "secondhand noise is emitted into the air(간접 소음이 대기에 방출된다)"의 내용이 되고, Ⓑ가 있는 뒤쪽의 내용은 "it travels on the air(it은 대기를 타고 이동한다)"가 된다. 이와 같은 비교 분석을 통해 Ⓑ의 it은 "secondhand noise"를 지시하고 있다는 사실을 알 수 있다. 다음으로 ⒸA의 it은 개인이나 그룹이 아닌 모든 이들에게 속해 있는 것이라고 말하고 있으므로, 이는 '간접 소음'이 아닌 공유재에 해당하는 '대기'가 된다는 것을 알 수 있다. 따라서 답은 ③이 된다.

---

23 빈칸 Ⓓ에 가장 적합한 것은?

① 게다가
② 이와는 반대로
③ 그럼에도 불구하고
④ 그래서, 그러므로

| 정답 | ②

| 해설 | 빈칸 앞부분을 보면 "소음을 낼 수 있는 무한대의 권리를 가진 것은 아님(do not have unlimited rights to broadcast noise)"을 명시하고 있으며, 빈칸 뒤의 내용에는 "공유재를 다른 이들과 조화롭게 사용할 의무가 있음 (have an obligation to use the commons in ways that are compatible with other uses)"을 명시하고 있다. 따라서 '누릴 권리'가 있는 것이 아니라 '지켜야 할 의무'가 있다는 내용이므로, 이런 역접의 관계를 잘 나타내 줄 수 있는 연결어구가 필요하다. 따라서 답은 ② 가 된다.

---

24 윗글의 내용과 일치하지 <u>않는</u> 것은?

① 간접 소음은 통제가 되지 않기 때문에 매우 불쾌할 수 있다.
② 간접 소음은 우리들이 만들어 내는 직접 소음처럼 해로울 수 있다.
③ 우리는 무심결에 다른 사람의 공유재 사용을 방해할 수 있다.
④ 우리는 소음 공해의 피해자가 아니라 가해자이다.

| 정답 | ④

| 해설 | ①의 경우는 본문의 "Secondhand noise is generally more troubling, however, because it is put into the environment by others, without our consent."을 통해 유추할 수 있으며, ②의 경우는 간접 소음이든 직접 소음이든 모두 해롭다는 내용("In both instances, noise is equally damaging physically.")을 통해 유추할 수 있다. ③의 경우도 본문 중 "Although they may do so unknowingly" 부분을 통해 다른 이들에게 부지불식간에 방해할 수 있다는 내용이 나온다. ④의 보기에서는 우리가 소음 공해의 피해자가 아니라 가해자라고 했는데, 본문에서는 상황에 따라서 피해자가 될 수도 있고 ("we experience noise generated by others"), 다른 상황에서는 피해자와 가해자가 동시에 될 수도 있다("we can be both the cause and victim of noise")고 했으므로 정답은 ④가 된다.

| 어휘 | **pervasive** ⓐ 만연하는, (구석구석) 스며드는   **transient** ⓐ 일시적인
define A as B A를 B라고 정의하다   **unwanted** ⓐ 불필요한
broadly ⓐⓓ 대체로, 대략적으로   **intrude into** 침입하다, 난입하다
unreasonably ⓐⓓ 지나치게, 불합리하게   **on some occasions** 어느 경우에는
noisy appliance 시끄러운 소리가 나는 가전제품   **equipment** ⓝ 장비

instance ⓝ 사례, 경우

consent ⓝ 동의

emit ⓥ 내뿜다, 방출하다

as one pleases 자기가 원하는 대로 하다

disregard ⓥ 무시하다

transparent ⓐ 투명한, 명백한

transitory ⓐ 일시적인

offensive ⓐ 불쾌한

irritating ⓐ 짜증나는

unintentionally ⓐⓓ 무심결에, 아무 생각 없이

physically ⓐⓓ 물리적으로

without one's consent 누구의 동의 없이

commons ⓝ 공유재 (cf. public goods ⓝ 공공재)

be compatible with 양립할 수 있는

bully ⓝ 약자를 괴롭히는 사람

transferable ⓐ 이동 가능한

transcendent ⓐ 초월하는, 초월적인

vexing ⓐ 짜증나게 하는

evasive ⓐ 얼버무리는, 회피하는

[25~27]

해석

노르만 왕들은 종종 영국인들을 전적으로 무시했지만, 헨리 1세의 경우 부인이 영국 사람이기에 예외로 약간의 영어를 말할 수 있었다. 물론 상류층 계급에선 프랑스어를 말하는 것이 아주 멋진 것이었음은 의심할 필요가 없다. 오늘날까지 대화에서 프랑스어를 사용하는 것은 지적 교양 또는 재치를 보여 주는 것으로 간주된다. 프랑스어가 사회·문화적 위상을 가졌다면, 라틴어는 종교와 학습의 주된 언어로 남았었다. 통속어인 영어는 일반인들의 말로 생존했다. 이러한 세 강력한 전통들의 융합은 kingly와 같은 단어에서 나타난다. 앵글로색슨은 이러한 개념을 표현하는 단어를 단지 하나만 가지고 있었는데, 단순히 king이란 단어에서 만들어 냈다. 노르만족 이후 세 가지 동의어인 royal, regal 그리고 sovereign이란 단어가 이 언어(영어)에 들어온다. 셋 또는 네 가지 다른 뉘앙스를 표현하거나 미묘한 구별을 하는 능력은 바로 노르만 정복 이후 rise-mount-ascend, ask-question-interrogate 또는 time-age-epoch와 같은 단어 그룹처럼 이 언어(영어)의 특징 중 하나이다.

25 ⓐ에 들어갈 가장 적절한 표현을 고르시오.

① 예

② 전문가

③ 전문 지식

④ 예외

| 정답 | ④

| 해설 | 논리적 반전을 이끄는 'although'를 활용한다. 노르만 정복 이후 왕들은 영어를 전적으로 무시했다고 했지만, 헨리 1세의 경우 아내가 영국인이었기에 영어를 사용한 '예외적' 왕임을 유추할 수 있다. 뒤에 이어지는 'some English'도 답의 근거로 활용할 수 있다.

26 밑줄 친 ⓑ와 ⓒ의 the language가 구체적으로 지시하는 쌍을 고르시오.

① 영어 – 라틴어

② 영어 – 프랑스어

③ 라틴어 – 프랑스어

④ 영어 – 영어

| 정답 | ④

| 해설 | 노르만 정복이 이후 앞에서 언급한 언어가 영어에 흡수되고, 그러면서 이런 영향으로 영어에선 미묘한 의미의 차이를 드러내는 동의어가 발생하게 되었다는 내용이다. 둘 다 영어를 지칭한다.

---

27 윗글의 내용에 가장 잘 부합하는 것을 고르시오.

① 헨리 1세는 다른 노르만족 왕과 같이 영어를 말할 수 없었다.

② 공공장소에서 프랑스어를 말하는 것은 수치로 여겨졌다.

③ 라틴어는 당시 교회와 학교에서 가장 위상이 높은 언어였다.

④ king이란 단어는 프랑스어에서 발생했다.

| 정답 | ③

| 해설 | 첫 번째 문장에서 헨리 1세는 영국인 아내로 인해 약간의 영어를 말할 수 있다고 했으니 ①은 틀린 진술이다. 프랑스어를 사용하는 것은 사회·문화적 위상을 드러낸다고 했으므로 ②는 옳지 못하다. 라틴어는 종교와 교육에서 주된 언어로 사용되었다고 했으므로 ③은 옳은 진술이다. ④ King은 영어에 해당하는 표현이다.

| 어휘 | **fashionable** ⓐ 부유층이 애용하는   **sophistication** ⓝ 교양

prestige ⓝ 특권   **vernacular** ⓝ 토착어, 고유어

capacity ⓝ 수용력   **savoir fair** 임기응변의 재치, 수완

principle ⓐ 주된   **vernacular** ⓝ 통속명, 일상어

synonym ⓝ 동의어   **shade** ⓝ 색깔, 명암, 빛깔의 뉘앙스

different shades of meaning 다양한 뉘앙스의 의미

[28~30] 국민대 2014

해석

인터넷상에서의 모유의 판매 및 기증을 촉진시키는 가내 산업이 우후죽순으로 생겨나고 있지만 월요일 발표된 한 연구는 이러한 규제되지 않는 새로운 시장에 대한 보건 전문가들의 우려를 확증하였다. 이 연구 보고서에 따르면 인터넷을 통해 구매한 모유는 살모넬라균을 포함한 각종 박테리아의 오염도가 매우 높았다. 검출된 양은 아이를 아프게 만들기에 충분할 정도였다. 컬럼비아 대학의 리처드 박사는 다음과 같이 말했다. "이번 연구 결과는 우려스럽습니다. 이런 행위는 잠재적으로 병을 유발할 수 있습니다. 친척들 사이라도 모유를 공유하는 것은 좋은 생각이 아닙니다." 모유가 신생아를 감염 및 질병으로부터 보호해 준다는 연구 결과가 쏟아지듯 발표된 이후 보건 담당자들은 갓 엄마가 된 여성들에게 조제분유는 버리고 모유를 먹여 아이를 키울 것을 권장했다. 하지만 이렇게 분유 대신에 모유를 먹이는 일은 어머니들에게 까다로운 과제가 될 것이다. 예를 들어 아이를 입양한 부모의 경우나 유방 절제술을 받은 부모는 종종 기증받거나 구매한 모유에 의존하게 된다.

---

28 다음 중 밑줄 친 ⓐ this가 가리키는 것은 무엇인가?

① 시장을 규제하기   ② 입양하거나 유방 절제술을 받기

③ 질병의 잠재적 원인을 차단하기   ④ 조제분유를 버리고 모유를 먹이기

| 정답 | ④

| 해설 | ⓐ this는 "까다로운 과제(difficult challenge)"이며, 그 뒤 문장을 보면 조제분유 대신에 모유를 먹이기가 쉽지 않은 사례를 열거하고 있다. 이 또한 "까다로운 과제"이다. 즉 this는 조제분유 대신에 모유를 먹이는 것을 가리킨다. 따라서 답은 ④이다.

29 다음 중 본문에 따르면 사실이 <u>아닌</u> 것은 무엇인가?

① 최근 연구 결과가 일부 부모들을 불안하게 만들었다.

② 모유는 아이들이 병에 걸리지 않게 막아 줄 수 있다.

③ 연구가 기증된 모유의 혜택을 입증했다.

④ 모유 공유 사이트에서 제공하는 몇 가지 샘플에는 위험한 수준의 박테리아가 함유되어 있다.

| 정답 | ③

| 해설 | 본문에 따르면 이번 연구는 기증된 모유가 오히려 아이들에게 병을 유발할 위험성이 있음을 증명하고 있다. 이는 ③과 정반대되는 내용이다.

30 다음 중 본문의 제목으로 가장 알맞은 것은 무엇인가?

① 모유를 찾고 계십니까? 조심하세요.

② 공급이 넘치는 상황입니까? 인터넷에서 판매하세요.

③ 위험을 감수하세요. 여러분의 자녀를 위해서입니다.

④ 모유를 먹여 아이를 키우지 마세요. 모유는 오염되어 있습니다.

| 정답 | ①

| 해설 | 아이는 조제분유 대신에 모유를 먹여 키워야 한다고 권장되지만 엄마가 직접 모유를 먹이는 것이 아니라 다른 사람으로부터 모유를 구매하거나 기증받는 것은 오히려 아이를 병에 걸리게 만들 수 있으므로 조심해야 한다는 것이 본문의 핵심이다. 따라서 답으로 가장 적절한 것은 ①이다.

| 어휘 | **cottage industry** 가내 공업[산업]

facilitate ⓥ 손쉽게 하다, (행위를) 돕다, 촉진하다

breast milk 모유

unregulated ⓐ 통제받지 않는, 규제[단속]되지 않은

detect ⓥ 발견하다, 간파하다, 검출하다

potential ⓐ 잠재적인

ailment ⓝ 불쾌, 우환, 질병

breast-feed ⓥ 모유로 기르다, 모유를 먹이다

unnerve ⓥ 불안하게 만들다

tainted ⓐ 더럽혀진, 오염된

spring up 갑자기 생겨나다, 우후죽순으로 생겨나다

donation ⓝ 증여, 기증

confirm ⓥ 확실히하다, 확증하다

contaminate ⓥ 더럽히다, 오염시키다

sicken ⓥ 구역질나게 하다, 병나게 하다

spate ⓝ (불쾌한 일의) 빈발, (말, 사건 따위의) 쏟아져 나옴

formula ⓝ 조제분유

mastectomy ⓝ 유방 절제술

demonstrate ⓥ 입증하다

| 연습 문제 | | 01 ① | 02 ② | 03 ② | 04 ③ |

01 밑줄 친 celibate와 의미가 가장 가까운 것을 고르시오.

> 여러 해 동안 학자들과 연구원들은 마치 수많은 자료들을 연구하면 천재들에 대해서 설명해 줄 것처럼 통계를 분석함으로써 천재들을 연구하는 일에 힘써 왔다. 1904년 해브럭 엘리스는 자신의 연구에서 대부분의 천재들은 아버지가 나이가 30세 이상이고 어머니가 25세 이하인 경우에서 나오고, 어릴 때는 신체가 약한 편이라고 밝혔다. 다른 많은 학자들은 천재들은 <u>독신주의자</u>(데카르트의 경우)거나, 아버지가 없는 사생아(디킨스의 경우)거나, 어머니가 없는 사생아(다윈의 경우) 등이라고 적었다. 결국 그 자료들은 아무것도 밝혀낸 것이 없는 셈이다.

① 절제하는, 금욕하는   ② 부모가 없는
③ 뒤죽박죽인, 난잡한   ④ 풍요로운

| 정답 | ①

| 해설 | celibate와 ① abstinent는 동의어 관계이다.

| 어휘 | **celibate** ⓐ 독신의, 절제하는, 금욕적인   **abstinent** ⓐ 절제하는, 금욕하는
promiscuous ⓐ 뒤죽박죽인, 무차별의

02 밑줄 친 ㉮ 'charge'와 의미상 가장 가까운 것은 다음 중 어떤 것인가?

> 아시아 사람들은 서구인들보다 몸짓을 훨씬 더 빈번히 그리고 창의적으로 사용한다. 이것은 특히 춤과 희곡에서 두드러지는데, 많은 극동 지역 국가에서는 춤과 희곡은 고도로 복잡하며, 손과 몸의 격식 있는 몸짓이 수백 가지에 달한다. 충분한 지식을 갖지 못한 서구인들에게는 이들 몸짓의 대부분은 외국어와 같다. 아시아의 춤과 희곡의 대부분은 종교적 배경을 갖고 있는데, 공연자의 몸짓은 관객에게 전해지는 정보와 감정의 힘으로 <u>충만해진다</u>.

① 비할 바 없는 용맹을 보이며 그 기병대는 적에게 돌진했다.
② 축제가 가까워 오면서, 공기가 흥분된 분위기로 충만해졌다.
③ 내부 고발자의 정보로 그는 횡령 혐의를 지게 되었다.
④ 감독은 비서에게 자신의 서신 왕래를 담당하도록 책임지웠다.
⑤ TV 자체에 문제가 있었으므로 난 수리 비용을 청구받지 않았다.

| 정답 | ②

| 해설 | 'charge'에는 여러 뜻이 있다.
     ① '돌진하다'라는 뜻이다.
     ② 'be charged with A'의 형태로 'A라는 감정에 가득 차다'라는 뜻이다.
     ③ 'charge A with B[doing B]'의 형태로 'A를 B라는 죄를 저질렀다고 기소 또는 고소하다'라는 뜻이다.
     ④ 'charge A with B'의 형태로 'A에게 B라는 임무를 맡기다'라는 뜻이다.

⑤ 'charge A for B'의 형태로 'A에게 B의 요금 또는 대금을 청구하다'라는 뜻이다.

| 어휘 | **far** ⓐ 훨씬 (비교급의 강조)   **frequently** ⓐ 자주, 빈번히
productively ⓐ 생산적으로   **particularly** ⓐ 특히
noticeable ⓐ 두드러지는   **formal** ⓐ 격식을 차린, 정식의, 의례를 갖춘
uninformed ⓐ 교육을 받지 않은, 충분한 지식이 없는
be charged with (감정으로) 충만한   **communicate to** ~에게 알리다, 전하다
unparalleled ⓐ 비할 바 없는, 견줄 나위 없는   **cavalry** ⓝ 기병대, 기갑 부대
whistle-blower ⓝ 내부 고발자   **embezzlement** ⓝ 횡령
correspondence ⓝ 서신 왕래   **defective** ⓐ 결함이 있는

[03~04]

해석

현대의 그리스는 보기 드물 정도로 다양한 영향의 집합체이다. 알렉산더 대왕의 시절부터 지금까지 비잔틴 제국은 말할 것도 없고, 로마인, 아랍인, 프랑스인, 베네치아인, 슬라브인, 알바니아인, 터키인, 이탈리아인들이 모두 여기 그리스에 왔다가 사라졌다. 그들은 모두 자신의 흔적을 남겼는데, 비잔틴인들은 수많은 교회와 수도원에, 베네치아인들은 펠로폰네소스 반도의 난공불락 성채에, 그리고 프랑크인들은 펠로폰네소스 반도뿐만 아니라 동쪽 에게해에 위치한 바위산 위의 성에 각각 그들의 흔적을 남겼다. 아마 가장 두드러진 것은 400년간의 오스만 제국 통치의 유산일 것인데, 제국의 통치는 음악·요리·언어·생활 방식 등에 이루 헤아릴 수 없는 영향을 끼쳤다. 덧붙여 왈라키아인·이슬람교도·유대인·집시 등 비중 있는 소수 민족들의 공헌과 지속적인 존재가 있음으로써 현대 그리스의 정체성 형성에 기여한 것들의 목록이 완성된다.

03 밑줄 친 ⓐ와 의미가 가장 가까운 것은?

① ~을 나쁘게 말하다
② ~는 말할 것도 없고
③ ~은 안중에 없다
④ ~을 가볍게 여기다

| 정답 | ②

| 해설 | ⓐ의 의미는 '~는 말할 것도 없고'이며 보기 중에서 ②와 의미상 가장 가깝다.

04 밑줄 친 ⓑ와 의미가 가장 가까운 것은?

① 지배하다   ② 원을 그리다
③ 완성하다   ④ 피해 가다

| 정답 | ③

| 해설 | ⓑ의 의미는 '~을 완성하다'이며 이는 보기 ③과 동일하다.

| 어휘 | **monastery** ⓝ 수도원   **impregnable** ⓐ 난공불락의, (신념이) 확고한
fortification ⓝ 축성술[학], 성채, 요새   **crag** ⓝ 험한 바위산

Aegean ⓐ 에게해의, 다도해의		**Ottoman Turkish** 오스만 제국의	
heritage ⓝ 세습[상속] 재산, 유산		**cuisine** ⓝ 요리, 요리법	
substantial ⓐ 상당한, 많은, 비중 있는		**minority** ⓝ 소수, 소수 민족	
Vlach ⓐ 왈카리아 사람의		**Muslim** ⓐ 이슬람교도의	
Jew ⓐ 유대인의, 히브리인의		**Hellenic** ⓐ (고대 또는 현대) 그리스 사람[말]의	
identity ⓝ 신원, 정체성		**round out** 완성하다, 마무리하다, 완전한 것으로 만들다	
nexus ⓝ 핵심, 연계		**remnant** ⓝ 나머지, 흔적, 자취	
to speak ill of ~을 나쁘게 말하다		**not to mention** ~은 말할 것도 없고	
to set at nought ~은 안중에 없다		**to make light of** ~을 가볍게 여기다	
circumvent ⓥ 피해 가다, 면하다			

실전 문제

01	②	02	④	03	②	04	④	05	①	06	②	07	①	08	④	09	③	10	②
11	②	12	③	13	④	14	②	15	②	16	①	17	③	18	④	19	⑤	20	①
21	②	22	③	23	④	24	③	25	②										

[01~02] 항공대 2015

> **해석**
>
> 월마트는 가능한 범위 내에서 최대한 할인을 받을 수 있도록 제조업체들로부터 직접 구매하는 기본적인 방안을 확립한 후, 세 가지 요소에 집요하리만치 집중했다. 첫 번째 요소는 제조업체들과 협력하여 이들이 비용을 최대한 줄일 수 있도록 하는 것이다. 두 번째 요소는 제조업체들이 세계 어디에 위치해 있든지 간에 제조업체들로부터 월마트의 물류센터까지 공급망을 구축하여, 가능한 공급 비용을 낮추고 공급 과정에서 마찰이 발생하지 않도록 한다. 세 번째 요소는 월마트의 정보 시스템을 지속적으로 개선하여 고객들이 무엇을 구매하는지 정확하게 파악한 후 이 정보를 모든 제조업체에 제공하여, 언제나 적시에 제대로 된 물품을 매대에 들여놓는 것이다.
>
> 월마트는 제조업체들로부터 물품을 직접 구매하고, 공급망을 운영하는 데 드는 비용을 낮추기 위해 지속적으로 혁신하고, 고객들에 관해 더 많은 사실을 배워서 재고 규모를 지속적으로 낮추는 방식을 통해 돈을 절약할 수 있다면, 가격 측면에서 경쟁사들을 항상 제압할 수 있을 것임을 신속하게 깨달았다. 아칸소주 벤턴빌에 본사를 둔 월마트에게는 다른 선택의 여지가 없었다.

01 본문에 따르면 다음 중 월마트가 가격 측면에서 경쟁사들을 제압할 수 있는 기회를 늘리기 위해 해야 할 일은 무엇인가?
① 월마트의 정보 시스템에 맞춰 고객의 정보 수준을 낮추기
② 재조업체들로부터 직접 구매하기
③ 창고에 보관하는 재고의 규모를 늘리기
④ 공급망을 가능한 복잡하게 하기

| 정답 | ②

| 해설 | 월마트가 돈을 절약하기 위해 그리고 가격 측면에서 경쟁사들을 제압하기 위해 선택한 방식은 '제조업체들로부터 물품을 직접 구매하기, 공급망 운영 비용을 낮추기, 낮은 재고 수준을 유지하기' 등이다. 따라서 답은 ②이다.

---

02 밑줄 친 (A)와 의미상 가장 가까운 것은 무엇인가?

① 조화롭게 　　② 유연하게 　　③ 고분고분하게 　　④ 끈덕지게

| 정답 | ④

| 해설 | (A) relentlessly는 문맥상 '집요하게'란 의미를 가지며, 보기 중에서 이와 의미상 가장 가까운 것은 ④이다.

| 어휘 |
deep discount 대폭[초특가] 할인
distribution center 유통[물류] 센터
feed ⓥ (충고 · 정보 등을) 주다
inventory ⓝ 재고
flexibly ⓐⓓ 유연하게
persistently ⓐⓓ 끈덕지게, 고집스럽게

relentlessly ⓐⓓ 집요하게, 가차없이
frictionless ⓐ 마찰이 없는
be stocked with ~을 갖추다, ~을 들여놓다
harmoniously ⓐⓓ 조화롭게
compliantly ⓐⓓ 고분고분하게, 비굴하게

[03~05]

해석

현대 영어권 국가들, 예를 들어 영국, 미국, 아일랜드, 호주, 뉴질랜드에서는 대부분 학교와 교육 기관들은 영어를 교육 수단으로 사용한다. 많은 분야, 전문직, 직업 등에서 영어의 실용적 지식이 요구되기 때문에 전 세계의 많은 국가들은 자국 경제의 경쟁력을 높이기 위한 수단으로 최소한 기본적인 수준의 영어 교육을 요구한다. 그렇지만 언어학자인 David Graddol에 따르면 영어의 세계적 확산은 만약 현재 상황을 바로잡을 계획이 즉시 실행되지 않으면 영국의 미래에 심각한 정치적, 경제적인 약점을 초래할 것이라고 한다. Graddol은 여러 언어를 사용할 수 있는 능력을 갖춘 다른 나라의 젊은이들이 영국의 젊은이들보다 다국적 기업이나 조직에서 경쟁적인 장점을 지닌 것이 입증되면서 영어라는 하나의 언어만을 사용하는 영국의 대학 졸업자들은 어두운 미래에 직면하게 될 것이라고 결론을 내렸다.

---

03 다음 중 밑줄 친 ⓑ를 대체할 수 있는 단어는?

① 요구하다 　　② 고치다, 시정하다 　　③ 줄이다
④ 깨닫다 　　⑤ 관련되다

| 정답 | ②

| 해설 | redress는 '바로잡다, 고치다, 시정하다'라는 의미로 remedy로 대체할 수 있다.

---

04 다음 중 적절한 제목은?

① 영어의 경쟁력 　　② 영어 교육의 중요성
③ 영국의 정치, 경제 분야에서 영어의 힘 　　④ 세계화 시대에서 영어의 미래
⑤ 영어의 힘

| 정답 | ④

| 해설 | 세계화 시대에는 영어는 필수적이어서, 영어만으로는 경쟁력이 없고 여러 언어를 사용하는 사람에게 밀릴 수 있다는 전망이다. 그러므로 미래의 영어는 어떠한지에 대해 얘기하는 ④가 정답이다.

05 밑줄 친 ⓐ와 ⓒ를 대체할 수 있는 적절한 것을 고르시오.

① 요구하다 – 우울한   ② 침수시키다 – 불확실한

③ 취소하다 – 우울한   ④ 반대하다 – 불공정한

⑤ 선택하다 – 장점이 있는

| 정답 | ①

| 해설 | mandate는 '요구하다'라는 뜻으로 require와 동의어이고, bleak는 '어두운, 쓸쓸한'의 의미로 dismal과 동의어 관계이다.

| 어휘 | **perceive** ⓥ 인식하다, 지각하다   **mandate** ⓥ 명령하다, 요구하다

predict ⓥ 예언하다, 예견하다   **monolingual** ⓐ 한 개의 언어만을 사용하는

bleak ⓐ 황폐한, 쓸쓸한, 어두운   **dismal** ⓐ 음울한, 황량한, 쓸쓸한

inundate ⓥ 범람시키다, 밀려들다   **grim** ⓐ 모진, 냉혹한

[06~07]

해석

오늘날 천문학책의 저자들에게 우주는 만만치 않은 곳이다. 저자와 편집자가 책을 인쇄하는 것보다 빠른 속도로, 우주 먼 곳에서의 발견과 지구상의 어느 누구도 본 적이 없는 놀라운 천체 사진들이 그들의 노력을 앞지르고 있기 때문이다. 승산 없는 경쟁일 수도 있지만, Mary K. Baumann과 공저자들은 지난 몇 년간 가장 인상적이고 흥미로운 천체 사진들을 수록한 What's Out There에서 최선의 노력을 다했다. 쉽고 짧은 설명이 달려 있는 사진들은 비교적 친숙한 우주의 모습뿐 아니라 베테랑 천문학자들도 놀랄 우주의 장관을 함께 담고 있다. 제목은 주제별이 아니라 알파벳순으로 배열되어 있기 때문에, 카드를 섞듯이 순서를 바꿔 읽을 수 있다. 예를 들어, 태양으로부터 두 번째 행성인 금성은 일곱 번째 행성인 천왕성 다음에 나온다. 천왕성은 가시 파장(visible wavelength) 에서 촬영된 가장 먼 은하계 사진인 허블 망원경의 눈부신 "울트라 딥 필드" 다음에 나온다.

06 밑줄 친 juxtapose에 가장 가까운 의미는?

① 공식적으로 행동하거나 발언하다

② 나란히 놓거나 가까이 두다

③ 나쁜 것을 조금 덜 나쁘게 만들다

④ 만족할 만한 방법을 찾다

| 정답 | ②

| 해설 | juxtapose는 "(대조나 비교를 위해) 병치하다[나란히 놓는다]"의 뜻이므로 ②가 적절하다.

07 윗글의 내용과 일치하지 <u>않는</u> 것은?

① 메리 바우만의 책의 순서는 주제별로 나열되어 있다.

② 우주 관련 분야에서 새 천문학책을 펴내기는 매우 어렵다.

③ 메리 바우만은 동료들과 함께 "저 먼 곳에 무엇이 있나"라는 제목의 책을 출판했다.

④ 메리 바우만의 책에는 태양에서 두 번째 행성인 금성이 천왕성 뒤에 소개된다.

| 정답 | ①

| 해설 | "Topics are presented in alphabetical order instead of thematically, effectively shuffling them like a deck of cards.(제목은 주제별이 아니라 알파벳순으로 배열되어 있기 때문에, 카드를 섞듯이 순서를 바꿔 읽을 수 있다.)"를 참조하면 소주제들이 알파벳순으로 정렬되었음을 알 수 있다.

| 어휘 |

astronomy ⓝ 천문학

overtake ⓥ 추월하다

eyepopping ⓐ 깜짝 놀랄 만한, 굉장한

coauthor ⓝ 공저자

accompany ⓥ 동반하다, 수반하다

juxtapose ⓥ 병치하다, 나란히 놓다

order ⓝ 순서

shuffle ⓥ 뒤섞다

Venus ⓝ 금성

dazzling ⓐ 눈부신, 화려한

visible wavelength 가시 파장

go to press 인쇄하다

far-out ⓐ 거리가 먼, 파격적인

unwinnable ⓐ 이길 수 없는

celestial ⓐ 천체의

in plain English 쉬운 말로

veteran ⓐ 전문가의, 퇴역의

effectively ⓐ 사실상, 효과적으로

deck of cards 카드 한 벌

Uranus ⓝ 천왕성

shot ⓝ 사진

[08~09] 한국외대 2015

해석

1990년대 초부터 할리우드는 영화 산업과 같은 의미로 통하고 있다. 오늘날 할리우드는 영화 제작자와 영화배우 지망생 그리고 영화 관련 직업에 종사하면서 캘리포니아주에서 성공을 꿈꾸는 사람들의 발상지가 되었다. 두 가지 특성이 혼합되면서 1910년대 초반에 영화 제작자들이 할리우드로 이끌리게 되었다. 첫 번째 특성은 캘리포니아 남부에 위치한 할리우드의 맑고 온화한 기후이다. 두 번째 특성은 다양한 풍경과 지형이다. 1950년대에는 TV 및 음반 제작사들이 <u>영화인들의 선례를 따르게</u> 되었다. 그 당시 할리우드는 이미 연예 산업의 중심지였다. LA 지역의 부동산 시장 및 생활비가 치솟게 되면서 수많은 영화사들이 비용 절약을 위해 교외 지역으로 이동하게 되었다. 그럼에도 불구하고 할리우드는 여전히 연예 산업의 상징적 중심지로 남아 있다. LA가 벌어들이는 소득의 상당 부분은 현재 관광업이 차지하고 있다. 영화사 방문 관광, 주요 건물, 유명인의 집 등이 여전히 전 세계에서 방문객들을 끌어 모으고 있다.

08 다음 중 밑줄 친 followed suit와 의미상 가장 가까운 것은 무엇인가?

① 무모한 짓을 하다

② 다른 이의 입장에 서다

③ 무임승차하다

④ 편승하다

| 정답 | ④

---

09 다음 중 맞는 내용은 무엇인가?

① 1950년대에 여러 TV 방송사들이 할리우드를 떠났다.
② 할리우드는 영화 업계에서 점차 지배력을 상실하고 있다.
③ 할리우드가 영화 업계에서 촬영지로 명성을 얻게 된 것은 날씨 덕분이다.
④ 여러 영화 제작자들은 높은 생활비 때문에 시내로 이주했다.

| 정답 | ③

| 해설 | "첫 번째 특성은 캘리포니아 남부에 위치한 할리우드의 맑고 온화한 기후이다(One was the sunny and mild climate of its southern California location)." 여기서 답은 ③임을 알 수 있다. 나머지 보기는 모두 본문과 정반대되는 내용을 담고 있어서 답이 될 수 없다.

| 어휘 | **synonymous** ⓐ 동의어의, 같은[비슷한] 뜻을 지닌   **mecca** ⓝ 메카, (～의) 발상지
would-be ⓐ ～이 되려고 하는, ～을 지망하는   **cinematic** ⓐ 영화의
blend ⓝ 혼합, 섞기   **geography** ⓝ 지형, 지리
follow suit 선례를 따르다   **skyrocket** ⓥ 급등하다, 치솟다
economical ⓐ 경제적인, 절약하는   **epicenter** ⓝ 중심지, 진앙지
account for (부분·비율을) 차지하다, ～의 이유가 되다
landmark ⓝ 주요 건물, 랜드마크   **ride for a fall** 무모한 짓을 하다
stand in other's shoes 다른 이의 입장에 서다   **have a free ride** 무임승차하다
get on the bandwagon 인기 있는 쪽에 가담하다, ～에 편승하다
dominance ⓝ 우세, 지배

[10~12] 국민대 2015

해석

> 미디어 업계의 다른 많은 영역과 마찬가지로 출판 업계는 인터넷의 성장과 함께 급격하게 새로운 구조로 전환되고 있다. 이미 온라인 소매상들은 책의 최대 판매업자에 속한다. 전자책은 전통적 의미의 책의 판매를 약화시키려는 조짐을 보이고 있다. 이에 대응하여, 출판사에서는 기존의 사업을 강화하려 노력하면서 전자책이 전체 판매의 훨씬 큰 규모를 나타낼 것으로 생각되는 미래에 대응하고 있다. 출판사에서 고민하는 점은 온라인 쇼핑으로 인해 소비자들은 온갖 종류의 책을 (시세보다) 낮은 가격에 구할 수 있을 거라고 기대하게 되었다는 점이다. 출판사는 또한 이러한 (가격의) 하향 곡선은 (살아남기 위해) 분투하면서 고생 중인 재래식 책 판매업체들을 더욱 낙담시킬 뿐만 아니라 이미 미미하기 그지없는 이들의 이윤 폭을 더욱 잠식할 것으로 우려한다. 상황이 개선되지 않을 경우 업계의 일부는 예측하기로 출판사는 음반 회사들과 비슷한 운명을 겪게 될 것이라고 예측한다. 음반 회사들은 애플이 개별 곡을 값싸게 온라인상에서 판매하면서 음악 업계를 완전히 뒤집어 놓자 이들이 그때까지 누렸던 번영은 서서히 사라지게 되었다.

---

10 다음 중 문맥상 제대로 사용된 것이 <u>아닌</u> 것은 무엇인가?

① Ⓐ   ② Ⓑ
③ Ⓒ   ④ Ⓓ

| 정답 | ②

| 해설 | 전자책이 확산되면 기존의 책의 판매는 '떨어질' 것이다. 따라서 판매를 끌어올린다는 의미를 지닌 ⓑ의 boost는 답으로 볼 수 없다.

---

11 밑줄 친 ⓐ <u>shore up</u>과 의미상 가장 가까운 것은 무엇인가?

① 삽으로 파다　　　　　　　　　　② 지탱하다
③ 근절하다　　　　　　　　　　　④ 청산하다

| 정답 | ②

| 해설 | ⓐ shore up은 '강화하다, 뒷받침하다' 등의 의미를 지니며, 보기 중에서 이와 의미상 가장 가까운 것은 ②이다.

---

12 밑줄 친 ⓑ <u>brick-and-mortar</u>와 의미상 가장 가까운 것은 무엇인가?

① 공장의　　　　　　　　　　　② 도매의
③ 오프라인의　　　　　　　　　④ 대규모의

| 정답 | ③

| 해설 | ⓑ brick-and-mortar는 "재래식의, 오프라인 거래의" 등의 의미를 지니며 온라인과 반대되는 의미를 갖는다. 따라서 답은 ③이다.

| 어휘 | **reshape** ⓥ 모양[구조]을 고치다　　　　　　　**distributor** ⓝ 판매업자, 유통업자
old-fashioned ⓐ 전통적인, 기존의, 구식의　　　**threaten** ⓥ (나쁜 일이 있을) 조짐을 보이다
shore up 강화하다, 뒷받침하다　　　　　　　**chunk** ⓝ 상당히 많은 양
fret ⓥ 조마조마하다, 안달하다, 고민하다
condition ⓥ (특정 조건에 반응을 보이거나 익숙해지도록) 길들이다[훈련시키다]
downward spiral 하향 곡선, 하향되는 악순환
margin ⓝ 마진, 이윤 폭　　　　　　　　　　**erode** ⓥ (서서히) 약화시키다[무너뜨리다], 잠식하다
struggling ⓐ 분투하는, 허우적거리는　　　　**dismay** ⓝ 실망, 낙담
fortune ⓝ 운, 숙명, 번영　　　　　　　　　**brick-and-mortar** ⓐ 재래식의, 오프라인 거래의
sustain ⓥ 지탱하다, 지속시키다　　　　　　**shovel** ⓥ 삽으로 파다
liquidate ⓥ 청산[정리]하다　　　　　　　**eradicate** ⓥ 근절하다, 뿌리 뽑다

[13~14]

제트기 제조사들은 기내에 첨단 정보 기술 서비스를 도입하고 있다. 목표는 바쁜 회사 임원들이 멀리 떨어진 사무실과 언제든 연락할 수 있도록 하는 것이다. 요즘 가장 인기 있는 서비스는 35,000피트 상공에서 이용하는 초고속 인터넷이다. 예를 들어, Gulfstream사의 Broadband MultiLink는 초당 3.5메가바이트의 데이터 전송 속도로 검색, 이메일, 주가 정보 서비스를 제공한다. 아 이러니한 것은 이것이 대부분의 가정에서 사용하는 인터넷보다 더 빠르다는 것이다.

그렇다면 노트북과 휴대폰으로 무장한 비즈니스 승객들에게 불가능한 서비스가 있을까? 비행 규정상, 천장의 샹들리에는 불가능하다. 특히 높이가 6피트밖에 되지 않는 객실이 그렇다. 샤워 시설을 갖춘 대리석 욕실을 기내에 설치하는 것도 선망의 대상이 되겠지만, 문제는 추가적인 배관 설비와 물, 대리석 때문에 비행기의 이륙 무게에 수백 파운드가 더해져서 비행 거리와 성능을 저해한다는 것이다. 다른 모든 시공 프로젝트들처럼, 결국 그것은 디자인을 택할 때 포기해야 하는 부분이다.

---

13 빈칸에 적절한 단어는 ＿＿＿＿＿＿＿이다.

① 패러독스
② 과장
③ 모순
④ 아이러니
⑤ 난제

| 정답 | ④

| 해설 | irony는 예상과 반대되는 의외의 상황에, paradox는 일면 모순적이지만 자세히 보면 이치에 닿는 상황에 사용한다. 기내 인터넷의 속도가 가정에서 사용하는 인터넷 속도보다 빠르다는 것은 상식과 반대되는 상황이므로 빈칸에는 ④ irony가 적절하다. ③ contradiction은 양립 불가능한 모순을 뜻하므로 예상과 반대된다는 의미의 irony와는 다르다.

---

14 밑줄 친 "out of bound"의 의미는 무엇인가?

① 호화로운
② 불가능한
③ 필수적인
④ 위협적인
⑤ 보람 있는

| 정답 | ②

| 해설 | 'out of bound'는 '경계를 벗어난, 불가능한'의 뜻이다. 뒤이어 기내 설치가 불가능한 샹들리에와 대리석 욕실들이 예시되었으므로 문맥상 밑줄은 '불가능한'을 의미한다는 것을 유추할 수 있다.

| 어휘 |

jetmaker ⓝ 제트기 제조사	equip A with B A에 B를 갖추다
information technology 정보 기술	goal ⓝ 목표
executive ⓝ 중역, 임원	be in touch with ~와 연락하다
far-flung ⓐ 멀리 있는	at all times 항상
deliver ⓥ 전송하다	browsing ⓝ 검색
stock price 주가	be likely to ~하는 경향이 있다, ~일 듯하다
out of bound 한계를 벗어난, 불가능한	high-flying ⓐ 높이 나는
road warrior 노트북과 휴대폰을 항상 가지고 다니는 현대인을 비유하는 표현	requirement ⓝ 요건, 필요조건
due to ~ 때문에	

hang ⓥ 매달다, 매달리다	chandelier ⓝ 샹들리에
out of the question 불가능한(cf. out of question 의심의 여지없이)	
cabin ⓝ 객실	marble ⓝ 대리석
enviable ⓐ 부러운, 선망의 대상이 되는	addition ⓝ 추가
aircraft ⓝ 비행기	downside ⓝ 불리한 면
plumbing ⓝ 배관	takeoff ⓝ 이륙
restrict ⓥ 제한하다	range ⓝ 1회 주유 후 주행 거리
performance ⓝ 성능, 성과	construction ⓝ 시공, 건축(물)
ultimately 囵 궁극적으로	tradeoff ⓝ 거래, 교환

[15~17]

해석

성공은 지루한 것이다. 성공이란 이미 할 수 있다고 알고 있는 것을 해낼 수 있다고 증명하는 것이다. 아니면 무언가를 처음으로 올바르게 한 것일 수도 있으며, 이 경우의 성공은 종종 문제가 있는 성공이 되기도 한다. 처음에 성공하는 것은 보통 <u>요행</u>이다. 이와는 달리 처음에 실패하는 것은 <u>예상된</u> 것이고, 이는 자연의 섭리라 할 수 있다.

실패야말로 우리가 배워 가는 방식이다. 나는 아프리카 표현에 훌륭한 요리사를 가리키는 말로 "많은 솥을 깨뜨린 사람"이 있다고 들은 적이 있다. 많은 솥을 깨뜨릴 만큼의 시간을 주방에서 보냈다면, 아마도 그는 요리에 대해 상당히 많은 것을 알고 있을 것이다. 한번은 주방장들과 늦게 저녁 식사를 가졌던 적이 있는데, 그때 그들은 칼에 베인 상처와 화상 자국을 서로 비교했다. 그들은 자신들의 실패가 그들에게 얼마나 많은 신뢰감을 주었는지 알고 있었다. 나는 일간지에 칼럼을 기고하며 산다. 매주 나는 어떤 칼럼이 그 주의 최악의 칼럼이 될 것이란 것을 알고 있다. 그렇다고 내가 최악의 칼럼을 쓰려고 하는 것은 아니다. 나는 매일 최선을 다한다. 그러나 매주 하나의 칼럼은 다른 칼럼들에 비해 질이 떨어지며, 가끔은 질이 확연히 떨어지기도 한다. 그러나 나는 그런 칼럼을 소중히 여기는 법을 배웠다. 일반적으로 성공적인 칼럼이 의미하는 것은 내가 잘 아는 분야를 다루고, 매번 잘 먹히는 요령을 사용하며, 이미 말하지 않아도 모두 공감하는 내용을 말하거나, 화려한 단어로 대중들이 공감하는 바를 아름답게 치장하는 것을 말한다. 열등한 칼럼들에서는 종종 이전에는 한번도 시도해 보지 않은 것을 성공시키기 위해 노력한다. 심지어는 내가 해낼 수 있다고 확신조차 서지 않는 것을 이루어 내기 위해 애쓴다.

15 ⓐ, ⓑ, ⓒ, ⓓ에 들어갈 적합한 것을 고르시오.

① 승리 – 패배 – 승리 – 예견된

② 성공 – 요행 – 실패 – 예상된

③ 업적 – 문제 – 실수 – 용서된

④ 인정 – 가짜 – 무시 – 견뎌 낸

| 정답 | ②

| 해설 | 본문은 성공을 보편적으로 사람들이 생각하는 것과는 달리 부정적으로 바라보면서 시작한다. 따라서 빈칸에는 성공이라는 뜻의 단어가 와야 하며, 두 문장이 'by contrast'로 연결되어 있으므로 뒤의 문장은 앞 문장과 대조를 이루어야 함을 알 수 있다. 이런 점에서 victory라는 말이 두 번 사용된 ①은 정답에서 제외된다. 또한 ④는 recognition과 ignorance가 성공과 관련이 없기 때문에 제외된다. ③을 대입해서 생각해 보면, '처음의 성취는 대개 문제가 있는 것이고, 처음의 실수는 용서되기 마련이다'라는 뜻이 되며, 뒤이어 이것이 자연의 순리라고 했는데, 이렇게 되면 처음의 성공은 항상 문제가 있는 것이라는 말이 되어 논리가 어색해진다. 정답은 ②로 '처음의 성공은 대개 요행이며, 처음 실패는 예상된 결과다'로 보는 것이 합리적이다.

16 ⓔ를 적합하게 풀어 쓴 표현을 고르시오.

① 어려움에도 불구하고 실행하다

② 연기하다

③ 받아들이다

④ 미루다

| 정답 | ①

| 해설 | ②와 ④는 비슷한 뜻이 되어 답이 될 수 없으며, 이에 대한 동의적 표현은 'pull off'가 아닌 'put off'이다. 'pull off'는 '힘든 것을 해내다'라는 뜻이므로 정답은 ①이 된다.

17 윗글의 내용과 잘 부합하는 표현을 고르시오.

① 주방장들은 자신들이 하는 일을 부끄러워했다.

② 나는 독자들의 칭찬을 받는 칼럼니스트가 되고 싶다.

③ 대개 처음 성공은 우연에 의한 이득을 보게 된다.

④ 나는 칼럼니스트로 실패자이다.

| 정답 | ③

| 해설 | ①의 경우 주방장들이 자신들의 실패(상처나 흉터)를 소중하게 생각하는 사람들로 나오기 때문에 본문과 맞지 않다. ②와 ④의 경우도 정답이 될 수 없는데, 본문에서 저자는 최선을 다해 글을 쓴다고 했으며, 그럼에도 질이 떨어지는 칼럼을 쓰는 경우가 있는데, 이는 새로운 것을 시도하려고 했기 때문이지 이를 의도한 것이 아니라고 설명하고 있다. 정답은 ③으로 본문의 도입부에 비슷한 내용이 나온다. 본문에서 필자는 성공보다는 실패의 중요성에 대해 역설하고 있다는 점을 상기한다.

| 어휘 | boring ⓐ 지루한

by contrast 반대로, 대조적으로

pot ⓝ 냄비, 솥

scar ⓝ 상처, 흉터

set out 계획하다

cherish ⓥ 소중히 여기다

work ⓥ 효과가 있다

preach to the choir 이미 잘 알고 있는 내용을 말하다(교회 성가대에게 목사가 설교하는 것이므로 '말하지 않아도 아는 얘기'를 의미함)

dress up 잘 차려 입히다; 보기[듣기] 좋게 하다

popular sentiment 대부분의 사람들이 생각하는 것, 민심

fluke ⓝ 요행

problematical ⓐ 문제가 있는

natural order of things 자연의 순리

chef ⓝ 요리사(특히 주방장)

credibility ⓝ 신뢰성

inferior ⓐ 열등한

tread ⓥ (길을) 걷다; 밟다

sentiment ⓝ 정서, 감정

pull off (힘든 것을) 해내다, 성사시키다

해석

직장 내 성별 다양성과 관련해 많은 수요가 있을 뿐만 아니라, 기업들은 직장 내 성별 다양성을 높이라는 압박도 받고 있다. "모든 상위 기업들은 다양성과 포용성을 확대하기 위해 최선의 노력을 다하고 있다."라고 윙(Wing)은 말했다. 물론 어떤 회사들은 단지 <u>사람들의 시선에</u> 자극을 받을 수도 있다. "기업들은 여성이 필요하다는 것을 알고 있다. 그렇게 하지 않으면 언론과 강성 지지자들로부터 망신을 당할 수 있다는 사실을 잘 알고 있기 때문이다."라고 과거 구글 파이버(Google Fiber)의 설립을 주도한 바 있는 잉거솔(Ingersoll)은 말했다.

하지만 현명한 기업들은 성별 다양성이 <u>자신들의 순이익</u>에 엄청난 자산이 될 수 있다는 것 또한 깨닫고 있다. 게임 산업을 예로 들어 보자. 게임 개발자 중 여성의 비율은 22퍼센트에 불과하지만, 비디오 게임을 즐기는 사람들의 50퍼센트는 여성이라고 유니티 테크놀로지(Unity Technologies)의 최고 인사 책임자인 엘리자베스 브라운(Elizabeth Brown)은 말했다. 따라서 게임을 만드는 사람들이 업계의 고객층을 대변해야 하므로 더 많은 여성 개발자를 고용하길 원하는 것은 회사 차원에서도 매우 이치에 맞는 것이라고 브라운은 말했다.

18 다음 중 밑줄 친 "by optics"가 의미하는 것은?

① 가식적인 허세 없이   ② 전반적인 외관상
③ 상호 동의에 의해서   ④ 대중들의 인식에 의해서
⑤ 진정으로 집중해서

| 정답 | ④

| 해설 | optic은 사람들의 '눈'을 의미한다. 여성을 고용하지 않으면 언론이나 강성 지지자들로부터 '망신'을 당할 수 있다는 내용을 통해, '대중들의 시선'을 의식해 여성을 고용하는 기업들도 일부 있다는 내용이 된다. 따라서 정답은 ④가 적합하다.

19 다음 중 밑줄 친 "their bottom line"가 의미하는 것은?

① 그들의 윤리적인 기준   ② 그들의 인건비
③ 그들의 기업 명성   ④ 그들의 인적 자원
⑤ 그들의 순이익

| 정답 | ⑤

| 해설 | 'bottom line'은 원래 손익 계산서에서 유래한 말로, 손익 계산서의 맨 밑에 위치하는 순이익(net profit)을 지칭한다. 여기에서 파생해 '핵심, 요점, 최종 결산 결과' 등으로도 사용된다. 여기서는 원래의 의미인 순이익을 지칭하며, 여성을 고용하는 것이 회사의 순이익에도 부합한다고 설명하는 대목이다. 따라서 정답은 ⑤가 된다.

| 어휘 | **on top of** ~뿐 아니라, ~ 외에
be committed to ~에 헌신하다, 전념하다
spur ⓥ 자극하다, 박차를 가하다
otherwise ⓐⓓ 만약 그렇지 않으면; 그 외에는; ~와는 달리
outspoken ⓐ 솔직한, 거리낌 없이 말하는
asset ⓝ 자산, 재산; 장점
represent ⓥ 나타내다, 대변하다, 대표하다

diversity ⓝ 다양성, 차이
inclusion ⓝ 포함
optic ⓝ 눈 ⓐ 눈의, 시력의

advocate ⓝ 옹호자, 지지자 ⓥ 옹호하다, 주장하다
bottom line 핵심, 요점; 최종 결산 결과, 수익
chief people officer 최고 인사 책임자

customer base 고객층

mutual consent 상호 동의, 양자 합의

criterion ⓝ (판단이나 결정을 위한) 기준 pl. criteria

human resource 인력, 인적 자원

pretension ⓝ 허세, 가식

perception ⓝ 인지, 인식, 지각, 이해

reputation ⓝ 명성

net profit 순이익, 순익

[20~22] 한성대 2017

해석

웨이트 리프팅에 관해 여러 낭설이 존재한다. 근육을 키우는 것과 관련한 낭설은 단백질을 많이 복용하는 것이 좋다는 것이다. 단백질은 필요하지만, 우리의 몸은 제한된 양만 흡수할 수 있고, 그 이후 나머지는 모두 제거한다. 근력 운동에 관한 다른 낭설은 매일 운동을 해야 한다는 것이다. 근육 조직은 힘든 운동을 한 후 회복하려면 적어도 48시간이 필요하므로, 같은 근육을 이틀 연속 사용하는 것은 과도한 훈련으로 아무런 이점도 제공하지 않는다. 웨이트 리프팅은 끈기와 결단이 필요하다. 일관성이 있어야 하며, 당장 결과를 눈으로 볼 수 없다고 해서 중도에 포기해서는 안 된다. 우리 몸은 때가 되면 근육이 생기게 되어 있다. 웨이트 리프팅, 심장의 유산소 운동 능력, 체중 감량 사이의 관계에 대한 여러 일반적인 오해가 존재한다. 웨이트 리프팅이 근지구력을 향상시킬 수 있다. 하지만 웨이트 리프팅은 심장의 유산소 운동 능력을 향상시키거나 체중을 줄이기 위한 최선의 방법은 아니다. 그러므로 근력 운동과 심장 강화 운동을 조합하는 것이 가장 좋다.

20 다음 중 빈칸 (A)에 올 수 있는 가장 적합한 것을 고르시오.

① 과부하가 걸리게 하다

② 접속하다

③ 운동하다, 생각해 내다

④ 분산시키다

| 정답 | ①

| 해설 | 근육을 키우기 위해 단백질을 섭취하는 것과 관련한 내용이다. 빈칸 이후의 내용에 "우리의 몸은 제한된 양(only so much)만 흡수할 수 있고, 나머지는 모두 제거한다."고 했으므로, 과도한 단백질 복용은 도움이 안 된다는 것을 알 수 있다. 따라서 '과도한 복용'에 해당하는 ①이 가장 유사한 뜻에 해당한다.

21 다음 중 (B) <u>takes</u>를 가장 잘 대체할 수 있는 것은?

① 향상시키다

② 요구하다

③ 추정하다

④ 동반하다

| 정답 | ②

| 해설 | (B)의 take는 '~을 필요로 하다'는 뜻이므로 ② requires가 정답이 된다.

22 다음 중 본문의 내용과 일치하지 <u>않는</u> 것은?

① 우리 몸이 흡수할 수 있는 단백질의 양은 제한되어 있다.

② 근육은 힘든 운동으로부터 회복하려면 적어도 이틀이 필요하다.

③ 웨이트 리프팅은 체중 감량을 위한 최선의 방법이다.

④ 근력 운동과 심장 강화 운동을 조합하는 것이 도움이 된다.

| 정답 | ③

| 해설 | ①은 본문의 "your body can absorb only so much, then it eliminates the rest."를 통해 알 수 있다. ② "Muscle tissue needs at least 48 hours to recover from hard exercise"에서 48시간이 필요하다고 했으므로 이틀에 해당한다. ④ 마지막 문장의 "it's best to combine weight training with a cardio program."에서 두 가지를 조합하는 것이 최선이라고 말하고 있다. 정답은 ③으로, "it's not the best way to improve cardiovascular fitness or to lose weight."에서 근력 운동이 체중 감량의 최선책은 아니라고 밝히고 있다.

| 어휘 |

myth ⓝ 허구, 신화, 낭설

muscle ⓝ 근육

absorb ⓥ 흡수하다, 빨아들이다

eliminate ⓥ 제외하다, 제거하다

tissue ⓝ (세포들로 이뤄진) 조직

commitment ⓝ 헌신, 전념, 공약, 약속, 언명, 위임, (범죄의) 실행

consistent ⓐ 한결같은, 일관된

misconception ⓝ 오해

muscle endurance ⓝ 근지구력

cardio ⓝ (달리기 등) 심장 강화 운동

log on ～에 접속하다

estimate ⓝ 추정, 추산; 평가, 견적 ⓥ 추산[추정]하다

exhausting ⓐ 진을 빼는, 기진맥진하게 만드는

weight-lifting ⓝ 웨이트 리프팅, 근력 운동

protein ⓝ 단백질

only so much 제한된 양

work out 운동하다; ～을 계획해[생각해] 내다

in a row (여러 번을) 잇달아[연이어]

in its own time 제때가 되면

cardiovascular ⓐ 심혈관의

combine A with B A를 B와 결합하다

overload on 과부하가 걸리게 하다

spread out 분산되다; 몸을 뻗다; 넓은 공간을 차지하다

accompany ⓥ 동반하다, 수반하다

beneficial ⓐ 유익한, 이익을 가져오는

[23~25] 단국대 2018

해석

만일 당신이 낮 동안에 졸음을 느낀다면, 심지어 지루한 활동을 하고 있는 중이라고 해도, 그것은 당신이 잠을 충분히 자지 못했기 때문이라고 전문가들은 말한다. 만일 당신이 자리에 눕고 나서 일상적으로 5분 이내에 잠이 든다면, 당신은 아마도 심각한 수면 부족에 시달리고 있는 것일 수 있다. 서구의 산업화 사회에서 널리 퍼진 관행인 "밤늦게 일하고 아침에 일찍 일어나 다시 많은 일을 하느라 몹시 지치게 되는" 행위가 너무도 심각한 수면 부족을 야기하며 그 결과 실제로는 비정상적인 수면이라고 할 수 있는 것이 이제는 거의 표준이나 다름없게 되어 버렸다. 많은 연구에서 수면 부족이 위험하다는 사실을 분명히 밝히고 있다. 수면 부족에 시달리는 사람들을 운전 시뮬레이션 장치를 이용해 검사를 해 보니 이들은 술에 취한 사람만큼이나 혹은 그보다 더 나쁜 운전 결과를 나타냈다. 뿐만 아니라 수면 부족은 술이 신체에 미치는 영향력을 증대시키는데, 그 결과 피로한 사람이 술을 마실 경우 충분히 휴식을 취한 사람보다 더 취하게 된다. 졸음은 잠들기 전 뇌가 거치는 마지막 단계이기 때문에, 졸음운전은 큰 재앙으로 이어질 수 있다. 카페인이나 다른 각성제로는 심각한 수면 부족의 영향을 극복할 수 없다. 미국 국립수면재단에 따르면, 당신이 눈의 초점을 계속 맞추는 것이 힘들 경우, 하품이 나오는 것을 멈출 수 없는 경우, 혹은 방금 전 몇 마일을 운전했던 것을 떠올리지 못할 경우, 당신은 안전 운전을 하기엔 너무 졸린 상태일 수 있다.

23 다음 중 밑줄 친 부분이 의미하는 것으로 적합한 것은?

① 목표 당성을 위한 열렬한 열망
② 극도로 동요된 상태
③ 갈등이 발생하기 전의 잠복기
④ 휴식을 거의 제공하지 않는 무자비한 일정

| 정답 | ④

| 해설 | 밑줄 친 "burn the candle at both ends"는 '밤늦게까지 일하고 다시 아침 일찍 일어나 많은 일을 처리하느라 몹시 지치다'라는 의미를 지닌다. 초의 양쪽 끝단에 불을 밝힐 경우 잠시 동안은 주변이 더 밝겠지만 초가 그만큼 빨리 소모되는 것을 빡빡한 일정을 소화하기 위해 무리하게 일하는 것을 비유적으로 표현한 것이므로, 정답은 ④가 된다.

24 다음 중 빈칸에 가장 적합한 것은?

① 덧문을 달다
② 방해하다
③ 확대하다
④ 분할하다, 나누다

| 정답 | ③

| 해설 | 빈칸 뒤에 접속사 so로 연결되어 있으므로, 인과 관계로 이어지고 있음을 알 수 있다. 따라서 결과에 해당하는 뒤 내용을 보면, 피곤한 사람이 술을 마시게 되면 휴식을 취한 사람이 술을 마시는 경우보다 더 impaired(손상된, 제기능을 못하는)하게 된다고 설명하고 있으므로, 더 큰 영향을 받는 것을 알 수 있다. 따라서 수면 부족(피곤)이 신체에 미치는 술의 영향을 더 증가시키는 것이므로, 정답은 ③ magnifies가 된다.

25 다음 중 본문을 쓴 목적으로 적합한 것은?

① 수면 부족에 대한 예방책을 제공하기 위해
② 충분한 수면을 취하지 않아 발생하는 신호나 위험에 대해 알리기 위해
③ 술이 수면 부족을 겪는 사람에게 미치는 영향을 논의하기 위해
④ 수면 부족이 서구 사회에서 흔한 이유를 설명하기 위해

| 정답 | ②

| 해설 | 첫 번째 문단에서는 사회에 만연한 수면 부족 현상에 대해 기술하고 있고, 두 번째 문단에서는 수면 부족의 위험성에 대해 설명하고 있다. 수면 부족이 음주보다 더 운전에 위험하다고 말하며, 졸음이 큰 재앙으로 이어질 수 있다고 경고하고 있으므로, 수면 부족으로 인해 발생하는 신호나 위험을 알리기 위해서라고 말한 ②가 정답이 된다.

| 어휘 | **drowsy** ⓐ 졸음이 오는, 졸리는 · **sleep deprivation** 수면 부족
burn the candle at both ends (밤늦게까지 일하고 아침 일찍 일어나며 많은 일을 하느라) 몹시 지치다
abnormal ⓐ 비정상적인 · **norm** ⓝ 표준, 기준, 규범
sleep-deprived ⓐ 잠이 부족한 · **simulator** ⓝ 시뮬레이터, 모의실험 장치
intoxicated ⓐ (술·마약에) 취한 · **fatigued** ⓐ 심신이 지친, 피로한

impaired ⓐ 손상된, 제 기능을 못하는

stimulant ⓝ 흥분제, 자극 물질

yawn ⓥ 하품하다 ⓝ 하품

agitation ⓝ 동요, 선동, 혼란

unrelenting ⓐ 끊임없는, 수그러들 줄 모르는; 용서 없는, 무자비한

afford ⓥ 주다, 제공하다; 여유가 있다

hamper ⓥ 방해하다

partition ⓥ 분할하다, 나누다

disaster ⓝ 재난

have trouble -ing ~하는 데 어려움을 겪다

ardent ⓐ 열렬한

latent ⓐ 잠복성의

shutter ⓥ 셔터를 달다, 덧문을 달다

magnify ⓥ 확대하다

preventive measure 예방책, 예방 조치

PART 03

논리적 이해

CHAPTER 01   순서 연결

CHAPTER 02   연결 구조

CHAPTER 03   문맥과 흐름

CHAPTER 04   전후 관계

CHAPTER 05   추론

CHAPTER 06   유사 추론

CHAPTER 07   어휘형 논리

CHAPTER 08   독해형 논리

| 연습 문제 | 01 | ① | 02 | ④ | 03 | ④ | 04 | ④ |

01 상자 안의 문장이 들어가기에 가장 알맞은 지점을 고르시오. 명지대 2014

> 이처럼 팬들은 엘비스를 매우 좋아했기 때문에 많은 이들은 엘비스가 죽었다는 사실을 받아들이지 않았다.

모두가 인정하는 로큰롤의 제왕 엘비스 프레슬리가 1977년 8월 16일에 사망하자 전 세계는 큰 충격에 빠졌다. 20세기의 슈퍼스타인 미국 출신의 가수 엘비스는 반짝이는 점프 수트와 허리께를 회전하는 춤과 함께 음악계의 전설이자 수많은 여자들의 가슴을 두근거리게 하는 동경의 대상이었다. 이처럼 팬들은 엘비스를 매우 좋아했기 때문에 많은 이들은 엘비스가 죽었다는 사실을 받아들이지 않았다. 일부는 엘비스가 세간의 주목으로부터 벗어나기 위해 은둔하게 되었다고 생각하며, 다른 이들은 엘비스가 외계인에 의해 납치되었다고 주장한다. 엘비스의 죽음을 둘러싸고 여러 가지 관심과 흥미가 이어지고 있으며, 엘비스가 때 이른 죽음을 맞은 이후 수백 건의 "목격" 사례가 보고되고 있다. 엘비스가 사망했다는 뉴스가 터진 직후 자신을 존 버로우스(Jon Burrows)로 지칭한 한 남성이 아르헨티나의 부에노스아이레스(Buenos Aires)로 향하는 편도 비행 편을 구매했다. 공교롭게도 존 버로우스란 이름은 엘비스가 여행할 때 사용하던 명칭이기도 했다. 이는 엘비스가 이제는 유명세로부터 벗어나고자 자신의 죽음을 가장했다는 소문을 촉발시켰다.

① ㉮   ② ㉯   ③ ㉰   ④ ㉱

| 정답 | ①

| 해설 | 주어진 문장은 엘비스의 죽음을 팬들이 인정하지 못했음을 말하고 있다. 따라서 주어진 문장 다음에는 엘비스가 죽지 않았다면 왜 모습을 드러내지 않는지에 관한 팬들의 추측이 제시되어야 한다. 그리고 그러한 추측은 ㉮ 다음부터 시작된다. 따라서 답은 ①이다.

| 어휘 | **undisputed** ⓐ 반박[이론]의 여지가 없는, 모두가 인정하는
heart-throb ⓝ 수많은 여자들의 가슴을 두근거리게 하는 남자(보통 배우나 가수), (연예인 등) 동경의 대상
sparkly ⓐ 반짝반짝 빛나는   **swivel** ⓥ 돌리다, 회전하다
hip ⓝ (허리와 다리가 만나는) 허리께[골반 부위]   **the spotlight** (세간·언론의) 주목[관심]
abduct ⓥ 유괴하다, 납치하다   **intrigue** ⓝ 흥미로움[흥미진진함]
sighting ⓝ 목격   **untimely** ⓐ 때 이른, 시기상조의
break ⓥ (뉴스가) 알려지다[터지다]   **fuel** ⓥ 부채질하다, 촉발하다

02 보기 가운데 ⓐ~ⓓ 문장의 적절한 순서는?

천재성이 특이한 것이라는 사실은 말할 필요도 없다.

ⓒ 하지만 천재성은 과연 천재성을 보유한 사람의 뇌가 다른 식으로도 특이하기를 요구할 정도로 특이한 것일까?

ⓑ 한쪽으로는 예술적 천재성을 보이지만 다른 쪽으로는 조현병과 조울병을 드러내는 것 사이의 관계에 관해 폭넓은 논쟁이 이어지고 있다.

ⓐ 하지만 서번트 증후군과 자폐증 사이의 관계에 관해서는 확실히 확립되어 있다.

ⓓ 서번트 증후군은 예를 들자면 자폐증을 앓는 형제가 수치를 기억하는 일에 놀라운 재능을 드러내는 영화인 "레인맨(Rain Man)" 같은 영화의 주제이다.

① ⓐ – ⓑ – ⓒ – ⓓ
② ⓐ – ⓓ – ⓒ – ⓑ
③ ⓒ – ⓑ – ⓓ – ⓐ
④ ⓒ – ⓑ – ⓐ – ⓓ

| 정답 | ④

| 해설 | 첫 문장은 천재성이 특이하다는 사실을 언급했다. 그 다음으로는 그 천재성이 어느 정도로 특이한 것인지를 묻는 ⓒ가 적합하다. ⓒ 다음에는 "뇌가 다른 식으로도 특이하다"에 해당되는 "조현병" 및 "조울병"이 언급된 ⓑ가 적합하다. ⓑ에서는 논쟁이 이어지고 있지만, 이와는 달리 "서번트 증후군"과 "자폐증" 사이의 관계는 명확하다는 ⓐ가 와야 한다. 그리고 마지막 ⓓ는 ⓐ의 예가 되니까 ⓐ 다음에 와야 한다. 이러한 요소를 감안했을 때 답으로 가장 적합한 것은 ④이다.

| 어휘 | **genius** ⓝ 천재성
schizophrenia ⓝ 조현병
savant syndrome 서번트 증후군
extraordinary ⓐ 놀라운

go without saying (아주 분명하므로) 말할 필요도 없다
manic-depression ⓝ 조울병
autism ⓝ 자폐증

---

03 다음 중 전체 문맥에 적합하지 <u>않은</u> 것을 고르시오. 가톨릭대 2016

테오티우아칸(Teotihuacan)은 서반구에 세워진 진정한 의미에서의 최초의 도심지 중 하나였고 전성기 때는 면적이 근 8평방 마일에 이르렀다. 달의 피라미드(Pyramid of the Moon) 및 다른 구조물로부터 회수된 귀중한 인공 유물을 통해 테오티우아칸이 여러 지역과 광범위하게 연결된 부유한 무역 도시임이 밝혀졌다. 알 수 없는 일이지만, 테오티우아칸은 서기 600년경에 갑작스러우면서도 격렬하게 붕괴하고 말았고 많은 이들이 도시를 등졌다. (이들은 몇몇 건축물이 무덤이었던 것으로 추정하고서, 그대로를 사자의 거리(Street of the Dead)라 칭했다.) 이들은 문자 기록을 거의 남기지 않았으며, 도시의 폐허와 한때 강력한 문화였음을 암시하는 흥미로운 단서만을 남겼다.

① [A]
② [B]
③ [C]
④ [D]
⑤ [E]

| 정답 | ④

| 해설 | [D]의 전후엔 테오티우아칸의 몰락에 관한 내용이 등장하는 반면에 [D]는 테오티우아칸의 어느 대로에 관한 내용이 담겨 있다. 즉 [D] 때문에 글의 흐름이 매끄럽지 않다. 따라서 답은 ④이다.

| 어휘 | **the Western Hemisphere** 서반구
artifact ⓝ 인공 유물
far-reaching ⓐ 광범위한
boulevard ⓝ 도로, 대로
intriguing ⓐ 아주 흥미로운

heyday ⓝ 전성기, 한창때
metropolis ⓝ 주요 도시
inexplicably ⓐⓓ 알 수 없는 일이지만
written record 문자 기록

04 상자 속 문장이 들어가기에 가장 적합한 곳을 고르시오.

이를 통해 고양이는 뇌우가 들이닥치기 전에 공기 중으로 들어가는 정전기에 반응하게 된다.

폭풍이 불기 전에 공기에 생기는 변화에 매우 민감하게 반응하는 생물체는 날씨의 변화를 예측할 수 있다. 예를 들어 새는 기압의 변화를 느끼고 낮게 날아간다. 마찬가지로 집파리는 이러한 변화를 감지하고 실내로 들어와서 폭우를 피한다. 그리고 고양이는 폭풍이 불기 전에 자신의 털을 다듬는 것으로 알려져 있다. <u>이를 통해 고양이는 뇌우가 들이닥치기 전에 공기 중으로 들어가는 정전기에 반응하게 된다.</u> 정전기는 고양이의 털이 서로 떨어지게 만들어서 고양이가 자신을 더럽다고 느끼게 만들고, 때문에 고양이는 자신의 몸을 핥아서 털을 다시 매끄럽고 깨끗하게 만든다.

① [A]
② [B]
③ [C]
④ [D]

| 정답 | ④

| 해설 | 주어진 문장만 보면 they가 무엇을 가리키는지 알 수 없지만 정전기와 관련된 것임은 알 수는 있다. 그리고 [D] 다음에 등장하는 the electricity가 바로 이 정전기에 해당된다. 그리고 주어진 문장의 in doing so는 [D] 앞 문장의 groom themselves에 해당된다. 즉 주어진 문장에서 they는 고양이를 의미하며, 주어진 문장은 고양이가 어떤 행동을 하는 이유에 해당하고, [D] 뒤 문장은 어떤 행동을 통한 결과를 의미한다. 따라서 답은 ④이다.

| 어휘 | **sensitive** ⓐ 민감한   **downpour** ⓝ 폭우
groom ⓥ (가죽·털 등을) 다듬다   **static electricity** 정전기
thunderstorm ⓝ 뇌우

실전 문제

01	①	02	②	03	⑤	04	③	05	③	06	④	07	①	08	②	09	③	10	②
11	④	12	④	13	①	14	④	15	③	16	①	17	②	18	①	19	④	20	③
21	③	22	④	23	①	24	②	25	③	26	④	27	③	28	④	29	①	30	②

[01] 서강대 2020

해석

Ⓑ 대부분의 사람들에게 모방과 수습의 기간은 오래 지속된다. Ⓓ 이때가 바로 자신의 힘과 자신의 목소리를 찾기 위해 노력해야 하는 시기이다. 이때가 바로 연습과 반복과 기술 숙달의 시기이다. Ⓒ 그러한 견습 생활을 거쳤던 사람들도 일부는 뛰어난 창조성에 오르지 못하고 기술적 숙달의 수준에 머물러 있을 수 있다. Ⓐ 재능은 있지만 파생적 수준의 일 처리가 주요한 혁신으로 도약하는 시기가 언제일지는 판단하기 어려울 수 있다. 창조적 동화, 즉 도용과 경험이 깊은 수준으로 뒤얽히는 것을 단순한 모방과 구별하게 해 주는 것은 무엇일까?

01 다음 문장을 가장 논리적인 지문이 되도록 재배열하시오.

① Ⓑ − Ⓓ − Ⓒ − Ⓐ

② Ⓐ − Ⓑ − Ⓒ − Ⓓ

③ Ⓓ − Ⓒ − Ⓐ − Ⓑ

④ Ⓒ − Ⓐ − Ⓓ − Ⓑ

| 정답 | ①

| 해설 | Ⓒ의 "such an apprenticeship"에서 such는 앞서 나온 단어를 지칭한다는 점에서 Ⓒ가 처음 올 수 없고, Ⓒ 앞에는 apprenticeship이 언급된 Ⓑ가 와야 함을 알 수 있다. 이 사실을 통해 정답은 ①이나 ②로 좁힐 수 있다. Ⓐ의 경우 마지막 내용이 "~을 구별하게 해주는 것은 무엇일까?"라고 질문을 던지고 있는데, Ⓐ가 맨 앞에 위치하는 ②의 경우 그에 대한 답이 뒤이어서 나오지 않는다. 따라서 정답은 Ⓐ의 물음이 제일 뒤로 배치되는 ①이 정답이 된다. 그리고 Ⓑ의 'a long time'을 Ⓒ에서 'It'으로 연달아 지칭하고 있다.

| 어휘 | derivative ⓐ 파생적인

distinguish A from B A와 B를 구별하다

intertwine ⓥ 서로 얽히게 하다

mimicry ⓝ 흉내

apprenticeship ⓝ 수습 기간, 수습직

ascend ⓥ 오르다, 올라가다

innovation ⓝ 혁신, 쇄신

assimilation ⓝ 동화, 융합, 흡수, 소화

appropriation ⓝ 도용, 전용

imitation ⓝ 모방

undergo ⓥ 겪다, 경험하다

[02] 한양대 2014

해석

가상 현실은 다양한 그리고 심지어는 다수의 신원과 신분 증명을 위한 열린 공간을 제공한다. 가상 환경하에서 사람들은 하나의 안정적이고 통합적인 대상이라는 입장에 국한되기보다 (연속적으로 또는 동시다발적으로) 다수의 신원을 취할 수 있다. 가상 환경하에서 이용자를 대변하기 위해 사용되는 그래픽 아바타에서 채팅방에서 사용되는 명칭이나 다수의 이메일 계정같이 단순한 것에 이르기까지 이 모든 것들은 가상 신원을 구축하고 유지하기 위해 사용될 수 있다. 가상 현실에서 신원은 실제 삶에서보다 훨씬 더 변화무쌍하고, 실제 삶과 마찬가지로 진정한 신원이자 자아를 구성하는 요소가 될 수 있다. (플라톤식 체제이든, 데카르트식 체제이든, 칸트식 체제이든 간에 이들 모든 체제에서 통합된 그리고 통합적인 대상이라는 개념이 공유되며 이들 개념의 존재는 지식과 행동 그리고 개인 신원의 구축의 기반이 된다.) 진행 중인 것이든 일시적으로 채택된 것이든 신원은 변경, 편집, 조작이 가능하며 심지어 완전히 파기하는 것도 가능하다. 따라서 가상 현실은 공간과 시간을 재현하는 것이 가능할 뿐 아니라 자아를 재현하는 것도 가능하다. 가상 현실 속 대상은 이러한 새로운 공간을 점유하면서 새롭게 만들어진다.

02 문맥상 글의 전체 흐름과 <u>관계없는</u> 문장을 고르시오.

①　　　　　②　　　　　③　　　　　④

| 정답 | ②

| 해설 | 본문은 가상 현실 속 이용자의 신원에 관해 논하고 있지만, ②는 철학적으로 공유되는 개념에 관해 논하고 있다. 즉 본문의 전체 흐름과 관계가 없는 것은 ②이다.

| 어휘 | **subject** ⓝ 대상, 소재   **handle** ⓝ 직함, 명칭

malleable ⓐ 잘 변하는, 영향을 잘 받는   **constitutive of** ~의 구성 요소를 이루는

Cartesian ⓐ 데카르트의   **Kantian** ⓐ 칸트의

ongoing ⓐ 진행 중인   **fabricate** ⓥ 날조하다, 조작하다

set aside 무효화하다, 파기하다

---

[03] 건국대 2020

해석

1860년 아브라함 링컨(Abraham Lincoln)의 대통령직 당선은 연방정부와 주정부의 상대적 권한에 대한 오랜 논쟁을 절정에 다다르게 했다. 링컨의 취임식이 있을 즈음에 남부 6개 주가 연방에서 탈퇴하여 남부연합국(Confederate States of America)을 결성했으며, 곧 남부의 5개 주가 추가로 뒤를 이었다. 이어서 발생한 북측과 남측 사이의 전쟁은 합법적인 정부를 가장 심각한 시험대 위에 올려놓았다. 4년간의 피비린내 나는 전쟁 이후, 연방은 보존되었고, 4백만 명의 아프리카계 미국 노예들은 해방되었으며, 한 나라 전체가 노예제도의 억압적 무게에서 해방되었다. 이 전쟁은 여러 다른 방식으로 조명될 수 있다. 두 지역적 하부문화가 겪어온 갈등의 최종적이고 폭력적 국면으로, 민주주의 정치 체제의 붕괴로, 수십 년 동안 지속된 사회개혁의 절정으로, 또는 미국의 인종 역사의 중추적 장 등으로 여겨질 수 있다. (전쟁 자체만큼 중요했던 것은 패배한 남부를 어떻게 재건할지에 대한 복잡한 문제였다.) 어떻게 해석되든, 남북전쟁은 위대한 영웅, 희생, 승리, 비극의 이야기로 우뚝 서 있다.

---

03 글의 흐름으로 보아, (A)~(E) 가운데 <u>어색한</u> 것은?

① (A)   ② (B)   ③ (C)   ④ (D)   ⑤ (E)

| 정답 | ⑤

| 해설 | (D)에서 남북전쟁은 여러 방식으로 이해될 수 있다고 말하고 있다. 그리고 마지막 문장에서 어떤 방식으로 해석되든(However interpreted) 남북전쟁은 어떠하다는 특징으로 글을 마치고 있으므로, 향후 남부의 재건이 중요했다는 (E)의 문장이 문맥과 어울리지 않는다. 따라서 정답은 ⑤가 된다.

| 어휘 | **presidency** ⓝ 대통령 직   **fester** ⓥ (상처 등이) 곪다, 부패하다

relative ⓐ 상대적인   **federal** ⓐ 연방의

by the time of ~할 때 쯤   **inauguration** ⓝ 취임식, 개시

secede ⓥ (정당, 교회 등에서) 탈퇴하다   **confederate** ⓐ 연맹에 속한, 연합한

constitutional ⓐ 헌법의, 입헌의   **severe** ⓐ 극심한

preserve ⓥ 보존하다, 유지하다   **oppressive** ⓐ 억압하는, 억압적인

violent ⓐ 폭력적인   **phase** ⓝ 단계, 국면

conflict ⓝ 갈등, 충돌   **regional** ⓐ 지방의, 지역적인

subculture ⓝ 하위문화   **pivotal** ⓐ 중추의, 중요한

tangled ⓐ 복잡한, 뒤얽힌   **reconstruct** ⓥ 재건하다

defeat ⓥ 패배시키다   **interpret** ⓥ 설명하다, 해석하다

sacrifice ⓝ 희생   **triumph** ⓝ 승리 ⓥ 승리하다, 기뻐 날뛰다

tragedy ⓝ 비극

해석

지금으로부터 수년 후 역사가들은 미국 역사에서 지금 시기를 일반 대중들 가운데 상당 부분의 사람들이 과장된 편견을 드러낸 시기이자 여러 정치 지도자들이 근시안적 태도를 보인 시기로 회고할 가능성이 높다. 진지한 시각에서 중동을 바라보는 사람들의 일치된 의견은 중동이 미국에 반감을 갖게 된 원인은 다양하고 다음의 사항과 관련이 있다는 점이다. 바로 이스라엘 및 팔레스타인에 대한 이스라엘의 팽창주의적이고 억압적인 정책에 대해 미국이 보이고 있는 무조건적인 지지, 중동 및 북아프리카 전역에 자리 잡고 있는 대표성도 부족하고 부패하였으며 억압적인 다수의 독재 정부를 미국이 지원하고 있다는 점, 그리고 수만 명의 민간인의 목숨을 앗아가는 드론 공격으로부터 수십만의 이슬람교도들의 목숨을 앗아가는 대규모 침공에 이르기까지 이슬람 세계에 대한 미국의 광범위한 군사적 개입 등이다. 팔레스타인 자치 정부 및 하마스 정부의 통치를 받는 주민들 가운데 거의 80퍼센트에 달하는 사람들은 미국을 "적"으로 여긴다. 중동의 미국 핵심 우방국인 이집트 · 요르단 · 터키 사람들의 경우, 이집트 및 요르단 사람들 가운데 약 85퍼센트 그리고 터키 사람들 가운데 약 73퍼센트가 이와 비슷한 의견을 갖고 있다. 여론조사에 따르면 미국을 가장 악감정을 갖고 바라보는 10개 국가들 가운데 7개 국가가 이슬람 국가이며, 미국을 가장 호의적으로 바라보는 10개 국가들 가운데 오직 1개 국가만이 이슬람 국가이다.

04 빈칸 Ⓐ에 가장 알맞은 것을 고르시오.

① 향기
② 예의
③ 반감
④ 화해

| 정답 | ③

| 해설 | 빈칸 뒤에는 중동이 미국에 대해 "반감"을 갖게 된 이유가 설명되어 있다. 따라서 빈칸에 적합한 것은 ③이다.

05 아래 문장이 들어가기에 가장 알맞은 곳을 고르시오.

"중동의 미국 핵심 우방국인 이집트 · 요르단 · 터키 사람들의 경우, 이집트 및 요르단 사람들 가운데 약 85퍼센트 그리고 터키 사람들 가운데 약 73퍼센트가 이와 비슷한 의견을 갖고 있다."

① [A]　　　　② [B]　　　　③ [C]　　　　④ [D]

| 정답 | ③

| 해설 | 주어진 문장은 중동에 위치한 미국의 우방국들이 어떤 견해를 갖고 있는지에 대한 통계 자료에 해당한다. 주어진 문장의 "이와 비슷한 의견(analogous opinion)"이 무엇을 가리키는지 생각해 볼 필요가 있다. 주어진 문장 이외의 통계 수치가 언급된 부분은 [B] 다음부터이며, 따라서 주어진 문장은 [A]를 제외한 곳에 들어올 수 있다. 주어진 문장에 "이와 비슷한 의견"이란 표현이 있는데, 이 말은 즉 주어진 문장 앞에 다른 통계 자료가 있음을 나타낸다. 따라서 모든 통계 자료의 가장 처음에 해당되는 [B]는 답이 될 수 없다. 남은 것은 [C] 아니면 [D]인데, [C]에 대입해 보면 "이와 비슷한 의견"은 앞서 언급된 '미국을 적으로 여기는 의견'을 가리키는 것임을 알 수 있다. 따라서 주어진 문장은 미국의 동맹국임에도 미국을 적으로 보는 인구의 비중이 상당함을 설명한 글임을 알 수 있다. 이 경우 우선 [C] 앞에서 미국과 적대 관계인 팔레스타인 자치 정부 및 하마스 정부 통치하의 국민들 사이에서 미국에 대한 반감이 어느 정도인지를 설명한 후 뒤이어 주어진 문장에서 적대국이 아닌 동맹국임에도 국민들이 얼마나 반감이 큰지를 설명하게 되면서 문장이 논리적으로 이어진다. 따라서 답은 ③이다.

06 본문과 일치하는 것을 고르시오.

① 미국과 중동 간의 반감은 가까운 미래에 점차 줄어들 것으로 예상된다.
② 이슬람 국가들은 미국에 대해 경멸적 감정을 갖고 있다.
③ 미국은 중동에 강력한 동맹국이 존재하지 않는다.
④ 중동에 대한 미국의 불균형적 개입은 중동 내 파열음의 원인 중 하나이다.

| 정답 | ④

| 해설 | "이스라엘 및 팔레스타인에 대한 이스라엘의 팽창주의적이고 억압적인 정책에 대해 미국이 보이고 있는 무조건적인 지지 (the United States' unconditional support of Israel and its expansionary and oppressive policies against the Palestinians)"는 ④에서 언급된 "중동에 대한 미국의 불균형적 개입"에 해당된다. 따라서 답은 ④이다.

본문 마지막 문장을 보면 중동 국가들이 품고 있는 미국에 대한 적개심은 상당함을 알 수 있고, 본문 어디에도 이런 적개심이 근시일 내에 줄어들 것이라는 내용은 찾을 수 없다. 따라서 ①은 답이 될 수 없다.

②의 "경멸적 감정(pejorative feeling)"은 깔보고 비판하는 감정에 해당되고 이는 "반감(animosity/antipathy)"과 는 의미가 좀 다르다. 또한 본문에 언급된 국가들은 중동 지역의 국가들인데, 이슬람 국가가 모두 중동에만 있는 것은 아니며 때문에 이슬람 국가가 모두 미국에 경멸적 감정을 갖고 있다고 보기는 어렵다. 따라서 ②는 답이 될 수 없다.

이집트 · 요르단 · 터키는 중동에 위치한 미국의 핵심 우방국이다. 따라서 ③은 답이 될 수 없다.

| 어휘 |

heighten ⓥ 과장하다, 증가시키다
shortsightedness ⓝ 근시안적임, 선견지명이 없음
animosity ⓝ 반감, 적대감
unconditional ⓐ 무조건적인
oppressive ⓐ 억압적인, 탄압하는
a host of 다수의
repressive ⓐ 억압적인, 탄압하는
intervention ⓝ 개입, 내정 간섭
whole-scale ⓐ 대규모의, 광범위한
qualify ⓥ (~라고) 보다[평하다]
redolence ⓝ 방향, 향기
rapprochement ⓝ 화해
pejorative ⓐ 경멸적인, 비난조의
asymmetrical ⓐ 비대칭적인, 불균형적인
stridency ⓝ 삐걱거림, 파열음

prejudice ⓝ 편견
consensus ⓝ 의견 일치, 합의
multifold ⓐ 여러 가지의, 다양한
expansionary ⓐ 팽창주의적인, 확대적인
prop up 지원하다, 받쳐 주다
unrepresentative ⓐ 대표[전형]적인 것이 못 되는
widespread ⓐ 광범위한, 널리 확산된
claim ⓥ (목숨을) 앗아가다
Palestinian Authority 팔레스타인 자치 정부
analogous ⓐ 유사한, 비슷한
comity ⓝ 예의
antipathy ⓝ 반감
confederate ⓝ 연맹, 동맹국
interference ⓝ 개입

해석

의학의 미래가 이처럼 밝게 보였던 적은 이전 어느 시기에도 존재하지 않았다. 심혈관 체계를 연구하고 있는 과학자들은 문제의 핵심에 조만간 근접할 수 있을 것이며, 심장 질환의 메커니즘을 더 이상은 불가해한 미스터리로 여기지 않을 것이라고 절대적으로 자신하고 있다. 암 과학자들은 암 연구를 어떻게 조직화하는 것이 가장 좋은 것인지에 대해 공개적으로 의견 일치를 보이지 못하고 있음에도 불구하고, 이들은 정상 및 종양 세포의 작동 방식에 대해 깊이 있게 이해하고 있으며, 이는 몇 년 전에는 상상할 수 없는 것이었다. 신경 생리학자들은 실험에서 모든 종류의 것들을 할 수 있으며, 뇌는 25년 전에 생각했던 것과는 전혀 다른 장기가 되었다.

요약하자면, 내 생각에 인간의 주요 질병은 접근 가능한 생물학적 퍼즐이 되었으며, 궁극적으로 해결할 수 있을 것으로 생각된다. 이런 생각에서 좀 더 나아가면 이제는 상대적으로 질병이 없는 인간의 사회를 생각해 보는 것이 가능해졌다. 이는 반세기 전만 하더라도 상상할 수 없는 개념이었다고 할 수 있다. 충분히 이상하게도, 이는 오늘날 종말론적인 어감을 내포한다. 만일 이런 일이 실현된다면 죽음을 우리는 어떻게 생각해야 하며, 이로 인한 인구의 증가는 또 어떻게 해야 하는가? 질병이 아니라면 대체 우리는 무엇으로 사망할 것인가?

---

07 빈칸 ㉠에 가장 적절한 것은?

① 심장　　　　② 폐　　　　③ 간　　　　④ 신장

| 정답 | ①

| 해설 | 앞에 심혈관(cardiovascular)이라는 단어가 등장하는데, 이는 심장(cardio)과 혈관(vascular)의 합성어로, 이 단어를 통해 심장(heart)임을 추측할 수 있다.

---

08 밑줄 친 ㉡에서 추론할 수 있는 것은?

① 신경 생리학자들은 면밀히 뇌의 형태에 대해 조사했다.
② 뇌 연구가 지난 25년간 급격하게 발전했다.
③ 이전보다 더 정확하게 뇌를 진단하는 것이 항상 가능한 것은 아니다.
④ 뇌는 특별한 장기로 신체의 다른 장기와 구별된다.

| 정답 | ②

| 해설 | 뇌가 25년 전에 생각되던 뇌와 다른 것이 되었다는 말이므로 뇌에 대해 인간이 더 많은 사실들을 알게 되었다는 뜻이다. 따라서 ②의 뇌 연구가 매우 진보했다는 내용이 적절하다.

---

09 다음 문장이 들어갈 가장 적절한 곳은?

충분히 이상하게도, 이는 오늘날 종말론적인 어감을 내포한다.

① ㉮　　　　② ㉯　　　　③ ㉰　　　　④ ㉱

| 정답 | ③

| 해설 | apocalyptic은 '종말론적인'이란 뜻의 단어로 종말을 의미하는 apocalypse에서 파생한 형용사이다. 마치 이런 말이 종말론

적인 느낌을 준다는 뜻이 된다. 인류가 질병으로 죽지 않게 된 것은 축복일 수 있지만, 이는 인류에게 또 다른 재앙이 될 수 있다는 말이므로, 충분히 이상하게 들릴 수 있다(oddly enough)고 표현하고 있다. 따라서 이 문장은 인류가 질병으로 죽지 않을 수 있다는 내용과 그럴 경우 발생할 재앙적인 예들 사이에 들어가는 것이 논리적으로 적절하므로 정답은 ③이 된다.

| 어휘 | **cardiovascular** ⓐ 심혈관의

regard A as B A를 B로 여기다

insight ⓝ 통찰력

neoplastic ⓐ 종양의

organ ⓝ 장기

drastically ⓐ 철저하게, 급격하게, 과감하게

entirely ⓐ 완전히, 아주

impenetrable ⓐ 불가해한, 관통할 수 없는

intimate ⓐ 정통한, 조예 깊은; 친밀한, 사적인

neurobiologist ⓝ 신경 생리학자

come about 발생하다, 일어나다

apocalyptic ⓐ 종말론적인, 세상에 종말이 온 듯한

[10~12] 국민대 2014

해석

몇 년 전에 나는 졸업 25주년 동창회에 참석했다. 나는 1959년 졸업 이후 반 친구 대부분을 만나지 못했다. 소수는 내가 과거 기억하던 그 모습 그대로 거의 변하지 않은 상태였다. 다른 이들은 내가 머릿속에 기억하고 있던 사진 속 모습과 일치하는 점을 거의 찾을 수 없을 정도로 나이가 너무 들어 보였다. 어디서 이런 차이가 나는 것일까? 왜 어떤 이들은 시간이 흐르면서 겉모습이 너무나 변했지만 그렇지 않은 이들도 있는 것일까? 달리 말하면 실제 연령과 생물학적 연령 간의 차이가 종종 발생하는 이유는 무엇일까? 나는 그 답이 유전학과 환경의 복잡한 상호 작용과 관련이 있다고 생각한다. 또한 나는 내가 검토한 증거를 기반으로 봤을 때 우리가 실제로는 이러한 요소를 어느 정도 통제할 수 있다고 생각한다. 나는 예순이든 아니면 어떤 중대 시점이든 인생의 어느 시기가 되면 노화가 우리를 불시에 덮친다는 시각에는 동의하지 않는다. 일부 의사들은 우리가 태어난 다음 성장하여 빠르게 성숙기에 접어든 다음 다소는 편안한 정체기에 진입하여 관성적으로 움직인 후 차차 하락하기 시작한다고 말한다. 의사들은 이런 하락 시기를 "노쇠"라 부르며 그 이전 시기와는 별개로 구분되는 시기로 취급한다. 하지만 나는 노화를 난소의 수정과 함께 시작되는 지속적이면서 필수적인 변화의 과정으로 보는 것이 더 유용함을 깨달았다. 노화라는 연속체 속에서 어디에 위치해 있든 건강과 행복을 극대화하기 위해 적절한 방식으로 사는 법을 배우는 것이 중요하다.

---

10 빈칸 ⓐ에 가장 적합한 것은 무엇인가?

① 가상의

② 실제의

③ 청소년의

④ 환경의

| 정답 | ②

| 해설 | 저자는 동창회에서 같은 나이임에도 어떤 친구들은 거의 변하지 않는데 어떤 친구들은 너무 나이 들어 보이는 이유가 무엇일까 궁금해했다. 즉 "실제 연령"과 "생물학적 연령" 간의 차이가 어떻게 나는 것인지를 궁금해한 것이다. 따라서 답은 ②이다.

---

11 다음 문장이 들어가기에 가장 적합한 위치는 어디인가?

의사들은 이런 하락 시기를 "노쇠"라 부르며 그 이전 시기와는 별개로 구분되는 시기로 취급한다.

① (A)　　　　② (B)　　　　③ (C)　　　　④ (D)

| 해설 | 주어진 문장에서 "이런 하락 시기(this period of decline)"가 무엇인지 생각해 보면, (C) 앞의 "차차 하락하는 시기(begin to decline)"를 가리키는 것임을 알 수 있다. 또한 (D)까지는 의사들이 가진 노화에 관한 시각을 말하고 있지만 (D) 이후부터는 저자가 가진 노화에 관한 시각을 말하고 있는데, 주어진 문장은 의사들의 시각과 같다. 즉 의사의 주장과 저자의 주장의 경계선인 (D)에 주어진 문장이 들어가는 것이 맞다. 따라서 답은 ④이다.

---

12 다음 중 본문에 따르면 사실인 것은 무엇인가?

① 저자는 고등학교 동창회에서 같은 반 친구 가운데 알아볼 수 있는 사람이 거의 없었다.
② 저자는 분명한 증거 없이 유전적 요소를 제어해서는 안 된다고 말한다.
③ 저자는 우리 신체의 쇠퇴는 특정한 시점에 도달하지 전까지는 시작되지 않는다고 추정한다.
④ 저자는 노화를 어머니가 우리를 임신한 시점부터 시작되는 지속적인 변화 과정의 일부라고 생각한다.

| 정답 | ④

| 해설 | "하지만 나는 노화를 난소의 수정과 함께 시작되는 지속적이면서 필수적인 변화의 과정으로 보는 것이 더 유용함을 깨달았다 (But I find it more useful to think of aging as a continuous and necessary process of change that begins at conception)." 따라서 답은 ④이다.

| 어휘 |

school reunion 동창회
coincidence ⓝ (우연의) 일치, 동시 발생
alter ⓥ 바꾸다, 변경하다
chronological ⓐ 시간 순서대로 된
biological age 생물학적 연령
genetics ⓝ 유전학, 유전적 특질
subscribe to 찬성하다, 동의하다
overtake ⓥ 따라잡다, 만회하다, (불쾌한 일이 사람에게) 불시에 닥치다
milestone ⓝ 이정표, (인생, 역사 따위의) 중대 시점
maturity ⓝ 성숙, 원숙
plateau ⓝ 고원, 안정기, 정체기
distinct ⓐ 별개의, 뚜렷이 다른
continuum ⓝ 연속, 연속체
hereditary ⓐ 유전적인, 세습되는

aged ⓐ 늙은, 나이 든, 오래된
outwardly ⓐ🅳 외견상, 겉으로는
discrepancy ⓝ 불일치, 차이, 모순
chronological age 생활 연령, 실제 연령
interaction ⓝ 상호 작용
factor ⓝ 요인, 요소

physician ⓝ 의사
coast ⓥ 순조롭게 나가다, 관성으로 움직이다
senescence ⓝ 노쇠
conception ⓝ (난소의) 수정
virtual ⓐ 사실상의, 가상의
conceive ⓥ 아이를 가지다[임신하다]

해석

컴퓨터 마우스를 클릭하고 이리저리 돌리는 행위와 연계된 훈련을 다른 분야로 전환할 수 있는 인간의 능력에 대한 연구 결과, 뇌는 마우스 조작 능력을 손을 필요로 하는 미세 운동 과업에 적용할 수 있다는 것이 드러났다. 코딩과 웨이가 주도하는 연구 팀에서 세 그룹의 사람들을 모집했는데, 하나는 중국 이주 노동자들로 컴퓨터를 사용한 경험이 없는 사람들이며, 다른 하나는 연령과 교육 수준은 비슷하지만 일하는 과정에서 컴퓨터를 써 본 경험이 있는 노동자들, 그리고 마지막으로 대조군 역할인 컴퓨터 사용에 능숙한 대학생들이었다. 모든 피실험자들은 2주간 훈련 기간을 거쳤으며 그 기간 동안 게임을 하기 위해 컴퓨터 마우스를 사용해야 했다. 연구진은 각 그룹을 대상으로 훈련 전후에 수많은 표준 운동 제어 테스트를 수행했다. 코딩과 웨이가 가장 관심을 가진 테스트는 일반화 가능성을 측정하는 테스트였다. 만일 컴퓨터 마우스의 사용법을 배운다면 마우스 사용을 위한 기술이 유사 운동 과업에 적용이 가능한 것인가? 피실험자가 익숙하지 않은 과업을 수행하는 능력을 측정하기 위해 연구진은 손이 덮개 밑에 숨겨져 있을 때 손가락의 위치를 제어하는 것같이 마우스와 아무 연관 없는 운동 기능을 검사했다. 훈련 기간 이전에는 컴퓨터 사용 경험을 지닌 이주 노동자들은 모든 과업에 있어 컴퓨터 관련 지식이 없는 쪽에 비해 더 잘 과업을 수행했다. 컴퓨터를 사용해 본 경험이 없는 사람들은 손의 움직임을 미세하게 제어하면서 움직이는 것에 특히나 어려움을 느꼈으며 특히 손이 숨겨져 있을 때 더욱 그러했다. 하지만 2주 동안의 훈련만으로도 과거 컴퓨터 이용 경험이 없던 이주 노동자들은 컴퓨터 마우스를 사용하고 마우스 사용 기술을 다른 미세 손 운동 기술에 적용하는 데 있어 대학생들에 비해 떨어졌다.

---

13 윗글의 주제로 가장 적합한 것을 고르시오.

① 운동 기술을 다른 익숙하지 않은 과업에 전환할 수 있는 가능성
② 컴퓨터 이용에 있어 운동 기술의 중요성
③ 과학 연구에 있어 운동 기술의 평가의 어려움
④ 운동 기술을 다루기 위한 뇌의 구조

| 정답 | ①

| 해설 | 본문의 핵심은 첫 문장인 "컴퓨터 마우스를 클릭하고 이리저리 돌리는 행위와 연계된 훈련을 다른 분야로 전환할 수 있는 인간의 능력에 대한 연구 결과, 뇌는 마우스 조작 능력을 손을 필요로 하는 미세 운동 과업에 적용할 수 있다는 것이 드러났다(A study of people's ability to translate training that involves clicking and twiddling a computer mouse reveals that the brain can apply that expertise to other fine-motor tasks requiring the hands)."이다. 그리고 실험 결과를 통해 과거에 컴퓨터를 써 본 적 없는 노동자들도 훈련을 받으면 낯설었던 과업도 수행이 가능하다는 것을 알 수 있다. 즉 마우스를 조작하는 능력은 익숙하지 않은 다른 미세한 손 운동 기술로 전환이 가능하다는 것이 본문의 주제이다. 따라서 답은 ①이다.

---

14 윗글의 흐름상 가장 적합하지 <u>않은</u> 것을 고르시오.

① (A)　　　　② (B)　　　　③ (C)　　　　④ (D)

| 정답 | ④

| 해설 | 본문의 핵심은 "과거 경험이 없던 사람도 훈련을 통해 익숙하지 않던 일도 능숙하게 하는 것이 가능해졌다"이다. 때문에 "2주 동안의 훈련만으로도(after just 2 weeks of training)" 과거 컴퓨터 이용 경험이 없던 이주 노동자들이 대학생들만큼 조작이 가능하다는 내용이 와야 문맥에 맞지 본문처럼 "떨어진다"는 내용은 맞지 않는다. just as well as로 바뀌어야 한다. 따라서 답은 ④이다.

어휘	twiddle ⓥ 빙빙 돌리다, 만지작거리다	expertise ⓝ 전문 기술
	fine-motor ⓐ 소근육의, 미세 운동의	match ⓥ 일치하다, 아주 비슷하다
	control group 대조군	proficient ⓐ 능숙한, 능한
	subject ⓝ 피실험자	a battery of 수많은
	motor control 운동 제어	generalizability ⓝ 일반화 가능성
	-naive ⓐ ~에 대한 지식이 없는	transferability ⓝ 전환 가능성

[15] 중앙대 2015

해석

사람들은 아스코르브산으로 불리는 비타민 C가 제공하는 혜택을 오래전부터 잘 알고 있다. 선원들은 괴혈병 예방을 위해 감귤류 과일같이 비타민 C가 풍부히 함유된 음식을 배에 싣곤 했다. 사람들은 오랫동안 매일 식단을 보완하기 위해 비타민 C를 섭취해 왔다. 그러나 사람들이 비타민 C를 보충제 형태로 섭취하긴 하지만 과학자들은 우리 신체에 과연 비타민 C가 얼마나 좋을지에 관해 논쟁하고 있다. 일부 학자는 비타민 C를 대량 섭취하면 흔한 감기는 치료할 수 있다고 본다. 다른 학자는 비타민 C가 암을 치료할 수 있다고 본다. 우리의 체내에서 비타민 C가 어떤 작용을 하는지에 관해서는 과학자들의 의견이 일치한다. 콜라겐은 세포끼리의 결속을 위해 필요한 물질이며, 콜라겐을 생성하기 위해서는 아스코르브산이 필요하다. (아스코르브산을 얻기 위한 또 다른 방법은 비타민이 강화된 가공식품으로부터 얻는 것이다.) 추가로 비타민 C는 물에서 용해되기 때문에 다른 수용성 비타민과 마찬가지로 비타민 C는 가스로 용해되는 다른 비타민이 체내에서 산화되는 것을 막는 데 도움이 된다. 우리의 신체는 아스코르브산을 생성할 수 없으므로 체외에서 획득해야 한다. 신선한 과일, 녹색 잎줄기채소, 조리된 야채 (조리가 덜 될수록 비타민 C가 더 풍부함), (토마토, 감자, 가지 등의) 가지속 채소에서 비타민 C를 획득할 수 있다. 문제가 되는 점은 과연 우리는 하루에 얼마나 많은 양의 비타민 C를 필요로 할지 여부이다. 어쩌면 여러분은 과학자들이 이 문제를 두고서도 논쟁을 벌이고 있다는 사실을 알게 되어도 놀라지는 않을 것이다.

15 윗글의 흐름상 가장 적합하지 **않은** 것을 고르시오.

① (A) ② (B) ③ (C) ④ (D)

| 정답 | ③

| 해설 | (C)는 비타민 C의 섭취 방법에 관해 말하고 있지만, (C) 앞 내용은 비타민 C의 효능에 관해 말하고 있다. 비타민 C의 섭취 방법에 관해서는 (C) 다음부터 언급되기 때문에, (C)는 본문의 위치보다는 (D)와 가까운 곳으로 이동하는 것이 적합하다. 따라서 답은 ③이다.

어휘	ascorbic acid 아스코르브산	citrus ⓝ 감귤류 과일
	scurvy ⓝ 괴혈병	down ⓥ (액체, 약 등을) 먹다[마시다]
	supplement ⓥ 보완하다, 추가하다	enriched ⓐ 강화된
	oxidize ⓥ 산화시키다	leafy vegetable 잎줄기채소
	nightshade ⓝ 가지속(屬) 채소	eggplant ⓝ 가지

해석

(a) 내일 창세기가 다시 쓰이게 될 것이다. 뮌헨에 위치한 유럽 특허청(European Patent Office)이라는 예상 밖의 장소에서 한 무리의 국제 공무원들이 살아 있는 동물은 자연계의 일부인지 아니면 인간의 재주로 인해 창조된 인공물, 즉 발명품인지 여부를 결정할 것이다.

(c) 문제가 되는 동물은 쥐인데, 보통의 쥐는 아니다. 이 쥐는 신이 아니라 인간에 의해 창조된 최초의 동물이다. 1984년 하버드 대학의 유전 공학자들은 실험 쥐의 유전자에 암호화된 형태로 존재하는 생물학적 지령을 조작하였다. 티모시 스튜어트(Timothy Stewart), 폴 패턴게일(Paul Patterngale), 필립 레더(Philip Leder) 이 셋으로 구성된 유전 공학자들은 실험 쥐의 DNA의 이중 나선 구조를 푼 다음에 쥐가 암에 걸려 죽게 만드는 유전자를 끼워 넣었다.

(d) 현재 하버드대학의 학장 및 특별 연구원들은 이 실험 쥐를 "발명품"으로 특허를 받기 원하며, 그 이유는 특허법상의 용어로 표현하면 종양의 발달 과정을 연구하기 위한 "산업상 이용 가능성"을 보유하고 있기 때문이다. 하버드 대학은 심지어 이 실험 쥐에게 하버드 온코마우스(Harvard Oncomouse)라는 상표를 붙였으며, 실험 쥐를 판매할 수 있는 독점권을 통해 수익을 얻고자 한다.

(b) 그리고 여기서 그칠 가능성은 없어 보인다. 암 연구에 사용되기 위해 고안된 "온코독(Oncodog)", "온코레빗 (Oncorabbit)", "온코멍키(Oncomonkey)" 등이 뒤이어 등장할 가능성이 크다.

(e) 특허는 지난 20년 동안 발전해 온 전 세계의 생명 공학 산업에서 매우 중요한 역할을 띠고 있다. 생명 공학 산업은 오로지 지적 재산을 보호할 목적으로만 한 해에 1억 달러 이상을 쓴다. 물론 지적 재산은 살아 있는 동물에 대한 특허보다 훨씬 더 광범위한 범위를 포괄한다.

16 위의 이야기를 논리적으로 올바른 순서에 맞춰 배열하시오.

① (a) − (c) − (d) − (b) − (e) 　　② (d) − (a) − (b) − (c) − (e)

③ (e) − (a) − (c) − (b) − (d) 　　④ (b) − (a) − (d) − (e) − (c)

| 정답 | ①

| 해설 | 본문은 인간에 의해 창조된 실험 쥐를 자연의 일부로 볼 것인지 아니면 인공물로 봐야 할 것인지에 관해 논하고 있다. 우선은 이 문제를 소개하고 있는 (a)가 맨 처음에 와야 하며 ⇨ 문제가 되고 있는 동물이 무엇이며 어떻게 만들어진 것인지 설명하는 (c)가 뒤에 등장해야 한다. ⇨ 다음으로 (d)에서는 하버드대학에서 실험 쥐를 창조했으며 실험 쥐에 "온코마우스"란 상표를 붙였음을 알 수 있다. ⇨ 그리고 이 "온코"란 용어는 쥐(마우스)뿐만 아니라 "여기서 그치지 않고" 개(독), 토끼(레빗), 원숭이(멍키)에도 상표 형태로 붙어 있음을 (b)를 통해 알 수 있다. ⇨ 마지막으로 (e)에서는 생명 공학 산업에서 특허가 어떤 중요성을 갖는지 말하고 있다.

| 어휘 | **the Book of Genesis** 창세기

setting ⓝ 환경, 장소

ingenuity ⓝ 기발한 재주, 재간, 독창성

ordinary ⓐ 보통의, 평범한

genetic engineer 유전 공학자

encode ⓥ 암호화[기호화]하다

double helix 이중 나선 구조

fatally ⓐⓓ 치명적으로

fellow ⓝ (대학의) 특별 연구원

in the language of ~의 말을 빌면, ~의 용어로 표현하면

rewrite ⓥ 고쳐 쓰다, 다시 쓰다

artifact ⓝ 인공물, 가공품

at issue 논쟁 중인, 문제가 되고 있는

invent ⓥ 발명하다, 고안[창안]하다

manipulate ⓥ 조종하다, 조작하다

unzip ⓥ 해결하다, 풀다

stitch ⓥ 꿰매다

doom ⓥ 운명 짓다, 불행한 운명[결말]을 맞게 하다

patent ⓥ 특허를 얻다[주다]

utility ⓝ 실용성, (산업상) 이용 가능성
exclusive ⓐ 독점적인
intellectual property 지적 재산

coin ⓥ (새로운 낱말, 어구를) 만들다
immensely ⓐ 무한히, 매우
range ⓥ (많은 다양한 것을) 포함[포괄]하다

[17~20] 명지대 2011

해석

내 생각에 사전의 첫 페이지의 내용을 마침표 하나까지 모두 메모장에 그대로 옮겨 적는 데 하루 종일 걸렸던 것 같다. 그런 후 큰 소리로 내가 메모장에 쓴 모든 내용을 혼자서 다시 읽었다. 계속 반복해서 혼자 큰 소리로 내가 손으로 쓴 글을 읽었다.

㉯ 다음 날 아침 그 단어들을 생각하면서 잠에서 깼다. 그리고 한순간에 그렇게 많은 글자를 썼다는 사실과 세상에 그런 단어가 존재하는지조차 몰랐던 단어들을 썼다는 사실을 깨닫고 스스로를 무척 대견스럽게 생각했다. 게다가 약간의 노력으로도 이들 단어 중 많은 단어들이 무엇을 의미하는지 기억할 수 있었다. 의미가 생각나지 않는 단어들은 다시 반복해서 익혔다. 재미있는 사실이 있는데, 사전의 첫 페이지에 있던 "aardvark(땅돼지)"라는 단어가 기억이 난다. 사전에는 땅돼지의 그림이 있었다. 땅돼지는 긴 꼬리에 긴 귀를 하고 있었으며 굴을 파는 습성을 지닌 아프리카의 포유류였으며, 개미핥기가 개미에게 하듯이 땅돼지는 혀를 내밀어서 흰개미를 잡아먹으며 산다는 것이었다.

㉰ 나는 너무도 매료된 나머지 하던 일을 계속했다. 사전의 다음 페이지 내용을 그대로 옮겨 적었다. 다음 장을 익히면서도 같은 경험을 하게 되었다. 매번 이어지는 페이지에서 나는 역사 현장의 인물과, 장소, 사건 등을 익혀 갔다. 사실 사전은 백과사전의 축소판과 같았다. 마침내 사전의 알파벳 A면을 메모장 전체에 채웠다. 그리고 알파벳 B로 넘어갔다. 이것도 처음 사전을 옮겨 적기 시작했던 방식 그대로 이뤄졌으며, 이런 식으로 사전 전체를 끝마치게 되었다. 이런 일은 훨씬 더 빠르게 이뤄졌다. 왜냐면 수많은 연습을 통해 필기 속도가 빨라졌기 때문이다. 메모장에 글을 적고 편지를 쓰면서, 이런 일을 하기 시작한 이후의 감옥에서 있었던 시간에 족히 백만 단어는 썼다고 생각된다.

㉮ 기본 어휘가 확장되면서 태어나서 처음으로 책을 골라 읽고 그러면서 책이 말하고자 하는 내용을 이해할 수 있게 된 것은 어쩌면 필연적이라고 생각한다. 많은 책을 읽은 사람이라면 새롭게 열리는 세계를 상상할 수 있을 것이다. 한 가지 말해 줄 게 있다. 그때부터 교도소를 출소하기 전까지 자유 시간이 생기면 항상, 내가 도서관에서 책을 읽는 것이 아니라면, 교도소의 침상에서 책을 읽었다. 당시 누군가가 쐐기로 책들에서 나를 떼어 내려고 시도했다 하더라도 성공하지 못했을 것이다. 편지를 주고받고, 방문객을 대하고, 독서를 하는 사이, 몇 달이 내가 교도소에 수감되어 있다는 생각도 잊은 채 흘렀다. 사실 그 이전 어느 순간에도 그때만큼 진정한 자유를 느낀 적이 없었다.

17 첫 문단 이후에 이어질 글의 순서로 가장 적절한 것은?

① ㉮ - ㉯ - ㉰
② ㉯ - ㉰ - ㉮
③ ㉯ - ㉮ - ㉰
④ ㉰ - ㉮ - ㉯

| 정답 | ②

| 해설 | 본문은 저자가 사전을 옮겨 적으며 글을 익히는 과정을 시간 순서대로 나열하고 있는 글이다. 따라서 어떻게 저자가 사전을 통해 글을 익혀 나갔는지를 추적하면 된다. ㉮에서는 책을 골라 읽을 수 있는 수준이 되었다고 나오며, ㉯에서는 이제 막 사전의 맨 첫 부분을 익히는 모습에 관한 글이며, ㉰에서는 A에서 시작해서 사전 마지막까지 학습한 내용에 관한 글이다. 따라서 정답은 ㉯ - ㉰ - ㉮ 순이 된다는 것을 알 수 있다.

18 윗글의 제목으로 가장 적절한 것은?

① 내가 사전을 옮겨 적기 시작한 이유
② 땅돼지(aardvark), 나의 백만 번째 단어
③ 미국 교도소에서의 언론의 자유
④ 필기를 향상시키기 위한 기초 내용

| 정답 | ①

| 해설 | 필자는 글을 모르던 사람이었을 것으로 추측되며, 자신이 쓴 글을 다시 해독해 읽는 데 시간이 많이 걸렸던 사람이다. 또한 어휘 또한 제한적으로 알고 있던 사람이다. 이런 그가 감옥에서 사전을 통해 글을 익히기 시작하면서 마침내 책을 골라 읽으면서 그 내용을 이해하게 되었고, 그러면서 새로운 세계를 경험하게 되었다는 내용을 담고 있으므로 이런 내용을 함축적으로 담고 있는 ①이 제목으로 적당하다.

---

19 빈칸 ㉠에 가장 적절한 것은?

① 감옥　　　　② 사전　　　　③ 개미들　　　　④ 책들

| 정답 | ④

| 해설 | 빈칸이 있는 부분은 본문 중에서 해석하기 좀 어려운 부분이다. 가정법 과거를 사용했고, 무엇인가를 서로 분리해 놓는 데 사용하는 쐐기(wedge)를 비유적으로 사용했다. 바로 앞의 내용을 보면 당시에는 남는 시간을 모두 책 읽기에 보냈기 때문에, 쐐기로 이것에서 필자를 분리하려 했어도 그렇게 할 수 없었을 것이라고 적고 있다. 따라서 독서와 관련 있는 ④ books가 정답이 된다.

---

20 밑줄 친 ㉡이 의미하는 바는?

① 같은 경험을 하는 것
② 처방대로 알약을 복용하는 것
③ 사전을 옮겨 적는 것
④ 인물, 장소, 사건을 배우는 것

| 정답 | ③

| 해설 | 이 문제의 정답은 밑줄 뒤의 "pick up handwriting speed(옮겨 적는 속도가 빨라지다)"를 통해 유추할 수 있다. 앞의 이유 때문에 그것이 수월해졌다고 했으므로, 그것은 사전을 옮겨 적는 것을 말한다. 따라서 정답은 ③이 된다.

| 어휘 |
punctuation ⓝ 구두점
suppose ⓥ 생각하다, 가정하다
broaden ⓥ 넓혀지다, 확장하다
bunk ⓝ 침대
correspondence ⓝ 서신, 편지
immensely ⓐⓓ 매우
spring to one's mind 갑자기 떠오르다
mammal ⓝ 포유류

tablet ⓝ 메모지, 편지지; 알약
inevitable ⓐ 필연적인
pick up a book 책을 고르다
wedge ⓝ 쐐기
imprison ⓥ 구속하다, 가두다
aardvark ⓝ 땅돼지
burrow ⓥ 굴을 파다, 굴에 살다
live off ~을 먹고 살다, ~을 착취해서 살다

termite ⓝ 흰개미
go on 계속해 나가다
pick up the speed 속도를 내다

stick out 내밀다
encyclopedia ⓝ 백과사전

---

21 상자 안의 문장 다음으로 이어지는 글의 순서를 올바르게 배열하시오. 인하대 2016

> 마우스는 1964년 더글러스 엥겔바트(Douglas Engelbart)에 의해 처음 개발되었다. 최초의 마우스는 나무로 된 몸통과 회로 기판 그리고 마우스가 사용되는 표면과 직접적으로 접촉하는 부분인 두 개의 금속 바퀴로 구성되어 있었다.

[C] 8년 후 빌 잉글리시(Bill English)는 "볼 마우스"로 알려진 것을 발명하여 최초 마우스의 설계를 더욱 개선하였다. 볼 마우스의 볼은 최초 마우스의 바퀴를 대체했고 어떤 방향에서도 움직임을 추적 관찰할 수 있었다. 볼은 두 개의 롤러와 접촉하고 뒤이어 롤러는 눈금이 달린 바퀴를 회전시켰으며 이는 방향과 속도를 나타내는 전기 신호로 변환되었다.

[B] 광 마우스는 그로부터 8년 후인 1980년에 개발되었고, 책상 위에서 이리저리 돌다 보면 종종 더러워 져서 구동에 악영향을 미치는 볼을 없애 버렸다. 그 다음 8년 동안 리사 M. 윌리엄스(Lisa M. Williams)와 로버트 S. 체리(Robert S. Cherry)가 발명한 광 마우스를 대상으로 특허 번호 4751505인 미국 특허가 발행되었다.

[A] 이 광 마우스는 17달러에 생산되어 35달러에 판매되었다. 그럼에도 불구하고, 10년이 지난 1998년경이 되어서야 광 마우스가 상업적으로 볼 마우스를 대체할 만한 유력한 대안이 되었고 일반 대중을 대상으로 한 소비 시장에 침투하여 진입할 수 있었다.

① [A] − [B] − [C]
② [B] − [A] − [C]
③ [C] − [B] − [A]
④ [B] − [C] − [A]
⑤ [C] − [A] − [B]

| 정답 | ③

| 해설 | 상자 안의 문장은 최초의 마우스 개발에 관해 말하고 있다. 최초의 마우스에는 바퀴가 달려 있었고, 그 다음에는 바퀴 대신 볼을 사용한 볼 마우스에 관한 내용인 [C]가 와야 하며, 이후 볼을 제거한 광 마우스가 등장했음을 말하는 [B]가 와야 한다. 마지막으로는 광 마우스에 대한 부연 설명이 이루어지는 [A]가 와야 한다. 따라서 답은 ③이다.

| 어휘 | shell ⓝ 케이스, 몸통
graduation ⓝ 도수, 눈금
affect ⓥ 악영향을 미치다
infiltrate ⓥ 침투하다, 침입하다

circuit board 회로 기판
represent ⓥ 대표하다, 나타내다
viable ⓐ 생존 가능한, 유력한

해석

서구 문명의 여명기부터 음악은 상당한 불안의 원인이 되어 왔으며 그 이유는 음악이 체제 전복적인 사고와 행동을 불어넣을 능력이 있기 때문이었다. 고대 그리스인들은 사람의 기질을 강화하거나 타락시키는 역량이 음악에 있는 것으로 보았다. 이들은 심지어 음계별로 각기 다른 도덕적 가치를 부여하기까지 했으며, 따라서 일부 음색은 공격성과 폭력을 야기하고 다른 일부는 고상한 행위를 조장하는 것으로 생각되었다. 플라톤은 영혼의 움직임과 음악의 리듬 간에 상관관계가 있다고 받아들였다. 플라톤은 음악을 피상적인 오락을 위한 수단이 아니라 그보다는 교육의 핵심 구성 요소라고 주장했는데, 교육의 목표는 격정을 자제하고 도덕적 기질을 강화하는 데 있었다. 따라서 음악은 개인적인 문제가 아니라 공공의 문제였다. "좋은" 음악을 함양하면 청자의 영혼이 더욱 정돈되며 따라서 더욱 윤리적이면서 훈육이 잘 된 시민이 만들어지는 반면에 "나쁜" 음악은 개인의 격정을 부추기며 따라서 공동체 내에서 불화를 조장한다. 플라톤은 새로운 유형의 음악의 도입은 국가 전체를 위태롭게 할 것이므로 반드시 피해야 한다고 주장했다. 그 이유는 음악 양식은 가장 중요한 정치 제도에 영향을 미치지 않고서 방해하는 경우는 없기 때문이었다. (정치제도에 부정적인 영향을 미친다: 저자 주) 플라톤은 이에 관해 기원전 360년에 글을 썼지만, 그의 기본적 전제는 여전히 지금 세상에도 울려 퍼지고 있다. 우리는 아마도 경찰의 폭력과 조직적 인종 차별에 대한 분노보다 힙합음악이 젊은이들로 하여금 법 집행관들에게 폭력적 행위를 가하게 만든다는 내용의 널리 확산된 믿음에서 플라톤의 기본적 전제의 자취를 감지할 수 있다.

---

22 아래의 문장이 들어갈 가장 알맞은 곳을 고르시오.

플라톤은 이에 관해 기원전 360년에 글을 썼지만, 그의 기본적 전제는 여전히 지금 세상에도 울려 퍼지고 있다.

① (A) ② (B) ③ (C) ④ (D)

| 정답 | ④

| 해설 | 플라톤의 "기본적 전제(basic premise)"는 음악을 오락 용도에 그치지 않고 교육의 핵심 요소로 본 것, 좋은 음악과 나쁜 음악을 구분한 것, 새로운 음악의 도입을 금지한 것 등이 있다. 즉 주어진 문장은 이 세 가지 전제가 제시된 다음에 위치해야 한다. 그리고 "여전히 지금 세상에도 울려 퍼지고 있다(still resonates in the contemporary world)"는 말은, 즉 주어진 문장 다음부터는 과거가 아닌 현재의 사례가 제시될 것임을 의미한다. 그리고 빈칸 (D) 다음부터는 현재 힙합 음악에 대한 사례가 제시되어 있다. 따라서 답은 ④가 된다.

| 어휘 |

profound ⓐ 엄청난, 상당한
subversive ⓐ 체제 전복적인
degrade ⓥ 저하시키다, 타락시키다
tone ⓝ 음조, 음색
correlation ⓝ 연관성, 상관관계
cultivation ⓝ 배양, 함양
inflame ⓥ 격앙시키다, 부추기다
imperil ⓥ 위태롭게 하다, 위험에 빠뜨리다
premise ⓝ 전제
compel ⓥ ~하게 만들다

anxiety ⓝ 불안, 염려
attribute A to B A를 B의 결과로[덕분으로] 보다
musical scale 음계
posit ⓥ 사실로 상정하다[받아들이다]
self-mastery ⓝ 극기, 자제
citizenry ⓝ 시민, 주민
discord ⓝ 불화
shun ⓥ 피하다
resonate ⓥ 울려 퍼지다
law enforcement officer 법 집행

해석

적절한 수분 섭취의 중요성은 아무리 강조해도 지나치지 않다. 그것은 피로를 막아 주고, 배고픔을 멀리하고, 신진대사를 활발하게 해 줄 수 있다. 또한 칼로리를 줄여 주는 것도 생각해 볼 수 있다. 매일 섭취하는 150칼로리의 탄산음료를 물 한 잔으로 대체한다면, 매주 1,000칼로리 이상을 절약할 수 있고 이것은 1년이면 15파운드의 체중 감소를 의미한다. 식사 전에 물 한 잔을 마시면 포만감을 주고 음식을 통해 칼로리를 덜 섭취하게 도와준다. 당신이 식단을 계획하는 것과 마찬가지로, 당신은 물 섭취를 계획할 수 있다. 이는 갈증이 수분 섭취의 필요성의 좋은 지표가 되지 못하는 나이 든 사람들에게 특히 중요하다. 또한 갈증이 배고픔으로 오인될 수 있기 때문에, 온종일 물을 마시는 계획을 세우면 불필요한 간식을 피할 수 있다. 마지막으로, 어떤 사람들은 단순히 맹물을 마시고 싶어 하지 않는다. ⑧ 만약 맹물이 끌리지 않는다면, 오렌지, 레몬, 오이와 같은 과일이나 채소 조각을 첨가해 향을 돋을 수 있다. ⓒ 그리고 탄산수가 또 다른 대안이 될 수도 있다. ⑩ 요즘 상점 진열대에는 맛이 첨가된 수많은 탄산수를 찾아볼 수 있다. ⓐ 이 중에서 자연스럽게 끌리는 것을 선택하면 된다.

23 다음 중 빈칸에 가장 적합한 것은?

① 적절히 수분을 섭취하는 것

② 지방 섭취를 줄이는 것

③ 식단을 계획하는 것

④ 몸에 좋은 간식을 먹는 것

| 정답 | ①

| 해설 | 본문에서는 물을 섭취하는 것과 갈증에 대해 말하고 있으므로, 적절히 수분을 섭취하는 것의 중요성에 대해 말하고 있다. 따라서 정답은 ①이 적합하다.

24 다음 중 가장 올바른 순서인 것은?

① ⓐ – ⑧ – ⓒ – ⑩

② ⑧ – ⓒ – ⑩ – ⓐ

③ ⓒ – ⑩ – ⓐ – ⑧

④ ⑩ – ⑧ – ⓐ – ⓒ

| 정답 | ②

| 해설 | 수분 섭취의 중요성에 대해 말하고 있는데, 맹물(plain water)을 마시는 것을 원하지 않을 경우에 대해 서술하고 있다. 그런 경우 대안으로 ⑧에서와 같이 과일이나 채소 조각을 넣을 수 있고, 아니면 ⓒ와 ⑩에서와 같이 탄산수를 마실 수도 있다고 말한다. 그리고 ⓐ에서는 이 중에서 원하는 것을 골라서 섭취하면 된다고 했으므로 가장 마지막에 위치한다. 따라서 정답은 ②가 적합하다.

| 어휘 | **cannot be stressed enough** 아무리 강조해도 지나치지 않다

ward off ~을 피하다, 막다   **fatigue** ⑪ 피로, 피곤

keep something at bay ~을 가까이 못 오게 하다, 저지하다

boost ⓥ 강화하다, 복돋다   **metabolism** ⑪ 신진대사

consume ⓥ 섭취하다   **translate to** ~로 연결되다, 바뀌다

fill up 포만감을 주다, 가득 채우다

thirst ⓝ 갈증

plain water 맹물, 담수, 민물

cucumber ⓝ 오이

carbonated water 소다수

hydrated ⓐ 수화한, 함수의

intake ⓝ 흡입, 섭취

indicator ⓝ 지표

unappealing ⓐ 매력 없는, 유쾌하지 못한

flavor ⓝ 맛, 풍미, 양념 ⓥ 맛을 내다

shelf ⓝ 선반

[25] 한양대 2018

해석

'친구'와 '우정'이라는 단어는 광범위한 인간관계를 서술하기 위해 사용된다. 문제를 더 복잡하게 만드는 것은, 우정이 나름의 방식으로 독립적인 관계로 발생하거나, 혹은 형제, 배우자, 부모와 자녀, 동료 사이에 형성되는 우정과 같이 진실함이 수반되는 다른 차원의 관계로 발생할 수 있다는 점에서 독특하다. 이러한 경우에 있어 우정은 관계의 필수적 부분이 아니다. 우정이 배제된 무수히 많은 그런 유대 관계가 존재한다. 우정은 항상 비슷한 개인 성향을 보이고 물질적 측면과 사회 문화적 측면의 가능성을 보이는 개인 간의 협상을 통해 도출된 애착이다. (인간의 삶에서 곳곳에 만연한 우정의 특성에도 불구하고 혹은 그러한 특성 때문에, 우정 그 자체의 필요성이 많은 연구자들을 지적으로 사로잡았다.) 우리는 사람 사이의 정서적 정당성의 진정성을 강요하거나 요구할 수 없다. 그리고 우정은 특정 상황에서 제한되거나, 금지되거나, 심지어 상상도 할 수 없는 것이 될 수 있다.

25 문맥상 글의 전체 흐름과 <u>관계없는</u> 문장을 고르시오.

①   ②   ③   ④

| 정답 | ③

| 해설 | 본문은 우정의 특성을 서술한 글로, ①의 경우 바로 앞에 등장한 '형제, 배우자, 부모와 자녀, 동료 사이에 형성되는 우정'에 대해 부연 설명하고 있다. 또한 ②와 ④는 우정의 특성을 나열하는 내용이다. ③에서는 연구자들이 우정에 대한 문제를 연구하게 된 원인을 설명하고 있지만 앞뒤 문맥에서 연구의 관점에서 바라본 우정이 등장하지 않고 있으므로, ③이 흐름과 무관한 내용에 해당한다.

| 어휘 | complicate ⓥ 복잡하게 만들다

sibling ⓝ 형제, 자매

devoid of ~이 없는

disposition ⓝ 성벽, 기질, 성향

captivate ⓥ 마음을 사로잡다

validity ⓝ 유효함, 타당성

free-standing ⓐ 단독으로 서 있는, 독립적인

spouse ⓝ 배우자

attachment ⓝ 애착, 애정

pervasive ⓐ 만연하는, 스며드는

genuine ⓐ 진짜의, 성실한, 진심에서 우러난

prohibit ⓥ 금지하다

해석

행동을 예측하는 유전적 지표가 반드시 설명할 수 있는 대상은 아니라는 것은 뇌의 복잡성 때문에 당연한 귀결이라고 할 수 있다. 즉 다시 말하면 DNA 지표와 정신 질환 간의 관계가 유전적 변이가 행동을 변화시키는 방식에 대한 이해로 이어질 수 있다고 반드시 생각할 수는 없다. 혹은 중간 과정에 대해 이해했다고 하더라도 전체적인 이해는 그런 중간 과정을 이해한 후 여러 해가 지나서 나타나게 될 것이고, 유전적 지표가 예측 변수로 사용되고 오랜 시간이 지난 후에야 나타나게 될 것이다. 우리는 아마도 어떤 사람의 뇌가 서로 유사하게 작동할지 예측할 수 있을 것이다. 하지만 그 이유를 설명하지는 못할 것이다. 그것은 마치 경찰이 빨간 차가 파란 차에 비해 더 빠른 속도로 주행한다는 사실을 주목하는 것과 같다. 아마도 경찰은 빨간 차에 더 많이 주목하게 될 것이다. 하지만 그 경찰은 예를 들어 빨간 차가 파란 차에 비해 더 좋은 엔진을 가지고 있다는 사실은 깨닫지 못할 것이다. 뇌의 복잡성이 서서히 풀리기 시작하고 있음에도 불구하고, 뇌 기능을 예측하게 하는 유전자 변형의 행동 메커니즘은 어떤 차들이 다른 차들보다 더 빨리 달리는 이유를 이해한 이후에도 해결되지 않고 미스터리로 남아 있을 가능성이 크다.

26 다음 중 본문의 문맥상 바르게 쓰이지 않은 것은?

① Ⓐ   ② Ⓑ   ③ Ⓒ   ④ Ⓓ

| 정답 | ④

| 해설 | Ⓐ의 경우 'not necessarily'가 '반드시 ~은 아닌'의 의미가 되며, 예측을 할 수는 있지만 반드시 설명할 수 있는 것은 아니라는 의미가 된다. Ⓒ의 경우 that 이하의 내용이 가능성이 있는 것인지(likely) 아니면 가능성이 없는지(unlikely)를 따져 보아야 한다. 전체적 내용이 뇌의 복잡성으로 인해 뇌의 메커니즘을 이해하는 것은 미래에도 어려울 것이라는 내용이 되어야 하므로 likely가 적합하다. 정답은 Ⓓ로 remain 뒤에는 부사(mysteriously)가 아닌 형용사(mysterious)가 와야 한다.

27 다음 중 글의 주제로 적합한 것은?

① 인간 DNA의 복잡성
② 유전적 변형에 근거해 인간의 행동을 예측하는 방법
③ 행동과 유전적 지표 간의 관계를 설명하는 것의 어려움
④ 교통 신호 위반을 예측하기 위해 유전자 정보를 사용하게 될 가능성

| 정답 | ③

| 해설 | 본문은 어떤 사람의 유전적 지표(genetic marker)를 통해 그 사람의 행동을 예측(predict)하는 것은 가능하지만 그 이유를 설명(explain)하는 것은 뇌의 복잡성 때문에 어렵다는 내용이다. 따라서 행동과 유전적 지표 간의 관계를 설명하는 데 어려움이 있다는 ③이 정답이 된다.

28 다음 중 빈칸 ⓐ에 올 수 있는 가장 적합한 것은?

① 차들의 속도가 제한 속도를 넘어서 있다
② 파란 차량이 빨간 차량에 비해 느리다
③ 빨간 색상으로 보이는 차량은 사실 핑크빛 노란색이다
④ 빨간 차가 파란 차에 비해 더 좋은 엔진을 가지고 있다

| 정답 | ④

| 해설 | 경찰에 대한 이야기는 앞부분의 "We may be able to predict ... but not be able to explain why."에 대한 예시에 해당한다. 즉 빨간 차가 파란 차보다 더 빠른 것을 '예측'할 수는 있지만 '설명'할 수는 없어야 하므로, 빈칸은 왜 그런지에 대한 '설명'에 해당하는 내용이 와야 한다. 즉 빨간 차가 파란 차보다 더 빠른 이유는 예를 들어 엔진이 더 좋기 때문이라는 식의 내용이 적합하므로 정답은 ④가 된다.

| 어휘 | **complexity** ⓝ 복잡성
explanatory ⓐ 이유를 밝히는; 설명하기 위한
psychiatric ⓐ 정신 의학[질환]의
alter ⓥ 바꾸다, 변경하다
comprehension ⓝ 이해력
unravel ⓥ (엉클어진 것을) 풀다, 이해하기 시작하다

genetic marker 유전적 지표
linkage ⓝ 연결, 결합
variation ⓝ 변화, 변형
intervening ⓐ (두 사건 · 날짜 · 사물 등의) 사이에 오는
figure out (생각한 끝에) ~을 이해하다[알아내다]
genetic variant 유전자 변형

[29~30] 중앙대 2017

해석

경기 순환의 한 국면으로 확장 국면(expansion phase)이 있다. 이 국면은 이중적이며, 회복과 번영이라는 두 측면을 갖고 있다. (확장 국면을 일으키는 것은 번영 그 자체가 아니라 번영에 대한 기대감이다.) 회복기에는 기존 설비가 계속 확장되고, 새로운 생산 시설이 생겨난다. 더 많은 사업체들이 생겨나며 기존의 사업체들은 확장된다. 다양한 분야에서의 발전이 이루어진다. 경제 성장의 미래에 대한 낙관론이 점점 증폭된다. 많은 자본이 기계류와 중공업에 투자된다. 고용도 증대된다. 더 많은 원자재가 필요하게 된다. 경제의 한 부분이 발전하면서 다른 부분들에 영향을 미친다. 예를 들어, 자동차 산업에서의 대규모 성장은 철강, 유리, 고무 산업의 확장을 가져온다. 도로도 필요하게 된다. 따라서 시멘트와 기계류 산업이 활기를 띠게 된다. 노동력과 원자재에 대한 수요는 농민을 포함하여 노동자와 원자재 제공업자의 번영을 가져온다. 이는 다시 구매력의 증대와 구매되고 판매되는 제품의 총량 증대를 가져온다. 이런 식으로 번영이 전체 인구의 다양한 부분들로 확산된다. 이 번영의 시기는 가시적인 종말도 없이 계속 확장될 수도 있다. 하지만 이 시기가 정점에 달하고 나선형의 상승을 그만두는 시기가 찾아온다. 이때가 바로 확장 국면이 끝나는 지점이다.

29 윗글의 흐름상 가장 적합하지 **않은** 것을 고르시오.

① (A)   ② (B)   ③ (C)   ④ (D)

| 정답 | ①

| 해설 | (B)와 (C)는 바로 앞의 "As one part of the economy develops, other parts are affected."에 대한 예시에 해당한다. (D)의 경우 바로 뒤에 이어지는 However 이하의 내용과 연결되어 있다. 정답은 (A)로, 실제 경제가 발전되고 성장하는 경제의 확장 국면을 일으키는 것은 번영 그 자체가 아닌 '번영에 대한 기대감'이라는 내용에서, '기대감'에 대한 사항이 내용 앞뒤에 등장하지 않는다.

30 윗글을 통해 추론할 수 있는 것으로 가장 적합한 것을 고르시오.

① 소비자가 시장에 대한 신뢰를 잃을 때 경기 침체가 발생한다.

② 확장 국면에서는 경제의 많은 부분이 상호 이익을 얻는다.

③ 보석과 같은 명품은 산업 확장에 영향을 받지 않는다.

④ 번영기에는 새로운 제품의 창출이 매우 중요하다.

| 정답 | ②

| 해설 | 본문의 "As one part of the economy develops, other parts are affected."에서 경제가 확장 국면에 있을 때, 경제의 여러 부분이 서로 긍정적 영향을 받으며 함께 발전한다고 설명하고 있으므로 정답은 ②가 된다.

| 어휘 | **phase** ⓝ 단계, 국면   **expansion phase** 확장 국면

twofold ⓐ 두 부분으로 된, 이중적인   **prosperity** ⓝ 번영

trigger ⓥ 유발하다, 방아쇠를 당기다 ⓝ 방아쇠, 계기, 도화선

optimism ⓝ 낙관주의   **capital** ⓝ 자본

stimulate ⓥ 자극하다, 격려하다   **supplier** ⓝ 공급자, 공급 회사

raw material 원자재, 원료, 소재

purchasing power 구매력(개인이나 단체가 어떤 재화나 용역을 살 수 있는 재력)

diffuse ⓥ 퍼뜨리다, 발산하다, 유포하다   **segment** ⓝ 단편, 조각, 부분

apparent ⓐ 명백한, 외관상의   **peak** ⓝ 절정, 정점, 최고조

spiral ⓥ 상승하다

CHAPTER 02

01 빈칸 ㉮와 ㉯에 들어가기에 가장 적합한 것을 고르시오.

> 경험주의라고도 불리는 실증주의(empiricism, positivism)는 19세기에 걸쳐 다소 침체되었으나, 논리의 초석을 다지는 작업을 통해 20세기 초반에 다시 화려하게 부활하게 된다. 많은 철학자들은 수학적 논리가 수학적 진실, 종합적 진술, 형이상학적 난센스 사이의 차이를 공식화하는 데 부족했던 도구를 자신들에게 제공할 것으로 믿었다. 게다가 논리는 진술(statement)과 관찰(observation), 증명으로 연결될 수 있는 절차(procedure) 사이의 관계를 분명하게 해 줄 수 있는 형식주의를 제공해 줄 것이라는 믿음을 주었다. 따라서 20세기의 실증주의는 종종 '논리 실증주의(logical empiricism, logical positivism)'라고 명명됐다. 이 시기에 지식층 사이에서 실증주의 철학이 폭넓게 매력을 발산할 수 있었던 데에는 의심할 여지없이 미국 역사상 그 어느 시기에도 당시만큼 과학적 방법과 결과에 대해 숭상했던 적이 없었다는 사실과 관련이 있다.

① 하지만 – 따라서   ② 그러므로 – 그럼에도 불구하고
③ 게다가 – 따라서   ④ 게다가 – 이와는 반대로

| 정답 | ③

| 해설 | 이 문제는 문장과 문장을 연결해 주는 transition에 대해 물어보고 있기 때문에 글의 흐름을 살펴서, 빈칸에 순접이나 역접, 양보 중 어떤 것이 적절한지를 파악해야 한다. 20세기 초반에 다시 부활한 실증주의에서 학자들은 수학적 논리(logic)가 그동안 부족했던 부분을 채워 줄 것으로 기대했다고 나온다. 첫 번째 빈칸 뒤에는 수학적 논리가 형식주의를 가져다줄 것이라는 믿음을 주었다고 나오는데, 이는 앞서 나온 내용과 동일한 의미를 지닌다는 것을 알 수 있다. 따라서 이곳에는 흐름상 ②, ③, ④가 올 수 있으며, 역접의 ①은 부적절하다. 두 번째 빈칸 뒤에는 20세기 실증주의가 '논리 실증주의'라고 불렸다고 나온다. 그 이유는 바로 앞서 나온 내용을 토대로 하기 때문에 이곳에는 '따라서'라는 의미의 ①, ③이 가능하다. 종합해 보면 ③만이 정답임을 알 수 있다.

| 어휘 | **empiricism** ⓝ 경험주의, 실증주의   **positivism** ⓝ 실증주의, 실증 철학
　　　be in retreat 후퇴하다   **apparatus** ⓝ 기구, 장치
　　　synthetic ⓐ 종합적인; 합성한, 인조의
　　　synthetic statement 종합 진술(사실일 수도 있고 사실이 아닐 수도 있는 문장을 의미함)
　　　analytic statement 분석 진술(설명하고자 하는 주어의 내용 속에 서술 부분이 이미 포함되어 있는 문장으로, 새로운 사실을 알려 준다기보다는 문장을 구성하는 요소들의 의미상의 관계를 나타냄)
　　　metaphysical ⓐ 형이상학의   **formalism** ⓝ 형식주의
　　　explicit ⓐ 분명한, 명쾌한, 명백한   **verification** ⓝ 확인, 증명, 입증
　　　logical positivism 논리 실증주의

02 다음 글을 두 단락으로 나누고자 할 때 가장 적절한 곳은?

영국에는 세금과 국민 보험(National Insurance)으로 비용이 지불되는 국민 건강 보험(NHS : National Health Service)이 있으며, 일반적으로 사람들은 의료비를 지불하지 않아도 된다. 모든 사람들은 일반 의학을 훈련받은 일반 개업의(GP)에게 본인이 거주하는 지역에서 치료를 받을 수 있다. 만약 병에 걸리면 그들은 일반 개업의의 진찰을 받기 위해 예약을 하거나, 집으로 내진을 요청할 수 있다. 어린이나 실업자, 60세 이상 노인이 아니라면 사람들은 의사의 처방전에 따른 약값의 일부를 지불해야 한다. 만약 필요하다면 일반 개업의는 환자들이 큰 병원에서 전문의의 진찰을 받을 수 있도록 이들을 대신해 예약을 잡아 준다. 중증의 환자라면 누구라도 구급차를 불러 병원에서 무료 응급 치료를 받을 수 있다. 비록 국민 건강 보험의 치료비가 무료지만 사람들은 종종 치료를 받기 위해 오래 기다려야 한다. 국민 건강 보험의 대기자 명단의 문제점을 두고 많은 정치인과 일반인들이 이 문제를 논의하고 있다. 일부 사람들은 사적으로 치료를 받거나 좀 더 빠른 치료를 받기 위해 '사설 기관의 치료'를 선택한다. 보통 이런 사람들은 개인 의료 보험을 든 사람들이다. 인구의 평균 연령이 점점 높아짐에 따라, 국민 건강 보험의 운영비는 점점 늘어나고 있으며, 사람들은 미래에는 의료비가 더 이상 무료로 지원되지 않을 수 있다는 점을 우려하고 있다.

① ㉮　　　　② ㉯　　　　③ ㉰　　　　④ ㉱

| 정답 | ③

| 해설 | 위 내용은 영국의 국민 의료 보험인 NHS에 대해 설명하고 있다. 비용도 저렴하며, 응급 상황일 때는 무료로 치료받을 수 있는 등의 여러 장점에 대해 나열하고 있다. 하지만 후반부의 내용은 NHS에 대한 문제점에 대해 설명하고 있다. 대기자의 수가 많아 장시간 기다려야 하거나, 노년층의 증가로 발생하는 막대한 비용이 발생한다는 것이 그런 문제점에 해당한다. 이런 내용상의 전환이 이루어지는 부분이 바로 ㉰ 부분이 된다.

| 어휘 | **National Health Service(NHS)** 국민 건강 보험　　　**National Insurance** 국민 보험
General Practitioner 일반 개업의　　　**prescribe** ⓥ 처방하다
go private 사설 의료 기관의 치료를 받다; 민영화하다; 개인적으로 이야기하다
private health insurance 개인 의료 보험

01	③	02	④	03	①	04	②	05	③	06	④	07	③	08	④	09	①	10	③
11	①	12	③	13	④	14	③	15	⑤	16	③	17	①	18	③	19	①	20	③

[01~02] 이화여대 2016

해석

배고픔과 식사 및 체중에 대한 다양한 연구 결과를 통합한 한 이론의 주장에 따르면 체중은 체중 조절점, 즉 유전적으로 설계된 체중을 대략적으로 유지하도록 하는 항상성 기제에 의해 통제된다. 체중 조절점 이론가들의 주장에 따르면 모든 사람에게는 유전적으로 프로그램된 기초 대사율이 존재하며, 사람의 지방 세포의 수 또한 정해져 있다. 기초 대사율이란 신체가 에너지를 얻기 위해 칼로리를 소비하는 비율을 의미하며, 지방 세포는 에너지 목적으로 지방을 저장하는 세포를 일컫는다. 지방 세포는 크기는 변할 수 있지만(지방 세포가 함유하고 있는 지방의 양이 변화한다는 의미), 수는 변하지 않는다. 체중이 감소하더라도 지방 세포는 (사라지는 것이 아니라) 신체 이곳저곳에서 암약하면서 다시 (지방을 흡수하여) 부풀어 오르게 될 기회를 기다릴 뿐이다. 체중 조절점 이론에 따르면 뇌에는 체중을 계속 파악하는 부위가 전혀 존재하지 않는다. 그보다는 신진대사와 지방 세포 및 호르몬 간의 상호 작용이 유전적으로 설계된 체중을 유지하도록 하는 역할을 한다. 살찐 사람이 다이어트를 할 경우, 신체는 에너지를 (그리고 비축된 지방을) 보존하기 위해 신체의 기능을 늦춘다. 마른 사람이 과식을 할 경우, 신체는 에너지를 소비하기 위해 기능을 높인다.

01 빈칸 [A]에 가장 알맞은 것은 무엇인가?

① 게다가　　　　　　　　　　　　② 또한
③ 그보다는　　　　　　　　　　　④ 따라서
⑤ 구체적으로는

| 정답 | ③

| 해설 | 빈칸 앞에서는 뇌에는 체중을 조절하는 부위가 존재하지 않음을 말하고 있고, 빈칸 뒤에서는 우리 몸에서 체중을 조절하는 역할을 하는 것은 뇌가 아니라 신진대사와 지방 세포 및 호르몬 간의 상호 작용임을 말하고 있다. 즉 빈칸을 기점으로 앞에 나온 내용과 뒤에 나온 내용이 다름을 알 수 있다. 따라서 빈칸에는 앞에 말한 내용과 다르거나 반대되는 말을 도입할 때 사용하는 접속사인 rather가 적합하다. 그래서 답은 ③이다.

02 위 본문에서 가장 잘 유추할 수 있는 것은 무엇인가?

① 유전적으로 마른 사람은 쉽게 살이 찔 수 있다.
② 지방 세포가 크기를 키우지 못하게 막는 방법은 수수께끼이다.
③ 인간은 유전적으로 비만이 되도록 설계되었다.
④ 인간은 생각한 것보다는 체중을 제어할 수 있는 수단이 그리 마땅치 않다.
⑤ 유전적으로 과체중이 되기 쉬운 사람이 체중을 줄이는 것은 불가능하다.

| 정답 | ④

| 해설 | "체중이 감소하더라도 지방 세포는 (사라지는 것이 아니라) 신체 이곳저곳에서 암약하면서 다시 (지방을 흡수하여) 부풀어 오르게 될 기회를 기다릴 뿐이다. 체중 조절점 이론에 따르면 뇌에는 체중을 계속 파악하는 부위가 전혀 존재하지 않는다. 그보다

는 신진대사와 지방 세포 및 호르몬 간의 상호 작용이 유전적으로 설계된 체중을 유지하도록 하는 역할을 한다(After weight loss, they just lurk around the body, waiting for the chance to puff up again. According to set-point theory, there is no single area in the brain that keeps track of weight. Rather, an interaction of metabolism, fat cells, and hormones keeps people at the weight their bodies are designed to be)." 여기서 지방 세포가 사라지지 않고 다시 부풀어 오를 기회를 기다린다는 소리는 살을 빼도 다시 찌기 쉽다는 의미이고, 뇌에서 체중을 조절하는 부위가 존재하지 않고 대신 상호 작용이 체중을 유지하는 역할을 한다는 것 또한 뺀 살을 유지하는 일이 쉽지 않음을 의미한다. 즉 인간이 체중을 제어하고 뺀 살을 유지하는 것은 근본적으로 쉽지 않음을 의미한다. 따라서 답은 ④이다.

| 어휘 |

integrate ⓥ 통합시키다

findings ⓝ (조사·연구 등의) 결과[결론]

set point 정해진 값, 설정값; 체중 조절점

mechanism ⓝ 메커니즘, 구조[기제]

basal ⓐ 기제[기초/토대]가 되는

basal metabolism rate 기초 대사율

lurk ⓥ 숨어 있다, 암약하다

keep track of ~을 계속 파악하다[기록하다]

reserve ⓝ 비축[예비](물)

predisposed ⓐ (특정한 질병에) 취약한[잘 걸리는/걸리기 쉬운]

diverse ⓐ 다양한

govern ⓥ 지배[좌우/통제]하다

homeostatic ⓐ 항상성의

roughly ⓐ 대략, 거의

metabolism ⓝ 신진대사, 물질대사

fixed ⓐ 고정된, 정해진

puff up 부어오르다[불룩해지다]

rather 더 정확히 말하면, 그보다는

specifically ⓐ 구체적으로는

[03~05] 단국대 2016

해석

언어는 민족을 나누는 경계 표지로서 기능하는 일이 빈번하다. 세계의 여러 지역에서는 한 개인의 모국어가 민족 집단의 정체성을 나타내는 가장 두드러진 지표이다. 미국 남서부 지방에서 호피(Hopi)족 및 나바호(Navajo) 족 원주민 구성원들은 언어만 가지고도 쉽게 구별이 가능하다. 하지만 두 집단이 공통된 언어를 공유한다는 사실이 두 집단이 동일한 정체성을 공유하고 있다는 의미는 아니며, 이는 두 집단이 다른 언어를 사용한다 해서 서로 뚜렷이 구분되는 정체성을 지니고 있다는 의미는 아닌 것과 마찬가지이다. 예를 들어 과거 유고슬라비아 연방 내의 세르비아인과 크로아티아인은 세르보크로아티아어를 말했다. 하지만 이들은 서로 간에 뚜렷한 차이가 존재했고 역사적으로도 적대적인 민족 집단이었다. 이와는 반대로 어떤 아일랜드인은 모국어로 게일어나 영어를 말할 수 있다. 독일 정부는 동유럽에서 온 독일 민족에 속하는 모든 난민들에게 자동적으로 시민권을 부여한다. 이러한 난민들이 독일 사회에 동화되는 데 어려움을 겪게 되는 요인은 많은 난민들이 폴란드어나 러시아어만을 할 줄 알기 때문이다. 따라서 독일 민족이 되기 위해서 꼭 독일어를 할 필요는 없는 것이다.

---

03 다음 중 본문에 따르면 사실인 것은 무엇인가?

① 호피족과 나바호족 구성원들은 같은 언어를 공유하지 않는다.

② 독일 시민권은 독일어를 할 줄 아는 사람들에게 자동적으로 주어진다.

③ 세르비아인과 크로아티아인은 같은 언어를 하기 때문에 공통된 정체성을 공유한다.

④ 모든 나라에서 모국어는 민족 집단의 정체성을 나타내는 가장 근본적인 단 하나의 지표이다.

| 정답 | ①

| 해설 | "호피(Hopi)족 및 나바호(Navajo)족 원주민 구성원들은 언어만 가지고도 쉽게 구별이 가능하다(Hopi and Navajo

members are readily distinguished by their language alone)." 이 말은 즉 호피 족과 나바호 족의 언어는 다르며 그렇기 때문에 언어를 통해 둘을 구분하는 것이 가능하다는 의미이다. 따라서 답은 ①이다.

독일 시민권은 독일어를 할 줄 아는 사람에게 주는 것이 아니라 "동유럽에서 온 독일 민족에 속하는 모든 난민들(all ethnic German refugees from Eastern Europe)"에게 자동적으로 주어지기 때문에 ②는 답이 될 수 없다. 세르비아인과 크로아티아인은 같은 언어를 말했지만 "하지만 이들은 서로 간에 뚜렷한 차이가 존재했고 역사적으로도 적대적인 민족 집단이었다(They are, however, distinct and historically antagonistic ethnic groups)." 따라서 ③은 답이 될 수 없다. "세계의 여러 지역에서는 한 개인의 모국어가 민족 집단의 정체성을 나타내는 가장 두드러진 지표이다(The native language of an individual is the primary indicator of ethnic group identity in many areas of the world)"는 것은 사실이지만, "하지만 두 집단이 공통된 언어를 공유한다는 사실이 두 집단이 동일한 정체성을 공유하고 있다는 의미는 아니며, 이는 두 집단이 다른 언어를 사용한다 해서 서로 뚜렷이 구분되는 정체성을 지니고 있다는 의미는 아닌 것과 마찬가지이다(However, just because two populations share a common language, it does not mean they share a common identity, any more than the fact that two populations speak different languages means that they have two distinct identities)"에서 알 수 있듯이 모국어가 가장 근본적인 유일한 지표는 아니며 동일한 언어를 말하는 두 집단이 동일한 정체성을 보유한다고는 할 수 없다. 따라서 ④는 답이 될 수 없다.

---

04 빈칸 Ⓐ에 가장 알맞은 것은 무엇인가?

① 따라서   ② 이와는 반대로
③ 결과적으로   ④ 우선

| 정답 | ②

| 해설 | 빈칸 앞에서는 다른 민족끼리 같은 언어를 사용하는 경우를 말하고 있고 빈칸 뒤에서는 한 국가 내에서 다른 언어를 사용하는 경우를 말하고 있다. 즉 빈칸을 기준으로 앞과 뒤가 서로 상반된 내용을 담고 있다. 따라서 답은 ②이다.

---

05 빈칸 Ⓑ에 가장 알맞은 것은 무엇인가?

① 칭찬하다   ② 은둔하다
③ 동화하다   ④ 비방하다

| 정답 | ③

| 해설 | 동유럽에서 온 독일 민족 소속 난민들에게 독일 정부는 독일 시민권을 부여하고 있지만, 이들 난민들은 독일어가 아니라 폴란드어나 러시아어만을 할 줄 안다. 여기서 이들이 독일 사회에 "동화하는 데" 어려움을 겪을 것으로 유추가 가능하다. 따라서 답은 ③이다.

| 어휘 | **ethnic** ⓐ 민족의, 종족의   **boundary marker** 경계 표지
indicator ⓝ 지표   **readily** ⓐⓓ 순조롭게, 손쉽게
distinct ⓐ 뚜렷이 다른[구별되는], 별개의   **antagonistic** ⓐ 적대적인
conversely ⓐⓓ 정반대로, 역으로   **grant** ⓥ 부여하다, 허용하다
citizenship ⓝ 시민권   **assimilate** ⓥ (국가·사회의 일원으로) 동화되다[동화시키다]
laud ⓥ 칭찬하다   **seclude** ⓥ 은둔하다, 고립시키다
calumniate ⓥ 비방하다, 중상하다

해석

시가나 파이프 담배가 궐련 담배보다 타르와 니코틴 농도가 더 높기는 하지만, 궐련 담배는 하루에 몇 개비씩만 피워도 시가나 파이프 담배를 많이 피우는 것보다 건강에 더 해롭다. 이유는, 궐련 담배를 피울 때는 연기를 마실 수밖에 없지만, 시가나 파이프는 의도적으로 담배 연기를 마시기가 더 어렵기 때문이다. 궐련 담배를 피우는 흡연자들은 담배 연기를 적극적으로, 깊게, 계속 들이마신다. 그러나 시가나 파이프 담배의 연기는 매우 독하기 때문에, 건강한 폐 속으로 직접 들이마시기가 더 어렵다. 하지만 궐련 담배를 파이프나 시가로 바꾸기만 해서는, 위험이 줄어드는 것이 아니라 오히려 커질 것이다. 당신은 담배 연기를 들이마시는 데 익숙하기 때문이다. 그 습관은 지속될 것이고, 결국 예전보다 훨씬 더 해로운 담배 연기를 들이마시게 될 것이다.

06 다음 중 빈칸 ⓐ, ⓑ, ⓒ에 가장 적절한 것은?

① 그러나 – 그럼에도 불구하고 – 그러나
② 그러나 – 그러나 – 그럼에도 불구하고
③ (비록) ∼이긴 하지만 – 그러나 – 그러나
④ (비록) ∼이긴 하지만 – 그러나 – 그러나

| 정답 | ④

| 해설 | 빈칸 ⓐ가 주절과 대조적인 내용의 종속절을 이끌기 위해서는 종속 접속사 Although가 필요하다. 빈칸 ⓑ가 위치한 문장은 "궐련 담배는 연기 흡입이 쉽다."는 앞 문장과 대조적으로 "파이프나 시가는 연기 흡입이 어렵다."는 문장을 이끌기 위해 역접 접속사가 필요하다. 빈칸 ⓒ가 위치한 문장은 "파이프나 시가는 연기 흡입이 어렵다."는 앞 단락과 대조적으로 "파이프나 시가로 담배를 바꿔도 흡입은 계속되므로 건강에 더 해롭다."는 경고가 이어지므로 역접 부사가 필요하다.

07 밑줄 친 the habit의 의미는?

① 시가 흡연
② 궐련 담배 흡연
③ 담배 연기를 적극적으로 들이마시는 것
④ 시가와 궐련 담배를 모두 흡연하는 것

| 정답 | ③

| 해설 | 궐련 담배가 더 해로운 이유는 담배 연기를 들이마시는 데 익숙해지기 때문이다. 따라서 궐련 담배 흡연자들은 시가나 파이프 담배로 바꿔도 담배 연기를 계속 들이마실 것이다. 문맥상 the habit은 ③ "담배 연기를 들이마시는 것"을 의미한다. 보기 ①을 선택하지 않도록 주의한다. "Cigarette smokers tend to inhale actively, deeply and constantly.", "This is because you have probably become accustomed to inhaling." 참조.

08 지문에 따르면, 다음 중 가장 해로운 것은 무엇인가?

① 시가 흡연   ② 궐련 담배 흡연
③ 시가 연기를 자발적으로 들이마시는 것   ④ 시가에서 궐련 담배로 바꾸는 것

| 정답 | ④

마지막 단락의 첫 문장에 착안한 문제이다. 모든 보기가 해롭다. 그러나 가장 해로운 것은 궐련 담배를 피우던 습관대로 니코틴과 타르 농도가 높은 시가나 파이프 담배의 연기를 들이마시는 것이다. 보기 ③을 선택하지 않도록 주의한다. "However simply switching to a pipe or cigars from cigarettes is likely to increase your risk instead of lessening it." 참조.

| 어휘 |

concentration ⓝ 농도	pose risk 위험을 제기하다
a number of 많은	inhale ⓥ 들이마시다
voluntarily ⓪ 자발적으로	tend to ~하는 경향이 있다
actively ⓪ 적극적으로, 능동적으로	constantly ⓪ 계속해서
harsh ⓐ 독한, 가혹한	breathe ⓥ 호흡하다
lung ⓝ 폐	switch to ~로의 전환
be likely to ~하기 쉽다	lessen ⓥ 감소시키다, 완화시키다
be accustomed to ~에 익숙하다	retain ⓥ 보유하다, 유지하다

[09~10]

해석

프로이드는 의사가 되기 위해 공부하던 중, 사람들이 생각하고 꿈꾸는 방식에 관심을 갖게 되었다. 그는 사람들에게 과거를 말하도록 함으로써 도우려 했다. 이 과정에서, 프로이드는 과거에서 비롯되는 무의식적인 사고가 행동에 영향을 미친다는 것을 발견했다. 이 무의식적 사고는 꿈에도 나타난다. 꿈속의 이미지들은 그 사람의 과거에 있었던 실제 이미지이거나, 삶 속에 등장하는 인물이나 사물의 상징일 수도 있었다.

그러나 1996년 캘리포니아에서 있었던 꿈 연구의 현대적인 꿈 해석의 결과에 따르면, 꿈은 뇌에서 아무런 기능도 하지 않는다. 연구진들은 사람들에게 매일 밤 기억나는 꿈과 낮에 있었던 일상적 일들을 기록하게 했다. 그 기록을 검토한 연구진들은 피실험자들의 꿈에는 그들과 연관된 스토리가 있고 이 스토리들은 그들의 낮 또는 삶에서 중요한 부분을 포함하고 있다고 밝혔다. 시간이 갈수록 이 꿈들은 개인의 성격이나 삶의 관심사들을 상당 부분 반영하기도 했지만 아직은 실제적인 심리적 기능이 확실히 발견되지 않았다.

09 다음 중 빈칸에 가장 적절한 것은?

① 그러나   ② 예를 들어
③ 결과적으로   ④ 더욱이

| 정답 | ①

| 해설 | 전후 단락의 관계를 확인한다. 꿈이 무의식적 사고와 관련 있다는 앞 단락과, 꿈이 뇌 기능(= 사고 = 심리적 기능)과 무관하다는 뒤 단락은 대조를 이루므로 역접을 나타내는 보기 ①이 논리적이다.

10 다음 중 제목으로 가장 적절한 것은?

① 대화 치료법   ② 프로이드의 대실수
③ 꿈의 의미   ④ 수면 중의 무의식

| 정답 | ③

| 해설 | 앞 단락은 프로이드가 해석한 꿈의 의미, 뒤 단락은 오늘날 밝혀진 꿈의 의미를 상술한다. 프로이드는 꿈의 의미를 무의식과 의식을 매개하는 중요한 상징으로 생각했지만 오늘날 꿈은 성격과 관심사를 반영하는 정도의 의미를 지닌다. 따라서 지문 전체의 내용을 포괄하는 보기는 ③이다. 꿈에 대한 프로이드의 관점을 반박하는 뒤 단락의 연구 결과를 비약해 보기 ②를 선택하지 않도록 주의한다.

| 어휘 | **unconscious** ⓐ 무의식적인
findings ⓝ 발견물, 연구 결과
function ⓝ 기능 ⓥ 기능하다
relate to ~와 상관있다
concern ⓝ 관심, 걱정
for sure 확실하게

show up 나타나다
point to ~을 시사하다, 가리키다
report ⓥ 보고하다, 밝히다
personality ⓝ 성격, 개성
psychological ⓐ 심리적인

[11~13]

해석

19살의 Bernie는 대학은커녕 고등학교도 졸업할 수 있을지 의심스러웠던 때가 있었다. 2학년 때 임신하자 그녀는 자퇴할까 잠시 고민했다. 그러나 Academy of Urban Planning으로 전학한 후, 그녀는 주 졸업 자격시험 5개를 모두 통과했는데 주 최고 성적으로 졸업하기 위해 한 과목은 재응시할 것이다. 그녀의 개인전의 전환점은 그녀가 재학 중인 학교의 전환점을 반영한다. 이 학교는 5년 전 Bushwick High School로 알려진 학교의 건물에 있다. Bushwick은 뉴욕의 4년 졸업률 최하위권 학교 중 하나로, 졸업률이 23퍼센트에 불과할 정도로 저조했고 교내는 폭력으로 가득했다. 그러던 5년 전, 뉴욕 시장 Michael Bloomberg가 뉴욕 학군들을 대상으로 전격적인 교육 개혁을 실시해 Bushwick은 4개의 더 작은 학교들로 분교되었다.

11 다음 중 빈칸에 가장 적절한 것은?

① ~은 말할 것도 없이
② ~은 말할 것도 없이 더
③ 훨씬 더
④ 어느 정도
⑤ 심지어 덜

| 정답 | ①

| 해설 | Bernie doubted that ~의 표현으로 연결되는 문장이므로, 부정적인 표현과 연결시켜야 한다. 그러므로 '말할 것도 없이'에 해당하는 much more와 much less 가운데 부정 표현과 어울리는 much less가 정답이다.

12 지문은 두 단락으로 나누기에 적절한 곳은 어디인가?

① (A)
② (B)
③ (C)
④ (D)
⑤ (E)

| 정답 | ③

| 해설 | (C)를 경계로 도입부와 주제부로 나누는 것이 글의 구조상 논리적이다. Bernie의 인생 전환이 도입이고, Bushwick 학교의 변모가 주제이다.

13 지문에 따르면, Bernie는 _____.

① 대학 입학 시험을 통과했다

② 고등학교 졸업을 포기했다

③ 다른 학교로 전학할 것을 고려 중이다

④ 더 좋은 점수를 위해 한 과목을 재응시할 것이다

⑤ Bushwick 고등학교에서 많은 것을 배웠다

| 정답 | ④

| 해설 | Bernie는 고등학교 졸업 시험을 통과했지만, 더 우수한 성적으로 위한 한 과목을 재응시할 것이다. "She is retaking one exam in the hopes of getting a diploma with the state's highest distinction." 참조. ⑤를 선택하지 않도록 주의한다. Bernie가 많은 것을 배우고 인생의 전환점을 맞을 수 있었던 곳은 Bushwick 고등학교가 아니라 Academy of Urban Planning이다.

| 어휘 |

sophomore ⓝ 2학년

briefly ⓐⓓ 잠시

transfer ⓥ 옮기다

graduation ⓝ 졸업

with distinction 우수한 성적으로

mirror ⓥ 비추다, 반영하다

house ⓥ 수용(보관)하다

dismal ⓐ 형편없는, 음울한

plague ⓥ 만연하다 ⓝ 전염병

pregnant ⓐ 임신한

drop out 자퇴하다, 중퇴하다

required ⓐ 의무적인

diploma ⓝ 졸업장, 수료증

turnaround ⓝ 전환

attend ⓥ 참석하다, 재학하다

graduation rate 졸업률

violence ⓝ 폭력

flurry ⓝ (한바탕 벌어지는) 소동

[14~16] 성균관대 2012

해석

우리나라가 TV와 함께 지내온 지 이제 50년이 넘었다. 우리는 예전에 예측된 바와 같이 다른 문화나 지구상의 생명의 기원 등에 관해 환상적으로 잘 알게 되지는 않는다. (A) 사람들은 TV 다큐멘터리에서 작품이 좋았다는 것을 제외하고 그 이상의 것은 많이 기억하지는 못한다. 애초에 다큐멘터리에서 다루는 주제에 관해 어느 정도 알던 사람들만이 다큐멘터리가 제공한 정보를 계속 간직할 뿐이다. (B) 어쨌든 다큐멘터리는 대부분의 사람들이 보고 싶어 하는 것은 아니다. TV는 TV 자신이 비추는 현재를 찬양할 때에만 가장 유명하다. TV가 이상적으로 생각하는 주제는 기억될 필요가 없고 즉시 교체되는 주제이며, 이런 주제에서 가장 중요한 것은 지금 일어나는 일과 그 다음에 바로 일어날 일이다. (C) 스포츠, 뉴스, 패널 게임, 경찰 프로, 장기 방영 중인 드라마, 시트콤 등은 방송 중인 순간에만 우리의 시선을 잡는다. (D) 밤 시간 시청률은 아무리 높았거나 낮았다고 한들 놀랄 만큼 잊어버려도 될 수준이다. TV는 잠시 눈 붙이는 수단이기도 하고 오락 수단이기도 하다. 우리의 도덕은 온전히 보존된다. (E) TV는 사람들이 시청하는 엄청난 양의 TV 프로그램 때문에 더욱 무력화된다. 물론 일부 TV 프로그램은 다른 프로그램에 비해 엄청나게 낫다. (F) TV에서 일하는 재능 있는 사람들도 있다. 하지만 좀 더 먼 관점에서 바라보면, 말하자면 3개월 동안 하루에 4시간 정도 TV를 시청해 보면, TV 프로그램 하나하나의 질은 출퇴근 시간대의 차 하나하나의 질과 마찬가지 수준이다.

14 위 본문이 세 부분으로 나뉘게 된다면 경계선으로 삼기 가장 좋은 부분은 어디인가?

① (A) and (C)　　　　　　　　　　② (B) and (C)

③ (B) and (E)　　　　　　　　　　④ (C) and (E)

⑤ (D) and (F)

| 정답 | ③

| 해설 | 처음부터 (B) 이전까지는 우리가 TV와 함께한 지 50년이 넘었고 다큐멘터리 같은 교양 프로도 존재하곤 있지만 실제 TV를 통해 우리가 많은 지식을 얻지는 못했다는 내용을 담고 있다. (B)에서부터 (E) 이전까지는 TV에서 주로 다루는 주제가 순간적이고 기억될 필요 없는 것들이라는 내용을 담고 있다. 마지막으로 (E)부터 마지막까지는 TV 프로그램의 양은 엄청나지만 품질은 그에 미치지 못하고, 오히려 양에 질식되고 있는 실정이라는 내용을 담고 있다. 이렇게 본문의 내용을 세 단위로 구분할 수 있으므로 답은 ③이다.

15 밑줄 친 표현은 여러분이 TV를 오래 보면 볼수록 ＿＿＿＿＿＿＿＿는 뜻을 내포한다.

① 더 많은 지식을 갖게 된다　　　　　② 도덕심이 더욱 약해진다

③ 더욱 들뜨게 된다　　　　　　　　④ TV의 콘텐츠는 더욱 중요해진다

⑤ TV의 콘텐츠는 덜 중요해진다

| 정답 | ⑤

| 해설 | 밑줄 쳐진 부분을 해석하면 "TV는 사람들이 시청하는 엄청난 양의 TV 프로그램 때문에 더욱 무력화된다"이다. 이 말은, 즉 TV 프로그램의 양이 엄청나게 많기 때문에 품질 좋은 프로그램이 더러 있더라도 양에 파묻히게 되고, 결국 프로그램의 품질은 그렇게 중요한 것이 아니게 된다는 의미이다. 따라서 답은 ⑤이다.

16 본문에 따르면 저자는 ＿＿＿＿＿＿＿＿＿＿＿＿고 주장한다.

① TV 산업은 프로그램을 만들 수 있는 더 똑똑한 사람들을 필요로 한다

② 많은 사람들은 TV 다큐멘터리를 외면하며 그 이유는 다큐멘터리에 도덕적 메시지가 담겨 있지 않기 때문이다

③ TV가 우리의 정신이나 사회를 바꾸지는 못하는 것으로 드러났다

④ TV는 앞으로 인간 문명에 더 큰 영향을 줄 것이다

⑤ TV는 도덕의 교육자로 더욱 성공할 것이다

| 정답 | ③

| 해설 | TV에서 다큐멘터리 같은 교양 프로그램을 방영하지만 우리의 지식이 엄청나게 늘어난 것도 아니었고, TV는 지금 우리의 시선을 잡을 수 있는 것에만 집중하고, 어쩌다 좋은 프로그램이 있긴 하지만 대부분을 차지하는 질 낮은 프로그램에 파묻히는 실정이다. 즉 TV는 오락 수단일 뿐이고 어떤 사회적이고 정신적 변화를 야기하는 매개체가 되지는 못했다. 보기 중에서 이를 잘 요약한 것은 ③이다.

| 어휘 | **well-informed** ⓐ 박식한, 잘 아는　　　　　**retain** ⓥ 유지하다

celebrate ⓥ 축하하다, 찬양하다

panel game 패널 게임(방송에서 여러 사람이 팀을 이뤄 하는 퀴즈 게임)

cop show TV의 경찰 쇼　　　　　　　　　**forgettable** ⓐ 특별한 구석 없는, 쉽게 잊혀질

intact ⓐ 온전한

infinitely ⓐ 무한히, 한없이

neutralize ⓥ 무효화시키다, 무력화시키다

gifted ⓐ 재능 있는

[17~18] 에리카 2014

해석

대부분의 역사가들은 게티즈버그 전투를 미국 남북 전쟁의 전환점으로 여긴다. 게티즈버그 전투 이전에는 로버트 E. 리 장군이 이끄는 남부 연맹군은 북부 연방군을 일련의 주요 전투들에서 때로는 상당한 격차를 내면서 물리쳤다. 하지만 이번 교전에서 남부 연맹군은 패배하고 쫓겨났다. 게다가 물질적 손실 이외에도 남부 연맹이 기세를 잃게 된 것이 더 중요한 점이었다. 북부 연방군이 주도권을 쥐게 되면서 (게티즈버그 전투 이후) 2년도 안 되어 마침내 남부 연맹군을 무찌르게 된다. 남부 연맹 지도자들은 북부 연합의 영토에 침공하여 북부의 전쟁 지속 의지를 분쇄하고 유럽 국가들이 남부 연맹을 독립 국가로 인정하도록 설득하려 했다. 그러기는커녕, 북부 연방의 전투 의지는 강화되었고 남부 연맹은 외국의 지원을 받을 수 있는 마지막 기회를 허비하고 말았다.

17 빈칸에 들어갈 가장 알맞은 것을 고르시오.

① 하지만 ‒ 그러기는커녕

② 하지만 ‒ 게다가

③ 게다가 ‒ 그러기는커녕

④ 게다가 ‒ 게다가

| 정답 | ①

| 해설 | 빈칸 (A)의 경우를 보면, 빈칸 앞에서는 내용은 남부 연맹군이 북구 연방군을 계속 무찔렀다는 내용이었지만 빈칸 뒤에서는 남부가 북부에 의해 패배당하여 쫓겨났음을 말하고 있다. 따라서 빈칸에는 역접을 나타내는 접속사 however가 적합하며, 그러므로 답은 ① 아니면 ②가 된다.

빈칸 (B)의 경우를 보면, 빈칸 바로 앞 문장이 게티즈버그 전투 이전에 남부 지도자들이 생각했던 것에 관해 말하고 있으며, 빈칸 바로 뒤 문장은 게티즈버그 전투로 인해 남부 지도자들이 생각했던 결과가 나오지 않았음을 말하고 있다. 즉 빈칸 다음에는 원래 의도와 상반되는 결과가 나왔던 것이다. 따라서 (B)에는 앞서 언급된 것과 상반되는 내용이 등장할 것임을 알려 주는 instead가 적합하다.

따라서 이 두 가지 요소를 조합해 보면 답은 결국 ①이다.

18 윗글의 내용과 맞는 것을 고르시오.

① 남부 연맹군은 게티즈버그 전투 이전에 북부 연방군을 완전히 무찔렀다.

② 유럽 국가들은 마침내 남부 연맹을 독립국으로 인정하게끔 설득되었다.

③ 게티즈버그 전투의 승리 덕분에 북부 연방군이 주도권을 잡기 시작했다.

④ 남부 연맹군이 북부 연방군의 영토에 침공한 것은 북부 연방군의 전투 지속 의지를 분쇄했다.

| 정답 | ③

| 해설 | 게티즈버그 전투로 인해 "북부 연방의 전투 의지는 강화되었고 남부 연맹은 외국의 지원을 받을 수 있는 마지막 기회를 허비하고 말았다(the Union's willingness to fight was strengthened and the Confederacy squandered its last chance for foreign support)." 즉 게티즈버그 전투 이후 주도권을 잡은 것은 남부가 아니라 북부였던 것이다. 따라서 답은 ③이다.

turning point 전환점   engagement ⓝ 교전
            Confederate ⓐ 남부 연맹의   Union ⓐ 북부 연합의
            Confederacy ⓝ 남부 연맹   squander ⓥ 허비하다, 낭비하다
            take the lead 앞장서다, 주도권을 잡다

[19~20] 에리카 2018

해석

매년 약 12만 개의 장기가 한 사람으로부터 다른 사람으로 이식되며, 이식되는 장기의 대부분은 간이다. 때로는 살아 있는 지원자가 장기 기증자인 경우도 있다. 하지만 일반적으로는 장기 기증자는 사고나 뇌졸중 또는 심장병의 희생자이거나 아니면 이러한 일이 없었더라면 건강했었을 사람의 생명을 끝내 버린 갑작스러운 사건의 희생자이다. 하지만 적합한 기증자가 부족한 관계로, 특히 자동차의 안전이 향상되고 응급 처치의 효과가 더욱 증대되면서, 위와 같은 장기의 공급은 제한을 받고 있다. 따라서 많은 이들은 이식을 기다리다 사망하고 만다. 연구자들은 이로 인해 아무것도 없는 상태에서 장기를 만들 수 있는 방법이 있을지를 두고 연구를 하게 되었다. 한 가지 유망한 접근법은 장기를 인쇄하는 것이다. 요즘은 3차원 인쇄를 통해 많은 것들을 만들 수 있으며, 따라서 신체 장기도 인쇄하지 못할 이유는 없는 것으로 보인다. 아직은 이러한 "바이오프린팅"은 대체로 실험적 단계에 머물러 있다. 하지만 바이오프린팅을 통해 인쇄된 조직은 이미 약물 검사 용도로 판매되고 있으며, 앞으로 수년 내에 이식 가능한 최초의 조직을 사용할 준비가 완료될 것으로 예측된다.

19 빈칸에 들어갈 가장 알맞은 것을 고르시오.

① 아직은   ③ 그럼에도 불구하고
② 대신에   ④ 그 결과

| 정답 | ①

| 해설 | 빈칸 앞에서는 3차원 인쇄로 장기를 출력하는 바이오프린팅이 장기 부족에 대한 유망한 해결책임을 알 수 있다. 하지만 빈칸 뒤를 보면 바이오프린팅이 대체로 실험적 단계에 머물러 있음을 알 수 있다. 즉 바이오프린팅은 '아직은' 완전히 실현되지 못한 방법에 불과하다. 따라서 답은 ①이다.

20 윗글의 내용과 맞는 것을 고르시오.

① 살아 있는 지원자의 장기만이 이식이 가능하다.
② 현재 바이오프린팅을 통해 인쇄된 장기가 인간에게 이식되고 있다.
③ 안전과 관련된 기술의 발전이 이식 목적의 장기의 공급을 감소시키고 있다.
④ 3차원 인쇄 기술은 연구자들이 바이오프린팅을 통해 인쇄된 이식 가능 조직의 가능성에 대해 탐구하게 하는 주된 요인이다.

| 정답 | ③

| 해설 | 자동차의 안전 향상과 응급 처치 효과 증대는 갑작스러운 사고로 인한 사망을 낮추고, 이는 이식에 적합한 건강한 장기의 공급에 악영향을 준다. 따라서 답은 ③이다.
        사고로 인해 뇌사 상태에 빠진 사람의 장기를 이식하는 것은 ①에서 말하는 것처럼 살아 있는 지원자의 장기만이 이식이 가능한 것과는 거리가 멀다. 따라서 ①은 답이 될 수 없다. 본문에 따르면 바이오프린팅은 아직 실험적 단계에 불과하고 따라서

②는 답이 될 수 없다. 연구자들이 바이오프린팅에 주목하는 이유는 3차원 인쇄 기술 때문이 아니라 기증 가능 장기가 부족해서 아예 직접 만들어 보겠다는 생각을 품었기 때문이다. 따라서 ④는 답이 될 수 없다.

| 어휘 | **organ** ⓝ 장기

donor ⓝ 기증자, 기부자

from scratch 아예 처음부터, 아무것도 없는 상태에서

as yet 아직[그때](까지)

bioprinting ⓝ 바이오프린팅; 세포층을 인쇄하여 조직을 만드는 과정

experimental ⓐ 실험적인, 실험을 기초로 하는

explore ⓥ 탐구하다, 분석하다

transplant ⓥ 이식하다

terminate ⓥ 끝내다, 종료하다

promising ⓐ 유망한, 장래가 기대되는

regarding ⓟⓡⓔⓟ ~에 관하여

01 밑줄 친 (A)~(E) 가운데, 문맥상 적절하지 <u>않은</u> 것은? 건국대 2018

> 정부 정책이 젊은 여성들이 재정적 지원을 다른 이들에게 의존할 수 있다고 가정하는 것은 위험하다. 첫째로, 일부 젊은 여성들은 가족과 연락을 하고 있지 않기 때문에, 또는 그들의 가족이 경제적으로 그들을 지원할 수 없거나, 지원을 원치 않기 때문에 가족에게서 지원을 받지 못한다. 둘째로, 배우자 혹은 가족 구성원으로서 같은 집에 거주한다는 것이 젊은 여성이 가정 재원에 있어 공정한 몫을 받고 있다는 것을 의미하지는 않는다. 가정 수입에 대한 여성의 낮은 기여는 그들이 자신을 위해 더 적은 돈을 받고 더 적은 가정 재원을 소비하고, 이는 빈곤으로 이어질 수 있다는 것을 의미할 수 있다. 셋째로 경제적 독립은 만약에 지원이 철회되거나 관계가 끝난다면 젊은 여성은 언제나 빈곤을 겪게 될 위험에 처해 있다는 것을 의미한다. 젊은 여성은 직장으로부터 혹은 사회보장 제도로부터 오는 그들 자신의 적당한 수입이 필요하다. 가장 취약한 젊은 여성들의 다수는 직장이 없거나 쉽게 직업을 가질 수 없다.

① (A)　　　　② (B)　　　　③ (C)　　　　④ (D)　　　　⑤ (E)

| 정답 |　④

| 해설 |　젊은 여성들이 경제적 지원을 받을 수 있다고 가정하고 경제 정책을 펼치는 것은 위험하다는 내용이다. (D)의 경우 if 절 이하의 내용은 경제적으로 독립한 여성들의 입장에서 매우 어려움을 초래하는 내용이다. 지원이 끊기거나 도움을 주는 관계가 끊긴다면 여성들은 '부'가 아닌 '빈곤'을 겪을 것이므로, (D)를 wealth가 아닌 poverty로 수정해야 한다.

| 어휘 |　**government policy** 정부 정책　　　　　**rely on** ~에 의지[의존]하다, ~을 필요로 하다
　　　　faire share 정당한 몫, 공정한 몫　　　　　**lower** ⓥ 낮추다, (가치 등을) 떨어뜨리다
　　　　contribution ⓝ 기여, 공헌, 기부(금), 기고(문)　　**withdraw** ⓥ 철수하다, 인출하다, 철회하다
　　　　adequate ⓐ 충분한　　　　　　　　　　**social security system** 사회보장제도
　　　　vulnerable ⓐ 취약한, 연약한; 상처를 입기 쉬운, 공격받기 쉬운

02 (A), (B), (C)의 각 네모 안에서 문맥에 맞는 낱말로 가장 적절한 것은?

한의학의 "증상과 징후"는 서양의학과는 다소 다른 의미를 가지고 있다. 그것들은 방대한 임상실험에도 불구하고 서양의학이 살펴보는 상대적으로 좁은 영역과는 다르다. 대신 한의학의 의사들은 시야를 넓혀 소변, 땀, 갈증 등과 같은 다양한 신체 기능에서 변화를 평가한다. 뿐만 아니라, 한의사는 얼굴·신체의 특정 징후에서부터 심리적·감정적 특징(이런 것들은 실제로 "증상"이나 "징후"가 아니며, 특정 부조화의 표출이다)에 이르는 임상증상을 고려한다.

	(A)	(B)	(C)
①	넓은 –	신체의 –	조화
②	넓은 –	정서의 –	부조화
③	좁은 –	정서의 –	부조화
④	좁은 –	신체의 –	조화
⑤	좁은 –	신체의 –	부조화

| 정답 | ⑤

| 해설 | 한의학과 서양의학을 서로 비교 및 대조하고 있다. 먼저 (A)를 보면, 서양의학에서 살펴보는 영역을 설명하면서 'despite its battery of clinical tests'라고 했으므로, 많다(a battery of)는 뜻과 대조되는 적다(narrow)의 의미가 와야 한다. 즉 한의학에서 생각하는 증상과 징후는 서양의학에 비해 더 넓다는 의미가 된다. (B)의 경우, 예시를 나타내는 such as 뒤에 내용이 모두 신체적 변화를 의미하므로 'bodily'가 와야 한다. (C)의 경우, 임상증상으로 나타나는 것은 몸에 어떤 부조화가 있다는 것의 신호이므로, disharmony가 와야 한다.

| 어휘 |

symptom ⓝ 증상
explore ⓥ (문제를) 조사하다, 탐구하다
clinical test 임상시험
bodily ⓐ 신체의
thirst ⓝ 갈증
clinical manifestation 임상증상, 임상소견
trait ⓝ 특징, 특성

sign ⓝ 징후, 조짐, 기색, 흔적
a battery of 일련의, 수많은
emotional ⓐ 정서의, 감정적인
urination ⓝ 배뇨 작용, 소변을 보는 것
take into account ~을 고려하다
range from A to B 범위가 A에서 B까지 이어지다
disharmony ⓝ 부조화, 불화

| 01 | ② | 02 | ⑤ | 03 | ② | 04 | ④ | 05 | ① | 06 | ① | 07 | ③ | 08 | ② | 09 | ⑤ | 10 | ① |

[01]

해석

요즘엔 전화를 하면서 길을 걷는 사람의 모습을 보는 것은 어디서나 접할 수 있는 광경이 된 나머지, 인류의 진화를 왜곡할 생각으로 유인원 같은 크로마뇽인의 모습 다음에 한 손을 귀 옆에 댄 현대인의 모습을 그려 넣어야 할 지경이다. 최근 언론 보도에 따르면 현재 미국 의사들은 소위 "휴대전화 엘보(Cell phone elbow)" 증후군에 대해 경고하고 있다. 의료 전문가들이 이 증후군을 두고 그와 같은 소란을 피운다는 것은 우스꽝스러운 일로 보인다. 테니스 경기 후 테니스 엘보(tennis elbow)로 인한 거듭된 고통으로 인해 매일 고생하는 사람들과 마찬가지로, 휴대전화로 잡담을 나누는 사람들은 손이, 특히 새끼손가락과 넷째 손가락이 아프거나 저리다고 투덜거린다.

01 밑줄 친 (A), (B), (C), (D) 중 쓰임이 적절하지 <u>않은</u> 것은 무엇인가?

① (A)   ② (B)   ③ (C)   ④ (D)

| 정답 | ②

| 해설 | 유인원에서 시작하여 인간이 되는 인간의 옆모습을 그린 진화도는 인류 진화를 묘사하기 위해 흔히 사용된다. 현생 인류의 조상인 크로마뇽인 다음 단계에 휴대폰을 든 인간의 모습을 집어넣는 것은 진화의 모습을 "왜곡"한 것이라기보다, 현재 상황을 "풍자" 내지는 "묘사"한 것으로 볼 수 있다. 따라서 답은 ②이다.

| 어휘 | **ubiquitous** ⓐ 어디에나 있는, 아주 흔한   **ape-like** ⓐ 유인원 같은
distort ⓥ 왜곡하다   **syndrome** ⓝ 증후군
farcical ⓐ 우스꽝스러운; 어리석은   **make a fuss** 소란을 피우다, 공연한 법석을 떨다
constant ⓐ 끊임없는, 거듭되는   **gab** ⓥ 수다를 떨다, 잡담을 나누다
grumble ⓥ 투덜거리다, 툴툴대다   **numbness** ⓝ 저림, 마비
pinky finger 새끼손가락   **ring finger** 약지, 넷째 손가락

해석

필립 거스톤(Philip Guston)의 예술적 언어와 시적 동기는 인간 존재의 비논리적이고 역설적인 현실을 더 잘 이해하고 파악하는 것을 추구한다. 화가의 임무는 '어떻게 표현해야 하는가'가 아니라 '어떻게 알 것인가'이다. 거스톤은 (A) 추상화를 포기한 후, 단순하고 직접전인 표현인 구상 미술(figurative painting)로 돌아왔다. 언뜻 보기에 어려운 도상화(iconography)로 보이는 것은 그의 어린 시절의 그림들(전구, 신발 밑창, 쓰레기통 뚜껑)을 종종 지칭하는 것으로, 이것들은 마치 피에로 델라 프란체스카(Pierro della Francesca)의 프레스코 화에서 가져온 요소처럼 보인다. 거스톤의 도상화는 (B) 기술적 논리를 통해 해석될 수 있는 단순한 표현이 아니다. 그것은 더 심오한 지식, 칼 융(Carl Jung)의 아니마(anima, 남성의 무의식 내에 존재하는 여성적 특성)와 관련이 있다. 거스톤의 비논리적 도상화는 기술적 표현이 아닌, 신화적 잠재의식의 기저에 있는 표현에 대해 말한다. 예지(divination)와 같이 (C) 비논리적으로 받아들여지는 것으로 스스로를 드러내는 직관과 같은 것을 말하고 있다.

02 윗글의 주제로 가장 적절한 것은?

① Philip Guston 시(詩)의 언어적 특징
② Philip Guston의 그림에 나타난 논리성
③ 추상예술과 구상예술의 철학적 배경
④ Carl Jung이 현대 예술에 미친 영향
⑤ Philip Guston 회화의 양식적 특징

| 정답 | ⑤

| 해설 | 회화를 그리는 필립 거스톤의 작품적 특성에 대해 기술하고 있으므로, 글의 주제는 ⑤가 된다.

03 (A), (B), (C)에 들어갈 말로 바르게 짝지어진 것은?

	(A)	(B)	(C)
①	추상화	기술하는	논리적으로
②	추상화	기술하는	비논리적으로
③	추상화	규범적인	논리적으로
④	구체화	규범적인	비논리적으로
⑤	구체화	규범적인	논리적으로

| 정답 | ②

| 해설 | (A)의 경우, 'figurative painting'이 구상 미술의 뜻을 이해하는 것이 중요하다. 구상화는 추상화(abstraction)의 반대로 실제 세계의 모습을 그리는 것을 말한다. 따라서 (A)에는 figurative painting의 반대인 'abstraction'이 와야 한다. 'concretion'은 구체화란 의미로, figurative painting과 유사한 의미를 지닌다. (B)의 경우, 거스톤의 그림은 단순히 있는 그대로를 재현한 그림(a simple representation)이 아니라고 설명한다. 이것은 심오한 의미를 담고 있다는 말로, 현상을 있는 그대로 기술하는 (descriptive) 논리로는 해석될 수 없다는 의미에서, (B)는 descriptive가 와야 한다. prescriptive는 당위를 설명하는 '규범적인'의 의미를 지닌다. (C)의 경우 거스톤의 그림은 기술적 표현이 아니라고 했으며, 예지(divination)와 같이 논리적으로 받아들여질 수 없는 어떤 것이라고 설명하고 있으므로, (C)는 '비논리적으로'에 해당하는 illogically가 적합하다. 종합하면 정답은 ②가 된다.

| 어휘 |

apprehend ⓥ 파악하다, 이해하다, 체포하다

paradoxical ⓐ 역설적인, 모순된

abandon ⓥ 포기하다

concretion ⓝ 구체화

at first glance 처음에는, 언뜻 보기에는

iconography ⓝ 도상학 (회화나 조각 등 미술 작품에서 일정한 종교적, 신화적 주제를 나타낸 표현 양식과 이에 대한 해석을 다루는 학문)

bulb ⓝ 전구

fresco ⓝ 프레스코 화법

interpret ⓥ (의미를) 설명[해석]하다

prescriptive ⓐ 규범적인, 지시하는, 권위적인

anima ⓝ (칼 융의 심리학) 아니마(↔ animus, 남성의 무의식 내에 존재하는 여성적 특성)

underlying ⓐ 기저에 있는, 근본적인

subconscious ⓐ 무의식의, 잠재의식의

epiphany ⓝ (어떤 사물이나 본질에 대한) 직관, 통찰, (동방 박사의) 예수 공현

manifest ⓥ 명백히 하다, 드러내다 ⓐ 명백한

illogical ⓐ 비논리적인, 터무니없는

represent ⓥ 대변하다, 대표하다; 재현하다

abstraction ⓝ 관념, 추상적 개념

figurative ⓐ (그림ㆍ조각이) 구상적인, 조형적인

sole ⓝ 발바닥, (신발ㆍ양말의) 바닥, 밑창

representation ⓝ 표시, 표현, 재현; 대표, 대리

descriptive ⓐ 기술적인, 서술하는

profound ⓐ 깊은, 심오한

mythical ⓐ 신화 속에 나오는; 가공의, 사실이 아닌

divination ⓝ 예측, 예지

[04~05] 국민대 2020

해석

현재의 대학 시스템은 훈련과 교육의 차이를 모호하게 만들었다. 대부분의 단과대학과 종합대학 관계자들은 예산 제약과 <u>불안한 고용시장</u>으로 야기된 경제적ㆍ문화적 불확실성에 대해 오늘날 기업의 모델에 기반을 두고 대학을 구축함으로써 대응해 왔다. 결과적으로, 많은 대학이 훈련을 전면에 내세우고 이를 교육이라고 불렀다. 학생들을 사회화할 수 있는 통일된 국가적 문화의 부족과 어떤 경우에도 독립적 교과과정을 운영할 수 있는 <u>교육철학</u>의 부재로, 전반적인 대학 시스템은 학생들이 졸업하자마자 취업 준비가 되어 있어야 한다는 <u>시장논리</u>에 사로잡혀 있는 실정이다. 이러한 필요성 아래, 단과대학과 종합대학들은 학생들이 경쟁적인 취업시장에 대비할 수 있는 교육 프로그램을 시행하는 것이 불가능했다. 대신에 대학의 리더들은 '우수성(excellence)'이라는 주문을 외치고 있는데, 이것은 대학의 모든 부분이 '제 기능을 수행(perform)'하고, 그들이 얼마나 지식과 자격을 갖춘 노동력을 기업 경제에 잘 전달하는지, 그리고 대학 행정부가 대학을 유지하기 위해 필요한 채용 및 자금 목표를 얼마나 잘 충족하는지에 따라 평가를 받는 것을 의미한다.

---

04 다음 중 맥락상 가장 일치하지 <u>않는</u> 것은?

① Ⓐ ② Ⓑ

③ Ⓒ ④ Ⓓ

| 정답 | ④

| 해설 | 글의 저자는 대학이 시장 논리에 따라 학생들에게 지식을 전달하는 것이 아닌 취업에 적합한 훈련을 제공하고 있는 상황을 비판하고 있다. 이러한 관점에서 Ⓓ가 포함된 문장인 "이러한 필요성 아래, 단과대학과 종합대학들은 학생들이 경쟁적인 취업시장에 대비할 수 있는 교육 프로그램을 시행하는 것이 불가능했다."에서 마지막 부분이 전체 내용과 일치하지 않게 된다. 학생들을 경쟁적인 취업시장에 대해서만 준비시킬 뿐 더 중요한 문제에 대해 관심을 두지 않고 있다는 내용이 되어야 하므로, Ⓓ의 'the competitive job market'을 'a world of great complexity'로 수정해야 한다.

05 다음 중 빈칸 ⓐ에 들어갈 가장 적합한 것은?

① 대신에   ② 사전에

③ 다행히도   ④ 그럼에도 불구하고

| 정답 | ①

| 해설 | 정답은 ①로, 〈not A but B〉와 유사한 〈not A instead B〉 구문에 해당한다. 대학에서 A(적합한 교육 프로그램을 제공하는 것)를 하지 않고 대신 B(우수성이라는 주문을 외치는 것)에만 치중하고 있다는 내용이 되어야 한다.

| 어휘 |

fudge ⓥ 얼버무리다; 날조하다, 조작하다

provoke ⓥ 도발하다, 유발시키다

constraint ⓝ 제약, 압박, 속박

institution ⓝ 제도, 기관

thrust ⓥ (거칠게) 밀다, 밀치다, 찌르다

unify ⓥ 통일하다

in any case 어쨌든, 어떤 일이 있어도

steer ⓥ 조종하다, 몰다

logic ⓝ 논리

upon -ing ~하자마자

imperative ⓝ 필요성

competitive ⓐ 경쟁을 하는, 경쟁력 있는

mantra ⓝ 기도, 명상 때 외는 주문

recruitment ⓝ 신규 모집, 채용

consistent ⓐ 한결같은, 일관된

administration ⓝ 관리직, 행정직; 행정부

budget ⓝ 예산, 비용

volatile ⓐ 휘발성의, 변하기 쉬운, 심하게 변동하는, 변덕스러운

on the model of ~을 거울삼아

to the fore 전면에

socialize ⓥ 사귀다, 사회화시키다

philosophy ⓝ 철학

be caught in ~에 빠지다, ~에 걸려들다

demand ⓥ 요구하다

graduation ⓝ 졸업

implement ⓥ 실시하다, 이행하다

chant ⓝ 연이어 외치는 구호

fulfill ⓥ 성취하다, 이행하다, 실행하다

funding ⓝ 자금 공급

proactively ⓐ 사전 대책을 강구해, 선제적으로, 미리

[06~07] 건국대 2015

해석

생각은 자유라는 말은 흔한 격언이다. 인간은 자신이 생각하는 것을 숨길 수 있는 한 자신이 선택한 것이 무엇이든 이를 생각하는 일을 결코 방해받지 않는다. 인간의 정신 작용은 오로지 자신의 경험의 경계와 상상력의 힘에 의해서만 제약을 받는다. 하지만 개인의 생각에 대한 이러한 천부적인 자유는 거의 가치가 없다. 만일 자신의 생각을 다른 이에게 전달하도록 허용되지 못할 경우 이는 생각하는 사람에게 있어 불만족스러운 일이며, 그 주변 사람들에게는 분명히 아무 가치가 없는 일이다. 게다가, 정신에 대해 영향력을 행사할 수 있는 생각을 숨긴다는 것은 극도로 까다로운 일이다. 만일 어느 한 사람이 사고 끝에 주변 사람들의 행동을 통제하는 사상이나 관습에 이의를 제기하게 되고, 주변 사람들이 가지고 있던 믿음을 거부하게 되고, 주변 사람들이 따르고 있는 것보다 더 나은 삶의 방식을 파악하게 될 경우, 그 사람은 만일 스스로의 추론을 통해 얻은 진실을 확신하고 있을 경우, 자신이 그들과는 다르며 그들의 견해를 공유하지 않는다는 것을 침묵으로든, 우연한 말이든, 일반적인 태도로든 무심코 드러내지 않을 가능성은 거의 없다. 소크라테스와 마찬가지로 일부는 오늘날 자신의 생각을 숨기는 대신에 죽음을 택했으며 일부는 오늘날에도 그러할 것이다. 따라서 생각의 자유는, 가치 있는 어느 의미에서든, 언론의 자유를 포함한다.

06 문맥상 적절하지 <u>않은</u> 것을 고르시오.

① ⓐ ② ⓑ ③ ⓒ ④ ⓓ ⑤ ⓔ

| 정답 | ①

| 해설 | ⓐ 다음을 보면, "만일 자신의 생각을 다른 이에게 전달하도록 허용되지 못할 경우 이는 생각하는 사람에게 있어 불만족스러운 일이며, 그 주변 사람들에게는 분명히 아무 가치가 없는 일이다(It is unsatisfactory, to the thinker himself if he is not permitted to communicate his thoughts to others, and it is obviously of no value to this neighbours)"라고 나와 있다. 이 말은 즉 개인적으로는 생각의 자유를 누릴 수 있지만 이를 다른 이에게 표현하지 못한다면 아무리 자유를 누리더라도 혼자만의 생각에 그치게 될 것이며 결국은 "아무 의미 없는" 또는 "가치 없는" 것에 불과할 것이라는 의미이다. 따라서 ⓐ는 of little value가 적합하다.

07 빈칸에 가장 적합한 것은 무엇인가?

① 집회 ② 종교
③ 언론 ④ 비판
⑤ 이동

| 정답 | ③

| 해설 | 빈칸 앞에서 "일부는 오늘날 자신의 생각을 숨기는 대신에 죽음을 택했으며 일부는 오늘날에도 그러할 것이다(Some have preferred, like Socrates, some would prefer to-day, to face death rather than conceal their thoughts)"라고 나와 있는데, 여기서 생각을 숨긴다는 것은 생각을 제대로 표현하지 않거나 숨긴다는 것을 의미한다. 따라서 생각의 자유는 생각을 제대로 표현하고 숨기지 않는 자유를 의미하며, 여기에는 "언론의 자유"라는 개념이 들어가게 된다. 따라서 답은 ③이다.

| 어휘 |

saying ⓝ 속담, 격언

conceal ⓥ 감추다, 숨기다

unsatisfactory ⓐ 만족스럽지 못한

regulate ⓥ 통제하다, 단속하다

be convinced of ~을 확신하다

betray ⓥ 무심코 노출시키다[드러내다], 나타내다

prefer ⓥ 택하다, 원하다

freedom of speech 언론의 자유

hinder ⓥ 저해하다, 방해하다

natural ⓐ 천부적인, 천성의

call ~ in question ~을 논박하다, ~에 이의를 제기하다

hold ⓥ (신념·의견 등을) 가지다

reasoning ⓝ 추론, 추리

chance ⓐ 우연한

conceal ⓥ 감추다, 숨기다

freedom of assembly 집회의 자유

해석

인공지능 기술은 사망한 음악가의 목소리를 복원하여 현대의 노래를 부르게 한다. 한 게임회사는 자사의 대표 게임의 사운드트랙을 위해 노래 경연대회를 방송한다. 한국의 음악계는 매체와 기술 및 업계가 하나로 수렴하면서 계속 진화하고 있다.

한국의 게임회사 넥슨은 아케이드 장르 스타일의 액션 게임인 던전앤파이터(Dungeon and Fighter)에 가장 어울릴 TV 경연대회 포맷을 채택했다. 넥슨은 다섯 개의 에피소드로 구성된 해당 시리즈는 유튜브 채널인 딩고뮤직(Dingo Music)에서 볼 수 있고 목요일 기준 시청 건수가 200만 뷰를 넘겼다고 밝혔다. 넥슨이 음악업계와 독특한 협업을 추구했던 것은 이번이 처음은 아니다. 넥슨은 과거에도 체코 내셔널심포니오케스트라(Czech National Symphony Orchestra)에서 유명 싱어송라이터인 요조에 이르기까지 다양한 음악가와 협업했다. 넥슨은 또한 클래식과 대중음악 모두를 다루는 콘서트를 준비 중에 있다.

인공지능의 사용 증가로 한국의 대중음악계가 활성화되고 있다. 음악 채널 Mnet은 최근에 "다시 한번"이란 인공지능 음악 프로젝트를 선보였고, 이 프로젝트에서는 사망한 아티스트들이 홀로그램과 인공지능 목소리 커버를 통해 모습을 드러낸다. 한국 방송사인 SBS도 인공지능과 인간 전문가 간의 경쟁을 방송했고, 여기서 이들은 1996년 31세의 나이로 사망한 전설적인 가수 김광석을 재창조하고자 했다. 한국의 한 음악 비평가는 다음과 같이 말했다. "과거의 음악 경연대회에서 경쟁에 초점을 맞췄더라면, 최근의 음악 프로그램은 신기술을 적용하고 게임 사운드트랙 같은 새로운 유형의 음악을 소개하는 등의 행동을 통해 보다 다양한 접근법을 취하고 있습니다. 이러한 새로운 시도는 계속하여 영향을 끼칠 것으로 예상됩니다."

---

08 본문의 전체 문맥과 맞지 <u>않은</u> 것은 무엇인가?

① Ⓐ   ② Ⓑ   ③ Ⓒ   ④ Ⓓ   ⑤ Ⓔ

| 정답 | ②

| 해설 | Ⓑ에서 말하는 게임회사와 음악계 간의 협업은 "관행적인" 것으로 보긴 힘들고 "파격적"이거나 "독특한" 것으로 볼 수 있다. 따라서 답은 ②이다.

---

09 인공지능 기술에 대한 저자의 견해는 무엇인가?

① 모호한   ② 의심스러운
③ 적대적인   ④ 불확실한
⑤ 유망한

| 정답 | ⑤

| 해설 | 본문에서는 "인공지능의 사용 증가로 한국의 대중음악계가 활성화되고 있다"고 언급되며, 이를 통해 한 음악 비평가는 "다양한 접근법을 취하게" 될 것임을 말하고 있다. 이런 시각은 인공지능 기술을 "유망한" 것으로 바라보고 있음을 나타낸다. 따라서 답은 ⑤이다.

10 본문의 주제는 무엇인가?

① 인공지능과 음악업계의 협업
② 사망한 음악가의 목소리를 되살림
③ 클래식과 대중음악의 조합
④ 옛날 대중가요의 재창조
⑤ 인공지능과 인간 전문가와의 경쟁

| 정답 | ①

| 해설 | 본문의 핵심은 "한국의 음악계는 매체와 기술 및 업계가 하나로 수렴하면서 계속 진화하고 있다"이며, 그 중 하나의 사례로 "인공지능과 음악업계의 협업"을 들 수 있다. 따라서 보기 중 ①이 본문의 주제와 관련이 깊은 것임을 유추할 수 있다.

| 어휘 |

deceased ⓐ 사망한
air ⓥ 방송하다
adopt ⓥ 채택하다
collaboration ⓝ 협업, 공동 업무
a wide range of 광범위한, 다양한
invigorate ⓥ 활성화하다
ambiguous ⓐ 모호한
hostile ⓐ 적대적인
promising ⓐ 유망한

contemporary ⓐ 동시대의, 현대의
convergence ⓝ 통합, 수렴
unconventional ⓐ 색다른, 독특한
collaborate ⓥ 협업하다, 공동으로 작업하다
feature ⓥ 특종으로 다루다, 중점 대상으로 삼다
diverse ⓐ 다양한
suspicious ⓐ 의심스러운
uncertain ⓐ 불확실한

연습 문제   01 ③   02 ④   03 ③

01 다음 중 본문 바로 앞에서 논의될 가능성이 가장 높은 것은 무엇인가?

> 또 하나 기억할 만한 더블 딥은 1980년대 초에 있었다. 1980년 Ronald Reagan의 당선 이후 경제는 불황에서 회복되기 시작했지만 여전히 두 자리 수의 금리와 인플레이션으로 곤란한 상황이었다. 당시 연방 준비 제도 이사회 이사장인 Paul Volcker는 초고금리를 유지하는 방식으로 인플레이션에 무자비한 공격을 가했고, 이는 소비자 지출을 약화시키고 투자를 억제하는 효과를 가져왔다. 그 결과, 인플레이션은 사그라졌지만, 경제는 1982년에 반등하기 전까지 다시 불황에 빠졌다.

① 더블 딥의 정의   ② 더블 딥의 원인
③ 더블 딥의 한 가지 사례   ④ 더블 딥의 문제점

| 정답 | ③

| 해설 | 둘 중에서 하나를 가리켜 one이라 하면 나머지 다른 하나는 the other라 한다. 따라서 본문 가장 첫 문장의 "또 하나 기억할 만한 더블 딥(The other memorable double dip)"에서 the other가 나왔다는 것은 본문 앞에서 one에 해당되는 '더블 딥'의 사례가 하나 제시되었음을 암시한다. 따라서 ③을 답으로 볼 수 있다.

| 어휘 | **memorable** ⓐ 기억할 만한, 기억에 남는
double-dip ⓝ 더블 딥; 경기가 회복할 조짐을 보이다가 다시 침체로 빠져드는 현상
recession ⓝ 불황   **hobble** ⓥ 방해하다, 다리를 절다
double-digit ⓐ 두 자리 수의   **relentless** ⓐ 무자비한, 가차 없는
sky-high ⓐ 아주 높은   **dampen** ⓥ 약화시키다, 기세를 꺾다
curtail ⓥ 축소시키다, 삭감시키다   **plunge** ⓥ 급락하다, (아래로 갑자기) 거꾸러지다
rebound ⓥ 반등하다

02 다음 글에 이어질 문장으로 가장 알맞은 것은? 국민대 2011

1588년까지 거슬러 올라가는 "스페인 죄수(Spanish Prisoner)"라는 사기는 인터넷상에서도 여전히 성행하고 있다. 원래 이 사기는 다음과 같다. 사기꾼들이 피해자(가 될 사람)에게 자신들이 신분을 속이고 스페인에 수감되어 있는 귀족을 알고 있다고 말한다. 수감되어 있다는 이 인물은 그의 신분이 밝혀지면 심각한 영향을 미칠 수 있기 때문에 밝힐 수 없으며, 그가 자신의 석방에 필요한 자금을 모으는 데 이들 사기꾼들에게 의지하고 있다는 식이다. 피해자들에게 이 자금의 일부를 자신들에게 보내 줄 것을 요청하며, 보내 주면 수감자가 풀려날 경우 상당한 보상을 해 주겠다고 약속한다. 하지만 피해자가 돈을 보내고 나면 또 다른 어려움이 생겼다고 말하면서, 추가로 돈이 더 필요하다고 말한다. 이런 일은 피해자의 돈이 바닥날 때까지 계속 되풀이된다.

① 보상해 준다는 큰돈은 그(피해자)의 욕망을 불타오르게 하는 수단이 될 것이다.
② 인터넷은 확실히 무임 승차자들의 온상이다.
③ 게다가 그는 보상해 준다는 큰돈을 착복할 것이다.
④ 비슷한 사기들이 인터넷상에서 벌어진다.

| 정답 | ④

| 해설 | 본문의 시작이 "~ is alive and well on the Internet"으로 되어 있는 것에 주의해야 한다. 시작을 이런 식으로 했기 때문에 스페인 죄수와 같은 오래전에 있었던 사기가 요즘 세상에서도 버젓이 벌어진다는 논지로 이어져야 한다. 따라서 답은 ④가 된다.

| 어휘 | **scam** ⓝ 신용 사기
victim ⓝ 피해자
aristocrat ⓝ 귀족(인 사람)
false identity 거짓 신분; 사람을 잘못 알아봄
reveal ⓥ 드러내다, 적발[폭로]하다(= disclose)
repercussion ⓝ (어떤 사건이 초래한, 보통 좋지 못한, 간접적인) 영향
rely on ~에 의지[의존]하다, ~을 필요로 하다
be rewarded 포상을 주다[받다]
stoke ⓥ ~에 불을 지피다
hotbed ⓝ (특히 범죄·폭력의) 온상
pocket ⓝ (제 것이 아닌 것을, 특히 돈을) 제 호주머니에 넣다, 착복하다
to boot 그것도 (앞서 한 말에 대해 다른 말을 덧붙일 때)
be played out 벌어지다, 펼쳐지다

con artist ⓝ 사기꾼
be in touch with 연락하고 지내다
be imprisoned 투옥되다, 감금되다
alleged ⓐ ~이라고들 말하는

secure ⓥ (특히 힘들게) 얻어 내다, 획득[확보]하다
turn over 넘기다, 주다, 맡기다
greed ⓝ 탐욕
freeloader ⓝ 남에게 얻어먹기만 하는 사람, 무임 승차자

03 본문 다음에 언급될 가능성이 가장 높은 것은 무엇인가?

> 매년 이 도시에서 약 5만 명의 사람들이 사망하고 있고, 사람들이 점차 오래 건강하게 살게 되면서 사망률이 계속 최저치에 근접하고 있다. 고인의 대다수에겐 사망 소식을 곧 듣고 장례식장에 눈물을 흘리며 모여들 친지와 친구들이 존재한다. 경건한 부고가 등장한다. 조문장이 쌓인다. 유명 인사가 사망하거나 무고한 사람이 살해당하는 비통한 사건이 발생할 경우 도시 전체가 눈물을 흘릴 것이다. 하지만 훨씬 소수의 사람들은 주목받지 못한 채 몸부림치다가 사망한다. 이처럼 쓸쓸한 형태의 죽음도 놀라울 정도의 활동을 야기할 수 있다. 때로는 이 과정에서 인생의 비밀이 밝혀지게 된다. 여기에 한 이야기를 들 수 있다.

① 유명인사의 삶의 비밀
② 장례식의 상세한 절차
③ 혼자 사망한 어떤 사람의 이야기
④ 감소하는 사망률의 원인
⑤ 친구나 친지를 상실함으로서 겪는 슬픔

| 정답 | ③

| 해설 | 본문 중반부까지는 도시의 죽음은 많은 사람들의 슬픔을 자아내는 사건임을 말하고 있지만 그 이후부터는 아무도 모르는 채 죽는 사람들도 있음을 말하고 있다. 그리고 그런 쓸쓸한 죽음도 의외로 큰 반향을 일으킴을 알 수 있다. 마지막 문장인 "여기에 한 이야기를 들 수 있다(Here's a story)"는 사망 당시에는 주목받지 못하고 쓸쓸하게 죽은 어떤 사람의 이야기가 존재함을 말하고 있고, 이 문장 다음부터는 그런 사람의 구체적인 사례가 등장할 것으로 유추 가능하다. 따라서 답은 ③이다.

| 어휘 | **mortality rate** 사망률
the deceased 고인
reverent ⓐ 경건한
sympathy card 조문장
unwatched ⓐ 주목받지 못하는, 무시된

graze ⓥ 스치다
passing ⓝ 죽음, 사망
death notice 사망 통지서, 부고
heart-rending ⓐ 가슴이 미어지는, 비통한
forlorn ⓐ 쓸쓸한, 황량한

01	①	02	④	03	①	04	③	05	④	06	③	07	①	08	④	09	④	10	②
11	②	12	④	13	②	14	①	15	④	16	②	17	②	18	①	19	④	20	②

[01~02] 항공대 2017

해석

사회 심리학에서 '정의로운 세상 가설(the just-world hypothesis)'이라고 불리는, 정의로운 세상에 대한 믿음이 만연해 있다는 사실이 수십 년 전 멜빈 러너(Melvin Lerner)에 의해 최초로 기술되었다. 러너의 주장에 따르면, 사람들은 세상이 예측 가능하고, 이해 가능하며, 결과적으로 잠재적으로 통제 가능하다고 생각하기 원한다. 혹은, 다른 학자의 말을 빌리면, 아주 어린 시절부터 우리는 '착하고 통제 가능한' 사람이 되도록 배운다. 거의 대부분 무작위적이고 통제하려고 하면 방해를 받는다고 느끼거나 좌절감을 느끼는 세상을 우리가 어떻게 다른 방식으로 항해해 갈 수 있겠는가? 정의로운 세상이 이해할 수 있고 예측할 수 있는 곳이기 때문에, 통제와 예측 가능성에 대한 욕망은 세상을 정의로운 곳으로 보려고 하는 경향을 낳는다. 규칙대로 행동하면 잘 될 것이고, 규칙을 따르지 않는다면 나쁜 일들이 벌어질 것이다. 정의로운 세상 가설에 따르면, 사람들은 자신이 받을 자격이 있는 것을 얻는다고 대부분 믿는다. 즉 좋은 사람은 보상을 받을 것이고 나쁜 사람은 벌을 받을 것이라는 것이다. 보다 중요한 사실은, 이런 현상이 반대로 작동한다는 것이다. 누군가가 잘 사는 것을 보면, 그런 사람을 관찰한 사람은 그 운 좋은 사람은 행운을 누릴 만한 무엇인가를 했음이 틀림없다는 판단을 내리는 사회 심리적 경향이 있다.

01 다음 중 본문의 제목으로 가장 적합한 것은?
① 정의로운 세상 가설의 심리적 기제
② 예측 가능성과 이해 가능성의 무의미함
③ 예측할 수 있는 행위의 불필요함
④ 보상에 대한 되돌릴 수 없는 욕망

| 정답 | ①

| 해설 | 본문에서는 세상은 무작위적이고 통제하려면 좌절감을 느끼는 곳이지만 사람들은 세상이 예측 가능하고, 이해할 수 있고, 통제할 수 있는 곳이라고 믿는 경향이 있다고 설명한다. 그런 것이 가능한 세상이 정의로운 세상이며, 세상은 정의로운 곳이므로 좋은 일을 하는 사람은 보상을 받고, 나쁜 일을 하는 사람은 벌을 받는다고 심리적으로 생각하는 경향이 있다고 설명한다. 이것은 '정의로운 세상 가설'이 작동하는 심리적 기제에 관한 내용이므로, 정답은 ①이 된다.

02 다음 중 본문의 마지막 문장 이후에 이어질 내용으로 적합한 것은?
① 게다가, 무작위적인 불운을 겪은 피해자들은 그들의 엄청난 성공을 누릴 만한 무엇인가 가치 있는 일을 했음에 틀림없다.
② 세상이 공평하다고 믿는 사람들은 환경의 다양한 가능성에 주목한다.
③ 성공은 성공한 사람에게서 많은 부정적 특성을 찾아내려는 노력을 촉진시킬 것이다.
④ 그 사람은 단지 관찰된 보상에 의해 더 좋은 사람이 된다.

| 정답 | ④

| 해설 | 착한 사람이 성공한다고 보는 것과는 반대로, 성공한 사람은 착한 사람일 것이라고 사람들은 생각하는 경향이 있다고 지적한다. 즉 관찰된 보상(성공)을 보면서 그들이 더 좋은 사람일 것이라고 생각한다는 앞 문장의 부연 설명에 해당하는 ④가 정답이 된다.

| 어휘 | **pervasiveness** ⓝ 온통 퍼짐, 만연함

predictable ⓐ 예측할 수 있는

controllable ⓐ 통제 가능한

thwart ⓥ 훼방 놓다, 방해하다, 좌절시키다

prosper ⓥ 번창하다, 성공하다

insignificance ⓝ 하찮음, 대수롭지 않음

irreversible ⓐ 되돌릴 수 없는

attribute ⓝ pl. 속성, 특질 ⓥ 돌리다, 탓으로 하다

hypothesis ⓝ 가설, 가정

comprehensible ⓐ 이해할 수 있는

navigate ⓥ 나아가다, 항해하다, 길을 찾다

frustrate ⓥ 좌절시키다

mechanism ⓝ 기제, 심리 과정

redundancy ⓝ 불필요한[쓸모없는] 중복[반복], 정리 해고

by virtue of ~에 의해서; ~ 덕분에[때문에]

[03~04] 한국외대 2015

> 해석

브래들리 윌슨(Bradley Wilson)은 모든 유형의 동물들이 취하는 작은 움직임에 관해 연구를 할 경우 과학자들은 동물의 감정 상태에 관해 새로이 이해할 수 있을 것으로 생각한다. 어떻게 이런 방식이 통할 수 있을지 보여 주고자 윌슨과 윌슨의 동료 연구원들은 코끼리와 인간이라는 매우 다른 두 종의 동물에게 소형 가속도계를 장착시켰다. 동물의 광범위한 움직임을 추적하는 행위는 과학자들 입장에서는 흔히 하는 일이다. GPS와 동작 탐지기를 이용하여 새와 장수거미게의 이동을 추적하는 것을 예로 들 수 있다. 하지만 윌슨은 동물이 어디로 이동하는지에는 관심이 없었다. 대신에 윌슨은 동물의 작은 움직임을 통해 어떻게 감정이나 내면의 상태가 드러나는지를 알고 싶었다.

우선 연구진은 코끼리를 관찰했으며, 목걸이에 달린 가속도계를 활용하여 코끼리의 움직임을 측정했다. 코끼리가 주변을 돌아다니면 관찰자는 코끼리가 "긍정적인" 이유 때문에 이동하는지 아니면 "부정적인" 이유 때문에 이동하는지 주목했다. 긍정적인 움직임이란 음식이나 뒹굴며 지내기 좋은 진흙더미 같이 호감을 느끼는 대상을 향해 이동하는 것을 의미한다. 반면에 무리 중에서 힘 센놈에게 쫓겨 다니는 것은 부정적인 움직임을 뜻한다. 연구진은 이러한 정보를 3차원으로 된 가속도계 데이터와 결합하면서 코끼리가 긍정적인 상태와 부정적인 상태에서 몸을 움직이는 모습에 커다란 차이가 있음을 발견했다.

---

03 윌슨의 실험 목적으로 가장 가능성이 높은 것은 무엇인가?

① 동물의 생각을 엿보기 위해 동물의 움직임을 관찰하기

② 동물의 움직임을 감시하기 위해 개발된 새로운 기기를 시험하기

③ 대형 동물의 긍정적 움직임과 부정적 움직임을 구별하기

④ 지적 능력을 활용하는 방식을 기준으로 다른 동물들과 비교하기

| 정답 | ①

| 해설 | 윌슨과 윌슨의 동료 연구원들은 "동물의 작은 움직임을 통해 어떻게 감정이나 내면의 상태가 드러나는지를 알고 싶었기 (wanted to know how their small-scale movements revealed their emotions or other internal states)" 때문에 가속도계를 활용하여 작은 움직임을 관찰하게 되었다. 따라서 답은 ①이다.

04 다음 중 저자가 본문 직후에 작성할 가능성이 높은 것은 무엇인가?

① 코끼리는 하루에 얼마나 이동할 수 있는가

② 연구진은 코끼리를 어떻게 추적할 수 있는가

③ 윌슨의 인간을 대상으로 한 실험의 결과

④ 실험에 있어 가속도계의 유용성

| 정답 | ③

| 해설 | 첫 번째 단락에서 연구 대상이 인간과 코끼리임을 밝혔고, 두 번째 단락에서는 코끼리를 대상으로 한 연구에 관해 설명하였다. 따라서 본문 다음 내용은 인간을 대상으로 한 연구에 관해 논할 것이다. 그러므로 답은 ③이다.

| 어휘 | **insight** ⓝ 통찰력, 이해, 간파

pocket-sized ⓐ 소형의

track ⓥ 추적하다

motion detector 동작 탐지기

giant crab 장수거미게

reveal ⓥ 드러내다, 밝히다

note ⓥ 주의하다, 주목하다

wallow in ~의 속에서 뒹굴다

dominant ⓐ 우세한, 지배적인

significant ⓐ 커다란, 중요한

intellect ⓝ 지적 능력

emotional state 정서 상태, 감정 상태

accelerometer ⓝ 가속도계

large-scale ⓐ 대규모의, 광범위한

migration ⓝ 이동, 이주

small-scale ⓐ 소규모의, 작은

collar ⓝ (개 등의 목에 거는) 목걸이

desirable ⓐ 바람직한, 호감 가는

chase away ~을 쫓아내다

herd ⓝ 떼, 무리

spy on 염탐하다, 몰래 감시하다

[05~07] 항공대 2016

해석

디지털 신호와 아날로그 신호에 관해 흔히 볼 수 있는 오해가 다수 존재한다. 그중에는 디지털은 불연속적인 것을 의미하는 반면에 아날로그는 연속적인 것을 의미한다는 오해이다. 이것은 사실일 때도 종종 있지만, 디지털 과 아날로그를 구분하기 위한 기준은 되지 못한다. 아날로그를 유사함, 즉 현실 세계와 유사하다는 의미로 생각해 보자. 만일 현실 세계의 사건이 불연속적인 것이라면 아날로그 세계의 사건도 불연속적일 것이다. 만일 물리적 과정이 연속적이라면, 아날로그적 과정 또한 연속적일 것이다. 하지만 디지털은 언제나 불연속적이다. 디지털은 수가 제한된 값 가운데 하나로, 보통은 둘 중 하나이고 때로는 셋이나 넷 또는 열 중 하나이다. 널리 퍼진 오해 중 하나는 디지털은 왠지 모르게 좋은 것이고 아날로그는 나쁜 것이라는 시각이다. 하지만 이는 전혀 사실이 아니다. 물론 디지털은 우리가 사용 중인 현대식 기계에는 적합하지만 아날로그는 어쩌면 미래에 등장할 기계에 더 적합할 수 있다. 그리고 아날로그는 분명히 말해 사람에게는 더 좋고 주된 이유는 소음으로 인한 영향 때문이다. 우리는 이 세계가 원하는 바에 부응하도록 진화되었다. 인간의 인지 능력이 어떻게 작동하는지 이해하고 싶다면, 빛의 세계와 소리의 세계가 어떻게 작동하는지를 이해하는 것으로부터 시작하는 편이 도움이 되며, 왜냐하면 눈과 귀는 이러한 물리적 신호의 본질에 적합해지도록 진화했기 때문이다.

05 다음 중 위 본문의 제목으로 가장 알맞은 것은 무엇인가?

① 디지털이 주는 이점

② 아날로그의 오작동

③ 아날로그의 공포

④ 아날로그에 대한 오해

| 정답 | ④

| 해설 | 본문은 디지털에 비해 아날로그가 오해를 받고 있으며, 어떤 고정관념에 노출되어 있는지를 말하고 있다. 따라서 답은 ④이다.

---

06 다음 중 사실이 <u>아닌</u> 것은 무엇인가?

① 현실 세계의 사건이 불연속적일 경우 아날로그 또한 불연속적이다.

② 현실 세계의 사건이 연속적일 경우 아날로그 또한 연속적이다.

③ 현실 세계의 사건이 연속적일 경우 디지털 또한 연속적이다.

④ 현실 세계의 사건이 불연속적일 경우 디지털 또한 불연속적이다.

| 정답 | ③

| 해설 | "하지만 디지털은 언제나 불연속적이다(Digital, however, is always discrete)." 이 말은 즉 현실 세계의 사건이 불연속적이든 연속적이든 상관없이 디지털은 어쨌든 불연속적이란 의미이다. 따라서 답은 ③이다.

---

07 다음 중 마지막 문장 다음에 올 만한 것으로 가능성이 가장 높은 것은 무엇인가?

① 이것이 의미하는 것은, 우리는 현실 세계의 일부가 되는 시스템이나 현실 세계와 유사한 시스템과 상호 작용을 가장 잘 할 수 있다는 것이다.

② 일상생활의 복잡성이 지속적으로 증가한 것이 엄청난 기회와 큰 슬픔을 가져온다.

③ 어느 정도의 속임수는 디지털을 통한 상호 작용을 원활하게 추구하는 데 있어 꼭 필요하다는 점에 주목하라.

④ 디지털이란 것이 지닌 진짜 문제는, 그것이 정확성에 대한 일종의 노예 상태에 빠진다는 것을 시사하며, 정확성은 인간의 자연스러운 활동과는 가장 거리가 먼 상태이다.

| 정답 | ①

| 해설 | 본문 마지막에서는 "인간의 인지 능력이 어떻게 작동하는지 이해하고 싶다면, 빛의 세계와 소리의 세계가 어떻게 작동하는지를 이해하는 것으로부터 시작하는 편이 도움이 되며, 왜냐하면 눈과 귀는 이러한 물리적 신호의 본질에 적합해지도록 진화했기 때문이다(If you want to understand how human perception works, it helps to start off by understanding how the world of light and sound works, because the eyes and ears have evolved to fit the nature of these physical signals)"라고 나와 있는데, 이 말은 즉 우리의 눈과 귀는 현실 세계에 존재하는 빛과 소리에 맞춰 진화했다는 내용이며, 이를 본문에 등장한 문구를 빌어 말하자면 "우리는 이 세계가 원하는 바에 부응하도록 진화되었다(We have evolved to match the world)"이다. 그런데 "이 세계"라 함은 "현실 세계"이기도 하고 "현실 세계"는 "아날로그를 유사함, 즉 현실 세계와 유사하다는 의미로 생각해 보자(Think of analog as meaning analogous : analogous to the real world)"라는 문장에서 유추할 수 있듯이 아날로그적인 세계이다. 따라서 우리는 이 세계가 원하는 바, 즉 아날로그적 현실 세계에 맞춰 진화를 했음을 유추할 수 있다. 따라서 이 다음에 와야 할 것은 마찬가지로 현실 세계에 관해 말하고 현실 세계와 유사한 것에 관해 말하는 것이어야 한다. 보기 중에서 이러한 조건에 부합하는 것은, "현실 세계의 일부가 되는 시스템이나 현실 세계와 유사한 시스템", 즉 아날로그적 시스템에 맞춰 상호 작용을 했고 그에 따라 진화를 이루었음을 말하는 ①이다.

| 어휘 |
misconception ⓝ 오해
this is the case 이것은 사실이다
analogous ⓐ 유사한
contemporary ⓐ 현대의, 동시대의 ⓝ 동시대인
perception ⓝ 인지

discrete ⓐ 별개의, 불연속적인
distinction ⓝ 차이, 구분
misconception ⓝ 오해
match ⓥ (필요에) 맞추다[부응하다]
fit ⓥ 적합하게 하다, 적응시키다

complexity ⓝ 복잡성, 복잡함

accuracy ⓝ 정확, 정확성

deception ⓝ 속임수

[08~09]

"적자생존"이라는 위험한 용어를 처음 사용한 사람은 Herbert Spencer였다. 그는 사회 진화론자로 알려진 많은 철학자들 중 하나였다. 그들은 빈곤층을 돕는 정책들이 무의미하다고 생각했다. 빈곤층은 분명 사회에 부적합하고 결국 주저앉게 되어 있기 때문이다. 100년간 진화론은 유난히 가혹하고 불편한 세계관, 게다가 명백히 옳지 않은, 최소한 전부 옳지는 않은 세계관과 관련 있었다. 사람들은 경쟁하지만 협력도 한다. 실패자를 밟는 것이 아니라 동정하고 도우려 한다. 인간은 Spencer의 생각처럼 개인 간의 경쟁이 아니라 사회적 상호 관계에 의존한다. 상호 작용은 때로는 적대적이고 가끔은 피비린내 나기도 한다. 그러나 많은 경우 상호 작용은 협력적이고, 그렇지 않은 경우에도 폭력보다는 교묘한 타협을 사용할 때가 더 많다. 이러한 관점은 위안이 된다. 경쟁과 협력이 함께할 수 있다는 것을 보여 주기 때문이다. Spencer의 또 다른 표현을 빌자면, 인간의 본성은 결코 치열하게 경쟁적이지 않다.

08 다음 중 사회 진화론자들의 주장이 <u>아닌</u> 것은?

① 사람들은 능력대로 보상받는다.

② 적자는 생존할 뿐 아니라 번영한다.

③ 부의 순위는 유전적으로 결정된다.

④ 사회는 인간이 진화하는 자연환경이다.

| 정답 | ④

| 해설 | 사회 진화론의 주장은 지문의 전반부의 '인간의 능력과 그에 따른 성취가 결정되어 있다는 결정론', 후반부의 '인간은 경쟁하는 존재라는 적자생존 논리'로 요약할 수 있다. ①, ③은 결정론, ②는 적자생존 논리를 반영하지만 ④는 사회 진화론의 주장과 무관하다.

09 다음 중 지문에 이어질 문장으로 가장 적절한 것은?

① 사회 진화론은 사회와 인간의 행동이 진화하는 방식을 규명해야 한다.

② Herbert Spencer야말로 사회 진화론의 폐해에 책임이 있는 인물이다.

③ 결과적으로, 사회 진화론의 현실 적용은 훨씬 더 성공적이었다.

④ 인간 본성은 오직 경쟁적이라는 사상에 기초한 사회는 곧 실패하게 되어 있다.

| 정답 | ④

| 해설 | 마지막 문장의 내용과 논리적 관계가 자연스러운 문장을 선택한다. 마지막 문장에서 인간 본성이 경쟁적이지 않다고 주장하고 있으므로, 경쟁을 강조하는 사회 진화론이나, 사회 진화론에 기초한 사회는 실패한다는 것을 유추할 수 있다. ①, ③은 사회 진화론의 실패와 무관한 내용이다. 지문의 주제는 사회 진화론의 오류와 실패이지 그 실패의 책임 소재가 아니므로 ②도 적절치 않다.

| 어휘 | **poisoned** ⓐ 독성의

band of 많은

survival of the fittest 적자생존

wasted ⓐ 낭비된, 헛된

measure ⑥ 조치, 정책
be doomed to ~할 운명이다
harsh ⑧ 거친, 가혹한
compassion ⑥ 동정
humanity ⑥ 인간, 인간성
confrontational ⑧ 대립하는
manipulative ⑧ 교묘하게 조종하는
reconciliation ⑥ 화해, 조화
red in tooth and claw 경쟁이 치열한

unfit ⑧ 부적합한, 무능한
sink ⑨ 가라앉다, 쇠퇴하다
collaborate ⑨ 협력하다
tread on ~을 밟아 뭉개다
interaction ⑥ 상호 작용
bloody ⑧ 유혈의, 피비린내 나는
comforting ⑧ 위안이 되는, 편안한
phrase ⑥ 구, 표현

[10~12] 한국외대 2012

해석

새해 결심 가운데 매년 첫 번째 자리를 차지할 가능성이 가장 높은 것은 "살을 빼는 것"이다. 살을 빼겠다는 결심이 계속 1위를 차지하는 원인은 아마도 대부분의 사람들은 실제로 살 빼는 것을 실패한다는 사실과 관련이 있을 것이다. 이러한 일이 벌어지는 이유는 단순하다. 자키식 교수에 따르면 섭취한 칼로리보다 더 많은 칼로리를 소비해야 한다는 사실은 모든 사람이 이해하고 있다. 하지만 "대부분의 사람들은 하루에 소비해야 할 칼로리가 얼마나 되는지를 알지 못한다." "사람들은 전혀 짐작도 못 하고 있다." 짐작하려면—아니면 최소한 정확한 측정치라도 얻으려면—실험실에 방문하거나 복잡한 과학 장비를 가동해야 했다. 과연 사람들이 이러한 접근법을 취할 수 있는 빈도가 과연 얼마나 될까?

하지만 지금은 신체 활동과 소비된 칼로리를 정확히 측정할 수 있게 고안된 간략화된 전자 모니터가 존재하며, 이 장비야말로 체중 감량을 위한 묘책이라 할 수 있다. 자키식 교수는 다음과 같이 말했다. "이런 모니터가 제 역할을 한다는 증거는 충분히 쌓여 있습니다." 모니터가 얼마나 잘 작동될지 여부는 모니터를 얼마나 많이 사용하느냐에 달려 있으며, 이는 결국 개인의 취향으로 귀결된다. 여러분은 놀이와 도전을 제공하는 것을 사용하고 싶은지, 그냥 숫자만 보고하는 것을 사용하고 싶은지, 아니면 눈에 잘 띄지 않는 것을 사용하고 싶은지? 우리는 가장 널리 사용되는 제품 가운데 네 개를 시험해 봤다.

10 본문에 따르면 살을 못 빼는 사람들이 많은 이유는 무엇인가?

① 살을 빼기 위한 기제를 이해하지 못한다.
② 하루에 얼마나 많은 칼로리를 소비하는지 알지 못한다.
③ 필요한 만큼 많은 칼로리를 소비하지 못한다.
④ 체중 문제에 관심을 보이지 않는다.

| 정답 | ②

| 해설 | 사람들은 섭취한 칼로리보다 많은 칼로리를 소비해야 살이 빠진다는 것은 알고 있지만, "대부분의 사람들은 하루에 소비해야 할 칼로리가 얼마나 되는지를 알지 못한다(most people don't know how many calories they burn a day)." 그리고 이를 측정하기도 힘들다. 이것이 사람들이 살을 빼는 데 어려움을 겪는 원인이다. 따라서 답은 ②이다.

11 다음 중 본문에서 언급되거나 암시된 것은 무엇인가?

① 의학 기술의 발달은 살을 못 빼는 사람들에게 어떤 문제가 있는지 진단하도록 돕는다.

② 소비된 칼로리를 측정하는 모니터의 효용성은 모니터의 사용 빈도에 달려 있다.

③ 사람들이 새해를 맞아 하기로 결심한 첫 번째 것은 살을 빼는 것이다.

④ 사람들은 체중 감량을 위한 기계 중에서 단순한 것보다 까다로운 것을 더 선호한다.

| 정답 | ②

| 해설 | "모니터가 얼마나 잘 작동될지 여부는 모니터를 얼마나 많이 사용하느냐에 달려 있다(How well a monitor works depends on how much it is used)." 따라서 답은 ②이다.

12 다음 중 본문 다음에 등장할 가능성이 가장 높은 것은 무엇인가?

① 살을 찌우기 위한 최고의 방법에 대한 소개

② 살을 빼기 위한 기제에 대한 설명

③ 살을 빼지 못하는 사람이 많은 이유에 대한 상세한 설명

④ 살을 빼기 위해 쓰이는 몇 가지 전자 모니터에 대한 설명

| 정답 | ④

| 해설 | 본문 마지막 문장에서 시중에서 널리 사용되는 네 종류의 전자 모니터에 관해 언급하겠다고 운을 띄웠으니, 본문 다음부터는 해당 모니터에 관해 서술하는 내용이 나와야 한다. 따라서 답은 ④이다.

| 어휘 | **persistence** ⓝ 지속됨

boil down to 결국 ~이 되다, ~으로 귀결되다

diagnose ⓥ 진단하다

description ⓝ 기술, 서술

silver bullet 묘책, 특효약

inconspicuous ⓐ 과시하지 않는, 눈에 잘 안 띄는

elaboration ⓝ 상세한 설명

[13~14] 인하대 2011

해석

비록 남부가 정치적으로는 미국의 일부이지만, 남부가 직면한 문제는 특유한 것이었고 남북 전쟁 이후 흑백 간의 투쟁은 본질적으로는 권력을 얻기 위한 투쟁으로서, 13개가 넘는 주에 걸쳐 수천만의 사람들의 생명이 걸린 투쟁이었다. 하지만 흑인들로부터 투표권을 막는 것만으로는 흑인들을 억제하기 충분치 않았다. 선거권 박탈 조치에는 평화(즉 완전한 복종)를 보장하기 위한 것뿐만 아니라 더 이상 (흑인들로 인한) 실질적인 위협이 부상하지 않도록 보장하기 위해 수많은 규칙, 금기, 처벌 등이 추가되어야만 했다. 만약 흑인들이 대부분의 백인 인구로부터 분리되어 (그들만의) 공동 영역에만 살았더라면, 이 같은 억압을 위한 프로그램은 그렇게 잔혹하고 폭력적인 행태를 취하지는 않았을 것이다. 하지만 이웃이었던 사람들끼리, 집이 인접한 사람들끼리, 농장의 경계가 인접한 사람들끼리 이 같은 전쟁은 벌어졌다. 그러므로 총과 선거권 박탈만으로는 이웃한 흑인들을 (자신들로부터) 거리를 두도록 하기엔 충분치 않았다.

13 윗글의 요지는 무엇인가?

① 남북 전쟁 이후 흑인과 백인은 함께 살았다.

② 흑인들을 떼어 놓기 위해 많은 조치가 취해졌다.

③ 흑인과 백인의 평화를 위해 총은 제거되어야 한다.

④ 선거권 박탈은 흑인에 대한 백인의 우위를 지키기 위한 좋은 방법이었다.

| 정답 | ②

| 해설 | 남북 전쟁 이후 미국 남부에서는 흑인과 백인을 분리하는 정책을 취했고 이는 흑인들의 복종을 통한 평화 보장을 위한 그리고 흑인들로 인한 위협으로부터 자신들을 보호하기 위한 조치였다. 이에 덧붙여 "총과 선거권 박탈만으로 는 충분치 않았다(Guns and disfranchisement … were not enough)"라는 문장을 통해 무력(= 총)과 선거권 박탈뿐 아니라 기타 여러 다양한 조치들이 흑인과 백인을 분리시키고자 취해졌다는 점을 유추할 수 있다. 따라서 ②를 답으로 볼 수 있다.

14 다음 중 본문의 바로 다음에 논의될 법한 사항이 <u>아닌</u> 것은?

① 무기로 흑인들을 폭력적으로 위협하기

② 흑인들을 사는 곳에서 백인들과 분리하기

③ 흑인들이 받는 교육의 양을 제한하기

④ 직종이나 직업에서 흑인의 참여를 제한하기

| 정답 | ①

| 해설 | "총과 선거권 박탈만으로는 충분치 않았다(Guns and disfranchisement … were not enough)"라는 문장에서 흑백 분리를 위해 무력과 선거권 박탈이 시행되었음을 알 수 있다. 따라서 '무력'에 해당하는 ①은 본문 바로 뒤에 나오면 중복이 되는 셈이므로 본문 바로 뒤에 등장하기엔 적절치 않다. 따라서 답은 ①이 된다.

| 어휘 |

peculiar ⓐ 특이한

range ⓥ (범위가) ~에 이르다

hold ~ in check ~을 억제하다

supplement ⓥ 보충하다, 추가하다

insure ⓥ ~을 보장하다

oppression ⓝ 억압

adjoin ⓥ 인접하다, 붙어 있다

reading ⓝ 읽을거리, 읽기 자료

residentially ⓓ 거주 지역에 관해

in essence 본질적으로는

ballot ⓝ 투표

disfranchisement ⓝ 선거권 박탈

panoply ⓝ 모음, 집합

submission ⓝ 복종

assume ⓥ (~한 양상을) 띠다, 취하다

turbulent ⓐ 사나운, 난기류의, 험난한

segregate ⓥ 분리하다, 차별하다

[15~16]

40년 전, 한 젊은 급진적 저널리스트의 선구적인 저서 *The Other America*는 "빈곤과의 전쟁"의 시발점이 되었다. 그 책에서 Michael Harrington은 당시 주장되던 풍요의 시대는 환상일 뿐이고, 미국의 번영 이면에는 수천만 명의 사람들이 오직 대대적인 정부 개입만이 해결할 수 있는 극심한 빈곤에 시달리고 있다고 경고했다. 오늘날의 신진 저널리스트들도 Harrington의 위업을 재연하기 위해, 현대 미국의 경제 시스템이 수백만 미국인들 에게는 효과가 없으며 오직 정부만이 그들을 빈곤으로부터 해방시킬 수 있다는 것을 알리기 위해 애쓰고 있다. 그러나 이 신진 저널리스트들은 Harrington보다 더 어려운 난관에 봉착해 있다. Harrington의 책이 출간된 이후로 범정부적으로 약 10조 달러가 빈곤 정책에 쓰였지만, 결과는 실망스러웠고 심지어 역효과도 있었기 때문이다. 지난 40년 동안, 수백만의 빈곤층은 이민자와 본토 미국인 모두 Harrington이 제시한 정부 정책에 의존하지 않고 빈곤에서 벗어났다.

15 지문에 따르면, 다음 중 사실이 <u>아닌</u> 것은?

① Michael Harrington은 빈곤에 대한 정부 개입을 요구했던 저널리스트이다.
② *The Other America*에 따르면, 많은 미국인들이 빈곤에 시달리고 있다.
③ 오늘날 저널리스트들은 Harrington의 주장에 영향을 받았다.
④ 정부의 빈곤 정책 덕분에 수백만 명이 빈곤에서 벗어났다.

| 정답 | ④

| 해설 | 마지막 문장에서, 수백만 명이 정부의 빈곤 정책의 도움 없이 빈곤에서 벗어났음을 알 수 있다. "millions of poor people, immigrants and native-born alike, have risen from poverty" 참조.

16 다음 중 이 단락 다음에 이어질 내용으로 적절한 것은?

① Harrington의 확고한 신념이 이뤄 낸 성취　②　Harrington의 주장에 대한 재평가
③ 미 정부 빈곤 정책의 성공 사례　④　미 정부의 노력이 경제에 미치는 긍정적 영향

| 정답 | ②

| 해설 | 이 글의 주제는 Harrington의 주장이 현실에서는 설득력이 없다는 것이다. "These new journalists face a tougher task than Harrington's" 참조. 따라서 다음 단락에서는 Harrington 주장의 문제점을 상술하는 '재평가, 재검토(reevaluation)'가 이어질 것이다.

| 어휘 | **radical** ⓐ 급진적인
pioneering ⓐ 선구적인
affluence ⓝ 풍요, 부유
surface ⓝ 표면
stuck ⓐ 갇힌
massive ⓐ 대규모의
strain to ~하기 위해 애쓰다
feat ⓝ 업적, 위업
disappointing ⓐ 실망스러운
immigrant ⓝ 이민자

ignite ⓥ 불붙이다, 촉발하다
proclaim ⓥ 선언(공표)하다
mirage ⓝ 신기루, 환상
prosperity ⓝ 번영
poverty ⓝ 빈곤
intervention ⓝ 개입
duplicate ⓥ 재연하다, 복제하다
convince ⓥ 설득하다
counterproductive ⓐ 역효과의
recourse ⓝ (도움을 얻기 위한) 의지, 부탁

해석

결과를 조종하는 또 다른 방법은 질문을 이용하는 것이다. 어휘는 긍정적, 부정적, 중립적 함의를 전달할 수 있다. 당신에게 "아름다운 Miss Piggy와 못생긴 Oscar 중 누구를 더 좋아하나요?"라고 묻는다면 어떨까? '아름다운'과 '못생긴'이라는 단어는 당신의 대답에 분명히 영향을 줄 것이다.

질문자의 외모도 응답자의 답변에 영향을 미친다. 정장을 입은 백인은 캐주얼 차림의 흑인과 똑같은 질문을 도심의 흑인 게토 지역 주민들이나 광고 회사의 백인 직원들에게 던져도 다른 답변을 얻어 낼 것이다.

또 다른 요인은 응답자의 기분이다. 기분은 의견에 영향을 준다. 현직 정치인이나 기존 정책에 대한 부정적인 답변이 필요할 때, 질문자는 흐리고 비 오는 날, 특히 월요일에 여론 조사를 실시한다. 사람들은 보통 이런 날 기분이 더 우울해지므로, 현재 상황에 만족하는 경향이 덜하기 때문이다.

대중을 쉽게 조종할 수 없다면, 정치 후보, 정부, 여타 공공, 민간 기관들이 매년 여기에 수십억 달러를 쓸 리도, 여론 조사가 그렇게 거대한 산업일 리도 없을 것이다. 하지만 그렇다면, 대중의 일부로서 당신과 내가 사회와 얼마나 일치하는지 보여 주어야 한다. 우리는 부적응자가 되고 싶지 않기 때문이다. 따라서 80퍼센트의 사람들이 X를 지지한다면, 당신과 나도 <u>역시 X를 지지할</u> 것이다.

17 다음 중 빈칸 (A)에 적절한 것은?

① 편안하다

② 역시 X를 지지하다

③ 불편하다

④ 여론 조사를 조작하다

⑤ 투표를 거부한다

| 정답 | ②

| 해설 | 사회(여론)와 일치한다는 것을 보여 주기 위해서는 다수의 의견에 동의해야 하므로 ②가 정답이다.

18 다음 중에서 사실이 아니거나 유추할 수 <u>없는</u> 것은?

① 민간 기관은 여론 조사에 많은 돈을 쓰지 않는다.

② 질문자는 일요일에 응답자로부터 더 호의적인 답변을 얻어 낼 것이다.

③ 정부 관료들은 유리한 결과를 얻기 위해 여론 조사를 조작한다.

④ 질문에 사용되는 단어들은 응답자의 답변에 영향을 미친다.

⑤ 응답자들은 질문자의 옷차림에 영향을 받는다.

| 정답 | ①

| 해설 | ①은 세 번째 단락의 "If the public were not so easily manipulated, candidates, governments and other public and private institutions would not be spending billions of dollars each year to do so."와 일치하지 않는다.

19 다음에 이어질 단락의 내용으로 가장 적절한 것은?

① 여론 조사의 테크놀로지를 이용하는 방법

② 표본을 추출하는 방법

③ 여론 조사의 중요성

④ 여론 조사를 조작하는 방법

⑤ 여론 조사를 분석하는 방법

| 정답 | ④

| 해설 | 지문은 대중의 의견이 외부적 요소에 쉽게 영향을 받으므로 여론은 쉽게 조종할 수 있다는 것이 요지이다. 글의 시작이 결과를 조종하는 또 다른 방법이 나오기 때문에, 앞의 단락에서는 여론 조사를 조작하는 방법이 상술되어야 논리적이다.

| 어휘 | **manipulate** ⓥ 조작하다, 조종하다

connotation ⓝ 함축, 숨의 의미

appearance ⓝ 외모

respondent ⓝ 응답자

ghetto ⓝ 빈민가

mood ⓝ 기분

conduct ⓥ 수행하다

be inclined to ~하기 쉽다

poll ⓝ 여론 조사

misfit ⓝ 부적응자

neutral ⓐ 중립적인

invariably ⓐ 변함없이

elicit ⓥ 유도하다, 도출하다

informally ⓐ 형식에 구애되지 않고

advertising agency 광고 회사

incumbent ⓐ 재임의, 현직의

fall on ~에 해당하다

candidate ⓝ 후보자

integrate ⓥ 통합하다

[20] 서강대 2017

해석

고등 교육 기관들은 의무 교육을 받을 나이가 지난 학생들을 돕는다. 미국에서는 고등 교육 기관에 소속된 학생들은 전통적·비전통적 학생들의 연령층이 매우 다양하며, 그들의 목표 또한 구체적인 직업 훈련에서부터 일반 교양 교육의 습득과 같은 일반적인 목표는 물론, 심화된 전문직 연구를 위한 특화된 준비에 이르기까지 다양하다. 이러한 각 학생 집단을 상대로 시행되는 이중 언어의 접근법의 역할과 범위는 상당히 다양하다. 미국의 성인들을 위한 일부 이중 언어 프로그램들은 정부의 특별 지원을 받을 자격이 있는 난민들과 같은 특수 계층의 사람들을 위해 단기간, 고도로 집중적인 직업 훈련을 제공하기 위해 개발되었다. 같은 모국어를 사용하는 영어 학습자들이 많은 곳에서는, 모국어 강의가 가능한 빨리 참가자들이 일자리를 찾을 수 있도록 돕는 것을 목표로 하는 비교적 단기의 프로그램의 일환으로 포함될 수 있다. 모국어 강의를 포함한 이런 이중 언어 프로그램들은 최근 이주민들이 가장 많이 정착한 지역에서 찾아볼 수 있다.

20 다음 중 본문의 내용 뒤에 이어질 내용으로 가장 적합한 것은?

① 하지만 그 기관들은 영어와 스페인어를 사용해 학위 프로그램을 제공한다는 점에서 실제로 이중 언어를 사용한다고 할수 있다.

② 모국어 강의를 포함한 이런 이중 언어 프로그램들은 최근 이주민들이 가장 많이 정착한 지역에서 찾아볼 수 있다.

③ 최근 한 연구 조사에 따르면, 대부분의 영어 학습자들이 학교를 영어 습득을 위해 정기적으로 이용하는 장소로 여긴다.

④ 학위를 위해 입학한 고등 교육 기관 소속 학생들은 제2언어로 진행하는 강의를 수강할 수 있을 것이다.

| 정답 | ②

| 해설 | 본문은 고등 교육 기관에서 사용하는 이중 언어 프로그램에 대해 설명하고 있다. 난민(refugee, immigrant)과 같은 특수 계층의 사람들을 위해 영어와 함께 모국어가 같이 교육되는 이중 언어 프로그램을 단기적으로 사용할 수 있다는 내용이다. 따라서 이런 이중 언어 프로그램이 최근 이민자들이 많이 정착한 지역에서 쉽게 찾아볼 수 있다는 ②의 내용으로 이어질 수 있다.

| 어휘 | **post-secondary institution** (대학과 같은) 고등 교육 기관

compulsory ⓐ 강제적인, 의무적인, 필수의   **range from A to B** 범위가 A에서 B까지 이어지다

occupational ⓐ 직업의, 직업과 관련된   **liberal education** 일반 교양 교육

bilingual ⓐ 2개 언어를 구사하는, 이중 언어의   **considerably** ⓐⓓ 상당히, 매우

short-term ⓐ 단기의, 단기적인   **vocational** ⓐ 직업과 관련된

refugee ⓝ 난민, 망명자   **qualify for** ~의 자격을 얻다

settlement ⓝ 정착   **immigrant** ⓝ 이민, 이주자

01 본문에서 유추할 수 있는 것은 무엇인가? 가톨릭대 2019

> 유능한 의사결정자들은 신중한 분석에만 의존하지 않는다. 그보다는 빠른 판단이나 직감을 통해 결론에 도달하는 방법인 직관 또한 활용한다. 직관에 의존하는 것은 마치 결정에 직면할 때 본능에 의존하는 것과 같다. 직관은 두뇌가 기억 속에 저장된 정보를 수집하고 이를 새로운 통찰력이나 해결책으로 포장할 경우 발생한다. 따라서 직관은 저장된 정보가 재조직된 또는 재포장된 것으로 여겨질 수 있다. 올바른 직관을 계발하는 데엔 매우 많은 정보가 저장되어야 하기 때문에 오랜 시간이 걸릴 수 있다.

① 직관은 지식이 시간이 흐름에 따라 축적되면서 함양될 수 있다.
② 직관은 근본적으로 타고난 또는 유전적으로 확정된 특성이다.
③ 결정을 내리는 데 있어 직관은 추론보다 더 중요한 요소이다.
④ 직관의 개념은 이해하고 설명하기 까다로운 것이다.

| 정답 | ①

| 해설 | "직관은 두뇌가 기억 속에 저장된 정보를 수집하고 이를 새로운 통찰력이나 해결책으로 포장할 경우 발생한다"는 말은 즉 직관은 머릿속에 정보와 지식이 쌓이고, 이렇게 쌓인 지식이 새로운 통찰력이나 해결책의 형태로 드러나면서 생성된다는 의미이다. 이는 보기 ①의 내용과 통하며, 따라서 답은 ①이다.

| 어휘 | **effective** ⓐ 유능한, 유력한
　　　 gut feeling 직감, 제육감
　　　 cultivate ⓥ 계발하다, 함양하다
　　　 inborn ⓐ 타고난, 선천적인
　　　 trait ⓝ 특성

　　　 intuition ⓝ 직감, 직관
　　　 develop ⓥ (지능 따위를) 계발(啓發)하다
　　　 essentially ⓐⓓ 근본적으로, 기본적으로
　　　 determined ⓐ 결정한, 확정한
　　　 reasoning ⓝ 추리, 추론

02 다음 중 본문에서 유추할 수 <u>없는</u> 것은 무엇인가?

> 외국인들이 계속 들어오는 것을 경비병들이 꺼려 하는 것은 이해가 될 만한 일이다. 한리(Hanle)에 위치한 국영 천문대로 향하는 얼마 안 되는 과학자들을 제외하면 대부분의 서양인들은 1962년에 있은 인도-중국 전쟁의 종결 이후 접근이 금지되고 있다. 중국의 첩자가 국경을 넘어 현재 분쟁 중인 국경 지대로부터 고작 12마일 떨어진 곳에 위치한 한리로 슬며시 들어올 수 있겠다는 두려움 때문에 인도 정부는 그 지역을 출입 금지 지역으로 선포했다.

① 한리는 인도 영토이다.
② 한리는 국경 부근에 위치해 있다.
③ 한리 사람들은 중국인들을 좋아하지 않는다.
④ 한리에는 서양인들이 많이 머물러 있다.
⑤ 한리에는 국영 천문대가 있다.

| 정답 | ④

| 해설 | "한리(Hanle)에 위치한 국영 천문대로 향하는 얼마 안 되는 과학자들을 제외하면 대부분의 서양인들은 1962년에 있은 인도-중국 전쟁의 종결 이후 접근이 금지되고 있다(Other than a handful of scientists bound for the government-run observatory in Hanle, most Westerners have been denied access since the end of the Chinese-Indian war of 1962)." 따라서 답은 ④이다.

| 어휘 | **reluctance** ⓝ 꺼려 함, 못마땅해함   **bound for** ~행의, ~로 향하는
observatory ⓝ 천문대, 관측소   **slip** ⓥ 슬며시 가다[오다]
disputed ⓐ 분쟁 중인   **off limits** 출입 금지의

03 다음 본문에 따르면, 사막에서의 삶에 적응하는 예로 유추할 수 있는 것은 무엇인가?

사막에서의 삶은 흥미로우면서도 다양하다. 비록 사막이 음식과 물을 찾기가 쉽지 않아서 매우 고된 장소이기는 하지만, 많은 동물이 사막에 살고 있다. 사막에는 물이 거의 없기 때문에 사막의 동물들은 이에 적응해 왔다. 낙타는 물을 마시지 않고도 며칠간 생존할 수 있다. 다른 동물들은 자신들이 섭취하는 곤충과 식물로부터 수분을 얻는다. 사막의 극단적인 기온 역시 사막에서의 삶을 힘겹게 만들 수 있다. 많은 사막의 포유류는 열과 냉기가 못 들어오게 하기 위해 두꺼운 가죽을 가지고 있다. 몇몇 사막의 동물은 야행성으로, 낮에는 자고 공기가 시원한 때인 밤에 사냥한다. 모든 사막이 다 똑같아 보이긴 해도, 실은 거기 사는 동물들만큼이나 다양하다.

① 딱정벌레의 육중한 껍질
② 포식자를 쫓아 버리는 코브라의 (우산 모양의) 목
③ 먹이를 붙잡기 위한 몽구스의 빠른 속도
④ 몸을 식히기 위해 열을 분출할 수 있도록 만들어진 고슴도치의 긴 귀

| 정답 | ④

| 해설 | 본문은 동물들이 사막에서 살아남기 위해 두 가지 전략을 채택했음을 설명하고 있다. "낙타는 물을 마시지 않고도 며칠간 생존할 수 있다. 다른 동물들은 자신들이 섭취하는 곤충과 식물로부터 수분을 얻는다.(Camels can survive for days without drinking. Other animals get their water from the insects and plants they eat.)"라 는 문장에서 우리는 사막의 동물이 물 없이도 적응하는 방법을 알 수 있다. 그리고 "많은 사막의 포유류는 열과 냉기가 못 들어오게 하기 위해 두꺼운 가죽을 가지고 있다. 몇몇 사막의 동물은 야행성으로, 낮에는 자고 공기가 시원한 때인 밤에 사냥한다.(Many desert mammals have thick fur to keep out the heat and the cold. Some desert animals are nocturnal, sleeping by day and hunting by night, when the air is cooler.)"라는 문장을 통해 우리는 사막의 동물이 사막의 혹독한 기온에 적응하는 방법을 알 수 있다. 그런데 보기 ①, ②, ③은 이 두 방법과는 별 관련이 없으므로 답이 될 수 없고, ④는 기온을 극복하는 방안의 예로 볼 수 있다. 따라서 답은 ④가 된다.

| 어휘 | **vary** ⓥ 다양하다   **punishing** ⓐ 고된, 지치게 하는
adapt ⓥ 적응시키다   **mammal** ⓝ 포유류, 포유동물
keep out 못 들어오게 하다   **nocturnal** ⓐ 야행성의
inhabit ⓥ ~에 거주하다, 살다   **scare off** 겁을 먹게 하다

실전 문제

01	①	02	①	03	④	04	①	05	③	06	④	07	②	08	③	09	④	10	①
11	②	12	①	13	④	14	②	15	④	16	①	17	③	18	④	19	③	20	④
21	②	22	④	23	②	24	④	25	③	26	②	27	④	28	③	29	②	30	④
31	①	32	④	33	②	34	④	35	②	36	③	37	④	38	④	39	①	40	④
41	①	42	②	43	②	44	③	45	④												

[01~02] 건국대 2015

해석

어느 누구도 매체 그 자체가 공격성을 유발한다고는 생각하지 않는다. 하지만 미시건대학(University of Michigan) 소속의 리어나르도 에론(Leonardo Eron)과 로웰 후스만(Rowell Huesmann)은 3학년 아이들을 성년에 이르기까지 추적 관찰한 22년간의 연구를 통해, 나중에 (성인이 되어) 표출시키는 공격성에 대한 가장 뛰어난 예측인자는, 가난·성적·편부모 가정·실제 폭력에의 노출보다는, TV를 통해 보여지는 온갖 참상을 어린 시절에 많이 접했을지 여부임을 발견했다. 에론은 다음과 같이 말했다. "물론 모든 청소년이 영향을 받는 것은 아닙니다. 폐암에 걸린 사람 모두가 담배를 피는 것은 아니며, 담배를 피는 사람 모두가 폐암에 걸리는 것은 아닌 것과 마찬가지입니다. 하지만 담배 업계 관계자를 제외하면 흡연이 폐암을 유발한다는 것을 부인하는 사람은 없을 것입니다." 가장 효과적인 연구 가운데 상당 부분은 아이들을 대상으로 수행되었으며, 이는 아이들이 가장 영향을 받기 쉬운 것으로 여겨지기 때문이다. 센터월(Centerwall)이 언급한 바와 같이 "나중에 청소년이나 어른이 되었을 때 매체에 대한 노출 수준에 차이를 주더라도 어떤 추가적인 효과가 나지는 않았습니다." 1960년대 초에 스탠포드대학의 앨버트 밴두러(Albert Bandura)는 아이들이 부모로부터 뿐만 아니라 TV를 통해서도 행동을 배운다는 것을 최초로 보여 주었다. 심리학자들은 TV에 등장하는 폭력이 아이들에게 어떻게 영향을 미치는지를 설명하기 위해 다음의 네 가지 학습 이론을 활용했다. 1) 아이들은 TV에서 본 것을 흉내 내며 특히 흉내 낸 행동이 보상을 받을 경우 더욱 그러하다. 2) TV 속에 폭력이 빈번하게 등장하는 것을 보고 폭력을 정상적인 것으로 받아들인다. 3) 실제 인간의 고통에 무감각하게 된다. 4) 아이들은 TV 속에 등장하는 이미지에 자극을 받으며, 이는 폭력적 반응을 촉발시킨다.

01 다음 중 위 본문에서 유추할 수 있는 것은 무엇인가?

① 매체는 모방 범죄를 야기할 수 있다.
② 흡연은 언제나 폐암을 유발한다.
③ 어린 시절에 겪은 가난은 나중에 등장하는 공격성과 관련하여 가장 중요한 역할을 한다.
④ 아이는 TV에 등장하는 폭력에 노출되면서 다른 사람들의 고통에 민감하게 된다.
⑤ 밴두러는 아이는 부모로부터 폭력적인 행동을 배우지 않는다고 생각한다.

| 정답 | ①

| 해설 | 본문에 따르면 아이들이 나중에 성년이 되어 공격성을 표출할 경우 이를 예측할 수 있는 예측 인자로 가장 적합한 것은 "TV를 통해 보여지는 온갖 참상을 어린 시절에 많이 접했을지 여부(a heavy childhood diet of TV carnage)"이다. 그리고 본문 마지막 부분에 제시된 네 가지 학습 이론을 보면, 아이들은 TV 속 폭력을 흉내, 즉 모방하며, 폭력을 정상적인 것으로 여기고, 그러면서도 폭력의 피해자가 되는 사람들의 고통에 둔감해지고, TV 속 이미지에 자극을 받아 폭력적 반응을 보이게 됨을 알 수 있다. 즉 TV 같은 매체가 폭력을 모방하면서 결국 범죄를 야기하게 되는 것이다. 따라서 답은 ①이다.

---

02 빈칸에 가장 알맞은 것을 고르시오.

① 영향을 받는   ② 미숙한

③ 반항적인   ④ 영향력 있는

⑤ 공격적인

| 정답 | ①

| 해설 | "나중에 청소년이나 어른이 되었을 때 매체에 대한 노출 수준에 차이를 주더라도 어떤 추가적인 효과가 나지는 않았습니다 (Later variations in exposure, in adolescence and adulthood, do not exert any additional effect)"라는 말은, 역으로 말하면 청소년이나 어른이 아니라 더 어렸을 때는 폭력 노출 수준에 차이를 줄 경우 효과가 크게 나타난다는 의미이다. 이 말은, 즉 어린아이들은 폭력에 노출될 경우 영향을 쉽게 받는다는 소리이다. 따라서 답은 ①이다.

| 어휘 | aggression ⓝ 공격성   predictor ⓝ 예측 변수, 예측 인자

carnage ⓝ 대학살, 참상

diet ⓝ 많은 양, (오락·독서 등에서의) 습관적인[지긋지긋한] 것

susceptible @ ~에 민감한, ~에 영향받기 쉬운   variation ⓝ 차이, 변화

exert ⓥ (권력·영향력을) 가하다[행사하다]   imitate ⓥ 모방하다, 흉내 내다

frequency ⓝ 빈도, 빈발   desensitize ⓥ 둔감하게 만들다, 무감하게 만들다

arouse ⓥ 자극하다, 자아내다   trigger ⓥ 촉발시키다, 촉진시키다

copycat crime 모방 범죄   rebellious @ 반항적인

[03~05] 숙명여대 2017

해석

의학적 사용에서 "위약(placebo)"은 치료되는 질병에 특정한 물리적 혹은 화학적 작용은 없지만, 순수한 물리적 메커니즘이라기보다는 심리적 메커니즘에 의해 증상에 영향을 주는 치료법이다. 윤리학자들은 위약이 의사에 의한 부분적 혹은 완전한 기만을 필연적으로 포함한다고 믿는다. 왜냐하면, 환자가 그 치료법이 특정한 효과를 가지고 있다고 믿는 것이 허용되기 때문이다. 그들은 위약이 약리 작용을 보이지 않는 것이 결코 아닌(엄격한 약리학적 관점을 제외하고) 의학계에 알려진 가장 강력한 약제 중 하나란 사실을 알지 못하는 것 같다. 위약은 약한 사람에게 힘을 주거나 혹은 강한 사람을 약하게 만들 수 있으며, 수면과 수유, 성적 패턴을 변화시킬 수 있으며, 광범위한 증상을 없애거나 유도할 수 있으며, 매우 강력한 약물의 효과를 모방하거나 없앨 수도 있다. 위약은 심지어 대부분 기관의 기능을 바꿀 수도 있다.

03 다음 중 본문을 통해 추론할 수 있는 것이 <u>아닌</u> 것은?

① "위약"은 환자의 심리에 근거한 치료법이다.

② 어떤 사람들은 "위약"이 거짓말이기 때문에 잘못된 것이라고 믿는다.

③ "위약"은 몇몇 환자에게 실제로 효과적인 방법이다.

④ "위약"은 환자의 물리적 상태에 영향을 주지 않는다.

⑤ 본문의 필자는 "위약"의 사용을 지지한다.

| 정답 | ④

| 해설 | ① 본문의 "given to affect symptoms by a psychologic mechanism"을 통해 위약은 환자의 심리에 근거한 치료법임을 알 수 있다. ② "Ethicists believe that placebos necessarily involve a partial or complete deception by the doctor"를 통해 윤리학자들은 위약이 의사들의 속임수라고 말한다. ③ 위약이 실제 효과가 있다는 것은 "among the most powerful agents known to medicine"에서 필자가 주장하는 부분이다. ⑤ 본문 후반부 내용을 통해 필자는 위약을 긍정적으로 생각한다는 것을 알 수 있다. 정답은 ④로, 위약은 물리적 작용에 의한 것은 아니지만 환자의 물리적 상태에 실제로 영향을 준다. 본문 후반의 "strengthen the weak or paralyze the strong ..." 이하의 내용을 통해 알 수 있다.

04 다음 중 밑줄 친 'inert'를 가장 잘 대체할 수 있는 것은?

① 게으른, 서서히 진행하는   ② 정서적인, 감정에 관한

③ 활기를 되찾게 된   ④ 유해한

⑤ 낙관적인

| 정답 | ①

| 해설 | inert는 '기력이 없는, 둔한, 비활성의, 약리 작용을 보이지 않는' 등의 뜻으로 'never'에 해당하는 'far from'과 함께 사용되어 위약이 약리 작용이 없는 것이 결코 아니라고 설명하고 있다. 즉 위약은 강력한 약이라고 다시 반복한다. 따라서 위약은 '치유가 더디거나 게으른' 약이 결코 아니라는 ① indolent가 동의어로 가장 적합하다.

05 다음 중 빈칸에 올 수 있는 가장 적합한 것은?

① 그러나   ② 그리고   ③ 왜냐하면

④ ~에도 불구하고   ⑤ ~하는 한

| 정답 | ③

| 해설 | 위약은 의사들이 행하는 일종의 사기(deception)라고 윤리학자들이 생각한다는 내용이 빈칸 앞에 위치하며, 빈칸 뒤의 내용은 윤리학자들이 그렇게 생각하는 이유에 대한 설명이므로, 정답은 ③ since가 적합하다.

| 어휘 |

placebo ⓝ 위약

psychologic ⓐ 심리의

partial ⓐ 부분인; 편파적인

unaware ⓐ 알지 못하는, 모르는

inert ⓐ 기력이 없는, 둔한; 비활성[불활성]의, 약리 작용을 보이지 않는

rigid ⓐ 엄격한, 융통성 없는, 단단한

agent ⓝ (특정한 효과·목적을 위해 쓰이는) 물질

induce ⓥ 설득하여 ~하게 하다; 유발[초래]하다

abolish ⓥ 폐지하다, 철폐하다

organ ⓝ (생물의) 기관

indolent ⓐ 게으른, 나태한; (질병이) 서서히 진행하는, 치유가 더딘

affective ⓐ 정서적인, 감정에 관한

detrimental ⓐ 해로운, 유해한

symptom ⓝ 징후, 증상

ethicist ⓝ 윤리학자, 도덕가

deception ⓝ 사기, 속임수

pharmacological ⓐ 약학의

paralyze ⓥ 마비시키다

mimic ⓥ 흉내 내다

alter ⓥ 바꾸다, 변경하다

rejuvenated ⓐ 활기를 되찾게 된, 다시 젊어 보이게 된

optimistic ⓐ 낙관적인

해석

구두 사회에서 매일 이루어지는 말뿐만 아니라 구전을 통한 이야기는 운율을 활용하는 경향이 있고, 이는 기억의 심리에 호소한다. 시의 운율은 운율 없는 산문보다 더 쉽게 기억된다. 마찬가지로 여러분은 수년 동안 듣거나 말한 적이 없더라도 어렸을 때 알던 간단한 시나 운문은 기억해 낼 수 있다. 이와 꼭 마찬가지로 여러분은 어렸을 때 교과서에서 읽은 것은 대부분 잊어버리며, 특히 생각을 전하기 위해 사용된 특정 표현은 잊어버린다. 노래 가사는 <u>놀랄 만큼 쉽게</u> 기억되고 떠오른다. 운율이 맞는 패턴은 더 기억이 쉽게 되기 때문에, 구전을 통한 이야기에서는 당연히 이 <u>두 방법</u>을 도입한다.

---

06 다음 중 본문에서 유추할 수 있는 것은 무엇인가?

① 모든 사람들은 과거 읽은 책을 기억해 낼 수 있다.
② 독서는 기억력을 빠르게 증가시킨다.
③ 청각 전통은 구전보다 더 중요하게 취급되어야 한다.
④ 노래 가사는 효과적으로 기억이 가능하다.

| 정답 | ④

| 해설 | "시의 운율은 운율 없는 산문보다 더 쉽게 기억된다(The rhymes and rhythms of poetry are remembered more easily than non-rhythmic prose)"는 점과 "운율이 맞는 패턴은 더 기억이 쉽게 된다(rhythmic, rhyming patterns are recalled more easily)"는 점에서, 노래처럼 운율이 있는 것이 없는 것에 비해 더욱 효과적으로 기억이 될 것임은 쉽게 유추할 수 있다. 따라서 답은 ④가 된다. ①과 ②의 경우, 우리는 "어렸을 때 교과서에서 읽은 것은 대부분 잊어버리기(have forgotten much of what you read in an earlier textbooks)" 때문에 ①에서 말하는 것처럼 과거 읽은 책을 쉽게 기억할 리도 없고 어렸을 때 읽은 책이 기억이 나지 않는 것이 현실인데 ②에서 말하는 것처럼 기억력을 빠르게 증가시킨다고 말할 수도 없을 것이다. 따라서 둘 다 답이 될 수 없다. ③의 경우, 본문에는 기억이 잘 되고 안 되고의 문제만 있을 뿐 중요성에 관한 내용은 없으므로 답으로 볼 수 없다.

---

07 다음 중 빈칸 ㉠에 가장 알맞은 것은 무엇인가?

① 매우 힘들게
② 놀랄 만큼 쉽게
③ 아주 짧은 시간 동안
④ 그것들이 좋도록

| 정답 | ②

| 해설 | 글에 운율이 섞이면 더 쉽고 효과적으로 기억이 가능하다. 따라서 빈칸에 들어가기 가장 알맞은 것은 ②뿐이다.

---

08 다음 중 ㉡의 '두 방법'과 의미가 가장 가까운 것은 무엇인가?

① 고등학교와 대학교
② 소설과 시
③ 운율
④ 구전과 청각 전통

| 정답 | ③

| 해설 | "운율이 맞는 패턴은 더 기억이 쉽게 되기 때문에(Since rhythmic, rhyming patterns are recalled more easily)" 당연히 구전을 통한 이야기에서는 운율을 도입했을 것이다. 따라서 답은 ③이 된다.

| 어휘 | **oral-tradition** ⓝ 구전

speech ⓝ 말

rhymes and rhythms 운율

prose ⓝ 산문

language ⓝ 표현, 언어

not surprisingly 당연히

for one's own good ~를 위해, ~좋으라고

narrative ⓝ 이야기

oral society 구두 사회

rhythmic ⓐ 운율이 맞는

rhyme ⓝ 운문

recall ⓥ 상기하다

recollect ⓥ 기억해 내다

[09~11] 동국대 2021

해석

직접 이룬 것은 과장하고 남에게 빚을 진 것은 부인하는 미국인들의 경향은, 식민지인들이 "사명을 띠고 황야로" 진출하여 무에서 풍요의 땅을 건설했다는 신화를 통해 성문화되어 있다. 하지만 실제로는 미국 동부의 식민지 주민들을 놀라게 할 만큼 사냥감과 식물 및 산딸기류 열매가 동부에 풍성하게 집중되었던 것은 "자연적인" 일이 아니었고, 아메리카 원주민들의 공동 농업 및 집단적 토지 활용 패턴을 통해 생성된 것이었다. 미국 북서부에서 초기 정착민들이 발견한 더글라스퍼 숲과 수많은 사슴 및 엘크 떼가 존재할 수 있었던 것은, 아메리카 원주민들에게 숲을 태우는 관행이 있었고 그 결과 산출량이 유지되는 숲의 천이 현상이 발생하여 이들 생물자원을 고갈시키는 일 없이 최대한 활용할 수 있었기 때문이다.

09 다음 중 빈칸 (A)에 가장 알맞은 것은 무엇인가?

① 도움이 되는

② 문명화된

③ 공격적인

④ 자연적인

| 정답 | ④

| 해설 | 빈칸 뒤를 보면, 식민지 사람들이 누린 풍족한 자연은 미리 살고 있던 원주민들의 덕분이었다. 즉 "자연적인" 것이 아니고 인위적인 것이었다. 따라서 답은 ④이다.

10 다음 중 빈칸 (B)에 가장 알맞은 것은 무엇인가?

① 최대화하다

② 완전히 파괴하다

③ 악화시키다

④ 파괴하다

| 정답 | ①

| 해설 | 생물자원을 고갈시키지 않는 한도 내에서 활용할 경우, 최선의 결과는 고갈되지 않는 한 "최대한" 활용하는 것일 것이다. 그 외 나머지 보기는 모두 자연에 악영향을 끼치는 것들이다. 따라서 답은 ①이다.

11 다음 중 본문에서 유추할 수 있는 것은 무엇인가?

① 미국 동부의 식민지 주민들은 유럽에서 사슴과 엘크를 데려왔다.

② 아메리카 원주민들은 경작 수단으로 숲을 태웠다.

③ 아메리카 원주민들은 각자 땅을 경작하는 것을 선호했다.

④ 미국인들은 자신들의 남의 도움을 통해 많은 것을 이룰 수 있었다고 굳게 믿는다.

| 정답 | ②

| 해설 | "아메리카 원주민들에게 숲을 태우는 관행이 있었고"는 ②의 근거가 되며, 따라서 답은 ②이다. ①은 본문에 언급되지 않은 내용이다. "아메리카 원주민들의 공동 농업 및 집단적 토지 활용 패턴을 통해 생성된 것이었다"는 ③의 내용과 반대이다. "직접 이룬 것은 과장하고 남에게 빚을 진 것은 부인하는 미국인들의 경향"은 ④의 내용과 반대이다.

| 어휘 |

overestimate ⓥ 과대평가하다

codify ⓥ 성문화하다; 체계적으로 정리하다

abundant ⓐ 풍부한

game ⓝ 사냥감

astonish ⓥ 깜짝[크게] 놀라게 하다

collective ⓐ 집단의, 단체의

sustained-yield ⓐ 수확량 유지의 (수확시에 줄어든 삼림·물고기 등의 생물 자원이 다음 수확 전에 불어나도록 관리하기)

succession ⓝ 천이 (어떤 생물 군락이 환경의 변화에 따라 새로운 식물 군락으로 변해가는 과정)

exhaust ⓥ 고갈시키다

devastate ⓥ 완전히 파괴하다

owe A to B A는 B 덕분이다, A를 B에 빚지다

on an errand 사명을 띤

concentration ⓝ 집중, 한곳에 모임

berry ⓝ 산딸기류 열매, −베리

husbandry ⓝ 농사

Douglas fir 미송, 더글라스퍼

civilized ⓐ 문명화된, 개화된

exacerbate ⓥ 악화시키다

[12~13]

> **해석**
>
> 수면은 당신이 생각하는 것보다 더 건강에 영향을 준다. 수면 시간이 적을수록 체질량 지수는 높아지는 경향이 있다. 연구에 따르면, 5시간 수면하는 사람들은 8시간 수면하는 사람들에 비해 체내 ghrelin(배고픔을 더 느끼게 하는 호르몬) 수치가 15퍼센트 높았고 leptin(배고픔을 억제하는 호르몬) 수치는 15퍼센트 낮았다. 게다가 수면은 뇌에 새로운 기억이 저장되는 데 중요한 역할을 한다. 피아노 음계 같은 복잡한 손가락 동작을 배운 한 실험의 피실험자들은 12시간 깨어 있던 경우보다 12시간 수면한 경우에 동작을 더 잘 기억해 냈다. 또한 숙면은 면역계를 강화한다. 수면 중 분비되는 melatonin은 항암 효과가 있는 항산화제이다. 야간 교대 근로자들은 유방암 발생률이 최대 70% 높을 수 있다. <u>수면 중에는 예방 물질 외에도 위벽 손상을 치료하는 물질이 분비된다.</u> 마지막으로, 어린 아이들은 더 많이 자야 한다. 단지 10대이기 때문에 생긴다는 우울증과 낮은 자존감은 사실 수면 부족과 관련 있다. 잠이 부족한 아이들은 사춘기에 음주와 마약을 할 가능성이 2배 더 높다.

---

12 다음 중 잠을 더 자야 하는 이유로 지문에 언급되지 않은 것은?

① 잠을 더 자면 체중이 감소한다.

② 잠을 더 자면 기억력이 좋아진다.

③ 잠을 더 자면 항암 효과가 있다.

④ 잠을 더 자면 노화를 늦출 수 있다.

⑤ 잠을 더 자면 정신을 건강하게 유지할 수 있다.

| 정답 | ④

| 해설 | 지문은 잠이 건강에 미치는 여러 가지 영향을 체중, 기억력, 면역력, 정신 건강 순으로 예시하고 있다. 직접 언급되지 않은 것은 노화와의 관계이므로 보기 ④가 정답이다. 기억력이 좋아지고 면역계가 향상되는 것을 노화 예방으로 비약하지 않도록 주의하자.

---

13 [I], [II], [III], [IV], [V] 중 다음 문장으로 대체할 수 있는 것은?

> 수면 중에는 예방 물질뿐 아니라 위벽 손상을 복구하는 물질도 분비된다.

① [I]　　　　　② [II]　　　　　③ [III]
④ [IV]　　　　　⑤ [V]

| 정답 | ③

| 해설 | 주어진 문장은 병과 관계된 내용이므로 수면이 면역계에 미치는 영향에 속하는 문장임을 알 수 있다. 또한 "in addition to preventive chemical"에서 앞 문장에 질병을 예방하는 물질이 예시되었음을 알 수 있다. 따라서 암을 예방하는 항산화 물질이 예시된 후 위치해야 논리적이다.

| 어휘 |

body mass index 체질량 지수	**piano scale** 음계
wakefulness ⓝ 각성, 잠들지 않은 상태	**boost** ⓥ 강화하다, 북돋다
immune system 면역계	**antioxidant** ⓝ 항산화제
night-shift ⓝ 야간 교대(근무)	**up to** ~ 최고 ~까지
breast cancer 유방암	**chemical** ⓝ 화학 물질
repair ⓥ 치료하다, 수리하다	**lining** ⓝ (인체 부위의) 내벽, 안감
secret ⓥ 분비하다	**depression** ⓝ 우울증
self-esteem ⓝ 자존감	**correlate with** ~와 상관 관계가 있다
sleep shortage 수면 부족	**adolescence** ⓝ 사춘기

[14~15] 한양대 2012

해석

사전은 승리를 "다른 사람과의 경쟁에서 이기고 성취의 대가로 상이나 보상을 받는 것"으로 정의한다. 하지만 내 삶에 있어 가장 의미 있는 승리는 다른 사람을 이긴 것이 아니었고 나는 아직도 성과에 대한 상이 없음에도 승리를 거뒀던 것을 기억한다.

내가 경험한 최초의 승리는 초등학교 체육 시간 때였다. 우리는 거의 매일 준비 운동으로 팔굽혀펴기와 스쿼트 스러스트를 한 다음에 이어달리기를 해야 했다. 비록 난 어렸을 때 천식을 앓고 있어도 경주에서 많이 이겼다. 몇 분 동안 가슴이 타는 듯 심하게 아팠지만 자랑스러운 기분이 들 만큼 뛸 만한 가치가 있었고, 다른 사람을 이겼기 때문이거나 상을 받았기 때문이 아니라 내가 나의 장애를 극복했기 때문에 자랑스러웠다.

나는 내가 지금 대학에 다니고 있는 사실을 승리로 여긴다. 대학에 가기 위해 나는 바깥과 내면의 많은 장애물을 극복해야 했다. 대학은 돈이 들고 나는 돈이 많이 없었다. 대학은 시간이 소요되고, 돌봐야 할 어린 아들이 있는 상황에서는 내겐 시간 또한 많이 없었다. 하지만 나는 이런 장애물을 극복했고 자신감의 부족이라는 더 큰 장애물도 극복했다. 나는 "포기하지 않아"라고 스스로에게 계속 말해야 했다. 그리고 이제 승리한 내가 여기 있다.

14 윗글의 제목으로 가장 알맞은 것을 고르시오.

① 천식을 극복하는 법
② 승리란 진실로 무엇을 의미하는가
③ 승리의 마법과 같은 힘
④ 대학에서 여러 가지 일들에 동시에 대처하기

| 정답 | ②

| 해설 | 저자는 스스로의 장애와 자신감 부족 같은 것을 극복하는 자신과의 싸움에서 승리를 거두었다. 즉 본문은 사전에 등장하는 "다른 사람과의 경쟁에서 이기는 것(achieving victory over others in a competition)"이나 "성취의 대가로 상이나 보상을 받는 것(receiving a prize or reward for achievement)"이 아닌 진정한 승리가 무엇인지에 관해 말하고 있다. 따라서 답은 ② 이다.

15 글쓴이의 발언이라고 추론할 수 <u>없는</u> 것을 고르시오.

① 나는 너무 쉽게 얻어지는 것을 신뢰하지 않는다.
② 절대 포기하지 않으면 자립을 이룰 수 있다.
③ 나는 다른 사람이 걸은 길보다 걷지 않은 길을 가겠다.
④ 나는 경쟁에서 강력한 도전자가 있을 때 거둔 승리를 더 좋아한다.

| 정답 | ④

| 해설 | 저자는 남과의 경쟁에서 이기는 것을 중시한 사람이 아니라서 ④는 추론할 수 없다.

| 어휘 | **achievement** ⓝ 성취
preparatory ⓐ 준비를 위한
squat thrust 두 손을 바닥에 짚고 두 다리를 쪼그렸다 폈다 하는 운동
asthma ⓝ 천식
obstacle ⓝ 장애물
self-reliance ⓝ 자립
contender ⓝ 도전자, 경쟁자

performance ⓝ 실적, 성과
push-up ⓝ 팔굽혀펴기
surmount ⓥ 극복하다
juggle ⓥ (두 가지 이상의 일을) 동시에 하다
tread ⓥ 발을 디디다, 걷다

인간은 영장류 가운데에서 해부학적으로 분류되며, 영장류 목은 유인원과 원숭이 및 여우원숭이를 포함한다. 현재 멸종되지 않은 수백의 영장류 종 가운데 인간만이 털이 없다. 털이 없는 포유류의 등장을 야기한 서식지의 유형으로는 두 가지가 있는데, 하나는 지하 서식지이며 다른 하나는 습한 서식지이다. 털이 없는 벌거숭이뻐드렁니쥐(Somalian mole rat)는 결코 지상으로 나가는 일이 없는 종이다. 털이 거의 또는 아예 나지 않는 인간 이외의 포유류는 모두가 고래나 돌고래처럼 헤엄을 치거나 하마와 돼지 및 맥처럼 진흙 속을 뒹군다. 코뿔소와 코끼리는 아프리카 대륙이 건조해진 시기부터 지상에서 발견되었지만, 과거에는 물기 많은 곳에서 살았던 흔적을 품고 있으며 기회만 되면 진흙이나 물에서 뒹군다.

인간의 털이 없어진 이유는 사바나에서 과열을 방지하기 위함이라는 설이 있다. 하지만 이러한 전략에 의지하는 포유동물이 달리 존재하지는 않는다. 머리카락으로 머리를 덮은 것이 태양열을 막는 역할을 했다. 때문에 사막에 거주하는 낙타조차도 털을 유지하고 있다. 또 다른 견해로는 땀의 냉각을 촉진하는 것이다. 하지만 다시 말하자면 수많은 종은 털을 잃을 필요 없이도 상당히 효율적으로 땀을 식힐 수 있다. 포유류 종에 대한 전반적인 조사 결과 하나의 일반적인 결론을 도출할 수 있다. 바로 털로 덮인 외피가 지상 포유류에게는 최상의 단열 효과를 제공하지만, 수중에서 얻을 수 있는 최상의 단열 효과는 털이 아니라 지방층이라는 점이다.

16 빈칸 (A)와 (B)에 가장 알맞은 것은 무엇인가?

① 지하의 – 젖은

② 얼은 – 습기 찬

③ 열대의 – 몹시 추운

④ 모래로 뒤덮인 – 풀로 덮인

| 정답 | ①

| 해설 | 빈칸이 들어 있는 문장의 다음 문장부터는 지하에 서식하는 벌거숭이뻐드렁니쥐와 습한 지역에서 서식하거나 틈만 나면 물기와 접하려 하는 여러 포유류 종에 대해 말하고 있다. 따라서 빈칸에는 "지하"와 "물기"와 관련된 단어가 와야 하며, 따라서 답은 ①이다.

17 본문을 통해 인간이 다른 영장류에 비해 털이 덜 난 이유는 무엇으로 유추할 수 있는가?

① 숲에 사는 유인원의 뒤를 이었다.

② 초창기의 조상이 물이 많은 지역에 살았다.

③ 뜨거운 사바나 환경에 적응해야 했다.

④ 조상은 신체를 건조하게 유지해야 했다.

| 정답 | ③

| 해설 | "인간의 털이 없어진 이유는 사바나에서 과열을 방지하기 위함이라는 설이 있다"와 "또 다른 견해로는 땀의 냉각을 촉진하는 것이다"는 인간의 몸에 털이 덜 난 이유로 본문에서 제시된 것들이다. 둘 다 더위와 관련이 있으며, 몸에 털이 덜 났기 때문에 더위에 더 잘 대처할 수 있는 것으로 유추할 수 있다. 따라서 답은 ③이다.

| 어휘 | **anatomically** ⓐ 해부학적으로   **primate** ⓝ 영장류

order ⓝ (동식물 분류상의) 목(目)   **ape** ⓝ 유인원

lemur ⓝ 여우원숭이   **naked** ⓐ 털 · 모피 등이 없는

habitat ⓝ 서식지

venture ⓥ (위험을 무릅쓰고 모험하듯) 가다

tapir ⓝ 맥

wallow ⓥ (진흙이나 물에서) 뒹굴다

retain ⓥ 유지하다, 보유하다

version ⓝ (어떤 사건에 대해 특정한 입장에서 밝힌) 설명[생각/견해]

facilitate ⓥ 용이하게 하다, 촉진시키다

mammalian ⓐ 포유류의

frigid ⓐ 몹시 추운

subterranean ⓐ 지하의

wallower ⓝ (진흙·모래 속을) 뒹구는 사람[동물]

trace ⓝ 흔적

resort to ~에 기대다[의지하다]

undeniable ⓐ 부인할 수 없는, 명백한

insulation ⓝ 단열

adapt to ~에 적응하다

[18~19] 홍익대 2011

해석

다른 무엇보다도, 그녀의 글을 읽은 많은 독자들에게 분노와 경외감을 갖게 했던 것은 Chua의 어머니로서의 자신감이었다. 그녀는 부모로서 취한 자신의 선택에 한 치의 망설임도 보이지 않았다. 그녀의 책이 출판된 이후, 세계 도처에서 이메일이 쏟아져 들어오고 있으며, 일부는 분노와 심지어 협박도 서슴지 않았지만, 대부분은 이메일은 부럽다거나 고맙다는 내용이라고 그녀는 말했다. "많은 사람들이 나에게 메일을 보내, 부모 자신들이 어렸을 때 좀 더 다그쳤더라면, 인생에서 좀 더 많은 일들을 이룰 수 있지 않았을까 생각한다고 말했다."고 Chua는 말했다. "또 다른 사람들은 내 책을 읽고 마침내 자신들의 부모를 이해할 수 있었으며, 왜 부모가 그런 일을 했었는지 이해하게 되었다고 말했다. 한 남자는, 책을 읽고 모친에게 꽃과 감사의 편지를 보냈는데, 모친이 전화해서 우셨던 일이 있었다고 편지에 적었다."고 덧붙여 말했다.

Chua가 "중국의 방식"의 미덕을 칭송하고 있지만, 그녀가 말한 이야기는 전적으로 미국의 이야기이기도 하기 때문이다. 이 이야기는, 그 같은 꿈들이 여전히 실현 가능한 미국이라는 나라에서 자신과 자신의 가족을 위해 보다 나은 삶을 만들기로 결심한, 치열하게 살아가는 이민자들의 이야기이다. "매일 밤 새벽 3시까지 일하시던 아버지의 모습을 기억한다. 그리고 8년이나 같은 신발을 신었던 그분의 모습을 기억한다."고 Chua는 말했다. "아버지와 어머니가 우리를 위해 치러야 했던 희생을 알기 때문에 나는 우리 가문의 이름을 드높이고 싶었고, 그래서 부모님이 자랑스럽게 생각하시길 원했다."고 덧붙였다.

근면 성실, 인내, 핑계를 용납하지 않는 것. 중국인이든 미국인이든, 이는 성공을 위한 보증 수표와 같은 것으로 감히 논박하기 어려운 내용이라고 할 수 있다.

18 다음 중 본문의 내용으로부터 유추할 수 <u>없는</u> 것은?

① Chua가 자신의 책에 대한 독자들의 반응에 대해 말하고 있다.

② Chua의 책은 부모와 자식 간의 관계에 관한 여러 문제들을 다루고 있다.

③ Chua는 자신의 책에서 "중국식 양육"에 대한 측면을 서양식 양육에 대한 측면과 비교하고 있다.

④ Chua의 책은 만장일치의 환호를 받고 있다.

| 정답 | ④

| 해설 | ①의 경우 자신의 책을 읽고 독자들이 보내온 메일에 대해 말하고 있으므로 적절하며, ②의 경우 책의 내용이 "maternal confidence"나 "choices as a parent" 등을 통해 양육(parenting)에 관한 내용이라는 것을 알 수 있다. 그리고 부모와 자식 간의 내용이라는 것을, Chua 자신의 사례와 모친에게 꽃과 편지를 보냈던 남성의 사례를 통해 짐작할 수 있다. ③의 경우는 "… though Chua hails the virtues of 'the Chinese way,' the story she tells is quintessentially American." 부분을 통해 추론할 수 있지만, 이에 대한 근거는 본문의 내용만으로는 다른 보기에 비해 약한 편이다. ④의 경우, 책을 읽고 독자들에

게서 분노(ire)와 존경(awe)을 동시에 불러일으켰다고 했기 때문에, 만장일치의 환호와는 전혀 달라 답은 ④가 된다.

---

19 본문의 저자는 아이들을 양육하는 Chua의 호랑이 엄마 방식이 민족성의 문제가 아니라 보편적 철학의 문제라고 결론짓고 있는데, 이에 대해 알 수 있는 보기는?

① 다그쳐서 하게 만드는 방식은 과거 미국인들도 종종 했던 방식이기 때문에
② 중국인 어머니들이 중국인일 필요는 없기 때문에
③ 아이들에게 최선을 기대하는 것이 성공한 민족 모두에게 발견되는 공통의 자극제이기 때문에
④ Chua가 이제 무엇인가를 열심히 집중해 노력하는 것과 무엇인가를 단숨에 해치우는 것과의 차이를 이해하기 때문에

| 정답 | ③

| 해설 | 이 문제는 본문의 마지막 문단인 "Hard work, persistence, no patience for excuses : whether Chinese or American, that sounds like a prescription for success …" 부분을 통해 알 수 있다. 열심히 일하고, 인내하고, 변명하지 않는 것이야말로 성공의 지름길인 것은 중국인이든 미국인이든 모두에게 해당되는 사실이란 의미이기 때문에 정답은 ③이 된다.

| 어휘 | **more than anything** 다른 무엇보다도
striking ⓐ 놀라운, 현저한
inspire ⓥ 영감을 주다
awe ⓝ 경외감
wistful ⓐ 동경하는, (지난 일을) 애석해하는
hail ⓥ 칭송하다, 환호하며 맞이하다
striver ⓝ 노력하는 사람, 싸우는 사람
uphold the family name 가문의 이름을 드높이다
prescription/recipe for success ⓝ 성공을 위한 처방, 성공을 위한 비결
address ⓥ 다루다, 고심하다
acclamation ⓝ 환호
dash sth off ～을 급히 휘갈겨 쓰다, ～을 단숨에 해치우다

maternal ⓐ 모성의, 어머니의
ambivalence ⓝ 양면 가치, 반대 감정 병존
ire ⓝ 분노, 노여움
pour in 쏟아져 들어오다
grateful ⓐ 고맙게 여기는
quintessentially ⓐⓓ 참으로, 철저히
sacrifice ⓝ 희생
persistence ⓝ 인내
unanimous ⓐ 만장일치의, 이구동성의
impetus ⓝ 자극제, 추진력

해석

2001년 9월 11일 오전 8시 46분 납치당한 비행기 한 편이 세계 무역 센터 북쪽 건물을 들이받았다. 오전 9시 3분에 두 번째 비행기가 남쪽 건물을 들이받았다. 충돌로 인한 화재 때문에 두 건물은 주저앉았는데, 남쪽 건물은 1시간 2분 동안 불탄 후에 주저앉았고 북쪽 건물은 남쪽 건물의 붕괴 후 23분 후에 주저앉았다. 이 테러 공격은 오사마 빈 라덴의 주도로 이뤄졌으며, 그는 미국을 위협해 사우디아라비아에 주둔한 미군의 철수와 이스라엘의 지원을 포기하는 것을 희망했고 과거 칼리프들이 다스리던 영토를 회복하게끔 모슬렘들을 단결시키길 희망했다.

그날 발생한 테러 공격은 이제 9.11이라 불리며, 다양한 영역의 주제에 관한 토론을 촉발하는 계기가 되었다. 9월의 그날 아침 정확히 얼마나 많은 사건이 벌어진 것일까? '한 건'을 답으로 주장할 수 있을지 모른다. 세계 무역 센터의 두 건물에 가해진 공격은 단일한 의제를 수행하려는 한 남자가 마음속에 구상한 단일 계획의 일부였다.

아니면 '두 건'을 답으로 주장할 수 있을지 모른다. 세계 무역 센터의 임차인인 Larry Silverstein에게 지불될 보험 배당금을 결정하기 위한 일련의 소송에 따르면 논란이 되는 보험 배당금 총액은 35억 달러이다. Larry Silverstein이 보유한 보험 증서는 파괴가 수반되는 "사건" 각 건당 최대 배상 금액을 명시하고 있다. 만약 9.11을 단일 사건으로 이뤄진 것으로 본다면, 그는 35억 달러를 받게 될 것이다. 만약 두 개의 사건으로 이뤄진 것으로 본다면, 그는 70억 달러를 받게 될 것이다.

20 본문에 따르면 다음 중 9.11 공격을 통한 오사마 빈 라덴의 목적이 <u>아닌</u> 것은 무엇인가?

① 이스라엘에 대한 미국의 정책을 바꾼다.
② 사우디아라비아에서 주둔하는 미군의 존재를 없앤다.
③ 모슬렘들을 단일 정치 체제하에 모이게 한다.
④ 알 카에다 테러 분자들의 활동을 지원한다.

| 정답 | ④

| 해설 | 본문에 따르면 오사마 빈 라덴이 9.11을 저지른 목적은 "사우디아라비아에 주둔한 미군의 철수(ending its military presence in Saudi Arabia)", 미국의 "이스라엘로의 지원을 포기(ending... its support for Israel)", "과거 칼리프들이 다스리던 영토를 회복하게끔 모슬렘들을 단결(unite Muslims in preparation for a restoration of the caliphate)" 등이 있다. 여기서 첫 번째 것은 ②에 해당되고, 두 번째 것은 ①에 해당되고, 세 번째 것은 ③에 해당된다. 따라서 ①, ②, ③ 모두 답이 될 수 없다. 그러나 본문에는 알 카에다에 관해서 언급된 사항은 전혀 없기 때문에 답은 ④가 된다.

21 다음 중 Sliverstein의 변호사가 주장할 가능성이 가장 높은 것은 무엇인가?

① 오사마 빈 라덴은 처벌되어야 한다.
② 9.11은 두 가지 사건으로 구성되었다.
③ Sliverstein은 9.11 사전 모의에 가담하지 않았다.
④ 미국의 법률 체제는 테러 분자들에게는 너무 관대하다.

| 정답 | ②

| 해설 | 세계 무역 센터의 임차인인 Larry Silverstein은 보험 계약상 9.11이 단일 사건이 아니라 두 개의 사건으로 취급되면 원래 받기로 했던 돈의 두 배를 더 받는다. 따라서 그나 그의 변호사는 9.11이 단일 사건이 아니라 두 가지 사건으로 구성되었다고 주장할 것이다. 그러므로 답은 ②가 된다.

22 다음 중 본문에서 언급되거나 암시되지 <u>않은</u> 것은 무엇인가?

① 9.11 공격을 통해 오사마 빈 라덴은 모슬렘 대부분의 지지를 얻게 되었다.

② 9.11은 사람들로 하여금 다양한 범주의 주제에 관해 토의를 하도록 유도했다.

③ Larry Silverstein은 세계 무역 센터 빌딩의 임차인이었다.

④ 9.11 때 먼저 무너진 것은 세계 무역 센터의 북쪽 건물이었다.

| 정답 | ④

| 해설 | 본문에서 "충돌로 인한 화재 때문에 두 건물은 주저앉았는데, 남쪽 건물은 1시간 2분 동안 불탄 후에 주저앉았고 북쪽 건물은 남쪽 건물의 붕괴 후 23분 후에 주저앉았다(The resulting infernos caused the buildings to collapse, the South Tower after burning for an hour and two minutes, the North Tower twenty-three minutes after that)"라는 문장을 통해 먼저 붕괴된 것은 남쪽 건물이고, 그 이후에 북쪽 건물이 붕괴했음을 알 수 있다. 따라서 정반대의 내용을 담은 보기 ④가 답이 된다.

| 어휘 | **inferno** ⓝ 화재

intimidate ⓥ 위협하다

restoration ⓝ 복원

caliphate ⓝ 칼리프가 다스리는 지역; 칼리프 정치와 종교의 권력을 아울러 갖는 이슬람 교단의 지배자

set off ~을 일으키다

service ⓝ 수행

leaseholder ⓝ 임차인

stipulate ⓥ 명시하다

comprise ⓥ ~로 이뤄지다

lenient ⓐ 관대한, 무른

mastermind ⓥ (계획하고) 조종하다, 지휘하다

military presence 군대 주둔

conceive ⓥ (마음속에) 품다, 구상하다

insurance payout 보험 배당금

insurance policy 보험 증권, 보험 증서

reimbursement ⓝ 변제, 상환, 배상

consist of ~로 구성된, 이루어진

stand to ~할 것 같다

[23~25] 서울여대 2014

해석

앞으로 두 세기 동안 가족은 어떤 전개를 맞이하게 될 것인가? 우리는 알 수 없지만, 만일 따로 조치를 취하지 않고 놔둘 경우 특정한 결과를 야기할 가능성이 높은 몇 가지 특정한 힘이 작용 중에 있음에 주목한다. 현대 문명화된 공동체에는 가족을 약화시킬 경향이 있는 몇 가지 것들이 존재한다. 그중 가장 주요한 것으로 아동을 향한 인도주의적 감정을 들 수 있다. 점차 많은 이들은 아동이 부모의 역경이나 심지어 원죄로 인해 도움 받을 수 있는 수준을 넘어 더 큰 고통을 받아서는 안 된다고 생각하게 되었다. 성경을 보면 고아의 운명은 매우 슬픈 것으로 묘사되며 과거에는 의심의 여지없이 실제로도 그랬다. 요즘은 고아는 다른 아동에 비해 별달리 더 큰 고통을 겪지는 않는다. 국가나 자선 기관이 점차 유기된 아동에게 매우 적절한 보살핌을 제공하는 추세가 더욱 확대될 것이며, 결과적으로 아동은 양심 없는 부모나 보호자에 의해 더욱 무관심하게 방치될 것이다. 점차 공공 자금으로부터 유기된 아동을 돌보는 비용이 너무 증가하게 되면서 이는 경제적으로 부유하지 못한 부모들이 자신의 자녀를 국가가 돌보도록 넘겨 버리는 기회를 활용하게 될 강력한 유인책이 될 것이다. 어쩌면 이는 결국에는 학교 교육과 마찬가지로 일정한 경제적 수준에 도달하지 못한 사람들 거의 모두에 의해 벌어질 것이다.

23 본문에 따르면 아동을 향한 인도주의적 감정은 다음의 결과를 낳게 된다.

① 부모가 자녀에게 너무 많은 돈을 쓴 나머지 가족을 약화시킨다.
② 결국에는 더욱 많은 수의 아동이 부모나 보호자에 의해 방치될 것이다.
③ 국가로 하여금 가난하거나 죄를 진 부모로부터 자녀를 강제적으로 떼어 놓게 할 것이다.
④ 국가의 재정 위기와 심지어는 국가의 파산을 야기할 것이다.

| 정답 | ②

| 해설 | 아동을 향한 인도주의적 감정으로 인해 "국가나 자선 기관이 점차 유기된 아동에게 매우 적절한 보살핌을 제공하는 추세가 더욱 확대될 것이며, 결과적으로 아동은 양심 없는 부모나 보호자에 의해 더욱 무관심하게 방치될 것이다 (There will be a growing tendency for the state or charitable institutions to give fairly adequate care to neglected children, and consequently children will be more and more neglected by unconscientious parents or guardians)." 이 말은, 즉 양심 없는 부모들은 자신들이 신경 쓰지 않아도 나라에서 알아서 자녀를 돌봐줄 것으로 판단하고 오히려 아이들에 대해 관심을 기울이지 않을 것이라는 의미이며, 결국 인도주의적 감정이 오히려 아동의 유기를 더욱 조장하게 될 것이라는 예측이다. 따라서 답은 ②이다.

24 저자는 다음의 사항을 제시하기 위해 성경을 언급했다.

① 과거의 고아와 그렇지 않은 아동의 생활 여건의 유사성
② 현재의 고아와 그렇지 않은 아동의 생활 여건의 차이점
③ 과거와 현재의 고아의 생활 여건의 유사성
④ 과거와 현재의 고아의 생활 여건의 차이점

| 정답 | ④

| 해설 | 성경에 제시된 고아의 삶과 실제 과거 고아의 삶은 비참했으나 현재는 그렇지 않다. 이는 즉 성경을 통해 과거와 현재의 고아의 삶을 서로 대비시키고 있는 것이다. 따라서 답은 ④이다.

25 다음 중 본문에서 암시된 것은 무엇인가?

① 현재 자녀 양육의 부담은 전적으로 국가 및 공공 기관이 지고 있다.
② 미래에 대부분의 부모는 자녀에게 적절한 보살핌을 제공해야 한다는 점을 알 만큼 제대로 교육을 받게 될 것이다.
③ 현재 국가는 일정한 경제적 수준에 도달하지 못한 가정을 위해 학교 교육을 책임진다.
④ 미래에 사실상 모든 부모는 학교 교육뿐만 아니라 양육에 있어서도 자녀를 국가에 넘길 것이다.

| 정답 | ③

| 해설 | "어쩌면 이는 결국에는 학교 교육과 마찬가지로 일정한 경제적 수준에 도달하지 못한 사람들 거의 모두에 의해 벌어질 것이다(probably this will be done, in the end, as now with schooling, by practically all who are below a certain economic level)." 이 말은 미래에는 일정한 경제적 수준에 미치지 못한 사람들은 직접 아이를 키우기보다 국가가 맡도록 할 것이며, 이는 현재 시점에서 집에서가 아니라 학교에서 아이를 가르치는 것과 마찬가지라는 의미로, ③과 같은 내용이다. 따라서 답은 ③이다. 참고로 ④는 모든 부모가 자녀 양육을 국가에 맡긴다는 것이 아니라 일정 경제적 수준에 도달하지 못한 부모가 자녀 양육을 국가에 맡긴다는 의미라서 실제 본문과는 거리가 있다.

development ⓝ 발달, 전개, 진행

at work 작용하는, (영향이) 미치는

humanitarian ⓐ 인도주의적인

lot ⓝ 운명, 숙명

tendency ⓝ 성향, 동향, 추세

neglected ⓐ 방치된, 유기된

unconscientious ⓐ 비양심적인, 지조가 없는

expense ⓝ 비용

be well off (경제적으로) 더 잘 살다

in the end 결국에는

be borne by ~이 부담하다

note ⓥ 주목하다, 알아차리다

unchecked ⓐ 억제하지[손을 쓰지] 않고 놔둔

misfortune ⓝ 불운, 역경, 불행한 일, 재난

orphan ⓝ 고아

adequate ⓐ 적당한, 충분한

consequently ⓐⓓ 결과적으로

guardian ⓝ 보호자, 후견인

inducement ⓝ 유인, 동기

avail oneself of ~을 이용하다, ~을 적절히 사용하다

practically ⓐⓓ 사실상

give over (양육권 등을 다른 쪽에) 이전하다[넘기다]

[26~28] 덕성여대 2018

해석

의료 분야에서 빅 데이터 혁명이 진행 중에 있다. 혁명은 정보 공급량의 엄청난 증가로부터 시작되었다. 지난 10년 동안 제약 회사는 수년간의 연구 및 개발 데이터를 의학 데이터베이스에 한데 모았고, 지불자 및 공급자는 자신들의 환자 기록을 디지털화했다. 한편 미국 연방 정부 및 기타 공공 부문 이해 당사자들은 임상 시험 데이터와 공공 의료 보험 프로그램 대상 환자들의 정보 등 자신들이 비축해 놓은 보건 부문의 광대한 지식을 개방하고 있다. 동시에 최근의 기술적 발전 덕분에 다수의 정보원으로부터 정보를 수집하여 분석하는 일이 용이해졌다. 이는 보건 분야에 있어 주된 이점이며, 왜냐하면 환자 한 명에 대한 데이터를 다양한 지불자, 큰 병원, 연구소, 개인 병원 등으로부터 얻을 수 있기 때문이다.

보건 부문 이해 당사자들은 가치 포착에 능통하고 이러한 목표 달성에 도움이 되는 여러 수단을 개발하였다. 하지만 전통적인 수단이 빅 데이터가 제공하는 통찰력을 항상 완전히 이용하는 것은 아니다. 예를 들어 단가 할인은 주로 계약 및 협상에 영향을 미치는 수단에 따라 결정된다. 그리고 보건 부문의 가치를 결정하는 다른 대부분의 기존 수단과 마찬가지로, 위의 수단은 환자의 치료 결과를 개선하는 것보다는 오로지 비용 절감에만 집중한다. 비록 이러한 수단은 앞으로도 지속적으로 중요한 역할을 맡겠지만, 이해 당사자들은 만일 가치에 대해 보다 전체론적이면서 환자 중심적인 접근법을 취했을 경우에만, 즉 보건 부문 지출액과 환자 치료 결과 이 두 요소에 동등하게 중점을 둔 경우에만 빅 데이터로부터 혜택을 볼 것이다.

26 본문의 저자에 따르면 수집 중인 대규모 데이터를 통해 가장 큰 혜택을 보는 쪽은 누구인가?

① 제약 회사

② 환자 개인과 환자 대상 보건 서비스 제공자

③ 미국 연방 정부

④ 의사와 병원 직원

| 정답 | ②

| 해설 | 최근의 빅 데이터 분야 발전으로 인해 대규모 데이터의 수집이 가능해졌고, 데이터 수집 및 분석도 용이해졌다. 이를 통해 이득을 보는 분야는 보건 분야이다("이는 보건 분야에 있어 주된 이점이며"). 보건 분야의 발전은 환자에게 있어서도 혜택이 되고, 환자를 상대하는 보건 서비스 제공자 입장에서도 혜택이 되는 것으로 유추할 수 있다. 따라서 답은 ②이다.

27 본문에서 가장 큰 데이터원으로 언급된 쪽은 누구인가?

① 미국 연방 정부 및 기타 공공 부문 이해 당사자

② 제약 회사

③ 공공 의료 보험 당국

④ 보건 부문 이해 당사자

| 정답 | ①

| 해설 | "미국 연방 정부 및 기타 공공 부문 이해 당사자들은 임상 시험 데이터와 공공 의료 보험 프로그램 대상 환자들의 정보 등 자신들이 비축해 놓은 보건 부문의 광대한 지식을 개방하고 있다." 여기서 가장 많은 데이터를 보유하고 있는 쪽은 "미국 연방 정부 및 기타 공공 부문 이해 당사자들"임을 알 수 있다. 따라서 답은 ①이다.

28 다음 중 본문에서 유추할 수 있는 것은 무엇인가?

① 빅 데이터 혁명은 환자들에게 침술같이 보다 전체론적이면서 대안적인 건강 옵션을 선택할 수 있게 할 것이다.

② 다수의 정보원으로부터 정보를 수집하여 분석하는 일은 항상 쉬웠다.

③ 빅 데이터 혁명은 비용 절감과 환자의 치료 결과 개선에 집중하는 보건 부문에 대한 보다 환자 중심적인 접근을 가능케 할 것이다.

④ 단가 할인 같은 전통적 수단의 활용은 더 이상 필요하지 않을 것이다.

| 정답 | ③

| 해설 | "이해 당사자들은 만일 가치에 대해 보다 전체론적이면서 환자 중심적인 접근법을 취했을 경우에만, 즉 보건 부문 지출액과 환자 치료 결과 이 두 요소에 동등하게 중점을 둔 경우에만 빅 데이터로부터 혜택을 볼 것이다." 이는 역으로 말하면 빅 데이터 혁명의 혜택을 보려면 이해 당사자들이 보다 환자 중심적 접근을 취해야 한다는 의미이기도 하다. 따라서 답은 ③이다.

| 어휘 | **vastly** ⓐⓓ 광대하게, 엄청나게

aggregate ⓥ 종합하다, 한데 모으다

clinical trial 임상 시험

advance ⓝ 발전, 진전

be versed in ~에 조예가 깊다, ~에 능통하다

take advantage of ~을 활용하다, ~을 이용하다

unit price 단가

well-established ⓐ 기존의, 확립된

acupuncture ⓝ 침술

pharmaceutical ⓐ 약학의, 제약의

store ⓝ 비축[저장](량)

in parallel 동시에

physician office 동네 병원, 개인 병원

lever ⓝ 지렛대, 수단

insight ⓝ 통찰력, 직관

leverage ⓝ (영향을 미치는) 수단

holistic ⓐ 전체론적인

해석

신용 거래는 역사적으로 지속적으로 사용되어 왔으며, 그 이유는 상인들이 고객의 부채 현황을 파악하기 위해 다양한 방안을 사용했기 때문이다. 예를 들어 18세기 영국에서는 할부 판매인들이 고객에게 옷을 팔고 그 대가로 매주 약간씩 옷의 금액을 지불받았다. 손님이 진 부채가 어느 정도인지 파악하기 위해 할부 판매인들은 긴 나무 막대기를 소지했는데, 막대기 한쪽에는 지불된 금액을 나타내는 표시가 되어 있고 다른 한쪽에는 아직 지불되지 않은 금액을 나타내는 표시가 되어 있다. 고대 및 중세 초기에는 부채 현황을 파악하기 위해 금속판이나 동전 같은 다른 유형의 신용 거래 수단이 사용되었다.

최초의 신용 카드는 1920년대에 미국에서 유래되었다. 그 당시의 번영하던 경제를 한껏 만끽하고 더 많은 고객을 위치할 수 있기를 바라는 마음을 품고 기업들은 고객들에게 카드를 발항하기 시작했으며, 고객들은 카드를 가지고 가게나 기업에서 구매를 하고 비용은 나중에 상환하는 방식이었다. 이런 카드는 발행한 상점에서만 사용이 가능하지만, 1930년대에 들어와서는 일부 회사들은 상대 업체의 신용 카드를 받기 시작했다. 이것이 바로 카드를 발행한 기업이 카드를 받은 상인에게 돈을 지불하는 제3자 결제의 최초 사례였다. 고객은 제3자 결제가 이루어진 다음에 카드 발행 업체에 돈을 지불하면 된다. 이후 제3자 결제는 은행 발행 신용 카드의 주요 운용 방식으로 자리 잡았다.

29 다음 중 본문의 제목으로 가장 알맞은 것은 무엇인가?

① 신용 카드 발행 기관의 유형
② 신용 거래의 역사
③ 다양한 모양의 신용 카드
④ 신용 거래의 대안

| 정답 | ②

| 해설 | 본문은 18세기 영국의 할부 거래에서부터 20세기 미국에서 최초 등장한 신용 카드에 이르기까지 신용 거래의 역사를 다루고 있다. 따라서 답은 ②이다.

30 다음 중 본문에 따르면 신용 거래 초창기의 신용 거래 수단으로 언급되지 <u>않은</u> 것은 무엇인가?

① 금속판
② 나무막대
③ 동전
④ 금

| 정답 | ④

| 해설 | 신용 거래 초창기의 거래 수단으로 언급된 것으로는 양쪽에 표시가 된 나무 막대기, 동전, 금속판 등이 있다. 하지만 금은 언급되지 않았으므로 답은 ④이다.

31 다음 중 본문에서 언급되어나 암시된 것은 무엇인가?

① 할부 판매인은 초창기 신용 역사에서 중요한 역할을 차지한다.
② 영국 은행인들이 최초로 신용 카드를 발명했다.
③ 은행은 기업보다 먼저 신용 카드를 발행했다.
④ 신용 역사의 초창기 때부터 제3자 결제가 사용 가능했다.

| 정답 | ①

| 해설 | 18세기 영국의 할부 판매인들이 고객들과 행한 거래 행태가 바로 현대적인 신용 거래의 원형이 되었다. 즉 이들이 초창기 신용

거래의 역사에 중요한 위치를 점했던 것이다. 따라서 답은 ①이다.

| 어휘 | **credit** ⓝ 신용 거래

tallyman ⓝ 할부 판매인

notch ⓝ 표시

third-party payment 3자 지급, 제3자 결제

keep track of ~을 파악하고 있다, ~을 기록하다

in exchange for ~의 대가로

pay back 돌려주다, 상환하다

[32~33] 중앙대 2016

해석

무언가를 하도록 합법적으로 허가를 받는 것과 실제로 그 무언가를 하는 것 간에 구분을 짓는 것이 중요하다. 모든 사람들이, 만일 원한다면, 2분 안에 1마일을 달리도록 허용하는 법이 통과될 수 있다. 하지만 그런 법이 사람들의 실질적인 자유를 증진시키지는 못할 것이며, 왜냐하면 달리도록 허용이 이루어져도 신체적으로 그렇게 달리는 것이 불가능하기 때문이다. 제한은 최소한으로 두고 가능성은 최대한으로 열어 놓는 것은 문제없다. 하지만 실제 세계에서 대부분의 사람들은 그들이 될 수 있도록 허용된 모든 것이 될 기회를 얻지 못할 것이며, 그들이 할 수 있는 것이 가능한 모든 것을 하지 못하게 억눌러져야 할 기회도 얻지 못할 것이다. 사람들의 실질적인 자유는 스스로가 선택한 것을 할 수 있는 수단과 능력을 실제로 갖고 있는지 여부에 좌우된다.

이러한 '실질적인 자유'라는 생각은 공정성의 고려와 다시 연계된다. 공정한 사회를 추구하는 것은, 롤스(Rawls)가 제의한 일종의 합의를 통해서이든 아니면 이득에 대한 공리주의적 평가를 통해서이든 간에, 실질적인 자유가 극대화된 사회를 추구하는 것과 동일하다. 부당한 대우를 받는 것은 인간의 가능성을 제약하는 것이며 따라서 공정한 몫의 자원을 보유했을 경우 가능했을 것들을 거부당하는 것과 같다. 가난은 단순히 돈이나 자원이 불충분한 것에 그치는 것이 아니라, 돈을 좀 더 보유한 사람이라면 자유로이 선택하여 할 수 있는 것들을 자유로이 할 수 없다는 것과 관련이 있다.

> **32** 윗글에서 빈칸에 들어가기에 가장 적합한 것을 고르시오.
> ① 공리주의적 시각에 대한 사회적 합의
> ② 스스로의 권리를 보호하는 법적 규제
> ③ 최소한의 제한으로 최대한의 혜택을 보기
> ④ 스스로가 선택한 것을 할 수 있는 수단과 능력

| 정답 | ④

| 해설 | 첫 번째 단락은 법률적 자유와 실질적 자유 간의 구분을 짓고 있다. 2분 안에 1마일을 달릴 수 있도록 법률적 자유가 주어졌더라도 이러한 자유를 누릴 수 있는 신체적 능력과 수단을 보유한 사람은 없기 때문에 "하지만 그런 법이 사람들의 실질적인 자유를 증진시키지는 못한다(That would not, however, increase their effective freedom)"고 저자는 말하고 있다. 즉 2분 안에 1마일을 달리도록 허용하는 것같이 이론상으로 허용되는 자유가 법률적 자유라면, 실질적 자유는 개인이 법률적 자유에 따라 허용되는 것 가운데 실제로 뭔가를 수행할 수 있는 자유를 의미한다. 따라서 빈칸에는 이러한 실질적 자유에 관해 말하는 ④가 적합하다.

33 윗글을 통해 추론할 수 있는 것으로 가장 적합한 것을 고르시오.

① 법을 통해 가능성을 극대화하는 것이 더욱 실질적인 자유를 얻는 데 기여한다.

② 실질적인 자유는 사회의 공정함을 증대시키는 것으로 강화될 수 있다.

③ 법은 종종 현실을 반영하지 못하며 따라서 개정이 필요하다.

④ 가난은 실질적인 자유를 키우는 것으로도 감소될 수 없다.

| 정답 | ②

| 해설 | "공정한 사회를 추구하는 것은 … 실질적인 자유가 극대화된 사회를 추구하는 것과 동일하다(The quest for a fair society… is at the same time a quest for a society in which effective freedom is maximized)." 이 말은 즉 실질적인 자유는 공정성의 추구를 통해 이룩할 수 있다는 의미이다. 따라서 답은 ②이다.

첫 번째 단락에서 법을 통해 가능성을 극대화하더라도 2분 안에 1마일을 달리도록 허용하는 법의 경우처럼 실질적 자유의 향상에 아무 기여를 하지 못하는 경우도 존재한다. 따라서 ①은 답이 될 수 없다. 본문 어디에도 법의 개정과 관련된 내용은 존재하지 않으며 따라서 ③은 답이 될 수 없다. "가난은 단순히 돈이나 자원이 불충분한 것에 그치는 것이 아니라, 돈을 좀 더 보유한 사람이라면 자유로이 선택하여 할 수 있는 것들을 자유로이 할 수 없다는 것과 관련이 있다(Poverty is not just a matter of having insufficient money or resources, it is also about not being free to do the things that people with more money are freely able to choose to do)." 여기서 돈을 가진 사람은 실질적 자유를 누리고 있고 돈이 없는 가난은 실질적 자유를 누리지 못하고 있음을 알 수 있다. 때문에 가난은 실질적 자유를 키우게 되면 감소할 수 있을 것이며, 이는 ④의 진술과는 정반대이다. 따라서 ④는 답이 될 수 없다.

| 어휘 | **effective** ⓐ 실질적인, 효과적인

restriction ⓝ 제한, 규제

fairness ⓝ 공정함, 공정성

utilitarian ⓐ 실용적인, 공리주의의

amend ⓥ 개정하다, 수정하다

physically ⓐ 신체적으로, 물리적으로

restrain ⓥ 저지하다, 억누르다

quest ⓝ 탐구, 탐색, 추구

deny ⓥ 거부하다, 거절하다

[34~36] 한성대 2017

해석

뉴욕 타임스가 유리 집에 사는 한 남자의 이야기를 특집 기사로 실었다. 그 남성의 집은 투명한 벽으로 이루어져 있다. 그는 자신의 모든 행위가 관찰될 수 있는 집에서 그 어떤 물리적 사생활도 갖지 않고 살기로 했다. 그는 모든 행위를 다른 사람들이 모두 볼 수 있는 공간인, 자신만의 파놉티콘(panopticon, 원형 감옥)을 만든 것이다. 제레미 벤담(Jeremy Bentham)은 감옥이 어떤 형태로 설계되어야 하는지에 대한 자기 생각을 묘사하면서 파놉티콘이라는 용어를 18세기 말에 처음으로 만들었다. 죄수의 감방은 원형으로 배치되어야 하며, 중앙에 감시탑이 위치한다. 원형의 중앙을 향하는 벽면은 모두 유리로 되어 있다. 이런 방식으로 모든 죄수의 감방은 간수의 감시 속에 놓이게 된다. 죄수는 감시를 받지 않고는 그 어떤 행위도 할 수 없다. 하지만 죄수는 감시탑을 볼 수 없다. 자신들이 감시를 받고 있다는 것을 알지만, 간수를 볼 수 없으므로 간수가 실제로 자신의 행동을 관찰하고 있는지는 알 수 없다. 사람들은 자신이 감시당하고 있다는 것을 아는 경우 평소와 다르게 행동한다. 이런 상황에서 사람들은 자신의 모습을 드러내 보일 가능성이 더 작다. 그 대신 사람들은 자신이 감시를 받는 경우 스스로 해야 한다고 생각하는 방식대로 행동하게 된다.

34 다음 중 빈칸 (A)와 (B)에 올 수 있는 가장 적합한 것을 고르시오.

      (A)   (B)

① 적극적으로 – 가능성이 더 크다

② 다르게 – 가능성이 더 크다

③ 적극적으로 – 가능성이 더 작다

④ 다르게 – 가능성이 더 작다

| 정답 | ④

| 해설 | 사람들은 감시를 받는다고 생각하면 평소와는 '다르게' 행동하므로 (A)에는 'differently'가 적합하다. (B)의 경우 'not A but B'에 해당하는 'not A instead B' 구문을 사용하고 있다. 이때 A와 B는 대조를 이룬다. B의 내용이 '스스로 해야 한다고 생각하는 모습'을 말하므로 '평소와는 다른 모습'이란 것을 알 수 있다. 따라서 A는 '평소의 모습'이 들어가야 한다. 다시 요약하면 "not '평소의 모습' instead '평소와 다른 모습'"의 구조를 보이므로 정답은 평소의 모습을 보일 가능성이 더 작다는 'less likely'가 와야 한다. 따라서 정답은 ④가 된다.

35 다음 중 파놉티콘에 대해 추론할 수 있는 것은?

① 파놉티콘은 감옥의 역학 구조 밖에서는 적용되지 않는다.

② 파놉티콘은 사회 통제를 위한 효과적인 수단이 될 수 있다.

③ 파놉티콘은 공공장소에서 정기적으로 사용되어야 한다.

④ 파놉티콘은 미래에 사생활을 확장할 것이다.

| 정답 | ②

| 해설 | 파놉티콘은 원형 감옥으로 중앙에 감시탑이 있어 죄수의 모든 행위가 감시의 대상이 된다. 하지만 파놉티콘 내에 위치한 죄수는 자신이 감시당하고 있다는 사실을 알고 있지만 언제 감시당하는지 알 수 없기 때문에 매 순간 행위가 위축될 수 있다. 따라서 파놉티콘이 '통제를 위한 효과적 수단'이 될 수 있는 것이므로, 정답은 ②가 된다.

36 다음 중 본문의 내용과 일치하는 것은?

① 뉴욕의 한 남성은 다른 사람들을 감시하기 위해 유리 집을 지었다.

② 파놉티콘이라는 용어는 수십 년 전에 제레미 벤담에 의해 만들어졌다.

③ 원래의 파놉티콘은 타워와 타워를 둘러싸고 있는 감방으로 이루어져 있었다.

④ 파놉티콘의 죄수들은 간수를 관찰할 수 있었다.

| 정답 | ③

| 해설 | ① 다른 사람을 감시하기 위한 것이 아니라 유리 집에 살고 있는 자신의 모습이 관찰의 대상이 된다. ② 18세기 말에 용어를 만든 것이므로, 수십 년 전이라고 할 수 없다. ④ 죄수가 간수를 관찰하는 것이 아니라 간수가 죄수를 관찰하는 구조이다. 정답은 ③으로 파놉티콘은 중앙에 감시탑(타워)이 있고, 그 주위를 원형의 형태로 둘러싼 여러 감방이 위치한 구조이므로, 보기 ③은 올바른 설명에 해당한다.

| 어휘 | **feature a story** 기사를 크게 다루다   **be filled with** ~로 가득차다

        transparent ⓐ 투명한, 명백한

panopticon ⑪ 파놉티콘, 원형감옥(제레미 벤담이 감옥 건축을 위해 고안한 일망 감시 장치)

coin the term 용어를 만들어 내다   **cell** ⑪ 감방; 세포

do nothing unobserved 감시를 받지 않고는 그 어떤 것도 할 수 없다, 모든 행위가 감시를 받는다

observer ⑪ 감시자, 목격자   **applicable** ⓐ 적용할 수 있는, 적절한

[37~38] 서강대 2020

해석

인도주의의 상품화가 가장 분명하게 그 모습을 드러내는 곳은 유명인사들의 UN 지지가 열광적으로 다시 부활하고 있는 모습에서 찾아볼 수 있다. 이는 오드리 헵번과 더 최근에는 안젤리나 졸리와 같은 유명 할리우드 스타들과 연관된 성공의 역사를 가진 인도주의적인 장르에 해당한다. 그러한 유명인사들의 지지는 항상 인도주의적 담론의 양면적 수행성에 의존해 왔으며, 이는 타인의 고통에 대한 유명인사의 증언인 '탈개성화(impersonation)'와 그러한 증언을 유명인사 자신의 독특한 아우라와 결합한 '개성화(personification)'를 혼합한 것이다. 하지만 현대의 지지 표현과 과거의 지지 표현이 차이를 보이는 지점은 전자가 유명인사의 '고백적(confessional)' 의사전달 구조를 중시하는 경향성에 있다. 유명인사 지지의 이전 형태였던 엄격한 형식성과는 달리, 고백적 수행성은 '거리를 둔 친밀감(intimacy at a distance)'에 달려 있다. 이는 연예인들의 삶의 사적인 영역에 우리가 간접적인 접근을 하는 것을 지칭하는 오늘날 대중문화의 주요 특징으로, 이러한 사적인 영역에 그들의 공적인 페르소나의 내재된 측면을 제공한다.

37 다음 중 본문을 통해 추론할 수 있는 것이 아닌 것은?

① 유명인사들은 대중 관객과 타인의 고통을 공유한다.

② 유명인사의 인도주의는 과거에 더 형식적이었다.

③ 오늘날 유명인사들은 자신의 공적인 페르소나를 사용해 자신의 죄를 고백한다.

④ 오늘날 할리우드 유명인사들은 자신의 증언에 자신들의 스타성을 불어넣는다.

| 정답 | ③

| 해설 | 유명인사들이 유엔이나 유니세프 같은 기구에서 인도주의 관련 대의명분을 지지하는 'celebrity advocacy'에 대해 말하고 있다. ①의 내용은 "the celebrity's testimony of the suffering of others"를 통해 알 수 있다. ②는 "Unlike the strict formality of earlier forms of celebrity advocacy" 부분을 통해 알 수 있다. ④는 "the infusion of such testimony with the celebrity's own distinct star aura" 부분에 서술되어 있다. 정답은 ③으로 본문에서 사용한 'confessional'이라는 뜻은 자신의 죄를 뉘우치는 참회적 성격이 아닌 자신이 직접 목격한 것을 고백하는 방식으로 타인의 고통을 대중들에게 전달하는 것을 말한다.

38 다음 중 빈칸 Ⓐ, Ⓑ, Ⓒ에 들어갈 가장 적합한 것은?

① Ⓐ 확산 – Ⓑ 불분명한 – Ⓒ 열린

② Ⓐ 확산 – Ⓑ 난해한 – Ⓒ 자유로운

③ Ⓐ 응집 – Ⓑ 퇴폐적인 – Ⓒ 미세한

④ Ⓐ 상품화 – Ⓑ 양면적인 – Ⓒ 간접적인

| 정답 | ④

| 해설 | Ⓐ의 경우, 인도주의가 연예인과 같은 유명인사와 결합되어 대중들에게 소개되는 방식인 '상품화'에 대해 말하고 있다. Ⓑ의 경우, 유명인사가 타인의 입장이 되어 타인의 고통을 증언하는 '탈개성화(impersonation)'와 그러한 증언을 유명인사 자신의 독특한 아우라와 결합해서 유명인사의 모습이 부각되는 '개성화(personification)'라는 양면적 특성을 지닌다는 내용이다. Ⓒ의 경우 앞에서 말한 '거리를 둔 친밀감(intimacy at a distance)'에 대한 설명으로 유명인사의 사생활에 직접 자유롭게 접근할 수 없고 거리를 둔 상태로 접근할 수 있다는 말은 다른 사람이 중간에 매개해서 간접적 방식으로 접근한다는 것을 의미한다. 따라서 'mediated'가 적합하다. 종합하면 정답은 ④가 된다.

| 어휘 |

humanitarianism ⓝ 인도주의, 박애주의

reinvigoration ⓝ 활기 회복, 기운 회복

celebrity advocacy 유명인사가 주창하는 명분·입장 등에 대해 적극적으로 지지하는 것

be associated with ～와 연관된

discourse ⓝ 담론, 담화

testimony ⓝ 증언

infusion ⓝ 주입, 투입

differentiate ⓥ 구별 짓다

articulation ⓝ 표현

privilege ⓥ 중시하다, 특권을 주다

formality ⓝ 형식에 구애됨, 틀에 박힘

rest upon ～에 달려 있다, 의지하다

refer to 지칭하다

inherent ⓐ 내재적인, 고유한, 선천적인

persona ⓝ [심리학] 페르소나(사회 역할이나 배우에 의해 연기되는 등장인물), 외적 인격(가면을 쓴 인격)

opaque ⓐ 글이 불분명한, 이해하기 힘든, 불투명한

abstruse ⓐ 난해한

decadent ⓐ 퇴폐적인

commodification ⓝ 상품화, 상업화

mediated ⓐ 간접적인, 매개적인

enthusiastic ⓐ 열정적인

performativity ⓝ 수행성

impersonation ⓝ 탈개성화, 흉내 내기, 인격화

personification ⓝ 개성화, 전형, 상징; 구현, 체현

aura ⓝ 아우라, 기운, 분위기

contemporary ⓐ 현대의

the former 전자

strict ⓐ 가혹한, 엄한

confessional ⓐ 고백의, 자백의, 참회의 ⓝ 고백, 참회

intimacy ⓝ 친밀함

render ⓥ 주다; ～이 되게 하다

proliferation ⓝ 증식, 확산

conglomeration ⓝ (상이한 물체의) 모임, 집합, 응집, 집성체

minute ⓐ 미세한, 사소한, 상세한

ambivalent ⓐ 상반(모순)되는 감정을 가진, 양면 가치적인

[39~40]

해석

에른스트 곰브리치(Ernst Gombrich)는 '질서의 감각(A Sense of Order)'에서 "우리가 아무리 규칙과 불규칙의 차이를 분석한다고 하더라도, 우리는 궁극적으로 미학적 경험의 가장 기본적인 사실, 즉 즐거움이란 지루함과 혼란 사이의 어딘가에 존재한다는 사실을 설명할 수 있어야 한다."라고 선언한다. 우리는 이미 인간이 얼마나 지속적인 갈등 속에 갇혀 있는가를 경험해 왔다. 즉 우리는 한편으로는 질서의 감각과 예측 가능성을 유지할 필요성을 추구하면서도, 다른 한편으로 그러한 안정성이 해체와 붕괴에 취약하다는 것을 인지하고 있다. 따라서, 여러 가닥의 의미를 한데 모을 강박적 필요성이 존재하며, 이를 통해 존재의 완전성을 유지하고 스스로에게 자신의 존재를 안심시킨다. 하지만 지속적으로 예측 가능한 상태에 있는 것은 지루함과 초조함으로 이어질 수 있다는 것도 사실이다. 감각의 부재의 경우에서와 같이 초연속성(super-continuity)이라고 불리는 것과 같은 완전한 자극의 부재 속에서 더 나쁜 것을 경험할 수 있다.

39 다음 중 본문의 제목으로 가장 적합한 것은?

① 중용의 가치

② 지각적 오류 및 개념적 오류를 예방하는 방법

③ 자동화된 창의성

④ 연속성에 대한 강박적 요구

| 정답 | ①

| 해설 | 규칙성은 질서와 예측 가능성, 완전성으로 이어지고, 이는 다시 지루함과 초조함을 유발한다. 이것이 극심해진 상태를 본문에서는 초연속성이라고 부르고 있으며, 이는 더 나쁜 경험으로 이어진다. 반면 불규칙성은 혼란을 유발한다고 말하고 있다. 이런 상황에서 본문은 "즐거움이란 지루함과 혼란 사이의 어딘가에 존재"하는 것이라고 설명하고 있다. 이것이 바로 ①에서 말한 중용(moderation)에 해당한다.

40 다음 중 본문을 통해 추론할 수 있는 것은?

① 격동의 시대에, 사람들은 풍부한 즐거움의 경험을 무시하는 경우가 많다.

② 일관성과 혼돈의 동시적 상황을 적절한 수준에서 수용하는 것이 필요하다.

③ 다양한 병립은 모순과 무질서로 이어진다.

④ 보다 일반적인 단편적 경험이 초연속성에 기여한다.

| 정답 | ②

| 해설 | 본문의 "여러 가닥의 의미를 한데 모을 강박적 필요성이 존재"한다는 내용을 통해 질서를 의미하는 '일관성'을 추구하면서도 이런 일관성이 지루함과 초조함으로 이어질 수 있기 때문에 질서의 반대적 속성인 '혼돈'도 함께 수용해야 한다고 말하고 있다. 따라서 정답은 ②가 된다.

| 어휘 | **analyse** ⓥ 분석하다

account for 설명하다; (~%를) 차지하다

boredom ⓝ 지루함, 권태

perpetual ⓐ 영구적인, 영속하는, 끊임없는

predictability ⓝ 예측 가능성

be vulnerable to ~에 영향을 받기 쉽다, 민감하다

dissolution ⓝ (결혼 생활의) 파경; (사업상 관계의) 해소; (의회의) 해산

collapse ⓝ (계획의) 좌절, 붕괴

compulsive ⓐ 자제가 힘든, 강박적인; 강제적인

thread ⓝ 실; (이야기 등의) 가닥, 맥락

restlessness ⓝ 초조함, 차분하지 못함

stimulation ⓝ 자극

moderation ⓝ 중용, 온건

turbulent ⓐ 몹시 거친, 사나운

coherence ⓝ 일관성, (문체, 이론 등의) 통일, 응집

incoherence ⓝ 앞뒤가 맞지 않음

ultimately ⓐ 궁극적으로, 결국

aesthetic ⓐ 미적인

confusion ⓝ 혼란

conflict ⓝ 갈등, 충돌

on the one hand 한편으로는

hence ⓐ 이런 이유로

draw together 한데 모으다

reassure ⓥ 안심시키다

absence ⓝ 부재

deprivation ⓝ 박탈, 상실

conceptual ⓐ 개념의, 구상의

accommodate ⓥ 수용하다

juxtaposition ⓝ 병렬, 병치

fragmentary ⓐ 파편의, 단편적인, 미완성의

해석

1937년 존 빈센트 아타나소프(John Vincent Atanasoff) 교수와 대학원생인 클리프 베리(Cliff Berry)에 의해 ABC[아타나소프-베리 컴퓨터(Atanasoff-Berry Computer)]의 개발이 시작되었다. ABC의 개발은 아이오와주립대학에서 1942년까지 계속되었다. ABC는 전자식 컴퓨터로 2진법 계산 및 불 논리 같은 디지털 계산을 위해 진공관을 사용했으며 CPU가 없었다. 1973년 10월 19일 얼 R. 라슨(Earl R. Larson) 미국 연방 판사는 J. 프레스퍼 에커트(J. Presper Eckert)와 존 모클리(John Mauchly)가 보유한 에니악[ENIAC; 전자식 숫자 적분 및 계산기(Electronic Numerical Integrator And Computer)]의 특허가 무효라는 판결을 내렸다. 이에 덧붙여 판사는 아타나소프를 전자식 디지털 컴퓨터의 발명가로 명명했다.

에니악은 1943년에 개발이 시작되었고 1946년이 되어서야 개발이 완료되었다. 에니악은 1,800평방피트의 공간을 점유했고, 18,000개 가량의 진공관을 사용했으며, 무게가 거의 50톤이나 되었다. 판사가 ABC를 최초의 디지털 컴퓨터로 판결했지만 여전히 많은 사람들은 에니악을 최초의 디지털 컴퓨터로 여기고 있는데, 그 이유는 완전한 기능을 발휘한 것이 에니악이었기 때문이다. 에니악은 발사체의 탄도를 계산할 목적으로 군에 의해 사용되었다. 현재 우리 주변 어디에서나 컴퓨터를 볼 수 있다. 휴대 전화에는 컴퓨터가 내장되어 있고, 수많은 신용 카드뿐만 아니라 대중교통 이용을 위한 교통 카드에도 마찬가지로 컴퓨터가 내장되어 있다. 현대식 자동차는 엔진, 브레이크, 등, 라디오를 제어하기 위해 몇 개의 컴퓨터를 보유하고 있다.

유비쿼터스 컴퓨팅의 등장은 우리 삶의 여러 측면을 변화시켰다. 과거에는 공장에서 반복적인 조립 업무를 수행하기 위해 사람들을 고용했지만, 현재는 이러한 작업은 컴퓨터로 제어되는 로봇에 의해 수행되고 있으며, 이들 로봇은 컴퓨터를 다룰 줄 아는 소수의 사람들에 의해 작동되고 있다. 책과 음악 및 영화는 종종 컴퓨터를 통해 소비되며, 책과 음악 및 영화의 제작에 있어 거의 항상 컴퓨터의 활용이 수반된다.

---

41 저자가 본문을 작성한 주된 목적은 무엇인가?

① 컴퓨터에 대한 간략한 역사를 소개함

② 컴퓨터의 특정 이용 사례에 대해 비판함

③ 컴퓨터의 중요성을 과소평가함

④ 디지털 컴퓨터의 기능을 정의함

| 정답 | ①

| 해설 | 저자는 ABC와 에니악의 개발 역사를 제시하는 것으로 시작하여 현재 컴퓨터가 어떤 기능을 수행하는지를 설명하는 식으로 컴퓨터의 간략한 역사를 소개하고 있다. 본문 마지막 단락에서 디지털 컴퓨터가 어떤 기능을 수행하고 있는지는 소개하고 있지만, 구체적 정의는 등장하지 않았다. 따라서 보기 중에서 답으로 가장 적합한 것은 ①이다.

---

42 빈칸 (A)에 가장 알맞은 것은 무엇인가?

① 감염   ② 등장   ③ 탈출   ④ 분기

| 정답 | ②

| 해설 | 본문 마지막 단락은 유비쿼터스 컴퓨팅이 "빈칸"한 이후 어떤 일이 벌어졌는지를 설명하고 있다. 본문에서 설명된 바는 없지만 유비쿼터스 컴퓨팅이란 "언제 어디서든 어떤 기기를 통해서도 컴퓨팅할 수 있는 것"을 의미한다. 빈칸이 들어간 문장 다음을 보면, 유비쿼터스 컴퓨팅을 통해 컴퓨터가 공장, 책, 음악, 영화 분야에서 필수적인 요소가 되었음을 알 수 있다. 즉 유비쿼터스 컴퓨팅이 "등장"한 덕분에 이 모든 것들이 가능해진 것이다. 따라서 답은 ②이다.

43 본문에 따르면 에니악은 어디서 쓰였는가?

① 휴대 전화기   ② 군대   ③ 자동차   ④ 대중교통

| 정답 | ②

| 해설 | "에니악은 발사체의 탄도를 계산할 목적으로 군에 의해 사용되었다(The ENIAC was used by the military to compute the trajectories of projectiles)." 여기서 답은 ②임을 알 수 있다.

44 본문에 따르면 다음 중 사실인 것은 무엇인가?

① ABC는 에니악이 발명되기 전까지 완성되지 않았다.

② 현재 공장에서는 반복적인 조립 업무를 극적으로 줄였다.

③ ABC는 에니악과 같은 수준으로 완전한 기능을 갖추지 못했다.

④ 에니악이 최초의 디지털 컴퓨터라고 말하는 사람은 소수에 불과하다.

| 정답 | ③

| 해설 | "여전히 많은 사람들은 에니악을 최초의 디지털 컴퓨터로 여기고 있으며 왜냐하면 완전한 기능을 발휘한 것이 에니악이었기 때문이다(many still consider the ENIAC to be the first digital computer because it was fully functional)." 이는 달리 말하면 ABC의 기능은 에니악에 미치지 못했음을 의미한다. 따라서 답은 ③이다. 그리고 이 문장은 에니악을 최초의 디지털 컴퓨터로 부르는 사람이 소수에 불과하다는 ④의 내용과 상반되며 따라서 ④는 답이 될 수 없다. ABC는 1937년에서 1942년 사이에 개발되었고 에니악은 1943년에서 1946년 사이에 개발되었다. 이는 ①의 내용과 일치하지 않으며 따라서 ①은 답이 될 수 없다. "과거에는 공장에서 반복적인 조립 업무를 수행하기 위해 사람들을 고용했지만, 현재는 이러한 작업은 컴퓨터로 제어되는 로봇에 의해 수행되고 있으며, 이들 로봇은 컴퓨터를 다룰 줄 아는 소수의 사람들에 의해 작동되고 있다(While factories used to employ people to do repetitive assembly tasks, those tasks are today carried out by computer-controlled robots, operated by a few people who know how to work with computers)." 여기서 공장의 반복 업무에 투입되는 사람이 줄었음은 알 수 있지만 이는 업무 자체가 줄어든 것으로는 볼 수 없다. 따라서 ②는 답이 될 수 없다.

45 다음 중 본문에서 유추할 수 있는 것은 무엇인가?

① ABC는 1937년부터 1946년까지 아이오와주립대학에서 개발되었다.

② 에니악은 데이터 센터라 불리는 거대한 건물을 점유했다.

③ 존 빈센트 아타나소프는 디지털 컴퓨터 장치에 대한 특허를 출원하지 않았다.

④ 법원에 따르면 에니악을 만드는 데 사용된 많은 아이디어가 ABC에서 유래했다.

| 정답 | ④

| 해설 | 판사가 에니악의 특허를 무효화하고 ABC를 최초의 디지털 컴퓨터로 판결한 이유는 ABC를 만드는 데 사용된 특허가 에니악에 도용되었기 때문일 것으로 유추할 수 있다. 따라서 답은 ④이다. 앞서 언급되었다시피 ABC의 개발 기간은 1937년에서 1942년으로, 따라서 ①은 답이 될 수 없다. 에니악이 거대한 공간을 점유했다는 내용은 본문에 있지만, 이 거대한 공간이 데이터 센터라 불리는 건물인지 여부는 본문에 언급된 바 없다. 따라서 ②는 답이 될 수 없다. 1973년 판결은 아타나소프가 특허를 출원했기 때문에 에니악의 특허와 충돌이 벌어졌고 그래서 판사가 판결을 내린 것으로 유추 가능하다. 따라서 ③은 답으로 볼 수 없다.

| 어휘 | vacuum tube 진공관

Boolean logic 불 논리

compute ⓥ 계산하다

projectile ⓝ 발사체, 발사 무기

advent ⓝ 도래, 등장

assembly ⓝ 조립

contagion ⓝ 감염

divergence ⓝ 분기, 일탈

file for a patent 특허를 출원하다

binary ⓐ 2진법의

invalid ⓐ 무효한, 효력 없는

trajectory ⓝ 탄도, 궤도

farecard ⓝ 교통 카드

repetitive ⓐ 반복되는, 반복적인

underestimate ⓥ 과소평가하다

exodus ⓝ 탈출

dramatically ⓐ 극적으로

derive from ～에서 유래하다[기인하다]

연습 문제   **01** ①   **02** ②   **03** ③

01 본문에서 내릴 수 있는 결론은 무엇인가?

> 이스라엘 건국 60주년을 맞이하며, 이스라엘 국민들은 축하할 일이 많아 보인다. 돌투성이 조그만 땅 위에 위치한 민주 국가 이스라엘은 전쟁과 테러로 인한 파괴를 견뎠고 이스라엘을 파괴하고자 맹세한 여러 적들도 견뎌 냈다. 하지만 오늘날 이스라엘 내의 분위기는 득의만만하기보다는 수심에 어려 있다. 이스라엘인들은 이란의 핵 공격 위협을 우려하고 있다. 이들은 헤즈볼라가 남부 레바논에서 미사일을 발사해 뿌려 댈 것이라 걱정한다. 또한 이들은 팔레스타인 자살 폭탄 테러범들이 텔아비브와 예루살렘의 버스나 카페에서 또 폭발할 것을 두려워한다.

① 이스라엘은 여전히 위험에 직면하고 있으며 평화와 거리가 멀다.
② 이스라엘은 진정한 국가라기보다는 모자이크와 가깝다.
③ 이스라엘인들에게 종교는 국가 정체성보다 중요하다.
④ 이스라엘인들은 자신들이 팔레스타인인들에게 그들만의 국가를 줘야 한다고 생각한다.

| 정답 | ①

| 해설 | 건국 60주년을 맞이한 이스라엘의 분위기를 "more pensive than jubilant(득의만만하기보다는 수심에 어려 있다)"고 묘사하고 있으며, 이란의 핵 공격 위협, 헤즈볼라, 팔레스타인 자살 폭탄 테러범 등을 그 이유로 들고 있다. 이를 통해 이스라엘의 현 상황은 평화와는 거리가 멀다는 것을 잘 알 수 있으며, 그러므로 보기 중에서 답으로 보기에 가장 적절한 것은 ①이 된다.

| 어휘 | **a patch of** 조그만   **ravage** ⓝ 파괴, 황폐
assortment ⓝ 모음, 종합   **pensive** ⓐ 수심 어린
jubilant ⓐ 의기양양한, 득의만만한   **in peril** 위험에 직면한
national identity 국가 정체성

02 다음 본문에서 주로 가정하고 있는 것은 무엇인가?

최근 파키스탄에 발굴된 유물이 고대의 위대한 도시 문화 중 하나인 수수께끼 같은 인더스 문명의 재평가를 위한 영감을 불어넣어 줬다. 인더스 문명은 고대 구대륙의 4대 위대한 문명 중 하나로, 다른 문명에는 메소포타미아 문명, 이집트 문명, 황허 문명 등이 있다. 인더스 문명에 관해서는 다른 세 문명에 관한 것보다 훨씬 덜 알려졌으며, 그 이유는 복구된 유물에서 발견되는 하라파 문자를 언어학자들이 아직 해독하지 못했기 때문이다. 이들 (인더스 문명의) 사라진 사람들과 그들의 사회 구조를 이해하고자 나와 내 동료들은 우리가 발견한 잡다한 유물과 발굴한 잡다한 유적지에서 실마리를 이끌었다. 이같이 노력을 쏟는 과정에서 하라파 문자로 쓰인 글이 전혀 쓸모없지는 않았다. 우리는 하라파 문자가 쓰인 용도의 맥락을 살펴서 (문자를) 이해할 수 있었다.

① 발굴지 내 유물이 발견된 지점은 그 유물의 사회적 중요도의 실마리가 된다.
② 문명을 이해하는 데 있어 문명의 언어를 해독할 수 있는 것은 큰 도움이 된다.
③ 고대 도시 문명의 사회 구조에는 공통점이 존재한다.
④ 유능한 고고학자는 연구 중인 문명의 언어를 배워야 한다.

| 정답 | ②

| 해설 | 우선 다른 고대 문명에 비해 인더스 문명에 관해 알려진 것이 많지 않은 이유로 "하라파 문자를 언어학자들이 아직 해독하지 못했기 때문(linguists have yet to decipher the Harappan script)"이라 말하고 있으며, 저자와 그 동료들은 아직 문자를 완벽히 해석하진 못했어도 어느 정도 문자가 유물에서 사용된 맥락을 살펴서 인더스 문명에 관해 "실마리를 이끌어 낼(have drawn clues)" 수 있었다. 따라서 문명의 이해를 위해 문명의 언어를 이해하는 일이 중요함을 유추할 수 있다. 그러므로 답은 ②가 된다. ①과 ③은 모두 본문과는 별 관련이 없기 때문에 답으로 보기 힘들다. ④의 경우, 연구 대상의 문명의 언어를 배우는 일은 당연히 중요하겠지만, 본문에 언급된 인더스 문명에서 사용된 언어는 아직 해독이 안 되어 배우고 싶어도 배울 수 없는 상황이다. 따라서 답으로 보기 힘들다.

| 어휘 | **excavate** ⓥ 발굴하다   **artifact** ⓝ 유물
inspire ⓥ 영감을 불어넣다   **reevaluation** ⓝ 재평가
enigmatic ⓐ 수수께끼의   **linguist** ⓝ 언어학자
decipher ⓥ 해독하다, 판독하다   **script** ⓝ 문자
vanish ⓥ 사라지다, 사라지게 하다   **clue** ⓝ 실마리
miscellaneous ⓐ 여러 종류의, 잡다한   **writing** ⓝ 글, 쓰기
glean ⓥ (정보·지식을) 얻다, 모으다   **insight** ⓝ 이해, 간파
effective ⓐ 유능한, 효과적인   **archaeologist** ⓝ 고고학자

다음 우화가 시사하는 것으로 가장 알맞은 것은?

어느 겨울 한 농부가 추위로 뻣뻣하게 굳은 뱀을 발견하였다. 뱀은 농부에게 "만약 당신이 나를 구해 배 속에 넣어 준다면, 당신 체온으로 나를 따뜻하게 할 수 있을 거예요."라고 얘기했다. 농부는 "만약 내가 그렇게 한다면 너를 나를 물 텐데." 그러자 뱀은 "당신이 내 생명을 구해 주는데 왜 그러겠어요?"라고 답했다. 농부는 뱀을 측은하게 여겨, 뱀을 구해 가슴 속에 넣어 주었다. 뱀은 빠르게 온기를 회복한 후에 자신의 타고난 본능을 되찾고는 그 은인인 농부를 물어 치명적인 상처를 가했다. 농부가 "오 이런, 왜 당신을 구해 준 나를 물었는가?"라고 울부짖었다. 그러자 뱀은 "당신은 나를 구할 때 내가 뱀인 것을 알았잖소."라고 답했다. 마지막으로 깊은 한숨을 쉬면서 농부는 "내가 악당을 구했으니 이렇게 당하는 것도 당연하지."라고 말했다.

① 어떤 것들은 행하기보다 말하기가 더 쉽다.
② 현명한 사람은 남의 불행으로부터 배운다.
③ 대단히 친절한 행동도 타고난 본성을 바꿀 수는 없다.
④ 자신이 놀림당하지 않으려면 남을 놀리지 마라.

| 정답 | ③

| 해설 | 뱀은 빠르게 온기를 회복한 후에 자신의 타고난 본능을 되찾고는 그 은인인 농부를 물어 치명적인 상처를 가했다는 내용에서 아무리 선하게 대한다 해도 악인의 본성을 바꿀 수는 없다는 이솝 우화의 내용이다.

| 어휘 | stiff ⓐ 뻣뻣한, 굳은   frozen ⓐ 언, 얼은
        take up 착수하다, 시작하다   benefactor ⓝ 은인
        mortal ⓐ 치명적인, 죽을 수 밖에 없는   scoundrel ⓝ 악당
        play trick on 놀리다

01	①	02	③	03	③	04	②	05	③	06	①	07	②	08	③	09	⑤	10	⑤
11	②	12	④	13	②	14	②	15	④	16	②	17	③	18	②	19	③	20	③
21	②	22	③	23	②	24	③	25	④	26	①	27	④	28	①	29	①	30	②

[01~02]

해석

외래 침입종은 과학적으로 수수께끼인 존재이다. 인간은 동물과 식물이 처음 진화했던 장소에서 수천 마일 떨어진 곳으로 동물과 식물을 이동시킨다. 이렇게 이동한 여러 종 가운데 대부분은 새로 생긴 고향에서 죽고 만다. 일부는 간신히 생존을 이어간다. 하지만 일부는 생태계의 악몽이 되어 토종을 능가한다. 과학자들은 이런 종이 어떻게 고향에서 멀리 떨어진 곳에서도 우월한 존재임이 입증되었는지 그 이유를 확신하지 못하고 있으며 다음과 같이 질문을 던진다. "토종은 자신들이 살고 있는 환경에 적응했고 외래종은 다른 환경으로부터 온 종인데, 어떻게 외래종은 토종이 살던 환경에 침입하여 살아갈 수 있는 것일까?" 생태학자들은 미국 북동부에 등장한 수많은 외래종이 동아시아에서 침입한 종임을 알게 되었다. 하지만 그 반대의 경우는 사실이 아니다 (미국에서 동아시아로 간 종은 살아남지 못했다). 이는 우연이 아니다. 이는 외래 침입종이 진화한 서식지와 관련이 있다. 세계의 일부 지역은 진화적 측면에서 인큐베이터와 같은 역할을 해서 다른 환경에서 번성할 수 있는 준비를 갖춘 우월한 경쟁종을 낳고 있다. 외래 침입 식물은 매우 다양한 종이 서로 경쟁 중인 서식지에서 진화할 가능성이 크다. 이러한 종들은 더욱 다양해지고, 진화하여, 결국에는 우월한 경쟁종이 되어 침입할 준비를 갖춘다.

---

01 본문에 따르면 다음 중 (A)의 답에 해당하는 것은 무엇인가?

① 외래종이 진화하는 장소에 좌우된다.
② 서식지의 천적과 관련이 있다.
③ 외래종은 우월한 유전적 구성을 갖춘 돌연변이인 경향을 보인다.
④ 외래종은 새로운 환경으로 향하는 도중에 빠르게 진화한다.

| 정답 | ①

| 해설 | "이는 외래 침입종이 진화한 서식지와 관련이 있다. 세계의 일부 지역은 진화적 측면에서 인큐베이터와 같은 역할을 해서 다른 환경에서 번성할 수 있는 준비를 갖춘 우월한 경쟁종을 낳고 있다(It has to do with the habitats in which invasive species evolve. There is evidence that some parts of the world have been evolutionary incubators, producing superior competitors primed to thrive in other environments)." 즉 일부 외래 침입종이 번성하는 이유는 해당 침입종이 살고 진화하던 서식지와 관련이 있는 것이다. 여기서 답은 ①임을 알 수 있다.

---

02 (B)에 가장 알맞은 것은 무엇인가?

① 곧바로 멸종하다   ② 진화적 지위
③ 우월한 경쟁종   ④ 생존하기엔 너무 복잡한

| 정답 | ③

| 해설 | 서식지에서 진화한 외래종은 이미 경쟁이 심한 곳에서 살다 보니 계속된 경쟁 끝에 더욱 다양해지고 계속 진화한다. 살아남기 위해 진화한 끝에 "우월한 경쟁종"이 되어 다른 곳에 이동하고 나서는 기존에 살던 토종을 능가하게 되는 것이다. 따라서 답은 ③이다.

| 어휘 | **invasive species** 외래 침입종, 생태계교란 생물
eke out 가까스로 살아가다, 겨우 (생계를) 이어나가다
outcompete ⓥ 다른 경쟁자들보다 훨씬 뛰어난
adapt ⓥ 적응하다
observe ⓥ (~을 보고) 알다
coincidence ⓝ 우연의 일치
prime ⓥ 준비시키다, 대비시키다
have to do with ~와 관련이 있다
makeup ⓝ 구성, 구조
niche=ecological niche ⓝ 생태적 지위; 특정 환경에서 생물종이 지니는 생태적 역할

barely ⓐⓓ 간신히, 가까스로
ecological ⓐ 생태계의
native ⓝ (동식물의) 토종[자생종]
exotic ⓝ 외래종
alien ⓐ 외래의, 외계의
habitat ⓝ 서식지
diversity ⓝ 다양성
mutation ⓝ 돌연변이
extinct ⓐ 멸종한

[03~04] 경기대 2011

해석

"있는 그대로 그려 달라."고 올리버 크롬웰이 화가 렐리에게 말했다. "만일 흉터나 주름을 빼고 그린다면 한 푼도 주지 않겠다"고 덧붙였다. 사소한 일화에서조차 크롬웰은 양식 있는 모습을 보여 주었다. (화가는) 그에게 일반적 특징을 지닌 얼굴과 매끈한 뺨을 그리려는 쓸데없는 일을 하려고 했지만, 크롬웰은 자신의 얼굴의 특징적인 것이 모두 사라지는 것을 원하지 않았다. 그는 자신의 얼굴에 세월과 전쟁, 잠 못 들었던 많은 밤들과 근심, 혹은 후회 등으로 인해 생긴 모든 결점들이 보이는 것에 만족해했다. 하지만 동시에 이런 얼굴의 결점들은 용기와 정책과 권위, 대중의 걱정에 의해 새겨진 것이라고도 생각했다. 위대한 인물들이 만일 어떤 것이 자신에게 가장 이득이 되는지 안다면, 이들이 자신의 마음을 초상화로 남기기를 원한 것은 어쩌면 당연한 일이다.

03 Cromwell이 어떤 식으로 묘사되기를 원하는지에 대해 그가 선택한 것을 본문의 저자는 어떤 느낌으로 바라보고 있는가?

① 해방, 자유, 이탈
② 냉소
③ 인정
④ 불쾌감, 혐오

| 정답 | ③

| 해설 | 본문 전반부에서 저자는 Cromwell이 "good sense(양식, 분별)"를 보여 주었다고 설명하고 있으며, 후반부에서는 Cromwell을 "great men(위인)"으로 묘사하면서, 외형의 얼굴이 아닌 내면의 마음이 그려지길 원했을 것이라고 생각하고 있다. 따라서 긍정의 느낌으로 Cromwell을 바라보고 있다는 것을 알 수 있으므로 정답은 ③이 된다.

04 본문에서는 화가들이 자신이 그림을 그리는 대상(subject)의 결점이나 불완전한 면을 감춘다면 이는 어떠하다는 것을 암시하는가?

① 사실적으로 그리는 이들보다 많은 돈을 받을 수 있다.

② 그림의 대상에게 사실상 호의를 베푸는 것이 아니다.

③ 그림의 대상이 갖고 있는 내면의 아름다움을 드러내는 것이다.

④ 화가 자신의 미적 선호도를 드러내는 것이다.

| 정답 | ②

| 해설 | 본문에 나오는 올리버 크롬웰은 아마도 얼굴에 상처나 흉터가 많았을 것으로 생각된다. 하지만 자신의 초상화에 그런 결점들이 모두 나타나기를 희망했으며, 그런 결점들 하나하나가 자신이 지나온 세월과 자신이 이루고자 했던 것들을 대변한다고 생각했다. 본문의 저자는 크롬웰의 그런 점을 높이 사서, 위인이라면 자신의 내면의 모습을 남기길 원할 것이라고 후반부에 말하고 있다. 그런 면에서 대상(subject)의 결점을 감춰 그리는 것은 대상에게 좋은 일이 아니라는 ②가 정답이 된다.

| 어휘 | **leave out** 제외하다, 무시하다

wrinkle ⓝ 주름

trifle ⓝ 하찮은 것, 사소한 일

countenance ⓝ 얼굴, 표정

feature ⓝ 특징, 얼굴 생김새

blemish ⓝ 흠, 결점, 얼룩; 오점

valor ⓝ 용맹, 용기

disengagement ⓝ 해방, 자유, 이탈

distaste ⓝ 불쾌감, 혐오

conceal ⓥ 감추다

do sb a favor ~에게 은혜를 베풀다, ~에게 호의를 베풀다, ~의 부탁을 들어주다

scar ⓝ 상처

shilling ⓝ (영국의 화폐 단위) 실링

good sense 양식, 분별

vain ⓐ 헛된, 쓸데없는

content ⓐ 만족한

remorse ⓝ 후회

in one's best interests ~에게 가장 이득이 되는

approval ⓝ 승인, 인정

subject ⓝ (그림·사진 등의) 대상; 실험 대상

해석

민간 설화의 목적 가운데 하나로 즐거움을 들 수 있겠지만, 이것만이 민간 설화의 유일한 기능은 아니다. 민간 설화가 오랫동안 살아남고 인간의 모든 사회에서 매우 널리 퍼진 원인은 민간 설화가 청중을 교육하기 때문이다. 민간 설화는 옳고 그름에 대한 지각이나 자립의 필요성같이 사회가 생존을 위해 필수적이라고 판단하는 가치를 서서히 주입시킨다. 민간 설화는 적절한 행동을 위한 표본을 제공하는 것 이외에도 자연계의 기원 및 의미에 관한 설명을 제공하며, 종종 이는 전통문화로부터 기인한다.

학자들은 여러 장소의 민간 설화 속에서 동일한 상황이 매우 빈번하게 반복된다는 사실에 매혹되었다. 신데렐라 이야기의 유사 버전의 수는 파악된 것이 3백 개가 넘는다. 동일한 이야기가 서로 멀리 떨어진 여러 사회에서 자연스럽게 등장한 것일 수도 있고, 아니면 여행자들에 의해 확산된 후 청자의 요구에 맞춰 각색된 것일 수도 있다. 이야기가 동일한 경우 이외에도, 동일한 주제가 되풀이해서 발견되기도 한다. 가장 흔한 주제 중 하나로 무력한 자가 강력한 자를 상대로 간교한 꾀를 무기로 활용하는 경우이다. 미국 남부의 아프리카계 흑인들의 민간 설화를 기반으로 조엘 챈들러 해리스(Joel Chandler Harris)가 지은 리머스 삼촌(Uncle Remus) 이야기 시리즈야말로 가장 좋은 사례이다.

리머스 삼촌 이야기 시리즈 가운데 가장 재밌는 것으로 토끼 형제(Brer Rabbit) 이야기를 들 수 있다. 이 이야기에서 토끼 형제는 여우 형제(Brer Fox) 때문에 위기에 빠진다. 토끼 형제는 자신을 사로잡은 여우 형제에게 절대로 자신을 찔레 가시덤불에 던지지 말아 달라고 간청했고, 그보다는 목을 매달거나 물에 빠뜨리거나 심지어 산 채로 가죽을 벗기는 편이 낫다고 말했다. 야비한 성격을 지닌 여우 형제는 곧바로 자신의 제물이 하지 말아 달라고 간청한 일을 한다. 물론 토끼 형제는 찔레 가시덤불에서 쉽게 탈출했고, 자기가 "찔레 가시덤불에서 나고 자랐다"고 외치면서 여우 형제를 놀리며 날쌔게 움직였다.

---

05 빈칸 (A)에 가장 알맞은 것은 무엇인가?

① ~의 여부에 따라
② 명목상의
③ 널리 퍼진
④ 익명인

| 정답 | ③

| 해설 | 민간 설화는 "오랫동안 살아남았고(have survived for so long)" 신데렐라 이야기처럼 여러 곳에서 비슷한 형태의 민간 설화가 등장한다. 이는 민간 설화가 오래 살아남아 전해질 만큼 "널리 퍼졌기" 때문이다. 따라서 답은 ③이다.

---

06 아래 문장이 들어가기에 가장 알맞은 장소는 어디인가?

신데렐라 이야기의 유사 버전의 수는 파악된 것이 3백 개가 넘는다.

① [1]
② [2]
③ [3]
④ [4]

| 정답 | ①

| 해설 | 신데렐라 이야기는 비슷한 내용의 민간 설화가 여러 곳에서 발견된 경우의 한 사례이다. 여기서 주어진 문장이 들어갈 장소는 비슷한 민간 설화가 여러 곳에서 발견되는 것과 관련된 곳이어야 함을 유추할 수 있다. 이를 감안하고 주어진 문장을 대입해 보면 가장 답에 가까운 것은 앞에서는 "여러 장소의 민간 설화 속에서 동일한 상황이 매우 빈번하게 반복된다는 사실(how

frequently the same situations recur in folk tales from many different places)"이 언급되고, 뒤에서는 왜 이런 일이 일어나는지를 "동일한 이야기가 서로 멀리 떨어진 여러 사회에서 자연스럽게 등장한 것일 수도 있고, 아니면 여행자들에 의해 확산된 후 청자의 요구에 맞춰 각색된 것일 수도 있다(erhaps the same stories appeared spontaneously in many distant societies, or perhaps they were spread by travelers and adapted to fit the needs of their listeners)"라고 설명한 [1]이다.

---

07 저자는 _____을 예로 들기 위해 토끼 형제의 이야기를 활용했다.

　① 민간 설화에서 다른 문화의 상황이 반복

　② 상대방보다 더 오래 살고 더 오래 가기 위한 주제로서 책략

　③ 민간 설화가 오락을 통해 어떻게 살아남았는가

　④ 아프리카계 미국인들의 자연계의 기원을 보여 주기

| 정답 | ②

| 해설 | 토끼 형제 이야기는 "무력한 자가 강력한 자를 상대로 간교한 꾀를 무기로 활용하는 경우(the use of guile as a weapon of the helpless against the powerful)"의 대표적 사례이다. 따라서 답은 ②이다.

---

08 본문에 따르면 다음 중 사실인 것은 무엇인가?

　① 민간 설화의 주제는 다른 어떤 주제에서도 반복되지 않는다.

　② 청중을 즐겁게 하는 것은 민간 설화의 주된 목적이다.

　③ 민간 설화는 청중을 교육하는 데 있어 유용하다.

　④ 민간 설화는 도덕적 지침을 제시하려 한 적이 없다.

| 정답 | ③

| 해설 | "민간 설화가 오랫동안 살아남고 인간의 모든 사회에서 매우 널리 퍼진 원인은 민간 설화가 청중을 교육하기 때문이다(The reason they have survived for so long and are so prevalent in all human societies is that they educate their audiences)." 여기서 ③이 답임을 유추할 수 있다. ①은 앞서 신데렐라 이야기를 통해 언급된 사항과 정반대이며, 따라서 답이 될 수 없다. ②는 민간 설화의 목적 중 하나로 언급은 되지만 본문 어디에도 주된 목적이라 언급된 바 없다. "민간 설화는 옳고 그름에 대한 지각이나 자립의 필요성같이 사회가 생존을 위해 필수적이라고 판단하는 가치를 서서히 주입시킨다(They seek to instill values that the society may consider imperative for its survival, such as a sense of right and wrong or the need for self-reliance)"에서 옳고 그름에 대한 지각은 도덕적 지침의 일종으로 볼 수 있다. 따라서 ④는 본문의 내용과 일치하지 않는다.

| 어휘 |

folk tale 민간 설화

instill ⓥ 스며들게 하다, 서서히 주입시키다

sense ⓝ 양식, 지각

derive from ~에서 유래하다[기인하다]

be struck by ~에 끌리다, ~에 매혹되다

spontaneously ⓐ 자발적으로, 자연스럽게

guile ⓝ 간교한 속임수[꾀]

brier patch 찔레 가시덤불

mean ⓐ 비열한, 야비한

prevalent ⓐ 일반적인, 널리 퍼진

imperative ⓐ 반드시 필요한, 필수적인

self-reliance ⓝ 자립, 자기 의존

folklore ⓝ 민속, 전통문화

recur ⓥ 다시 일어나다, 반복되다

adapted ⓐ 번안된, 각색된

clutch ⓝ 위기

skin ⓥ (동물의) 가죽을 벗기다

disposition ⓝ 성격, 기질

promptly ⓐ 즉각적으로, 지체 없이

mock ⓥ 조롱하다, 놀리다

contingent ⓐ ~의 여부에 따라

anonymous ⓐ 익명인

trickery ⓝ 속임수, 책략

recurrence ⓝ 반복, 재발

extricate ⓥ 탈출시키다, 해방시키다

scamper ⓥ 날쌔게 움직이다

nominal ⓐ 명목상의, 이름뿐인

exemplify ⓥ 예를 들다

outlast ⓥ ~보다 더 오래 살다[오래 가다]

[09~11]

해석

20대 초반이었을 때, 나는 몇 가지 건강 음식만 먹는 다이어트를 해 본 적이 있다. 3주 후에는 8파운드 감량이 라는 목표에 거의 다 가섰다. 그러나 그 이후의 일은 기대했던 것만큼 달콤하지 않았다. 어느 날 밤, 나는 다이어트를 포기하고 그동안 먹고 싶었던 모든 음식들을 마구 먹어 치웠다. 그 2주 동안 나는 그 어느 때보다 많이 먹었다. 당연히, 곧 8파운드가 다시 찐 것은 물론이고 2파운드 가 더 늘었다. 이것은 너무나 자주 듣던 흔한 "다이어트와 폭식의 반복"이었다. 음식에 대한 나의 무모한 탐닉은 단조롭고 제약 많 은 다이어트의 직접적 결과였다. "누군가에게 치즈 케이크를 먹어서는 안 된다고 말한다면, 그들이 가장 먹고 싶은 것은 치즈 케이 크가 될 겁니다."라고 허버트 박사(Dr. Hubbert)는 말한다. 치즈 케이크를 먹고 나면 그들은 "이런, 오늘도 망쳤네. 그러니까 매일 망 치는 게 낫겠어."라고 말한다. 보스턴 소재 터프츠(Tufts)대학의 연구진들은 20세에서 80세 사이의 건강한 남녀 71명이 6개월간 먹 은 모든 것들을 자세히 기록한 보고서를 연구했다. 야채, 과일, 도정이 되지 않은 곡물 같은 영양가 높은 다양한 음식을 매일 섭취한 사람들은 더 마른 경향이 있었다. 연구진들이 발견한 사실은, 사람들이 야채 같이 몸에 좋은 음식들을 다양하게 섭취하면 과자, 사 탕, 감자칩 같은 저영양, 고칼로리 음식을 덜 먹는다는 것이다. 전반적으로, 이들은 음식 섭취량을 의도적으로 줄이지 않고도 더 적 은 칼로리를 섭취한다.

09 다음 중 지문의 중심 주제는 무엇인가?

① 제한적인 다이어트의 중요성

② 고칼로리 음식의 위험성

③ 장기적인 체중 감량 트레이닝의 효과

④ 장기적인 체중 감량의 이점들

⑤ 고영양 음식 섭취의 중요성

| 정답 | ⑤

| 해설 | 지문의 후반부에 상술된 연구 결과에서, 체중 감량을 위해서는 음식 섭취의 제한이 아니라 "영양가 높은 음식 섭취가 더 효 과적"이라는 주제를 찾을 수 있다. "People who routinely ate a variety of nutrient-dense foods such as vegetables, fruits, and whole grains tended to be lean." 참조.

10 다음 중 지문에 언급된 과학자들이 동의할 주장으로 가장 적절한 것은?

① 식사 후에 운동해라.
② 제한적인 다이어트를 계속해라.
③ 고칼로리 음식을 많이 섭취해라.
④ 음식의 유혹을 이겨 내라.
⑤ 영양이 풍부한 음식을 다양하게 섭취해라.

| 정답 | ⑤

| 해설 | 주제를 완성하는 문제이다. 지문에 상술된 연구 결과는 "영양가가 높은 다양한 음식들을 섭취하는 것이 중요하다."는 것이므로 ⑤가 주제와 일치한다. 음식의 유혹을 견디는 것은 잘못된 다이어트 방식이므로 ④를 선택하지 않도록 주의한다.

11 다음 중 지문의 구성을 가장 잘 나타낸 것은?

① 한 이론에 대한 서로 다른 의견들을 제시한다.
② 문제점을 설명한 후 가능성 있는 해결책을 논의한다.
③ 문제점에 대한 두 개의 해결책을 제시하고 수용한다.
④ 일반적인 아이디어를 먼저 제시한 후 여러 개의 예시를 보여 준다.
⑤ 권고 사항을 분석한 후 반박한다.

| 정답 | ②

| 해설 | 이 글은 전반부에 잘못된 다이어트 방식의 문제점을 제시한 후, 후반부에 그 해결책을 제시하는 구조이다. 지문에 예시가 있기는 하지만 글의 구조를 결정하는 지배적인 전개 방식은 아니므로 ④를 선택하지 않도록 주의한다.

| 어휘 | **be limited to** ~에 한정되다
progress ⓝ 진전, 과정
gorge on ~을 게걸스럽게 먹어 치우다
no surprise that ~은 당연하다
put on 몸무게가 늘다
cycle ⓝ 주기, 반복
indulgence ⓝ 탐닉, 하고 싶은 대로 함
restrictive ⓐ 제한적인
may as well ~하는 것이 낫다
detailed ⓐ 자세한
a variety of 다양한
whole grain 도정을 하지 않은 곡물
lean ⓐ 마른
calorie-dense ⓐ 고열량의
consume ⓥ 섭취하다
restrict ⓥ 제한하다

reach ⓥ 도달하다
abandon ⓥ 포기하다
miss ⓥ 그리워하다, 놓치다
regain ⓥ 다시 얻다
binge ⓝ 폭식, 폭음
brazen ⓐ 뻔뻔한, 놋쇠의
boring ⓐ 지루한, 단조로운
blow ⓥ 망치다, 실패하다
provide ⓥ 제공하다
routinely ⓓ 일상적으로
nutrient-dense ⓐ 영양가가 높은
tend to ~하는 경향이 있다
desirable ⓐ 바람직한, 좋은
overall ⓐ 전체적으로, 종합적으로
consciously ⓓ 의식적으로
intake ⓝ 섭취(량)

해석

우리 가운데 대부분은 긍정적 태도가 건강을 향상시키고 질병으로부터의 회복 속도를 높인다는 사실을 알고 있다. 하지만 이것이 과연 반대로도 작용할까? '체화된 인지'는 우리가 행동하는 방식이 어떻게 우리가 사고하는 방식과 느끼는 방식에 영향을 미치는지 기술하기 위해 심리학자들이 사용하는 용어이다. 이 매력적인 분야에 관한 초창기 연구를 보면, 이로 연필을 수평으로 물고 있으면 미소를 짓는 데 사용되는 근육이 활성화되기 때문에 우리의 뇌에 쾌락 신호를 보내게 되는 반면에 잔주름을 펴기 위해 보톡스 주사를 맞은 사람들은 시술 후 행복감을 더 느끼게 된다는 것이 입증되었다. 만일 마사지를 받는 동안 울어 본 경험이 있다면 근육이 단순히 조직과 섬유질이 합해진 것은 아님을 알게 될 것이다. 근육에는 우리의 정서적 삶에 대한 섬세한 흔적이 담겨 있으며 정신의 작용을 통한 영향력 없이도 감정을 불러일으킬 수 있는 역량이 존재한다. 우리의 몸은 감정의 시초가 되며 정서적 경험의 강력한 공동 창조자가 될 수 있다. 그리고 이를 입증하는 연구도 존재한다.

12 다음 중 빈칸에 가장 적합한 것은 무엇인가?
　① 거울
　② 주인
　③ 저장소
　④ 시초

| 정답 | ④

| 해설 | 본문의 핵심은 "마음이 몸에 영향을 주는 것처럼 몸도 마음에 영향을 준다"이다. 이를 감안하고 문제를 보면, 빈칸에는 "우리의 몸은 감정이 생겨나게 만드는 역할을 할 수 있다"는 취지에서 ④가 적합하다.

13 다음 중 본문의 주제에 대한 적절한 예가 아닌 것은 무엇인가?
　① 용기가 없을 때는 팔을 활짝 펴라.
　② 기분이 좋지 않을 때는 행복한 추억을 떠올려라.
　③ 외롭다는 기분이 들면 뜨거운 물로 목욕하라.
　④ 창의성을 발휘해야겠다면 춤 강습을 받으라.

| 정답 | ②

| 해설 | 본문은 마음이 몸에 영향을 주고 몸도 마음에 영향을 미친다는 내용을 담고 있다. 이를 감안하고 보기를 보면, ②는 몸과는 관계없이 정신적인 내용만을 다루고 있지만 나머지는 몸을 통해 정신적 효과를 얻는 내용을 다루고 있다. 따라서 답은 ②이다.

| 어휘 | **the other way around** 반대로, 거꾸로
fascinating ⓐ 대단히 흥미로운, 매력적인
laughter lines 잔주름
delicate ⓐ 섬세한, 미묘한
executive ⓐ 집행의, 운영의
reservoir ⓝ 저수지, 저장소

embodied cognition 체화된 인지
horizontally ⓐⓓ 수평으로
amalgamation ⓝ 합동, 합병
engender ⓥ 낳다, 불러일으키다
originator ⓝ 시초, 창시자
timid ⓐ 소심한, 용기가 없는

[14~18] 덕성여대 2011

감기에 잘 걸리게 하는 또 다른 주요 요인은 바로 나이(age)이다. 인디애나(Indiana)공중보건대학에서 실시한 연구를 보면, 일반인에게 잘 들어맞는 것으로 보이는 상세한 내용들이 제공되어 있다. 유아들은 감기에 가장 잘 걸리는 집단으로, 생후 1년간 평균 6차례 이상 감기에 걸린다. 3세까지는 남아들이 여아들에 비해 감기에 더 잘 걸리며, 3세 이후에는 여아들이 남아들보다 감기에 더 걸리기 쉽고, 십 대 소녀들은 1년에 평균 3번 감기에 걸리는 반면 십 대 소년들이 1년에 2번 감기 걸린다.

성인이 될수록 감기의 발병률은 계속 감소한다. 건강한 노인들은 1년에 한두 번일 정도로 감기에 거의 걸리지 않는다. 20대에서, 그것도 여성의 경우에서, 예외를 찾아볼 수 있는데 이들은 감기 감염률이 높다. 왜냐면 이 나이대의 사람들은 대부분 어린아이가 있기 때문이다. 30대나 40대까지 출산을 미뤄 뒤늦게 어린아이를 키우는 사람들도 갑자기 감기 감염률이 증가한다.

또한 이 연구에서는 경제력도 중요한 역할을 한다는 사실이 밝혀졌다. 수입이 증가하면 가정에서 감기에 걸리는 빈도가 감소한다. 최저소득층 가정은 최고소득층 가정보다 감기 발병률이 대략 1/3 정도 높다. 저소득층 사람들은 부유층이 사는 공간보다 더 비좁은 장소에서 살 수밖에 없으며, 이렇게 밀집해서 생활하기 때문에 감기 바이러스가 이 사람에서 저 사람으로 옮겨질 기회가 증가한다. 저소득은 또한 식단에도 악영향을 줄 수 있다. 불충분한 영양 섭취가 감기 감염률에 어느 정도 영향력을 끼치는지 아직 명확하게 밝혀지지는 않았지만, 불충분한 식단이 일반적으로 감기의 저항력을 약화시키는 것으로 추정된다.

14 다음 중 첫 번째 문단의 'particulars'와 의미가 가장 가까운 것은?

① 사소한 문제들   ② 특정 사실들
③ 작은 차이들   ④ 개인들

| 정답 | ②

| 해설 | particular는 형용사로 '특정한'의 의미이며, 명사로 사용되면, '특정한 사실이나 상세한 사실'을 의미한다. 따라서 정답은 ②가 된다.

15 본문에서 논의된 연구에서 저자가 주장하는 것은 무엇인가?

① 연구에는 많은 모순이 있다.
② 연구는 아동에 대해 전문으로 다루고 있다.
③ 연구는 그 분야의 이전 연구 결과들과 모순된다.
④ 연구의 결과는 대체로 사람들과 관련 있는 것으로 생각된다.

| 정답 | ④

| 해설 | 본문에서 말한 연구 내용에 모순이 있다고 생각된다면 해당 부분을 제대로 이해하지 못한 결과이며, 이전 연구와 모순된다는 내용은 본문에 등장하지 않는다. 그리고 이 글은 감기의 발병률에 대해 서술하고 있는 것으로 아이들을 대상으로 진행한 연구는 아니다. 따라서 정답은 ④가 되며, 이 부분은 본문 첫 번째 문단의 "... seem to hold true for the general population." 이라는 부분을 paraphrasing한 것이다.

16 본문의 두 번째 문단에 있는 내용이 뒷받침해 주고 있는 사실은?

① 남성은 여성보다 감기에 걸리기 쉽다.

② 어린아이들은 부모에게 감기를 옮긴다.

③ 추운 기후에서 사는 사람들은 따뜻한 기후에 사는 사람들보다 감기에 더 자주 걸린다.

④ 어린아이가 없는 사람들은 아이가 있는 사람들보다 감기에 쉽게 걸린다.

| 정답 | ②

| 해설 | 두 번째 문단을 보면, 성인(maturity)이 될수록 감기에 덜 걸리는 것이 일반적이지만, 예외적으로 어린아이를 키우는 집단(20대 여성들, 뒤늦게 아이를 가진 30~40대 사람들)에서는 감기 발병률이 갑자기 높아진다고 했으므로, 이는 감기에 쉽게 걸리는 아이들을 통해 어른들도 감기에 걸리게 된다는 것을 함축하고 있다. 따라서 정답은 ②가 된다.

17 저자가 마지막 문단을 서술한 주요 목적은 무엇인가?

① 어떻게 감기 바이러스가 전염되는지 설명하기 위해서

② 부족한 영양 섭취가 감기를 유발한다는 것을 증명하기 위해서

③ 수입과 감기에 걸리는 빈도의 상관 관계를 설명하기 위해서

④ 연구에 참가한 사람들의 수입 분포를 설명하기 위해서

| 정답 | ③

| 해설 | 마지막 문단에서 핵심이 되는 단어는 economics와 income이다. 감기에 걸리는 비율이 경제적인 측면과 무관하지 않다는 내용을 서술하고 있기 때문에 정답은 ③이 된다.

18 'cramped'라는 단어와 의미상 가장 가까운 것은?

① 값싼　　　　　② 붐비는　　　　　③ 침울한　　　　　④ 간단한

| 정답 | ②

| 해설 | 저소득층은 부유층보다 더 cramped한 장소에서 살 수밖에 없으며, 이런 crowding으로 인해 감기 바이러스가 더 쉽게 옮겨 간다고 설명하고 있다. 따라서 cramped는 crowding과 관련 있는 뜻이라는 것을 알 수 있으며, 의미상으로는 '비좁은'의 뜻이 된다.

| 어휘 | **play a part/role in** ~에 관여하다, ~에 역할을 수행하다

susceptibility ⓝ 병에 걸리기 쉬움　　　　**A is susceptible to B** A가 B에 걸리기 쉽다

reveal ⓥ 밝히다, 드러내다　　　　**particular** ⓝ 자세한 사실

hold true for ~에게 해당하다, 유효하다, 들어맞다　　　　**cold-ridden** ⓐ 감기에 시달리는, 감기로 고통 받는

maturity ⓝ 성인, 성숙　　　　**infection** ⓝ 감염

frequency ⓝ 빈도　　　　**the upper end** 최상위층

cramped ⓐ 비좁은; 경련을 일으킨　　　　**quarter** ⓝ 주거, 숙소

adversely ⓐⓓ 불리하게　　　　**influence** ⓥ 영향을 주다

inadequate ⓐ 불충분한　　　　**be suspected of** ~의 혐의를 받다

distinction ⓝ 차이　　　　**inconsistency** ⓝ 모순

specialize in ～을 전공하다, ～을 전문적으로 다루다　　contradict ⓥ 부인하다, 반박하다

apparently ⓐⓓ 보기에, 외관상으로는, 명백히　　relevant ⓐ 관련 있는, 적절한

distribution ⓝ 분배, 분포

[19~21] 단국대 2015

해석

결정을 내리는 데 도움이 될 장단점의 목록을 작성해 본 적이 있다면 당신은 도덕적 추론에 있어 공리주의적 방식을 사용한 셈이다. 주요 윤리 이론 중 하나인 공리주의는 어떤 행위가 도덕적으로 옳은지 아니면 그렇지 않은지를 결정하는 핵심 요소는 바로 행위의 결과라고 상정한다. 의도가 좋은가 나쁜가는 중요하지 않으며, 중요한 것은 행동의 결과가 좋은가 나쁜가 여부이다. 공리주의자에게 있어 행복은 인류의 궁극적 목표이자 최상의 도덕적 선이다. 따라서 어떤 행위 때문에 엄청난 불행이 존재한다면, 그러한 행위는 도덕적으로 잘못된 것이라고 할 수 있다. 반면에 만일 어떤 행위 때문에 엄청난 행복이 존재한다면, 그러한 행위는 도덕적으로 옳은 것이라 할 수 있다.

공리주의자들은 우리가 어떤 행동을 취하기 전에 있을 법한 결과를 신중하게 따져 봐야 한다고 생각한다. 만일 그 행위가 우리나 다른 사람들을 행복하게 만드는 결과를 낳을 것인가? 그 행위로 우리나 다른 이가 불행해질 것인가? 공리주의자들에 따르면 우리는 최대 다수의 최대 행복을 달성할 수 있는 일을 하겠다는 선택을 해야 한다. 하지만 이는 결정하기 힘들 수 있으며, 그 이유는 때로는 어떤 행위가 단기적으로는 행복을 야기하지만 장기적으로는 불행을 야기할 수 있기 때문이다. 공리주의의 또 다른 문제점은 공리주의는 다른 사람을 목적 달성을 위한 수단으로 이용하는 것과 한 사람이나 소수의 사람의 행복을 다수의 사람들의 행복을 위해 희생시키는 것을 허용할 수 있는 것으로, 그리고 심지어는 필요한 것으로 여긴다는 데 있다.

---

19 본문에 제시된 공리주의의 정의에 따르면 다음 중 "배고픈 아이들을 위해 빵을 훔치기"에 관해 사실인 것은 무엇인가?

　① 의도가 좋으므로 도덕적으로 옳다.

　② 다른 사람의 권리를 침해하므로 도덕적으로 그릇되었다.

　③ 긍정적인 결과를 낳기 때문에 도덕적으로 옳다.

　④ 절도는 불법이므로 도덕적으로 그릇되었다.

| 정답 | ③

| 해설 | 공리주의적 관점에서는 행위의 의도는 중요치 않으며, 행위의 결과가 어떠한지가 중요하다. 그리고 공리주의적 관점에서는 "최대 다수의 최대 행복"이 가장 중요하다. 이 점을 감안하고 보면, 배고픈 아이들을 위해 빵을 훔치게 되면 많은 배고픈 아이들이 빵을 먹고 행복을 느끼는 긍정적 결과를 낳게 된다. 즉 많은 이에게 행복을 안겨다 준 행위이므로 도덕적으로도 옳은 행위라 할 수 있다. 따라서 답은 ③이다.

---

20 다음 중 본문에 따르면 공리주의적 원칙을 가장 잘 설명한 것은 무엇인가?

　① 우리는 언제나 다른 이를 먼저 생각해야 한다.

　② 우리는 다른 이에게 자신의 의도를 분명히 밝혀야 한다.

　③ 우리는 대부분의 사람들을 행복하게 해 줄 일을 해야 한다.

　④ 우리는 우리 자신에게 최대한의 행복을 가져다줄 일을 해야 한다.

| 해설 | 공리주의적 관점에서 가장 중요한 것은 "최대 다수의 최대 행복"이다. 따라서 답은 ③이다. 참고로 ④가 답이 될 수 없는 이유는, 공리주의적 관점에서는 우리뿐만 아니라 다른 모든 이의 행복을 추구해야 하기 때문이다.

---

21 본문의 주제는 무엇인가?

① 삶에 있어 희생은 필요하다.

② 도덕적 결정을 내리기 위해 공리주의를 활용하는 것은 항상 쉬운 일만은 아니다.

③ 장기적 결과가 단기적 결과보다 더 중요하다.

④ 장단점의 목록을 작성하는 것은 중요한 결정을 내리는 데 있어 가장 효과적인 기법이다.

| 정답 | ②

| 해설 | 공리주의는 최대 다수의 최대 행복을 추구하는 것을 목표로 하지만, 어떤 행위가 최대 다수의 최대 행복을 달성할 수 있을지 결정하는 것은 쉬운 일이 아니며, 그 이유는 다음의 두 가지이다. 1. 어떤 행위는 단기적으로는 행복을 야기하지만 장기적으로는 불행을 야기할 수 있다. 2. 사람을 목적 달성의 수단으로 이용하고 다수를 위해 소수를 희생할 수 있다. 이를 보면 공리주의의 활용은 쉬운 문제가 아님을 알 수 있다. 따라서 답은 ②이다.

| 어휘 | **pros and cons** 장단점, 찬반양론

reasoning ⓝ 추론

utilitarianism ⓝ 공리주의

posit ⓥ (주장·논의의 근거로 삼기 위해 무엇을) 사실로 상정하다[받아들이다]

irrelevant ⓐ 무관한, 중요하지 않은

determine ⓥ 결정하다

violate ⓥ 침해하다

utilitarian ⓐ 공리주의의, 실용적인 ⓝ 공리주의자

ethical ⓐ 윤리적인

weigh ⓥ (결정을 내리기 전에) 따져 보다, 저울질하다

acceptable ⓐ 허용되는, 받아들일 수 있는

[22~26]

해석

저명한 개발 경제학자이자 세계 은행의 전 수석 경제학자인 니콜라스 스턴(Nicholas Stern)은 과장을 즐기는 인물이 아니다. 그런데도 그는 "향후 몇십 년간의 인류의 행동이 이번 세기 후반과 그 다음 세기 경제와 사회 활동에 미칠 심각한 피해는 20세기 전반의 1, 2차 세계 대전과 경제 공황이 미친 피해를 합친 것과 비슷한 규모일 것이다."라고 말했다. 그가 최근에 발표한 "Stern Report"는 이 경제적 사회적 피해를 최소화하는 방법을 제시한다. 그의 핵심적인 주장은, 이산화탄소 배출 감축 조치를 위해 지금 큰 비용을 쓰면, 이후에 막대한 이익을 얻을 수 있다는 것이다. 그러나 그는 기후 변화(흔히 "지구 온난화"로 알려져 있다.)로 인한 피해를 예방하기에는 너무 늦었다는 경고도 하고 있다. 따라서 그가 생각하는 현실적인 목표는 2050년까지 대기 온실가스 수치를 500~550피피엠으로 안정화하는 것이다. 이 수치는 산업화 이전 시대의 온실가스 수치의 2배이고, 현재 수치인 430피피엠과 비교가 된다. 온실가스 배출량을 그 수준으로 안정화시키기 위해서만도, 2050년까지 모든 국가는 국내 총생산당 배출량을 평균 4분의 3 줄여야 한다. 이러한 변화에 드는 비용은 전 세계 국내 총생산의 약 1퍼센트에 달할 것이다. 이 1퍼센트는 일종의 투자로 볼 수 있다. 이러한 조치를 취하지 않았을 때 발생하는 비용은 상상을 초월할 정도로 막대하기 때문이다.

22 밑줄 친 given to hyperbole을 대신할 수 있는 것은 _____.

① 아첨을 좋아하다.

② 거짓말을 하는 경향이 있다.

③ 과장에 익숙하다.

④ 애매모호함을 좋아하다.

| 정답 | ③

| 해설 | 두 번째 문장에서 스턴은 환경 파괴로 인한 피해가 천문학적 규모가 될 것이라고 주장한다. 이러한 경고가 과장이 아니라는 전제가 앞 문장에 있어야 그의 주장이 설득력을 얻을 수 있다.

23 "Stern Report"에 따르면, 대기 중 온실가스의 지속적인 증가는 반드시 _____ 한다.

① 증가되어야   ② 중단되어야

③ 반박되어야   ④ 부인되어야

| 정답 | ②

| 해설 | 이 글의 주제는 온실가스 배출량을 감축하는 데 비용을 아끼지 말자는 것이다. 따라서 "Stern Report"의 주장도 대기 중 온실가스 증가를 억제해야 한다는 것임을 유추할 수 있다. "His central argument is that spending large sums of money now on measures to reduce carbon emissions will bring dividends on a colossal scale."에서 알 수 있다.

24 "Stern Report"의 주장에 따르면, 이 문제(환경 문제)에 대한 투자는 _____을 가져올 것이다.

① 곧 일어날 재난   ② 감당할 수 없는 빚

③ 막대한 수익   ④ 예측 불가능한 문제들

| 정답 | ③

| 해설 | 지문의 문장 "His central argument is that spending large sums of money now on measures to reduce carbon emissions will bring dividends on a colossal scale."을 이해했는지 묻는 문제이다. "이산화탄소 감축을 위한 투자가 이후에 막대한 배당금(이익)을 가져온다."는 뜻이므로 보기 ③이 적절하다.

25 지문에 따르면, 오늘날 대기 중 온실가스 수치는 _____.

① 사실상 몇 세기 전의 온실가스 수치와 같다   ② 위협적으로 증가했다

③ 이미 안정화되었다   ④ 어떤 조치가 취해지든 당분간 계속 증가할 것이다

| 정답 | ④

| 해설 | 스턴은 온실가스 배출량 감축을 주장하고 있지만 동시에 환경 변화의 결과(온실가스 배출)를 막을 수는 없다고 경고했다. 그렇기 때문에 현실적인 목표로서 이산화탄소 배출량의 안정화를 제안하고 있다. 즉 어떤 조치를 취하건 온실가스 수치가 증가하는 것은 막을 수는 없다는 것을 유추할 수 있다. "However, he warns that we are too late to prevent any deleterious consequences from climate change" 문장을 근거로 볼 수 있다.

26 지문의 마지막 문장이 의미하는 것은 _____.

① 지구 온난화를 막지 않으면 엄청난 재난이 닥칠 것이다
② 탄소 배출은 어떤 수단으로도 제한할 수 없다
③ 누구도 이 제안을 받아들일 준비가 되어 있지 않다
④ 탄소 배출을 감축하는 데 드는 비용은 미미하다

| 정답 | ①

| 해설 | 마지막 문장은 "지금 당장 온실가스 감축에 비용을 투자하지 않는다면 그로 인해 초래될 비용(cost)이 막대하다"는 의미이다. 비용을 투자하지 않는 것은 "uncontrolled global warming"으로, 초래될 막대한 비용은 "untold disaster"를 은유한 것이다.

| 어휘 | **distinguished** ⓐ 저명한, 탁월한
hyperbole ⓝ 과장, 허풍
scale ⓝ 규모
depression ⓝ (경제) 침체, 공황
minimize ⓥ 최소화하다
sum ⓝ 합계, 총액
carbon emission 이산화탄소 배출(량)
colossal ⓐ 대규모의
aim for 목표하다
atmosphere ⓝ 대기, 공기
gross domestic product 국내 총생산(GDP)
investment ⓝ 투자
take action 조치를 취하다

be given to ~에 빠지다, 곧잘 ~하다
disruption ⓝ 교란, 파괴
associate ⓥ 결합하다, 교제하다
prescription ⓝ 처방
argument ⓝ 주장
measure ⓝ 조치
dividend ⓝ 배당금, 상금, 수익
deleterious ⓐ 피해를 주는
stabilization ⓝ 안정화
compare with ~와 비슷하다, 견줄 만하다
quarter ⓝ 4분의 1
cost ⓝ 비용, 희생

[27~28] 서울여대 2014

해석

벤저민 프랭클린(Ben Franklin)에서 호레이쇼 앨저(Horatio Alger)와 오프라 윈프리(Oprah Winfrey)에 이르기까지 미국의 영웅들은 항상 자수성가한 인물로 혼자 힘으로 세상을 헤치고 나아가는 사람들이다. 부모의 발자국을 따르는 행위는 항상 부끄러움의 원천이었다. 하지만 실제로는 선조의 선례를 연구하는 일은 매우 좋은 생각이며, 이는 선조의 삶의 궤적을 연구하는 과정에서 드러난 바 있다. 여러분은 함께 공유되는 재능, 기질, 관심사 등을 기반으로 무엇을 해야 할지에 관해 실마리를 감지할 수 있다. 의대생 가운데 많은 수가 의사 부모를 두고 있는 이유나 농부나 소방사의 혈통이 가문 내에서 대대로 내려오는 이유에 대한 설득력 있는 이유가 좋은 연줄을 두고 있는 것 이외에도 존재할 수 있다. 하지만 여러분은 무엇을 하지 말아야 할지에 관해서도 마찬가지로 강력한 신호를 발견할 수 있다. 만일 여러분의 어머니가 사무실에 하루 종일 앉아 있는 것을 매우 싫어할 경우, 여러분은 경영대에 가는 것에 관해 망설일 수 있다. 반면에 루이(Louie) 삼촌이 건설 노동자로서 몸이 일찍 쇠약해졌다면, 사무직은 그렇게 나쁜 선택은 아닐 것이다.

27 다음 중 저자가 제안할 의견으로 가장 가능성이 높은 것은 무엇인가?

  ① 부모의 발자국을 따르기

  ② 자신의 일에 관해 망설이기

  ③ 자수성가한 사람의 인생을 추구하기

  ④ 선조들이 어떻게 인생을 살았는지에 관해 연구하기

| 정답 | ④

| 해설 | "하지만 실제로는 선조의 선례를 연구하는 일은 매우 좋은 생각이다(But, actually, it's a great idea to study the example of your ancestors)." 이러한 언급으로 미루어 보건대 저자는 선조의 선례를 연구하라고 제안할 가능성이 높다. 따라서 답은 ④이다.

28 다음 중 빈칸에 가장 알맞은 것은 무엇인가?

① 무엇을 하지 말아야 할지	② 무엇을 공유하지 말아야 할지
③ 무엇에 능숙한지	④ 무엇을 하고 싶은지

| 정답 | ①

| 해설 | 빈칸 뒤에 제시된 어머니의 사례는 '무엇을 하지 않아야 겠다고' 결심한 사례이며, 삼촌의 사례는 '무엇을 해야 겠다고' 결심한 사례이다. 따라서 답은 ①이다.

| 어휘 |

self-made ⓐ 자수성가한	**stride** ⓥ 성큼성큼 걷다, 헤치고 나아가다
on one's own 혼자 힘으로	
follow in a person's footsteps 남의 발자국을 따라가다, 남의 선례를 따르다	
reveal ⓥ 드러내다, 알리다	**clue** ⓝ 실마리, 단서
disposition ⓝ 성질, 기질, 경향	**compelling** ⓐ 설득력 있는, 주목하지 않을 수 없는
connection ⓝ 인맥, 연줄, 연줄이 닿는[있는] 사람[기관]	**connections** ⓝ 인척, 먼 친척
run in (성질·특징이) (혈통에) 전해지다, 유전되다	**despise** ⓥ 경멸하다, 몹시 싫어하다
think twice 망설이다, 재고하다	**wear out** 못쓰게 되다, 지치다

[29~30] 성균관대 2014

해석

"만약 이 문제가 전적으로 내게 달려 있다면, 나는 담배를 통한 세수가 0이 될 정도로 담배세를 인상할 것"이라고 2002년 마이클 블룸버그 시장이 고함치듯 부르짖었다. 뉴욕시의 투지 넘치는 시장인 그는 이후 담배세를 여러 번에 걸쳐 인상했다. 담배세 인상을 통한 효과는 제한적이었기 때문에 그는 새로운 것을 시도했다. 그는 최근에 담배의 할인 판매와 상점에서 노출하여 진열하는 것을 불법화할 것을 제안했다. 이러한 조치가 의회의 승인을 받을지 여부는 두고 봐야 한다. 하지만 블룸버그 시장이 금지 조치를 더 많이 추진하는 것은 옳은 조치로 볼 수 있다. 미국에서 수행된 대규모의 여론 조사를 기반으로 파리경제대학의 아벨 브로더가 발표한 논문에 따르면 흡연 금지 조치는 효과가 있을 뿐 아니라 실제로 흡연자들을 행복하게 만들어 준다. 정부는 식당과 술집에서 담배를 피우지 못하게 함으로써 의지가 약한 사람들에게 금지하지 않았더라면 할 수 없었던 일, 즉 금연을 할 수 있는 핑계를 제공하는 셈이다. 추가적인 혜택을 말하자면, 금지 조치는 흡연자의 배우자 또한 행복하게 만드는 것으로 보인다.

29 본문에 따르면 시장이 취한 조치는 무엇인가?

① 금연 관련 법을 강화하려 했다.

② 높은 담배세에 관해 여전히 회의적이다.

③ 길거리 흡연을 금하는 법을 제안했다.

④ 정치적 야망 때문에 담배세에 관한 자신의 입장을 번복했다.

⑤ 담배 회사의 압력에 굴복했다.

| 정답 | ①

| 해설 | 블룸버그 시장은 흡연율을 낮추기 위해 담배세를 인상하고 담배의 진열과 할인 판매를 제한하는 법을 제정했다. 따라서 답은 ①이다.

30 브로더의 연구는 다음의 사실을 나타낸다.

① 금지 조치가 금연에 많은 영향을 미치지 못한다.

② 금지 조치가 흡연의 의욕을 꺾는 하나의 방법으로 기능한다.

③ 미국의 흡연자들은 담배 가격 상승을 신경 쓰지 않는다.

④ 흡연자들은 비흡연자들에 비해 더 행복하다.

⑤ 흡연자의 배우자는 흡연보다 음주가 덜 해롭다고 생각한다.

| 정답 | ②

| 해설 | "정부는 식당과 술집에서 담배를 피우지 못하게 함으로서 의지가 약한 사람들에게 금지하지 않았더라면 할 수 없었던 일, 즉 금연을 할 수 있는 핑계를 제공하는 셈이다(By not allowing them to light up in restaurants and bars, governments give weaker-willed individuals an excuse to do what they otherwise cannot: stop smoking)." 즉 금연을 위한 조치는 흡연의 의욕을 꺾고 금연의 핑계를 제공하는 셈이다. 따라서 답은 ②이다.

| 어휘 | **thunder** ⓥ (큰 소리로) 고함치다, (천둥소리같이) 으르렁대다

combative ⓐ 전투적인, 투지 넘치는

discount ⓥ 할인 판매하다

skeptical ⓐ 회의적인

discourage ⓥ 의욕을 꺾다, 좌절시키다

outlaw ⓥ 불법화하다

extensive ⓐ 대규모의

give in to ~에 굴복하다

| 연습 문제 | 01 ③ | 02 ③ | 03 ④ |

01 다음 중 빈칸에 가장 알맞은 것은 무엇인가?

쉬지 않고 계속되는 TV 광고가 잘 나타내듯이 미 인구 통계국에서는 진정 여러분이 지금쯤이면 인구 조사 설문지를 반송해 줄 것을 바라고 있다. 하지만 실제로 우리는 미국의 인구 통계의 미래가 어떤 모습일지 기본적인 모습을 파악하기 위해 인구 통계 조사 결과가 나오기까지 기다릴 필요도 없다. 핵심어는 "(인구가) 증가함"이다. 2050년이 되면 이 넓은 미국이란 나라에 1억 명이 더 거주하게 될 것이며, 그 결과 미국의 총 인구는 4억이 넘을 것이다. 러시아, 독일, 일본보다 출산율이 50퍼센트 이상 높고, 중국, 이탈리아, 싱가포르, 한국 그리고 거의 모든 동유럽 국가보다 훨씬 높은 출산율을 지닌 미국은, 인구가 정체 중이고 결국에는 감소할 운명으로 보이는 (미국의) 전통적인 경쟁국들 사이에서 이질적인 존재가 되었다.

① 고령화 사회   ② 세계의 조언자

③ 분리된 것   ④ 실패

| 정답 | ③

| 해설 | 본문에 따르면 미국의 인구는 계속 늘어나기 때문에, "인구가 정체 중이고 결국에는 감소할 운명으로 보이는(all of whose populations are stagnant and seem destined to eventually decline)" 경쟁국들과는 다른 존재가 될 것이다. 따라서 보기 중에서 '다른 존재'를 나타낼 만한 것으로는 ③을 들 수 있다.

| 어휘 | **nonstop** ⓐ 멈추지 않는, 쉬지 않고 계속되는   **questionnaire** ⓝ 설문지

demographic ⓐ 인구(통계)의   **operative word** 가장 중요한 말, 요점

stagnant ⓐ 정체된, 침체된   **destined** ⓐ ~할 운명의, ~하도록 정해진

outlier ⓝ 문외한, 분리된 것, 벗어난 것

02 다음 중 빈칸 (A)에 가장 알맞은 것은 무엇인가? 가천대 2020

로마에 위치한 스페인 광장(Piazza di Spagna)은 오랜 시간 동안 이탈리아 젊은이들의 만남과 휴식의 장소였다. 또한 스페인 광장은 오드리 헵번(Audrey Hepburn)과 그레고리 펙(Gregory Peck)이 주연한 고전 영화 "로마의 휴일(Roman Holiday)"의 낭만적인 배경이 되었다. 이와는 대조적으로 베를린 중앙의 베벨 광장(Bebelplatz)은 역사의 상처를 담고 있다. 1933년 나치는 나치 정권 하에서 금서로 지정된 2만 권이 넘는 책을 베벨 광장에서 불태웠다. 독일의 시인 하인리히 하이네(Heinrich Heine)는 베벨 광장에 새겨진 기념비에 다음과 같은 글을 남겼다. "그자들은 책을 태우는 장소에서 최후에는 사람도 태운다."

① 전파된   ② 신성하게 된

③ 금지된   ④ 합금된

| 정답 | ③

| 해설 | 나치가 책을 태운 이유는 그 책들이 나치 정권 하에서 "금지된" 책이기 때문이다. 따라서 답은 ③이다.

| 어휘 |

embrace ⓥ 포괄하다, 받아들이다	**ban** ⓥ 금지하다
memorial ⓝ 기념비	**engrave** ⓥ (나무 · 돌 · 쇠붙이 등에) 새기다
ultimately ⓐⓓ 궁극적으로, 최후에	**propagate** ⓥ 전파하다, 선전하다
sanctify ⓥ 신성하게 하다, 축성하다	**alloy** ⓥ 합금하다

03 각 빈칸에 가장 알맞은 것을 고르시오.

세컨드 라이프, 페이스북, 마이스페이스, 트위터 등 우리의 디지털 세계가 확장되면서 우리가 시간을 보내는 방법뿐 아니라 우리가 정체성을 구축하는 방법 또한 변화되고 있다. 매사추세츠공과대학(MIT)의 교수인 셰리 터클(Sherry Turkle)은 곧 출간되는 자신의 책인 "Alone Together"에서 400명이 넘는 아이와 그 부모들의 소셜 미디어와 휴대폰의 활용도에 관해 인터뷰를 했다. 터클 교수는 특히 젊은 층들 사이에서 점차 자아가 <u>내적으로</u> 구축되는 대신에 <u>외적으로</u> 만들어진다는 것을 발견했다. 즉 (소셜 미디어상의) 일련의 프로필이 대중의 반응에 따라 장식되고 개선된다는 것을 말한다. 터클 교수는 "여러분은 트위터 나 페이스북에서 자신이 누구인지 진정한 모습을 표현하고자 합니다. 하지만 여러분은 또한 다른 사람들이 소비할 무언가를 창조하고 있으므로, 점차 스스로가 여러분의 청중의 인기에 맞춰 상상하고 영합하고 있음을 발견하게 됩니다. 때문에 여러 분이 <u>스스로</u>의 진정한 자아를 드러내고 있어야 할 순간이 (청중에게 하는) 연기가 됩니다. 여러분의 심리가 연기되는 것입니 다."라고 설명했다.

① 부정적으로 – 긍정적으로　　　　② 긍정적으로 – 부정적으로
③ 내적으로 – 외적으로　　　　　　④ 외적으로 – 내적으로

| 정답 | ④

| 해설 | 본문에서는 "일련의 프로필이 대중의 반응에 따라 장식되고 개선된다(a series of profiles to be sculptured and refined in response to public opinion)"를 문제 해결을 위한 가장 핵심 부분으로 선정할 수 있다. 여기서 개개인 의 온라인상의 프로필이 외부의 영향에서 자유로울 수 없음을 유추할 수 있다. 여기에 덧붙여 글의 저자는 "하지만 여 러분은 또한 다른 사람들이 소비할 무언가를 창조하고 있으므로, 점차 스스로가 여러분의 청중의 인기에 맞춰 상상하 고 영합하고 있음을 발견하게 됩니다.(But because you're also creating something for others' consumption, you find yourself imagining and playing to your audience more and more.)"라는 말을 통해 온라인상의 프 로필은 청중의 취향에 맞게 제조되고 있음을 암시한다. 따라서 온라인상에서 개인의 자아는 '내적으로 구축되는' 것이 아니라 '외적으로 만들어진다는' 의미에서 ④가 답임을 알 수 있다.

| 어휘 |

expansion ⓝ 확장	**identity** ⓝ 신원, 정체성
self ⓝ 자아	**profile** ⓝ 프로필
sculpture ⓥ 조각하다, 장식하다	**refine** ⓥ 개선하다, 가다듬다
play to your audience 청중에 맞춰 영합하다	**be supposed to** ~하기로 되어 있다
internally ⓐⓓ 내적으로	**externally** ⓐⓓ 외적으로

실전 문제

01	②	02	①	03	③	04	①	05	④	06	④	07	④	08	①	09	③	10	④
11	③	12	②	13	②	14	③	15	③	16	⑤	17	⑤	18	②	19	①	20	⑤
21	③	22	①	23	④	24	②	25	①	26	②	27	④	28	④	29	③	30	①

[01~02] 가천대 2018

> 해석
>
> 완벽하게 깨끗한 차는 없다. 미국의 한 자동차 잡지는 '합리적 가격의 클린 디젤은 말이 안 되는 목표였다'는 전직 폭스바겐 임원의 고백을 실었다. 연료로 구동되는 차량이 환경에 이로움을 줄 수 있는 방법은 존재하지 않는데, 폭스바겐은 마치 이를 기술로 극복할 수 있는 것처럼 위장해 환경에 대한 죄책감을 덜어 보려고 했으며, 소비자와 차량 제조업체들은 이 같은 청정차 신화를 퍼트렸다. 어쩌면 우리도 청정 디젤이 이치에 맞지 않는다는 합리적 의심을 가졌을 수 있다. 하지만 우리는 힘 좋고 연비 좋고 명망 높은 독일 차를 타면서 동시에 환경 친화적이라고 주장하면서 (이런 합리적 의심에) 모른 척 눈감았을 수도 있다. 부정직한 폭스바겐을 질타하는 동시에 우리 또한 소비자 인식을 돌아볼 필요가 있다.

01 다음 중 빈칸 Ⓐ에 들어갈 가장 적합한 것은?

① 남용하다
② 유익하다
③ 오염시키다
④ 양성하다

| 정답 | ②

| 해설 | 첫 문장에서 'no completely clean vehicle'이라고 했고, 바로 뒤에서 합리적 가격의 청정 디젤 엔진은 '비현실적'인 목표라고 했으므로, 빈칸에는 'completely clean'의 내용이 들어가야 한다. 차량이 완벽히 깨끗하다는 것은 무공해 청정 차량임을 의미하므로, 환경을 이롭게 한다는 ②가 정답이 된다.

02 다음 중 빈칸 Ⓑ에 들어갈 가장 적합한 것은?

① 눈이 먼
② 예민한
③ 공평한
④ 마음속을 꿰뚫어 보는 듯한

| 정답 | ①

| 해설 | 'turn a blind eye'가 숙어로 '안 좋은 일에 대해 눈을 감아 버리다, ~을 못 본 체하다'의 뜻이므로, ①이 정답이 된다. 디젤 차량이 깨끗할 수 없다는 것을 알면서도 그런 사실을 못 본 체했다는 내용으로, 소비자들의 인식에도 문제가 있다고 비판하는 내용이다.

| 어휘 | **confession** ⓝ 자백, 고백
reasonable ⓐ 타당한, 사리에 맞는, 합리적인
fuel-powered ⓐ 연료로 구동되는
overcome ⓥ 극복하다
guilt ⓝ 죄책감

executive ⓝ (기업의) 경영진
unrealistic ⓐ 비현실적인
fabricate ⓥ 꾸며 내다, 날조하다; 제조하다, 규격대로 만들다
mitigate ⓥ 누그러뜨리다, 완화하다
myth ⓝ 신화; 허구, 낭설

make sense 이치에 맞다; 의미가 통하다[이해가 되다]	efficient ⓐ 능률적인, 유능한; 효율적인
environmentally friendly 친환경적인	condemn ⓥ 비난하다
dishonesty ⓝ 부정직, 불성실; 부정, 사기	reflect on 심사숙고하다, 반성하다, 되돌아보다
consumer awareness 소비자 인식	
abuse ⓥ 학대하다; 남용하다, 오용하다; 욕을 하다 ⓝ 학대; 남용, 오용; 욕설	
contaminate ⓥ 오염시키다, 더럽히다	cultivate ⓥ 재배하다, 경작하다, 양성하다
keen ⓐ 예민한, 민감한; 열정적인, 예리한, 갈망하고 있는	
impartial ⓐ 공평한	penetrating ⓐ 마음속을 꿰뚫어 보는 듯한

[03~04] 서울여대 2017

해석

오랜 시간이 흘렀지만 내가 애머스트칼리지(Amherst College)에 입학 허가를 받았다는 사실을 알았을 때 나의 첫 반응을 생생히 기억한다. 그때 나는 "대학 입학처에서 틀림없이 엄청난 실수를 했을 거야"라고 생각했다. 나는 대부분의 학생이 대학에 진학하지 않았던 롱아일랜드 고등학교를 졸업했고, 그래서 애머스트칼리지에 가면 나보다 더 교육을 잘 받고 더 교양을 갖춘 또래 학생들의 상대가 되지 않을 것이고 뛰어난 교수들에게 갈기갈기 난도질당할 것이라고 확신했다. 놀랍게도 나는 우수한 학업 성적으로 대학을 마칠 수 있었다. 하지만 나는 사기꾼이라는 느낌을 완벽히 이겨 낼 수는 없었다. 몇십 년이 흐른 후 대학 동창회에서야 나는 내 또래의 많은 학생들이 정확히 같은 방식으로 느꼈다는 사실을 알게 됐다. 어느 정도 자격을 갖췄는지와는 무관하게, 대학의 많은 신입생은 대학에서 성공할 지력과 뛰어난 사교성을 충분히 갖고 있다는 사실을 스스로 의심한다. 이와 같은 실패에 대한 두려움이 가난한 학생들과 소수 인종의 학생들, 그리고 이민 첫 세대의 학생들에게 더 큰 충격을 준다. 시험에 낙제하거나, 교수가 자신의 이름을 불러 질문을 던지지 않으면 이곳이 과연 내가 있을 곳인가에 대한 불안감이 확인될 수 있다. 계속되는 의심은 자기 확신으로 발전하면서 학생들이 중도에 그만둘 가능성을 늘어난다.

03 다음 중 밑줄 친 "being an impostor"이 의미하는 것은?

① 끔찍한 성적을 받은 것
② 비현실적인 목표를 설정하는 것
③ 운으로 대학에 입학한 것
④ 불리한 조건을 가지고 있는 것

| 정답 | ③

| 해설 | 본문의 저자는 입학 허가를 받고 틀림없이 대학 입학처에서 실수를 한 것이라고 생각했다. 그다지 좋지 않은 고등학교를 졸업해서 자신이 이런 대학에 입학할 자격이 있는지에 대해 의심했던 것을 마치 사기를 쳐서 입학할 수 있는 것에 비유한 것이므로, ③이 정답이 된다.

04 다음 중 빈칸에 올 수 있는 가장 적합한 것은?

① 중퇴하다
② 도움의 손길을 뻗다
③ 특권 의식을 느끼다
④ 교수에게 도전장을 내밀다

| 정답 | ①

| 해설 | 대학 신입생들은 실패에 대한 두려움이 많고, 특히 가난하고, 소수 인종이며, 이민 첫 세대인 경우 그 영향이 더 심하다. 따라서 이런 두려움이 실제인 것으로 확인이 되면, 의심이 자기 확신으로 바뀌면서 부정적인 결과를 가지고 올 가능성이 커지게 된다. 따라서 그런 두려움과 의구심을 떨치지 못하고 중도에 퇴학한다는 ①이 정답으로 적합하다.

| 어휘 | **vividly** ad 생생하게

admission office 대학 입학처 cf. **admission officer** 대학 입학 사정관

overmatch ⓥ 능가하다, 이기다, 압도하다, 물리치다

slice something to ribbons ～을 갈기갈기 찢다(= cut/tear something to ribbons)

to one's surprise 놀랍게도

impostor ⓝ 남의 이름을 사칭하는 자, 사기꾼

peer ⓝ 동료, 또래 친구 ⓥ 응시하다

credential ⓝ 훌륭한 경력, 자격; 성적 증명서, 자격 증명서; 신임장 ⓥ 신임장[자격증]을 주다

freshman ⓝ 신입생

hit hard 심한 타격을 주다

call on (이름을 불러서) (학생에게) 시키다

self-reinforcing ⓐ 자기 강화의

be admitted to ～에 입학[입원, 입장]하다

sophisticated ⓐ 정교한, 세밀한, 세련된

fare well 잘 되어 가다, 성공하다

class reunion (졸업 후의) 동창회

adeptness ⓝ 숙련, 뛰어남

flunk ⓥ 낙제하다, (시험에) 떨어지다

confirm ⓥ 확인하다, 확증하다

drop out 중퇴하다

[05~06] 한국외대 2020

해석

고집 센 한 노부인이 도로 한 가운데를 걷는 바람에 교통에 상당한 혼란을 야기했고 노부인 또한 작지 않은 위험에 처했다. 노부인에게 보행자는 인도로 가야 한다고 지적했지만, 노부인은 "난 내가 걷고 싶은 데로 걸어갈 거야. 우리에겐 자유가 있어"라고 답했다. 자유가 보행자에게 도로 한가운데를 걸어도 된다는 권리를 부여한다면 그러한 자유의 끝에는 보편적인 혼란이 있을 것이라는 생각이 그 노부인에게는 들지 않았다. 요즘 세상은 그 노부인처럼 자유에 도취할 위험이 있고, 따라서 우리는 도로 규칙이 어떤 의미를 갖는지 스스로에게 상기하는 편이 좋다. 도로 규칙은 모든 이의 자유가 보존되려면 각각의 자유는 축소되어야 한다는 것을 의미한다. 혼잡한 교차로에 서 있던 경찰관이 도로 한가운데로 들어가 손을 내밀 경우, 경찰관은 압제의 상징이 아니라 자유의 상징이된다. 당신은 서두르는 중에 이런 상황이 벌어졌다면 자신의 자유가 짓밟혔다고 생각할지도 모른다. 그러다 만일 당신이 합리적인 사람이라면, 심사숙고 끝에 만일 경찰관이 당신을 방해하지 않았더라면 다른 아무도 간섭하지 않았을 것이고 그 결과 교차로가 광분 상태가 되어 건너갈 수 없는 지경이 될 것이라는 결론을 내릴 것이다. 당신은 당신의 자유를 실현시키는 역할인 사회 질서를 누리기 위해 개인의 자유를 축소하는 조치에 따른 것이다.

05 다음 중 본문의 주제는 무엇인가?

① 세상은 요즘 자유에 도취했다.

② 개인의 자유는 항상 사회적 혼란으로 이어진다.

③ 경찰은 비합리적인 운전자를 위해 필요하다.

④ 당신은 사회적 질서를 위해 자유를 양보해야 한다.

| 정답 | ④

| 해설 | 본문은 어떤 노부인의 경우처럼 자유를 빌미로 혼란을 야기해서는 안 되며, "모든 이의 자유가 보존되려면 각각의 자유는 축소

되어야 한다"는 원칙에 의거하여 "자유를 실현시키는 역할인 사회 질서를 누리기 위해 개인의 자유를 축소하는 조치"에 따라야 함을 강조한다. 즉 "사회적 질서를 위해 자유를 양보해야" 함을 말하고 있다. 따라서 답은 ④이다.

---

06 다음 중 (A)와 (B)에 가장 알맞은 것은 무엇인가?

① 거부당한 – 거부　　　　　　　　② 할당된 – 할당

③ 보장된 – 보장　　　　　　　　　④ 축소된 – 축소

| 정답 | ④

| 해설 | (A): 도로상에서 모두가 자유로이 자기 맘대로 움직이게 할 경우 도로는 광분 상태에서 혼란과 함께 엉망이 될 것이다. 본문의 취지와 함께 생각해 보면 모든 이의 자유가 보존되려면 각각의 자유는 어느 정도 제한 및 "축소"되어야 할 것이다. (B): 도로의 경우와 마찬가지로 자유를 현실화하려면 사회 규칙에 따라야 하고 사회 규칙의 성립을 위해서는 개인의 자유를 "축소"하는 조치에 따라야 한다. 따라서 빈칸에 적합한 것은 "축소시킨다"는 의미의 curtail 및 명사형인 curtailment이다.

| 어휘 |

stubborn ⓐ 고집 센, 완강한

sidewalk ⓝ 보도, 인도

entitle ⓥ 자격[권리]를 주다

just as well ~하는 편이 좋다

outrage ⓥ (법률 · 정의 · 인도 등을) 어기다, 짓밟다

reflect ⓥ 깊이 생각하다, 심사숙고하다

frenzied ⓐ 광분한, 광란의

curtailment ⓝ 축소, 단축

allot ⓥ 할당하다, 배당하다

to the confusion of ~에 혼란을 야기하는

occur to ~에게 생각이 떠오르다

drunk ⓐ (특정한 감정 · 상황에) 도취한

curtail ⓥ 축소[삭감/단축]시키다

reasonable ⓐ 합리적인

interfere with 방해하다

submit to ~에 따르다[복종하다]

compromise ⓥ 타협하다, 양보하다

[07~09] 국민대 2010

해석

다윈(Darwin)의 진면목은 진화론을 주장했다는 데 있지 않다는 것을 우리는 알고 있다. 왜냐하면 그보다 앞서 수십 명의 과학자들이 그런 주장을 했기 때문이다. 그의 특별한 기여는 진화가 어떻게 작동하는지에 관한 그의 저술과 그의 이론의 참신성에 기인한다. 다윈 이전의 진화론자들은 생물 내부에 존재한다고 생각한 완벽함을 지향하는 경향 혹은 생물의 내재된 진화 방향 등에 기초한 말도 안 되는 내용들을 제안했다. 다윈은 개체 간의 즉각적인 상호 작용을 토대로 자연적이고 실험 가능한 이론을 주장했다. 자연 선택설(natural selection)은 이성적으로 작동하는 경제를 옹호했던 경제학자 아담 스미스(Adam Smith)의 근본 주장과 같은 혁신적인 생물학으로의 전이라고 할 수 있다. 즉 자연의 균형과 질서는 고차원적이거나 외부의(신의) 통제로 기인한 것이 아니며, 또한 전체에 직접적으로 작용하는 법칙이 존재해서 이로부터 기인한 것이 아니라, 개체들 간에 서로의 이익을 위해 투쟁하는 과정에서 (자연스럽게) 생겨나게 된 것이라는 것이다.

07 빈칸 ㉮에 들어갈 가장 알맞은 것은?

① 자선, 자비

② 고안품, 장치, 계략

③ 기부

④ 기여, 공헌, 기부

| 정답 | ④

| 해설 | 빈칸 바로 앞 문장을 보면 빈칸 ㉮와 상관 관계가 있는 단어는 "uniqueness"란 것을 알 수 있다. 왜냐면 앞 문장의 'reside in' 과 'rest upon'은 '〜 하는 데 있다'는 뜻의 같은 의미로 사용되었기 때문이다. 쉽게 얘기해서 다윈의 뛰어난 점(uniqueness) 은 '앞 문장'에 있는 것이 아니라 '빈칸이 들어간 문장'에 있다는 뜻이 된다. 그런 의미에서 빈칸은 긍정의 의미를 지닌 단어가 와야 한다. ②의 contrivance는 고안품, 계획, 연구 등의 뜻으로 사용되어 답이 될 수 있을 것 같지만 contrivance는 부정 의 의미, 즉 책략이나 계략 등의 의미를 지닌 단어이다. 영영 사전에 보면 "something that is artificial or does not seem natural, but that helps something else to happen — usually used to show disapproval"이라고 나온다. 나머지 보 기는 charity, donation, contribution으로 모두 다른 사람들을 도와준다는 의미를 포함하고 있다. 하지만 이 문장에서는 Darwin이 인류사에 '기여'하고, '공헌'한 점을 말하고 있으므로, 이런 의미를 내포하고 있는 단어는 'contribution'만 해당한다. 따라서 답은 ④가 된다.

08 빈칸 ㉯에 들어갈 가장 알맞은 것은?

① 이전, 이동

② 운동, 움직임, 이동

③ 거래

④ 변경, 개조

| 정답 | ①

| 해설 | 이 문제는 "a creative _____ to biology"에 알맞은 단어를 찾는 것이다. 본문의 필자는 다윈이 주창한 자 연 선택설(natural selection)이 원리상 경제학자 아담 스미스의 주장과 비슷하다고 말하고 있다. '보이지 않는 손(invisible hand)'에 의해 경제가 이성적으로 작동하는 것과 같이 생물의 진화도 신의 섭리에 의해 작동하는 것이 아니라 개체 간의 투쟁 이 결국 진화를 이끌고 있다고 설명하고 있다. 하지만 이전의 학자들은 이런 태도를 취하지 않았다는 것을 알 수 있다(internal perfecting tendencies and inherent directions). 따라서 생물학이 이전의 단계에서 다윈이 주창한 새로운 단계로의 전이 (transfer)가 일어났다고 보는 것이 맞으므로 답은 ①이 된다. ② movement와 ④ alteration도 비슷한 의미라고 생각할 수 있지만 답이 되기에는 불분명하다. ②의 movement는 단순히 '움직임이나 운동' 등을 뜻하는 단어로 A에서 B로 옮겨져 왔 다는 내용을 포함하지 않는다. ④의 alteration은 영영 사전에서 "a small change that makes someone or something slightly different, or the process of this change"라고 설명하고 있으며, 변경이나 개조의 의미이다. 다윈의 학설이 생물 학을 조금 변경한 것이라고 하면 전체적인 맥락과 크게 벗어나게 된다.

09 윗글의 다윈에 대한 설명으로 가장 알맞은 것은?

① 개체 간 즉각적인 상호 작용을 한다는 그의 이론은 실행 불가능하고, 시험해 볼 수 없는 것이다.

② 그의 진화론에 대한 발상은 매우 독특하고 창의적이었다.

③ 그의 자연 선택설은 아담 스미스의 이성적인 경제와의 비유를 통해 체계화되었다.

④ 그는 모든 개체에 직접적으로 작용하는 법칙이 있어서 이로부터 자연의 질서가 발생했다고 생각했다.

| 정답 | ③

| 해설 | 먼저 ①과 ④는 명백히 다윈의 생각이 아닌 것을 본문을 통해 확인할 수 있다. ②에 보면 그의 진화론에 대한 발상이 독창적(unique)이고 창의적(creative)이라고 했지만, 본문에서 필자는 creative하지만 unique하진 않다고 본문의 첫 문장에서 밝히고 있다.(Darwin's uniqueness does not reside in his support for the idea of evolution.) 왜냐하면 진화론을 주장한 이들은 다윈 이전에도 있었기 때문이다. 따라서 답은 ③으로 다윈의 이론이 아담 스미스의 이론과 유사한 점이 있다는 사실을 본문의 후반부에 제시하고 있다. 콜론(:) 이후에 제시된 내용은 다윈의 자연 선택설과 아담 스미스의 국부론(Wealth of Nation)에 모두 해당하는 말이다. 따라서 다윈이 아담 스미스의 이론에서 아이디어를 유추(analogy)해 자신의 이론을 체계화시켰다고 볼 수 있다.

| 어휘 | **reside in** ~에 거주하다, 속하다, 존재하다

precede ⓥ 앞서다

rest upon ~에 달려 있다(여기서는 앞에 나온 reside in과 비슷한 의미로 사용됨)

novel ⓐ 새로운 ⓝ 소설

scheme ⓝ 계획, 음모

inherent ⓐ 내재의, 고유의, 타고난

an argument for ~에 찬성하는 주장

order ⓝ 질서

divine ⓐ 신성한

contrivance ⓝ 고안품, 장치, 계략

contribution ⓝ 기여, 공헌, 기부

transaction ⓝ 거래

formulate ⓥ 공식화하다, 체계화하다

scores of 수십 명의, 수십 개의

unworkable ⓐ 쓸모없는, 실행할 수 없는

perfect ⓥ 완성하다, 수행하다

advocate ⓥ 옹호하다, 지지하다

rational ⓐ 이성이 있는, 합리적인

external ⓐ 외부의

charity ⓝ 자선, 사랑, 자애

donation ⓝ 기부

transfer ⓝ 이전, 이동

alteration ⓝ 변경, 개조

해석

인간이 만든 오염 물질이 자연에 미치는 영향은 먹이 사슬로 인해 크게 증폭될 수 있다. 먹이 사슬은 일반적으로 약한 개체들이 더 강한 개체들에게 잡아먹히는 사다리 구조의 연쇄 과정이다. 가장 면밀히 연구된 예는 살충제의 영향이다. 살충제로 농작물 수확은 크게 증대된 반면 엄청나게 많은 물고기와 야생 동물들이 죽었다. 예를 들어, 캐나다의 뉴브런즈윅(New Brunswick)주에서는 전나무 새싹을 갉아먹는 나방 유충을 방제하기 위해서 1에이커당 겨우 0.5파운드의 DDT를 살포했을 뿐인데도 미라미치강(Miramichi River)의 어린 연어 연간 어획량의 거의 두 배를 전멸시켰다. 이 과정에서 지표에 남아 있던 DDT는 빗물에 씻겨 내려와 호수와 강의 플랑크톤에게 들어갔다. 물고기는 DDT에 오염된 플랑크톤을 먹는다. 물고기의 체내에서 이 살충제는 계속 축적되기 때문에, 처음 플랑크톤에 흡수된 DDT 양은 물고기를 먹은 새에 이르면 농도가 몇 배가 더 증가하고 결국 새는 죽거나 생식을 멈추게 된다.

10 밑줄 친 (A)와 의미가 가장 가까운 것은?

① 통렬한
② 수반되는
③ 순응적인
④ 뚜렷한

| 정답 | ④

| 해설 | 살충제로 인한 생태계 파괴가 심각하다는 앞 문장의 내용을 상술하는 문장으로, 죽은 물고기와 야생 동물이 매우 많았다는 내용이다. 따라서 밑줄의 "spectacular(눈부신, 현저한, 대단한)"는 "conspicuous(눈에 띄는, 현저한)"와 의미가 가장 비슷하다.

11 다음 중 빈칸 (B)에 적절하지 <u>않은</u> 것은?

① 전멸되었다
② 근절되었다
③ 포기되었다
④ 없어졌다

| 정답 | ③

| 해설 | 살충제로 인한 생태계 파괴의 예시이므로 빈칸은 어린 연어 연간 어획량의 거의 두 배가 "전멸되었다(완전히 사라졌다)"는 내용으로 완성한다. 보기 ③은 문맥에 맞지 않는다.

12 다음 중 빈칸 (C)에 적절한 것은?

① 극복할 수 없는
② 축적되는
③ 팽창되는
④ 탁한

| 정답 | ②

| 해설 | 빈칸은 이후에 이어지는 내용의 원인이 되도록 완성한다. DDT는 플랑크톤 안에 '축적'되기 때문에 먹이 사슬 위쪽으로 올라갈수록 DDT 양은 '몇 배로 배가' 된다.

| 어휘 | **pollutant** ⓝ 오염 물질, 오염원
amplify ⓥ 증폭시키다
serial ⓐ 연쇄의, 연속의
creature ⓝ 생명체

vastly ⓐ 거대하게
food chain 먹이 사슬
process ⓝ 과정, 절차
typically ⓐ 일반적으로, 전형적으로

ascending ⓐ 위를 향하는, 상승하는	**pesticide** ⓝ 살충제
sharply ⓐd 급격하게	**crops** ⓝ 농작물
spectacular ⓐ 눈부신, 대단한, 현저한	**wildlife** ⓝ 야생 동물
province ⓝ 주, 지방	**application** ⓝ 살포, 사용
spruce ⓝ 전나무	**bud worm** ⓝ 버드웜(싹을 갉아먹는 나방의 유충)
annihilate ⓥ 전멸시키다	**eradicate** ⓥ 근절시키다
obliterate ⓥ 없애다, 지우다	**salmon** ⓝ 연어
wash off 씻어 내다	**stream** ⓝ 강, 개울, 시내
tainted ⓐ 오염된	**concentrate** ⓥ 농축되다
original ⓐ 원래의	**dose** ⓝ 1회 투약(복용)량, 소량
multifold ⓐ 몇 배의	**strength** ⓝ 강도
reproducing ⓝ 번식, 생식	

[13~14] 한양대 2020

해석

의사결정의 과학적·기술적 특성과 안보 지향적, 의학적 대응에 초점을 맞추는 것은 정치적-민주적 대결 가능성의 축소를 의미하지만, EU의 역할 확대(및 광범위한 초국적화)는 지배자와 피지배자 사이의 거리를 증가시키고 있다. 요약하면, 공공보건에서의 의사결정의 민주적 정당성과 책임성이 특히 통치에 대한 시민의 참여 측면에서 훨씬 더 어려워 보인다. 이것을 더욱 큰 문제로 만드는 것은, 이런 일이 과학적·기술적 지식과 이런 맥락과 관련한 전문 지식이 우세한 시점에서 벌어지고 있다는 점이며, 리스크의 규모와 특성에 대한 불확실성과 무지는 그들이 점점 더 큰 피해를 보고 있다는 것을 의미한다. 공중 보건 규제의 주요 수신인임에도 불구하고, 그리고 그 시행에 관여하고 있음에도 불구하고, EU 시민권자 또는 공식적으로 EU 시민은 아니지만 그럼에도 불구하고 EU의 통치에 영향을 받는 사람들의 역할은 다소 불투명하다.

---

13 빈칸에 들어갈 가장 적절한 것은?

① 정치적 입법
② 통치에 대한 시민의 참여
③ EU 통치의 안보 문제
④ EU의 초국가적 차원
⑤ 중앙집권적 통치의 정당성

| 정답 | ②

| 해설 | 본문은 보건과 관련한 의사결정에서 EU 시민들의 참여가 부족하다는 점을 지적하고 있다. 예를 들어 본문의 "increases the distance between governance and the governed(지배자와 피지배자 사이의 거리를 증가시키고 있다)"는 내용은 피지배층이 참여할 여지가 줄어들고 있다는 설명이며, 후반부의 "the role of the EU's citizenry ... is rather opaque(EU 시민들의 역할이 불투명하다)"는 내용 또한 시민들이 제대로 참여할 수 없다는 내용을 말하고 있다. 따라서 빈칸은 '통치에 대한 시민의 참여'가 부족해 문제가 되고 있다는 내용인 ②가 적합하다.

| 정답 | ③

| 해설 | 본문은 EU의 거버넌스(통치)가 증가하면서 EU 시민들의 참여는 줄어드는 상황을 지적하고 있다. 따라서 ③에서 말한 EU의 규제로 대중들의 정치적 민감성이 증가한 것이 아니라 그 반대로 정치적 민감성이 줄어들었다고 보아야 하므로 정답은 ③이 된다.

| 어휘 |
contestation ⓝ 논쟁, 주장, 논점
governance ⓝ 지배권력; 통치, 관리
legitimacy ⓝ 합법성, 적법, 타당성
at a time when 바로 ~한 시기에
dominant ⓐ 지배적인, 유력한, 주요한
addressee ⓝ 수신인
be implicated in (범죄에) 연루되다; (나쁜 일에 대한) 책임이 있다
implementation ⓝ 이행, 실행; 완성, 성취; 충족
opaque ⓐ 글이 불분명한, 이해하기 힘든, 불투명한

transnationalisation ⓝ 초국적화
the governed 국민, 피통치자
accountability ⓝ 책임 (있음), 의무
expertise ⓝ 전문 지식
undermine ⓥ 손상시키다, 약화시키다
regulation ⓝ 통제, 단속, 규제
citizenry ⓝ 시민들, 주민들
implication ⓝ 영향, 결과

[15~16]

해석

> 통계가 허위를 사실이라고 주장할 때 통계는 오용된다. 통계학은 사회적으로 중요한 역할을 하기 시작하면서부터 오용되어 왔다. 우발적 오용인 경우도 일부 있지만 그 외에는 통계를 오용하는 사람의 이익을 위한 의도적 오용이다. 관련된 통계적 근거가 사실이 아니거나 오용되는 것을 통계적 오류라 한다. 통계의 오류라는 함정은 지식 탐구에 매우 해로울 수 있다. 예를 들어, 의학에서 오류가 수정되려면 수십 년이 걸리고 많은 인명이 희생될 것이다. 통계의 오용은 빠져들기 쉬운 덫이다. 사실 확인에 신중한 전문 과학자, 심지어 수학자와 전문 통계학자들조차도 매우 간단한 통계적 방법에 속을 수 있다.

| 정답 | ③

| 해설 | 'take＋시간(시간이 ~만큼 걸리다)'와 'cost＋대가(~을 대가로 지불하다, 희생시키다)' 용법을 묻는 문제이다. '수십 년이 걸리

다'와 '인명을 희생시키다'는 의미를 전달하기 위해서는 ③이 적절한 표현이다.

---

16 다음 중 지문의 제목으로 가장 적절한 것은?

① 통계 오용의 목적
② 통계적 오류의 기원
③ 통계 오용의 유혹
④ 통계적 주장에 대한 지식
⑤ 통계 오용의 위험성

| 정답 | ⑤

| 해설 | 전반부인 도입에는 통계 오용의 정의, 후반부인 주제에는 통계 오용에 속기 쉽다는 내용이 담겨 있다. "The false statistics trap", "Misuses can be easy to fall into."에서 제목을 유추할 수 있다.

| 어휘 | misuse ⓝ 오용, 남용
falsehood ⓝ 허위, 거짓
accidental ⓐ 우연한, 우발적인
perpetrator ⓝ 행위자, 범죄자
misapplied ⓐ 오용된
trap ⓝ 덫, 함정
correct ⓥ 수정하다, 바로잡다
fall into ~에 빠지다
fool ⓥ 속이다

statistical ⓐ 통계적인
play a role 역할을 하다, 참여하다
purposeful ⓐ 의도적인
involved ⓐ 관련된
constitute ⓥ ~이 되다, 구성하다
quest ⓝ 추구
decades ⓝ 수십 년
statistician ⓝ 통계학자

[17~18] 성균관대 2010

해석

죽은 이들이 산 자의 일상생활에 큰 힘을 미친다고 믿어졌다. 불만스러워하는 조상님들은 후손들에게 병이나 재앙을 불러올 수 있었고, 따라서 많은 수의 갑골은 불행한 조상님들의 혼을 달래기 위한 의도의 인신 공양과 관련이 있다. 허난성의 어느 한 고분군의 경우, 발굴을 통해 대부분에 산 제물로 바쳐진 희생자들이 담겨 있는 1,200곳이 넘는 제물 구덩이를 드러냈다. 언젠가 한 고고학자는 나에게 상나라의 의식 중에 사람이 죽임을 당하는 방식을 60개 이상 셀 수 있었다고 했다. 하지만 그는 또한 내게 이 일은 어디까지나 의식이지 살인과 파괴적 행위가 아니었다고 상기시켜 주었다. 상나라 사람들 관점에서는 인간의 희생은 단지 놀랄 만큼 잘 조직된 시스템의 일부일 뿐이었다. 상나라 사람들은 엄격한 역법을 준수했고, 여기에는 특정 조상님에게 바쳐지는 특정 제의일이 있었다. 이것들은 거의 과학적 탐구의 결과로 봐도 될 정도로 자세했다. 예를 들어, 점성술사는 지금 살아 있는 왕의 치통이 어떤 조상님 때문인지 판단하기 위해 끈기 있게 갑골에 70개의 갈라진 자국을 내었다.

---

17 빈칸에 가장 적절한 것은 무엇인가?

① 먹이다
② 보호하다
③ 숭배하다
④ 흔들다
⑤ 위로하다

| 정답 | ⑤

| 해설 | 본문은 고대 중국의 (은으로 불리기도 하는) 상나라에서 발견되는 갑골에 관한 이야기이다. "unhappy ancestors could cause illness or disaster among the living(불만스러워하는 조상님들은 후손들에게 병이나 재앙을 불러올 수 있었으며)" 따라서 "human sacrifices(인신 공양)"이 이루어졌음을 알 수 있다. 이 점을 미루어 볼 때 결국 불만스러워하는 조상님들을 "appease(위로)"하기 위해 인간을 제물로 바쳤음을 알 수 있으며 따라서 ⑤가 답이 된다.

---

18 본문에 따르면, _____고 믿어졌다.

① 내세가 현세보다 더 중요하다
② 사람들의 현재 삶은 조상님의 뜻에 달려 있다
③ 죽음은 사람들에게 행복을 가져다준다
④ 사람들은 영원히 살 수 있다
⑤ 조상님들은 언제나 우리를 돕기 위해 계시다

| 정답 | ②

| 해설 | 본문을 전체적으로 봤을 때 결국 제사나 인신 공양 같은 모든 행위가 조상님을 위로하기 위한 것임을 알 수 있다.
②의 경우, 상나라 사람들이 조상님을 위해 인신 공양을 하던 이유는 결국 불만스러워하는 조상님들이 자신들에게 해코지를 할까 봐 두려웠기 때문이며, 결국 살아 있는 자의 삶이 돌아가신 조상들에 의해 좌우된다는 의미가 된다. 따라서 답은 ②가 된다.
①의 경우, 본문 어디에도 내세에 관한 내용은 없으므로 답이 될 수 없다. ③의 경우, 인신 공양은 제의적 목적이지 그 외에 기쁨을 가져다주기 위한다는 내용은 없기 때문에 답이 될 수 없다. ④의 경우, 본문과는 관련이 없는 내용이므로 답이 될 수 없다.
⑤의 경우, 조상님들은 "후손들에게 병이나 재앙을 불러올 수 있었던(cause illness or disaster among the living)" 존재이기 때문에 답이 될 수 없다.

| 어휘 |
oracle bone 갑골(甲骨)
sacrifice ⓝ 산 제물
spirit ⓝ 혼, 영혼
excavation ⓝ 발굴, 굴착
archaeologist ⓝ 고고학자
mayhem ⓝ 대혼란, 파괴적 행위
devote A to B A를 B에 바치다
to the point of ~라고 해도 좋을 만큼
stir ⓥ ~을 뒤섞다, 흔들다
afterlife ⓝ 사후 세계, 내세

refer to ~와 관련이 있다; 적용하다
sacrificial ⓐ 제물의, 희생의
complex ⓝ 단지, 복합 단지, 군
uncover ⓥ 덮개를 열다, 드러내다
Shang ⓝ 상(商)나라
from one's perspective ~의 관점에서는
meticulous ⓐ 세심한, 꼼꼼한, 자세한
diviner ⓝ 점쟁이, 점성술사
appease ⓥ ~을 위로하다, 달래다
be up to ~의 책임이다, ~에게 달려 있다

[19~20]

해석

진화생물학은 항상 논란의 중심에 있다. 논란의 중심에 서게 된 주된 이유는, 다윈(Darwin)의 이론이 종교적 전통에 뿌리를 둔 인간의 기원에 대한 초자연적 설명과 직접적으로 상반되며 이러한 초자연적인 종교적 설명을 완전히 자연에 근거한 설명으로 대체시키기 때문이다. 철학자인 대니얼 데닛(Daniel Dennett)은 진화를 일종의 "만능 산(universal acid)"이라 칭하면서 "거의 모든 기존 개념을 부식시키고, 뒤이어 혁명적인 세계관을 낳으며, 그 결과 오래 전에 획기적인 발견으로 취급되었던 것들은 아직은 식별은 가능한 수준으로 남아 있지만 근본적인 면에서 과거와는 차이가 나고 마는" 결과를 낳는 것으로 보았다. 이처럼 기존의 관념을 좀먹는 아이디어를 두려워한 나머지 미국에서는 하나님이 성경의 창세기에 묘사된 바와 같이 현재의 형태로 생명을 창조했다고 믿는 우파 복음주의 기독교인들이 주로 진화에 반대한다.

19 내용상 빈칸에 들어가기에 가장 적절한 것은?

① 좀먹는   ② 구성주의적인
③ 공동의   ④ 동시대의
⑤ 경멸하는

| 정답 | ①

| 해설 | 진화론은 "만능 산(universal acid)"이며 기존의 아이디어를 변화시키는 것으로 취급된다. 산은 물체를 부식시키며, 아이디어가 산성이라면 이 아이디어는 기존의 것을 "좀먹는" 것이라 유추할 수 있다. 따라서 답은 ①이다.

20 윗글의 내용과 가장 잘 부합하는 것은?

① 미국의 기독교인들은 이제는 다윈이 옳다고 믿지 않는다.
② 다윈은 한동안 우파 복음 선교사들로부터 찬사를 받았다.
③ 데닛은 인류의 기원을 화학을 통해 설명했다.
④ 다윈의 이론은 인간 기원에 대한 초자연적 설명을 뒷받침하는 것으로 드러났다.
⑤ 데닛에 따르면 "만능 산"은 기존의 개념을 완전히 새로운 세계관으로 변모시킨다.

| 정답 | ⑤

| 해설 | 데닛이 말하는 만능 산은 "거의 모든 기존 개념을 부식시키고, 뒤이어 혁명적인 세계관을 낳는" 것이다. 여기서 답은 ⑤임을 유추할 수 있다.

①은 no more(이제는)란 표현 때문에 미국의 기독교인들이 과거에는 다윈을 믿었다는 내용이 되는데, 이는 본문의 내용과는 거리가 있다. ② 또한 본문에서는 찾을 수 없는 내용이다. ③에서 데닛이 산에 비유하여 설명한 것은 인류의 기원이 아니라 진화론 같은 아이디어이다. ④에서 다윈의 이론은 초자연적 설명을 뒷받침하는 것이 아니라 "대체한다(replace)".

| 어휘 | **evolutionary biology** 진화생물학
account ⑩ 설명, 해석
eat through 부식시키다
in the wake of ~에 뒤이어, ~의 결과로
landmark ⑪ 주요 지형지물, 랜드마크; 획기적 사건[발견/발명품 등]
recognizable ⓐ (쉽게) 알[알아볼] 수 있는, 식별 가능한

contradict ⓥ 모순되다, 상반되다
replace A with B A를 B로 대체하다, B가 A를 대신하다
just about 거의 (다)

corrosive ⓐ 부식성의, 좀먹는

evangelical ⓐ 복음주의의   constructivist ⓐ 구성주의적인

collaborative ⓐ 공동의   contemporary ⓐ 동시대의

contemptuous ⓐ 경멸하는   evangelist ⓝ 복음 선교사

account for 설명하다

[21~23] 단국대 2014

해석

한 영국 심리학자의 연구에 따르면 셰익스피어, 모차르트, 피카소 같은 천재들이 "천부적인 재능을 갖추었다"고 하거나 선천적인 재능을 보유하고 있다는 개념은 <u>근거 없는 믿음</u>에 불과하다. 엑세터대학의 마이클 하우 교수와 그의 동료들은 예술 및 스포츠 분야에서 달성한 뛰어난 성과를 점검한 후 탁월함은 기회, 격려, 훈련, 동기 부여, 자신감, 그리고 무엇보다도 연습을 통해 결정된다는 결론을 내렸다. 이 이론은 기존의 믿음으로부터 근본적으로 <u>단절</u>된 것으로 전 세계 학자들로부터 갈채를 받았다. 이 이론은 또한 교사 및 부모에게 상당한 영향을 미쳤는데, 특히 천부적인 재능을 갖추었다고 생각되지 않는 아이들은 성공을 위해 필요한 격려를 받지 못하고 있기 때문이다. 연구 저자들은 "높은 수준의 능력을 달성하기 위해서는 재능이라 불리는 선천적인 가능성을 보유해야만 한다는 널리 퍼진 믿음"을 자신들의 연구의 출발점으로 삼았다. 연구 저자들은 이 믿음이 옳은지 여부를 규명하는 일이 중요하다고 했으며 그 이유는 그 믿음이 선별 절차와 훈련에 영향을 미치는 사회적이면서 교육적인 결과를 야기하기 때문이다. 하지만 기량이 뛰어난 예술가들과 수학자들 그리고 정상급의 테니스 선수들과 수영 선수들을 대상으로 수행된 연구에 따르면 부모의 격려 이전에 성공할 가능성을 초기에 신호로 보여 준 경우는 거의 존재하지 않았다. 수천 시간을 진지한 훈련에 쏟지 않고서 최상위 수준의 업적을 달성한 경우는 전혀 존재하지 않았다. 음악이든, 수학이든, 체스든, 스포츠든 어떤 분야에서 특별한 재능을 갖추고 있다고 여겨진 사람들도 오랜 기간 동안의 교육과 연습을 필요로 했다.

21 다음 중 본문의 제목으로 가장 알맞은 것은 무엇인가?

① 천재는 부모가 만든다

② 천재는 재능이 필요하다

③ 연습이 천재를 만든다

④ 동기 부여가 천재를 약속한다

| 정답 | ③

| 해설 | 본문은 천재성 유무와는 관계없이 연습과 훈련이 없이는 성공을 달성할 수 없음을 강조하고 있다. 따라서 답은 ③이다.

22 다음 중 빈칸 (A)와 (B)에 가장 적합한 것은 무엇인가?

① 근거 없는 믿음 – 단절   ② 진실 – 원칙

③ 구상 – 확인   ④ 추정 – 증거

| 정답 | ①

| 해설 | (A) : 본문은 천부적인 재능을 갖춘 것이 이름을 날리는 필수적인 요건은 아님을 말하고 있다. 따라서 셰익스피어, 모차르트, 피카소 같은 천재들이 원래 선천적인 재능을 갖추었기 때문에 결국 성공하여 후대에 이름을 날리게 되었다는 견해는 '근거 없는 믿음'에 불과한 것이다.

(B): 하우 교수의 연구 결과는 '천재는 연습과 노력을 통해 만들어진다'이며 이는 기존의 '천재는 재능이 있어야 한다'는 믿음과는 상반되는 것이다. 즉 전통과의 '단절'인 것이다. 따라서 답은 ①이다.

23 다음 중 본문에 따르면 사실이 <u>아닌</u> 것은 무엇인가?

① 하우 교수는 예술 및 스포츠 분야에서 거둔 뛰어난 성과를 설명해 주는 몇 가지 요소를 제시했다.
② 전 세계의 많은 학자들은 하우의 이론이 제기한 교육학적 영향을 환영했다.
③ 하우의 이론은 자녀 양육에 있어 부모의 격려가 중요함을 강조한다.
④ 교육과 연습을 필요로 하지 않는 특별한 재능을 갖추고 있는 사람들은 많이 존재한다.

| 정답 | ④

| 해설 | "음악이든, 수학이든, 체스든, 스포츠든 어떤 분야에서 특별한 재능을 갖추고 있다고 여겨진 사람들도 오랜 기간 동안의 교육과 연습을 필요로 했다(Even those who were believed to be exceptionally talented — whether in music, mathematics, chess, or sports — required lengthy periods of instruction and practice)." 이 말은 ④의 견해와는 정반대되는 의미이다. 따라서 답은 ④이다.

| 어휘 |

genius ⓝ 천재, 비범한 재능
possess ⓥ 소유하다, 보유하다
myth ⓝ (많은 사람들의) 근거 없는 믿음
performance ⓝ 성과, 성취
motivation ⓝ 자극, 동기 부여
break with ~와의 단절[분열]하다
academic ⓝ 대학 교수, 학도, 학자
implication ⓝ 영향, 결과, 함축
widespread ⓐ 광범위한, 널리 퍼진
establish ⓥ (사실을) 규명하다[밝히다]
promise ⓝ 장래성, (성공할) 가능성
exceptionally ⓐⓓ 특별히, 예외적으로
conception ⓝ 구상, 이해
presumption ⓝ 추정
account for ~을 설명하다

gifted ⓐ 타고난[천부의] 재능이 있는
innate ⓐ (능력, 성질 등이) 타고난, 선천적인
outstanding ⓐ 두드러진, 뛰어난
excellence ⓝ 우수, 뛰어남, 탁월함
most of all 그중에서도, 무엇보다도
applaud ⓥ 갈채를 보내다, 칭찬하다
significant ⓐ 중대한, 중요한
not least 특히
potential ⓐ 잠재력, 가능성
accomplished ⓐ 숙달한, 기량이 뛰어난
achievement ⓝ 업적, 성취
instruction ⓝ 교수, 교육, 지시
confirmation ⓝ 확인
proof ⓝ 증거
pedagogical ⓐ 교육학의

해석

> 스위스 시계의 평균 가격은 685달러이다. 중국산 시계는 평균 2달러 정도 하지만 시간을 확인하는 데는 스위스 시계와 큰 차이가 없다. 그렇다면 스위스 시계는 도대체 어떻게 살아남을 수 있을까? 지난 2년간 스위스의 시계 수출은 32퍼센트가 증가해 233억 달러 규모에 이른다. 수요가 가장 큰 시장인 중국이나 미국, 싱가포르에서 수요가 감소하긴 했지만, 시계를 사랑하는 아랍 지역이나 유럽에서 그 감소한 부분만큼 높여 주고 있다. 아무도 스위스 시계를 시간을 확인하려고 사지 않는다. 스위스 시계의 매력은 <u>무형의</u> 것으로, 정교한 세공과 아름다운 디자인이 바로 그것이다. 뛰어난 시계 제조 기술이 다른 곳에서는 거의 사라져 가고 있지만, 스위스에서는 번성한다. "스위스산(Swiss-made)"은 세계에서 가장 가치 있는 브랜드 중 하나가 되었다. 최근 스위스 정부는 "스위스산" 시계의 기준을 더 <u>엄격하게 정하려고</u> 하는 것 같다. 현재는 시계 가치의 50퍼센트 이상이 스위스에서 생산이 된 것이 아니면 스위스산이라고 주장할 수 없다. 스위스 시계 생산자들은 이 기준을 60퍼센트로 올리려 하고 있다.

24 다음 중 밑줄 친 Ⓐ slack과 가장 가까운 의미에 해당하는 것은?

① 호황   ② 휴지, 휴식   ③ 공급   ④ 수요

| 정답 | ②

| 해설 | slack은 느슨하고 부진한 것을 의미하는데, 여기서는 바로 앞 내용에서 '수요가 감소한 것'을 지칭한다. 따라서 수요가 감소한 것을 수요가 멈춘 것인 휴지(pause, break)의 뜻으로 생각할 수 있으므로 정답은 ②가 된다.

25 다음 중 빈칸 ⓐ에 올 수 있는 가장 적합한 것은?

① 무형의   ② 있을 법하지 않은
③ 멈출 수 없는   ④ 참을 수 없는

| 정답 | ①

| 해설 | 콜론(:) 뒤의 내용과 빈칸 ⓐ의 내용은 일치해야 한다. 스위스 시계의 매력은 시간을 확인하는 것이 아닌 정교한 세공과 아름다운 디자인이라는 뜻으로, '시간'을 '유형'의 것으로 보고 '정교함과 아름다움'을 '무형'의 것으로 본 ①이 정답이 된다.

26 다음 중 빈칸 ⓑ에 올 수 있는 가장 적합한 것은?

① 명료하게 하다   ② 엄격하게 하다
③ 규정하다   ④ 선포하다

| 정답 | ②

| 해설 | '스위스산'에 대한 기준이 무엇인지 '엄격한' 규정을 제시하고 있는 것을 알 수 있다. 현재는 시계 가치의 50퍼센트 이상이 넘어야 스위스산이며, 이 기준을 시계 생산자들은 더 올려 줄 것을 요구하고 있다. 따라서 빈칸의 정답은 '더 엄격하게 하다'는 ② tighten이 적합하다. ① clarify는 "to make something clearer or easier to understand"의 의미로 '분명하지 않은 것을 더 분명하고 이해하기 쉽게 한다'는 뜻으로 쓰일 때 사용된다. 따라서 기준이 불분명한 것이 아니라 정해진 기준을 좀 더 엄격하게 규정해 가는 것이므로 이 경우는 clarify보다 tighten이 더 적합하다.

| 어휘 | **on earth** (의문문을 강조하여) 도대체   **survive** ⓥ 살아남다, 생존[존속]하다

demand ⓝ 수요	**dip** ⓥ (아래로) 내려가다[떨어지다]; (액체에) 살짝 담그다
slack ⓝ 느슨한 부분 ⓐ 느슨한, 부진한 ⓥ (하는 일에) 해이해지다[태만해지다]	
allure ⓝ 매력	**fine watchmaking** 명품 시계 제작
all but 거의	**die out** 멸종되다, 자취를 감추다
thrive ⓝ 번창하다, 잘 자라다, 무성해지다	**be about to** 막 ~하려는 참이다
definition ⓝ 정의	**component** ⓝ 구성 요소
craft ⓥ (특히 손으로) 공예품을 만들다, 공들여 만들다 ⓝ 공예, 기술; 술책	
canton ⓝ (스위스 등의 국가에서 지역을 나눈) 주	**threshold** ⓝ 문지방, 한계점
boom ⓝ (사업 · 경제의) 붐, 호황 ⓥ 호황을 맞다, 번창[성공]하다	
recess 쉼, 휴가, 휴식, 휴지, 방학	**intangible** ⓐ 만질 수 없는, 무형의
improbable ⓐ 있을 법하지 않은, 참말 같지 않은	**inexorable** ⓐ 멈출[변경할] 수 없는, 거침없는, 냉혹한
insufferable ⓐ 참을[견딜] 수 없는	**clarify** ⓥ 명료하게 하다, 분명히 하다
tighten ⓥ 조이다, 더 엄격하게 하다	**stipulate** ⓥ 규정하다
proclaim ⓥ 선포하다, 선언하다	

[27~28] 건국대 2020

해석

여자아이들은 일반적으로 더 빨리 말하고, 더 빨리 읽는 것을 배우고, 더 적은 학습 장애를 가지고 있다. 예일대 신경학 교수들에 따르면, 그 이유는 그들이 글을 읽거나 다른 언어적 활동을 참여할 때 뇌 양쪽의 신경 영역을 모두 사용하기 때문일 것이라고 말한다. 이와는 대조적으로 남성은 좌뇌의 신경 영역만 사용한다.

이러한 접근 방식은 여성들이 논리적인 좌뇌의 추리력을 사용하도록 해 줄 뿐만 아니라 우뇌의 감성과 경험도 사용하도록 허용해 줌으로써 여성들에게 이점을 줄 수 있다. 성인으로서, 여성들은 남성들보다 언어적으로 더 능숙한 경향이 있다. 시간이 정해진 시험에서, 여성들은 남성들에 비해 같은 문자로 시작하는 더 많은 단어들을 생각해 내고, 더 많은 동의어를 나열하고, 더 빠르게 색이나 모양에 대한 명칭을 생각해 낸다. 여성들은 심지어 알파벳 글자를 더 빨리 암기한다.

그러나 여성들의 뇌가 양쪽 반구에서 언어를 처리하는 능력은 훨씬 더 큰 이점을 제공한다. 그것은 바로 뇌졸중이나 뇌 손상을 입은 여성들이 더 쉽게 회복할 수 있도록 도와주는 것이다. 한 신경학자는 "여성들은 말을 하거나 글을 읽을 때 남성보다 더 많은 수의 뉴런을 활성화시키기 때문에, 뇌의 일부가 손상되더라도 남성보다 덜 취약해진다."라고 말한다. "의료계에서 우리는 뇌졸중을 앓고 있는 여성이 남성보다 언어 능력을 더 많이 회복하는 경향이 있다는 사실을 관찰하고 있으며, 그들이 양쪽 반구의 뉴런을 사용하는 것이 그 이유일 것이다."라고 덧붙였다.

27 윗글의 빈칸에 들어갈 말로 가장 적절한 것은?

① 정상적인   ② 간결한   ③ 나태한
④ 능숙한   ⑤ 유익한

| 정답 | ④

| 해설 | 앞에서 계속 여성들이 남성보다 더 언어적으로 뛰어나다고 말하고 있으며, 그 이유를 여성들이 좌뇌와 우뇌를 모두 사용하기 때문이라고 밝히고 있다. 따라서 빈칸에는 여성들이 언어적으로 남성들보다 더 뛰어나다는 내용이 와야 하므로, 정답은 ④ adept가 된다.

28 윗글의 내용과 일치하지 <u>않는</u> 것은?

① 언어 활동을 할 때 여성들은 뇌의 양 측면을 사용한다.

② 여성들은 남성들보다 알파벳 글자들을 더 빨리 암기한다.

③ 여자아이들은 남자아이들보다 일반적으로 더 일찍 말을 시작한다.

④ 남성들은 말할 때 여성들보다 더 많은 수의 뉴런이 활성화된다.

⑤ 여성들은 뇌가 손상되더라도 남성들보다 회복이 용이하다.

| 정답 | ④

| 해설 | 정답은 ④로, 세 번째 문단의 "women activate a larger number of neurons than men when they speak or read"에서 더 많은 수의 뉴런을 활성화하는 측은 여성이라고 밝히고 있다.

| 어휘 |

disorder ⑪ 질병, 무질서, 혼란

neural ⓐ 신경(계통)의

verbal ⓐ 말의, 구두의

hemisphere ⑪ 반구

verbally ⓐ 언어적으로

come up with (아이디어, 돈을) 생각해 내다, 떠올리다, 만들어 내다

significant ⓐ 중대한, 의미심장한, 주목할 만한

injury ⑪ (마음의) 상처[피해]

vulnerable ⓐ 취약한, 연약한; 상처를 입기 쉬운, 공격받기 쉬운

regain ⓥ 다시 얻다

sluggish ⓐ 느린, 게으른, 나태한

instructive ⓐ 유익한

neurology ⑪ 신경학

engage in ~에 참여하다

draw on 이용하다, 의지하다

approach ⑪ 접근법, 처리 방법

synonym ⑪ 동의어

stroke ⑪ 뇌졸중 ⓥ 쓰다듬다, 어루만지다

concise ⓐ 간결한, 간명한

adept ⓐ 능숙한, 숙련된, 정통한

[29~30] 건국대 2020

해석

사람들이 자신의 말을 남들이 경청하고 있다고 느끼면, 그들은 당신을 높이 평가하고, 당신의 견해를 생각해 보고, 당신과 협력하는 등의 방식으로 당신의 호의에 보답할 가능성이 크다. 그러나 적극적인 경청에는 노력이 필요하다. 무엇보다도 말과 행동 모든 측면에서 말하는 이가 이야기하는 것에 전적으로 집중하면서, 그 순간에 머물러야 한다. 만약 여러분의 마음이 방황하고 있다면, 그것을 알게 된 즉시 <u>재빨리 돌아가야</u> 한다. 가장 중요한 것은, 상대방이 어디로 가고 있는지 안다고 생각하지 말아야 하는 것이다. 당신이 예상하지 못했던 것을 들을 수 있도록 열린 자세를 가져야 한다. 다음으로, 당신이 듣고 있다는 것을 말하는 이에게 보여줘야 한다. 눈을 마주치고, 고개를 끄덕이고, 'Uh-huh'나 'Yeah'와 같은 짧은 동의를 표하고, 그들의 말을 바꿔 말하거나 질문을 던지면서 이런 일을 할 수 있다. 이러한 신호는 일부 꾸며낸 것일 수 있지만, 말을 하는 많은 사람들이 적극적인 청자와 <u>거짓</u> 청자의 차이를 감지할 수 있다는 사실을 주의해야 한다.

29 다음 중 빈칸 ⓐ에 들어갈 가장 적합한 것은?

① 잘못을 인정하다

② 곤경에서 빠져나가다

③ 재빨리 돌아가다

④ 앞으로 나서다

| 정답 | ③

| 해설 | 경청이란 말하는 순간에 몰입하는 것이라고 했다. 그리고 상대방의 말을 듣다 다른 생각을 하는 것(If your mind wanders)을 알게 된다면 즉시 경청하던 순간으로 돌아가야 한다는 뜻이 적합하므로, 정답은 ③이 된다.

---

30 다음 중 빈칸 ⓑ에 들어갈 가장 적합한 것은?

① 가짜의
② 신중한
③ 긍정적인
④ 참회하는

| 정답 | ①

| 해설 | 말하는 사람들은 다른 이가 자신의 말을 경청하는지 아니면 경청하지 않거나 경청하는 척하는지 알 수 있다는 내용이 와야 한다. 따라서 앞의 active(적극적인)에 대조를 이룰 수 있는 ① phony(가짜의)가 정답이 된다.

| 어휘 | **return** ⓥ (호의 등을) 되돌려 주다, 화답하다

favour ⓝ 특혜

entertain ⓥ (생각 · 희망 · 감정 등을) 품다, 생각해 보다, 고려하다; 즐겁게 해주다

a point of view 관점, 견해

active listening 적극적인 경청

physically ⓐⓓ 신체적으로, 몸짓으로

snap back 재빨리 제자리로 돌아가다, 회복하다

demonstrate ⓥ (행동으로) 보여 주다

acknowledgement ⓝ 인정

fudge ⓥ 조작하다, 지어내다, 속임수를 쓰다

own up 인정하다, 자백하다

come forward (도움 등을 주겠다고) 나서다

positive ⓐ 긍정적인

be likely to ~하기 쉽다

think highly of ~를 높이 평가하다

cooperate ⓥ 협력하다

verbally ⓐⓓ 언어적으로

wander ⓥ 헤매다, 돌아다니다

assume ⓥ 추정하다

nod ⓥ (고개를) 끄덕이다

paraphrase ⓥ 바꾸어 쓰다, 바꾸어 말하다

phony ⓐ 가짜의, 허위의

get away ~에서 떠나다, 빠져나가다

prudent ⓐ 신중한

penitent ⓐ 죄를 뉘우치는

연습 문제   01 ① 02 ① 03 ③

01 빈칸에 들어갈 적당한 것을 고르시오.

> 더욱 많은 연구에 따르면 TV의 주된 위험은 TV가 전하는 메시지가 아니라 TV라는 매체 그 자체에 있다는 것이, 즉 TV를 보는 것 자체에 위험이 있을 수 있음이 나타나고 있다. 매사추세츠주 Bedford에서 정신 생리학자 토마스 멀홀랜드(Thomas Mulholland)와 햄프셔(Hampshire)대학의 TV 심리학 교수 Peter Crown은 TV를 보는 아이와 어른의 머리에 전극을 부착했다. 멀홀랜드(Mulholland)는 신나는 쇼를 보는 아이들이 높은 집중력을 보이리라 생각했다. 놀랍게도 정반대의 사실이 증명되었다. TV를 보는 동안에 실험 대상의 알파파 출력이 증가했는데, 이는 그들이 "그냥 어둠 속에 조용히 앉아 있는" 것마냥 수동적인 상태에 있음을 나타낸다. 이것이 암시하는 바는 TV 시청은 <u>집중력 상실을 숙련시키는 훈련 과정</u>이 될 수 있다는 것이다.

① 집중력 상실을 숙련시키는 훈련 과정　　　　② 아이의 집중력을 향상시키기에 효과적인 매체
③ 아이들이 적절히 본다면 유용한 기계　　　　④ 아이들에게 메시지를 정확히 전달하기 위해 중요한 매체

| 정답 | ①

| 해설 | TV를 보는 아이들이 "높은 집중력(high attention)"을 보여 줄 것으로 예상했던 것과는 달리 "정반대의 사실이 증명(the reverse proved true)"되었고 또한 "수동적인 상태(in a passive state)"에 있었음을 미루어 볼 때, 보기 중에서 빈칸에 들어가기에 가장 적절한 것은 높은 집중력과 반대되는 inattention이라는 단어가 들어간 ①이다.

| 어휘 | **medium** ⑪ 매체　　　　　　　　　　**psycho-physiologist** ⑪ 정신 생리학자
　　　　psychology ⑪ 심리학　　　　　　　**electrode** ⑪ 전극
　　　　output ⑪ 출력　　　　　　　　　　**implication** ⑪ 암시
　　　　art ⑪ 기술, 숙련, 기교　　　　　　　**inattention** ⑪ 부주의, 집중력 없음

02 빈칸에 들어갈 적당한 것을 고르시오.

신경 경제학자(neuro-economist)들이 새로운 기술을 이용해 뇌 속의 뉴런의 활동을 추적하고 있으며, 이를 통해 감정이 우리의 구매 선택에 어떤 영향을 미치는지 연구하고 있다. 예를 들어, 긍정적 흥분 상태일 때는 사람들이 앞으로 기대되는 이익에 대해 생각하고 위험 부담을 즐기는 경향이 있다. 하지만 비용을 생각할 경우, 사람들은 뇌의 다른 영역을 사용하며 더 불안한 모습을 보인다. 이를 통해 한 가지 알 수 있는 것은, 사람들이 일관되거나 이성적인 결정을 내리는 것은 아니라는 것이다. 이는 MRI나 CT 같은 의료 장비를 통해서도 확인할 수 있는데, 장비들을 통해 사람들은 <u>자신의 선택을 뇌의 각각 다른 영역으로 보내 구분한다는</u> 사실을 확인할 수 있다. 이 같은 경험적 증거를 통해 신경 경제학자들은 뇌가 소위 기대 효용(expected utility)이라고 하는 단일화된 평가를 하는 것이 아니라, 위험과 수익을 각각 따로 평가한다는 결론을 도출했다.

① 자신의 선택을 뇌의 각기 다른 영역에 보내 구분 지었다.
② 현재 자원을 뇌의 특정 반구에 통합시켰다.
③ 구매 선택이 가져오는 위험과 이익에 대한 중요도를 잘못 계산했다.
④ 뉴런을 적절히 할당하기 위해 중앙 집중화된 명령과 통제를 내렸다.

| 정답 | ①

| 해설 | 빈칸 바로 앞 내용을 보면 사람들은 어떤 선택을 해야 할 경우 이성적인(rational) 판단에 따라 행동하지 않는다고 했으며, 빈칸 바로 다음 내용을 보면 사람들은 위험과 수익을 각각 별개의(separately) 방식으로 평가한다고 했으므로 동일한 내용이라는 것을 유추할 수 있다. ①을 보면 뇌의 각기 다른 부분에서 특정 선택을 구분 지어(compartmentalize) 내린다는 내용이기 때문에 빈칸의 앞뒤 문맥과 일치해 정답이 된다.

| 어휘 | **neuro-economist** ⓝ 신경 경제학자   **trace** ⓥ 추적하다
arousal ⓝ 흥분, 각성   **prospective** ⓐ 예상되는
consistent ⓐ 일관된   **rational** ⓐ 이성적인
corroborate ⓥ 확증하다, 입증하다   **empirical** ⓐ 경험적인
assess ⓥ 평가하다   **risk and return** 위험과 수익
expected utility [경제] 기대 효용(행동의 귀결이 불확실한 상황에서 합리적인 경제 주체의 판단은 결과에 관한 효용의 기대치에 입각하여 이루어진다는 이론)
compartmentalize ⓥ 구분하다, 구획하다   **integrate** ⓥ 통합하다
weight ⓝ 중요도   **allocate** ⓥ 할당하다, 배분하다

03 빈칸에 들어갈 적당한 것을 고르시오.

유전자의 차이로 인해 생각과 행동의 차이가 생기게 되고 이를 가장 인상적으로 잘 보여 주는 것이 쌍둥이에 관한 연구이다. 일란성 쌍둥이(모든 유전자를 똑같이 공유한다)가 이란성 쌍둥이(유전자의 절반만을 공유한다)보다 훨씬 더 닮았다. 일란성 쌍둥이가 태어나자마자 헤어져 서로 떨어져 성장했어도 같은 부모 아래, 같은 집에서 성장했을 때와 같은 결과를 보인다. 또한, 마찬가지로 유전자의 절반을 공유하는 피를 나눈 형제자매는 타인과 마찬가지 수준으로 유전자를 전혀 공유하지 않은 입양한 형제자매보다는 훨씬 닮았다. 실제로, 입양한 남매는 닮은 점이 거의 없다. <u>유전자의 영향은 0에 수렴한다</u>는 대안적 주장에 대한 실험이 이루어졌고 결국 받아들여지지 않았다.

① 모든 것은 유전을 통해 결정된다.
② 우리는 타고난 정신 능력을 갖고 태어난다.
③ 유전자의 영향은 0에 수렴한다.
④ 우리는 천성과 양육의 산물이다.

| 정답 | ③

| 해설 | 본문의 핵심은 '유전자를 공유하는 정도에 따라 서로 닮는다'는 연구 결과이다. 다시 말하면 가장 많이 공유한 일란성 쌍둥이의 경우부터 전혀 공유하지 않은 입양한 경우를 비교하면 유전자를 공유한 정도에 따라 서로 닮는다는 결과가 도출된다. 이에 대한 '대안적(alternative)' 연구라 함은 '유전자는 서로 닮는 정도와 상관이 없다'일 것이다. 따라서 빈칸에 들어갈 것은 ③이다.

| 어휘 | **gene** ⓝ 유전자   **make a difference** 차이를 만들다
dramatic ⓐ 극적인, 인상적인   **demonstration** ⓝ 입증, 보여 줌
identical twin 일란성 쌍둥이   **fraternal twin** 이란성 쌍둥이
biological ⓐ 피를 나눈   **sibling** ⓝ 형제자매
adoptive ⓐ 입양한   **alternative** ⓐ 대체의, 대안의
heredity ⓝ 유전   **innate** ⓐ 선천적인
faculty ⓝ 능력

실전 문제

01	①	02	④	03	④	04	③	05	③	06	④	07	①	08	③	09	①	10	③
11	①	12	④	13	④	14	②	15	④	16	②	17	④	18	①	19	④	20	②
21	①	22	③	23	⑤	24	⑤	25	①										

[01~02] 한국외대 2020

해석

과학은 이해하기 힘든 분야로, 특히 실제 사실이 아닌 수많은 "사실"이 떠돌아다닐 때 더욱 그러하다. 여러분은 아마도 중국의 만리장성이 달에서 볼 수 있는 유일한 인공 구조물이라는 소리를 들어봤을 것이다. 흥미로운 점은, 이러한 근거 없는 믿음은 적어도 "리플리의 믿거나 말거나(Ripley's Believe It or Not!)"란 만화에서 만리장성을 "인류의 가장 장대한 건축물이자 인간이 달에서 눈으로 볼 수 있는 유일한 것"이라고 한 1932년 이후 계속되었다. 물론 1932년은 기계가 달에 착륙하기 근 30년 전의 시기로, 이 주장은 터무니없는 소리였다. 이제 우주인들은 고도가 낮을 때를 제외하면 실제로는 만리장성이 우주에서도 보이지 않는다고 확인해 줬다. 심지어 비교적 낮은 높이에서도 실제로는 도로와 비행기 활주로가 만리장성보다 더 잘 보이며, 왜냐하면 도로와 활주로의 색은 만리장성과는 달리 지면에 뒤섞여 구분이 가지 않거나 하는 일이 없기 때문이다. 하지만 그렇다고 만리장성 같은 주요 지형지물이 인상적이지 않다는 것은 아니며, 왜냐하면 만리장성은 이제껏 만들어진 것 가운데 가장 큰 장벽이기 때문이다.

---

01 본문에 따르면 다음 중 만리장성에 대해 사실인 것은 무엇인가?

① 만화에서 언급되었다.
② 1962년 우주인들이 달에서 만리장성을 봤다.
③ 만리장성은 우주의 높은 고도에서 보인다.
④ 만리장성은 지면과 쉽게 분간이 가능하다.

| 정답 | ①

| 해설 | 본문에 따르면 "리플리의 믿거나 말거나(Ripley's Believe It or Not!)"란 만화에서 만리장성을 "인류의 가장 장대한 건축물이자 인간이 달에서 눈으로 볼 수 있는 유일한 것"이라고 언급했다. 따라서 답은 ①이다. 인간이 달에 착륙한 해는 1969년이며, 따라서 ②는 답이 될 수 없다. "이제 우주인들은 고도가 낮을 때를 제외하면 실제로는 만리장성이 우주에서도 보이지 않는다고 확인해줬다"에서 ③은 답이 될 수 없음을 알 수 있다. "심지어 비교적 낮은 높이에서도 실제로는 도로와 비행기 활주로가 만리장성보다 더 잘 보이며, 왜냐하면 도로와 활주로의 색은 만리장성과는 달리 지면에 뒤섞여 구분이 가지 않거나 하는 일이 없기 때문이다"에서 ④는 답이 될 수 없음을 알 수 있다.

---

02 (A)에 가장 알맞은 것은 무엇인가?

① 널리 공유된 근거 없는 믿음은 믿지 말아야 한다.
② 아무도 만리장성이 어떻게 지어졌는지 파악하지 못했다.
③ 이러한 기묘한 사실은 과학적으로는 사실이다.
④ 만리장성 같은 주요 지형지물은 인상적이지 않다.

| 정답 | ④

| 해설 | 빈칸이 들어간 문장의 바로 앞까지를 보면 만리장성이 우주에서 보인다는 소리는 사실이 아님을 알 수 있다. 그런데 빈칸이 들어간 문장은 however로 시작되므로, 빈칸이 들어간 문장은 앞서 언급한 사실과 상반된 내용이 들어갈 것임을 알 수 있다. 그리고 빈칸 뒤를 보면 만리장성이 "이제껏 만들어진 것 가운데 가장 큰 장벽"임을 알 수 있다. 여기서 빈칸의 내용을 추측해 보면, 비록 만리장성이 우주에서 보일 정도로 큰 건축물은 아니지만 어쨌든 지금까지 인류가 만든 건축물 가운데 가장 큰 장벽인 것은 사실이므로, 보이지 않는다고 한들 이것이 "만리장성 같은 주요 지형지물이 인상적이지 않다"는 의미는 아니다(it does not mean)라고 유추할 수 있다. 따라서 답은 ④이다.

| 어휘 | **especially** @ 특히
float around (소문 등이) 떠돌아다니다, (소문, 뉴스 등을) 많은 사람이 언급하다
myth ⓝ 근거 없는 믿음   **mighty** @ 장대한, 웅장한
altitude ⓝ 고도   **blend into** (구분이 가지 않게) ~에 뒤섞이다
landmark ⓝ 랜드마크, 주요 지형지물   **weird** @ 기이한, 기묘한

[03~04] 에리카 2014

해석

> 살이 반복적으로 찌고 빠지는 사람은 신진대사가 영구적으로 그리고 장기적으로 변화한다. 이런 사람들의 신진대사는 느려지고 따라서 다른 사람들보다 식품 에너지를 덜 섭취한다. 그 결과 식품 속 잉여 에너지는 지방 형태로 저장된다. 이는 즉 속성 다이어트는 문제를 오히려 더 키우는 결과를 낳는다는 것을 의미한다. 쥐 실험에 따르면 식사를 과도하게 적게 주는 것과 과도하게 많이 주는 것을 반복할 경우 신진대사율이 낮아지는 결과가 나왔다. 낮은 신진대사율은 쥐가 평소 필요한 것보다 더 적은 음식량으로 살이 더 쉽게 찌도록 만들었다. 추가적으로 고등학교 레슬링 선수들을 대상으로 한 연구에 따르면 일부 선수들은 레슬링 시즌 중에 열 번이나 체중을 줄였다가 늘리곤 하는 것을 알 수 있었다. 비시즌 중에 이들은 체중이 변하지 않는 사람보다 살이 찌지 않았지만 이들의 신진대사율은 상당히 낮았다. 이것이 암시하는 것은 속성 다이어트를 했다가 살이 다시 찌는 사람들은 <u>살을 빼기가 점점 힘들어진다</u>는 것이다.

03 빈칸에 들어갈 가장 알맞은 것을 고르시오.

  ① 속성 다이어트를 반복한다.
  ② 상당히 쉬운 체중을 조절한다.
  ③ 신진대사 비율을 계속 낮추기를 고대한다.
  ④ 살을 빼기가 점점 힘들어진다.

| 정답 | ④

| 해설 | "낮은 신진대사율은 쥐가 평소 필요한 것보다 더 적은 음식량으로 살이 더 쉽게 찌도록 만들었다(The lower rate enabled the rats to gain weight more easily, with less food than they would ordinarily need)." 여기서 쥐뿐만 아니라 신진대사율이 낮은 사람 또한 다른 사람에 비해 같은 양을 먹어도 살이 더 쉽게 찔 것으로 유추 가능하다. 그리고 레슬링 선수 중에서 시즌 중에 열 번이나 체중이 늘었다 줄었다 하는 사람, 즉 속성 다이어트를 하는 사람의 신진대사율도 상당히 낮았다. 신진대사율이 낮다는 것은 살이 더 쉽게 찐다는 의미이며, 역으로 말하면 살을 빼기가 쉽지 않다는 의미이기도 하다. 따라서 답은 ④가 가장 적합하다.

04 윗글의 내용과 맞는 것을 고르시오.

① 인간과 쥐는 살이 쪘다가 빠지기를 반복한다.

② 고등학교 레슬링 선수들은 비시즌 동안에 속성 다이어트를 하도록 권장된다.

③ 신진대사율은 살을 빼는 능력과 관련이 있다.

④ 식사를 과도하게 적게 주는 것과 과도하게 많이 주는 것을 반복하는 것이 쥐의 신진대사에 영향을 미치지는 않는다.

| 정답 | ③

| 해설 | 본문은 신진대사율과 체중과의 관계에 대해 논하고 있으며, 특히 신진대사율이 낮으면 살이 쉽게 찐다는 것을 말하고 있다. 여기서 신진대사율과 살을 빼는 능력 간에는 서로 관계가 있음을 알 수 있다. 따라서 답은 ③이다.

| 어휘 | **repeatedly** ⓐ 되풀이하여, 반복하여   **metabolism** ⓝ 신진대사

excess energy 잉여 에너지, 과잉 에너지   **crash dieting** 속성 다이어트

self-defeating ⓐ 자멸적인, 문제를 오히려 더 키우는   **alternate A with B** A와 B를 서로 번갈아 나오게 하다

implication ⓝ 암시, 함축

[05~07]

해석

베개를 폭신하게 하고 이불을 잘 덮어라. 감기 예방은 잠을 더 자는 것만큼이나 쉬울 수도 있다. 한 연구진은 건강한 성인들에게 800달러를 지급하고 코에 감기 바이러스를 뿌린 후, 호텔에서 5일간 지켜보며 그들이 감기에 걸리는지 확인했다. 일상적으로 8시간 수면하는 사람들은 7시간 이하 혹은 잠을 설치는 사람들보다 감기에 덜 걸렸다. 이 보고서의 대표 저자이자 피츠버그(Pittsburgh)의 카네기멜론(Carnegie Mellon)대학에서 스트레스가 건강에 미치는 영향을 연구 중인 쉘던 코헨(Sheldon Cohen)는 "잠을 더 잘수록, 더 건강하고, 감기에도 덜 걸립니다."라고 말했다. 그 이전의 연구에서는 수면이 세포 수준의 면역력을 강화한다는 것이 밝혀졌다. 로스앤젤레스 (Los Angeles)의 캘리포니아대학교(University of California)에서 면역 반응을 연구하는 마이클 어윈 박사(Dr. Michael Irwin)에 따르면, 이번 연구는 경미한 수면 장애로도 병에 걸릴 위험이 커진다는 것을 시사하는 최초의 연구이다. 그는 이 연구에 직접 참여하지는 않았지만 "연구의 메시지는 규칙적인 수면을 취해야 한다는 겁니다. 그것은 건강에 매우 중요하니까요."라고 말했다. 물론 겨울에는 재채기하는 친척이나 동료들을 피하기는 어려울 것이다. 월요일자 내과 의학 자료집(The Archives of Internal Medicine)에 실린 보고서에서, 연구 팀은 이 같은 상황을 재연해서 피험자들을 흔한 감기 바이러스인 코감기 바이러스(rhino virus)에 노출시켰다. 그 결과, 대부분의 피험자들은 감기에 걸렸다. 그러나 모두에게 감기 증상이 나타나지는 않았다.

05 지문의 주제는 무엇인가?

① 독감은 곧 정복될 것이다.

② 수면은 인체의 면역 반응을 변화시킬 수 있다.

③ 수면은 감기 예방에 도움이 된다.

④ 겨울에는 운동을 더 오래하는 것이 중요하다.

| 정답 | ③

| 해설 | 규칙적인 수면을 취하는 것이 감기 예방에 도움이 된다는 것이 이 글의 주제이다. "The longer you sleep, the better off you are, the less susceptible you are to colds," 참조. ②는 ③에 비해 지나치게 포괄적인 주제이므로 선택하지 않도록 주의한다.

06 "slept fitfully"라는 표현과 의미가 가장 비슷한 것은 "_____"이다.

① 숙면을 취했다　　　　　　　　　　② 즉시 잠들었다

③ 취한 상태로 잠들었다　　　　　　　④ 잠을 설쳤다

| 정답 | ④

| 해설 | 'sleep fitfully'는 '잠을 설치다'는 뜻이다. 보기 ④의 'toss and turn'은 '뒤척이다'의 뜻이므로 가장 의미가 비슷하다.

07 다음 중 지문 마지막 부분의 빈칸에 가장 적절한 것은?

① 그러나 모두에게 감기 증상이 나타나지는 않았다.

② 모두가 실제로 감기에 걸렸다.

③ 당시 그들 중 대부분이 잠을 덜 잤다.

④ 그러나 그들의 주변 사람들이 감기의 원인이다.

| 정답 | ①

| 해설 | 지문의 주제를 완성하는 문제이다. 규칙적인 수면이 면역을 강화하고 감기에 덜 걸리게 하므로, 면역력이 강한 사람들은 감기에 걸리지 않았을 것이다.

| 어휘 | **fluff up** 솜을 부풀려서 풍성하게 하다　　　**pull up** 당기다

common cold 감기　　　　　　　　　　　　**habitual** ⓐ 습관적인, 늘 하는

be likely to ~하는 듯하다, ~하기 쉽다　　　**sleep fitfully** 잠을 설치다

be susceptible to ~에 취약하다, (병 등에) 잘 걸리다　　**boost** ⓥ 촉진하다, 강화하다

immune system 면역 체계　　　　　　　　**cell** ⓝ 세포

sleep disturbance 수면 장애　　　　　　　**response** ⓝ 반응, 응답

be involved in ~에 참여하다, 개입하다　　　**maintain** ⓥ 유지하다

regular ⓐ 규칙적인　　　　　　　　　　　**critical** ⓐ 중요한, 결정적인

stay out of ~로부터 떨어져 있다, 피하다　　**sneezing** ⓐ 재채기하는

relative ⓝ 친척　　　　　　　　　　　　　**mimic** ⓥ 모방하다

condition ⓝ 상황, 상태, 질환　　　　　　　**expose A to B** A를 B에 노출시키다

rhino virus 코감기 바이러스　　　　　　　**be infected with** ~에 감염되다

[08~09] 성균관대 2016

해석

아름다운 사람들에게도 함정은 있다. 예를 들어 매력적인 남성은 더 나은 리더로 간주될 수 있지만, 암묵적인 성차별적 편견은 매력적인 여성에게 불리하게 작용할 수 있으며, (오히려 아름다움 때문에) 권위가 필요한 고위직에 고용될 가능성을 줄어들게 만든다. 그리고 여러분의 예상처럼, 외모가 뛰어난 남녀 모두 시기와 질투를 받는다. 한 연구에 따르면, 당신이 같은 성별의 누군가와 인터뷰를 하면, 당신이 그들보다 더 매력적이라고 판단하면 당신을 고용할 가능성이 적다. 더 걱정스러운 사실은 아름답거나 잘생기면 의학적 치료에 해가 될 수도 있다. 우리는 좋은 외모를 건강한 것과 연관시키는 경향이 있는데, 잘생긴 사람이 병에 걸리면 그 병이 심각한 것으로 간주되는 경향이 줄어든다는 것을 의미한다. 예를 들어, 의사들이 통증을 치료할 때, 의사들은 보다 매력적인 사람들을 덜 신경 쓰는 경향이 있다.

08 다음 중 빈칸 Ⓐ에 가장 적절한 것은 무엇인가?

① 뛰어난 외모는 인생에서 성공을 가져다준다.

② 호감 가는 외모는 마법의 효과가 있다.

③ 아름다운 사람들에게도 함정은 있다.

④ 아무리 뛰어난 아름다움이라도 나쁜 성격을 보완해 줄 수는 없다.

⑤ 아름다움은 피상적인 것일 뿐이다.

| 정답 | ③

| 해설 | 빈칸에 주제문이 등장하며, 뒤에 오는 'for instance'를 통해 예시가 오는 것을 알 수 있다. 뛰어난 외모가 오히려 도움이 되지 않을 수 있다는 예시가 나오고 있으므로 정답은 ③이 된다.

09 다음 중 빈칸 Ⓑ와 Ⓒ에 가장 적절한 것은 무엇인가?

① 더 적은 – 더 적은　　　　　　　　　② 더 적은 – 더 많은

③ 더 많은 – 더 적은　　　　　　　　　④ 가장 많은 – 더 많은

⑤ 더 많은 – 가장 많은

| 정답 | ①

| 해설 | Ⓑ의 경우, 바로 앞의 "work against attractive women"을 통해 뛰어난 외모가 부정적으로 작용한다는 것을 알 수 있으므로 고용될 확률이 떨어진다는 내용이 와야 하고, Ⓒ의 경우 앞의 "illnesses are often taken less seriously"을 통해 앞서의 경우와 마찬가지로 뛰어난 외모가 부정적으로 작용해 의사들로부터 치료를 제대로 받지 못한다는 내용이 나와야 하므로, 빈칸 모두 less가 적합하다.

| 어휘 | **implicit** ⓐ 암시된, 내포된

prejudice ⓝ 편견

authority ⓝ 권한, 지휘권

jealousy ⓝ 질투[시기](심), 시샘

take something seriously 심각하게 여기다

pitfall ⓝ (눈에 잘 안 띄는) 위험[곤란], 함정

beauty is only skin deep 아름다움은 피상적인 것일 뿐이다(사람의 성격이 더 중요하다는 뜻)

sexist ⓐ 성차별주의자의

work against ~에 반대하다; ~에 불리하게 되다

run into 직면하다

recruit ⓥ 모집하다[뽑다]

work one's magic 놀라운 방법으로 ~을 성취하다

make up for 벌충[만회]하다

해석

사상 처음으로 전 세계의 여러 지역에서 외국인이라는 것이 완전히 정상적인 상태로 취급되게 되었다. 외국인이라는 것은 키가 크거나, 뚱뚱하거나, 왼손잡이인 것을 독특한 특징이라 하지 않는 것처럼 더 이상 독특한 것이 아니다. 아무도 베를린에 프랑스인이 있거나, 런던에 짐바브웨인이 있거나, 파리에 러시아인이 있거나 뉴욕에 한국인이 있다고 눈살을 찌푸리지 않는다. 많은 사람들이 기회만 주어진다면 조국을 벗어나 다른 나라에 살고 싶다고 하는 이 현상은 정치 및 철학 분야에서 오래전부터 확립된 합의점인 '인간이라는 동물은 집에 있는 편이 가장 낫다'는 명제를 무의미한 것으로 만든다. 인간은 사회적 동물이기 때문에 특정한 사회에 속해야 한다고 추정해 왔던 것이 철학의 오류였다. 분명히 말하자면 많은 사람들은 집과 고향에 있을 때 가장 안도한다. 하지만 고국에서 억압을 느끼고 외국에서 해방감을 느끼는 사람들의 경우는 어떠한가?

이들의 선택은 해가 갈수록 점차 쉬워지면서 동시에 어려워지고 있다. 쉬워진다는 이유는 산업 및 교육의 세계화가 국경을 짓밟아 무너뜨리기 때문이다. 어려워진다는 이유는 지금처럼 세계화된 세상에서는 도착했을 때 자신이 완전히 외국인이 된 것 같다는 느낌을 주는 곳이 거의 남아 있지 않기 때문이다.

---

10 빈칸 ⓐ에 가장 알맞은 것은 무엇인가?

① 긍정적인
② 터무니없는
③ 독특한
④ 취약한

| 정답 | ③

| 해설 | 외국인이라는 것이 정상적인 상태로 취급된다는 말은 딱히 '독특한' 것도 아니라는 의미이다. 따라서 답은 ③이다.

---

11 빈칸 ⓑ에 가장 알맞은 것은 무엇인가?

① 인간이라는 동물은 집에 있는 편이 가장 낫다.
② 때로는 말도 안 되는 의견으로 합의할 때도 있다.
③ 인간의 욕망은 언제나 자가당착적이다.
④ 외국에서 사는 것은 인간의 본성 차원에서 좋은 일이다.

| 정답 | ①

| 해설 | 빈칸 뒤를 보면, 기존 철학에서는 인간은 사회적 동물이므로 어딘가에 소속되어 있으려 한다고 봤지만 이를 본문에서는 오류로 보고 있다. 즉 과거에는 집을 떠나 외국에 사는 것은 특이한 일이었지만 이제는 기회만 주어진다면 조국을 벗어나 다른 나라에 살고 싶어 하며 이는 "모국에 사는 것이 최고다" 내지는 "외국에 나가지 않고 모국에 살고 싶어 한다"는 생각과 정반대되는 것이다. 따라서 빈칸에는 따옴표 안의 내용과 유사한 의미의 것이 와야 하며, 보기 중에서 이에 해당되는 것은 ①이다.

12 빈칸 ⓒ와 ⓓ에 가장 알맞은 것은 무엇인가?

	ⓒ		ⓓ
①	편안한	–	당혹스러운
②	쾌활한	–	유쾌하지 못한
③	불만족스러운	–	불쾌한
④	억압적인	–	해방감을 주는

| 정답 | ④

| 해설 | 빈칸 앞 문장을 보면 외국이 아니라 집과 고향에 있을 때 가장 편안해하는 사람은 아직 많이 있음을 알 수 있다. 그러나 the others가 가리키는 사람들은 문맥상 집과 고향에 있을 때 편안함을 느끼는 사람들이 아닌 '다른 사람들'이다. 이런 사람들에게는 집은 편안한 존재라기보다는 '불만족스럽거나 억압적으로' 느껴질 것이며, 외국에서 외국인으로 지내는 것은 '억압 대신 해방감을 주는' 일일 것이다. 따라서 답은 ④이다.

| 어휘 |
distinctive ⓐ 독특한
make nonsense of ~을 무의미한 것으로 만들다
consensus ⓝ 의견 일치, 합의
oppressive ⓐ 억압하는, 억압적인
liberate ⓥ 해방시키다, 자유롭게[벗어나게] 해 주다
trample ⓥ 짓밟다
self-contradictory ⓐ 자기모순적인, 자가당착의
agreeable ⓐ 기분 좋은, 쾌활한

raise an eyebrow 눈살을 찌푸리다
long-established ⓐ 오래전부터 확립된
feel at ease 안심하다, 안도하다
foreignness ⓝ 외래성, 이질성
exercise ⓥ 행하다, 이행하다
ludicrous ⓐ 터무니없는
disconcerting ⓐ 당황케 하는, 당혹스러운
disagreeable ⓐ 무례한, 유쾌하지 못한

[13~14] 가톨릭대 2019

해석

우리가 어른이 되어 하는 일 가운데 다수는 어린 시절 우리가 모방을 통해 흡수한 것을 바탕으로 한다. 우리는 흔히 우리가 특정한 방식으로 행동하는 이유가 그러한 행동이 어떤 도덕적 원칙의 추상적이며 고상한 규정과 일치하기 때문이라고 생각하지만, 실제로는 우리의 모든 행동은 우리 내면 깊이 몸에 배었지만 오랫동안 '잊고 지낸' 순전히 모방적인 일련의 흔적에 충실할 뿐이다. (C) 사회가 자신의 관습과 신념을 바꾸기가 매우 힘든 것은 바로 이런 흔적에 변경할 수 없이 충실하기 때문이다. (B) 순전하고 객관적인 지성의 적용에 기반한 흥미롭고 뛰어나게 이성적인 새로운 생각과 마주할 때에도, 사회 공동체는 가정에 기반을 둔 오래된 자신의 습관 및 편견에 여전히 매달린다. (A) 이는 이전 세대가 축적한 경험을 신속하게 집어삼키는 시기이며 필수적으로 겪는 시기인, 청소년기의 '압지' 시기를 무사히 치르기 위해 우리가 져야 할 십자가이다. 우리는 귀중한 사실과 함께 편향된 의견도 받아들여야 한다. 다행히 우리는 모방적 학습 과정에 내재된 이러한 약점에 대해 강력한 해결책을 보유하고 있다. 우리는 날카롭게 갈고 닦은 호기심과 탐구하고자 하는 강한 욕구를 품고 있는데, 이는 다른 성향에 대한 반작용적 역할을 하며, 엄청난 성공을 이룰 수 있는 잠재력을 지닌 균형을 생성한다. 문화는 모방을 통한 반복에 예속된 결과 너무나 융통성 없이 변하거나, 너무나 대담하고 무분별하게 탐구적일 경우에만, 곤경에 처해 허우적거릴 것이다. 두 욕구 사이에서 균형을 잘 잡는 문화가 번성할 것이다. 모방과 호기심 간의 그리고 맹종하며 생각 없이 모방하는 것과 점진적이면서 이성적인 실험 간의 완벽한 균형을 점차적으로 습득해 가는 사회는 운이 좋은 사회이다.

13 다음 중 본문의 순서로 가장 적합한 것은 무엇인가?

① (A) – (B) – (C) ② (B) – (A) – (C)
③ (C) – (A) – (B) ④ (C) – (B) – (A)

| 정답 | ④

| 해설 | 밑줄 쳐진 부분 바로 앞 문장의 "모방적인 흔적(imitative impressions)"을 these impression로 받은 (C)가 먼저 와야 한다. (C)에서는 사회가 자신의 관습과 신념을 바꾸기 힘들다는 사실이 언급되며, (C) 다음에는, (C)에서 언급된 "관습과 신념을 바꾸기 힘들다"는 내용을 부연해 설명하는 차원에서, 흥미롭고 이성적인 새로운 생각이 등장함에도 불구하고 여전히 "가정에 기반을 둔 오래된 자신의 습관 및 편견에 매달린다"는 내용이 등장하는 (B)가 와야 한다. 마지막으로 남은 것은 (A)인데, (A)에서는 앞서 언급된 오래된 습관과 편견은 마치 십자가를 지듯 감당해야 함을 말하고 있으며, 이런 감수해야 한다는 말은 첫 번째 단락의 마지막 문장의 내용인 "편향된 의견도 받아들여야 한다"와 뜻이 통한다. 즉 첫 번째 단락의 마지막 문장 앞에 (A)가 와야 함을 알 수 있다. 따라서 답은 ④이다.

14 빈칸에 가장 알맞은 것은 무엇인가?

① 권위에 거역하는 것을 꺼리다
② 너무나 대담하고 무분별하게 탐구적인
③ 금기로 인한 과중한 부담에 압도되다
④ 본래 역할을 할 수 없을 정도로 지나치게 민주화가 이루어지다

| 정답 | ②

| 해설 | 빈칸이 들어간 문장은 문화가 곤경에 처하는(flounder) 경우를 A or B 구조로 제시하였고, 그 다음 문장에서는 A와 B 둘 간의 균형을 잘 잡는 문화가 번성한다고 말하고 있다. 여기서 A에 해당하는 "모방을 통한 반복에 예속된 결과 너무나 융통성 없이 변하는(too rigid as a result of its slavery to imitative repetition)" 것과 B에 해당하는 것은 서로 양 극단에 위치하는 것이리라 유추 가능하다. 보기 중에서 B에 해당하는 것은 융통성이 없는 것과 정반대되는 "너무나 대담하고 무분별하게 탐구적인" ②이다.

| 어휘 |
imitative ⓐ 모방적인
accord with ~와 일치하다, ~와 부합하다
code ⓝ 규칙, 규정
impression ⓝ 인상, 느낌; 흔적
obedience ⓝ 복종, 충실, 순종
cling to ~을 고수하에, ~에 매달리다
juvenile ⓐ 청소년의, 유치한
mop up 없애버리다, 집어삼키다
inherent ⓐ 내재하는, 타고난
sharpen ⓥ (논쟁·쟁점 등을) 더 분명히 하다, (기량 등을) 갈고 닦다[연마하다]
intensify ⓥ 격렬해지다, 강화하다
rigid ⓐ 융통성 없는, 엄격한
daring ⓐ 대담한, 앞뒤를 헤아리지 않는
exploratory ⓐ 탐구적인, 캐기 좋아하는

absorption ⓝ 흡수, 몰두
lofty ⓐ 고귀한, 고상한
ingrained ⓐ 뿌리 깊은, 깊이 몸에 밴
unmodifiable ⓐ 변경할 수 없는
brilliantly ⓐⓓ 뛰어나게, 훌륭히
sail through 무사히 치르다, 순조롭게 통과하다
blotting paper (잉크 글씨의 잉크를 닦아내는) 압지
antidote ⓝ 해독제, 해결책

tendency ⓝ 성향, 기질
slavery ⓝ 예속
rashly ⓐⓓ 성급하게, 무분별하게
flounder ⓥ 곤경에 처하다, (곤경에 처해) 허우적거리다

gradual ⓐ 점진적인

slavish ⓐ 노예 같은, 맹종하는

progressive ⓐ 진보적인, 점진적인

dominate ⓥ 압도하다, 억제하다

acquisition ⓝ 습득, 획득

unthinking ⓐ 생각 없는, 무모한

disobey ⓥ 불복하다, 거역하다

[15~17]

해석

표현주의가 무엇이었는지를 밝히는 것보다 표현주의가 아닌 것을 밝히는 편이 더 쉽다. 분명히 말해 표현주의는 일관성 있는 단일 개체는 아니다. 꾸준히 발전 중인 "표현주의자"들의 통일된 무리 같은 것은 존재하지 않는다. 하지만 프랑스의 "야수파"나 "입체파"라는 별명이 붙은 소수의 화가들과는 달리, 결과적으로는 예술 분야에 걸쳐 이런저런 유형의 표현주의자들의 수는 매우 많았다. 독일 표현주의는 1933년 나치 독재 정권에 의해 완전히 소멸되었다. 하지만 독일 표현주의가 가장 찬란했던 시기인 1910~20년대는 이후 반향을 지속시킨 유산을 후대에 남겼다. 일부 예술가들은 표현주의의 특징인 자아 성찰이 지닌 정치적 위험성을 인식하였기 때문에, 표현주의가 지닌 정치 참여나 더 폭넓은 사회 개혁에 대한 가능성을 탐구하는 데 더 전념하였다. 하지만 유토피아적인 열망과 예술이 구원의 기능을 갖고 있다고 보는 시각과 관련해 상당한 위험이 존재한다는 점을 감안하면, 표현주의가 절망, 환멸, 위축을 야기할 가능성 또한 크다.

15 윗글의 내용과 일치하지 <u>않는</u> 것은?

① "야수파"로 불린 한 무리의 화가들의 통일된 정체성

② 표현주의의 예술적 측면으로서의 정신적인 자기 성찰

③ 사회 개혁에 대한 표현주의자들의 예술적 영향

④ 야수파 및 입체파와 관련이 있는 표현주의의 예술적 양식

| 정답 | ④

| 해설 | 입체파나 야수파는 표현주의와 대비를 위해 제시되었을 뿐, 그 외 서로 간의 관련성에 관해 언급된 사항은 본문에 존재하지 않는다. 따라서 답은 ④이다.

16 다음 중 문맥상 빈칸 ⓐ에 들어갈 가장 알맞은 어구는?

① 표현주의자들의 정신적 이상을 향한 갈망은 목적을 넘어서서 너무나 컸다

② 예술 분야에 걸쳐 이런저런 유형의 표현주의자들의 수는 매우 많다

③ 표현주의자들은 자신들의 예술적 이해관계를 넘어서 같은 깃발 아래에서 통합되도록 노력했다

④ 표현주의자들의 예술적 양식은 다른 집단의 예술적 양식과 거의 구분되지 않았다

| 정답 | ②

| 해설 | 입체파나 야수파는 소수 집단이었고 앞서 문제에서 언급된 바와 같이 표현주의와 어떤 예술적 양식을 공유하지는 않는다. 이들과 "다른(unlike)" 입체파는 소수 집단이 아니라 "다수"일 것으로 추측이 가능하며, "표현주의자들의 통일된 무리 같은 것은 존재하지 않는다(There was no such thing as a unified band of Expressionists)"는 말은, 즉 표현주의자들은 어떤 통합된 예술 유형을 추구하지는 않는다는 점을 알 수 있다. 이 두 가지 측면을 고려했을 때 답으로 가장 적합한 것은 ②이다.

17 다음 중 빈칸 ⓑ에 들어갈 가장 알맞은 단어는?

① 지성주의　　　　　　　　　　② 불만감

③ 불안　　　　　　　　　　　　④ 반향

| 정답 | ④

| 해설 | 빈칸 ⓑ 바로 앞 문장에서 독일 표현주의가 나치에 의해 1933년에 막을 내렸다는 것을 알 수 있다. 하지만 1910년대~20년대 사이의 "가장 찬란했던 시기(most incandescent phase)"가 남긴 "유산(legacy)"이 무엇인지를 생각해 보면, 현재완료구문(have caused)과 함께 '1920년대 이후 계속'을 의미하는 ever since가 사용되었으므로 독일 표현주의의 유산이 지금까지도 "반향(reverberations)"을 일으키면서 지속되는 유산을 남긴 것으로 추측할 수 있다. 따라서 답은 ④이다.

| 어휘 |

establish ⓥ 밝히다, 확립하다　　　　　　　Expressionism ⓝ 표현주의

coherent ⓐ 일관성 있는　　　　　　　　　on the march 진행 중인, 행군 중인

Fauve ⓝ 야수파 화가　　　　　　　　　　Cubist ⓝ 입체파 화가

dub ⓥ 별명을 붙이다　　　　　　　　　　hue ⓝ 유형

one or another 이런저런　　　　　　　　incandescent ⓐ 눈부시게 밝은

reverberation ⓝ 반향　　　　　　　　　inwardness ⓝ 내성, 자기 성찰

aspiration ⓝ 열망

ascribe A to B A를 B의 탓[덕]으로 돌리다, A를 B에 속하는 것으로 생각하다

redemptive ⓐ 구원하는　　　　　　　　　disillusionment ⓝ 환멸

atrophy ⓝ 위축　　　　　　　　　　　　facet ⓝ 측면, 양상

implication ⓝ 영향　　　　　　　　　　affinity ⓝ 친밀감, 관련성

intellectualism ⓝ 지성주의　　　　　　　malaise ⓝ 불만감, 불쾌감

insecurity ⓝ 불안

[18~20] 한국외대 2018

해석

화장품의 역사는 적어도 6,000년에 걸쳐 이어지고 있으며 화장품은 지구상의 거의 모든 사회에 존재한다. 화장품의 고고학적 증거는 이집트와 그리스에서 시작된다. 고대 로마에서는 일부 여성이 피부 미백 목적의 메이크업 공식을 발명한 것으로 알려져 있다. 1990년대에는 주로 '밤의 숙녀들'이 여전히 메이크업을 했기 때문에 메이크업은 인기가 없었다. 1910년경에 발레 스타들과 극단의 스타들 덕분에 미국과 유럽에서 메이크업이 유행하기 시작했다. 세계 2차 대전 기간에는 화장품의 기본 재료가 전쟁 물자 공급을 위해 전용되었기 때문에 화장품의 공급이 달렸다. 얄궂게도, 당시는 립스틱과 파우더 및 페이스크림의 사용에 제약이 있었던 시절이지만 역으로 수요는 가장 높았고 전후시기를 대비하여 대부분의 실험이 진행되었다. 왜냐하면 화장품 개발업체들은 전쟁 이후 화장품의 경이적인 유행이 찾아올 것이라는 올바른 예측을 했기 때문이다. 1960년대에서 1970년대에 페미니즘의 영향을 받은 많은 여성들은 여성의 열등한 사회적 지위를 고착화하여 여성을 단순한 성적 대상화하는 화장품의 역할에 반대를 표했다. 현대식 메이크업은 주로 여성이 하고 있지만 점차 많은 수의 남성들이 자신의 용모를 강화하기 위해 화장품을 바르고 있다. 화장품 브랜드에서는 특히 남성을 위해 만들어진 컨실러 같은 제품을 내놓고 있다. 하지만 이를 둘러싸고 논란이 벌어지고 있는데, 왜냐하면 많은 사람들은 메이크업을 하는 남성은 전통적인 성역할을 등한시하고 있다고 생각하기 때문이다. 하지만 다른 이들은 이러한 현상을 현재 진행 중인 성평등의 신호로 받아들이고 있으며 왜냐하면 이들은 여성에게 화장품을 바를 권리가 있다면 남성에게도 그럴 권리가 있다고 생각하기 때문이다.

18 다음 중 (A)와 (B)에 가장 알맞은 것은 무엇인가?

① 얄궂게도 – 반대하다

② 사실은 – 고수하다

③ 슬프게도 – 대체되다

④ 자연스럽게도 – 상응하다

| 정답 | ①

| 해설 | (A): 전쟁 때문에 많은 물자가 전시 품목 생산으로 전용되어 화장품 공급이 달리고 사용에 제한이 있었지만, 그 시기에 공교롭게도 수요도 높고 실험도 많이 진행되었다는 것은 "얄궂은" 내지는 "아이러니한" 상황으로 볼 수 있다.

(B): 페미니즘의 영향을 받은 여성들은 화장품이 여성의 열등한 사회적 지위를 고착화하여 여성을 단순한 성적 대상화하는 역할을 한다고 생각했으므로 자연히 "반대했을" 것이다.

이러한 점들을 고려했을 때 답으로 가장 적합한 것은 ①이다.

19 (C)에 가장 알맞은 것은 무엇인가?

① 남성은 여성을 위해 화장품을 구매해야 한다

② 남성은 계속 남자다운 모습을 보이는 한 자유로이 화장품을 살 수 있다

③ 남성은 남성용 화장품을 오래 전부터 구매하고 있다

④ 여성에게 화장품을 바를 권리가 있다면 남성에게도 그럴 권리가 있다

| 정답 | ④

| 해설 | 성평등을 추구하는 관점에서 남자와 여자 모두 동등한 권리를 보유하고 있다. 따라서 여성에게 화장품을 사서 바를 권리가 있다면 당연히 남성에게도 화장품을 사서 바를 권리가 있는 것이다. 그러므로 답은 ④이다.

20 본문에 따르면 다음 중 사실이 <u>아닌</u> 것은 무엇인가?

① 1910년대에는 배우들이 메이크업의 인기에 기여했다.

② 피부 미백을 위한 공식은 처음 그리스에서 등장했다.

③ 남성 전용 컨실러가 존재한다.

④ 세계 2차 대전 이후 화장품이 크게 유행했다.

| 정답 | ②

| 해설 | "고대 로마에서는 일부 여성이 피부 미백 목적의 메이크업 공식을 발명한 것으로 알려져 있다(It is known that some women in ancient Rome invented makeup formulas to whiten the skin)." 여기서 피부 미백 공식은 그리스가 아니라 로마에서 처음 등장한 것임을 알 수 있다. 따라서 답은 ②이다.

"1910년경에 발레 스타들과 극단의 스타들 덕분에 미국과 유럽에서 메이크업이 유행하기 시작했다(Around 1910, makeup became fashionable in the United States and Europe owing to the influence of ballet and theater stars)"는 ①의 근거가 된다. "화장품 브랜드에서는 특히 남성을 위해 만들어진 컨실러 같은 제품을 내놓고 있다(Cosmetics brands are releasing products such as concealers especially created for men)"는 ③의 근거가 된다. "왜냐하면 화장품 개발업체들은 전쟁 이후 화장품의 경이적인 유행이 찾아올 것이라는 올바른 예측을 했기 때문이다(This is because cosmetics developers rightly predicted that the war would result in a phenomenal boom afterwards)"는 ④의 근거가 된다.

| 어휘 |

영어	뜻	영어	뜻
span ⓥ	(얼마의 기간에) 걸치다[걸쳐 이어지다]	archaeological ⓐ	고고학의
date from	~으로부터 시작되다	makeup ⓝ	화장품, 메이크업
ingredient ⓝ	재료, 성분	divert ⓥ	(돈·재료 등을) 전용[유용]하다
experimentation ⓝ	실험	phenomenal ⓐ	경이적인, 놀랄 만한
object to	~에 반대하다	features ⓝ	이목구비(의 각 부분), 용모
ongoing ⓐ	진행 중인	adhere to	~을 고수하다, ~을 충실히 지키다
yield to	~으로 대체되다	correspond to	~에 해당[상응]하다, ~와 일치하다
masculine ⓐ	남자다운, 남성적인	exclusively ⓐⓓ	독점적으로, 전용의

[21~23] 숙명여대 2020

해석

이스터 섬을 찾는 대부분의 방문객들은 화산암으로 조각되어 섬에 흩어져 있는 거대한 조각상인 887개의 모아이 석상을 보기 위해 그곳을 방문한다. 원주민들은 모아이를 자신들의 선조와 현존하거나 죽은 강력한 족장을 표현한 것이라고 여겼다. 그러나 끔찍한 내전이 끝난 후, 모아이 석상 중 극히 일부만이 온전한 상태로 남아 있고, 다수는 땅속에 반쯤 묻혀 있다. 한 가지 의문이 존재한다. 평균적인 조각상의 무게가 코끼리보다 더 나가는 상황에서, 어떻게 그것들을 옮길 수 있었을까? 작가 에릭 폰 데니켄(Eric von Däniken)은 이 조각상들이 외계인들이 우주에서 가져온 물질을 이용해 만든 것이 틀림없다고 주장했다. 당연히 역사학자들은 이 주장에 대해 회의적이다. 모아이가 현재 장소로 끌려 온 것일 수 있다는 주장이 더 신빙성이 있다. 모아이 석상을 끌고 온다는 것은 엄청난 작업으로, 석상 중 다수가 채석장에 남겨진 것을 설명해 준다. 그러나 모든 역사가들이 동의하는 것은 아니며, 모아이 석상의 수수께끼는 풀리지 않은 채로 남아 있다.

---

21 다음 중 본문의 제목으로 가장 적합한 것은?

① 신비한 모아이
② 가장 큰 조각상
③ 아름다운 이스터 섬
④ 훌륭한 건축양식
⑤ 모아이의 정체성

| 정답 | ①

| 해설 | 본문은 이스터 섬에 놓여 있는 모아이 석상에 대해 말하고 있으며, 거대한 석상을 누가 어떻게 만들어 놓은 것인지 의문에 싸여 있다고 말한다. 즉 신비에 싸여 있는 모아이 석상이라는 의미에서 제목으로 ①이 적합하다.

---

22 다음 중 빈칸에 들어갈 가장 적합한 것은?

① 거대한 조각상은 얼마나 오래되었나?
② 화산암으로 887개의 조각상을 조각한 사람은 누구인가?
③ 어떻게 그것들을 옮길 수 있었을까?
④ 왜 그들 중 다수가 절반이 묻혀 있는가?
⑤ 원주민들은 왜 거대한 조각상을 만들었을까?

| 정답 | ③

바로 앞의 'with the average statue weighing more than an elephant' 내용을 통해, 엄청나게 무거운 석상을 '어떻게 옮길 수 있었을까?'라고 묻는 ③이 적합하다는 것을 알 수 있다.

23 문법적으로 잘못된 것을 고르시오.

① ⓐ   ② ⓑ   ③ ⓒ   ④ ⓓ   ⑤ ⓔ

| 정답 | ⑤

| 해설 | 주어는 '수수께끼'를 뜻하는 'the riddle'이고, 이것이 풀리지 않은 상태로 남겨져 있다는 의미이므로, '해결되지 않은'을 의미하는 unsolved가 와야 한다.

| 어휘 |

enormous ⓐ 거대한
volcanic ⓐ 화산의
representation ⓝ 표현, 재현
fraction ⓝ 부분, 일부
alien ⓝ 외계인
conceivable ⓐ 상상할 수 있는
immense ⓐ 광대한, 거대한, 막대한
quarry ⓝ 채석장
architecture ⓝ 건축학, 건축 양식
feasible ⓐ 실현 가능한

carve ⓥ 조각하다, 깎아서 만들다
scatter ⓥ 산란시키다, 흩뿌리다
devastating ⓐ 황폐시키는, 파괴적인, 압도적인
intact ⓐ 온전한, 손상되지 않은
skeptical ⓐ 의심 많은, 회의적인
drag ⓥ 끌고 가다
account for 설명하다
riddle ⓝ 수수께끼, 불가사의
identity ⓝ 신원, 정체성

[24~25] 이화여대 2016

해석

미국 내에서 보육은 여전히 두 가지 계급으로 나뉜다. 적절한 소득을 보유한 사람들은 대체로 자신들의 미취학 자녀를 위해 일류 보육 서비스를 구매한다. 적절한 소득을 보유하지 못한 사람들은 사회 정책을 결정짓는 정치적이고 경제적인 요소에 휘둘리게 된다. 빈곤 계급과 차상위 빈곤 계급 및 노동자 계급은 때로는 훌륭한 보육 서비스를 누리기도 하지만, 긴 대기자 명단과 불충분한 교사 대 아동 비율 그리고 보육 교사의 높은 <u>이직률</u> 등에 직면하는 경우가 자주 존재한다. 미국 국립 교육 통계 센터(National Center of Education)에서 발표한 통계 자료에 따르면 1982년 가구 소득이 25,000달러 이상인 가정의 세 살에서 네 살 아이 아동 가운데 53퍼센트가 미취학 아동을 위한 프로그램을 받던 반면에 가구 소득이 25,000달러 미만인 아이들 가운데 29퍼센트만이 미취학 아동을 위한 프로그램을 받았다. 추가로, 1982년 대졸자 어머니를 둔 세 살 아동 가운데 대략 절반가량 그리고 네 살 아동 가운데 72퍼센트가 미취학 아동을 위한 프로그램을 받고 있었다. 다른 인간 서비스 분야와 마찬가지로 보육에 있어서도 <u>비용을 감당할 수 있을지 여부와 이용이 가능할지 여부</u>가 핵심 요소가 되었다.

24 빈칸 [A]에 가장 알맞은 것은 무엇인가?

① 증가   ② 유입
③ 철수   ④ 생산량
⑤ 이직률

| 정답 | ⑤

| 해설 | 빈칸 앞 형용사 rapid와 함께 열거된 것들은 모두 저소득층이 겪고 있는 보육 서비스의 문제점에 해당한다. 이를 감안하고 보기의 단어를 빈칸에 대입해 보면 적절한 것은 "보육 교사의 이직률이 높다"는 의미에서 ⑤의 turnover이다. rapid는 원래는 '신속한, 빠른'의 의미이고 turnover는 '이직률'을 의미하며, rapid turnover는 '빠른 이직률', 즉 사람이 빨리 빠져나가고 다른 사람으로 대체된다는 의미라서 우리말로는 '높은 이직률'에 가깝다.

---

25 빈칸 [B]에 가장 알맞은 것은 무엇인가?

① 비용을 감당할 수 있을지 여부와 이용이 가능할지 여부가 핵심 요소가 되었다
② 많은 사람들은 보육의 중요성에 대해 여전히 애증이 엇갈리는 태도를 보인다
③ 보육에 대한 대우가 사회마다 크게 다르다
④ 정부는 노동자 계급에 속한 부모를 재정적으로 지원할 책임이 없다
⑤ 정부와 가정은 동반자 관계를 형성한다

| 정답 | ①

| 해설 | 본문에 따르면 보육 서비스의 양극화는 각 가정에서 비용을 감당할 수 있을 만한 재력을 보유하고 있을지 여부에 좌우된다. 또한 대졸자 어머니를 둔 자녀 가운데 미취학 아동을 위한 프로그램을 받는 비율이 높다는 것은 달리 말하면 어머니의 교육 수준에 따라 서비스 이용 가능성에 차이가 존재한다는 의미이다. 즉 "비용을 감당할 수 있을지 여부와 이용이 가능할지 여부(affordability and accessibility)"가 보육에 있어 핵심 요소가 된 것이다. 따라서 답은 ①이다.

| 어휘 |

adequate ⓐ 충분한, 적절한
at the mercy of ~에 휘둘리는, ~앞에서 속수무책인
determine ⓥ 결정하다
inadequate ⓐ 불충분한, 부적당한
affordability ⓝ 구입할 능력이 됨, 비용을 감당할 수 있음
accessibility ⓝ 접근성, 접근[이용/입장]이 가능함
pullout ⓝ (자금의) 회수, (군대의) 철수
ambivalent ⓐ 반대 감정이 병존하는, 애증이 엇갈리는

preschool ⓐ 미취학의 ⓝ 유치원, 보육원
more often than not 자주, 대개
turnover ⓝ 이직률
influx ⓝ 밀려닥침, 유입
turnout ⓝ 참가자의 수; 생산량

MEMO

MEMO

여러분의 작은 소리
에듀윌은 크게 듣겠습니다.

본 교재에 대한 여러분의 목소리를 들려주세요.
공부하시면서 어려웠던 점, 궁금한 점,
칭찬하고 싶은 점, 개선할 점, 어떤 것이라도 좋습니다.

에듀윌은 여러분께서 나누어 주신 의견을
통해 끊임없이 발전하고 있습니다.

에듀윌 도서몰 book.eduwill.net
- 부가학습자료 및 정오표: 에듀윌 도서몰 → 도서자료실
- 교재 문의: 에듀윌 도서몰 → 문의하기 → 교재(내용, 출간) / 주문 및 배송

에듀윌 편입영어 핵심유형 완성 독해

발 행 일	2022년 10월 19일 초판
편 저 자	홍준기
펴 낸 이	권대호
펴 낸 곳	(주)에듀윌
등록번호	제25100-2002-000052호
주 소	08378 서울특별시 구로구 디지털로34길 55
	코오롱싸이언스밸리 2차 3층

www.eduwill.net

대표전화 1600-6700

업계 최초 대통령상 3관왕,
정부기관상 18관왕 달성!

2010 대통령상

2019 대통령상

2019 대통령상

대한민국 브랜드대상
국무총리상

서울특별시장상

과학기술부장관상

정보통신부장관상

산업자원부장관상

고용노동부장관상

미래창조과학부장관상

법무부장관상

여성가족부장관상

과학기술정보통신부
장관상

문화체육관광부
장관상

농림축산식품부
장관상

2004
서울특별시장상 우수벤처기업 대상

2006
산업자원부장관상 대한민국 e비즈니스대상

2007
정보통신부장관상 디지털콘텐츠 대상
산업자원부장관 표창 대한민국 e비즈니스대상

2010
대통령 표창 대한민국 IT 이노베이션 대상

2013
고용노동부장관 표창 일자리 창출 공로

2014
미래창조과학부장관 표창 ICT Innovation 대상

2015
법무부장관 표창 사회공헌 유공

2017
여성가족부장관상 사회공헌 유공
2016 합격자 수 최고 기록 KRI 한국기록원 공식 인증

2018
2017 합격자 수 최고 기록 KRI 한국기록원 공식 인증

2019
대통령 표창 범죄예방대상
대통령 표창 일자리 창출 유공
과학기술정보통신부장관상 대한민국 ICT 대상

2020
국무총리상 대한민국 브랜드대상
2019 합격자 수 최고 기록 KRI 한국기록원 공식 인증

2021
고용노동부장관상 일·생활 균형 우수 기업 공모전 대상
문화체육관광부장관 표창 근로자휴가지원사업 우수 참여 기업
농림축산식품부장관상 대한민국 사회공헌 대상
문화체육관광부장관 표창 여가친화기업 인증 우수 기업

2022
농림축산식품부장관상 대한민국 ESG 대상

에듀윌 편입영어

핵심유형 완성 독해

전과정 학습로드맵 제공

월별 학습계획 및
학습방법 제공

무료 진단고사

나의 위치에 맞는
전문 학습매니저의 1:1 학습설계

실시간 알림 서비스

최신 편입정보
알림 서비스

강의용 PDF 제공

편입 스타터팩을 위한
강의용 PDF 제공

고객의 꿈, 직원의 꿈, 지역사회의 꿈을 실현한다

펴낸곳 (주)에듀윌 **펴낸이** 권대호 **출판총괄** 김형석
개발책임 우지형, 윤대권 **개발** 윤관식
주소 서울시 구로구 디지털로34길 55 코오롱싸이언스밸리 2차 3층
대표번호 1600-6700 **등록번호** 제25100-2002-000052호
협의 없는 무단 복제는 법으로 금지되어 있습니다.

에듀윌 도서몰 book.eduwill.net
• 부가학습자료 및 정오표: 에듀윌 도서몰 → 도서자료실
• 교재 문의: 에듀윌 도서몰 → 문의하기 → 교재(내용, 출간) / 주문 및 배송